Royal Commission on
Electoral Reform and
Party Financing

Commission royale sur
la réforme électorale et
le financement des partis

CANADA

FINAL REPORT

VOLUME 1

This is Volume 1 of the *Final Report* of the Royal Commission on Electoral Reform and Party Financing. The Report is published in four volumes:

Royal Commission on
Electoral Reform and
Party Financing

Commission royale sur
la réforme électorale et
le financement des partis

CANADA

*R*EFORMING
*E*LECTORAL
*D*EMOCRACY

*V*OLUME 1

FINAL REPORT

The Report is available in both official languages as a set or as individual volumes.

Available in Canada through
Associated Bookstores
and other booksellers

or by mail from
Canada Communication Group – Publishing
Ottawa, Canada K1A 0S9

Catalogue No. Z1-1989/2-1-1991E
ISBN 0-660-14245-7 (vol. 1)
       0-660-14244-9 (set)

Canadian Cataloguing in Publication Data

Canada. Royal Commission on Electoral Reform and Party Financing

Reforming electoral democracy : final report

Chairman: Pierre Lortie
Partial contents: vol. 3: Proposed legislation; –
v. 4: What Canadians told us.
ISBN 0-660-14244-9 (set);
0-660-14245-7 (vol. 1); 0-660-14246-5 (v. 2);
0-660-14247-3 (v. 3); 0-660-14248-1 (v. 4)
DSS cat. nos. Z1-1989/2-1991E (set);
Z1-1989/2-1-1991E (vol. 1); Z1-1989/2-2-1991E (v. 2);
Z1-1989/2-3-1991E (v. 3); Z1-1989/2-4-1991E (v. 4)

1. Elections – Canada. 2. Election law – Canada. 3. Advertising,
Political – Canada. 4. Campaign funds – Canada. 5. Voter
registration – Canada. I. Title.

JL193.C35 1991   324.6'0971   C91-098741-6

The Royal Commission on Electoral Reform and Party Financing and the publishers wish to acknowledge with gratitude the permission of the following publishers and individuals to reprint and translate in this Final Report material from their works:

The Globe and Mail; The New York Times Company; Andrew Sancton, University of Western Ontario and Canadian Political Science Association, *Canadian Journal of Political Science*; University of Toronto Press.

Royal Commission on
Electoral Reform and
Party Financing

CANADA

Commission royale sur
la réforme électorale et
le financement des partis

TO HIS EXCELLENCY
THE GOVERNOR GENERAL IN COUNCIL

MAY IT PLEASE YOUR EXCELLENCY

We, the Commissioners, appointed by Order in Council dated 15th November 1989, as revised and amended on 3rd October 1990, to inquire into and report on the appropriate principles and process that should govern the election of members of the House of Commons and the financing of political parties and of candidates' campaigns

BEG TO SUBMIT TO YOUR EXCELLENCY THIS REPORT.

Pierre Lortie, Chairman

Pierre Wilfrid Fortier

William Knight

Robert Thomas Gabor

Lucie Pépin

November 1991

171, rue Slater St., Suite 1120
P.O. Box/C.P. 1718, Stn./Succ. "B"
Ottawa, Canada K1P 6R1

(613) 990-4353 FAX: (613) 990-3311

500 Place D'Armes
Suite 1930
Montreal, Canada H2Y 2W2

(514) 496-1212 FAX: (514) 496-1832

CONTENTS

~

Following is the complete Table of Contents for volumes 1 and 2 of the *Final Report* of the Royal Commission on Electoral Reform and Party Financing.

VOLUME 1

VOLUME 2

1

THE OBJECTIVES OF
ELECTORAL DEMOCRACY

INTRODUCTION

IN NOVEMBER 1989, when the Royal Commission on Electoral Reform and Party Financing was established, East Germans and West Germans, along with the entire democratic world, were celebrating the freedom symbolized by the dismantling of the Berlin Wall. As we completed our work in the fall of 1991, peoples of central and eastern Europe and from what used to be the Soviet Union were taking tentative steps toward an uncertain future as citizens of rebuilt or burgeoning democracies. As these events demonstrate, the political order determines the degree to which economic and social freedoms, as well as social and economic justice, prevail. An equitable socioeconomic order cannot be built on an inequitable political order.

The people of Canada were not unaffected by these historic developments in freedom and democratic government. Canadians looked with new appreciation on their democratic society and its political and economic rights and its freedoms. But even as they did so, many Canadians made it clear at the Commission's public hearings that in evaluating the processes of our electoral democracy they have found it lacking in several crucial respects. These Canadians are demanding that electoral reform not merely tinker with the electoral law; they are demanding that electoral reform focus on the broader and central purposes of electoral democracy.

Furthermore, the current challenges to democratic governance in Canada are not restricted to struggles over federal constitutional arrangements, critical as they may be to our future as members of a Canadian polity. Canada is not merely a federation; it is also, as the *Canadian Charter of Rights and Freedoms* states, a "free and democratic society". What makes us free and democratic are precisely those matters of electoral democracy that the Commission was privileged to address on behalf of Canadians.

Our mandate concerned the most basic of democratic rights – the right to vote, to be a candidate and to participate in free and open elections. Electoral reform, therefore, goes to the heart of the democratic process. It requires that we re-examine our electoral laws and practices to ensure that they fully and truly reflect common values – the basic passions and beliefs that determine how we harness the most powerful forces in a political society and how we order our collective life to achieve a free and democratic society.

HISTORICAL CONTEXT

This is not the first time in recent years that the electoral system has been the subject of study and reform. Since 1960, there have been at least four notable series of changes or proposals for change. The first series introduced the *Electoral Boundaries Readjustment Act* in 1964, which established an independent and impartial process for drawing the boundaries of federal constituencies. This process was removed from the purview of Members of Parliament and conducted instead by an electoral boundaries commission for each province, chaired by a judge of the superior court of the province.

Other major events of the 1960s were the 1964 appointment of the Committee on Election Expenses – the Barbeau Committee – and its 1966 report. Created in response to the rapidly rising cost of general elections, particularly for political parties, the Barbeau Committee proposed controlling election spending by limiting the amount of media advertising parties could purchase and the amount candidates could spend on advertising.

The election spending limits that emerged in the *Election Expenses Act* of 1974 were the product of further study by the Chappell parliamentary committee. (Canada, House of Commons 1971) The regulatory framework that ensued was much more extensive than that envisaged by the Barbeau recommendations. It limited expenditures by both candidates and parties, restricted election spending by other individuals and groups, regulated the timing and amount of paid advertising, and introduced tax credits for political contributions as well as partial reimbursement of election expenses incurred.

The last milestone in electoral reform in the past 30 years was the *White Paper on Election Law Reform*. (Canada, Privy Council Office 1986) Proposing comprehensive reform of the *Canada Elections Act*, the main objectives of the white paper were to extend the vote to more Canadians, to make the voting process more convenient, and to modernize the administration of elections. The white paper also proposed restricting government advertising during an election campaign, requiring more information to accompany published opinion poll results, and removing the restrictions on certain categories of voters to be candidates for election to the House of Commons.

The white paper was based on recommendations made by the chief electoral officer of Canada in 1984 and 1985 and by the broadcasting arbitrator. But the legislative proposal that would have implemented many of the white paper reforms, Bill C-79, died on the order paper with the call of the 1988 general election.

In acknowledging the crucial role of electoral reform in the democratic process, we must reconsider what Aristotle understood as authentic politics. Ethics and politics, he argued, are one and the same enquiry. Each demands that we ask: "How ought we to order our life together?"

This new focus on the ethical dimensions of political culture and practice has a particular salience in the Canadian context. The Charter gave rise to new expectations about the legitimate claims of citizens. It also transformed the basic structures of governance. Citizens no longer have to rely on parliamentarians or political parties to have their claims included on the decision-making agenda. Citizens can now pursue their constitutional claims through the courts.

These changes are not merely hypothetical. On several critical issues related to electoral democracy, Charter challenges have resulted in court decisions that have altered the basic electoral law. Citizens have also used the ethical principles implied by the Charter to evaluate many election-related practices, especially by political parties, and they have found these practices wanting. As these evaluations make clear, practical reforms must proceed from ethical principles; ethics is not merely a concern of democratic theory.

THE COMMISSION'S MANDATE
The mandate given to the Commission on 15 November 1989 required us

> to inquire into and report on the appropriate principles and process that should govern the election of members of the House of Commons and the financing of political parties and of candidates' campaigns, [including, but not so as to limit the generality of the foregoing, issues such as]
> (a) the practices, procedures and legislation in Canada;
> (b) the means by which political parties should be funded, the provision of funds to political parties from any source, the limits on such funding and the uses to which such funds ought, or ought not, to be put; [and]
> (c) the qualifications of electors and the compiling of voters' lists, including the advisability of the establishment of a permanent voters' list.

Our mandate did not refer to the Senate of Canada. The Senate is very much part of our system of parliamentary government, but, because its members are appointed, it is not part of electoral democracy. Senate reform could affect how seats in the House of Commons are assigned to the provinces. At present, the distribution of seats attempts to reconcile the constitutional principle of proportionate representation – that is, the representation of provinces on the basis of their population – and the constitutional provision whereby a province cannot have fewer seats in the Commons than it has senators. This approach to representation in the House of Commons has been necessary because of dissatisfaction with the way the Senate has fulfilled its role as a second chamber of Parliament that represents provinces as the constituent units of the Canadian federation. In its constitutional proposals released in September 1991, the government of Canada endorsed an elected Senate based on an equitable representation of provinces. (Canada 1991)

Until the Senate is reformed to reflect the federal principle of representation within Parliament, the assignment of Commons seats to provinces must be based on more than proportionate representation. Our recommendations to redistribute Commons seats therefore assume that the Senate remains largely unchanged. We do indicate, however, the implications of a reformed Senate for redistribution.

THE COMMISSION'S APPROACH

We began by consulting former and present senior federal and provincial officials involved with different elements of the electoral system, as well as political party officials. From these consultations we learned the main concerns of those most involved with the current election law. Shortly after, we invited some 75 scholars from across Canada to prepare papers on what they considered the major issues of electoral reform and the research projects that would be necessary to address them. Many of those who responded were also invited to a seminar at which they discussed the major issues with us, with a group of knowledgeable, experienced representatives from the larger political parties and with election officials from across Canada.

At the same time, we asked Canadians for briefs and submissions. The response was enthusiastic. Nearly 900 briefs and submissions were received: 233 from groups and associations; 195 from political practitioners and organizations; and 466 from election administrators and private citizens.

We originally scheduled 28 days of sittings in 25 cities across Canada between March and June 1990. To accommodate the heavy demand for hearings, however, in most cities we added evening sessions, and in several cities we had to schedule extra days of hearings. In total, we held 42 days of hearings in 27 cities. The record of this testimony extends to some 14 000 pages.

Our extensive research program responded not only to the advice we received from scholars, political practitioners and election administrators, but also to the issues raised in our public hearings. The research program ensured that we were informed on federal electoral and political practices, including the financing of political parties and candidates. Throughout, we added an historical perspective, to place the contemporary experience within the Canadian political tradition. We also recognized that any examination of Canadian electoral democracy would not be complete without examining the experience of the provinces and territories, and other western democracies. Our research projects thus incorporated comparative studies on the major topics of enquiry. Because of the experience of the United States in election finance regulation and the role of money in electoral politics, we had two major meetings in the United States. The first was a joint session with the Federal Election Commission in Washington, DC. In this session we considered the U.S. regulatory regime from a Canadian perspective. The second was a workshop organized jointly with the Joan Shorenstein Barone Center on the Press, Politics and Public Policy and the Institute of Politics, John F. Kennedy School of Government, Harvard University. This workshop brought together political and media practitioners from the United States and Canada to consider current U.S. efforts to reform its electoral process, including lessons that could be drawn for Canada.

In addition to the Commission's research co-ordinators and analysts, some 180 researchers from 28 Canadian universities, the private sector and, for several projects, from universities and institutes abroad, were engaged in research. We were fortunate that our research program was able to attract some of the foremost scholars in Canada and abroad. Their studies, published along with our report, will contribute to a greater knowledge and understanding of electoral democracy in Canada and abroad.

Because we wanted the benefit of the experience and advice of those most familiar with the workings of the *Canada Elections Act* and provincial and territorial electoral laws, we also met during the past two years with the chief electoral officers across the country and consulted regularly with the registered national political parties. Our research projects benefited from their co-operation: they provided access to information that allowed us to analyse their structures, operations and financial practices.

The third major phase of our work consisted of symposiums and workshops in which preliminary research findings were evaluated by those with practical experience in election campaigns, political parties and the media. We also held symposiums with election officials on election administration, and with local party officials on managing campaigns under the current electoral law. In all symposiums we sought consensus on what were the major electoral reform issues and options.

Early in our public hearings, several witnesses spoke of the serious underrepresentation of Aboriginal people in the House of Commons. Aboriginal people have never been represented in proportion to their numbers in Canada – although they make up 3.5 per cent of the population, only 12 self-identified Aboriginal people have been elected to the more than 10 500 House of Commons seats available since Confederation – nine of them since 1960.

Among those proposing more effective Aboriginal representation was Senator Len Marchand, who in 1968 became the first Indian person elected to the House of Commons. Senator Marchand proposed that the Commission consider remedying this underrepresentation through the establishment of Aboriginal constituencies. Among others, New Zealand and the state of Maine have set aside seats for Aboriginal people in their legislatures – four seats for the Maori in New Zealand and two seats for the two Indian nations in Maine. Many Aboriginal persons who appeared at our public hearings referred to these examples to support their requests for direct representation in the House of Commons.

Toward the end of our hearings, several interveners from Aboriginal organizations urged more substantive consultations on Aboriginal issues than had taken place during our hearings. A representative of the Native Council of Canada recommended that the Commission establish a joint working committee with representatives of Aboriginal organizations to develop proposals for Aboriginal representation in the House of Commons.

To ascertain the views of Aboriginal leaders on the general concept of Aboriginal constituencies, we asked Senator Marchand to co-ordinate a series of consultations based on his brief. These consultations took place in

January 1991. Aboriginal leaders responded positively and requested a second round of consultations to discuss a more detailed proposal. This proposal would outline the implications of Aboriginal constituencies and how they could be established. This request led to the establishment of a Committee for Aboriginal Electoral Reform, chaired by Senator Marchand, and composed of Ethel Blondin, Willie Littlechild, Jack Anawak and Gene Rheaume, who with Senator Marchand represent five of the nine living Aboriginal persons who have been elected to the House of Commons since 1960. This Committee of Aboriginal leaders developed a concrete proposal that would guarantee a process for creating Aboriginal constituencies rather than guaranteeing a specific number of seats. The proposal was published in the Aboriginal press, and the Committee then conducted extensive consultations with Aboriginal people across Canada during May, June and July of 1991. The Committee's report on these consultations was presented to the Commission and made public on 18 September 1991. Its report is reproduced in Volume 4 of our report.

THE OBJECTIVES OF ELECTORAL REFORM

In considering how to reform the electoral process it became clear that we could not approach our task as a technical exercise, simply reforming disparate items in the electoral law. Rather, we needed to clarify the fundamental objectives of electoral democracy and propose reforms to meet these objectives. Two major studies aided our efforts to define these fundamental objectives. The first was an ethicological analysis identifying the values underlying the briefs and submissions we received. (Fortin 1991 RC)* The second was a major national survey of Canadian attitudes on electoral practices and reform proposals. (Blais and Gidengil 1991 RC) We then formulated six objectives and used them to assess the current federal electoral law and political practices and to develop our reform proposals.

Securing the Democratic Rights of Voters

The Canadian record on securing the democratic rights of voters – the most essential characteristic of an electoral democracy – is relatively good. Three factors in Canada's electoral law affect how we participate in the voting process.

First, the constitutional right of citizens to vote is guaranteed in the *Canadian Charter of Rights and Freedoms*. Electoral law, however, qualifies this right. Limiting the right to vote is not necessarily contrary to the Charter. The Charter allows limits on rights if they are prescribed by law and can be demonstrably justified as reasonable in a free and democratic society. Under the Charter, the onus has shifted to the state to justify exclusions; the right to vote is a constitutional right of citizens, not a privilege. Any

---

* In references to Royal Commission research studies, the date is followed by the initials RC.

limits on the right to vote must therefore be justified; Parliament no longer has the authority to set arbitrary limits. To secure the right of citizens to vote, this standard must be applied in assessing the limitations in the *Canada Elections Act*.

Second, to be eligible to vote a citizen must be registered. This statutory requirement serves two fundamental purposes: it ensures that only qualified voters vote and that they do so only once. Voter registration thus promotes the integrity of the vote.

Registering voters in a country the size of Canada is a major undertaking. Canada's current law and approach assume that because the state is responsible for voter registration more citizens are registered; this assumption is validated by comparative assessment. The vast majority of eligible Canadians are registered at every federal election.

At the same time, however, Canada's voter registration does disfranchise some voters, either because of provisions in the *Canada Elections Act* or because of administrative shortcomings. Moreover, changing lifestyles and increased mobility, among other factors, have made it more difficult to meet previous standards of completeness. The federal registration system is also not as open as it could be, nor is it as open as many provincial systems. If we do not want voter registration to be an obstacle to citizen participation in voting, reforms are clearly necessary.

The third factor affecting how we participate in the voting process is the degree to which voting is accessible. Under our current law and practice, voting is relatively accessible for the majority of voters. For many, however, the system is less friendly. Statutory and administrative requirements can impose unreasonable burdens and unjustified restrictions. Voting in ways other than at a polling station on election day is treated as an exception to the norm and made unnecessarily complicated. We need to treat these other ways of voting as extensions of the normal voting process, rather than as exceptions to be tolerated only in special circumstances.

Enhancing Access to Elected Office

The laws governing the right to be a candidate determine the degree to which a political society is open or closed to the claims of its citizens to stand as candidates. By this measure, the Charter gives each citizen the right to be qualified for membership in the House of Commons, subject only to such reasonable limitations prescribed by law as are demonstrably justified in a free and democratic society. The *Canada Elections Act* requires a candidate to be a qualified voter and imposes several other qualifications. With few exceptions, however, candidacy is open to virtually all voters.

Yet when we consider the extent to which citizens have equitable access to candidacy, the Canadian electoral process appears far less open. In particular, women have been, and remain, greatly underrepresented among those nominated as candidates and elected to the House of Commons. In 1988, for instance, women were only 19 per cent of all candidates and only

13 per cent of those elected. Aboriginal people and members of visible minority groups are also underrepresented. Since 1960, there have been only nine self-identified Aboriginal persons elected. Members of visible minority groups represented 2 per cent of MPs following the 1988 election, although people from visible minority groups constitute slightly more than 6 per cent of the population.

Representation is fundamental to the concept of parliamentary democracy. In one sense, representation in governance identifies those represented, designates representatives and legitimizes institutional processes for securing agreements and resolving conflicts. In another and more fundamental sense, representative governance incorporates a society's definition of itself as a political community. Distinctions about who has a legitimate claim to political power are established in elections. In the process, a society pronounces whether it is open or closed to the claims of its citizens to stand as candidates for elected office, regardless of their sex, ethno-cultural heritage or financial resources. In this respect, a society is explicitly representing itself. In so doing, it reveals a great deal about its political culture and values.

Canada does not formally require candidates and, by extension, those elected to the House of Commons to reflect the nation's socio-demographic reality. Indeed, our theory and practice of representation reject any such notion that the process of selecting candidates or the electoral system itself should ensure that our society is reflected in those who are chosen as candidates or elected. Rather, representation promotes free and open competition for candidacy and election so that the best will be chosen as candidates and the best candidates will be elected.

At the same time, Canadian political parties acknowledge that Parliament should be an assembly of representatives whose legitimacy is endorsed by the degree to which the parties provide access to various segments of the population. In recruiting and selecting candidates, the large, national political parties have sought to ensure a measure of representativeness in their standard-bearers. Individuals from various language, ethno-cultural and religious communities have been recruited as candidates. Moreover, Canadian prime ministers since Sir John A. Macdonald have embraced the principle of representativeness when appointing cabinet ministers.

Despite these efforts, however, the large, national political parties have not extended this practice to several segments of the Canadian population. This virtual exclusion, particularly of women, from the corridors of political power is no longer acceptable. It is not merely a matter of political symbolism; elected representatives will not and cannot effectively represent the full range of Canada's interests if they do not reasonably reflect its society. To this extent, the electoral system fails to secure the best persons to sit in the House of Commons.

One of the challenges of electoral reform is thus to help reduce the systemic or structural barriers to candidacy without compromising the elements that constitute its strengths. This is no simple task: Canada is not alone in this shortcoming, and several factors beyond political practices are at play.

Promoting the Equality and Efficacy of the Vote

Securing the rights of voters and enhancing the effective representation of Canadian society are necessary but insufficient conditions to ensure the equality and efficacy of the vote. The equality and efficacy of the vote are meant to achieve distinct but related goals. The equality of the vote is meant to ensure that the value of each vote is reasonably equal across territorially defined constituencies within a province. The efficacy of the vote means that voters who identify themselves as members of a 'community of interest' can influence the outcome of the vote whenever the community is a majority or significant minority in a territorially defined constituency. This objective has been used to justify drawing constituency boundaries such that members of rural, ethno-cultural and minority language communities have been able to influence the outcome of elections where they are concentrated. This, in turn, enhances the likelihood that the community would be represented by one of its own, and its parliamentary representation would thereby be more effective because its interests would be more clearly defined.

Equality and efficacy of the vote are fundamental objectives of an electoral democracy that aspires to the quality of representation that Canadians deem necessary for effective and legitimate representative governance. These two objectives have long been recognized in the assignment of House of Commons seats to provinces and in the drawing of constituency boundaries within provinces.

To achieve representation by population as a method of representing Canadians as members of provincial communities, the principle of proportionate representation was adopted at Confederation. This principle was the basis for assigning House of Commons seats to provinces and is entrenched in the constitution. Departures from this constitutional principle have been required, however, because the Senate has not proved an effective second chamber for regional representation. The assignment of Senate seats to provinces provides proportionately greater weight to smaller provinces than their population would warrant, and the Senate's powers are considerable. But because senators are appointed rather than elected, the Senate lacks the democratic legitimacy necessary to act as a check on the elected House of Commons.

The principle of proportionate representation in the Commons has therefore been compromised by a constitutional provision and by successive formulas for assigning House of Commons seats to provinces. The equality of the vote has been diminished accordingly. Although some restrictions must be maintained on the principle of proportionate representation, in the absence of a reformed Senate, the restrictions should be the least severe necessary to achieve proportionate representation. This is not the case with the present formula for assigning seats.

The efficacy of the vote as a fundamental objective of electoral democracy in Canada has also been recognized since Confederation. Partisan politics played a major role in drawing constituency boundaries until an independent process was adopted in 1964. Nonetheless, to the extent that representational principles mattered, the objective of representing communities of interest in drawing constituency boundaries was paramount. In the 1964 reform, equality of the vote was given enhanced status, but the criterion of community of interest was maintained. In a 1986 amendment, the representational objective of community of interest was given still more importance.

We recommend that the current representational system, with members of the House of Commons elected from single-member constituencies based on the plurality of votes cast in a constituency, be maintained. This system of representation performs best when constituency boundaries are drawn to achieve equality and efficacy of the vote. Relative equality in the number of voters in each constituency in a province is required not only to preserve the constitutional right that each vote be of equal value, but also because large variations in the size of constituencies tend to produce a legislature at significant variance with the distribution of the popular vote. Such occurrences undermine the legitimacy of Parliament and of the government. Moreover, boundaries can be drawn to adhere reasonably closely to equality of the vote and still promote efficacy of the vote. There is a widespread assumption that voter equality must inevitably be diminished by representing communities of interest, but the Canadian record since 1964 demonstrates that this need not be the case. The most relevant international comparison, with Australia, confirms that equality and efficacy are not necessarily contradictory. Voter equality in Australia requires that constituencies be within 10 per cent of state electoral quotients (compared with Canada's present standard of 25 per cent), yet communities of interest are still adequately acknowledged in drawing electoral boundaries.

The major exception to this generalization pertains to the Aboriginal people of Canada. Many factors, including their dispersal in most parts of the country and the practices of electoral boundaries commissions, have resulted in less than due consideration of their distinct identity when drawing constituency boundaries. More important, however, as shown at our public hearings and in subsequent consultations, many Aboriginal people would prefer direct representation based on Aboriginal constituencies. This would acknowledge that Aboriginal peoples, as the First Peoples of this land, have a status different from all other Canadians.

There is a compelling case for changing the *Canada Elections Act* to guarantee Aboriginal voters the right to create Aboriginal constituencies in one or more provinces where numbers warrant. By establishing a process for creating Aboriginal constituencies, rather than providing a guaranteed number of Aboriginal seats, Aboriginal constituencies would be created only when and where Aboriginal voters themselves chose this alternative to voting in the constituencies where they reside. This process would also be compatible with the equality of the vote in Canada, since Aboriginal constituencies would be required to conform to the electoral quotients in each province. Through this process, Aboriginal constituencies could also be efficiently incorporated into our representative system of parliamentary government.

Consultations with Aboriginal leaders and communities, based on a specific proposal, indicate that there is sufficient support for establishing a process for creating Aboriginal constituencies that would meet the requirements of our traditions and constitutional principles. At the same time, our research indicates that this process would not depart from the traditions of representation in Canada. Nor would it depart from the principles that we recommend should govern the drawing of constituency boundaries in provinces, particularly the principle of equality of the vote.

Equally important, there are four major reasons why a process to create Aboriginal constituencies is in the interest of all Canadians. First, Aboriginal peoples have a unique status under Canada's constitution. Second, they have always expressed a desire to preserve their distinct identity rather than assimilate with Canadian society. Third, Parliament has special and exclusive responsibilities for Indian and Inuit peoples on matters that for other Canadians are provincial responsibilities. It is therefore essential that Aboriginal peoples be present in the House of Commons to speak for their interests. Fourth, the claims of Aboriginal peoples, as the First Peoples of this land, to effective representation, as defined by the Supreme Court of Canada, are unique.

Contrary to some opinion, Aboriginal constituencies would not 'ghetto-ize' Aboriginal peoples or isolate their representatives in Parliament. These constituencies and their MPs would be distinct but fully a part of the Canadian electorate and its representation in the House of Commons. Aboriginal voters who choose to vote in Aboriginal constituencies would vote for candidates who spoke not only to their specific interests, but also to national policies from an Aboriginal perspective. In this way, Aboriginal peoples could participate more fully in Canadian political life without having to assimilate and thus deny their distinct identity. Such direct representation would also send an important message to the international community about the participation of Aboriginal peoples in the Canadian polity and confirm their unique place in and contribution to the development and history of our country.

Strengthening Political Parties as Primary Political Organizations

Canadian experience, as well as that of other countries, demonstrates that a competitive political party system is an essential complement to the institutions of government. In this sense, political parties are primary political organizations.

Politics is inherently adversarial because basic human passions – including self-interest and the pursuit of power – are at play. The fundamental task of governance in a free and democratic society is to restrain these passions. Citizens may organize themselves for political purposes into organizations such as interest groups or pressure groups. But only political parties can reconcile and accommodate diverse and competing interests to reach agreement on public policy. The objective of democratic institutions is thus to channel these passions so that society can reach agreement while protecting the rights of minority groups.

Contemporary populism, as it is called, challenges many basic assumptions that underlie our representative and parliamentary government and give prominence to political parties as primary political organizations. Populist critiques of contemporary representative government, and the role of parties within it, draw attention to several shortcomings in our current practices. At the same time, calls for non-partisan democratic politics to achieve consensus create an illusion about our capacity to restrain and order basic human passions. Where formally organized political parties do not compete for political power, the result is the dominance of factions or special-interest groups. Competition is not eliminated; rather, it occurs in different arenas and takes different forms. The pressure of competition in different forms does not rule out democratic government or political freedoms, but the capacity for organized democratic participation and political control by the public is reduced accordingly.

Under our system, competitive parties have organized the political processes of democratic parliamentary government. Although it is possible to have *representative* government without political parties, as is the norm in municipal government in Canada, *responsible* government requires political parties. Parties ensure that the government accounts for its policies and programs in the House of Commons and that at general elections voters can pass judgement on the government's record. Not surprisingly, then, Canadians acknowledge that political parties are primary political organizations in a parliamentary system.

At the same time, Canadians have become increasingly critical of how our large, national political parties are structured, how they operate and the extent to which they are accessible to Canadians in general and their adherents in particular. Our parties are seen as having shortcomings in the way they recruit and select their leaders and candidates for the House of Commons; also questioned are the opportunities their membership has to engage in political discourse and meaningful political participation. These shortcomings have resulted in national parties that lack a broad basis of membership and that tend to exclude certain segments of the body politic.

Many factors explain these shortcomings. The impact of modern communications technologies, especially television, has focused public attention on party leaders. Technological developments have also enabled, if not forced, parties to conduct highly centralized election campaigns through the mass media and to use other means, such as polling, to tap into public opinion. In the process, party membership has declined in importance, other than for periodically selecting candidates and leaders. The role of the membership in selecting candidates and leaders has also been tainted, however, by practices that most Canadians consider need reform. Finally, this state of affairs has been paralleled, if not caused, by the proliferation of special-interest groups. Many political activists, who previously would have pursued their public policy interests through a political party, now participate in advocacy and interest groups.

Despite the shortcomings of political parties and the challenge of special-interest groups, parties remain the primary political organizations for recruiting and selecting candidates for election to the House of Commons, for organizing the processes of responsible parliamentary government, and for formulating policy that accommodates and reconciles competing regional and socio-economic interests. As legitimate as interest groups are in a free and democratic society, by their nature they cannot perform these crucial functions. Accordingly, our democratic politics can be healthy and ethically sound only when political parties perform their essential functions in ways that are, and are seen to be, consistent with democratic principles and processes. It is therefore imperative that electoral reform address the fundamental objective of strengthening political parties as primary political organizations.

Promoting Fairness in the Electoral Process

Although fairness in the electoral process is not an entirely contemporary concern, fairness as a fundamental value of electoral democracy has become more prominent over time. Fairness in a free and democratic society presupposes a foundation of justice, in which the equality of citizens to participate in governance requires a fair opportunity to influence political institutions and public policy. This foundation of political justice is reflected in the principle of 'one person, one vote' and section 15 of the *Canadian Charter of Rights and Freedoms*, which declares that "every individual is equal before and under the law". At the same time, the rights and freedoms guaranteed by the Charter are subject to reasonable limits that can be "justified in a free and democratic society". The assumption here is that justice as fairness, among other fundamental values that are important to our society, must temper the unbridled exercise of individual rights and freedoms.

The way democratic theory, democratic institutions and constitutional law have evolved testifies to the degree to which fairness is now regarded as fundamental. Fairness does not override basic freedoms, for that would imply that freedoms are not contained within the concept of justice. But, in certain circumstances, fairness may justifiably restrict certain freedoms in the pursuit of justice itself.

Electoral laws promote fairness only to the extent that voters have a reasonable opportunity to assess the choices presented to them by those who seek elected office. This condition requires that election discourse not be dominated by those whose resources enable them to overwhelm the efforts of others to present their case to the electorate. If discourse is dominated by those with the greatest resources, the equality of voters and the freedom to make choices about who should govern are impaired.

Elections are unlike the economic marketplace where fundamental rights and freedoms do not presuppose that individuals are equal. In the marketplace, fairness merely prescribes equal opportunity to participate; it does not restrict the ability of individuals or groups to accumulate resources and use them to advance their economic interests. In sharp contrast, the electoral process is predicated on the equality of the vote and of the right to be a candidate. This equality is granted so that each voter has the same opportunity to influence the outcome of elections.

It is important to emphasize that over the course of our political history we have progressively asserted the primacy of political equality. For instance, changes to Canadian electoral law have removed inequalities in the right to vote – in particular, disqualifications from the franchise based on property, sex and race. Through efforts to draw constituency boundaries that recognize equality of the vote, we have further asserted the fundamental value of 'one person, one vote'.

At the same time, we have also progressively adopted measures that acknowledge that the right to vote can be politically meaningful and the equality of voters assured only if the electoral process itself is fair. Our independent and impartial system to register voters and administer the vote thus promotes fairness, as well as the integrity of the electoral process. Later, rules governing radio broadcasting were introduced to promote fair allocation of time so that candidates and parties would not be overwhelmed by those with greater financial resources and voters would be given the opportunity to hear and assess different points of view.

In 1974, the *Canada Elections Act* was reformed to limit the election expenses of candidates and registered political parties, place restrictions on independent election spending by individuals and groups, add tax credits for political contributions, and partially reimburse with public funds the election expenses of registered parties and candidates. This broadening of fairness explicitly recognized the role of money in election campaigns.

Canadians not only accept but also strongly support fair election spending. Spending limits on parties and candidates, restrictions on independent expenditures by individuals and groups, and regulated access to the broadcast media serve to ensure that electoral contests are not determined primarily by disparities in the financial resources of competing candidates, parties or other interested individuals and groups.

To promote fairness, the foundations of the current system must be preserved. Its scope must be extended, however, to acknowledge that access to elected office includes the rules governing the nomination of candidates by political parties. By ignoring this dimension of the electoral process, the current electoral law undermines fairness. Our rules governing access to registered party status under the *Canada Elections Act* and the basis for providing public funding and access to the broadcast media must also be reformed to enhance fairness in election discourse.

Fairness also demands reform of the election finance regime. This regime provides for partial public reimbursement of the election expenses of candidates and parties. It also regulates election expenses of parties, candidates, and other individuals and groups. Reforms to public funding through reimbursements are required to ensure that public funds received by parties and candidates reflect their electoral support. Reforms are also needed to clarify the scope of election expenses to provide a fairer system of documenting election finance. Further, the law must be comprehensible to the thousands of volunteers who participate in our electoral process.

Finally, fairness demands that the election finance regime limit the ability of candidates, parties, and other individuals and groups to incur election expenses. Election expenses, therefore, must be defined to include the cost of any goods or services used during an election to promote or oppose, directly or indirectly, the election of a candidate or the program or policies of a candidate or party, or to approve or disapprove of an action advocated or opposed by a candidate, party or party leader.

At the same time, limits on election expenses must extend to other individuals and groups to ensure fairness. If only candidates and parties were limited in their election spending, 'independent expenditures' could give direct or indirect advantage to one or more candidates or parties. This would jeopardize the fairness that the electoral finance regime promotes. This is not merely a hypothetical outcome.

The unfettered spending by individuals and groups in the 1988 general election was a result of deficiencies in the *Canada Elections Act* combined with 1984 decisions that rendered inoperative the provisions in the Act on independent expenditures. The Act prohibits independent expenditures to directly promote or oppose candidates or parties; however, it permits independent expenditures that promote 'issues' as long as such advertising does not directly promote or oppose a candidate or party. Although this section of the Act was not in force in the 1988 general election, that election conclusively demonstrated that allowing unlimited independent election spending on 'issues' would not have adequately addressed the issue of fairness. No meaningful distinction can be drawn between the promotion of a 'partisan' position, on the one hand, and an 'issue' position, on the other. Any position on an election issue will inevitably be linked, directly or indirectly, to candidates or parties.

Fairness is a pressing, legitimate concern of the electoral process. Any law limiting election spending must be linked to the fundamental principle of fairness and, at the same time, impinge on the freedom of expression as little as possible. Such a law could not be justified if it ruled out independent expenditures completely. On the grounds of fairness, as well as freedom of expression, individuals and groups should be able to participate in an election campaign, to enrich electoral debate. This is not the same, however, as spending freely to affect the outcome of the election.

The challenge, therefore, is to draft a law that upholds the objective of fairness while meeting constitutional tests and judicial standards. Without such a law, the role of money in electoral competition would be unrestrained. We have seen the consequences of the U.S. electoral experience with no restraints on election spending and conclude that it is imperative that Canada not travel the same road. Our traditions and basic values, which are affirmed through the electoral process, are at stake at this critical juncture: they must be preserved and promoted. Our recommendations are designed to promote fairness in the electoral process by limiting the election expenses of candidates, parties, and other individuals and groups. These limits ensure a fair expression of opinions and views from all quarters, partisan and otherwise, and healthy and vigorous competition between those seeking office.

Enhancing Public Confidence in the Integrity of the Electoral Process

The integrity of the electoral process must be enhanced if Canadians are to be fully confident that their democratic rights are secure. Among other things, integrity means that any undue influence from financial contributions to candidates and parties is curtailed, that the policies and practices of the media in election coverage and political advertising do not manipulate voters, that elections are administered independently and impartially, and that the election law is effectively and reasonably enforced.

The Canadian requirement of full disclosure of contributions to candidates and political parties, and their expenditures, inspires public confidence. Inherent in disclosure are the principles of transparency and accountability. These principles must apply to the financial affairs of candidates, nomination and party leadership contestants, Members of Parliament, parties and registered constituency associations. These financial affairs must be open to public scrutiny. To achieve this objective, disclosure must be broad, provide timely reports, ensure sufficient information and produce information in a format that facilitates public access and media coverage.

Limits on the size and sources of political contributions are also part of the election finance laws of some provinces and countries. At issue is whether the integrity of the electoral process requires one or more of these limits in addition to spending limits and full disclosure. The need for such limits must also be assessed against the rights of individuals and groups to contribute financially to the electoral process, as well as against the need for candidates and parties to conduct competitive and informative election campaigns.

For candidates, political parties and voters, the media are an essential component of election campaigns. Candidates and parties rely on the media to communicate their campaign messages to voters, and voters receive much of their information about elections from the media. Although the role of the news media has changed over time, with the advent of new technologies and the evolution of the party system, news coverage has never been regulated. Even before the enshrining of press freedom in the *Canadian Charter of Rights and Freedoms*, the independent role of the news media was recognized. At the same time, the importance of news coverage to parties, candidates and voters was generally accepted, especially in the television age. News organizations have traditionally accorded considerable importance to election coverage, although concerns have been expressed that this commitment is declining.

With the emergence of radio broadcasting came a recognition that parties needed some form of direct access to voters. Parties began to purchase broadcasting time in the 1920s and the Canadian Broadcasting Corporation (CBC) developed regulations for free-time election broadcasting in the 1930s. The purpose of the CBC regulations was to ensure fair access to broadcasting time for all recognized parties. Except for a ban on 'dramatization' in party broadcasts, which was in force from 1936 to 1968 (Boyer 1983, 370), the regulations have focused on questions of time allocation and access rather than content. In addition, the regulations provided for a blackout on campaign advertising at the beginning and end of campaigns and a ban on advertising on broadcast outlets outside the country to preserve the integrity of the rules regarding time allocation and expenditure limits. Content has been essentially a matter for the parties and controversy has focused primarily on the allocation of time among the parties.

The reporting of public opinion polls during campaigns has also been controversial in recent elections. These concerns involve the validity of polls, their effect on media coverage of campaigns, the quality of media reporting of polls, the publication of 'polls' that do not meet accepted professional standards, and the effect of polls on the decisions of voters and voter turnout. What must be addressed are the responsibilities of pollsters and the media for the accuracy, reliability and availability of polling data and the right of voters to acquire information relevant to the election.

Public confidence in any democratic system of representative government demands efficient election administration and impartial enforcement of the electoral law. Since 1920, elections have been administered and the election law enforced under the general supervision of the chief electoral officer of Canada, an independent officer appointed by the House of Commons.

Since that time the office of the chief electoral officer, now known as Elections Canada, has functioned, and has been seen to function, impartially. It has also become known for its effectiveness and commitment to providing world-class service to Canadian voters. The effectiveness and cost efficiency of elections administration have been hampered, however, by many provisions in the *Canada Elections Act* that do not recognize current realities or changes in technology. The Act must be sufficiently comprehensive to ensure the integrity of the electoral process and its immunity to pressures from the government of the day. At the same time, the Act must be sufficiently flexible to accommodate current realities and continuing technological change. Election administrators provide one of the most essential public services in a democracy, and their effectiveness should be facilitated, not impeded, by electoral law.

The enforcement provisions of the election law must inspire confidence in the integrity of the process. The current law patently does not do so. It fails to distinguish properly between election fraud and administrative infractions. Amendments to the *Canada Elections Act* have greatly added to the offences under the Act that are administrative in character and relate primarily to election and party finance. Moreover, most alleged offences concern the Act's administrative requirements.

Minor administrative infractions under the Act should not be treated as criminal offences. As the Commissioner of the Royal Canadian Mounted Police (RCMP) indicated clearly at our public hearings (Ottawa, 13 March 1990),* the RCMP's current procedures for investigation and for prosecution before the regular courts convey a misleading message to the public and thereby undermine public confidence in the integrity of the electoral system. For this reason, and because the rules to enforce the *Canada Elections Act* treat those who are investigated or prosecuted for administrative infractions inappropriately and thus unfairly, the current rules lead to unsatisfactory enforcement. When offences are prosecuted before the courts, the onus on the prosecution is increased, and very few complaints are prosecuted. The enforcement of administrative requirements, especially those affecting candidates and registered parties, thus demands reform.

THE ISSUE OF PROPORTIONAL REPRESENTATION

Although our mandate encompasses the way in which Canada organizes its electoral system for choosing members of the House of Commons, we decided at the outset to retain the single-member constituency, plurality voting system (sometimes referred to as 'first-past-the-post'). The Royal Commission on the Economic Union and Development Prospects for Canada – the Macdonald Commission – considered alternatives to our present system, including proportional representation, in its report (Canada, Royal Commission 1985) and research studies. (Irvine 1985) But so far none of these alternative systems has been placed before the House of Commons. We therefore do not recommend changes to this aspect of the electoral system, even though several interveners raised this issue at our public hearings.

Compared with our present electoral system, a proportional representation system would mean that the membership of the House of Commons would reflect more closely the relationship between votes cast for each political party and the number of seats won by each party, both nationally and in each region or province. As Table 1.1 indicates, countries that use proportional representation systems and have more than two competitive political parties achieve greater proportionality nationally between votes cast for parties and seats won.

---

* Transcripts of testimony before the Royal Commission are cited by the city where the hearing took place and the date.

Measured against countries that use proportional representation, Canada does well nationally. Our system does less well, however, in ensuring proportionality at the level of regions and provinces. In the recent past, for instance, each of the three largest political parties secured a reasonable percentage of the popular vote in a province only to find itself with few, if any, MPs in the House of Commons from that province. (Cairns 1968; Seidle 1988) An argument in favour of proportional representation, therefore, is that by having MPs better reflect their party's popular vote in each province, parliamentary caucuses would generally be more regionally representative than under our current system.

Table 1.1
Index of proportionality in recent elections

Electoral system	Country (election year)	Proportionality index
Single-member plurality systems	Canada (1988)	86
	Great Britain (1987)	80
	New Zealand (1987)	88
	United States (1988)	93
Proportional representation systems (various types)	Ireland (1987)	91
	Belgium (1987)	94
	Israel (1988)	96
	Federal Republic of Germany (1987)	99
	Denmark (1987)	96
	Sweden (1988)	96
	Italy (1987)	95

Source: The data on the party votes and seats are from the Inter-Parliamentary Union and National Election results reported in *Electoral Studies.*

Note: The proportionality index is the difference between the percentage of votes received and the percentage of seats won by each party, summed across the parties and normalized by adding both gains and losses in proportionality. It has a range from 0 to 100; the closer the index is to 100, the more each party's percentage of the vote approaches its percentage of seats won. The index as used here is a modification of an index for the 'deviation from proportionality' as applied by Taagepera and Shugart (1989, 104–5), and formally is:

$$\text{Proportionality index} = 100 - \frac{\sum |s_i - v_i|}{2}$$

where:
s_i is the percentage of seats won by party i,
and
v_i is the percentage of votes received by party i.

Although such a change to the electoral system could not guarantee that national political parties in the House of Commons would be more responsive to representing and reconciling regional interests, including different interests within a region, than is now the case, it would increase the likelihood of this result. It would also help mitigate the public perception that particular provincial and regional interests, at times, are inadequately represented in the caucuses of the largest parliamentary parties and in the cabinet.

This being said, the rate of legislative turnover in the House of Commons indicates that the present electoral system is responsive to changes in voters' preferences. During the period from 1979 to 1988, when four general elections took place, on average 24.9 per cent of MPs seeking re-election were defeated. In contrast, during the same period, the rate of defeat for members of the United States House of Representatives was 6 per cent. Moreover, the rates of defeat in the last two Canadian federal elections – 39.7 and 26.6 per cent, respectively – were considerably higher than in the 1979 and 1980 elections (20.3 and 15.0 per cent, respectively) (adapted from Atkinson and Docherty 1991).

In countries with a proportional representation system, political parties most often establish the order of the lists of candidates, which affects the likelihood of a particular candidate being elected. In some cases, voters have no choice but to support the party list as presented. Where the law allows voters to indicate a preference within a list, only a small proportion do so; sometimes the parties discourage voters from taking this step and, in effect, altering the order of candidates. (Bogdanor 1985, 9) The Canadian electoral system allows much greater scope for voters to judge the merits of particular candidates. The resulting responsiveness to voter preference is one of our system's greatest strengths.

A second argument in favour of proportional representation is that it promotes the representation of major segments of the population or groups that are not geographically concentrated, such as women or ethno-cultural communities. Women, for instance, tend to have greater representation in countries that use proportional representation. Contrary to what some have claimed, however, the international experience clearly indicates that this outcome is the consequence of political parties adopting male-female quotas or other measures of strengthening the position of women candidates. In countries that use proportional representation but whose parties do not take such action, the representation of women is similar to the Canadian record or worse.

Compared with our present electoral system, proportional representation would require MPs to be elected from multi-member constituencies, rather than single-member constituencies. Under proportional representation, each multi-member constituency would have a much larger population and cover a much larger geographical area than is now the case, if the House of Commons were to remain the same size. To achieve a sufficient degree of proportionality between votes cast and seats won by each party, such a system would require that each constituency elect five or more MPs and therefore be at least five times its present size in population and territory. This would mean that virtually all medium-sized cities – Calgary, for example – would each form one constituency, electing at least five members. Prince Edward Island and Newfoundland would be one constituency each; Nova Scotia, New Brunswick, Manitoba and Saskatchewan would have at most two constituencies each. Constituencies in the rural areas of the larger provinces would cover most of each province's non-urban territory. These larger constituencies would present many difficulties to Members of Parliament who must act on behalf of their constituents.

A better regional balance in the caucuses of national parties – perhaps the most compelling case for proportional representation in Canada – could be achieved by using such a system. But there is an alternative to having such a system apply to elections for the House of Commons. The Macdonald Commission presented a persuasive case that a Senate elected by a proportional representation system could achieve this goal. (Canada, Royal Commission 1985; Aucoin 1985) An elected Senate, as in Australia, would inevitably have elections based on political parties. At the same time, a Senate elected by a proportional representation system would better ensure that the parliamentary caucuses of national parties, including MPs and senators, represented the various regions. In addition, a more equitable distribution of Senate seats to the provinces would provide the less populated provinces with a greater influence in the parliamentary caucuses of national parties. The issues of how an elected Senate might be chosen and the distribution of Senate seats are among those the government of Canada has referred to a special joint committee, which began hearings on its constitutional proposals in autumn 1991.

THE ORGANIZATION OF OUR REPORT

In Volume 1, we devote a chapter to each of the above six objectives. In these chapters, we assess the performance of the current electoral law and procedures to determine how well the objectives are being met. This assessment, in turn, suggests where reform is needed and leads to our recommendations.

Volume 2 takes a more specialized approach to the mechanics of the electoral system, detailing specific legal and administrative changes required to implement our recommendations in Volume 1.

Recommendations in volumes 1 and 2 fall into two broad categories: recommendations to change electoral law and recommendations directed to participants in the electoral system – political parties, election officials, the media and polling organizations. The second category of recommendations is intended to convey to participants what we heard from Canadians about the electoral process: their experiences and their proposals for reform.

Volume 3 recommends changes to electoral law in the form of a draft legislative proposal for a new Canada Elections Act. In Volume 4, we present an overview and a sampling of the assessments and opinions offered at our public hearings. This volume also summarizes the presentations and discussions at our symposiums and seminars and contains the entire report of the Committee for Aboriginal Electoral Reform.

If all our proposals are adopted, there will be no increase in total costs to the federal treasury. We have identified a number of areas where costs can be reduced. Among other things, expenditures can be reduced in the registration process, where there is unnecessary duplication by the federal government in conducting enumerations in some provinces. Public money is also wasted in the way in which the vote-at card is distributed to voters and in the printing of voters lists. The savings arising from our proposed changes to these activities would cover the costs of our initiatives to improve the institutions of our electoral democracy. Finally, our proposal to reduce the length of campaigns will reduce the costs for all concerned.

The sizeable task set out before our Commission would have been impossible to complete without the highly competent and dedicated people who agreed to join us. We were most fortunate to be assisted by such an outstanding team. The high calibre of assistance we received from all our staff – research co-ordinators and analysts, librarians, editors, translators, and administrative, clerical and secretarial personnel – is worthy of acknowledgement and praise; their names are listed in Volume 4, and we extend our thanks to all of them.

While it is difficult to single out any individual contribution in light of the remarkable efforts of so many, we would be remiss not to record our special gratitude for the work of the senior members of the team who were so critical to the success of the enterprise: Guy Goulard, Executive Director; Peter Aucoin, Director of Research; Jean-Marc Hamel, Special Adviser to the Chairman; Jules Brière, Senior Adviser, Legislation; Richard Rochefort, Director of Communications and Publishing; and Maurice Lacasse, Director of Finance and Administration.

We are also grateful for the co-operation we received from political parties when conducting our research projects and symposiums, the assistance given us by federal, provincial and territorial election offices, the invaluable research undertaken by specialists from universities and the private sector, and the contribution of individuals and groups who appeared at our public hearings.

CONCLUSION

The six objectives we have adopted to develop recommendations for electoral reform go to the heart of Canadian electoral democracy. In so doing, they address how best to secure the constitutional rights of Canadians, as individuals and as members of communities. They also address how best to secure the fundamental democratic values of the Canadian polity.

In many parts of Canada's electoral law and electoral process, these objectives lead to conclusions on electoral reform that are relatively straightforward. They easily meet the tests of common sense and practicality, and they respond to public concerns. In some instances, however, the issues involve trade-offs among fundamental values and are therefore highly contentious. Precisely because so much is at stake in any comprehensive reform, we have recognized and addressed the presence of conflicting values in examining the six objectives which should underlie the reform of our electoral democracy. Our goal was also to enhance the legitimacy of the Canadian House of Commons and of our institutions of governance. Legitimacy is a most important resource, if only for the economy it allows in the use of all the others.

"Our constitution is named a democracy, because it is in the hands not of the few but of the many," Thucydides explained to the ancient Athenians. It remains the cardinal rule today. The genius of a free and democratic people is manifested in its capacity and willingness to devise institutions and laws that secure fairness and equitable opportunities for citizens to influence democratic governance.

Our recommendations, adopted unanimously, ensure that the Canadian electoral process truly reflects the Canadian ideals of a free *and* democratic society.

2

THE DEMOCRATIC RIGHTS
OF VOTERS

THE RIGHT TO VOTE

THE *CANADIAN CHARTER of Rights and Freedoms* gives every citizen the right to vote subject only to such reasonable limits prescribed by law as can be demonstrably justified in a free and democratic society. The *Canada Elections Act* requires that qualified voters be at least 18 years old; it also disqualifies certain categories of citizens. The Charter introduced a new dimension to the franchise by making it a constitutional right of citizenship; this means that any disqualifications in the elections act must be justified under the Charter. Thus the onus of the argument has been shifted. No longer must a case be made to *extend* the franchise; rather, each restriction on the right to vote must be demonstrated to be justified in a free and democratic society.

We do not underestimate the impact of the Charter; but the right to vote must also be seen in the context of the historical evolution of representative governance and the individual rights implicit in it. The experience of the United States, with its long history of judicial review and a bill of rights, demonstrates that constitutional entrenchment of individual rights does not automatically override all legislative restrictions on such rights, including the right to vote. Canadians' experience with extending the franchise testifies to how we have transformed our political culture since Confederation, even though the right to vote was not enshrined in a written constitution.

This increasingly inclusive approach to the franchise has had the effects that many early proponents of democratic reform hoped for and predicted. Contrary to some early fears, extended political participation has not resulted in mob rule or debilitating factionalism, however imperfect our structures and policies have been. On the contrary, successive extensions of the franchise at various times in our history have corrected many injustices.

We do not therefore see the Charter guarantee as a threat. The Charter does not imply that rights are absolute; limitations can be imposed under certain conditions. We therefore assessed the current exclusions in the electoral law in a manner that respects the Charter as an integral part of our constitutional values but recognizes the need to uphold the dignity of democratic citizenship in relation to the significance of the franchise for the Canadian political community.

Our public hearings provided ample evidence that changes in the franchise are required. We heard many presentations about the need to enfranchise

Canadians who are now disfranchised for one reason or another. These interveners affirmed that the franchise is a matter of utmost political significance. The legitimacy of our political system rests on the franchise, for it is the principal means for the governed to express their consent; it should therefore be as inclusive as necessary to provide this essential legitimacy. We must thus assess each limitation as a question that goes to the heart of what we consider to be a free and democratic society.

We acknowledge that preserving this quality of our society demands some restrictions on the right to vote. For instance, it is inappropriate for very young children to have this right because they cannot make informed, rational and free choices about who should represent them.

Beyond the exclusion of young children, however, who should and should not vote is open to debate. In answering this question, a society is expressing its most fundamental beliefs about who should participate in the electoral process. This is vividly expressed in our history. At Confederation, the electoral law excluded the vast majority of citizens, primarily on the bases of economic class, sex and race. Removing these exclusions required that concepts of democratic citizenship be redefined. By our current standards, these former exclusions patently belong to history.

Past struggles to extend the right to vote were characterized by conflicting political values and vested political interests. The exclusion of non-propertied men, all women, and members of various racial groups was partly a function of political culture. It was also a function of the perceived partisan advantages in excluding certain categories of citizens.

By comparison, the present exclusions appear to have few, if any, significant partisan dimensions; rather, they stem from political principles and values. They are no less easy to resolve for this, but at the least they can be considered as questions of the public interest in franchise reform.

To address these exclusions, we must consider the meaning of the vote – the right of franchise – within representative democratic government. This requires examination of the basic values inherent in the idea of political representation.

Representation as Consent

Representative Government as Indirect Democracy
Our system of government is essentially an 'indirect' democracy. Citizens do not govern themselves directly; instead, they elect representatives to govern them. In this way, the consent of citizens is secured, however indirectly and imperfectly.

Between elections, these representatives have a mandate to govern – to make and administer laws – subject legally only to the constitutional distribution of authority between the different branches and orders of government and to the constitutional rights of citizens. Indeed, under the law, candidates for the House of Commons are barred from signing pledges that would restrict their freedom of action if elected.

The right of citizens to elect their governors is partly a matter of securing the legitimacy of the political system. It is also a matter of ensuring the representation of interests in the governing of society. The right to elect representatives is thus fundamental to a free and democratic society. Other rights, such as freedom of expression and association, are no less important as a consequence, but they flow from the political sovereignty of the people, as expressed most effectively in the right to vote.

Indirect Democracy and Citizen Risks

In choosing representative government, citizens restrict their participation in the governance of their society; they transfer the authority to govern to their representatives. In large societies, this is the only practical means to secure orderly and efficient government while allowing for a measure of citizen participation. The fact that citizens can elect and 'retire' these representatives at regular intervals serves to hold them responsible and accountable for what they do. Thus elections become the critical method of reconciling order with freedom.

But conferring a mandate to govern presents significant risks for citizens. (Smith 1991 RC) Chief among them are the tyranny of the majority over minorities, the abuse of power by elected representatives, and the undermining of the public good by excessive factionalism among citizens and their representatives. Debate about whose consent should count in the workings of representative government has thus focused on the theory and practice of the franchise.

Minimizing Risks

There are several ways to minimize the risks inherent in representative government. Frequent elections are one way. Where concern about these risks was high, elections are more frequent than in states where elected representatives were accorded greater deference. This is illustrated by the contrast between the two-year terms of members of the U.S. House of Representatives and the maximum five-year term of members of the British House of Commons.

A second way to minimize risks is to extend the election of officials to the executive and even the judicial branches of government; hence the contrast between the U.S. and Canadian traditions, for instance.

A third way is to make the executive branch responsible to the elected legislative branch and publicly accountable for its policies and programs through legislative debate and scrutiny. This is the case in the parliamentary system. Alternatively, the executive and legislative branches may have separate powers, so that each acts as a check on the other, as in the presidential-congressional system.

A fourth way to minimize risks is to allow citizens to initiate the recall of their elected representatives between elections; some U.S. states have this provision. A fifth way, found in a few political systems, is to permit citizens to initiate referendums on matters of public policy, with legislators bound by the result. Finally, in some political systems, the legislators themselves may put matters to a referendum and be bound by the result. Recall and referendums are discussed in Volume 2 of our report.

Even in political systems that use these devices of 'direct' democracy, elected representatives remain primary in the governing process. The rise of the modern administrative state has served to ensure this, and nowhere has it been more evident than in systems where the executive branch has control over the legislative branch through cohesive political parties. This is clearly the experience in Canada.

The Evolution of the Franchise

Democratic citizenship under representative government implies the right to vote – the right to have a say in what values and interests are given priority in formulating public policy. At issue is the exercise of political power. In Canada, the franchise has been characterized by a complicated evolution of qualifications and disqualifications driven primarily by evolving public opinion on who should vote.

Regulation of the Franchise

At Confederation, no agreement could be reached about qualifications for the franchise. As a consequence, and in what was meant to be a temporary measure, the existing qualifications in each of the original provinces were used for federal elections. This situation remained until *The Electoral Franchise Act* of 1885.

From 1867 to 1885, the provinces varied in their approach to the franchise. In all cases there were property or income qualifications; only white males over the age of 21 who met these conditions were eligible to vote. In all provinces, however, property or income qualifications were set at a level that enabled the majority of male heads of households to qualify. It has been estimated that, by 1882, those who could vote made up approximately 16 per cent of the population in Quebec, Nova Scotia and New Brunswick, and 20 per cent of the population of Ontario. In Manitoba, the low property qualification and the primarily male population meant that 35 per cent of the population had the vote, whereas in British Columbia the relatively small number of white males meant that only 11 per cent of the population was eligible to vote, as seen in Table 2.1.

In 1885, Parliament adopted *The Electoral Franchise Act*. The Act reflected the concerns of Sir John A. Macdonald's Conservative government that Liberal-governed provinces were using their control over the federal franchise to expand the right to vote in ways that advanced Liberal interests, particularly in moves to enfranchise urban artisans and wage earners. The new federal law therefore set the property qualification at a level above the provincial average, thereby restricting the franchise slightly. This first attempt at a federal franchise did little to promote uniformity in the right to vote. Not only did it establish variations in the property requirement from city to city, it also granted special concessions to maritime fishermen in its definition of property (defining fishing equipment as real property) and enfranchised only those Indian persons living east of Manitoba.

Table 2.1
Percentage of total population enfranchised, selected federal general elections, by province, 1867–1940

Province	1867	1882	1891	1900	1911	1917	1921	1930	1940
Ontario	16.5	20.2	26.4	27.1	27.4	39.4	58.6	55.2	61.8
Quebec	16.1	16.6	20.1	21.1	22.7	20.6	44.8	47.0	54.0
Nova Scotia	14.0	15.1	22.1	24.8	27.8	29.7	56.2	53.8	58.1
New Brunswick	15.2	16.9	21.1	27.3	28.7	29.9	52.7	50.7	55.1
Manitoba		34.8	30.3	27.9	21.4	29.3	41.8	46.9	58.2
British Columbia		11.0	13.3	21.9	21.2	38.4	44.0	48.0	57.8
Prince Edward Island		*	22.1	*	*	33.3	52.9	53.4	58.2
Saskatchewan					28.9	22.9	44.0	44.5	53.8
Alberta					28.6	32.5	46.5	41.6	53.2

Source: Ward 1963, 211–32.

*Not available.

By 1898, universal suffrage for Caucasian males had been adopted in all but two provinces for provincial elections. A Liberal federal government, however, was unable to reconcile the expectation of universal suffrage for males in much of the country with opposition from Quebec and Nova Scotia. The government escaped the dilemma by allowing the defini-tion of the franchise to revert to the provinces. The result was universal manhood suffrage for whites in all provinces except Nova Scotia and Quebec.

The 1917 *War-time Elections Act* was introduced by the government of Sir Robert Borden in alliance with a wing of the Liberal Party not adverse to military conscription. The Act reasserted federal control over the franchise for federal elections. Among other things, this paved the way for the 1920 *Dominion Elections Act*, which established the first genuinely uniform federal franchise.

Female Suffrage

Two years previously, in 1918, Parliament had passed legislation adopting universal female suffrage (again with the exception of Indian persons living on reserves). This action also followed the wartime exigency; women who served or had close relatives in the forces were granted the right to vote under the *Military Voters Act, 1917* and the *War-time Elections Act* respectively.

Before 1836, women who met the property qualifications in the British North American colonies had the right to vote, although there is no evidence that this right was exercised except in Quebec. (Cleverdon 1974, 214) Between 1836 and 1851, however, the colonies all passed laws explicitly disfranchising women; these laws continued in force following Confederation. By the end of the last century, the women's suffrage movement had arisen in Canada, as it had in Great Britain and the United States. Canadian women formed organizations such as the Canadian Suffrage Association, the Women's Christian Temperance Union, the National Council of Women, and the Women's Institutes to advocate extending the franchise to women.

By 1917, all the western provinces and Ontario had given women the vote. (Cleverdon 1974, 105) Pressure was mounting on Parliament to ensure that women who were enfranchised provincially would also be able to vote federally, given that the franchise was still defined by provincial law, and to extend this right to women in Quebec and the maritime provinces. Facing an election fought on the issue of conscription for wartime military service, the Borden government considered its options, including the enfranchisement of women. To maximize the number of female voters sympathetic to conscription, the government decided to grant the franchise to the close female relatives of men in active military service – much to the dismay of many suffragist organizations, which saw no reason to limit the extension of the franchise in this manner.

Owing its re-election in large part to newly enfranchised women, the government acted quickly to extend the franchise fully. Thus the franchise for women was enacted in 1918, with only a handful of MPs objecting on the grounds that women's "sanctified ... place" was in the home. (Ward 1963, 230)

Ethnicity and Race

At various times and for various intervals access to the vote has been denied on the grounds of ethnic or racial origin. The 1885 *Electoral Franchise Act,* for example, defined 'person' to exclude Chinese and Mongolians. This did not change until 1898, when the Liberal government's *Electoral Franchise Act* stated that the federal franchise would extend to all persons disqualified provincially because they belonged to some "class". The 1917 *War-time Elections Act* excluded from voting naturalized British subjects born in an enemy country and naturalized after 1902. The franchise was not extended to Canadians of Japanese descent until 1948.

The 1920 *Dominion Elections Act,* which finally put the federal franchise fully within the control of Parliament, did not provide for full universal suffrage. Rather, it disfranchised anyone disfranchised by provincial laws because of their racial origin, unless they were war veterans. This meant that Canadians of Japanese, Chinese and East Indian descent in British Columbia and Canadians of Chinese origin in Saskatchewan were denied the vote.

Other groups were disfranchised indirectly. Doukhobors and Mennonites were effectively disfranchised when conscientious objectors were denied the vote in 1917, a provision that was not repealed until 1955.

Some provinces also used language qualifications to discriminate against members of certain ethnic groups. (Qualter 1970, 11–12)

Aboriginal People

Aboriginal people – with the exception of the Métis, who have never been singled out in either federal or provincial electoral law – were denied the vote for many decades. The franchise for the Inuit was never seriously considered in the first several decades after Confederation. Because of their geographic isolation, they simply were not given the opportunity to vote. In 1934, however, Parliament added to the list of those disqualified "every Esquimau person, whether born in Canada or elsewhere". This provision was repealed in 1950.

The denial of the vote to Indian persons was accomplished in a more complicated but no less effective manner. From 1867 to 1885 and 1889 to 1917, this took the form of provincial property qualifications and express prohibitions in provincial statutes. From 1885 to 1898, Indian males not living on a reserve who met the relevant provincial property qualification and resided east of Manitoba could vote in federal elections. This limited right to vote was the result of a compromise amendment by the Conservative government to its own reform bill, following Prime Minister Macdonald's efforts to secure the right to vote for all Indian males who could meet the normal property qualification. The opposition to Macdonald's original proposal is well illustrated in the following exchange in the Commons between Macdonald and David Mills, a former minister responsible for Indian affairs:

> Mr. Mills. What we are anxious to know is whether the hon. gentleman proposes to give other than enfranchised Indians[1] votes.
> Sir John A. Macdonald. Yes.
> Mr. Mills. Indians residing on a reservation?
> Sir John A. Macdonald. Yes, if they have the necessary property qualification.
> Mr. Mills. An Indian who cannot make a contract for himself, who can neither buy nor sell anything without the consent of the Superintendent General – an Indian who is not enfranchised?
> Sir John A. Macdonald. Whether he is enfranchised or not.
> Mr. Mills. This will include Indians in Manitoba and British Columbia?
> Sir John A. Macdonald. Yes.
> Mr. Mills. Poundmaker and Big Bear?
> Sir John A. Macdonald. Yes.
> Mr. Mills. So that they can go from a scalping party to the polls. (Canada, House of Commons, *Debates*, 30 April 1885, 1484)

In 1917, the *Military Voters Act* extended the franchise to Indian persons on active service, and the 1920 *Dominion Elections Act* guaranteed the continuation of this right to veterans. But the Act also disqualified Indians living on reserves. In 1944, the wartime amendments to the *Dominion*

Elections Act gave the vote to Indian persons who had served in the forces and to their spouses. In 1950, another amendment gave the vote to Indian people who were willing to waive their tax-exempt status with respect to personal property. Finally, in 1960, the government of John Diefenbaker introduced an amendment to the elections act to secure universal suffrage for Indian people.

The Franchise and Democratic Citizenship

This brief history of the franchise shows that exclusions have been justified, explicitly or implicitly, on the basis of criteria developed over time in relation to the meaning of democratic citizenship. This evolution reflected similar developments that transformed democracies in Europe and the United States.

Interests at Stake

Before universal male suffrage was adopted, the definition of democratic citizenship assumed that the interests to be represented in government were first and foremost economic in character. Those who did not own property lacked a valid claim to participate in the election of representatives; they were deemed not to have a sufficient stake in the governance of society. At best, those without property had their interests, such as they were, represented by legislators elected by property owners. All citizens might then be considered to be 'represented', but not in the direct manner of those with the right to vote.

Struggles to expand the franchise were thus efforts to redefine the meaning of democratic citizenship. Demands for universal male suffrage in the last century and the first decade of this century required a new understanding of the interests at stake in representative government – a shift from an economic definition to a definition of individuals as members of a political community.

Although much more was involved, women were also excluded from the franchise for reasons associated with an economic definition of political rights. The property criterion was used to deny them the right to vote; few women owned property, and women were considered 'property' themselves – the property of their fathers or husbands. As such they were 'represented' by the electoral choices of their male relatives.

Indian people were also denied the right to vote partly for this reason; those living on reserves did not have personal title to their land and were exempt from taxes on real or personal property. For these two reasons, among others, they were considered not to have a sufficient stake in the Canadian political system. As Richard Bartlett has noted, this second factor constituted "a curious reversal of the slogan 'no taxation without representation' to 'no representation without taxation'." (Bartlett 1980, 164)

Although Indian persons living on reserves were denied the right to vote until 1960, they were entitled to vote if they had been on active duty in either of the two world wars or in the Korean conflict. The Department of Indian Affairs, commenting on this extension of the right to vote in 1917, pointed out that "owing to the large number of Indians who have enlisted in the Canadian Expeditionary Force, ... it has been contended, and justly so, that men who render service of such a nature to their country should be entitled to the fullest rights of citizenship". (Canada, Department of Indian Affairs 1918, 20) The Department went on to note that fully 35 per cent of the male Indian population of military age had enlisted during the First World War.

The treatment of certain racial minorities also had an economic dimension. This was especially the case with workers brought to Canada from Asia, who were seen as a threat to working-class interests; their exclusion from the franchise was as much an effort to deny them full participation in Canada's economic life as it was a denial of their right to participate in politics.

The significance of the property criterion was reinforced by the property qualifications imposed on candidates for election to the House of Commons. Property qualifications for those appointed to the Senate were even stricter, as the Senate's perceived role was in part to protect the rights of property.

Over time, this criterion was increasingly at odds with political sentiment in Canada and abroad. The evolution of political opinion first lowered the property qualification, then caused it to be removed altogether. This step acknowledged that property possession was no longer considered an indicator of the capacity to be a good citizen. Eliminating property qualifications redefined the understanding of democratic citizenship in a profound way. Citizens could now vote as a matter of political right, not as a function of their economic stake in society's governance.

At the same time, the idea of a stake in society remains a cornerstone of democratic citizenship, reflected in the fact that the right to vote is extended to citizens, not to all residents of Canada. That right is also limited, with only a few exceptions, by the provision that Canadian citizens who wish to exercise their franchise must live in Canada.

Rational and Informed Vote

The second major criterion respecting the franchise – albeit one that has always been more implicit than explicit in our electoral law – is that voters be qualified to cast a rational and informed vote. By this standard, children are not given the franchise. Adults judged to be mentally ill or mentally disabled have been denied the vote. Indian persons have been denied the right to vote on this ground: they were considered 'uneducated'. The rationale has also been used as one of many reasons to deny prisoners the right to vote; prisoners were considered incapable of casting an informed vote because they are isolated from society. In each case, the assumption was that voting requires the exercise of independent judgement and the capacity to engage in political discourse with other citizens.

The most numerous group excluded by this criterion was women. Even removing the property qualification for males did not bring about universal suffrage. Simply put, men did not consider women their intellectual equals. Women's struggle to secure the franchise required that they transform the political culture, changing its definition of democratic citizenship by overcoming sexist assumptions about their fitness as persons. This was no easy task, as illustrated by how long it took the women's suffrage movement to achieve its goal.

It is obvious that the criterion of a rational and informed vote can no longer be used to discriminate on the basis of sex. The current electoral law continues to use this criterion to exclude certain categories of citizens, however, including those under the age of 18 and those who are "restrained of [their] liberty of movement or deprived of the management of [their] property by reason of mental disease".

Responsible Citizenship

The traditional criteria for determining who should vote also reflected the view that those who do not conform to the norms of responsible citizenship – or what Jennifer Smith calls "the right conduct of politics in representative regimes" – should be disqualified from voting. Smith argues that representative government requires "an enormous degree of trust and civility among citizens"; the law therefore should encourage "the view that the vote is a serious responsibility of citizens. It means discouraging anything that would bring the vote into disrepute, or devalue it in citizens' eyes." (Smith 1991 RC)

This criterion has been used to disqualify citizens who are in prison and those convicted of offences against the election law. In these cases, one general and one particular, citizens are disqualified on the grounds that by violating the law, they have forfeited the right to participate as responsible citizens in the electoral process while they are incarcerated or for a specific period. The latter disqualification depends on the type of offence against the electoral law; the disqualification of prisoners makes no such distinction. This is unlike the law in some countries, such as France, Belgium and Australia, where disqualification varies with the type of offence or the length of the sentence. A justification for Canada's law is that law breakers should not be able to elect law makers; but there is no relationship between the conviction and the disqualification. Rather, all those serving a prison sentence at the time of an election are disqualified.

Impartiality

For reasons quite different from the first three, some public officials are disqualified from voting. They include the chief electoral officer, the assistant chief electoral officer, the returning officer for each constituency, and judges appointed by the Governor in Council, with the exception of citizenship judges. The rationale for these disqualifications is twofold.

Election officers are disqualified on the grounds that there must be, and must be seen to be, no conflict of interest or partisan behaviour on the part of those with executive and administrative responsibilities in conducting elections. Public confidence and trust in the integrity of the electoral process has been deemed sufficient justification for denying the vote in these cases. Judges have been disqualified on the grounds that the independence and impartiality of the judicial branch require that judges not be involved, or be seen to be involved, in partisan politics.

In the past, one other criterion cut across all four of the criteria just discussed: people who were under the care and responsibility of others. They included Indian persons, who were deemed to be wards of the state being prepared for citizenship; prisoners, who were in custodial care; women, who were considered the property of or were in the care of fathers or husbands; children, who were cared for by parents; and persons with mental disabilities, who were often confined to institutions. In other words, there was a generic category of individuals who were not considered autonomous, self-directing persons. Indian people, for example – and revealingly – were often compared to children. Hence the exclusion of these categories of persons at various times. It seemed logical that those who were being looked after by society should not or could not simultaneously participate in the governance of society. The extension of the franchise to some of these groups was in part a repudiation of paternalism.

Conclusion

The four criteria for determining who should vote – holding a stake in the governance of society, the ability to cast a rational and informed vote, conforming to the norms of responsible citizenship, and maintaining impartiality – remain the cornerstones of electoral law. Each provides a benchmark against which to assess whether an exclusion from the franchise is justified in a free and democratic society. The need for an explicit justification is a constitutional requirement because of the *Canadian Charter of Rights and Freedoms*. The Charter does not negate the value of these criteria. Rather, it requires that their use be justified explicitly and that the electoral law be formulated precisely to cover only the categories of persons meant to be excluded.

THE SECRECY OF THE VOTE

Before dealing with exclusions from the franchise, we wish to consider an important omission from the constitution – the secrecy of the vote.

Canadians now take the secret ballot for granted, but a secret ballot was not always the rule. The first three federal elections (1867, 1872 and 1874) were conducted with an open ballot, except in New Brunswick. At the time, many considered this to be "the manly, British way of exercising the franchise", although as J.M. Beck notes, everyone was well aware that open voting "facilitated the bribery of voters and the coercion of employees by their superiors and of civil servants by the government". (Beck 1968, 1)

Following the 1874 general election, provision was made for a secret ballot; since then Canadians have been able to vote in secret. The United Nations *International Covenant on Civil and Political Rights*, to which Canada is a party, establishes the right of every citizen "to vote ... at ... elections which ... shall be held by secret ballot, guaranteeing the free expression of the will of the electors". The *Canada Elections Act* recognizes this right implicitly; it is an offence for anyone present at the time of voting or at the counting of ballots to violate the secrecy of the vote. It also charges election officials with ensuring the secrecy of the vote. However, neither the *Canada Elections Act* nor the Charter proclaims the right to a secret ballot. It is appropriate, therefore, that our first recommendation concerning the right to vote affirm this essential dimension of the franchise.

Recommendation 1.2.1

We recommend that the *Canada Elections Act* state that the right to vote entails the right to a secret ballot.

DISQUALIFIED VOTERS

We now return to the disqualifications in the *Canada Elections Act*. Those disqualified from voting are the chief and assistant chief electoral officers; returning officers; judges appointed by the Governor in Council (except citizenship judges); prisoners; those "restrained of [their] liberty of movement or deprived of the management of [their] property by reason of mental disease"; and those "disqualified from voting under any law relating to the disqualification of electors for corrupt or illegal practices". In addition, with only a few exceptions, voters whose ordinary residence is not deemed to be in Canada, or voters in Canada who have no residence, cannot be registered and therefore cannot vote.

Election Officials

The chief electoral officer, assistant chief electoral officer and returning officers are disqualified, although the returning officer may be called upon to cast a tie-breaking vote in a constituency election following a judicial recount.

The traditional rationale for denying the vote to the chief and assistant chief electoral officers is that these officials have executive authority to make rulings with respect to enforcing and implementing the electoral law. This includes the registration of parties, the reimbursement of parties and candidates, enumeration and the revision of voters lists, the administration of the election, and the counting of the vote. To ensure integrity and credibility in electoral contests, election officials must be seen to be committed to fair electoral practices and indifferent to the outcome.

Thus, disqualification was based on the need for impartiality. In practice, however, this exclusion is symbolic and not justifiable in the context of the functions actually exercised. In four provinces – Quebec, Ontario, Alberta and British Columbia – the chief and deputy chief electoral officers have the right to vote, as does the deputy in every other province except Saskatchewan.

In Chapter 7, we recommend the creation of a Canada Elections Commission made up of six commissioners, with the chief electoral officer as chair. The exclusion of these seven election officers from the vote would not be justified given the experience in other Canadian jurisdictions, nor would it be justified for any other officer of the Commission. It is clear that voting is a private act and does not entail participation in partisan activities that could impair the integrity of the election process.

Recommendation 1.2.2

We recommend that all members and officers of the Canada Elections Commission, including the chief electoral officer, be qualified to vote.

The case for denying returning officers the vote was based in large part on the need for a mechanism to decide the outcome when an election remained tied following a judicial recount. The returning officers' tie-breaking vote is not secret: it is a public act. If they had the right to vote in the first instance, a tie-breaking vote would be their second vote.

The tie-breaking provision has been used just four times since Confederation and only once in this century, yet it denies almost 300 Canadians the right to vote. Al Dahlo, returning officer for North Vancouver, stated at our hearings, "I'm asking [the Commission] on behalf of myself and 294 other returning officers to consider us.... I think we deserve the right to vote." (Vancouver, 17 May 1990)

We consider this disqualification unreasonable. Returning officers can vote in Quebec; this has not raised doubts about their impartiality. Finally, the tie-breaking vote has rarely been required.

Recommendation 1.2.3

We recommend that returning officers be qualified to vote.

A new mechanism is therefore required to deal with a tie vote. If the vote were still tied after a recount, a special second election involving all candidates should be held. The electorate would then decide the matter. Such events would be rare; it is not reasonable to disqualify all returning officers because of events that occur so seldom.

Recommendation 1.2.4

We recommend that, in the event that an election remains tied after a recount, a special second election involving all candidates be conducted within three weeks of the recount.

The rules that should govern the conduct of such elections are discussed in Volume 2.

Judges

Some 800 judges are affected by the current exclusions in the elections act. These provisions were declared invalid by a Federal Court of Canada judgement shortly before the 1988 general election, following an uncontested statement of claim by two judges of the Federal Court. (*Muldoon* 1988) Judges are permitted to vote in provincial elections in Ontario, Quebec, British Columbia, Newfoundland, New Brunswick and Prince Edward Island, as well as in Great Britain, Australia, New Zealand, the United States, Germany and France.

The case for denying judges the vote rests on the assumption that members of the judicial branch should be, and should be seen to be, impartial. This flows from the need to ensure the independence of the judiciary from the executive and legislative branches in adjudicating the law. Given that partisanship is the fundamental dynamic of the executive and the legislature in both their selection and operation, the case for judicial independence and impartiality is sound.

But disqualifying judges ignores the fact that voters cast their ballots in secret as an act of citizenship. Because judges would exercise the franchise in secret, no compromise of their impartiality or independence arises, whatever the personal preferences of any individual judge. No public interest, including the need to preserve the independence of the judiciary, is served by disqualifying them.

Voting must not be confused with partisan activities. In stating that voting by judges does not undermine the independence of the judiciary, we are not implying that they should participate in political campaigns in any way, including making financial contributions to parties or candidates.

We should also note that voting by judges would not compromise their independence in deciding cases involving the election law. The *Judges Act* and judicial codes of conduct are sufficient guides to appropriate behaviour by members of the bench. It follows that no judge could be involved in a case concerning an election in a constituency in which she or he had cast a vote.

Recommendation 1.2.5

We recommend that judges be qualified to vote.

Persons with Mental Disabilities

The *Canada Elections Act* disqualifies "every person who is restrained of his liberty of movement or deprived of the management of his property by reason of mental disease". This provision was declared invalid in a 1988 judicial decision. According to Madam Justice Reed of the Federal Court of Canada,

> paragraph 14(4)(*f*) as presently drafted does not address itself only to mental competence or capacity in so far as that quality is required for the purposes of voting.
>
> It is more broadly framed than that. It denies people the right to vote on the basis of "mental disease". This clearly will include individuals who might suffer from a personality disorder which impairs their judgment in one aspect of their life only. There may be no reason on that basis to deprive them of the right to vote. What is more, paragraph 14(4)(*f*) does not deny all persons suffering from mental disease the right to vote, but only those whose liberty of movement has been restrained or whose property is under the control of a committee of estate.... The limitation ... is in that sense arbitrary. If it is intended as a test of mental competency, it is at the same time both too narrow and too wide. (*Canadian Disability Rights Council* 1988, 624–25)

This case requires that we reconsider the assumption that all persons with mental disabilities are incapable of casting a rational vote and that a person unable to make informed decisions in certain areas is also unable to make them in other areas.

The current disqualification clearly belongs to history, a history in which our understanding of mental illness and its effects was seriously deficient and the social stigma attached to mental illness was based on this ignorance. Mental illness no longer implies a necessary deficiency in the capacity to know one's political interests or to make choices on the basis of them; nor does it necessarily mean an impaired ability to act as a rational and informed voter in relation to the public interest. By itself, being deprived of the management of property does not mean that a person's exercise of the franchise would jeopardize the freedoms of other citizens or undermine the public interest in democratic government. Canada's election law contains no provisions requiring otherwise eligible voters to demonstrate any minimal standard of mental ability, knowledge or literacy.

Yet some citizens are clearly incapable, because of mental incapacity, of exercising the franchise in a way that meets the standard of a rational and informed vote. The integrity of the vote and the dignity of citizens who cannot function as voters for reasons of mental incapacity demand that there be some restrictions on the franchise. As Madam Justice Reed stated, she had "no doubt that ... a requirement of mental competence or judgmental capacity" (*Canadian Disability Rights Council* 1988, 624) might constitute a demonstrably justifiable limitation on the right to vote.

The franchise status of persons with mental disabilities varies among the provinces and in other countries. Across Canada, there is no consistent standard. In Quebec, only persons under curatorship are disfranchised. In Saskatchewan, those declared criminally insane under a Lieutenant Governor's warrant cannot vote. The Manitoba law disqualifies persons declared to be mentally disordered by order of the Court of Queen's Bench and whose custody has been assigned under the *Mental Health Act*. Newfoundland and Ontario have no restrictions. The other provinces have legislative provisions similar to the federal law. The U.S. states, which control the federal franchise, have laws that range from allowing all such persons to vote, to excluding only those declared 'incompetent' by the courts, to excluding all judged to be 'insane'.

Abroad there are variations as well. Great Britain, for example, distinguishes between patients in mental hospitals on a voluntary basis, who are entitled to vote, and involuntary patients, who cannot vote. In Germany, persons placed under trusteeship without their consent, those committed to a psychiatric hospital by virtue of the criminal code, and those confined in a psychiatric hospital, in accordance with procedures prescribed by law, for reasons of mental illness or mental deficiency, are excluded from voting.

Many groups representing persons with mental disabilities, senior officials of psychiatric institutions, and persons residing in such institutions testified at our public hearings about the experience in provincial elections where the franchise has been extended. Their testimony demonstrated clearly that the present exclusion casts too wide a net. At the same time, they cautioned that certain persons are vulnerable; care must be taken to safeguard their dignity and ensure that they are not subject to undue influence by over-zealous partisans or hospital employees. Close co-operation between the returning officer and hospital officials is required to alleviate potential problems.

Modern mental health legislation in Canada[2] embodies three guiding principles to define the notion of mental incapacity. These principles are (1) the recognition of 'incapacity' as a relative term that depends upon the specific context in which it is used – that is, the ability of a person, by reason of his or her mental state, to carry out a particular type of activity or make a particular type of decision; (2) the need to limit intervention only to the extent commensurate with the individual's degree of ability; and (3) the need for fair and due process defined expressly in law and meeting the standards of the Charter. A procedure must (a) give the person an opportunity to be heard and informed of all decisions taken in his or her regard; (b) rely on a determination made by a judge based on objective medical and social criteria; and (c) include a mechanism for review of the decision. Our recommendation takes these three principles into account.

Further, persons who have been deemed by the court to lack the capacity to understand the nature and consequences of their actions within the norms of society should not be entitled to vote. If their incapacity has been judged to be so, then they must be deemed to lack the ability to make a rational and informed vote. This restriction would apply to persons committed to a psychiatric hospital as criminally insane. This follows the practice in several countries, including Australia and Germany.

Recommendation 1.2.6

We recommend that the following persons not be qualified to vote in federal elections:
(1) a person subject to a regime established to protect the person or the person's property, pursuant to the law of a province or territory, because the person is totally incapable of understanding the nature and consequences of his or her acts; and
(2) a person confined to a psychiatric or other institution as a result of being acquitted of an offence under the *Criminal Code* by reason of insanity.

Prisoners

The *Canada Elections Act* disqualifies as a voter "every person undergoing punishment as an inmate in any penal institution for the commission of any offence" (section 51(e)). This provision was declared invalid most recently by Justice B.L. Strayer of the Federal Court of Canada in *Belczowski* (1991) on the grounds that the provision is too broad. The decision has been appealed. Other cases, including *Sauvé* (1988), have found the provision to be justifiable under section 1 of the Charter. The decisions of the different courts appear to be proceeding in contrary ways; in the absence of new legislation, therefore, the validity of the provision, as it stands, can be resolved only by a decision of the Supreme Court of Canada.

The federal disqualification of prisoners is comparable to provisions in provincial law; the exceptions are Quebec and Newfoundland, where prisoners were given the right to vote in 1979 and 1985 respectively. Prisoners, including inmates in federal prisons, also voted in the 1980 Quebec referendum. By virtue of judicial decisions, prisoners also have the right to vote in provincial elections in Ontario and Manitoba. Alberta's election law allows remand prisoners to vote, and this right was granted to remand prisoners in Saskatchewan by judicial decision. The *Canada Elections Act* does not disfranchise remand prisoners; but it does not contain the provisions that would allow them to cast a vote.

Prisoners have the right to vote in some countries, including Italy, Sweden, Norway and Denmark, but not in many others, such as Great Britain, France, Switzerland and Greece. France also disqualifies some convicted persons who are not in prison. In the United States, all prisoners have the right to vote in some states, and some prisoners have that right in other states; but in the majority of states prisoners are disqualified from voting, in some cases for life. In Australia, the right to vote is removed only from persons convicted of treason or of crimes punishable by sentences of five years or more.

Three main arguments for denying prisoners the vote have been advanced in cases where this disqualification has been challenged in the courts. The first concerns the administrative requirements of prisons to maintain security. The second relates to the capacity of prisoners to cast an informed vote. The third involves the criterion of a decent and responsible citizenry.

The first argument can no longer justify this disqualification, now that several jurisdictions have given prisoners the vote and have demonstrated that prisoners can vote without any threat to prison security. Moreover, in at least two explicit references to this matter, judicial opinion has declared that administrative reasons, including security, are not a sufficient justification for denying the right to vote. (*Gould* 1984; *Lévesque* 1985) Finally, officials from Correctional Service Canada, who assisted provincial officials in Quebec with provincial elections and the 1980 referendum, and from Newfoundland and British Columbia made it clear in their presentations before the Commission that neither security nor the good order of the institution is jeopardized when prisoners vote. (Dyotte, Brief 1990; Office des droits des détenu-e-s, Brief 1990; Frontenac Law Association, Brief 1990)*

The second ground for disqualifying prisoners proceeds from an understanding of the franchise as demanding an informed voting decision. This argument assumes that prisoners should be disqualified because they are denied access to the information and public discourse necessary to cast an informed vote. This argument was accepted by Mr. Justice Taylor of the British Columbia Supreme Court in *Jolivet* (1983), although not by other courts. In our view this objection is no longer relevant, even if it once was. Prisoners can now learn about politics through the printed and electronic media, to which they normally have access. Moreover, there are no administrative or security reasons related to their imprisonment that would deny inmates access to printed materials from candidates or parties.

The most crucial question is clearly the third objection, namely that prisoners have violated the law and thus have demonstrated that they are unwilling to abide by the norms of responsible citizenship. As Madam Justice Van Camp of the Supreme Court of Ontario put it in the *Sauvé* case (now under appeal), prisoners have "disqualified themselves".

> [I]t seems to me that Parliament was justified in limiting the right to vote with the objective that a liberal democratic regime requires a decent and responsible citizenry. Such a regime requires that the citizens obey voluntarily; the practical efficacy of laws relies on the willing acquiescence of those subject to them. The state has a role in preserving itself by the symbolic exclusion of criminals from the right to vote for the lawmakers. So also,

---

* Briefs submitted to the Royal Commission are identified in the text only. They are not listed in the list of references at the end of this volume.

the exclusion of the criminal from the right to vote reinforces the concept of a decent responsible citizenry essential for a liberal democracy. (*Sauvé* 1988, 238)

This argument makes several invalid assumptions about the disqualification as it is now phrased in the *Canada Elections Act*. The first is that all prisoners, in violating the law, also violate the social foundations of liberal democracy. The second is that all who have violated the law have been sentenced to prison. Neither assumption can be supported.

First, many prisoners have not been convicted of a criminal offence. In 1989–1990, for instance, 21 per cent of admissions to provincial institutions were for violations of provincial or municipal laws.

Second, many prisoners are inmates for relatively minor offences, even if under the *Criminal Code*. Statistics Canada's data for 1989–1990 indicate that 28 per cent of admissions to provincial institutions were for failure to pay a fine; 43 per cent of the sentences being served were for less than 30 days and 38 per cent were for one to six months. (Canada, Statistics Canada 1990a, 67–68)

Third, remand prisoners, that is, those awaiting trial, are incarcerated. A count of inmates in provincial institutions during that period also showed that more than 4000 prisoners, that is, 22 per cent of the total population, were on remand and had not been convicted. (Landreville and Lemonde 1991 RC) In our society, a person is considered innocent until proven guilty, and these people should therefore not be denied the vote simply because they are incarcerated.

Finally, many who have violated the law are not in prison as a consequence. Their sentences may include probation or a fine but not incarceration.

Disqualifying all prisoners ignores the possibility that someone sentenced for a substantial period, but released on bail pending an appeal, may vote. It also overlooks the fact that someone in prison for a minor offence may be deprived of the vote, while someone convicted of a major crime may vote if released on parole just before an election is called.

In all these cases, there is no principled relationship between the violation of the law and the disqualification from voting. Rather, the relationship is between incarceration and disqualification. Moreover, this relationship is 'fortuitous' in its timing, as noted by Justices Bowlby and Monnin in the *Grondin* (1988) and *Badger* (1988) judgements respectively. As the John Howard Society of Alberta pointed out, several courts have declared that the disqualification of all prisoners from voting "surely casts too wide a net". (Brief 1990, 13) In so doing, the present law is unequal in its treatment of prisoners, who are only one of the categories of law breakers.

The objective of punishing law breakers is not so important that it should override the basic right to vote; this argument is well accepted. It is difficult nevertheless to interpret the present law as meaning other than that those incarcerated are denied the vote for punitive reasons. Indeed, the *Canada*

Elections Act states that the disqualification includes "every person undergoing *punishment* as an inmate ..." (emphasis added). If this were other than punishment pure and simple, the logic of the argument would disqualify everyone convicted of breaking the law, regardless of the sentence.

The disqualification must also be viewed in the context of evolving correctional policies here and abroad. The policy of Canada's Correctional Service is to provide for inmates "as normal an environment as the circumstances of security will allow and to safeguard [their] rights and dignity as a human being and as a member of Canadian society". (Canada, Correctional Service Canada 1985) Maintaining prisoners' rights, beyond those necessarily restricted as a consequence of being in prison, has been a consistent policy of the Correctional Service over the past two decades.

The scope of the current disqualification is clearly too broad. It fails to distinguish between types of offences and thus disqualifies persons who have committed offences that cannot in any way be considered significant violations of the essential norms of responsible conduct in a liberal democratic state. In terms of Canadian jurisprudence, this blanket disqualification cannot meet the proportionality test laid down in *R. v. Oakes* (1986), because the disqualification is not proportional to any intended objective. In Justice Strayer's view, the current provision is too blunt an instrument. Implicit in this argument is that the restriction would be acceptable if it were proportional to the offence.

Without minimizing the gravity of the offences committed by a number of prisoners, allowing some prisoners to vote would not undermine public confidence in the value of the vote or threaten the interests of other citizens. This would perhaps require an additional degree of tolerance on the part of some citizens toward those in prison. But tolerance has always been an important feature in extending the franchise, and we have concluded that the cause of Canadian democratic politics will be advanced as a result of a more generous approach to the franchise in this as in other cases.

Allowing prisoners to vote would also serve to highlight the importance of the right to vote. As Justice Bowlby pointed out in the *Grondin* (1988, 430) case, "[T]he right to vote is so firmly entrenched in the Canadian Charter that, unlike other protected rights and freedoms, it is excluded from the override power afforded to parliament and the legislature by s. 33(1) of the Charter." He went on to say that enfranchising prisoners would promote the principal goal of incarceration, the rehabilitation of prisoners.

The average number of persons imprisoned in Canada on any given day is about 29 600. The average number of persons on probation, parole or mandatory supervision is approximately 79 000. Of those in prison, about 18 100 are in provincial institutions, serving sentences of less than two years; the remainder, roughly 11 500, are serving longer sentences in federal penitentiaries. Of those in federal penitentiaries, approximately 60 per cent have no previous record of a federal prison sentence. Of all prisoners, 93 per cent are serving sentences of less than 10 years. (Canada, Correctional Service Canada 1990; Canada, Statistics Canada 1990a)

Confinement in prison is meant to be the extent of punishment; the rights and freedoms of prisoners are to be limited only to the degree necessary to effect confinement. Extending the punishment to include disfranchisement is a limitation on democratic rights that is clearly a legacy of the past – a tradition that, at times, paid insufficient attention to democratic rights and to the need to limit them only for demonstrably justified reasons.

Limiting the right of prisoners to vote is justified, however, where the offences committed constitute the most serious violations against the country or against the basic rights of citizens to life, liberty and security of the person, including murder, kidnapping, hostage taking, treason, and certain sexual offences. Our tradition defines heinous crimes against persons or the country as those offences that are punishable by life imprisonment. Persons convicted of these crimes are considered to have gone beyond the pale of civilized behaviour.

People convicted of offences for which the maximum sentence is life imprisonment and who have been sentenced to prison for a period of 10 years or more have clearly violated the social contract. Society is therefore justified in disqualifying them from voting for the duration of their sentence.

This disqualification is rationally connected to the specific limitation on an individual's right to vote, because persons convicted of these crimes have offended the very foundations of a civilized political community. In so doing, they have declared themselves unwilling to participate in civil society in ways that respect the most fundamental rights of others or the basic character of the political system. Second, this disqualification is a minimum impairment of the right to vote. It is limited to the period of incarceration; prisoners disqualified from voting would regain this right upon release from prison. Third, and most important, the disqualification is proportional in terms of its purpose and effect. It removes the vote only from persons whose criminal behaviour has seriously violated the fundamental criteria of democratic citizenship.

We conclude that there are no demonstrably justified reasons for disqualifying the vast majority of prisoners. At the same time, those convicted of treason or of the most serious offences against individuals should be disqualified during the time they are in prison.

Recommendation 1.2.7

We recommend that persons convicted of an offence punishable by a maximum of life imprisonment and sentenced for 10 years or more be disqualified from voting during the time they are in prison.

Canadians Living Abroad

Voters not resident in Canada cannot exercise their franchise because there is no provision for registering them to vote. The exceptions to this general exclusion are members and certain employees of the Canadian forces, federal public servants and their spouses and dependants living abroad with them. Canadians live abroad for many reasons, including their occupation or that of their spouse or parents; in many cases their presence abroad contributes to the direct benefit of Canada or Canadian interests and ideals. As CUSO stated, "it would be a tremendous step forward to grant Canadians who are helping to promote Canada's image as a leader in foreign aid the right to the choice of government at home". (Brief 1990, 2) Nor is it the case that all Canadians living abroad have severed their ties to Canada.

We conclude that the administrative difficulties of serving voters living abroad do not constitute an acceptable justification for disfranchising these citizens. The United States, France, Germany, Australia, and Great Britain make provision for voters living abroad to be registered and to vote, as do Quebec and Alberta. In all these cases it has been recognized that with modern telecommunications and the international press, the argument that citizens living abroad cannot be informed about public affairs at home no longer applies. Moreover, with increasing globalization of the world economy, the number of Canadians travelling and living abroad will likely increase in the coming years.

At the same time, we think it reasonable and fair to expect Canadians not resident in Canada to demonstrate their continuing attachment to the Canadian polity if they wish to participate in its political processes. The question is what criteria would be both meaningful and practical. Given our objective of securing the democratic rights of citizens as voters, we should not impose any requirement that citizens return to Canada at some date, testify that they intend to return at some prescribed or undefined time, or maintain an attachment to Canada. Rather, as is the case with much of what we do in the electoral process, we should trust these Canadians. We should assume that they continue to have a stake in Canada and keep themselves sufficiently informed as citizens. In other words, we should not attempt to impose on citizens living outside Canada conditions that are not imposed on those residing in Canada.

We can, however, require citizens abroad to testify that they have not become involved in another political system. To meet this criterion, citizens living abroad should be required to certify that they have not voted in a foreign election at the national level since leaving Canada. Citizens living abroad would then be allowed to vote in federal elections.

Recommendation 1.2.8

We recommend that eligible voters not resident in Canada be qualified to vote in federal elections, provided they certify that

they have not voted in a foreign national election since becoming a non-resident.

Age of Voting

The *Canada Elections Act* stipulates that to be a qualified voter a citizen must be at least 18 years of age. The only exceptions to this age requirement are Canadian forces personnel who are regular members, reserve members on full-time training or active service, or members of the special force. These persons are qualified to vote even if they have not attained the age of 18. Since 17-year-olds are accepted into the Canadian forces, members of the forces who are 17 years old constitute a special category of voters.

Until 1970, the right to vote was limited to those who were at least 21 years of age. On 23 October 1969, the government of Pierre Elliott Trudeau announced its intention to introduce legislation to lower the voting age to 18, although there had been no strong public demand for such a change. The law setting the minimum voting age at 18 was passed virtually unanimously the following year.

Three arguments were put forward at that time. The first focused on the extent to which those to be enfranchised had a stake in the governance of society. The second concerned the extent to which they could be expected to exercise a mature and informed vote. The third concerned their level of participation in activities of citizenship.

These same criteria apply today, although the Charter has shifted the onus of the argument. In 1969, a case had to be made to extend the franchise. Now, a case must be made to restrict the franchise. However, as John Courtney stated at our hearings, "the whole issue is such an arbitrary one that you define what you consider to be a reasonable age, and you have to make a case for it". (Saskatoon, 17 April 1990)

One consideration arising because of the Charter is discrimination against 17-year-old civilians. According to one legal scholar, "This is discrimination with respect to those under 18 years of age who are not in service as members of the forces. It would be difficult to support such discrimination by applying the criteria identified in section 1 of the Charter." (Garant 1991b RC) Given this inconsistency, the question arises whether the voting age should be lowered to 17 for all citizens or raised to 18 for those in the forces to ensure equality before the law.

The second consideration arises from the Charter's requirements concerning limitations on rights. The Canadian Bar Association made several points in its brief to the Commission.

> It might readily be assumed that 18 is a reasonable minimum age at which to attribute the responsibility of voting.... These apparently reasonable assumptions might not readily withstand scrutiny under section 1 of the *Charter*.... If justification is to be based on the fact that the act of voting requires a certain mental capacity, evidence should be available to support

> the proposition that an 18 year old has sufficient capacity, while a 17 year old does not. Although it might be clear that a two year old is incapable, it is difficult to draw rational distinctions between individuals who are 17, 18 or 21.... It is not ... clear that [developmental psychology] would support the age of 18 as an appropriate dividing line. (Brief 1990, 13–14)

Developmental psychology theory has identified six distinct stages in the development of moral judgement capacity. (Kohlberg 1958) Kohlberg's stages are intended to classify individuals according to their level of cognitive awareness and acceptance of responsibility. Between 16 and 20, adolescents are generally at stage 4, which is characterized by a recognition of authority and social order. The adolescent is able to make a moral judgement on the basis that proper action consists in carrying out a duty to respect authority and to maintain the established social order. (Cloutier 1982)

The Canadian Bar Association also questioned the pertinence of tying the voting age to the age of majority:

> The second ground of potential justification for disqualifying citizens below the age of 18 is general policy objectives.... These policy grounds might include a social consensus supporting the notion of an "age of majority".... However, fewer and fewer powers, privileges and responsibilities are tied to the so-called age of majority.... The right to vote ... is specifically guaranteed by the *Charter*.... Restrictions on *Charter* rights must be directed toward objectives which are "pressing and substantial"; it is far from clear that support of a general notion of "age of majority" constitutes such an objective. (Brief 1990, 14)

Given these conclusions, the three criteria raised in the 1969 debate must be considered once again. The choice of any particular age is to some extent arbitrary. The decision should, however, be broadly justifiable on the basis of defined criteria.

The first criterion pertains to the degree to which citizens under the age of 18 have a sufficient stake in the community. The nature and extent of 'adult' responsibilities entrusted to those under 18 are considerable. In 1990, for instance, almost 50 per cent of Canada's 700 000 16- and 17-year-olds were in the work force; close to 50 per cent of 16-year-olds filed income tax returns. Rights and responsibilities are also conferred on 16-year-olds under provincial laws on social and employment policy. The ability to obtain a driver's permit is one example.

The second criterion is the ability to exercise a mature and informed vote. Several interveners at our hearings suggested that young men and women today are more mature and better informed than their predecessors. Research tells us that by the age of 15 or 16, most young people have acquired a view of the social and political world that is not significantly different from the perceptions and understanding of adults. In addition, although the amount and depth of civics education vary between and within provinces, courses are now generally offered in high schools across the country. (Pammett and Myles 1991 RC) Moreover, as with the rest of the population, today's youth have more sources of information on current affairs than was the case even two decades ago. Thus, in terms of political competence, 16 could be just as defensible an age as 18.

The third criterion, responsible citizenship, raises the question of whether young people generally act responsibly when they participate in public affairs. There is no evidence to suggest that they act otherwise. Research on their political attitudes indicates that they tend to be less cynical about the political process and are more likely than older persons to have a sense of political efficacy – a feeling that participating in the political process is meaningful and worthwhile. (Pammett and Myles 1991 RC)

When the voting age was lowered from 21 to 18 in 1970, extension of the franchise did not work to the benefit of any one political party over time. Extending the franchise to citizens under 18 years of age could serve to reinforce the belief that participation counts and the notion of civic responsibility. (Environics 1990) Moreover, since the majority of 16- and 17-year-olds would still be living at home when they cast their first vote, they might be more likely to vote than would those who were slightly older but living away from home.

These arguments for lowering the voting age to 16 constitute the best case for this proposal, but they are not sufficiently compelling. Ultimately, any decision on the voting age involves the judgement of a society about when individuals reach maturity as citizens. Under most statutes, a person is not considered an adult until age 18; for example, a person under 18 is not an adult for purposes of criminal proceedings unless special application is made under the *Young Offenders Act*. Further, a minor requires parental consent for many important decisions, including applying for citizenship, getting married and seeking certain medical interventions. As expressed many times at our hearings, there remains a strong conviction that the time has not come to lower the voting age. This is also the conclusion of every other democracy with the exception of Brazil and Nicaragua.

Since Confederation, the franchise has undergone regular change to include an ever-increasing number of Canadians. As our society continues to evolve, it is possible that a lower voting age will become the focus of stronger demands by those concerned and greater support on the part of Canadians, particularly if the law is changed to eliminate the need for parental consent on certain important decisions. The voting age is not specified in the constitution and is therefore relatively easy to change. We therefore conclude that the voting age should be set at 18 years of age but that Parliament should revisit the issue periodically.

Recommendation 1.2.9

We recommend that the voting age be set at 18 years of age.

Non-Citizens

People living in Canada who are not Canadian citizens are not entitled to vote, a provision that conforms with the Charter. Given the criterion of a stake in Canadian political life and the risks citizens take in representative democracies, it is not only appropriate but also entirely reasonable that this restriction continue to apply.

Those who wish to participate in Canada's political life must commit themselves to a permanent stake in our governance and share in its risks; they have an obligation to seek Canadian citizenship. The right conduct of politics in representative governance implies that the vote is significant to citizens. This demands that only citizens possess the franchise.

Recommendation 1.2.10

We recommend that the right to vote extend only to Canadian citizens.

VOTING IN CANADA

Introduction

The exercise of the franchise is one of the critical elements in maintaining public support for our form of government. Through voting, voters participate, however indirectly, in the nation's governance, giving their consent to the institutional arrangements for exercising political power. Voting is also the most efficient and effective way for the vast majority of citizens to register their political views and indicate changes in their preferences. Through the vote, citizens choose who should represent them in the House of Commons and thus which party will form the government. Voter turnout is therefore a basic measure of citizens' confidence in the political system and, ultimately, of the health of the polity.

As one of the bases of democratic government, the right to vote must not be impeded by the law or by administrative measures used to register voters or conduct the vote; nor should it be undermined by the absence of appropriate remedial measures. A principal objective of electoral reform is thus to ensure that all voters who wish to exercise their constitutional right to vote have a reasonable opportunity to do so.

Not all voters vote at every election. This pool of non-voters averages about 25 per cent of the electorate at any given federal election. Yet studies of voting behaviour reveal only a small hard core of perennial non-voters; those who never vote are estimated at perhaps 5 per cent of the electorate. Much more common, therefore, and accounting for most of those who fail to vote in any given election, are the occasional non-voters.

Our primary interest in voter turnout is a practical one. People fail to turn up at the polling booth for a variety of reasons. For some it may be a lack of interest in the election or in politics generally; others may find it difficult to vote that particular day because of travel or illness. We need to determine, to the degree possible, what percentage of occasional non-voters would vote if existing legal or administrative impediments were removed.

The Canadian Record

Voter turnout in federal elections, as measured by the percentage of registered voters who actually cast a ballot, has averaged around 75 per cent since 1945. There have been significant fluctuations from election to election, as shown in Table 2.2. Turnout has been as low as 67.9 per cent, in the early 1950s, and as high as 80.6 per cent, in 1958. Turnout can be affected by a variety of factors, including weather or the time of year. The elections of 1953 and 1980, for example, took place at the height of the summer holiday season and in the middle of winter respectively; this is thought to have affected turnout in both instances. Overall, however, as depicted in Figure 2.1, voter turnout peaked at about 80 per cent in the period 1958 through 1963, then declined gradually thereafter.

Table 2.2
Turnout rates for general elections, 1945–1988
(per cent)

General election (date)	Turnout
1945 (June 11)	76.3
1949 (June 27)	74.8
1953 (August 10)	67.9
1957 (June 10)	75.0
1958 (March 31)	80.6
1962 (June 18)	80.1
1963 (April 8)	80.3
1965 (November 8)	75.9
1968 (June 25)	75.7
1972 (October 30)	76.7
1974 (July 8)	71.0
1979 (May 22)	75.8
1980 (February 18)	69.3
1984 (September 4)	75.3
1988 (November 21)	75.3
Post-war average	75.3

Source: Canada, Chief Electoral Officer (various), using reported voter registration and vote totals.

Contrary to popular belief, Canada's voter turnout rate does not stand up well to international comparisons. Canadians' apparent satisfaction with the current turnout rate relates no doubt to the favourable comparison with the lower rate in the United States. In fact, however, Canada's turnout rate has been consistently below the international average over the past four decades, as shown in Table 2.3. Further, as is evident in Table 2.4, which ranks 33 countries by turnout during the 1980s, Canada's record is even less impressive than that of several of the newer democracies.

Table 2.3
Turnout rates, Canada and other democratic countries, decade averages[a]

Decade	Canada	All other democracies	Voluntary voting democracies	Voluntary voting democracies excluding Switzerland, United States
1940s	75.0	82.1	78.6	81.8
1950s	73.3	82.7	79.3	82.0
1960s	77.3	83.1	80.1	82.9
1970s	74.7	81.5	79.1	83.0
1980s	73.3	80.6	78.2	82.6
N		(17/18)[b]	(13/15)[b,c]	(11/13)[b,c]

Source: Canada, Chief Electoral Officer (various); for other countries, see Table 2.4.
[a]Turnout based on registration figures, except for the United States (voting-age population).
[b]France included as of the 1960s.
[c]The Netherlands included as of the 1970s.

Moreover, and more troubling, Canada's turnout rate is slipping further behind the international average. (Black 1991 RC; Jackman 1987) The growing gap is clearly evident in Figure 2.1, which summarizes comparative trends in voter turnout rates in Canada and in other democracies, some of which have compulsory voting. Given that Canada is roughly comparable in socio-economic terms to the countries of western Europe, virtually all of which have better turnout rates, there is a reasonable basis for inferring that our institutional arrangements are contributing to our lower turnout rate.

Voter Turnout: Institutional Factors

Studies of differences in voter turnout have increasingly identified institutional factors as accounting for major variations. Several studies have demonstrated that certain constitutional provisions, political system characteristics, and electoral law features in combination provide a better explanation for differences in turnout than do factors associated with political culture, such as attitudes, values and beliefs. (Jackman 1987; Blais and Carty 1990;

Table 2.4
Turnout rates, Canada and 32 other democracies, 1980s

Rank		1980s
1	Australia	94.3*
2	Belgium	93.8*
3	Austria	91.5
4	New Zealand	90.5
5	Bahamas	90.5
6	Italy	89.8*
7	Iceland	89.2
8	Sweden	89.1
9	Luxembourg	88.1*
10	Germany	87.3
11	France	86.2
12	Denmark	86.1
13	Venezuela	84.3
14	Netherlands	83.4
15	Norway	83.1
16	Greece	82.0*
17	Mauritius	80.1
18	Israel	79.0
19	Costa Rica	78.9*
20	Finland	78.2
21	Barbados	77.3
22	Jamaica	77.1
23	Portugal	76.8
24	Botswana	76.0
25	Ireland	74.2
26	United Kingdom	74.0
27	Spain	73.4
28	**Canada**	**73.0**
29	Japan	71.4
30	India	62.0
31	Trinidad and Tobago	58.8
32	United States	54.3
33	Switzerland	47.5

Source: Black 1991 RC.

*Compulsory voting.

Figure 2.1
Turnout rates, Canada and other democracies, decade averages

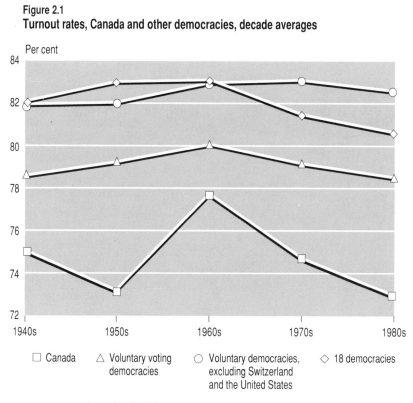

Source: Adapted from Black 1991 RC.

Lijphart 1990; Black 1991 RC) Even studies that argue that political culture is the primary determinant readily acknowledge that institutions matter a great deal. (Crewe 1981)

The structure of institutions, laws, and political organizations in democratic states clearly affects the way people behave. Different institutional arrangements establish different opportunities and costs for individuals exercising their right to vote and for political parties mobilizing the vote. Different outcomes are thus the result of different incentive systems. Institutional arrangements and administrative practices are not neutral in their effect on people's propensity to exercise their right to vote, even when they share values about political participation.

Comparative research is especially useful in this regard. The factors found to be most important in explaining differences relate to the electoral system, the party system, the legislative-executive structures of government, and the basic electoral law.

Research has found that to the degree the electoral system promotes proportionality in translating party votes into party seats in the legislature, turnout rises. The average turnout in systems with some form of proportional representation (PR) is 82 per cent, compared to 73.6 per cent for plurality systems like Canada's. PR systems vary in the degree to which they translate votes proportionally into seats, but they generally enjoy greater turnout. (Blais and Carty 1990) Such systems appear to offer an incentive for voters to vote and, equally important, for parties to mobilize their voters. Conversely, where there is not (or does not appear to be) a high correlation between votes cast for a party candidate and the seats a party obtains, the incentive to vote and to mobilize voters declines accordingly.

Second, the incentive for voters to vote and for parties to mobilize voters is partly a function of the degree to which a competitive party system is operating. Where only one party is strong, the parties have less incentive to commit resources and to mobilize as many voters as possible; their supporters also have less incentive to vote. Many voters will consider the outcome of an election a foregone conclusion and will not bother to vote, whether because their preferred choice has a safe seat or because voting for other parties' candidates would be voting for a lost cause.

Third, in political systems where several competitive political parties can secure some representation in the legislature, voter turnout is likely to suffer somewhat if governments tend to be formed through coalitions built by legislative leaders rather than as a direct consequence of the election result. Although parties in these circumstances may have a high incentive to mobilize the vote, voters have somewhat less incentive because they do not see themselves as determining directly which party will form the government. (Jackman 1987)

Conversely, in systems with only two strong parties, voters have a greater sense of participating directly in determining which party forms the government. The effect of a multi-party system in depressing voting turnout is not strong, however. (Blais and Carty 1990) Furthermore, in multi-party systems where there is greater ideological variety represented in the legislature, particularly when newer groups such as environmentalists are represented directly, turnout tends to be higher. (Crepaz 1990)

Fourth, other factors being equal, political systems with a single legislative chamber tend to have higher turnout than political systems with two legislative chambers. In one-chamber systems, voters have a greater chance of affecting government policies through their electoral choices than do voters who select two sets of legislators. Those voters know that public policies will likely be the result of compromises worked out between the leaders of the two legislative chambers. For similar reasons, turnout in national elections in federal systems is adversely affected by the division of power between the two orders of government.

There is also compelling evidence that giving voters ready access to advance polls well before election day and generally making voting as easy as possible contribute to higher turnout. In Sweden, for example, any eligible voter is entitled to vote up to 24 days in advance of the election simply by visiting a local post office. Since the early 1980s, more than a third of Swedish voters have consistently used this system. (Black 1991 RC) In

New Zealand, polling stations are set up in unconventional settings, such as race tracks, shopping malls, and other places where there are likely to be large crowds. The two countries, both non-compulsory systems, enjoy turnout rates that are well above average. In Texas, experiments with non-traditional polling locations, such as retail areas, and the use of mobile polls have resulted in increases in turnout averaging 18 to 22 per cent. (Cooper and Christe 1991)

Two further measures clearly enhance voter turnout. The first pertains to the day of the election. Canadian elections are held on a Monday, unless it is a federal or provincial holiday, in which case the election is held on the Tuesday. Many European countries hold their elections on Sunday, resulting in higher turnout. We encountered some support for voting on Sunday during our hearings, but others were quite adamant that voting should not take place on Sunday for religious or other reasons.

The second measure that increases voter turnout is a compulsory voting law, as found in Greece, Australia, Belgium, Luxembourg, Italy and Costa Rica. In none of these cases, however, does turnout reach 100 per cent, because valid excuses are numerous, sanctions are not severe, and the law is not vigorously enforced. The rationale for compulsory voting is essentially threefold: voting is a civic duty; the legitimacy of government is enhanced; and candidates and political parties are not required to spend limited campaign time and resources to get out the vote. In these countries, compulsory voting is predicated on compulsory registration. (Australia, Queensland 1990)

The Canadian electoral system has relied on voters' voluntary participation to secure the consent of citizens to the outcome of elections. Canadian electoral law has required neither compulsory registration nor compulsory voting. In our tradition, the state has assumed responsibility for registration, but people have the right not to be enrolled on the voters list. Even if they are enrolled, they have the right not to vote.

Although every effort must be made to ensure that voters are registered and are able to vote if they wish to do so, the public interest in electoral democracy need not extend to a requirement that citizens vote. The Canadian approach has assumed that voters have the right not to vote, and we agree with this view.

Moreover, compulsory voting laws are rarely enforced effectively or equitably because citizens must be given the benefit of the doubt when they explain why they did not vote. The Australian experience is relevant here; only those who admit that they did not vote and offer no reasonable excuse, or who refuse to reply to requests for a reason, are prosecuted and fined. This means that the law is enforced only on people who do not want to vote or who do not know that they could easily offer an acceptable excuse. In the first instance, people are prosecuted because of a decision that ought to be a free choice; in the second instance, they are prosecuted because they are ignorant of the law.

Compulsory voting would be unacceptable to most Canadians, given our understanding of a free and democratic society, and unfair to other Canadians, who may not fully understand their rights. Compulsory voting would run counter to the tradition of the vote as a right to be exercised freely; for this reason, its enforcement would also be problematic. Moreover, efforts to apply the law fairly and reasonably might very well lead to prosecutions only of those who reject the idea of compulsory voting. Without a civic culture to support the principle of compulsory voting, this solution could be worse than the problem.

In summary, research demonstrates the significant effects of institutional factors on voter turnout. Some factors, related to the structure of the political system, lie outside the realm of electoral law. Others may be more readily amenable to electoral reform but must also be rejected for reasons unrelated to voter turnout. But research does support the general premise that institutional reform at the micro level – such as voter registration systems and voting arrangements – does affect turnout. These factors fall within our mandate and principal objectives.

Voting and Non-Voting: Determinants

Canadians' voting behaviour varies by province, constituency, and individual characteristics. Examining these non-institutional characteristics helps determine why some voters do not vote; this in turn may suggest how administrative procedures should be designed, modified, or eliminated to improve voter turnout, as well as the extent to which such changes might be expected to improve turnout. Knowing why some voters do not vote is an important prerequisite to changing the electoral law. If we discover, for example, that many non-voters are simply not interested in elections, it is unlikely that administrative changes will have much impact. But the converse might very well be the case.

Provinces and Territories

There are significant provincial variations in voter turnout at federal elections, as shown in Table 2.5. The average turnout in the three most recent federal elections ranged from about 64 per cent in Newfoundland to 83 per cent in Prince Edward Island. Turnout in the other Atlantic provinces was slightly above the national average, while turnout in Quebec and Ontario was slightly below. Turnout in Manitoba was also slightly below average, while in Saskatchewan it was slightly above. Alberta was at the low end of the range, but not as low as Newfoundland.

It has also been argued that the availability of early returns from eastern Canada may help depress turnout in the western provinces. Because the polls close at 8 p.m. local time, voters in western Canada may learn of the national outcome before the polls close and be discouraged from voting. However, in the two provinces most affected, Alberta and British Columbia, turnout in provincial elections is nearly the same as or lower than in federal elections. Moreover, in the parts of Saskatchewan located in the mountain time zone (the same zone as Alberta), turnout in federal elections is higher than the Canadian average and consistent with the higher turnout for the province as a whole.

Table 2.5
Average voter turnout, federal, provincial and territorial elections, 1980–88

	Average federal voter turnout	Average provincial and territorial voter turnout
Ontario	74.3	60.8
Quebec	73.0	77.7
Nova Scotia	74.3	72.5
New Brunswick	74.6	82.0
Manitoba	72.3	70.9
British Columbia	76.0	77.4
Prince Edward Island	83.0	82.1
Saskatchewan	75.7	83.1
Alberta	68.3	55.6
Newfoundland	63.7	78.7
Yukon	75.0	78.4
Northwest Territories	68.7	70.6
Average federal turnout	73.2	

Source: Various reports from federal and provincial chief electoral officers.

More careful constituency-by-constituency analysis of the time zone factor fails to yield statistically significant results. Overall, our research suggests that the putative time zone effect is not a particularly important determinant of non-voting in western provinces. (Eagles 1991b RC) In the absence of statistically significant results, however, there are no doubt a number of western Canadians who resent being reminded of the electoral weight of central Canada, and some of them may have decided on occasion not to vote for that reason.

Moreover, voters in western Canada generally may feel that their votes count for less because the election outcome has so often been determined before their votes are cast. For example, in the 1980 election, by the time the Ontario results were announced, it was clear that the Liberals had won enough seats to form the government. Had the results been announced from west to east, however, Canadians would have had to wait until the Prince Edward Island results were broadcast to learn who would form the government. One cannot help but feel that this would have conferred an entirely different meaning on the vote for western Canadians.

Constituency Characteristics

The context in which elections take place includes both the socio-economic characteristics of constituencies and the political dynamics of constituency contests. Research shows that differences in this context are associated with differences in voter turnout. Using aggregate data, contextual factors can be measured by establishing a statistical profile of federal constituencies. For example, Statistics Canada data can be used to determine, among other things, the proportion of low-income families in each constituency, the percentage of residents who are university graduates, or the proportion of the labour force working in professional, administrative and managerial occupations.

Several socio-economic factors have been shown to correlate directly with voter turnout. First, as the mean income of a constituency increases, so does voter turnout. Second, the occupational profile of a constituency has some influence; turnout is higher in constituencies with a significant percentage of professionals and white collar workers. Third, population mobility has a significant impact: the more stable a constituency's population, the higher the turnout. Finally, other factors being equal, turnout tends to be lower in constituencies with substantial Aboriginal populations. (Eagles 1991b RC)

Research has also shown that factors such as the level of campaign expenditures, the closeness of the constituency contest, and the presence of a smaller party or independent candidates – factors one might think would raise the level of interest in a local campaign or make individual votes seem more critical to the outcome – in fact have little independent impact on differences in voter turnout across constituencies. (Eagles 1991b RC)

Although specific events or issues in a given election may increase or suppress turnout, the general conclusion from research conducted for the Commission is that the socio-economic profile of a constituency is more strongly correlated with voter turnout than are factors such as local campaign expenditures. This is in line with similar research in other countries.

These characteristics are simply associated or correlated with turnout. With aggregate data we can never establish with absolute certainty the exact causal linkages between contextual factors and turnout and how they work at the individual level. The effect of socio-economic status, for example, likely reflects the aggregate of individual characteristics. In addition, however, the overall milieu of the constituency may affect turnout, so that even better-off individuals residing in an economically depressed constituency may be less likely to vote than they would be if they lived elsewhere. The effects on turnout may therefore be the result of a combination of these factors.

Voters and Non-Voters: Socio-Demographic Characteristics

The general relationship between socio-economic factors and voter turnout at the aggregate level is confirmed through survey research of the voting behaviour of random samples of Canadian voters. As shown in Table 2.6, survey data for 1984 (the most recent year for which data are available) pertaining to age, family income, marital status, occupation and religion have a distinct effect on turnout. Other factors being equal, voters are more likely than non-voters to be older, married and better educated; to be employed and to have a higher family income; to have been born in Canada; to be in a white collar occupation or a homemaker; and to belong to one of the main religious groupings. (Pammett 1991 RC; MacDermid 1991 RC) In the past in Canada, as in many other countries, there was a distinct gender gap: women were less likely to vote than men. In recent years, however, this gap has closed considerably. (Canadian National Election Study 1984, 1988)

Table 2.6
Demographic correlates of voters who voted, 1984

Age					
18–21	22–29	30–39	40–49	50–59	60+
63%	71%	83%	85%	88%	88%

Family income (thousands of dollars)					
Under 10	10–15	15–20	20–30	30–40	40+
74%	77%	79%	81%	82%	86%

Marital status		
Single	Widowed, separated, divorced	Married
70%	77%	84%

Occupation					
Student	Unemployed	Blue collar	Clerical/ sales	Homemakers	Professional/ business
68%	70%	77%	81%	82%	85%

Religion				
Other	None	Jewish	Roman Catholic	Protestant
71%	72%	78%	82%	82%

Source: Adapted from Pammett 1991 RC.

Note: Percentages indicate the proportion in each category who voted. For example, 63 per cent between the ages of 18 and 21 voted; 37 per cent in this age group did not vote.

Of all of these factors, the most important determinant is age. Regardless of other characteristics, older voters tend to vote more regularly than younger voters. When socio-economic characteristics are combined with provincial factors, it can be shown that specific sub-groups in the population are either much more likely or much less likely to vote. Voter turnout for young unmarried students with no religious affiliation living in British Columbia is about 40 per cent. By contrast, voter turnout for members of a group such as married, middle-aged, well-educated, Protestant or Catholic professionals living in Prince Edward Island is about 90 per cent. Thus, beyond the basic categories, the variation in turnout can be quite dramatic.

Voters and Non-Voters: Attitudinal Factors

Voters and non-voters are also characterized by differences in political atti-tudes. As shown in Table 2.7, voters are more likely than non-voters to believe that their own vote affects the outcome of elections, to read about politics, to be interested in an election, and to be interested in politics generally.

Table 2.7
Attitudinal correlates of voters who voted, 1984

	Vote doesn't matter		
Strongly agree 63%	Agree 70%	Disagree 83%	Strongly disagree 92%
	Reads about politics		
Often 91%	Sometimes 85%		Seldom/never 73%
	Interested in election		
Very interested 95%	Fairly interested 93%		Slightly/not interested 67%
	Interested in politics		
Very interested 98%	Fairly interested 92%		Not very interested 79%

Source: Adapted from Pammett 1991 RC.

Note: Percentages indicate the proportion in each category who voted. For example, 63 per cent who strongly agreed with the statement that their vote doesn't matter voted in the 1984 election, while 37 per cent of this group did not vote.

These findings are not unexpected, but they do show that voters and non-voters have different attitudes about electoral democracy and that non-voters are more likely to be disengaged from the political process. In particular, responses to the question about the importance of the vote show whether respondents are fundamentally disenchanted with, or alienated from, the political system.

Reasons for Non-Voting

In addition to their socio-economic and attitudinal characteristics, it is important to know why non-voters did not vote in a given election. This is especially important for understanding the motives of occasional non-voters, who make up a much larger group than the perennial non-voters. Through survey research, the reasons for not voting can generally be identi-fied. They may involve a rejection of electoral politics, perhaps only for a spe-cific election; alternatively, an administrative inconvenience or impediment may have been the reason – the voter was not registered or found it too difficult to leave the house or get to the polling station.

Thus two types of self-professed non-voters emerge. The first are those who are too busy or uninterested to cast a ballot. These we will call the 'uninterested' non-voters. The second group includes voters who were not registered and thus were unable to vote, or who were away or ill, especially on election day, and could not cast a ballot. These we will call the 'administratively disfranchised' non-voters (ADNVs). In other words, not all non-voters are alienated or uninterested in the electoral process. The act of voting entails costs in time and effort. There may well be a significant number of citizens who find it too difficult or costly to cast a ballot in a particular election.

Survey data on people who did not vote in the 1974, 1980 and 1984 elections show that 53 per cent, 56 per cent and 43 per cent respectively claimed to be away, sick, or unenumerated, as shown in Table 2.8. In short, about half were busy/uninterested non-voters and about half intended to vote but did not for the reasons just noted.

Table 2.8
Reasons for non-voting, 1974–1984
(per cent)

	1974	1980	1984
Away	38	39	23
Sick	13	13	9
Busy	10	2	19
Uninterested	37	40	39
Unenumerated	2	6	11
Total	100	100	100
N	(437)	(182)	(483)

Source: Pammett 1991 RC, based on Gallup Polls and Canadian National Election Study (1974, 1980, 1984).

As Table 2.9 shows, administratively disfranchised non-voters are more likely to be single, younger and less educated than those who vote; at the same time, they are more likely to be older, married and better educated than non-voters classified as uninterested. For example, only 18 per cent of people who voted are between 18 and 25 years old, compared to 45 per cent of uninterested non-voters. Similarly, 25 per cent of voters are university-educated, versus only 12 per cent of uninterested non-voters.

Moreover, as Table 2.10 indicates, the administratively disfranchised, while less positive than voters about the political and electoral process, are nonetheless more positive than the uninterested non-voters. For example, 26 per cent of the busy/uninterested agreed strongly with the statement that their vote doesn't matter, compared to only 6 per cent of those who voted.

It is reasonable to conclude that 50 per cent of administratively disfranchised non-voters would likely vote if certain obstacles were removed.

As a result, the overall turnout rate would increase by almost 4.5 percentage points. Further, if we also assume that roughly 25 per cent of uninterested non-voters, especially those who were too busy, would also vote if access to the vote were made easier, turnout would increase by an additional 3 percentage points. Taken together, therefore, these two increases could conceivably improve turnout in federal elections by more than 7 percentage points. (Pammett 1991 RC)

Table 2.9
Comparing voters, ADNVs and uninterested non-voters
(per cent)

	Voters	ADNVs	Busy/ uninterested
Age 18–25	18	35	45
Marital status Married	72	57	48
University education	25	16	12

Source: Data provided to the Commission by Jon Pammett, based on National Election Studies and Gallup Polls.

Note: Each cell represents the percentage of voters, ADNVs, and uninterested non-voters for each socio-demographic category, e.g., 72 per cent of voters are married versus 48 per cent of the uninterested.

Table 2.10
Comparing voters, ADNVs and uninterested non-voters
(per cent)

	Voters	ADNVs	Busy/ uninterested
Vote doesn't matter Strongly agree	6	15	26
Political reading Often	46	28	11
Interest in election Very interested	38	17	6
Interest in politics Very interested	19	13	6

Source: Data provided to the Commission by Jon Pammett, based on National Election Studies and Gallup Polls.

Note: Percentages show proportion in each category who concurred with the indicated response category for each of the attitudinal items mentioned in Table 2.7.

The survey data therefore show that, although non-voters who claim to have been administratively disfranchised are generally less interested in politics than those who did vote, they are not as politically disengaged as those who simply declare themselves uninterested in voting. The fact that they did not vote at a given election does not necessarily represent a rejection of the electoral process. Rather, it reflects the fact that some were not registered and others could not vote because of other factors, such as being away or ill.

Individuals who are reasonably motivated will usually find ways of overcoming obstacles and voting. Those less motivated, however, may be unwilling or unable to overcome the same barriers; thus they could well be deterred from voting despite an initial inclination to do so. These are voters who have voted in the past and will likely do so again in the future, though the chances of their doing so are likely contingent on easy access to the voting process.

This interpretation suggests that reforms to make the registration and voting processes more open and accessible will increase the likelihood of these non-voters casting ballots. The objective of electoral reform must be to eliminate or at least to reduce significantly the barriers to and costs of voting as long as the integrity of the process is not jeopardized.

MAKING THE REGISTRATION AND VOTING PROCESSES VOTER-FRIENDLY

Introduction

Registration and voting must facilitate voter turnout if the right to vote is to be secured. Both processes stand in need of major reform. The registration system needs to be revamped fundamentally to ensure that, insofar as possible, it is accessible to those wishing to register and its coverage of qualified voters is complete and accurate. The voting process also needs to be updated to remove rigidities and complexities, to bring voting methods into line with the best practices of electoral systems elsewhere in Canada and abroad, and generally to make the process voter-friendly while preserving the integrity of the vote.

Given the procedural character of the registration system and the voting process, the reforms we propose are necessarily detailed. In this chapter, therefore, we outline the principles and general direction of the reforms we consider essential. A more detailed discussion and specific recommendations are provided in Volume 2 of our report.

The Registration of Voters

The registration of voters serves two fundamental purposes: it determines the eligibility of voters to vote, and it prevents them from voting more than once. In these ways, registration is a regulatory mechanism to ensure the integrity of the vote. Assembling voters lists for each constituency also assists candidates and parties in canvassing voters and encouraging their supporters to vote. In these indirect ways, voters lists are an important instrument for mobilizing voters, thereby promoting political participation and voting.

Canada's approach to the registration of voters consists of three phases:

1. An enumeration or census of voters, administered by returning officers in each constituency using specially appointed enumerators for each polling division.

2. Revision of the preliminary lists produced by the enumeration. This is structured as an appeal process; those not enumerated may apply to be registered, corrections may be made, and objections to those on the preliminary lists may be raised.
3. In rural polling divisions, those not on the voters list can register and hence vote on election day at their polling station if another registered voter from the same polling division vouches for them.

The enumeration process is marked by two major characteristics. First, it is initiated by the state through a nation-wide enumeration carried out by enumerators under the direction of returning officers in each constituency. Second, enumeration is conducted only after an election is called. In both respects the Canadian approach is unique among democracies.

Keeping the onus on the state to seek out voters and enrol them on a voters list was strongly supported at our public hearings. Canadians do not favour any move toward a system where the onus rests on individual voters to register or to ascertain whether they are on the voters list. The experience in the United States, for example, has demonstrated that voluntary registration entails major obstacles to voting. (Courtney and Smith 1991 RC) On a practical level, voluntary registration is not an effective device to secure a meaningful right to vote. Ongoing struggles to reform the U.S. system attest to the deficiencies of voluntary registration. Great Britain, to take another example, has also experienced shortcomings in using a system of essentially voluntary registration. A 1987 study revealed that in 1981, 2.5 million eligible voters were not on the register and another 2.6 million people were wrongly included. (Pinto-Duschinsky and Pinto-Duschinsky 1987)

We conclude that the registration system should continue to be based on state responsibility and should be conducted in a manner predicated on trust. These features are a solid foundation upon which to reform registration in ways that maintain the integrity of the electoral process and improve its capacity to provide more complete and accurate lists of voters.

Reforming Registration

The present registration system is inadequate in several respects. Enumeration fails to register many voters, especially in major urban areas. Among those frequently missed by enumeration are homeless people or people living temporarily in shelters, students living away from home who wish to vote in their home constituency, voters with hearing or reading deficiencies, and voters who are fearful of unannounced visitors or visits from government officials.

Second, the revision process, whereby those not registered by enumeration can be enrolled on the voters list, is too complex, cumbersome and limited to serve this vital purpose effectively. Third, voters not on the voters list are permitted to register and vote on election day only in rural polling divisions, as defined by the *Canada Elections Act*. This procedure is not available to those in urban polling divisions; if they have not been registered through enumeration or revision, they cannot vote.

These shortcomings have administratively disfranchised a significant number of voters. This need not be so; several reforms could eliminate these obstacles. As discussed more fully in Volume 2, they include changes in enumeration and revision and the extension of election-day registration to all voters.

At the same time, enumeration is not the only effective way to compile preliminary voters lists, nor is it always the most cost-efficient. For the 1980 general election, for example, the chief electoral officer decided that there was insufficient time to conduct an enumeration; he determined, however, that the final voters lists for the 1979 election, held nine months previously, would constitute satisfactory preliminary lists, which could be revised by a special registration drive. This approach cost a great deal less than conducting a new enumeration. It also resulted in fewer complaints than usual – and a large majority of these could have been avoided if voters in urban polling divisions had been able to register on election day.

The 1980 experience demonstrated that a properly managed revision can produce lists of high quality when reasonably complete lists of voters already exist. Two provinces, Ontario and British Columbia, maintain continually updated lists of voters. In Ontario, the lists are maintained by the Ministry of Revenue and are used for municipal and school board elections. In British Columbia, the lists are maintained by Elections British Columbia and are used for provincial, municipal and school board elections. With appropriate co-operation and technical modifications, these lists could be purchased and used by Elections Canada as preliminary lists for federal elections, thus eliminating the expense of enumeration in these two provinces. As outlined in Volume 2, our studies indicate that this approach is feasible and worth pursuing.

Except for British Columbia, provinces and territories do not maintain continually updated lists for provincial elections; they conduct enumerations to compile preliminary lists during the election period. Alberta conducts its enumeration outside the election period on a three-year cycle. Newfoundland does so at the discretion of the provincial cabinet.

In every case, then, voters lists are available at some point and could be used as preliminary federal lists if they were sufficiently current, assuming the co-operation of the agencies responsible for registration and the possibility of making the necessary technical modifications. Chief electoral officers from across Canada recognize the duplication of effort that exists and acknowledge that it serves no public policy or public interest purpose.

Giving the chief electoral officer the authority to use provincial or territorial lists as preliminary lists would constitute a useful reform. Provinces and territories could also use final federal voters lists as their preliminary lists for elections if the federal lists were still current. Given that the cost of the last federal enumeration was just over $27 million, while the total cost of all provincial enumerations for the most recent elections was approximately another $30 million, such a measure would result in considerable savings to Canadians. Moreover, such an approach on the part of Elections Canada could serve as an incentive for one or more provinces and territories to maintain continually updated lists, since their use by all levels of government would justify the initial investment and the ongoing cost of maintenance.

The Voting Process

For the vast majority of registered voters, the voting process is simple and accessible. On election day, they go to the assigned polling station, usually located relatively close to home, give their name and address to a deputy returning officer, receive a ballot, go to a voting booth and mark the ballot in secret, fold it so it remains secret, and return the folded ballot to the deputy returning officer, who places it in the ballot box.

The *Canada Elections Act* is deficient, however, in instances where a voter, for one reason or another, is unable to exercise the franchise in this simple and straightforward manner. Although the Act does make some provision for voters who cannot vote in this manner, both its underlying philosophy and its specific provisions are less than voter-friendly. Voting other than on election day is not equally available to all voters, and for some this alternative is not available at all. Moreover, to use these and other exceptional procedures, a voter must be well informed about the details of the election law and must know well in advance that he or she will require their use in order to vote.

To achieve our objective of securing the democratic right of voters to vote, the philosophy that underlies the voting process must be changed. Elements of the process that have until now been considered exceptions must become extensions of the normal voting process. In addition, the alternatives available to voters must be expanded to include procedures in use elsewhere in Canada or in other countries that have been shown to enhance access to the vote and to increase voter turnout. Finally, the Act must be simplified to ensure that these new provisions, as well as changes in existing provisions, can be understood and used easily by voters, candidates and their agents, and election officials.

The following alternatives to voting at a normal polling station on election day are provided in the Act: the advance poll; voting in the office of the returning officer; voting by proxy; voting at a mobile poll; and voting by special ballot. However, these alternatives apply only in limited circumstances and for narrowly defined categories of voters.

Advance polls enable voters to vote before election day on three specified days. However, this opportunity is not readily accessible in many rural polls, especially in remote areas. The same shortcomings, especially the lack of accessibility, apply to the provision allowing voters to vote at the returning officer's office (essentially another form of advance voting) on certain days prior to election day.

An alternative to voting in person on election day is the proxy vote. Registered voters who meet certain conditions can appoint another registered voter to vote on their behalf at the first voter's assigned polling station. This means that the voter's vote is not secret; nor can the voter be guaranteed that the proxy vote will be cast as instructed. In any event, the rules governing this procedure are so complex and demanding that it is used infrequently.

The Act also provides for the use of mobile polls, but only in very restricted circumstances. Mobile polling stations move to where voters are located and remain there only for the period necessary to conduct the vote. At polling stations established in hospitals, for example, the station may be closed for short periods to take the ballot box to patients confined to bed. Mobile polls may also be used for Canadian forces and public service voters living abroad.

Except for members of the Canadian forces and public servants posted abroad, and their spouses and dependants living with them, there is no provision to allow voters living abroad to obtain a ballot and then to tender the ballot in person to an election official or return it by mail. Finally, there are no provisions to allow voters with disabilities to vote using a special ballot.

Reforming the Voting Process

The *Canada Elections Act* must be adapted to expand and modify current voting procedures – including reforms to ensure that the special needs of certain voters are met – to make the exercise of the franchise as accessible as possible while still providing the safeguards necessary to ensure the secrecy of the vote and the integrity of the voting process. Our recommendations, presented in detail in Volume 2, are designed to produce a voting process with two basic components: ordinary voting and the special ballot.

Ordinary Voting

We propose that the ordinary voting procedures for voting at a voter's assigned polling station and at advance polls be extended to include voting at temporary mobile polling stations in many more circumstances than now provided for in the Act. Mobile polling stations would be similar in all respects to regular and advance polling stations, except that they would be available only for a period sufficient to conduct the vote at specified locations, such as nursing homes or communities in remote areas. In this manner, they would be a useful complement to regular and advance polling stations. We also propose that the provisions governing advance polls be made more flexible and broadly available. Any voter who has reason to believe that it would be difficult to vote at an ordinary polling station on election day could vote at an advance poll. For maximum convenience, advance polls would be open for two days spread over two weekends.

Special Ballot

We also propose to extend the use of the special ballot. The special ballot is now available only to members of the Canadian forces in Canada, Canadian forces personnel abroad and public servants posted abroad and their spouses and dependants living with them. This method of voting is extremely flexible, in that it allows voters to vote without having to appear at a polling station. The voter receives a ballot, marks it and returns it in person to an election official or by post to an election office. Several countries, including Australia, Germany, Great Britain, the United States and the Netherlands, as well as the provinces of Quebec, New Brunswick, Manitoba, British Columbia, Saskatchewan and Alberta, successfully use this kind of ballot, commonly referred to as a postal ballot.

Time Off for Voting

The *Canada Elections Act* provides that every employee who is a qualified voter shall have four consecutive hours to vote during the hours the polls are open on election day. If an employee's hours of work do not allow for these four consecutive hours, the employer is to provide time off at regular pay for the period necessary to meet this requirement. If an employer is required to provide time off for voting under this requirement, the hours provided may be arranged at the convenience of the employer. It is an offence for an employer to fail to abide by these provisions.

The rationale for the four-hour provision, first introduced in the 1920 *Dominion Elections Act*, is to ensure that every voter has a reasonable opportunity to cast a ballot on election day. The provision thus contributes to the objective of securing the constitutional right to vote. Every province but Prince Edward Island has a provision for employees to have time off to vote, as do most other democracies.

The obligation of employers is to ensure that employees have four consecutive hours in which to vote. This does not necessarily require them to provide four hours during working hours. Rather, time off is combined, if necessary, with time when employees would not normally be working – so long as the four hours are consecutive during the time polls are open.

At the same time, employers should not be required to pay employees for four hours of time off; a maximum of two hours of time off at regular pay should be sufficient in all but a few circumstances. For instance, employees who work 12-hour shifts that encompass the hours of voting on election day, and who cannot vote within a two-hour period, could use the special ballot or vote at an advance poll. In the case of workers who are paid on an hourly, piece work, or other basis and who normally work during the period of time off work provided to vote, they should be paid the equivalent of what they would normally earn, for up to two hours of the time off work for voting.

Employers and employees should reach an agreement regarding time off for voting. Employees should give adequate advance notice to their employers regarding when they intend to vote, but employers should retain the right to determine when time off would be taken by employees and should not be required to pay employees for time that they would not normally be working.

The right to time off for voting does not apply to certain categories of voters working in the transportation sector if they are eligible to vote by proxy or are not working in the constituency where they are registered to vote and it would take them more than four hours to travel to their polling station. Given the changes we recommend, voters in these circumstances would now be able to vote by special ballot or at an advance poll. In addition, there should be an exemption for employees who work too far away from their polling station to be able to vote during the hours that the polling station is open, as giving them time off work would impose a requirement on employers without achieving the purpose of the Act. These voters should also use the special ballot or vote at an advance poll. Finally, election officials should be excluded from this provision, given their responsibilities on election day.

Recommendation 1.2.11

We recommend that

(a) **every employee who is a qualified voter have four consecutive hours to vote on election day;**

(b) **employers be required to provide whatever time off is necessary to provide for these four consecutive hours at the convenience of the employer;**

(c) **employers be required to provide regular pay for time off for voting to a maximum of two hours; and**

(d) **this provision not extend to persons working as election officials on election day, Canada Elections Commission employees, or employees who, by reason of their employment, are too far from their polling station to be able to vote on election day during the hours the polling station is open.**

NOTES

1. An enfranchised Indian was one who had given up his Indian status.

2. *An Act respecting the Public Curator and Amending the Civil Code and other legislative provisions* (S.Q. 1989, c. 54); *Mental Patients Protection Act* (R.S.Q. P-41); *Mental Health Act* (R.S.O. 1980, c. 262); *Mental Incompetency Act* (R.S.O. 1980, c. 264); *Interpretation Act* (R.S.O. 1980, c. 219); *Dependant Adults Act* (R.S.A. 1980, c. D-32); *Mental Health Act* (R.S.A. c. M-13.1); *Mental Health Act* (R.S.M. 1970, c. M110); *Mental Health Act* (R.S.B.C., c. 256); *Neglected Adults Welfare Act* (S.N. 1973, No. 81); *Infirm Persons Act* (R.S.N.B. 1973, c. I-8); *Mental Health Act* (R.S.P.E.I. 1974, c. M-9); *Incompetent Persons Act* (R.S.N.S. 1967, c. 135); *Mentally Disordered Persons Act* (R.S.S. 1978, c. M-14); *Mental Health Act* (R.S.N. 1971, No. 80); *Mental Health Services Act* (S.S. 1984-85-86, c. M-13.1); *Mental Health Act* (R.S.N.B. 1973, c. M-10); *Mental Health Act* (S.N.W.T. 1985, c. 6); *Mental Health Act* (R.S.Y. 1986, c. 115); *Mentally Incompetent Persons' Estates Act* (R.S.N. 1971, No. 234); *Dependant Adults Act* (S.S. 1989-90, c. D-25).

3

ACCESS TO ELECTED OFFICE

INTRODUCTION

THE CHARTER STATES that every citizen has the "right ... to be qualified for membership" in the House of Commons, subject only to such reasonable limits prescribed by law as can be demonstrably justified in a free and democratic society. The qualifications established for membership are set out in the *Constitution Act, 1867* and the *Canada Elections Act*.

These qualifications are important for two reasons. First, they determine the eligibility of citizens to be candidates. Second, they set the requirements that must be met by citizens who wish to be candidates. In each case, the right to be a candidate must be considered in the context of parliamentary government and the norms that should govern this fundamental question of access in a free and democratic society.

The right to be a candidate ensures that representative government is by citizens. Canadians elect members to the House of Commons directly. By contrast, the prime minister and the cabinet – the ministers of the Crown in whom executive authority is vested by the constitution – are not elected directly. They are selected through Canada's system of responsible government. Nor are members of the judiciary selected by direct election; they are appointed by the prime minister under the Crown's executive authority. Finally, the second house of Parliament, the Senate, is appointed by the executive. The only direct link between Canadians and these organs of government, therefore, is through their representatives in the House of Commons. Under the constitution, these members are elected for a maximum of five years.

Canadian elections are primarily contests between the candidates of political parties; citizens who wish to be serious contenders for election to the House of Commons must therefore secure a party nomination. In 1988, for example, non-affiliated candidates represented 9.8 per cent of all candidates and received less than 1 per cent of the total vote. (This group of candidates included independent candidates and those who represented parties that had failed to meet the registration requirements.) (Bertram 1991 RC) Thus the right of citizens to be candidates can be exercised effectively only to the extent that the nomination process of political parties provides fair access.

The question of candidacy therefore revolves around two groups of issues: the qualifications for candidacy found in constitutional and electoral law, and the processes political parties use to select candidates for election to the House of Commons. The first constitutes the formal or legal foundations of candidacy, the second the *realpolitik* of candidacy. Our mandate requires that we examine both.

THE RIGHT TO BE A CANDIDATE

The *Canada Elections Act* requires that candidates be qualified voters. However, this is not a sufficient condition. The right to vote and the right to be a candidate are not one and the same. The former confers the right to participate in choosing elected representatives; the latter confers the right to be a candidate for elected office. This distinction arises because there are different responsibilities and obligations associated with the exercise of each right. Candidates and members of the House of Commons have responsibilities and obligations that go beyond those of voters, precisely because they are presumed to act on behalf of other citizens. This distinction has long been recognized in Canada's electoral law and that of other democracies.

The Evolution of Qualifications

As with the right to vote, the laws governing the right to candidacy for federal elections have had a chequered history. At Confederation, agreement could not be reached on a federal law to govern qualifications for candidacy or membership in the House of Commons. There was agreement, however, that senators should be barred from election to the Commons, and a provision to this effect was included in the *British North America Act, 1867* (now known as *Constitution Act, 1867*). As a consequence, provincial laws concerning candidacy prevailed, as they did for the franchise, and candidacy requirements varied across the country.

Provinces had certain common requirements: candidates had to be British subjects, male and at least 21 years old. Every province had a property qualification greater than that required of voters, although the dollar amount varied from province to province. By Confederation, every province had also accepted that judges could not be members of the legislative branch and therefore could not be candidates. In addition, persons holding government contracts could not be members of the House of Commons; neither could public officials. Because ministers received a salary from the Crown in addition to their stipend as MPs, they met the definition of public official. Members appointed to ministerial posts therefore had to resign their seats and seek re-election as candidates holding a ministerial portfolio, to obtain the approval of voters for this deviation from the principle. Finally, persons convicted of corrupt or illegal election practices were excluded from candidacy for specified periods of time.

Provincial rules on 'dual' representation were not uniform. In Ontario and Quebec, members of the provincial legislature were eligible to be candidates for and members of the House of Commons. But New Brunswick and Nova Scotia had taken legislative action on dual representation. In New Brunswick, members of the provincial legislature could be candidates for election to the House, but they had to resign their provincial seat before they could sit in the Commons. Members of the Nova Scotia legislature could be neither members of the House of Commons nor candidates for election to the Commons.

Finally, it was possible to be a candidate in more than one constituency, but a person could not hold more than one seat in the House of Commons. If elected in more than one constituency, the member had to choose which seat to hold.

Parliament began to legislate on matters affecting candidacy and membership in the House of Commons in 1873. That year a private member's bill to disqualify members of provincial legislatures as candidates for the House of Commons was enacted. In the first House of Commons, members of the Ontario and Quebec legislatures held seats while retaining their provincial seats. In fact, a majority of both provincial cabinets held Commons seats. (Ward 1963, 65) The entry of Manitoba into Confederation in 1871 brought two more members of a provincial legislature to the House of Commons. The bipartisan agreement to end this early practice recognized the need for MPs to be independent of the provincial order of government.

In 1874, federal law eliminated the property qualification for candidates. This brought Canadian law into line with contemporary British and U.S. practice and acknowledged that the qualification had not been enforced.

In 1878, federal laws tightened the provisions on government office holders and contractors to ensure the independence of the House of Commons from government. The 1878 statute also disqualified as candidates sheriffs, clerks of the peace, county Crown attorneys and registrars in recognition of their responsibilities for administering federal elections (which were still conducted by the provinces). Other than this provision, provincial public officials were not, and have never been, disqualified by federal law from candidacy for the House of Commons.

Although multiple candidacies were never common, there were several instances in which candidates, particularly prominent political figures, contested two seats, notably Sir Wilfrid Laurier and Sir George-Étienne Cartier. Sir John A. Macdonald even contested three seats in a single general election: two in September 1878 and a third in October, since at that time, polling day did not have to be held on the same day across the Dominion. (Ward 1963, 81) Of the 14 cases in which a candidate won two seats, 12 involved party leaders. The rationale for this practice was, first, to provide a safe seat for the party leader; the second reason was to have the party leader contest a seat previously held by the other party. Needless to say, the practice required a number of by-elections following the general election. (Ward 1963, 81–82)

In 1919, federal legislation required that "members elected in two districts ... had to choose one of them or be penalized for it, unless it could be established that one of the candidatures was without their knowledge" (Ward 1963, 80–81)

The same year, the electoral law was amended to extend the right to be a candidate to women, coinciding with the extension to them of the right to vote.

In 1931, the provision requiring ministers appointed following an election to resign their seats and seek re-election was repealed. This requirement had caused inconvenience to more than one government; it had also been an important factor in the constitutional crisis of 1926. Repeal of the provision made ministers an "absolute [exception] to the general rule that an office of emolument disqualifies for the House of Commons". (Ward 1963, 97)

In 1948, the election law stipulated for the first time that candidates be qualified voters, although it did not require that candidates reside in the constituency where they sought election. In 1970, the law required that voters be Canadian citizens. In 1982, the Charter entrenched the right of every citizen to be qualified for membership in the House of Commons and thus to be a candidate, subject to the requirement that disqualifications must be prescribed by law and must constitute reasonable limits that can be demonstrably justified in a free and democratic society.

As the right to seek membership in the House of Commons evolved, federal law established more firmly the independence of Parliament from the executive branch and from the provincial order of government. At the same time federal law maintained the practice of disqualifying certain categories of persons as candidates. Some are disqualified by virtue of the public offices they occupy, and some are disqualified because they have been convicted of offences under the *Canada Elections Act*.

Qualifications for Candidacy

Prospective candidates must be eligible to sit in the House of Commons. Eligibility is defined by electoral law, constitutional law and other requirements.

Some disqualifications are based on the office a prospective candidate already holds. Sometimes the nature of the office is incompatible with both membership and candidacy. In other cases, eligibility to be a candidate should be considered separately from eligibility to sit in the House of Commons; the offices in question may be incompatible with membership in the House, but not incompatible with candidacy. This crucial distinction is not found in the current electoral law. If this distinction were applied, it would be necessary for a successful candidate to resign from the office in question only after the election, before taking a seat in the House.

In addition, there may be some categories of persons who should not be eligible for candidacy because their circumstances would not permit them to fulfil the responsibilities of candidates or the representative obligations of a member of the House of Commons.

Finally, the elections act requires that candidates be qualified voters. This is a reasonable and necessary condition for candidacy since it establishes who is a member of the polity.

Recommendation 1.3.1

We recommend that only qualified voters be eligible to be candidates.

Incompatibility of Offices

Certain official positions are incompatible with candidacy and membership in the House of Commons. The three categories of persons affected by this criterion are senators, judges and election officers.

Senators   The *Constitution Act, 1867* states that senators "shall not be capable of being elected or of sitting or voting as a Member of the House of Commons" (s. 39). Senators are already Members of Parliament, and the constitution makes it clear that the two houses of Parliament have separate functions, powers and responsibilities in the legislative process.

Separating the memberships of the upper and lower legislative chambers was an important development in the reforms that culminated in responsible government in the late 1840s. Along with other reforms, this separation served to ensure the independence of the lower house from the executive branch under the authority of the colonial governor.

Separating the two houses also brought Canadian practice into line with the British tradition. The peers of Parliament, that is, members of the House of Lords, have always been disqualified from sitting in the House of Commons. This reflects the distinct and separate status of the House of Lords and the different representative roles of members of the two houses. Consequently, peers are disqualified from standing for election to the House of Commons. A 1960 controversy confirmed this traditional disqualification and led subsequently to the *Peerage Act 1963*, which made it possible for a hereditary peer to disclaim a peerage and thus to be a candidate for election to the Commons. Anyone holding a life peerage (the equivalent of a senator in Canada) would be obliged to renounce the peerage before seeking a seat in the House of Commons.

Because the reason for disqualifying senators as candidates is fundamental to the Canadian constitution, we see no cause to alter this disqualification.

Recommendation 1.3.2

We recommend that senators be disqualified as candidates for election to the House of Commons while they hold office.

Judges   The *Canada Elections Act* provides that judges appointed by the Governor in Council, other than citizenship judges appointed under the *Citizenship Act*, are not qualified to vote. They are thereby disqualified as candidates. A Federal Court of Canada decision has declared this disqualification from voting invalid. Moreover, we recommend that judges should have the right to vote. We see no conflict with their independence or impartiality implied by this right. It is a right of citizenship, exercised in secret.

It does not follow, however, that judges should have the right to be members of the House of Commons. The independence of the judicial branch is a fundamental principle of our system of government and requires that membership in the judiciary be separate from membership in the legislative branch.

Moreover, the principle of independence, along with the principle of impartiality, also requires that judges not be eligible to be candidates for election to the House of Commons. Candidacy, even for candidates who are independent of any political party, implies partisanship. This is clearly contrary to the basic idea of impartiality. Judges must be and must be seen to be impartial.

Recommendation 1.3.3

We recommend that judges, including federal, provincial and territorial judges, other than citizenship judges be disqualified as candidates for election to the House of Commons while they hold office.

Election Officers   The chief electoral officer, the assistant chief electoral officer and returning officers are not qualified to vote and are thereby disqualified as candidates. We recommend that these officials be given the right to vote. This is an act of citizenship and is exercised in secret. No conflict with the impartiality of election officers is implied by giving them the right to vote.

Candidacy is by definition a public act of partisanship, however, and requires different criteria to preserve impartiality. The impartiality expected of permanent election officers, of the members and managerial and professional staff of the Canada Elections Commission that we recommend in a subsequent chapter, and of officials appointed for each election demands that they be disqualified as candidates. There is clear and obvious incompatibility between their functions and candidacy. They cannot be both impartial officials responsible for conducting elections and participants in the electoral contest.[1]

Recommendation 1.3.4

We recommend that election officers, members of the Canada Elections Commission and the Commission's managerial and professional staff be disqualified as candidates for election to the House of Commons while they hold office.

Compatibility with Candidacy

Some persons occupy official positions or have official relationships with government that are incompatible with membership in the House of Commons but not incompatible with candidacy. This applies, for example, to members of provincial legislatures and territorial councils, public servants and other public employees, and persons holding contracts with the federal government.

Provincial Legislators and Territorial Councillors Members of provincial legislatures and territorial councils are disqualified as candidates for the House of Commons while they hold office. Dual representation was abolished in 1873, under federal legislation prohibiting members of provincial legislatures from even being candidates for election to the House of Commons.

We see no reason to return to dual representation. The constitution divides legislative authority between the federal and provincial orders of government, and the federal and provincial legislatures have independent authority over matters within their jurisdictions. Moreover, it is well established in constitutional law that neither Parliament nor a provincial legislature may delegate its assigned powers to the other. This fundamental constitutional fact means that the two orders of government must be distinct and independent of each other. It follows that membership in Parliament and in provincial legislatures should be separate.

The same logic applies to territorial councils, although they do not have the same independence from Parliament. Territorial governments are responsible for representing the interests of their citizens on matters authorized by federal law. For this reason territorial councillors should not be qualified to sit on a territorial council and in the House of Commons at the same time. Members of municipal councils are not covered by the *Canada Elections Act*. We do not believe that this constitutes a gap in the law, given that municipal governments fall within provincial jurisdiction.

Federal law need not, however, disqualify members of a provincial legislature or territorial council from seeking election at the federal level if they wish to bring to the House of Commons policy issues or concerns pertaining to the province or territory they represent. The functions of candidacy do not entail the functions of an elected representative in the House of Commons. If elected, however, these members would have to resign their provincial or territorial seat before taking a seat in the House of Commons, as the *Canada Elections Act* now requires. Allowing these members to be candidates could result in a rise in the number of by-elections if they won but turned down a seat in the Commons; the likelihood of this outcome is small. Candidates in this position would be forced by public pressure to declare their intentions well before election day. This should also remove any conflict of interest between being a member of a provincial legislature or territorial council and being a candidate.

Recommendation 1.3.5

We recommend that

(a) **members of provincial legislatures and territorial councils be qualified as candidates for election to the House of Commons but be required to resign their seat in a provincial legislature or on a territorial council if elected; and**
(b) **the *Parliament of Canada Act* be amended accordingly.**

Public Officials   A wide range of public officials are excluded from candidacy by the *Canada Elections Act*. The Act states that every person is ineligible "who accepts or holds any office, commission or employment, permanent or temporary, in the service of the Government of Canada at the nomination of the Crown or at the nomination of any of the officers of the Government of Canada, to which any salary, fee, wages, allowance, emolument or profit of any kind is attached, during the time he so holds that office, commission or employment". Ministers are exempt from this provision, as are members of the Canadian forces on active service as a consequence of war, and members of the Canadian forces reserve who are not on full-time service other than active service as a consequence of war. Public servants and other public sector employees who have been granted a leave of absence to seek a nomination and be a candidate are also exempt from this provision. These public officials perform functions under the executive authority of the Crown, as represented by ministers. They cannot be members of the executive branch and the legislative branch at the same time, given their separate and distinct responsibilities. Their functions as officials within the executive branch are incompatible with membership in the House of Commons.

As the current law implies, however, there is no reason to exclude these officials from candidacy if they obtain a leave of absence to seek a nomination and contest an election. The impartiality and neutrality expected of public officials relates only to the performance of duties specific to their position. It ought not to imply that they are denied the right to seek a nomination candidacy or be a candidate. Moreover, given the provisions of the law with respect to leaves of absence, such persons are not rendered incapable of performing the duties of a public official in an impartial and neutral manner following an unsuccessful nomination or electoral effort.

The *Canada Elections Act* covers all public employees who are considered public servants under the *Public Service Employment Act*, as well as individuals employed by government agencies and corporations subject to the *Canada Labour Code*. It does not encompass order-in-council appointees, who are not entitled to leaves of absence. The law specifies, however, that public employees must be granted a leave of absence by the employer or the employer's agent (such as the Public Service Commission) before seeking a nomination or contesting an election. If it is judged that the future effectiveness of an employee under the authority of the Public Service Commission may be impaired by contesting a nomination or an election, the request may be denied. On the other hand, employees whose employers are subject to the *Canada Labour Code* are entitled to a leave of absence.

Three questions arise. First, should the right to take a leave of absence (rather than the right simply to *apply* for leave) be an entitlement? Second, should public employees at all levels, including those appointed by order in council, be entitled to this right? Finally, should leaves of absence extend beyond the election campaign period to cover employees elected to the House of Commons?

Public employees in six provinces are entitled to a leave of absence to participate in electoral politics: British Columbia (non-management employees); Alberta (all non-management personnel); Manitoba (all employees except deputy ministers and designated staff); Ontario (all but senior staff); Saskatchewan (all employees); and Quebec (all but deputy ministers, assistant deputy ministers and associate deputy ministers). In British Columbia and Manitoba, moreover, leave can be extended for five years if the candidate is elected. New Brunswick law provides that a leave of absence *may* be granted. This also applies to management personnel in British Columbia, whereas Alberta and Ontario make no provision for senior management.

The right of citizens employed by the Crown to be candidates for election to the House of Commons should be limited only where it can be demonstrated that the public interest in an impartial and neutral public service would be seriously impaired by the exercise of this right. The principles of an impartial and neutral public service are described in a *Statement of Principles Regarding the Conduct of Public Employees*, published in 1986 by the Institute of Public Administration of Canada, which is an independent national association of public administrators from all orders of government. The statement makes it clear that impartiality and neutrality are required of public servants while in office. These principles do not require that public servants have a non-partisan personal history. Rather, impartiality and neutrality are to be judged on the basis of performance while in the employ of the state.

This interpretation conforms with federal administrative practice. Many federal public service officials were once members of ministers' 'exempt' staff – staff appointed by and serving ministers as partisan aides. The converse is also true. Departmental officials are often seconded to a minister's office for short periods; this is common practice in several countries, including Great Britain and France. Further evidence of the possibility of impartial and neutral public service from people with partisan connections is the tradition of appointments to the rank of deputy minister of persons from outside the public service; they may have links to the prime minister or the party in power, but they are expected to eschew partisan politics while occupying a public service position. Moreover, to the extent that the public interest is served by the election of people with extensive knowledge of and attachment to the public sector, we should not be discouraging public servants from seeking office if that is their desire or requiring that they give up their livelihood to do so.

If public service impartiality and neutrality do not require that public servants, even at the highest levels, have no political past – even an immediate past – it follows that all public employees should be entitled to exercise the right to seek nomination as a candidate and to be a candidate, provided they take a leave of absence. This would be a leave of absence as an employee of the Crown, not leave from a particular position. The employee would be entitled to a position at an equivalent level if she or he returned; the guarantee would not extend to a return to the same position.

The professionalism of the public service is the basis on which this right can be reconciled with impartiality and neutrality. To imply otherwise is to belie federal practices and traditions. Certainly, in individual cases there may be tensions between individual public servants who exercise this right and their political masters in the government of the day. But these tensions are present in any event, as ministers may suspect the loyalties of officials promoted to their current positions by a previous government or by procedures beyond the control of ministers.

At the same time, we acknowledge that public servants have no right to tenure as public employees beyond the time necessary to seek a nomination or be a candidate. In our view, the right to be a candidate should not entail any protection of an individual's position in the federal public service or as a member of the board or staff of a commission, agency or Crown corporation following an election. If elected to the House of Commons, the individual's employment with the Crown should be deemed terminated. Public service employment legislation might provide for a leave of absence before or after the election period, as is the case in other jurisdictions, but this entitlement should not be inherent in the right to be a candidate.

Recommendation 1.3.6

We recommend that

(a) **federal public service employees and members of the boards and staff of commissions, agencies and Crown corporations have the right to a leave of absence, following the issue of the writ, to seek a nomination and to be a candidate in a federal election;**

(b) **if the individual is not nominated, this leave of absence expire seven days after the nomination date; if the individual is a candidate, it expire seven days after a candidate has been declared elected;**

(c) **public servants on such a leave of absence continue to receive the non-salary benefits to which they are regularly entitled; and**

(d) **this not preclude any agreement between the above-noted employees and their employer about a leave of absence before or after the writ period.**

Persons Holding Contracts with Government   Every person holding a contract with the federal government is disqualified from being a candidate.

The rationale for this is the need to avoid conflict of interest if a contractor becomes a member of the House of Commons. The potential conflict of interest concerns a Member of Parliament, not a candidate. If persons holding contracts with the government were elected, they would merely have to bring the contractual relationship with the government into line with the rules governing the conduct of MPs. Current provisions with respect to the letting of contracts with government require that their dealing be a matter of public record. We do not, therefore, see any reason to exclude any such person from being a candidate.

Recommendation 1.3.7

We recommend that the disqualification from being candidates of voters holding contracts with the government be removed.

Ineligibility
Finally, some categories of persons may be declared ineligible to be candidates because they cannot meet the requirements of candidacy or membership in the House of Commons; those who cannot fulfil the conditions of membership in the House should not be eligible to be candidates. They include people legally deprived of the right to manage their affairs, Canadian citizens who are foreign residents, and certain prisoners and persons who have been convicted of corrupt or illegal practices under the *Canada Elections Act*.

Legal Capacity   The right to be a candidate requires that a citizen be able to meet certain legal conditions that have been imposed on candidacy to protect the integrity of the electoral process. Candidates state under oath that their nomination papers are in order, that they consent to the nomination and that they have attested to the financial reporting documents submitted to the chief electoral officer by them or on their behalf by their official agent. Candidates must be legally responsible for actions taken during a campaign and be able to be prosecuted if the Act is contravened. Those who have been legally deprived of the right to manage their property and persons under the age of 18 cannot perform these functions of candidacy or accept the legal responsibilities entailed. It follows that these persons cannot meet the statutory requirements to be candidates, even if some of them are qualified as voters.

Given the strong public interest in the integrity of electoral law as it pertains to the conduct of candidates, all candidates must be able to act with full legal authority and responsibility.

Recommendation 1.3.8

We recommend that voters who have been legally deprived of the right to manage their property be ineligible to be candidates.

Canadians Living Abroad   We recommend that voters living abroad be entitled to vote. Canadian voters living abroad are effectively disfranchised at present, but they are eligible to be candidates.

To promote the aims of electoral contests and protect the integrity of the electoral process, it is justified to require that persons who wish to be candidates be residents of Canada at the time their nomination is filed. Meeting this condition should serve as evidence that such candidates intend to take part actively in the election process and, if elected, to represent their constituents in Parliament. However, the Act should retain the current provision that states that members of the Canadian forces on active service as a consequence of war have a right to candidacy.

Recommendation 1.3.9

We recommend that any voter not a resident of Canada on the date on which her or his nomination is filed be ineligible to be a candidate, unless a member of the Canadian forces on active service as a consequence of war.

Prisoners   We recommend in Chapter 2 of this volume that, with some exceptions, prisoners be entitled to vote. The question of their eligibility as candidates and members of the House of Commons thus arises. The law does not address this question; prisoners are disqualified from voting and are therefore ineligible to be candidates. During our public hearings, many groups argued in favour of extending the right to vote to prisoners, but they drew a distinction between the right to vote and the right to be a candidate.

The rationale for excluding prisoners from candidacy and membership in the House of Commons is twofold. First, MPs are expected to represent their constituents and serve them in their dealings with government. Although prisoners might be able to perform some of these functions, it is obvious that they could not represent their constituents in Parliament from prison. Second, candidates must be able to participate in the election campaign to provide the electorate with the opportunity to assess their candidacy and to engage in a dialogue with them. Thus, persons serving sentences that overlap with the electoral period would be unable to carry out these necessary functions.

The right of prisoners to be candidates must be balanced with the public interest in effective representation and operation of the House of Commons. The public interest requires that members of the House of Commons fulfil their duties on behalf of their constituents, including their legislative functions.

At issue is whether voters would elect a prisoner given that the responsibilities of MPs require their presence in the House and its committees along with direct service to constituents and that these responsibilities cannot be discharged at a distance. It might seem reasonable to let normal conditions and requirements apply and allow the electorate to decide. However, Members of Parliament must provide representation for all constituents in their constituencies – not only their supporters but also those who did not vote for them. Voters who voted for someone other than the winning candidate have every right to expect their MP to represent them in Parliament and to provide the services expected of an MP. In Canada, those voting against the elected candidate usually constitute the majority of voters in a constituency. Those who voted against a winning candidate who was a prisoner sentenced to a lengthy period covering all or a substantial part of the average term of Parliament would find themselves without an MP to represent them in Parliament or provide these services.

In Quebec, the law allows prisoners to be candidates if they are serving a sentence of less than two years. The prisoner must meet all conditions of candidacy; beyond that, the decision is left to the voters. This rationale was used in *MacLean* (1987). The dispute centred on an individual who had been convicted of a criminal offence and who, by provincial law, was prohibited from being a candidate for five years. The decision was that, under section 3 of the Charter, the law could not prohibit his candidacy. The choice, said the court, was to be made by the voters.

In Australia and Great Britain, prisoners are not eligible to be candidates if they are convicted and imprisoned for more than one year. In France, prisoners are effectively barred from candidacy through a disqualification to enrol and hence to vote.

However, in assessing who should have the right to candidacy, it must be emphasized that those seeking election to the House must also be able to fulfil certain crucial functions during the campaign period. These include participating in public debates and meeting with constituents, responsibilities that even a person serving a short sentence could not carry out if it coincided with the electoral period. Hence it is reasonable and appropriate that those unable to perform these essential functions of candidacy be ineligible to be a candidate. Obviously, these restrictions would not apply to those on parole.

Recommendation 1.3.10

We recommend that any prisoner who is serving a sentence that includes the period from nomination day to election day be ineligible to be a candidate.

The rules of the House of Commons, however, do not demand removal of an elected member who is subsequently imprisoned. An MP can be serving a sentence for any offence and still remain a member of the House of Commons. To ensure that the representational needs of constituents are met, MPs who are sentenced to prison for more than six months should be required to resign their seat.

Recommendation 1.3.11

We recommend that the *Parliament of Canada Act* be amended to require that any sitting member sentenced to prison for six months or more resign his or her seat.

Persons Convicted of Corrupt or Illegal Practices　Persons convicted of corrupt practices under the *Canada Elections Act* are excluded from candidacy for seven years; those convicted of illegal practices are ineligible for five years.

Although we propose removing the concepts of corrupt and illegal practices from the elections act, we believe that the courts should still be able to impose penalties for conviction of certain serious offences; among the penalties would be exclusion from standing as a candidate at the next election. This would ensure that when this penalty was imposed, there would be a rational connection between the offence and the limit on the right to candidacy. This provision is required to fulfil a fundamental requirement of the electoral law – securing the integrity of the electoral process.

Recommendation 1.3.12

We recommend that the penalties for conviction of serious election offences include the provision that a judge can disqualify a person from being a candidate at the next election.

Conditions of Candidacy

Elections are conducted under rules designed to foster and secure the public interest in representative government. The public interest includes the need to ensure that the right to candidacy is not abused in ways that diminish public confidence in electoral contests or in the enforcement of election law.

Simultaneous Candidacies

The *Parliament of Canada Act* prohibits a person from seeking candidacy for election to the House of Commons in more than one constituency at the same time. Given the ambit of this provision, it properly belongs in the *Canada Elections Act*.

Recommendation 1.3.13

We recommend that

(a) **the *Canada Elections Act* prohibit a person from being a candidate for election in more than one constituency at the same time; and**
(b) **the *Parliament of Canada Act* be amended accordingly.**

Nomination Requirements

Electoral laws in democratic countries invariably require that prospective candidates demonstrate that they have a degree of support for their candidacy from other citizens. This does not necessarily require selection and nomination by a political party. It does, however, require nomination by a specified number of voters living in the constituency in which nomination is sought. This requirement is justified by the need to have elections contested only by candidates who have already demonstrated that they represent the political preferences of some voters.

Electoral law also invariably requires that candidates certify, and be legally able to certify, that they will fulfil the legal obligations of candidates. These obligations are imposed to uphold the integrity of the electoral process and to assure the polity of effective enforcement of the electoral law. Moreover, given that elections are conducted largely at public expense, it is reasonable to ensure abuses do not occur.

Persons who are unable or unwilling to meet these conditions must forgo their right to be a candidate. The conditions should not impose an unreasonable burden on citizens seeking to exercise this right; but at the same time it is not unreasonable that there be conditions. A balance must be struck between the right of candidacy and the public interest in fair and orderly elections.

The *Canada Elections Act* requires prospective candidates to secure nomination by 25 eligible voters living in the appropriate constituency and to pay a deposit of $200. The deposit is refunded if the candidate is elected or receives at least 15 per cent of the valid votes cast. The 25 signatures are required to demonstrate that prospective candidates have a measure of public support for their candidacy. The deposit seeks to ensure that the person's candidacy is serious and related directly to the electoral process.

These conditions are not adequate. The deposit is unfair in that it penalizes too many candidates; the number of votes needed to claim reimbursement of the deposit is often too high for all but the winner and the runner-up. Serious independent candidates, and even candidates from registered political parties, often lose their deposit with no public purpose being served.

The deposit is also ineffective because, at $200, it is hardly a financial deterrent to a frivolous candidate. Many people consider it an acceptable price for the publicity that goes along with being a candidate. The deposit was originally set at $50 in 1874 and then increased to $200 in 1882; it was an effective deterrent for that time. Adjusted for inflation, the deposit would now be set at $2500.

The public interest in setting conditions on candidacy is twofold. First, there is a legitimate public interest in the integrity and effectiveness of electoral competition. Candidates should be required to demonstrate that they are serious. At the same time, financial obstacles should not be used to discourage candidacy. Rather, the seriousness of a candidacy should be measured by the test of public support. Nomination by voters, rather than self-nomination, is meant to demonstrate public support. Given the expansion of the franchise and the average size of constituencies, however, 25 signatures are not an adequate reflection of public support.

The requirement that a candidate be nominated by 25 voters was set in 1874, when the average number of voters in a constituency was less than 5000. (Ward 1963, 214) The average number of voters in a constituency today is about 60 000 – a twelvefold increase. Taking these figures into consideration, and accounting for the time required to obtain signatures in support of a nomination and the current geographic size of most constituencies, we conclude that a tenfold increase in the number of signatures required should be sufficient to serve the intended purpose. Except in constituencies now classified as Schedule III districts (which we suggest renaming as 'remote constituencies'), a candidate for nomination should be required to obtain 250 signatures of voters in that constituency; in remote constituencies, 100 signatures should be sufficient.

Further, given the distances that someone might have to travel to comply with the Act's requirements for filing the nomination documents in person with the returning officer, we propose to allow the transmission of nomination documents to be carried out by facsimile or by filing them with any official designated by the returning officer. The official may then transmit the documents by whatever means possible, including facsimile, to the returning officer with the original documents mailed at the same time. Interveners before the Commission stressed the need for such flexibility, particularly in larger constituencies.

Unlike the situation in 1874, when political parties were not recognized in election law, most candidates today are selected and endorsed by political parties that are themselves registered under the *Canada Elections Act*. Under the conditions for registration, political parties are required to demonstrate that they are continuing political organizations with a substantial base of support among the electorate.

Their status as registered political parties means that they have a legitimate claim to nominate candidates through constituency associations. For candidates nominated and confirmed by the party leader in this way, the requirement to obtain signatures is redundant.

Recommendation 1.3.14

We recommend that

(a) in the case of candidates of registered constituency associations, the signatures of a member of the executive and the official agent of the constituency association be required, certifying that the nomination has been made in accordance with the constitution of the association;

(b) in all other cases, the number of signatures required for nomination be 250 voters in that constituency, except in remote constituencies, where the number required be 100; and

(c) the returning officer be permitted to accept, as an original document, nomination papers received via facsimile.

The second public purpose served by conditions on candidacy is ensuring the integrity of the electoral process and protecting public investment in the conduct of elections and the support of electoral campaigns. In this latter respect, for instance, candidates are required to declare under oath that they will meet the Act's financial reporting requirements. Candidates who fail to fulfil their obligation to report on contributions and expenses undermine the integrity of the system and impose additional costs on the public treasury by forcing Elections Canada to initiate enforcement procedures.

The candidate's $200 deposit does not cover the expense of enforcement, nor is it a deterrent to candidates who do not fulfil their obligations. In 1988, 92 candidates, or 6 per cent, failed to file their election expense returns by the deadline, and considerable expense had to be incurred to enforce the law. At the same time, the deposit imposes a penalty on candidates who do meet their obligations but do not obtain sufficient votes for reimbursement.

Only those who do not meet their obligations under the law should be penalized. The cost to a candidate of failing to comply should therefore correspond to the costs resulting from this failure. Elections Canada estimates that the current cost of enforcement is a minimum of $1000. The deposit is not to deter frivolous candidates; this objective is achieved by requiring public endorsement for a nomination. Instead of making a deposit, therefore, candidates should post a performance guarantee that would be refunded or cancelled if they met their obligations under the *Canada Elections Act*. This performance guarantee could also be posted for the candidate by supporters or an organization such as a constituency association or party. Under these new conditions, we do not believe the size of the performance guarantee would be a serious hindrance to candidates who intend to abide by the requirements of the law.

Recommendation 1.3.15

We recommend that candidates be required to provide a performance guarantee of $1000, the guarantee to be cancelled or fully refundable to candidates who meet their obligations to file reporting documents in accordance with the requirements of the *Canada Elections Act*.

Candidates Who Fail to File a Report
In Volume 1, Chapter 7, we recommend changes to the reporting requirements of the *Canada Elections Act*. Currently, winning candidates who fail

to submit the required reporting documents lose the right to sit or vote in the House of Commons until the conditions are fulfilled. This provision, which was first introduced in the *Dominion Elections Act* of 1920, should be retained. Further, submission of the necessary reporting documents should be a condition for candidacy at the next election. These requirements are necessary to protect the integrity of the electoral process and constitute a reasonable limitation on the right to be a candidate. The reporting requirements for candidates are not onerous; in fact, most candidates comply within the prescribed period.

We recognize that this requirement places an explicit limitation on the Charter right to be qualified for membership in the House of Commons. However, given that the reporting requirement is not onerous – and the potential impact on the integrity of the electoral process is severe – a much greater burden is placed on the public interest. The lack of such a rule creates the possibility of abuse that can never be contained. We therefore conclude that limiting the right of those who have demonstrated unequivocally their unwillingness to abide by the minimal legal requirements of candidacy is reasonable and justified in a free and democratic society.

Recommendation 1.3.16

We recommend that

(a) the requirement in the *Canada Elections Act* to submit the required reporting documents or lose the right to sit or vote in the House of Commons until the conditions are fulfilled be retained; and

(b) candidates who have not complied with the *Canada Elections Act* reporting requirements for a previous election by the deadline for filing nominations in a subsequent election be ineligible to be candidates at that election.

Right to a Leave of Absence

Public sector employees whose employer is subject to Part III of the *Canada Labour Code* have the right to a leave of absence to seek a nomination and to be a candidate during the election period. This is not simply the right to apply for leave but an entitlement; the employer must grant the leave. In Quebec, a similar provision applies to all employers in the province. These provisions recognize that the right to seek nomination and be a candidate is diminished to the extent that some citizens are unable to do so because of the terms of their employment.

The need to expand the opportunities for people from the private sector to become involved in political life led to the funding of the Institute for Political Involvement, a national non-partisan organization whose membership included large and small companies, business associations and private individuals. The Institute has prepared *A Model Corporate Policy on Political Leave for Employees* (1981) that draws upon the best practices of existing corporate policies.

The model recommends that regular employees be entitled to a leave of absence to run for office, to return to the position they occupied or an equivalent, and to continue to participate in pension plans and other benefit plans while on leave of absence. Such provisions recognize that in many instances a person could not run for office unless the employer granted a leave of absence. They are of greatest benefit to employees whose financial and family circumstances would make them hesitant to assume the risk involved in running for office if they were required to resign. By protecting employment, such measures promote accessibility to candidacy and, ultimately, a more representative House of Commons.

Analogous provisions are found in Canadian law for jury duty. Five provinces – Newfoundland, Quebec, Ontario, Saskatchewan and Alberta – recognize in law that the performance of certain citizens' public responsibilities takes precedence over the rights of employers with respect to employees.

The right to candidacy is so fundamental that it is not subject to the notwithstanding clause of the Charter. The objectives of the *Canada Elections Act* should take precedence over federal or provincial laws governing employer-employee relationships. To the extent that the right is exercised during a very limited period, the provision is not a major intrusion into labour law, and it pertains directly to a central objective of the electoral process. This provision does not constitute an invasion of provincial jurisdiction.

Seeking a nomination and being a candidate are fundamental acts of citizenship and should be treated as such when an individual's employment status affects his or her capacity to undertake them once the writ has been issued. The recommended provision in the *Canada Elections Act* for the electoral period does not preclude any agreement between employers and employees about a leave of absence before or following the writ period.

Recommendation 1.3.17

We recommend that

(a) **every employer, on receiving written notice, grant a leave of absence following the issue of an election writ to an employee seeking nomination and candidacy in a federal election;**
(b) **if the individual is not nominated, this leave of absence expire seven days after the nomination date; if the individual is a candidate, it expire seven days after a candidate has been declared elected;**
(c) **employees on such a leave of absence continue to receive the non-salary benefits to which they are regularly entitled; and**

(d) this not preclude any agreement between employees and employers about a leave of absence before or after the writ period.

The Right to Representation – By-Elections

When a vacancy occurs in the House of Commons between general elections, and the chief electoral officer has received a warrant for the issue of a writ from the Speaker of the House of Commons, the Governor in Council has six months to set a date for a by-election. This provision in the *Parliament of Canada Act*, coupled with the lack of a maximum campaign period for by-elections, means that residents of a constituency where an MP resigns or dies may be deprived of representation for a potentially lengthy period. In four instances in 1977–78, for example, constituents were without an MP for more than a year.

Some flexibility is required in setting a date for a by-election, but this requirement must be balanced against the fundamental right of Canadians to representation. Thus we believe that the deadline for calling and holding a by-election should be set at no more than 180 days from the day the Speaker of the House is informed of the vacancy. This would mean that the maximum period that constituents could be without a representative in the House would be six months, which as we discuss elsewhere is the maximum length of time a constituency should remain unrepresented. Further, the same restrictions on the length of the electoral period that apply to general elections should also apply to by-elections.

The only exceptions would be when a vacancy occurs within six months of the expiration of the time limit for the duration of the House of Commons or when a general election has been called. In both these situations the general election takes precedence over the by-election.

Recommendation 1.3.18

We recommend that

(a) the provision pertaining to the issue of a writ for a by-election be deleted from the *Parliament of Canada Act*;
(b) the *Canada Elections Act* require that a by-election be called and held within 180 days of the day the Speaker of the House of Commons is informed of the vacancy;
(c) the recommended election period of 40 to 47 days apply to by-elections;
(d) if a vacancy occurs within six months of the expiration of the time limit for the duration of the House of Commons, the provisions pertaining to the issue of the writ for the by-election not apply; and

(e) if a writ has been issued ordering a by-election to be held on a date after the dissolution of Parliament, the writ be deemed to have been superseded and withdrawn.

REPRESENTATION

Representation in the House of Commons

A generally accepted principle is that every Canadian voter should have an equal opportunity to seek a candidacy for election to the House of Commons. Membership of the House of Commons should therefore provide, on average and over time, a relatively accurate reflection of Canadian society. Although the principles of electoral democracy do not demand that citizens be represented in the House of Commons in a manner that mirrors Canadian society, neither do they assume that citizens will be represented by a political class whose membership is restricted to certain segments of society. All things being equal, the House of Commons should reasonably reflect the country's diversity. All things are not equal, however, if obstacles to participation inhibit and, in certain cases, deter members of certain groups in Canadian society from seeking candidacy.

Sex, race, ethnicity and physical ability must not determine who can enter the political arena. The issue of representation takes on an important symbolic aspect since it contributes to the extent to which Canadians identify with their representative institutions; people who are consistently underrepresented may feel alienated and thus reject institutions that do not allow for the accommodation of their identity. (Breton 1986) The composition of the representative body also affects the type of issues that receive public attention, the priority attached to them on the public agenda, and how and when they receive consideration. This is not to suggest that all matters of public policy have different salience for different demographic segments of society, that opinion on public policy will always divide along demographic lines, or that normative or ideological considerations cannot unite individuals from different segments of society. At the same time, however, MPs elected only from a limited subset of Canadians cannot be said to represent our society fully in all its important dimensions. In this sense, a profile of MPs as a body over time constitutes a valid indicator of the openness, equity and fairness of our electoral process.

An examination of membership in the House of Commons reveals that major segments of Canadian society are underrepresented. Many of these segments have been demanding greater access to the political process for a long time. Over the past two decades, however, particularly in the debate leading to the adoption of the Charter, these demands have achieved greater prominence. Moreover, the Charter has provided a new focus for their demands and a new language of constitutional and political discourse with which to articulate them. (Cairns 1991) This was clearly evident in our public hearings generally and at our symposium on women's participation in federal politics in particular.

Women are the most underrepresented segment of Canadian society. They account for more than 50 per cent of the electorate, yet in 1980 only 5 per cent of MPs were women. In 1984 women accounted for just 9.9 per cent of MPs, and by 1988 the figure had risen to 13.2 per cent (see Table 3.1). Women are underrepresented by 74.1 per cent relative to their demographic weight. In other words, they are only 25.9 per cent of the way to attaining proportional electoral representation. As the Canadian Advisory Council on the Status of Women told us, "Despite modest improvements in the participation of women in public life since the Royal Commission on the Status of Women reported in September 1970, twenty years later we must conclude, as did that Commission, that 'the voice of government is still a man's voice'." (Brief 1990) Not surprisingly, an attitudinal survey has shown that women are consistently less likely to find current arrangements acceptable. (Blais and Gidengil 1991 RC)

Ethno-cultural communities have also been traditionally underrepresented in the House of Commons. It appears, however, that some of these communities have greatly increased their representation. The difficulties inherent in this type of analysis will be discussed later in this chapter.

Using 1986 census mid-term projections, members of ethno-cultural groups reporting either single or multiple origins other than French, British or Aboriginal constituted 21.7 per cent of the population. At the same time, 16.3 per cent of MPs were from these groups (see Table 3.2). Excluding members of visible minorities, who face specific and distinct situations in seeking membership in the House of Commons, the electoral representativeness of ethno-cultural groups exceeds 90 per cent.

Table 3.1
The election of women to the House of Commons, 1980–88

Year	Party		Percentage of MPs	Percentage of population	Percentage of electoral representation
1980	Lib.		8.0		
	PC		1.9		
	NDP		6.0		
		Total	5.0	50	10.0
1984	Lib.		12.5		
	PC		9.0		
	NDP		13.3		
		Total	9.9	51	19.4
1988	Lib.		15.7		
	PC		12.4		
	NDP		11.6		
		Total	13.2	51	25.9

Source: Young 1991a RC.

On the other hand, the situation of visible minorities, who are also defined according to ethno-cultural characteristics, poses a challenge. Defined as "persons, other than aboriginal peoples, who are non-Caucasian in race or non-white in colour", visible minorities accounted for about 6 per cent of the population in 1988 but 2 per cent of MPs, which places their electoral representation at 32 per cent. (Canada, Employment and Immigration Canada 1991, 25) There is some evidence of change as succeeding generations – the children and grandchildren of immigrants – are integrated into the Canadian political community. This does not, however, alter the fact that some communities have remained virtually excluded from the federal political process, despite a longstanding presence in Canada.

Table 3.2
The election of ethno-cultural groups to the House of Commons, 1984–88

Year	Party	Percentage of MPs from ethno-cultural minorities (visible minorities excluded)	Percentage of MPs from visible minorities only	Percentage of population Ethno-cultural minorities (visible minorities excluded)[a]	Visible minorities only[b]	Percentage of electoral representation Ethno-cultural minorities (visible minorities excluded)	Visible minorities only
1984	Lib.	22.5	0.0				
	PC	13.3	0.0				
	NDP	10.0	10.0				
	Total	14.5	1.1	15.4	6.3	94.2	17.5
1988	Lib.	19.3	3.6				
	PC	13.0	0.0				
	NDP	9.3	7.0				
	Total	14.3	2.0	15.4	6.3	92.9	31.7

Source: Adapted from A. Pelletier 1991 RC.

[a]The criterion used is ethnic origin. Ethno-cultural minorities here exclude British, French and Aboriginal (single and multiple origins).

[b]This percentage results from a special compilation of Statistics Canada census data that combined criteria such as ethnic origin, birthplace and mother tongue to determine if an individual is a member of a visible minority. See Canada, Statistics Canada 1990d.

Aboriginal persons make up about 3.5 per cent of the population of Canada. Since 1960, when Indians living on reserves received the vote, there have been only nine self-identified Aboriginal MPs. Currently, Aboriginal persons make up about 1 per cent of MPs – for a rate of electoral representation of 28.6 per cent. Given the special status of Aboriginal peoples in Canada, the question of their electoral representation is discussed separately in Chapter 4.

Persons with disabilities have also faced major barriers to nomination and election to the House of Commons. Many of the barriers that impede access by other underrepresented groups have also deterred participation by persons with physical disabilities. For example, the Canadian Association of the Deaf pointed to the escalating cost of seeking nomination: "For the average able-bodied person, [the cost of seeking a nomination for one of the larger political parties and running for political office] is a very expensive gamble to undertake. For a deaf or otherly-disabled person, it is quite frankly prohibitive." (Brief 1990, 3) Persons with disabilities who wish to run for office must incur greater costs than those borne by others, over and above the costs associated with the normal use of assistive devices. Recommendations outlined later in this chapter address the obstacles identified by representatives of persons with disabilities and should help to increase their presence in the electoral process.

These shortcomings in representation have roots in our institutions and in our social and economic structures. It is thus important to understand the sources of these problems as they affect each group to determine whether and to what extent it is possible for electoral legislation to alter these structures and thereby promote more equitable representation.

The Electorate and Voting Preferences

The issue of underrepresentation requires an assessment of whether discrimination exists in Canada's political system and, if so, an indication of what its sources might be. The most obvious starting point is to ask whether these representational deficits result from discrimination by voters against candidates from the underrepresented groups.

We do not have sufficiently strong evidence to answer this question definitively for all groups, but the hypothesis does not appear to be borne out in the case of women. Public opinion polls, survey research on voting behaviour and aggregate analyses of voting patterns do not indicate that voters discriminate against women candidates. Voters do not show a particular preference for male politicians, nor do they appear to vote disproportionately for male candidates. As one study concluded, in similarly placed competitive circumstances women and men appear to perform equally well in election contests. (Hunter and Denton 1984)

This finding may not apply to all underrepresented groups. Representatives of several visible minorities were clear on this point: they affirm that racial discrimination is present in our political system, and that it contributes to the relative exclusion of minorities from elected office. (Simard 1991 RC) Representatives of these groups nonetheless agreed with representatives of women's groups that we should also look for answers earlier in the electoral process, in particular in the candidate selection process. Any discrimination by the electorate is unlikely to be overcome if members of underrepresented groups are unable to reach the starting blocks.

Candidacy and Representation

Evidence from our hearings and research suggests that the process of nominating candidates constitutes the most formidable barrier to members of underrepresented groups. This is especially true in constituencies where nominated candidates of particular political parties have a good chance of being elected.

The candidate selection process is particularly important because of the high turnover of MPs, through either the defeat or the retirement of the incumbent. This means that there are numerous opportunities for political parties to nominate candidates representing the full diversity of Canadian society and who have a reasonable chance of election. The character and impact of barriers to party nominations therefore warrant examination. The process of candidate selection is addressed in detail in Chapter 5. Other parts of the process, however, have a demonstrable effect on underrepresented groups. These are the focus of this chapter.

Systemic Discrimination

In assessing the underrepresentation of certain segments of society, it is neither useful nor appropriate to assign blame to specific individuals or associations. No factor in the nomination process can be singled out to explain the persistent underrepresentation of some segments of society. Systemic discrimination exists in our society, and there is no reason to believe that political structures are any exception. Measures to address these systemic factors are thus required. This approach assumes that pervasive cultural attitudes and institutional practices have a great impact on certain groups, even if society succeeds in eradicating overt discrimination.

The concept of systemic discrimination, though now widely accepted, is relatively recent. The 1971 U.S. Supreme Court judgement in *Griggs* accepted that the impact of a discriminatory action, rather than its motive, must be used to determine whether discrimination has occurred. The court ruled that when statistical data demonstrated that specific groups were dramatically underrepresented in particular occupations, this outcome, rather than proof of an intention to exclude specific groups, constituted sufficient evidence to conclude that systemic discrimination was present and that remedies were required.

The concept of systemic discrimination is equally well established in Canadian human rights legislation and jurisprudence. The objective of the Canadian human rights legislation is to prevent discrimination rather than punish wrongdoing. This promotes the goal of equal opportunity for each individual to achieve "the life that he or she is able and wishes to have". The 1987 decision of the Supreme Court of Canada in *Action Travail des Femmes* clearly indicated that the emphasis on discriminatory effects rather than intent was central to the *Canadian Human Rights Act*. In other words, the Supreme Court judgement underscored that a focus on whether there was intent to discriminate did not adequately deal with the many instances where the effects of policies and practices are unintentionally discriminatory.

This discrimination does not necessarily mean lack of compliance with the law; rather, it often signals that unintentional – or systemic – factors are at play. Discrimination often emanates from deeply ingrained cultural attitudes and practices; they may be unintentional or unacknowledged, but they systematically devalue members of certain social groups. Moreover, section 15(2) of the Charter on affirmative action programs provides that "any law, program or activity that has as its object the amelioration of conditions of disadvantaged individuals or groups"would not constitute a contravention of the equality rights guaranteed in section 15(1). This is an explicit recognition that equal laws can result in inequality if applied to persons in unequal circumstances.

This approach to discrimination acknowledges that societies and institutions adopt laws and practices that may have unintended or undesired effects on particular groups and that, when these effects can be shown to have occurred, positive steps can reduce and eliminate their discriminatory dimensions. In examining the underrepresentation of women and others in Canadian politics, we have therefore given considerable weight to the outcome of processes such as candidate selection and elections.

Ethno-Cultural Minorities and Participation in the Political Process

Relatively little research has been devoted to the political integration of racial and ethno-cultural minorities in Canadian society. A clear understanding of this situation is complicated by the difficulties associated with defining ethnic identity and using Statistics Canada census data. The definition of ethnicity is generally accepted to be based on objective criteria such as shared language, religion and culture and on subjective criteria that identify these characteristics. Furthermore, the identity of an ethnic group results from its relations with other groups, that is, the notion of 'we' and 'they'. Thus, as a result of these interactions, the boundaries of ethnicity tend to evolve over time.

To determine the size of the Canadian ethno-cultural population, the census relies on self-identification to classify individuals into ethno-cultural groups. As a result, two individuals belonging to the same ethno-cultural community according to objective criteria would not necessarily be classified as belonging to the same ethno-cultural group if they responded differently to the census questionnaire. A second limitation in the data is that the choice of variables that refer to the objective and subjective criteria and the questions used to collect census data have undergone significant changes over time, which some people have suggested could ultimately affect the validity of meaningful comparisons. However, as Herberg observed, "the degree of comparability is not so variant that it seriously interferes with the use of census statistics relating to a particular ethnic factor". (1989, xviii)

A final methodological point worth noting in assessing the performance of ethno-cultural communities in the electoral system is determining who is an ethno-cultural candidate or MP. In the research conducted for us, the classification of a candidate or an MP as belonging to an ethno-cultural group relied on a set of multiple criteria including place of birth, religion, language, ancestry and participation in an ethnic association. (A. Pelletier 1991 RC) It is important to note that our research assumed, based on this classification, that the individual still identifies himself or herself as an ethnic individual, which (1) may not necessarily be the case and (2) may not be related to his or her desire to act as a representative or spokesperson for ethno-cultural groups.

From the early days of Confederation until the 1960s, members of many ethnic and racial groups were virtually barred from entering the country by an "explicitly racist and restrictive immigration policy". (Stasiulis and Abu-Laban 1991 RC) Further, and for almost as long a time, many racial groups were excluded from politics through the denial of the franchise or exclusion from candidacy. In some cases, these exclusions lasted until the middle of this century.

Our public hearings and research revealed that many ethno-cultural groups have profound feelings of alienation in both their access to the vote and their participation in political parties and elected office. These findings echo the report of the parliamentary committee on the participation of visible minorities in Canadian society (Canada, House of Commons 1984), which lamented the low rate of political participation among members of visible minorities. It stressed the lack of information on the electoral process, the desire of visible minority groups to engage in greater participation and the desire of parties to include them to a greater extent in their activities.

Participation in the Electoral Process
Interveners and members of visible minorities interviewed in the course of our research emphasized several factors to explain their absence from the electoral process. Chief among these was that the current enumeration process misses many members of visible minority groups because of language barriers and the hesitancy or reluctance of members of these communities to participate in a process they do not fully understand. Even if members of visible minority groups are enumerated, language difficulties and lack of understanding of the electoral process still act as impediments to voting. As Deborah Wong told us at our public hearings, "Language barriers and cultural differences ... may tend to alienate ethnic minorities from ... Canadian society, and maybe the democratic process as well.... I am concerned about them being part of our system and feeling comfortable, as well as making sure they understand the electoral process and voting." (Calgary, 22 May 1990) To overcome some of these problems, we recommend in Volume 2, chapters 1 and 2, several changes to registration and voting.

To participate in the electoral process, a voter should be a citizen. Canadian citizenship is obtained after three years of residence. This prerequisite to participate in the electoral process is liberal compared with that of many countries. This prerequisite remains important as a necessary transition period to permit new immigrants to become more familiar with the Canadian political culture. This period should be perceived as the first step to increase the political competence of members of ethno-cultural groups regarding the Canadian political system. Simard concluded, based on extensive interviews with members of several visible minority communities, that it was necessary to increase the political competence of members of visible minorities – that is, to develop a better knowledge of the Canadian political system and the electoral process – to increase their participation in the voting process. (1991 RC) As she pointed out, the lack of political competence of visible minorities may be accentuated by linguistic barriers, lack of information, individual level of motivation, as well as by some internal factors such as religious differences and economic disparities or by the undemocratic background of the immigrant. This analysis underscores the importance of the role that education can play.

In this regard, an examination of the written information provided to immigrants seeking Canadian citizenship is revealing. Overall, it suffers from a lack of comprehensive description of our electoral process; of the democratic values embodied in our electoral laws, which channel and give substance to the behaviour and actions of political parties, candidates and Members of Parliament; and of the rights of citizens and the democratic responsibilities they are expected to fulfil.

Clearly, the education and language skills of prospective citizens have a direct bearing on these issues; but this does not remove the onus from immigration policies and programs to give prospective citizens the means to understand their new political structure and electoral system. Our obligation to new immigrants should not end with the decision to admit them to the country. Indeed our survey of citizenship judges revealed that better, more comprehensive and systematic educational programs for immigrants would facilitate and hasten their participation in the electoral process.

Our recommendations aim to enhance the participation of new Canadians in the registration and voting process. This objective would be much easier to achieve, however, if greater and more systematic efforts were made to give new Canadians the opportunity to acquire a better understanding of the process right from the beginning of their lives in Canada.

Representation Within Political Parties and the House of Commons

Although many presentations to the Commission focused on making the vote more accessible to members of ethno-cultural communities, increased representation of visible minorities within political parties and in the House of Commons was also a concern.

Even after the right to vote and to stand for election was granted to ethno-cultural groups, the number of MPs from these groups remained small and their influence limited. This limitation is vividly captured in the tragic situation faced by two Jewish MPs of the 1930s, Sam Jacobs and Sam Factor, whose efforts to open Canada's borders to victims of Naziism were ignored by the King government. (Abella and Troper 1982, 14–15)

Between 1867 and 1964, fewer than 100 of the thousands of MPs elected were of an ethnic origin other than French, British or Aboriginal. Those few elected were largely of German, Ukrainian or Jewish origin. During this period, only two MPs were from visible minority groups. (Canada, Royal Commission 1970a, 282) Since 1965, representation of ethnic groups has been rising steadily: 121 MPs of other than English, French or Aboriginal origin have served in Parliament. Of these, more than 70 per cent were of Jewish or northern and eastern European origin (see Table 3.3). This is explained in large part by: (1) the demographic weight of Canadians of European descent, which exceeds 60 per cent, (2) the fact that for the most part they immigrated before 1967, and (3) the fact that, for many, their cultural heritage, political background and language helped accelerate their integration into Canadian society.

Table 3.3
Members of the House of Commons from ethno-cultural groups, by origin, 1965–1988

Ethnic origin	Number of MPs
Southern European	22
Northern and Eastern European	72
African and Arab	5
Asian, Indian, Filipino	3
Latin-American, Haitian	2
Black	2
Jewish	13
Australian, New Zealander	2
Total	121

Source: A. Pelletier 1991 RC.

In the period 1965–1988, 10 of the 121 MPs from ethno-cultural groups were from visible minority communities. (A. Pelletier 1991 RC) The Canadian situation compares favourably with that in England where no member of a visible minority has been elected since the Second World War. (Anwar 1986, 98) In the 1983 British general election there were 18 candidates from visible minorities but none were elected. (Anwar 1986, 104; Fitzgerald 1983, 394) In Canada, there were 29 candidates from visible minorities in the last general election and six became MPs. The representation of visible minorities in the United States more closely resembles our own situation. In 1991, the electoral representativeness – that is, how the percentage of elected officials from the minority group compares with the percentage of that group in the general population – of Blacks in the House of Representatives stood at 50 per cent and that of Hispanics at 33 per cent. (Interviews with Joint Center for Political Studies, Washington, DC; Congressional Black Caucus, Washington, DC)

Over the past decade, the three largest political parties have demonstrated increased sensitivity to the cultural diversity of the electorate, and to the need to include members of all ethno-cultural groups in their ranks and among their candidates. The Liberal and New Democratic parties have set up permanent internal structures for representing ethno-cultural groups, with a mandate to increase the participation of minorities in their party. All three parties have nominated greater numbers of candidates from racial and ethno-cultural minorities, in many instances in constituencies where the relevant group is present in large numbers.

In general, ethno-cultural groups are now relatively well represented in the House of Commons. Visible minorities, however, remain an exception. To what is this exception attributable? Several factors have been suggested: latent or overt racism; the cost of pursuing a nomination; negative media coverage; and the lack of sufficient party support. We cannot underestimate the impact of these factors; they obviously limit the ability of members of visible minorities to participate fully in the electoral process. In particular, we must highlight the role of the media in reinforcing the exclusion of visible minorities from the wider political process. In her research, Eileen Saunders found a clear pattern of exclusion in media coverage: "(i) minorities are underrepresented in the media; (ii) when present, minorities are represented in a limited range of roles, and those are usually characterized by their marginal status; (iii) minorities are represented as being different, whether in terms of basic personality characteristics or general aptitude for particular social roles; and (iv) alternative or oppositional definitions of their situation, emanating from minority groups themselves, receive little play in the media". (Saunders 1991 RC)

Some factors, such as the marginalization of visible minorities in media coverage, are unacceptable, and sustained efforts to change them are required. Others, however, must be assessed against the backdrop of the changing composition of Canadian society.

A recent report from the Economic Council of Canada documents how Canada is rapidly becoming much more ethnically diverse. (Economic Council of Canada 1991) During the 1980s, Canada received 1.25 million immigrants, most of whom were members of visible minorities. Since the mid-1960s, the pattern of immigration has shifted dramatically, as shown in Table 3.4. Although Europeans once dominated immigration, the emphasis has now shifted to immigration from Asia, the Caribbean, and Central and South America.

New immigrants face major cultural, political, social and economic change: finding work and a position in Canadian society naturally takes precedence over an interest in political participation. Research shows that there must be a certain degree of social mobility within a group to favour the emergence of ethno-cultural candidates. As Wolfinger pointed out: "Middle-class status is a virtual prerequisite for candidacy for major office; an ethnic group's development of sufficient political skill and influence to secure such a nomination also requires the development of a middle class". (1974, 49) This factor contributes to understanding the representative strength of ethno-cultural communities, especially those of European origin whose class status, according to the 1986 census, is comparable to that of French and English Canadians. Some visible minority groups, because of their more recent immigration, have not achieved comparable economic status. We also must acknowledge that social and economic integration do not in themselves lead to political integration. The lack of political interest, at least at the outset, is reinforced by the fact that some immigrants may be disinclined to participate in politics. This is particularly true of those from countries with oppressive political regimes or non-democratic political cultures. Further, and closely related to social integration and political participation, two-thirds of visible minority group members are first-generation Canadians. Thus, it is clear that the process of adaptation and integration of Canada's new immigrants into the social fabric will generally be characterized by a transition period.

This transition period should be seen as a collective phenomenon that does not preclude the nomination of first-generation members of cultural groups. For instance, between 1965 and 1988, only 28 per cent (34/121) of MPs from ethno-cultural groups were born outside Canada. In 1984, this rate stood at 32 per cent (14/44) and in 1988 it rose to 42 per cent (20/48). For MPs from visible minorities, this rate was 40 per cent (4/10) between 1965 and 1988 and 67 per cent (4/6) in 1984 and 1988. (A. Pelletier 1991 RC) This individual pattern does not, however, obviate the prerequisite for a transition period. The fact that there is a high rate of ethno-cultural MPs born outside Canada is a good indication that they are facing fewer barriers than in the past. The period between immigration into Canada and nomination as a candidate will vary from one individual to another and depend on ethnic origin, age and other factors such as economic and social factors.

Table 3.4
Immigration patterns for Canada, 1986
(per cent)

Country / region of birth	Percentage of total	Period of immigration
Europe	62.3	65% before 1967
Asia	17.7	44% after 1978
United States	7.2	—
Caribbean and Bermuda	5.0	59% between 1967 and 1977
Central and South America	3.8	62% after 1978
Africa	2.9	56% between 1967 and 1977
Oceania	0.9	68% between 1967 and 1977
Other	0.2	—
Total immigrant population	3 908 150	

Source: A. Pelletier 1991 RC. Adapted from Statistics Canada 1986 census data.

Table 3.5
Representation of visible minorities in the House of Commons, 1965–1988

Election	Census	Visible minorities only		
		MPs (N)	MPs (%)	Population (%)
1988	1986	6	2.0	6.3
1984	1986	3	1.1	6.3
1980	1981	4	1.4	3.9
1979	1981	3	1.1	3.9
1974	1971	3	1.1	2.3
1972	1971	2	0.8	2.3
1968	1971	2	0.8	2.3
1965	1961	0	0.0	2.0
—	1951	—	—	1.9
—	1941	—	—	1.2
—	1931	—	—	1.1
—	1921	—	—	1.2
—	1911	—	—	1.3
—	1901	—	—	1.4
1965–1988	—	10	—	—

Sources: A. Pelletier 1991 RC; Canada, Statistics Canada 1990d; and 1961, 1971 and 1981 census data.

Note: The 1984 and 1988 figures are based on the 1986 census, which for the first time provided a defini-tion for visible minorities. For all other censuses, because there is no special compilation of data on visible minorities, we used only the ethnic origin criterion; here we excluded British, French, Aboriginal and European (single and multiple origins, which are compiled only for the 1981 census). If the same methodology were used for the 1986 census, the percentage of visible minorities in the population would be 5 per cent rather than 6.3 per cent.

Collectively, the political integration of members of visible minorities appears to span roughly one generation. As Table 3.5 shows, the 1988 rep-resentation of visible minorities in the House of Commons (2.0 per cent) cor-responds to their representation in the Canadian population at the time of the 1965 general election. In other words, between 20 and 25 years elapsed before visible minority groups achieved representation equal to their demographic weight in 1965 in the House. This gap was more accentuated previously. Thus although current figures point to their underrepresentation, the situa-tion should be seen in the context of the political integration process and the time required to complete it. Moreover, the years needed to achieve representation in proportion to numbers appear to be shrinking. As noted by Stasiulis and Abu-Laban, "some of the barriers that are associated with immigrant status in a new country disappear or lessen for second and fur-ther generations". (1991 RC) Their research suggests that the second genera-tion does not encounter barriers to participation in political parties and that the party youth organizations tend to reflect the diversity of the institutions (such as universities) in which they are situated. This accelerated integration is also imputable to an increased openness in Canadian society, including on the part of political parties and the electorate the heightened willingness and interest of members of visible minority communities to participate in the political process of their new society, and the growing number of visible minority MPs who serve as role models.

This pattern by no means suggests that difficulties for members of visible minority groups in seeking representation can be dismissed on the grounds that, over time, they tend to disappear. We must recognize that the dynamics of political integration appear to be hastening the inclusion of members of visible minorities in the political process as they did for members of other ethno-cultural groups. Unrelenting efforts to eradicate racism from our society must be sustained. At the same time, ensuring that members of visible minorities have full access to the voting process, become more familiar with the Canadian political system, benefit from less biased media coverage and have access to a fairer nomination process is crucial in improving their participation. The electoral reforms we propose, taken in their entirety, should eliminate many of the barriers confronting members of minority communities, and facilitate and promote their access to the democratic process.

Women and Underrepresentation

Profile of Women Candidates and MPs in the 1988 Election

Women are clearly underrepresented in the House of Commons, but it is not so clear how to assess the relative importance of the barriers that are said to explain this inequity. Any attempt to redress the current situation should be based on a solid empirical assessment of the effect of these barriers. A description of the current situation is a useful starting point.

What can be said about the background of the women in the House of Commons – their education, their occupation and their political experience? How does this profile differ from that of the men in the House, from that of women who ran unsuccessfully for a seat, from that of women active in municipal politics or from that of women in general? Our analysis is based on a comparison of the biographical profiles of candidates for the three largest political parties who contested a seat in the 1988 election with the profiles of all members of the House of Commons. Although not discussed here, it is clear that differences exist among the parties in the educational, professional and other characteristics of the candidates and elected members.

Women and Men in the House of Commons   A much larger proportion of male as compared with female MPs are married (95 per cent compared with 68 per cent) and, on average, male MPs have more children (indeed, a major percentage of female MPs have no children). The age profiles of men and women in the House are generally similar, although more female MPs are concentrated in the 40–49 category than in the younger or older groups. The professional and educational backgrounds of male and female MPs are also similar. Virtually the same percentage of men and women in the House have a university degree. In their training and professional profiles, relatively more female MPs have a degree in the social sciences and relatively fewer a degree in engineering. There are relatively fewer lawyers among the female MPs but more with a background in business. Both groups of MPs appear to have had similar levels of experience in politics at the provincial and municipal levels.

Women Candidates for the House of Commons   Compared with women MPs, unsuccessful female candidates in the 1988 election were younger and had slightly fewer children. The unsuccessful candidates had a similar profile for university training, with a somewhat greater emphasis on studies in social sciences and less on economics and business administration. They also had a somewhat different professional profile, with fewer in law and business and more in education, administration and social services. The unsuccessful candidates more closely resembled the profile of the general population of female professionals. A final important difference concerned the lack of political experience for unsuccessful candidates. Less than 1 per cent of these women had a background in municipal politics (compared with 8 per cent for female MPs), and only 9 per cent had experience at the provincial level (compared with 15 per cent for female MPs).

MPs and the General Population   To what extent are the members of the House representative of the population in general? In several respects, the profile of MPs differs considerably from that of the general population. For example, and perhaps not surprisingly, the 25–39 age group is substantially underrepresented in the House, and the 40–49 group is overrepresented. One interesting difference between women and men is that women over the age of 50 are underrepresented among female MPs, and men over 50 are overrepresented among male MPs.

Roughly 65 per cent of the working-age population is married, with only a small difference between men and women. The percentage of married women MPs is roughly similar; but the proportion of married men MPs is much higher, underscoring the availability of strong family support for men and the difficulties facing women in combining a political career with family responsibilities.

It is difficult to compare the occupational profile of MPs with that of the general population. There are no MPs who fall into the occupational category of workers or clerks, who constitute approximately 60 per cent of the general male and female labour force. On the other hand, 13 per cent of female MPs and 15 per cent of male MPs are lawyers; yet lawyers make up only a fraction of 1 per cent of the total population. Overall, it is clear that the law and business categories are overrepresented in the House, among both women and men MPs, with underrepresentation among male MPs of the agriculture–fisheries category, and of the health care category among women MPs.

Barriers to Entry

Witnesses before the Commission and our research studies identified several barriers impeding women's access to candidacy and to the House of Commons. Some of these barriers relate to broad social phenomena; as important as these factors are, they do not lend themselves to solutions by institutional or legal reform of the electoral system. For example, a frequently cited factor is the effect of sex role socialization: women have been socialized to see politics as an unsuitable, even undesirable, vocation. This is reinforced by the relative scarcity of female role models. A recent survey of adolescents revealed that young men were much more interested in politics than were young women. This distinction begins as early as high school when almost 50 per cent of males, but only 33 per cent of females, indicate an interest in politics. (Hudon et al. 1991 RC)

Among the structural barriers identified, however, two are paramount. The first is the cost of the nomination process; the second is the lack of concerted efforts by political parties to support women seeking nominations. Although the two are clearly interrelated, we analyse them separately.

Financial Barriers   During our hearings, at the symposium on women in federal politics and in surveys, women identified cost as the most formidable obstacle to nomination. The impact is usually greater on women because they are generally at a financial disadvantage relative to men, and particularly because women are more likely to find themselves in an expensive contested nomination: 47 per cent of women faced contested nominations, compared with 31 per cent of men in the 1988 election. (Erickson 1991 RC) They also receive fewer and smaller donations than men. As Judy Erola, a former federal cabinet minister, stated at our research symposium on women in federal politics: "I think we have to move ... to make donations to nominations legitimate tax credits.... In that way you are going to be able to get women to donate to women. They still don't make enough money but, if they can get a tax credit, they are more likely to do so." (Symposium on the Participation of Women in Federal Politics, 1 November 1990)

Women appear to lack the professional or social contacts needed to build financially competitive campaign organizations. This is illustrated by the characteristics of official agents; according to research conducted for the Commission by R.K. Carty (1991a RC), female candidates are less likely than men to have a professional as their official agent. The author of a study of women candidates for the Liberal Party in the 1988 election concluded: "The obstacles that women in the Liberal party faced in the 1988 election are systemic rather than openly discriminatory. The financial burden of an expensive nomination campaign ... [creates] more of an obstacle for women than for men ... who on the average have a higher income and more access to campaign funds [and] are in a better position to finance an expensive nomination." (Leduc 1990, 43)

This conclusion was confirmed by Janine Brodie in a survey of 47 women candidates for the three largest parties in the 1988 election. Funding outweighed all the other factors that these women considered major barriers to nomination and to candidacy. In fact, more than 90 per cent of these women suggested that Parliament should set limits on the amount spent during nomination contests; some 80 per cent suggested that the limit be less than $5000. (Brodie 1991 RC)

One factor that imposes an unequal financial burden on women seeking elected office is the cost of child care. Taxpayers can deduct the cost of child care required to earn income from employment or a business or to take an occupational training course. The deduction is not permitted, however, in the expenses incurred to seek nomination or be a candidate. For candidates responsible for the care of their children, child care is a necessary expense – one that they must incur if they wish to seek nomination and election.

Party Support   Over the past two decades, and further to the recommendations of the Royal Commission on the Status of Women in Canada (1970b), women's groups inside and outside political parties have pressured parties to become more representative. The three largest parties have responded in some measure to these demands. Women's commissions are now guaranteed representation on the governing bodies of each of the party organizations, as well as at policy and leadership conventions. The NDP has given its governing bodies the mandate of equal representation of women and men. All three parties have established funds to assist women once they are nominated: the Ellen Fairclough Foundation of the Progressive Conservative Party (1983), the Judy LaMarsh Fund of the Liberal Party (1984), and the Agnes MacPhail Fund of the New Democratic Party (1986). These funds provide modest assistance – between $500 and $1500 – to women candidates, many of whom have used the grant for child care expenses. The leaders of these three parties have also given increased attention to women's issues, including specific policies for women in the parties' electoral platforms, and participated in the televised 1984 leaders debate on issues of concern to women.

Since 1989 the Ontario NDP has had affirmative action guidelines for nominating and electing members of specific target groups. The objective was to set aside a specific group of 'priority' constituencies of which 75 per cent would be targeted for candidates from affirmative action groups: women, members of visible minorities, persons with disabilities and Aboriginal people. In the 1990 Ontario election, 27 per cent of the NDP members elected were women, double the percentage of women in the House of Commons.

At its 1991 convention, the federal New Democratic Party became the first large national party in North America to adopt a policy to promote the nomination of women candidates in a specified number of constituencies. The objective of the policy is to have women candidates in at least 50 per cent of constituencies.

Despite these initiatives, and in some cases strong statements by the leaders of all three of these parties on the importance of attracting more women into the political process, progress has been slow. This is true for the participation of women within political parties and the number of women seeking candidacy. The national leaders have called for broader representation, but local associations often appear reluctant to field women candidates. (Brodie 1991 RC) Constituency associations have considerable influence in the selection of candidates. Initiatives by the leadership to nominate women candidates are sometimes opposed by the executive of local associations on the pretext that such a decision would be "undemocratic". This tends to occur in relatively safe constituencies, hence compounding the problem.

The ideal index of local party support for women candidates would be to compare the number of women who ran for nomination to the number who became candidates and to the number who were elected. Unfortunately, statistics on the former are not available. A good index is the propensity of parties to nominate women in 'losing' or 'unwinnable', as opposed to 'safe' or 'winnable', constituencies. Lynda Erickson reports that in 1988, 30 per cent of all female candidates stood for election in constituencies considered winnable for their party, compared with 51 per cent of all male candidates. (1991 RC) These figures, based on a party's past performance in a constituency, are lower than the figures provided by constituency associations to assess the electoral chances of a candidate in their constituency. According to the local associations, 62 per cent of women candidates were in winnable seats, compared with 67 per cent of male candidates. Comparisons of the number of women candidates and the number of women elected in recent elections appear to indicate that in the Progressive Conservative and Liberal parties, the gap is shrinking. In 1988, women represented 12.5 per cent of all candidates for the Progressive Conservatives and 12.4 per cent of that party's MPs (see Table 3.6). This is attributable in part to the strength of the party's electoral victory; but the success of women candidates for the Liberals suggests that the national parties are making concerted efforts to nominate more women in winnable constituencies.

Women's Role in Political Parties   Within political parties, women continue overwhelmingly to occupy the lower rung or pink-collar positions. As shown in Table 3.7, except in the case of constituency secretary, women rarely account for more than 30 per cent of executive positions, election campaign managers or candidates' agents. This confirms the conclusion of previous research on women's party involvement: the higher the position, the fewer women occupy it; and the more competitive the party in the constituency, the fewer the number of women involved in the local party association. As Bashevkin concludes, "Women's numerical representation in [political institutions] tends to be inversely related to both the level of party activity and to the competitive position of a party organization." (1991 RC)

Table 3.6
Women: candidates and elected, general elections of 1980, 1984 and 1988

Year	Party		Women candidates (N)	Women candidates as percentage of all candidates	Women elected (N)	Women elected as percentage of all elected
1980	Lib.		23	8.2	12	8.0
	PC		14	5.0	2	1.9
	NDP		32	11.4	2	6.0
		Total	69	8.2	16	5.0
1984	Lib.		45	16.0	5	12.5
	PC		23	8.2	19	9.0
	NDP		64	22.7	4	13.3
		Total	132	15.6	28	9.9
1988	Lib.		51	17.3	13	15.7
	PC		37	12.5	21	12.4
	NDP		84	28.5	5	11.6
		Total	172	19.4	39	13.2

Source: Young 1991a RC.

Table 3.7
Sex of constituency association and campaign position holders, 1988 election
(per cent)

	Male	Female
Constituency association president	80	20
Constituency association treasurer	67	33
Constituency association secretary	32	68
Election campaign manager	72	28
Election candidate's agent	79	21

Source: Carty 1991a RC.

Entry to Politics   Another troubling question is why so many fewer women than men seek nomination. Several factors appear to be at work here.

Based on the socio-economic analysis presented earlier, it is clear that family responsibilities, still shouldered largely, and as a prime responsibility, by women, deter many competent and interested women from seeking office at least until their children are older. A second factor is that women tend to have less employment security and thus face a greater potential impact if they lose their bid for public office at the nomination stage, as a candidate or following one term in office. As the Canadian Advisory Council on the Status of Women noted, "One of the most obvious financial costs associated with running for elected office is the risk to employment. Many women cannot afford to gamble their jobs on the chance of winning an election." (Ottawa, 11 June 1990)

Finally, it is clear that some women are deterred by the differential media treatment they receive as political contenders. Our research showed that although the coverage of women in politics has improved over the last two decades, it remains stereotyped, focusing much more often on women's appearance, personal life and opinions about specific issues such as abortion. (Robinson and Saint-Jean 1991 RC)

Comparative Experiences   Women's persistent underrepresentation in politics has prompted different reactions in several countries to redress the problem.

The United States, for instance, is an international leader in affirmative action to increase the participation of women and racial minorities in educational institutions and the workplace; it has not, however, adopted a similar approach to improving its political representation, despite a very weak record in electing women. Women currently make up only 5 per cent of members of Congress and 18 per cent of state legislators. Given the vast sums of money required to contest an election in the United States, attempts to achieve better balance in the representation of women have come largely through the efforts of private groups and political action committees, which have raised money for prospective candidates. They include Americans for Democratic Action, the National Organization of Women, the National Political Congress of Black Women, the National Women's Political Caucus Victory Fund, the Women's Fund and the Fund for a Feminist Majority. Despite their efforts, such groups have been unable to reverse the historical legacy of underrepresentation of women in U.S. politics.

The most stringent measures and highest proportion of women among elected representatives are found in the Scandinavian countries. Many have attributed the strong showing of women in these countries (see Table 3.8) to their electoral system, which is based on proportional representation. Many advocates of proportional representation claim that it increases women's representation. International comparisons reveal, however, that the relationship is more complex than this.

Although some countries with proportional representation systems, including Sweden, Denmark and Norway, have a higher proportion of women representatives, others, including Italy, Belgium and Spain, have a smaller percentage of women representatives than countries with a plurality system. The evidence shows that proportional representation is neither a necessary nor a sufficient condition for achieving more equitable representation. The evidence from countries where women are now a strong force in elected politics is that the presence of mandatory requirements within political parties, as an explicit and immediate corrective to the historical underrepresentation of women, has been the principal cause of greater women's representation.

Table 3.8
Female representation in lower houses of legislature, international comparisons, 1988

Country	Percentage
United States	5.3
Australia	6.1
Great Britain	6.3
France	6.4
Spain	6.4
Portugal	7.6
Belgium	8.5
Switzerland	10.2
Italy	12.8
Canada	**13.2**
New Zealand	14.4
West Germany	15.4
Netherlands	20.0
Denmark	29.0
Sweden	30.9
Finland	30.5
Norway	34.4

Source: Data supplied to the Commission by Janine Brodie.

In Norway, for example, the number of female legislators jumped from 15.5 per cent in 1975 to 34.4 per cent in 1985 after the Norwegian Labour Party adopted a rule in 1983 requiring that at least 40 per cent of each sex be represented in all nominations and all elections. The Swedish Democratic Party followed Norway's example with the adoption of a 40 per cent rule. There, too, the results were immediate. Between 1975 and 1985, the proportion of women in the Swedish lower house increased by 10 per cent.

The social democratic parties of Denmark and Germany adopted mandatory requirements for representation on party electoral lists. Socialist parties in Portugal, Austria and Belgium have adopted a 25 per cent minimum, and their counterparts in France and Italy adhere to a 20 per cent rule. Last year, the French socialists increased their mandatory requirement for the representation of women to 30 per cent.

These findings suggest that it is the presence of mandatory requirements, rather than a proportional representation system, that has made a discernible difference in female representation in European politics. At the same time, it is also the case that proportional representation systems help national parties ensure women's representation because they can generally exert control over the lists of candidates. If the national parties decide to, they can present a slate of candidates that includes a minimum proportion of women. In other words, proportional representation provides a tool that may facilitate the election of women, but its success requires that a political party be committed to gender equality in representation. The decentralized approach to nomination in Canada makes it more difficult to ensure this objective is realized, because it requires the full commitment and co-operation of local associations. Nominations, moreover, generally result from open conventions; such a competitive process does not lend itself easily to pre-ordained results.

Toward Equitable Representation

Experience in Canada and elsewhere demonstrates that providing equal rights in constitutional law does not in itself secure fair and equitable outcomes, even when the aptitudes of the contenders are comparable. Of course, when individuals of varying aptitude and interests are provided with similar opportunities, disparities will result. In certain domains, such as the economic sphere, liberal societies accept this outcome, although they often adopt policies in the pursuit of equality. In the political sphere, however, the gap that exists between equality on the one hand and fairness and equity on the other must be closed. Formal equality under the law does not automatically erase systemic discrimination. Recognizing this fundamental reality, many countries now adhere to the principle that it may be necessary to treat some groups differently to achieve a greater measure of political equality. As the Supreme Court of Canada noted in an important Charter case, "... the interests of true equality may well require differentiation in treatment". (*R. v. Big M Drug Mart* 1985)

Canada's obligation to pursue political equality stems from at least two sources: our international obligations as a member of the United Nations and a signatory of international rights agreements and our own constitutional provisions in the Charter.

The *International Covenant on Civil and Political Rights*, a document drawn up under the auspices of the United Nations, has been in force for Canada since 19 August 1976, when Canada became a signatory after unanimous agreement of the provinces and the federal government. Article 3 of the Covenant provides that:

> The States Parties to the present Covenant undertake to ensure the equal right of men and women to the enjoyment of all civil and political rights set forth in the present Covenant.

And article 25 provides that:

> Every citizen shall have the right and the opportunity, without any of the distinctions mentioned in article 2 [race, colour, sex, language, political or other opinion, national or social origin, property, birth or other status] and without unreasonable restrictions:
> (a) To take part in the conduct of public affairs, directly or through freely chosen representatives;
> (b) To vote and to be elected at genuine periodic elections....

A second United Nations document is the *Convention on the Elimination of All Forms of Discrimination Against Women*, to which Canada became a signatory on 9 January 1982. The Convention provides in article 7 that:

> States Parties shall take all appropriate measures to eliminate discrimination against women in the political and public life of the country and, in particular, shall ensure, on equal terms with men, the right:
> ...(b) To participate in the formulation of government policy and the implementation thereof and to hold public office and perform all public functions at all levels of government.

Special measures are an acceptable means of achieving equity in representation. Section 15 of the Charter provides that:

> 1. Every individual is equal before and under the law and has the right to the equal protection and equal benefit of the law without discrimination and, in particular, without discrimination based on race, national or ethnic origin, colour, religion, sex, age or mental or physical disability.
> 2. Subsection (1) does not preclude any law, program or activity that has as its object the amelioration of conditions of disadvantaged individuals or groups including those that are disadvantaged because of race, national or ethnic origin, colour, religion, sex, age or mental or physical disability.

Section 15 of the Charter provides for the possibility of special measures to address problems of systemic discrimination, and the Supreme Court of Canada has approved employment equity remedies to redress historical inequities resulting from systemic discrimination.

Parliament has also enacted legislation such as the *Employment Equity Act*, whose purpose is to promote equity in the workplace. The Act states that the principle of employment equity "means more than treating persons in the same way but also requires special measures and the accommodation of differences". Further, at the federal level and in some provinces, companies with a certain number of employees must implement an employment equity program to bid on government contracts.

The Supreme Court of Canada has also linked equality principles to the idea of representation in the legislature. (*Carter* 1991) The Court has recognized that the values and principles animating a free and democratic society – including equality – place effective representation at the heart of the guarantees in section 3 of the Charter.

The Court stressed that respect for individual dignity and social equality, and the need to recognize cultural and group identity and enhance the participation of individuals in the electoral process, all have a bearing on the interpretation of the section 3 guarantees. All of these concerns support measures that would enhance the participation of women in elected assemblies.

These precedents, the understanding of equality on which they are based, and the substantial body of evidence on the underrepresentation of certain groups in Canada's legislatures require that we consider positive steps for the right to candidacy. The persistent underrepresentation of certain groups can be positively linked to the practices of national political parties, particularly their local constituency associations, which function as gatekeepers of access to candidacy for most Canadians who belong to or share the values of these parties. Despite efforts in good faith by people in these parties to correct representational imbalances, the results have come up short; we are thus left to conclude that other forces must be at work. The absence of effective provisions for the nomination of candidates is a regrettable shortcoming of the current electoral law.

In Chapter 5, we consider the role of political parties in greater detail. We consider their status under the law and their public responsibilities for the health of our democratic system. It is our objective to strengthen the role of political parties as the primary political organizations of democratic representative government. In pursuing this objective, we recognize their essentially volunteer character. At the same time, as organizations registered under electoral law that receive substantial public financial support, political parties have public responsibilities in some critical respects. They are not state institutions, but neither are they purely private.

One of the most critical functions of political parties is to recruit, select and nominate candidates. This process has a major impact on the extent to which Canadians' equal right to candidacy is realized. To secure a meaningful right to candidacy, electoral law must address certain critical aspects of candidacy, including the cost of seeking a nomination and the selection process itself. These include the following matters.

The Financing of Nomination Contests

The cost of seeking a nomination is considered a barrier to candidacy for those underrepresented in the electoral process. Political parties are not equally competitive in all federal constituencies across Canada; each party has a reasonable chance of electoral success in only some constituencies. Party nominations in these constituencies are naturally more appealing, and therefore more competitive, than in constituencies where a party is weak. If the selection process is to ensure better representativeness among candidates, there must be reasonable opportunities to secure nominations in competitive constituencies. In other words, steps are required to ensure that nomination is accessible in constituencies where there is a chance of being elected.

Research shows that in constituencies where a party is competitive, substantial sums of money and other resources are often needed to win a nomination. Other things being equal, individuals who do not have access to a network of contributors have less capacity to wage a competitive nomination campaign. (Carty and Erickson 1991 RC) In these instances, the candidate selection process cannot be said to be fair to all prospective contenders.

Candidate selection thus stands in contrast to the electoral process. The Canadian experience since 1974 has demonstrated that costs can be checked effectively by electoral law through limits on campaign expenditures by candidates and political parties. Equally important, as discussed in Volume 1, Chapter 6, this experience has also shown that the competitive character of the electoral process is not diminished by such limits; if anything, competition has been stronger since 1974. Our experience with tax credits for political contributions demonstrates further that fair and reasonable access to the financial resources necessary to mount an effective campaign can be enhanced while the responsibility of candidates to secure the funding necessary to conduct a campaign is maintained.

The lessons of this experience, together with evidence from provinces with similar provisions, are instructive as we consider how to attack systemic discrimination in the political process. To date, Canada's electoral law has not drawn on these lessons to enhance fairness in nomination contests, and the political parties and their local associations have been slow to respond to pressure from within. Only 15 per cent of local associations in the 1988 survey had set spending limits on nomination races. The *Canada Elections Act* does not apply to nomination contests;[2] no spending limits are imposed, and those seeking a nomination cannot issue tax receipts to their contributors.

Competition has a dramatic effect on the level of expenditure. Commission research shows that in constituencies that were highly competitive or when competition intensified, the level of expenditure was much higher than in less competitive constituencies. (Heintzman 1991 RC) Further, the absence of spending limits means that an individual seeking a nomination cannot estimate precisely, or even approximately, how much money will be needed to wage a competitive campaign. This uncertainty is a deterrent to many who might wish to seek nomination. As MP John Manley told the Commission, the possibility that they will have to spend large amounts of money to contest a campaign is a "deterrent factor to people ... who are not in a position to raise a lot of money.... I think [the selection process] is too important just to be left to the parties and that limits should be imposed and disclosure of contributors should be part of that as well." (Ottawa, 13 June 1990) One other function of spending limits during general elections is to ensure that the search for funds is not the dominant concern of the candidate during the campaign; the same holds true for nomination contests.

The financial obstacles to candidacy prevent many from seeking nomination. As a result, the principle of fairness is compromised. In addition, only a few individuals from certain segments of Canadian society have the necessary resources, or access to them, to offer themselves as nominees for candidacy. Canadians therefore have less opportunity to choose their representatives from among individuals who are more broadly representative of society; their choices are limited unnecessarily.

To remove the financial barriers to effective representation, reform is required on four fronts: (1) expenditure limits in nomination contests; (2) public financial support; (3) specific financial barriers to candidacy, that is, child care costs and the cost of assistive devices for persons with physical disabilities; and (4) party mechanisms to achieve broader representation in the recruitment process.

Expenditure Limits   Limits should be set on expenditures incurred by those seeking the nomination of a registered local party association. These limits should allow for competitive campaigns but at the same time ensure that access to financial resources not be the principal determinant of a successful nomination bid. Precisely how the law should be designed and administered, including disclosure provisions, is outlined in other parts of our report. Here we simply state our basic policy objective of promoting effective representation by securing fairness in the nomination contests of registered constituency associations.

Recommendation 1.3.19

We recommend that limits be set on spending by all persons seeking the nomination of a registered constituency association during the nomination period.

Public Financial Support   Especially for people underrepresented in the electoral process, fairness requires that there be public financial support for seeking the nomination of a registered constituency association. This can be achieved by one or both of two basic measures. The most direct method is to reimburse the campaign expenditures of those seeking a nomination. Electoral candidates are reimbursed a percentage of their expenditures if they achieve a certain threshold of electoral support. The indirect method is to give those seeking a nomination of a registered constituency association the right to issue tax receipts for financial contributions to their campaigns. Under current law, contributions to electoral candidates benefit from this provision.

On the basis of Canadian experience with these two methods of public funding for elections, we conclude that the first method would be much more costly to the public treasury than the second method, assuming that the general features of both applied as an extension of the current system. Equally important, the cost of reimbursing expenditures would be driven largely by the expenditure decisions of those seeking nomination in light of their access to resources. In other words, the ability to spend would be rewarded. Although reimbursement is essential in general elections, because of the costs of campaigning in constituencies that average 60 000 constituents, the need to reimburse nomination expenses is less pressing and less important from the perspective of fairness.

By contrast, the cost of a tax receipt approach would be driven primarily by the number of persons contributing to nomination campaigns. Assuming a ceiling on the amount credited for tax purposes, the incentive would be to obtain relatively small contributions from many supporters. Those who are now underrepresented, especially women, would clearly benefit from such a measure. This could also raise the number of Canadians who make political contributions and thus take part in the electoral process.

On the basis of these considerations, presented in greater detail in Volume 1, Chapter 6, we conclude that extending the tax credit system for political contributions to nomination campaigns is the best method to promote equitable representation at a reasonable cost to the public treasury.

Recommendation 1.3.20

We recommend that contributors to the campaigns of those seeking the nomination of a registered constituency association be eligible for tax receipts issued by an authorized officer of the association.

Tax Measures

(a) Child Care Expenses: A major cost facing many candidates seeking election, and one that imposes an unequal burden on women seeking elected office, is the cost of child care. At present, a taxpayer is permitted to deduct child care expenses, subject to certain restrictions and maximum amounts, from income earned from employment, from carrying on a business, or from scholarships, research grants or training allowances. A person is not permitted to claim a tax deduction for child care expenses incurred to seek nomination or to be a candidate. For those who are responsible for the care of their children, child care is a necessary expense while they seek nomination or election as a candidate. As we have noted previously, the activity of seeking nomination and election are civic undertakings of the highest order in an electoral democracy. This should be recognized by acknowledging in the *Income Tax Act* that child care expenses incurred to seek nomination or election are a legitimate tax deduction.

Recommendation 1.3.21

We recommend that the *Income Tax Act* be amended to include, in the list of activities for which such expenses are tax deductible, child care expenses incurred by the primary caregiver when she or he is seeking the nomination of a registered constituency association during the nomination period or election as a candidate during the writ period.

(b) Expenses Incurred for Assistive Devices: Many disabled Canadians face major expenses for medical technical devices. The Canadian Association of the Deaf "estimates that a deaf Canadian could expect to pay $10 000 for assistive devices in one year". (Brief 1990, 3) To ensure that disabled people have equal access to the electoral process and are not unfairly constrained by the additional expenses they must incur, some changes are necessary.

Money paid to an attendant who assists a disabled person, enabling him or her to perform employment duties, carry on a business or conduct research, is deductible (subject to certain limits) or eligible for the medical expense credit when no income is earned during the period for which the tax relief is claimed. These provisions for attendant care should be broadened to include the services of an attendant for a disabled person seeking candidacy or elected office.

The *Income Tax Act* also allows transportation services as a medical expense credit but only if the travel is for medical reasons. Travelling expenses incurred in seeking a nomination or during the writ period do not qualify for this credit.

If persons with disabilities are to be able to contest nominations and elections equally, some form of financial assistance is required to help with the cost of assistive devices. Although we are proposing a vote-based reimbursement, we recognize that disabled persons may have to incur major expenses for technical assistive devices to enable them to carry out campaign activities.

We therefore propose that candidates who obtain at least 1 per cent of the vote be reimbursed 75 per cent of their expenses incurred during the election period for assistive devices related to their specific needs in conducting an election campaign (such as special vehicles for candidates with mobility impairments), for expenses totalling a maximum of 30 per cent of their spending limit.

Recommendation 1.3.22

We recommend that

(a) the *Income Tax Act* be amended to broaden the definition of attendant care to include the services of a person required

to assist a disabled person to perform the functions necessary to seek the nomination of a registered constituency
association during the nomination period or to be a candidate during the writ period; and

(b) candidates who have obtained at least 1 per cent of the
vote be reimbursed 75 per cent of their expenses incurred
during the election period for assistive devices related to
their specific needs in conducting an election campaign, for
expenses totalling a maximum of 30 per cent of their overall spending limit.

Improving Candidate Selection   The three measures just proposed affect
individuals seeking nomination. The first two would affect political parties
administratively, but none would promote different behaviour by the parties
themselves. To remedy the underrepresentation of certain groups, particularly that of women, the behaviour of party and constituency association
executives must be altered to achieve more equitable representation through
the recruitment process.

As a general policy, the three largest parties encourage the use of search
committees in constituencies where there is no incumbent. Information supplied by these three parties indicates that the composition of search committees differs from one party to another: in the Progressive Conservative Party
a search committee can consist of between three and 30 members, with no
specific requirements as to its composition; in the Liberal Party, search committees consist of five or six members, including at least one woman; and in
the NDP, they consist of an unspecified number of members, but, whatever
their number, they must respect gender parity. The process for identifying
the ideal candidate is relatively unstructured in all three parties, relying for
the most part on the executive committee's knowledge of the community.
In selected constituencies, opinion surveys may be conducted to develop a
profile of the candidate with the best chance of electoral success.

The three parties rely to some extent on centralized information to identify potential female candidates. Both the Progressive Conservatives and the
NDP keep a central registry of potential women candidates, and the Liberals
have a resource directory containing the names of persons who can help
identify candidates at the local level.

By comparison with other countries, recruitment by our parties, including the identification of prospective candidates, is neither rigorous nor
systematic. The parties also fall short of the best private sector practices
for executive searches. Effective search processes, in which the characteristics of the ideal candidate are identified in advance and potential candidates gauged against this standard, generally lead to the identification of
more individuals who would qualify as representative candidates.

At present, close to 50 per cent of constituency associations say they use
a search committee. (Carty and Erickson 1991 RC) Further, about 7 per cent

of local associations without an incumbent asked the national or provincial level of the party to assist in identifying potential candidates. We do not have definitive evidence that local associations with search committees always identified the best candidates, but the evidence does indicate that search committees are a powerful tool in encouraging women to run for nomination. In constituencies with a search committee, women contested 43 per cent of the nominations and won 30 per cent of them; in the absence of a search committee, women contested 27 per cent of the nominations and won 16 per cent of them. Equally important, most of the women who were encouraged to run did so in constituencies where they had a good chance of winning. (Carty and Erickson 1991 RC)

In cases in which the constituency association received help from the party in identifying candidates, women candidates were more likely to be selected. Carty and Erickson report that 40 per cent of the Liberal and NDP associations that received help in identifying potential candidates nominated women, compared with 22 per cent that sought no outside assistance. (1991 RC)

The evidence suggests that the presence of formal search committees and assistance from national parties in identifying prospective candidates broaden the recruitment process. Compared with the traditional approach, the use of these mechanisms, especially in combination, is more likely to lead to nomination contests and candidates that represent a broader range of the Canadian mosaic.

Recommendation 1.3.23

We recommend that the by-laws and constitutions of registered political parties require the establishment of formal search committees and commit the parties to processes that demonstrably promote the identification and nomination of broadly representative candidates.

NOTES

1. The *Canada Elections Act* renders ineligible for candidacy sheriffs, clerks of the peace and judicial district Crown attorneys while they hold office. This provision is an anachronism and has been for more than a century. The ineligibility of these officials dates from the time in the early years of Confederation when election administration was largely under provincial government management and these officials were used as returning officers and election officials. Given their roles in election administration, these officials were rendered ineligible for candidacy by federal electoral law. Once the appointment of returning officers was vested with the federal government in 1882, this provision became obsolete. It has been overlooked each time federal legislation was revised, however. There is no reason for its continued inclusion in the Act.

2. There is one exception. Under section 214(1), the *Canada Elections Act* limits the amount that can be spent on notices of nomination meetings: 1 per cent of the amount the candidate was entitled to spend on 'election expenses' for the immediately preceding general election. This applies only to nominations that take place during the writ period.

4

EQUALITY AND EFFICACY OF THE VOTE

INTRODUCTION

T HE RIGHT TO VOTE and the right to be a candidate for election to the House of Commons are necessary but not sufficient conditions to ensure that the electoral law promotes both the equality of the vote and effective representation. How we assign Commons seats to provinces and draw the constituency boundaries within provinces can also affect the degree to which we realize these two objectives. Equality of the vote is secured if the assignment of seats to provinces conforms to the principle of proportionate representation and if the drawing of constituency boundaries conforms to the principle of representation by population. Effective representation is secured if constituency boundaries are drawn to recognize the various communities of interest that exist within a province.

In this chapter we examine and assess the processes and principles for assigning Commons seats to provinces and territories and for drawing constituency boundaries within provinces and territories. Although the two processes are related, that is, the boundaries of federal constituencies are drawn only after the number of seats for a province or territory has been determined, they are independent. We therefore present our recommendations for each in sequence. The two processes are sometimes referred to collectively as "redistribution". For clarity, we restrict this term to the assignment of seats to provinces. We use the term "boundaries readjustment" to refer to the process of drawing constituency boundaries.

THE ASSIGNMENT OF SEATS TO PROVINCES

Parliament and Federalism

Canada's federal system means not only that citizens are subject to two orders of government, each with its own jurisdiction, but also that citizens are represented in Parliament on the basis of their membership in both the national and a provincial political community.

As in all western federal systems, the representation of citizens as members of two political communities requires a "bicameral" federal legislature – a legislature with two chambers. One chamber – in Canada, the House of Commons – represents citizens as members of the national political community. The second – in Canada, the Senate – represents citizens as members of a provincial political community. The constitution requires that seats in the House of Commons be assigned to provinces on the basis of their proportionate populations. In contrast, the constitution requires that seats in the Senate be assigned to provinces in a manner that gives disproportionate (but not equal) representation to the less populous provinces. This distribution of Senate seats is meant to give the less populous provinces greater representational weight to counter the weight of the more populous provinces in the House of Commons. In this way, the Senate is based on a 'federal' principle of representation.

The original assignment of Senate seats in 1867 reflected this federal principle by creating three equal 'divisions', each with 24 seats: Quebec, Ontario and the maritime provinces (Nova Scotia and New Brunswick, each with 12 seats). Prince Edward Island was added to the maritime provinces division when it entered Confederation. It received four of the division's seats; Nova Scotia and New Brunswick each lost two. Manitoba was given two Senate seats when it became a province; British Columbia was given three; and Alberta and Saskatchewan were each given four. In 1915, the number of divisions was increased to four; in the new western provinces division, the four western provinces each received six seats. Newfoundland was given six seats on entering Confederation in 1949. The Northwest Territories and the Yukon received a seat each in 1975, so the current total of assigned seats is 104 (not counting eight senators appointed in 1990 under the terms of the *Constitution Act, 1867*, section 26). This allocation is shown in Table 4.1.

The Senate of Canada, unlike second chambers in other federal systems, including Australia, the United States and Germany, has not effectively realized the federal principle of representation. Although the less populous provinces have a disproportionate number of seats, thus meeting this criterion of the federal principle, its members are neither elected (as in Australia or the United States) nor appointed by the governments of the constituent units of the federation (as in Germany). Rather, Canadian senators are appointed by the federal government (formally by the Governor General on the advice of the prime minister). This means that they have neither the legitimacy of popular election nor the legitimacy of appointment by provincial governments. Without the necessary political legitimacy, the Senate has not been able to use its considerable formal legislative powers in defence of the less populous provinces against the will of the House of Commons.

Because the Senate as an institution fails to adequately realize the federal principle of representation in Parliament, the assignment of Commons seats to provinces subsequent to the original plan has had to accommodate demands from the less populous provinces for greater representation than they would be entitled to according to proportionate representation. The members of the House of Commons, accordingly, have been forced by the politics of federalism to use formulas that compromise the constitutional principle of proportionate representation. As the then President of the Privy Council, Ramon Hnatyshyn, acknowledged in speaking to the proposed representation legislation in 1985,

> The relative imbalances which exist today and have long been accepted as necessary compromises on the principle of absolute representation by population will remain.... In a Parliament with only one elected House, our system has come to recognize the need of finding ways of ensuring adequate regional representation in the elected body. (Canada, House of Commons, *Debates*, 1 October 1985, 7186)

Table 4.1
Allocation of Senate seats
(by province and territory)

Province / territory	Seats
Ontario	24
Quebec	24
Nova Scotia[a]	10
New Brunswick[a]	10
Prince Edward Island[a]	4
Manitoba[b]	6
British Columbia[b]	6
Saskatchewan[b]	6
Alberta[b]	6
Newfoundland	6
Yukon	1
Northwest Territories	1

Note: This allocation does not include eight senators appointed in 1990 pursuant to the *Constitution Act, 1867*, section 26.

[a]These three provinces form the maritime provinces division.
[b]These four provinces form the western provinces division.

Although the Senate of Canada did not come within our mandate, it is obvious that, should a reformed Senate effectively realize the federal principle, the formula for assigning seats to provinces could then adhere much more strictly to the principle of proportionate representation. As in Australia, this might still include a minimum floor for provincial representation as well as the assignment of Commons seats to the federal territories without unduly undermining the principle of proportionate representation.

The House of Commons and Proportionate Representation

Proportionate representation was adopted at the outset as the principle governing the assignment of seats to provinces in the House of Commons. Before Confederation, representation by population had been the subject of persistent controversy among political leaders in the province of Canada. The Confederation settlement was possible largely because it divided the province into two separate provinces – Ontario and Quebec – and adopted proportionate representation as the basis for assigning Commons seats. This solution ended a long and bitter dispute over representation in the united legislature of the province of Canada, where Upper Canada and Lower Canada had had an equal number of seats since 1840, despite having unequal populations.

The first House of Commons was based on an agreement among the Fathers of Confederation that secured proportionate representation in the distribution of seats to the four original provinces. It was mainly because of this adherence to proportionate representation that Prince Edward Island refused to become a province in 1867; it would have received five seats, which it regarded as inadequate. (Ward 1963)

The *Constitution Act, 1867* (then the *British North America Act*) contained a formula (section 40) that gave a fixed number of seats to one province, Quebec, and then assigned seats to other provinces according to their population relative to Quebec's population/seat ratio. Quebec not only wanted to have its number of seats guaranteed at 65, the number chosen, but also had the advantage of a comparatively stable population and had neither the largest nor the smallest population.

The 1867 formula also contained a provision minimizing the effect on any province whose population might subsequently decline relative to Canada's total population. A province would not lose seats until its population had declined relative to the total population of Canada by more than 5 per cent since the previous census. Thus began the Canadian tradition of minimizing the effects of declining relative population on representation.

Proportionate Representation and the Representation of Provinces

The entry of three new provinces in the decade following Confederation required a departure from proportionate representation. The political bargains struck when Manitoba (1870), British Columbia (1871) and Prince Edward Island (1873) entered Confederation resulted in each receiving greater representation than they would have been entitled to under proportionate representation. In at least the first two cases, the accommodation was considered a temporary measure, given their rates of population growth.

Manitoba, with a population that would not have warranted a single seat, received four, along with a guarantee that this number would be protected until after the 1881 census and the subsequent redistribution. British Columbia, which would have been entitled to one seat, received six and was guaranteed this number permanently. Prince Edward Island received six seats when it entered Confederation in 1873; a strict application of proportionate representation would have given the province only five seats – the same number it considered too low in 1867. In this case, however, and for unknown reasons, no guarantee of seats was provided.

Canada, 1912

Based on these precedents, the Northwest Territories was given four seats in 1886, instead of the two it would have received on the basis of its population (it encompassed the present-day territories as well as what is now Alberta, Saskatchewan and part of northern Manitoba). Following the creation of Alberta and Saskatchewan in 1905, however, the number of seats they received (seven and 10, respectively) was justified on the basis of population. On being admitted to Confederation in 1949, Newfoundland received seven seats on the same basis.

In each of these cases, the political bargains struck at the time a province or territory entered Confederation required consideration of both the principle of proportionate representation and the demand for a disproportionate number of seats in the House of Commons. This consideration did not always result in the overrepresentation of smaller provinces, as is shown by the cases of Alberta, Saskatchewan and Newfoundland.

Various rules have also been used to protect provinces from the effects of declining relative populations. The first, as noted above, was in the 1867 formula: a province would not lose seats until its population had declined relative to the total population of Canada by more than 5 per cent since the previous census.

The maritime provinces were the first to suffer a loss of seats. In 1892, Nova Scotia lost two, and New Brunswick and Prince Edward Island lost one each. Although their populations had not declined absolutely, they had declined as a proportion of the national population since the 1881 census.

When these provinces incurred further losses at the turn of the century, they began to press for special consideration through both the political and the judicial process. Although the provinces were not successful in the courts, the eventual political outcome was the 1915 constitutional amendment guaranteeing a province no fewer seats in the Commons than it had senators. The immediate effect of this "senatorial floor" provision was to guarantee Prince Edward Island four Commons seats – the same as the number of senators it received on joining Confederation. This was one seat more than it would have been allocated under the 1867 formula after the 1911 census.

The first major overhaul of the redistribution formula took place following the Second World War. The original formula had resulted in three provinces maintaining seats solely on the basis of the 1867 provision protecting provinces from a loss of seats. The most significant consequence was that the largest province, Ontario, had maintained its original 82 seats; its population had declined relative to the national population since 1867, but never by more than the specified 5 per cent between two censuses.

Without the formula's protection, Ontario would have lost one seat following the 1920 census, another three after 1931 and a further four after 1941, giving it a total of 74 instead of 82. At the same time, Quebec maintained its share of Commons seats at 65. As Norman Ward notes, "The demand for fair representation, which had been so familiar a cry in the mouths of Upper Canadian statesmen before Confederation, was logically taken over in 1946 by Quebec." (Ward 1963, 53)

The result was the adoption of a completely new formula in 1946 and its implementation in the 1947 redistribution. The formula established a fixed number of seats in the House of Commons – 255, which was raised to 262 with the entry of Newfoundland. The total population of Canada was divided by the number of seats, not counting the seat assigned to the Yukon and Mackenzie Territories, to obtain a quota; seats were then assigned to provinces by dividing their population by the quota, with the 1915 senatorial floor provision still applying. The result was that all provinces except Prince Edward Island, whose seats were protected by the senatorial floor provision, had their number of seats determined by their share of the population.

The 1946 redistribution formula was amended in 1952. First, no province would lose more than 15 per cent of the seats to which it had been entitled at the time of the previous redistribution. This provision was added to avoid a 25 per cent seat loss by Saskatchewan (from 20 to 15 seats) following the 1951 census.

A second amendment provided that no province would have fewer seats than a province with a smaller population. This was required because Alberta would have had fewer seats than Saskatchewan, given the 15 per cent clause, even though Saskatchewan had a smaller population.

In 1974, the formula was altered once again, as population changes had introduced deviations. The objective this time was to ensure that the smaller provinces maintained their number of representatives while increasing adherence to the principle of proportionate representation. Achieving this required abandoning the idea of a fixed number of Commons seats. If no province was to lose seats from one redistribution to the next, the number of seats had to rise with real population growth. The 1974 formula was used just once, following the 1971 census, and the House expanded from 264 to 282 members. (Balinski and Young 1981)

After the 1981 census, a redistribution was begun as required by the 1974 formula, but it was aborted when the House of Commons failed to complete its consideration of the reports of the electoral boundaries commissions. The formula had produced a House of Commons with 310 members. More significant, perhaps, were projected increases in the size of the House if the formula were maintained indefinitely. The number of seats was projected to be almost 400 at the turn of the century – an increase of 40 per cent over 30 years. The result was a new formula: the *Representation Act, 1985*.

The *Representation Act, 1985* sets out the formula used for the redistribution carried out in 1986:

1. Starting with 282 seats (the number of Commons seats in the 33rd Parliament), three are set aside for the two federal territories (two for the Northwest Territories and one for the Yukon).
2. The total population of the 10 provinces is divided by 279 to establish a national quotient.
3. The population of each province, as established at the decennial census, is divided by the quotient to determine the number of seats to which each province is entitled.
4. If a province's number of seats by this calculation is less than what it was in the 33rd Parliament (following the 1976 redistribution), the former is "topped up" to the latter.

In 1986, this resulted in a House of Commons with 295 seats, 12 of which were top-ups, as shown in Table 4.2.

The *Representation Act, 1985*: An Evaluation

The *Representation Act, 1985* substantially modified the principle of proportionate representation to an extent never before experienced. The consequences of the 1985 Act and the 1915 senatorial floor provision for proportionate representation are amply illustrated by the fact that under its first application, six of the 10 provinces had more seats than they were entitled to under proportionate representation (see Table 4.3). If current population projections hold, that number will increase to seven after the next redistribution, when Newfoundland will fall into this category. This would leave only Ontario, Alberta and British Columbia with seats determined solely on the basis of population; all three would be proportionately underrepresented in relation to the other provinces.

Table 4.2
Allocation of House of Commons seats
(by province)

	Seats prior to 1985 Act	1981 population	Quotient	Population divided by quotient (rounded)	Assigned seats	Adjustment
Ontario	95	8 625 107	87 005	99	99	0
Quebec	75	6 438 404	87 005	74	75	+1
Nova Scotia	11	847 442	87 005	10	11	+1
New Brunswick	10	696 403	87 005	8	10*	+2
Manitoba	14	1 026 241	87 005	12	14	+2
British Columbia	28	2 744 467	87 005	32	32	0
Prince Edward Island	4	122 506	87 005	1	4*	+3
Saskatchewan	14	968 313	87 005	11	14	+3
Alberta	21	2 237 724	87 005	26	26	0
Newfoundland	7	567 681	87 005	7	7	0
Total	279	24 274 287		280	292	+12

Source: Canada, Elections Canada 1986, 17.

*Guaranteed by 1915 senatorial floor provision.

The intention behind the 1985 Act is not without merit. We heard from many Canadians who supported the right of smaller provinces to their present level of representation in the House of Commons. Because there are only 10 provinces and because the Senate inadequately realizes the federal principle, it is unlikely that Prince Edward Island – with a population that merits only one seat in the House of Commons on the basis of proportionate representation – could be persuaded or made to accept such minimal representation.

Australia, for instance, sets the floor at five seats for each state in their federal House of Representatives, even though there is an effective Senate with equal representation for each state. Although the floor for state representation in the U.S. House of Representatives is one seat, the provision of two senators per state in the more powerful Senate adequately compensates the six states with only the minimum one seat in the House of Representatives.

Because our redistribution formula has compromised the principle of proportionate representation, Canadian constituencies deviate from the national electoral quotient to a much greater degree (14.3 per cent) than either U.S. or Australian constituencies (6.4 per cent and 4.4 per cent, respectively; see Appendix A). In 1991, for example, Saskatchewan will have 40 per cent more seats than it is entitled to by proportionate representation.

Put another way, a Member of Parliament from British Columbia will represent, on average, 25 000 more people than a Member from Saskatchewan. The guarantee that no province's seats will ever fall below the number it had in 1976 cannot be justified with reference to any principle of representation.

Table 4.3
Share of House of Commons seats and share of population, 1981, 1991
(by province)

	1981		1991	
	Percentage of seats	Percentage of population	Percentage of seats	Percentage of population
Newfoundland[a]	2.4	2.3	2.4	2.2
Nova Scotia[b]	3.8	3.5	3.7	3.4
Prince Edward Island[b]	1.4	0.5	1.3	0.5
New Brunswick[b]	3.4	2.9	3.4	2.7
Quebec[b]	25.7	26.5	25.3	25.4
Ontario	33.9	35.5	34.7	36.8
Manitoba[b]	4.8	4.2	4.7	4.1
Saskatchewan[b]	4.8	4.0	4.7	3.7
Alberta	8.9	9.2	8.8	9.4
British Columbia	11.0	11.3	11.1	11.9

Source: Adapted from Canada, Statistics Canada 1990b.

[a]Denotes protected province in 1991 only.
[b]Denotes protected province.

If current demographic projections are accurate, the application of the 1985 formula will increase the inequality among provinces over time because the size of the House can increase only to top up the seats of provinces that would otherwise lose seats (Table 4.4). The formula is thus a recipe for increasing the inequality among provinces. Discriminating against provinces with populations that are growing relative to national population growth can only cause unnecessary friction within our country.

In short, the formula errs in two ways: it fails to give sufficient weight to the constitutional principle of proportionate representation; and its restriction on increases in the number of Commons seats, which works to penalize the provinces experiencing population growth, is not related to any principle of representation.

A Return to Our Roots
Within the current constitutional provisions for redistribution, assigning seats to provinces requires a formula that respects both the principle of

proportionate representation and the 1915 senatorial floor guarantee. Of the several formulas that have been used to redistribute Commons seats since 1867, the one that came the closest to ensuring proportionate representation was the original formula of 1867.

Table 4.4
Prospective allocation of House of Commons seats: current formula, 1991, 2001, 2011
(by province and territory)

	Percentage of population[a]			Seats by population			Adjustment[b]			Total seats			Percentage of seats[c]		
	1991	2001	2011	1991	2001	2011	1991	2001	2011	1991	2001	2011	1991	2001	2011
Newfoundland	2.2	2.0	1.8	6	5	5	1	2	2	7	7	7	2.4	2.3	2.3
Prince Edward Island	0.5	0.5	0.4	1	1	1	3	3	3	4	4	4	1.3	1.3	1.3
Nova Scotia	3.4	3.2	3.1	9	9	9	2	2	2	11	11	11	3.7	3.6	3.6
New Brunswick	2.7	2.5	2.4	8	7	7	2	3	3	10	10	10	3.4	3.3	3.3
Quebec	25.4	24.8	24.4	71	69	68	4	6	7	75	75	75	25.3	24.8	24.7
Ontario	36.8	37.2	37.5	103	104	105	—	—	—	103	104	105	34.7	34.4	34.5
Manitoba	4.1	3.9	3.9	11	11	11	3	3	3	14	14	14	4.7	4.6	4.6
Saskatchewan	3.7	3.6	3.6	10	10	10	4	4	4	14	14	14	4.7	4.6	4.6
Alberta	9.4	10.0	10.4	26	28	29	—	—	—	26	28	29	8.8	9.3	9.5
British Columbia	11.9	12.4	12.6	33	35	35	—	—	—	33	35	35	11.1	11.6	11.5
Northwest Territories										2	2	2			
Yukon										1	1	1			
Total				278	279	280	19	23	24	300	305	307			

Source: Adapted from Canada, Statistics Canada 1990b.
[a]Percentage of the total population of 10 provinces; excludes the Yukon and NWT.
[b]Seats added to bring provincial number to senatorial floor or last distribution less one.
[c]Percentage of seats of 10 provinces; excludes three for the Yukon and NWT.

If we returned to this formula, we would need to meet three requirements in order to adhere to the intent of its original provisions. As in 1867, (1) one province must be selected as the base province, (2) the number of seats to be assigned to the base province must be established, and (3) a provision must be included to cushion the loss of seats for provinces with declining relative populations. In addition, because the senatorial floor guarantee must also be respected – and given the current distribution of Senate seats to provinces – there must be a provision that no province have fewer Commons seats than a province with a smaller population. In practical terms, this latter provision is required because Manitoba and Saskatchewan are each guaranteed only six Senate seats, whereas Nova Scotia and New Brunswick each have 10 Senate seats, even though these two maritime provinces have smaller populations than the two western provinces.

The original provision to cushion provinces with declining relative populations against loss of seats must be modified because, as noted previously, it protected the seats of a large province, namely Ontario, rather than those of the smaller provinces as was originally intended. If increases in the total number of Commons seats are to be kept to a minimum, this provision should simply limit the loss of seats at any one redistribution to one.

Under the 1867 formula, Quebec was the base province. If the House of Commons is to remain reasonably close to the size it is now, only four provinces can be candidates for the base province: Alberta, British Columbia, Ontario and Quebec. The projected relative population declines of the others would produce a national quotient that would increase the size of the House of Commons significantly.

If either Alberta or British Columbia, the two fastest growing provinces, became the base, there would be an increase in the number of protected seats, including those in Ontario, after the redistribution of 2001. At the same time, of course, the number of seats assigned to the base province would remain the same (Table 4.5). Ontario's projected population growth over the next 20 years is expected to be closest to the national average, but using Ontario as the base would also increase the number of protected seats. Just as at Confederation, Quebec is the most appropriate base.

Table 4.5
Prospective allocation of House of Commons seats: proposed formula, 1991, 2001, 2011
(effect of using various provinces as the base)

Base province (number of constituencies)	Total number of members[a]			Protected constituencies			Percentage of protected constituencies		
	1991	2001	2011	1991	2001	2011	1991	2001	2011
Alberta (26)[b]	291	286	282	14	26	30	4.8	9.1	10.6
British Columbia (33)[b]	291	288	284	15	21	23	5.2	7.3	8.1
Ontario (103)[b]	292	292	291	14	15	16	4.8	5.1	5.5
Quebec (71)[b]	292	299	300	14	12	10	4.8	4.0	3.3
Quebec (75)[c]	303	310	314	8	6	7	2.6	1.9	2.2

Source: Adapted from Canada, Statistics Canada 1990b.

Note: See appendices D and E for the assignment of seats to each province under each scenario.

[a]Total number excludes three seats guaranteed to the Territories.

[b]Number of constituencies provinces would be entitled to under present system after 1991.

[c]Current number of constituencies assigned to Quebec.

Using an allocation of 71 Quebec seats as the base (the number of seats Quebec would merit under proportionate representation if the present formula were applied to the 1991 census) would also result in a significant, albeit slightly declining, number of protected seats. Using 75 Quebec seats (its current number) would increase adherence to proportionate representation by reducing the number of protected seats substantially at first and even further over time (Table 4.6). Table 4.5 summarizes these results and compares the effect of using different provinces as the base.

Table 4.6
Prospective allocation of House of Commons seats, 1991, 2001, 2011
(formula using Quebec as the base, with 75 seats)

Province	Percentage of population[a]			Seats by population			Adjustment[b]			Total seats			Percentage of seats[c]		
	1991	2001	2011	1991	2001	2011	1991	2001	2011	1991	2001	2011	1991	2001	2011
Newfoundland	2.2	2.0	1.8	6	6	6	—	—	—	6	6	6	2.0	1.9	1.9
Prince Edward Island	0.5	0.5	0.4	1	1	1	3	3	3	4	4	4	1.3	1.3	1.3
Nova Scotia	3.4	3.2	3.1	10	10	9	—	—	1	10	10	10	3.3	3.2	3.2
New Brunswick	2.7	2.5	2.4	8	8	7	2	2	3	10	10	10	3.3	3.2	3.2
Quebec	25.4	24.8	24.4	75	75	75	—	—	—	75	75	75	24.8	24.2	23.9
Ontario	36.8	37.2	37.5	109	113	115	—	—	—	109	113	115	36.0	36.5	36.6
Manitoba	4.1	3.9	3.9	12	12	12	1	—	—	13	12	12	4.3	3.9	3.8
Saskatchewan	3.7	3.6	3.6	11	11	11	2	1	—	13	12	11	4.3	3.9	3.5
Alberta	9.4	10.0	10.4	28	30	32	—	—	—	28	30	32	9.2	9.7	10.2
British Columbia	11.9	12.4	12.6	35	38	39	—	—	—	35	38	39	11.6	12.3	12.4
Northwest Territories										2	2	2			
Yukon										1	1	1			
Total				295	304	307	8	6	7	306	313	317			

Source: Adapted from Canada, Statistics Canada 1990b.
[a]Percentage of the total population of 10 provinces; excludes the Yukon and NWT.
[b]Seats added to bring provincial number to senatorial floor or last distribution less one.
[c]Percentage of seats of 10 provinces; excludes three for the Yukon and NWT.

Using 75 Quebec seats as the base would restore the primacy of proportionate representation, thereby enhancing the equality of the vote among all Canadians. Some provinces would lose seats as a consequence of declining relative populations, but the losses would be cushioned. For provinces with growing relative populations, the number of Commons seats would rise to accommodate proportionate representation. But the projected increase would be reasonable (Table 4.7).

Table 4.7
Projected House of Commons size, 1991, 2001, 2011

	1991		2001		2011	
Formula	Quotient	Seats	Quotient	Seats	Quotient	Seats
Current formula	97 793	300	105 491	303	113 201	300
1867 modernized	90 560	306	97 148	313	101 979	317

Source: Adapted from Canada, Statistics Canada 1990b.

Recommendation 1.4.1

We recommend that section 51 of the *Constitution Act, 1867* be amended to embody the following principles:
(1) Quebec be assigned 75 seats, and other provinces be assigned seats on the basis of the ratio of their population to the population of Quebec; and
(2) if necessary, additional seats be assigned to provinces to ensure that
    (i) the senatorial floor guarantee is respected;
    (ii) no province loses more than one seat relative to the previous redistribution; and
    (iii) no province has fewer seats than a province with a smaller population.

The Question of Senate Reform

Senate reform could clearly affect the principles and objectives of the redistribution formula we recommend. Our proposals assume that the distribution of Commons seats will meet the dual requirements of proportionate representation and the federal principle. Should the Senate be reformed in ways that effectively realize the federal principle, the need for the distribution of Commons seats to depart from proportionate representation to secure this principle would diminish accordingly. Were this to occur, we recommend that the redistribution of seats in the House of Commons be conducted on the basis of proportionate representation, with the single proviso that each province be entitled to a minimum of four seats in order to secure meaningful provincial representation in the House of Commons. There would still be a need for representation of the territories. Consequently, the Yukon and the Northwest Territories should continue to have one seat and two seats, respectively.

DRAWING CONSTITUENCY BOUNDARIES

Introduction

Once the number of seats for each province is determined by the redistribution formula, the boundaries of the electoral constituencies in each province must be drawn. Boundaries are geographic; electors select their Members of Parliament to represent them as constituents of a local community or contiguous communities.

Representation of Community

This territorial approach to representation can be traced to the origins of parliamentary government in Great Britain, where the Crown summoned individuals to represent local communities in what became the House of Commons. The English term "commons" derives from the French term *commune*, meaning local community. The House of Commons was thus established as a legislative assembly of representatives from territorially defined communities.

With the advent of elections, the territorial approach was maintained; represented in the House of Commons were the shared interests of those residing in territorially defined communities, even though the vast majority did not have the right to vote.

Representation by Population

The ascendancy of modern democratic theory in the eighteenth and nineteenth centuries challenged the prevailing concept of representative government by asserting that individuals were the sole source of the state's political legitimacy. Authorities therefore had to govern with the consent of individuals as expressed through democratic elections.

This philosophy of representation demanded an equality of the vote, expressed in the call for "one man, one vote" or "representation by population". To achieve equality, reformers demanded not only an expanded franchise, but also constituencies that were relatively equal in population, making the value of each vote more or less equal. This understanding of representation conflicted with the traditional idea that individuals were represented solely as members of their territorially defined communities, regardless of population.

Comparable Population

Major electoral reforms followed acceptance of this new idea of representation, but the nineteenth-century reforms did not entirely transform the system of representation. Rather, the system was altered gradually so that its structure reflected both the traditional preference for representation based on territory and the new democratic principle of representation by population.

To reconcile the traditional and new understandings of representation, the boundaries of constituencies were drawn in light of population, but variations in constituency populations were accepted to accommodate local communities of interest. In both Great Britain and Canada, before and after Confederation, this meant drawing electoral boundaries to respect existing county and municipal boundaries as much as possible. Constituencies were not to be randomly constructed territorial groupings of roughly equal numbers of individuals.

The territorial approach to representation did not assume that each local community would have separate representation. It did imply, however, that within the bounds of "comparable population", communities of interest should be contained within a single electoral constituency so that their members would have a fair chance of influencing the outcome of the election. Deviations from population equality could therefore be justified by community of interest considerations.

The Processes and Outcomes of Boundaries Readjustment

For almost a full century following Confederation, Members of Parliament determined the boundaries of electoral constituencies. Unlike the constitutional provisions governing the assignment of seats to provinces, representation by population or comparable population was not enshrined in the electoral boundaries law. Without constitutionally prescribed objectives and criteria to govern the drawing of boundaries, members of the House of Commons, and thus the governing party, had great latitude in determining the factors used in drawing boundaries; the matter was governed by ordinary statute and thus subject to a simple majority in the House of Commons.

Parliamentary Boundaries Readjustment

From Confederation on, it was recognized that the drawing of electoral boundaries could not be other than partisan so long as Parliament readjusted the boundaries of constituencies. During the Confederation debates, the idea of an independent judicial authority for drawing electoral boundaries was discussed but not accepted.

The first three times Parliament redrew electoral boundaries (1872, 1882 and 1892), the government submitted a bill with its proposals for electoral boundaries. A new practice was established in 1903, that of having a select Commons committee consider the government's proposed boundaries. Although the governing party had a majority on this committee, opposition members did have a greater opportunity to affect the final design.

Several criteria, in addition to representation by population, were used to justify Parliament's decisions on electoral boundaries. Among the most important were adherence to municipal and county boundaries, continuation of prior electoral boundaries, and the need to design rural constituencies of manageable geographic size.

The priority attached to these criteria, especially the last one, could only result in varying constituency populations. The common rationale for the third criterion was that rural constituencies deserved special consideration given "the problems of accessibility, transport, and communications". (Qualter 1970, 94) Representing rural constituents, it was argued, as well as campaigning in rural areas, required that rural constituencies be as small as possible. This usually meant that they were also smaller in population than urban constituencies. If this meant overrepresentation of rural areas, it was argued, it was offset in part by the then-current practice of rural areas being represented by MPs who lived in urban areas.

In addition, the overrepresentation of rural areas ensured that local communities of interest were recognized adequately when boundaries were drawn. This did not always result in separate representation for all such communities, but it did mean that communities could be incorporated in constituencies where other communities shared their interests. Thus, politicians could address the question of representation of minority groups at the time of boundaries readjustment. The same objectives were also applied to boundaries in urban communities, although here the pressure to recognize communities of interest was usually less intense in part because the acceptance of larger populations in urban constituencies normally meant that there were more possibilities for boundary readjustment, and therefore such demands could be accommodated more easily.

Of course, differences in population were not always the major criterion. Partisan gerrymandering was also a driving force behind the drawing of boundaries. Attempts to secure partisan advantage invariably sacrificed both representation by population and the representation of communities of interest whenever a departure from one or the other suited the governing party. Although gerrymandering did not always secure partisan advantages – in some cases it actually backfired – the effect was to diminish the priority attached to legitimate principles of representation.

Between the first readjustment of boundaries in 1872 and reform of the process in 1964, the combination of these forces resulted in a smorgasbord of constituency designs and populations. Not surprisingly, departures from representation by population and representation by community had inconsistent effects on constituency design. Urban and rural constituencies varied greatly in both geographic configuration and population. There were several rural constituencies with larger populations than urban constituencies in the same province! As Norman Ward concluded in his study of boundaries readjustment between 1872 and 1948, "It is indisputable that [boundaries readjustment] has so far taken place with reference to none but the vaguest of principles." (Ward 1963, 46)

Reforming the Boundaries Readjustment Process
Gerrymandering during the first three boundaries readjustment exercises led the Liberals, then in opposition, to demand reform. The Liberal demand, however, was for a bipartisan, not an independent, process. Having come to power prior to the 1903 exercise, Sir Wilfrid Laurier's Liberal government

initiated reform by referring boundary design to a select committee of the House of Commons. From the 1930s on, proposals for an impartial judicial authority were advanced prior to each exercise.

Following an unsuccessful attempt to redraw electoral boundaries after the 1961 census and redistribution, the *Electoral Boundaries Readjustment Act* of 1964 established an independent and impartial process. The Act introduced an electoral boundaries commission for each province. These commissions are responsible for drawing federal electoral boundaries. Each commission is headed by a judge chosen by the province's chief justice. When a second Northwest Territories seat was established in 1975, the Act was amended: the territorial electoral boundaries commission is headed by a judge of the Court of Appeal or the Supreme Court of the Northwest Territories, appointed by the chief justice of the Court of Appeal. All 11 commissions include two other members selected by the Speaker of the House of Commons, but these persons cannot be members of the Senate, the House of Commons or a provincial or territorial legislature.

Electoral boundaries commissions are appointed after each decennial census. Using census data, the chief electoral officer determines the assignment of seats to provinces and the distribution of population within each province. Using this information, each commission draws an initial map outlining the new boundaries of constituencies in its province. Following publication of the map, the commission holds public hearings on its proposed boundaries. After considering public interventions, a commission may revise its map. It then sends the map to the chief electoral officer, who transmits it to the Speaker of the House of Commons.

Following the 1986 amendments to the *Electoral Boundaries Readjustment Act*, these proposed boundaries can be the subject of hearings before a Commons committee. (Under the original Act, debate was confined to the House.) After this stage, the commissions consider any objections raised by MPs, then submit their final reports. A "representation order", proclaimed by the Governor in Council, then gives effect to the new constituencies for the entire country. This order cannot change the boundaries drawn by the commissions, but the new boundaries do not come into effect until one year after the order is issued. If an election is called before one year has passed, the old electoral map must be used.

The 1964 *Electoral Boundaries Readjustment Act* enshrined the principle of comparable population in federal law for the first time. The Act required the commission for each province[1] to design constituencies so that the population of each corresponded "as nearly as may be to the electoral quota for the province". This quota, known as the electoral quotient, is determined by dividing a province's population by the number of seats it was assigned in the most recent redistribution.

The Act provided an allowance for deviations from the electoral quotient: a 25 per cent variation above or below the quotient is permitted. This allowed commissions to depart from the electoral quotient where

(a) special geographic considerations, including in particular the sparsity or density of the population of various regions of the province, the accessibility of those regions or the size or shape thereof, appear to the commission to render such a departure necessary or desirable; or

(b) any special community or diversity of interests of the inhabitants of various regions of the province appears to the commission to render such a departure necessary or desirable. (*Electoral Boundaries Readjustment Act*, s. 15(2))

The Act was amended in 1986 by the *Representation Act, 1985* to give even greater weight to community of interest objectives. As a result of these amendments, commissions are now required to design constituencies with populations "as close as *reasonably* possible" to a province's electoral quotient (emphasis added).

In addition, boundaries commissions are now required (rather than merely permitted) to consider

(i) the community of interest or community of identity in or the historical pattern of an electoral district in the province; and

(ii) a manageable geographic size for districts in sparsely populated, rural or northern regions of the province. (*Representation Act 1985*, s. 6)

Commissions may also depart from the quotient to respect (i) or to maintain (ii). Finally, commissions were given discretion to depart from a province's quotient altogether in circumstances they deemed "extraordinary". In such cases, they would not be constrained by the maximum variation of 25 per cent above or below the quotient.

Independent Boundaries Readjustment: The Record

The 1964 *Electoral Boundaries Readjustment Act* contained several significant innovations. Recognizing that Members of Parliament were in a conflict of interest, it removed the drawing of electoral boundaries from partisan politics. It also established comparable population as the basis for drawing boundaries, albeit tempered by a generous deviation if needed to accommodate community of interest or geographic size. The subsequent amendments in 1986 sought an even more effective representation of communities of interest.

The 1964 Act was based on the Australian model of independent boundaries readjustment. (Courtney 1988) The Australian experience is highly relevant to Canada because Australia is also a federation and its size and population distribution are comparable to Canada's. Australia's approach emphasizes representation by population, but it also recognizes the importance of community of interest considerations. Australia allowed for these concerns initially by permitting population variations of 20 per cent above or below the quotient in each state; the allowable variation has since been reduced to 10 per cent.

The original Bill that preceded Canada's 1964 legislation recommended a 20 per cent variation, but after parliamentary debate, it was increased to 25 per cent. This means that the population of a constituency at the lower limit might be only 60 per cent of the population of a constituency at the upper limit.

The record since 1964 reveals mixed results with respect to the objectives of the original Act and its subsequent amendments. One positive result is that the provincial commissions collectively moved in the general direction of enhancing comparable population in the exercises of 1966, 1976 and 1987. Each of these resulted in more constituencies that were closer to meeting provincial quotients than in the previous exercise (Table 4.8).

Table 4.8
Seats above and below provincial quotients, 1952–1987

Year (total seats)	Variations from quotient					
	>25%	20–25%	15–20%	10–15%	5–10%	0–5%
1952 (263)	35 (91)	11 (28)	13 (33)	13 (33)	13 (33)	17 (45)
1966 (262)	N.A.	11 (28)	17 (45)	24 (63)	26 (68)	22 (58)
1976 (279)	N.A.	9 (25)	24 (68)	27 (75)	21 (59)	19 (52)
1987 (292)	2 (5)	6 (18)	10 (30)	16 (48)	29 (85)	36 (106)

Source: Royal Commission Research Branch.

Note: Percentages may not add to 100 because of rounding.
Bracketed numbers are the number of seats.

At the same time, however, movement toward population equality *within* provinces has been uneven (Table 4.9). Five provinces have moved toward greater equality; in the other five, the movement has been toward greater variation from the province's quotient.

Moreover, the 1986 amendments appear to have reduced adherence to equality in representation. In his analysis of boundary readjustments since 1966, Andrew Sancton compared the proposals of the 1983 boundaries commissions (which were aborted when the House of Commons did not complete debate on their reports) with those of the 1987 commissions at the same stage in the process, that is, the report to Parliament stage. (Sancton 1990) This comparison shows that there was movement away from population equality between the 1983 and 1987 proposals (Table 4.10). Seven of the 10 commissions had moved farther away from their province's quotient, and the movement was significant.

Table 4.9
Gini scores of constituency populations, 1966, 1976, 1987
(by province)

Province	1966	1976	1987	Variation 1966–87
Ontario	0.077	0.080	0.051	-0.026
Quebec	0.060	0.081	0.072	+0.012
Nova Scotia	0.061	0.073	0.073	+0.012
New Brunswick	0.071	0.098	0.098	+0.027
Manitoba	0.104	0.060	0.035	-0.069
British Columbia	0.058	0.071	0.063	+0.005
Prince Edward Island	0.100	0.037	0.042	-0.058
Saskatchewan	0.081	0.054	0.013	-0.068
Alberta	0.086	0.068	0.077	-0.009
Newfoundland	0.086	0.074	0.140	+0.054

Source: Sancton 1990, 453.

Note: Perfect equality is represented by a score of 0, where each constituency's population equals the provincial quotient; greater inequality is portrayed as the score increases from 0 to 1.

Table 4.10
Gini scores of proposed electoral constituency populations at the report to Parliament stage, 1983, 1987
(by province)

Province	1983	1987	Variation 1983–87
Ontario	0.041	0.051	+0.010
Quebec	0.059	0.070	+0.011
Nova Scotia	0.044	0.073	+0.029
New Brunswick	0.088	0.098	+0.010
Manitoba	0.042	0.035	-0.007
British Columbia	0.044	0.067	+0.023
Prince Edward Island	0.055	0.042	-0.013
Saskatchewan	0.011	0.011	0.000
Alberta	0.058	0.077	+0.019
Newfoundland	0.106	0.167	+0.061

Source: Sancton 1990, 455.

Note: Perfect equality is represented by a score of 0, where each constituency's population equals the provincial quotient; greater inequality is represented as the score increases from 0 to 1.

A specific consequence of the 1986 amendments was that three commissions used the provision enabling them to create electoral constituencies with populations beyond the ±25 per cent variation. The three commissions were Newfoundland's, with two such cases; Quebec's, with two; and Ontario's, with one. In Newfoundland, for example, Labrador was given its own seat: its population is 61.4 per cent below the province's electoral quotient. As a result, the average population of the other constituencies was almost 90 000 – larger than that of any other province. Newfoundland's most populous constituency, St. John's East, with a population 28.8 per cent above the quotient, had more than three times the population of its least populous constituency, Labrador.

Commissions have considerable discretion in approaching their task. Having a commission for each province, rather than a single commission for Canada, has its merits, of course. Most important is a commission's capacity to weigh community characteristics that may justify departures from population equality. Were there no objectives other than population equality, a national commission might be sufficient.

At the same time, however, the record suggests that even in instances where variations from population equality are roughly similar, a different outcome can result. This is illustrated by the approaches taken by the most recent commissions in Saskatchewan and Manitoba.

The Saskatchewan commission achieved the lowest variation of any province, with all its constituencies within 5 per cent of the quotient. As John Courtney, one of its commissioners, stated at our public hearings, "What we were placed in the position of doing was trying to conciliate these different demands [territory and population]. So the conclusion that we reached as the fairest way for the whole province was to go as closely as we could to the arithmetic mean." (Saskatoon, 17 April 1990) The Manitoba commission achieved the second lowest population variation, but it was also able to accommodate a significant number of community of interest considerations: with one metropolitan area with over 60 per cent of the provincial population and fewer population centres of any size in rural areas, the commission for this province could more easily accommodate communities of interest than Saskatchewan. As might be expected, the Saskatchewan commission received a large number of objections to its proposals, whereas the Manitoba body received relatively few.

In some provinces, particularly those where the number of constituencies did not change, commissions have simply taken the path of least resistance, changing the boundaries as little as possible to meet the letter, if not the spirit, of the law. At our public hearings Condé Grondin characterized the most recent New Brunswick commission as "showing an unwillingness to change or to go against the pattern that had been set up by the Commission in 1964 [even though] they were very much aware that the ridings in New Brunswick were departing to a greater degree from the so-called idea of one person, one vote". (Fredericton, 19 March 1990) Grondin argued that New Brunswick could in fact do more to meet the objective of comparable population while also accommodating communities of interest.

We conclude that the drawing of constituency boundaries since 1964 has had mixed success in securing equal and efficacious representation. The principal reason for this outcome is the law itself. The *Electoral Boundaries Readjustment Act*, as amended by the *Representation Act, 1985*, gives mixed, even confusing, signals to electoral boundaries commissions and to citizens. (Sancton 1990) On one hand, the law appears to require commissions to advance the equality of the vote: constituencies are to be designed with populations "as close as reasonably possible" to the provincial quotient. On the other hand, they are required to "consider" community of interest criteria in designing constituencies and in deviating from the provincial quotient. These provisions appear to require that the commissions advance the efficacy of the vote. But to confuse matters even further, commissions may depart from the quotient altogether in "extraordinary" circumstances. Lack of consistency under these conditions is not surprising.

The crux of the problem is that boundaries commissions have interpreted the law in different ways. (Courtney 1988) As we have already seen, this was dramatically evident in the contrasting approaches of the Saskatchewan and Newfoundland commissions in the last boundaries readjustment.

Population comparability and community of interest need not and should not be regarded as contradictory. Even with no variation from population equality, as represented by an electoral quotient, infinite variations on a province's electoral boundaries are possible. The challenge is to draw boundaries that detract from neither voter equality nor community of interest.

We believe that reform can meet both objectives. Reform requires that equality and efficacy be situated in the context of our parliamentary institutions and electoral system.

Toward Equality and Efficacy of the Vote

At our public hearings, two competing schools of thought on electoral reform were well represented. The first, based on strict adherence to representation by population, is part of our political tradition. It occasioned political struggle prior to Confederation and became the basis for assigning seats to the provinces of the Dominion created in 1867. "Rep by pop" was only one of several factors in drawing electoral boundaries during the long period when MPs carried out this task, but it was given primacy in the 1964 *Electoral Boundaries Readjustment Act*.

The second school of thought, which emphasizes the representation of communities of interest, has an equally long history. The original scheme for drawing electoral boundaries recognized the primacy of existing county and municipal boundaries, and throughout the period when Parliament performed this task, claims of community of interest were acknowledged as legitimate influences on constituency design. The 1986 amendments reasserted the fundamental significance of such factors.

Given this tradition, what are we to make of these competing claims? The right to an equally *weighted* vote is clearly an individual right. But the right to an equally *effective* vote is no less an individual right, even if it takes expression through a community of interest. The apparent contradiction between equality of representation and quality of representation derives, we suggest, from an inadequate appreciation of the dynamic relationship between the equality and the efficacy of representation. We must therefore consider a third approach to the drawing of electoral boundaries, one that does not consider the equality and effectiveness of representation to be contradictory principles. To appreciate this third approach to drawing electoral boundaries, we must situate these two principles in our system of representative democracy.

Equality of the Vote

Representation by population has long been acknowledged in our political tradition. This principle seeks to advance the equality of the vote by asserting the *equal value* of each vote. In a system where legislators are elected from geographically defined constituencies, this means not only a universal franchise, with each elector having only one vote, but also constituencies designed with roughly equal populations.

Canada's use of single-member constituencies reflects the localized character of our political culture. (Smith 1985; Courtney 1985) As a result, despite various nationalizing forces within our political and party systems, maintaining an electoral democracy based on representation of local communities has strong roots in our political tradition. (Bakvis 1991)

Canadians value the personal representation made possible by having a locally chosen MP, making the single-member constituency preferable to the geographically larger multi-member constituencies required by electoral systems such as "proportional representation". Canadians approach their MP for assistance, even if they have not voted for the winner. If anything, Canadians seem to want their MPs to be even more locally oriented than they are now. (Blais and Gidengil 1991 RC) The disciplined public face that parties maintain tends to mask the amount of local advocacy that goes on within parliamentary parties. (Thomas 1991 RC)

At the same time, of course, nationalizing forces – especially the *Canadian Charter of Rights and Freedoms* in recent years – influence the political system. Adopting the Charter signified acceptance of certain national political norms, including democratic and equality rights. One focus for promoting these rights has been constituency design; the major focus here has been the principle of representation by population, based on the objective of the equality of the vote.

Three major court decisions on representation by population and the design of constituencies have given new salience to this principle. Courts in both British Columbia and Saskatchewan (*Dixon* 1989; *Reference re Provincial Electoral Boundaries* 1991) ruled that provincial boundaries readjustment legislation or practices violated the Charter's section 3 guarantee of the right to vote by diluting the equality of the vote between constituencies. In the *Dixon* case Justice McLachlin stated that the Charter guaranteed citizens "relative equality of voting power"; the Saskatchewan Court of Appeal referred to "relative or substantial equality" of voting power. Neither decision mandated absolute mathematical equality, and both recognized that geography, particularly remoteness and sparsity of population, were mitigating factors in determining boundaries. Justice McLachlin reaffirmed this approach in writing the majority opinion of the Supreme Court of Canada in *Carter* (1991). (The Supreme Court heard this case under the name *Carter v. Saskatchewan (Attorney General)*.)

The Saskatchewan *Reference* case and its appeal to the Supreme Court of Canada (the *Carter* case) attracted national attention because the issue pitted the principle of voter equality against what was alleged to be partisan gerrymandering by the Saskatchewan government. The alleged gerrymandering resulted from two dimensions of Saskatchewan's *Electoral Boundaries Commission Act* as well as from the constituency boundaries produced by the provincial boundaries commission under this Act. This Act mandated a quota for the number of seats to be given to urban and rural areas of the province and increased the allowed deviation from the provincial quotient from 15 per cent to 25 per cent. The quota meant that urban areas, by legislative design, were to be underrepresented, given the number of seats for urban areas in relation to the urban population of the province. Conversely, rural areas, where the governing party was traditionally well represented, were to be overrepresented.

The electoral boundaries drawn by the Saskatchewan provincial commission in 1988 under the above legislation resulted in a Gini score of 0.081. This was farther from meeting the criterion of equality of the vote than achieved by the previous commission in 1980, with a Gini score of 0.048. It was also on the high side of inequality when compared with federal electoral boundaries commissions for the 10 provinces in 1987 – only Newfoundland and New Brunswick at 0.140 and 0.098, respectively, produced electoral maps with greater inequality of constituency populations. Moreover, the federal boundaries commission for Saskatchewan in 1987 produced a map with a Gini score of 0.013, coming closer to representing equality of the vote than any of the federal commissions for the 10 provinces. These comparisons indicate the extent to which the 1988 Saskatchewan provincial commission departed from recent experience and trends toward the equality of the vote both in Canada generally and in Saskatchewan in particular. In anticipation of an unsuccessful appeal of the *Reference* decision, a second Saskatchewan map was drawn in 1991, following new legislation. This map resulted in a Gini score of 0.031, very much in line with the trend toward equality of the vote.

The Saskatchewan Court of Appeal in the *Reference* case decided that voter equality was required by the Charter and that any deviations from voter equality could be justified only on practical grounds. The Court did not accept the government's claim that rural areas necessarily required overrepresentation in the legislature. It also decided that the provision whereby constituencies could have populations up to 25 per cent above or below the provincial electoral quotient was unjustified.

The public perception of the decision of the Supreme Court of Canada (*Carter* 1991) on the appeal of this case was complicated by two factors. First, the Saskatchewan government responded to the Court of Appeal decision by enacting new legislation, and its boundaries commission then produced a new electoral map for the province with all but two northern constituencies falling within 5 per cent of the electoral quotient. This was taken to be an admission that voter equality could be achieved if pursued as a matter of public policy. Second, the questions put to the Supreme Court of Canada merely asked whether the original map, rather than the legislation on which it was based, was unconstitutional because it infringed on Charter rights in a manner that could not be justified.

A crucial fact overlooked by most, perhaps all, commentators was the precise wording of the two questions put to the Supreme Court. The two questions considered by the Supreme Court were:

> "(a) Does the variance in the size of voter populations among those con-
> stituencies ... infringe or deny rights or freedoms guaranteed by the
> *Canadian Charter of Rights and Freedoms*? If so, in what particulars? Is
> any such limitation or denial of rights justified by section 1 of the
> *Canadian Charter of Rights and Freedoms*?
>
> (b) Does the distribution of those constituencies among urban, rural and
> northern areas ... infringe or deny rights or freedoms guaranteed by
> the *Canadian Charter of Rights and Freedoms*? If so, in what particulars?
> Is any such limitation or denial of rights or freedoms justified by sec-
> tion 1 of the *Canadian Charter of Rights and Freedoms*?" (*Carter* 1991, 30)

The first question was answered in the negative. The Supreme Court stated that absolute equality in the size of constituencies was not required by the Charter; "effective representation", it argued, allows for some devia-tion from the electoral quotient to represent communities of interest and other non-population factors. The Court also stated that a 25 per cent devia-tion was not unreasonable. With the exception of the two northern con-stituencies that even the Saskatchewan Court of Appeal had accepted, all southern constituencies, urban and rural, were within the 25 per cent per-mitted deviation from the electoral quotient. This latter fact was almost totally ignored in coverage of this decision.

The Supreme Court also answered the second question in the negative. It did so on the grounds that the electoral map produced by the original boundaries commission was based on legislation that recognized the increased population of urban areas, such that the number of seats allocated for urban areas had increased from the previous boundary readjustment a decade earlier. Second, it argued that the resulting difference between the seat/population ratio for urban areas and that for rural areas was not so large that it infringed on voter equality. Rural areas were overrepresented by 2.6 per cent; urban areas were underrepresented by 3.7 per cent (the two numbers were not identical because of the accepted overrepresentation of the two northern constituencies).

The majority decision of the Supreme Court of Canada in this case thus adhered to the Canadian tradition: absolute voter equality was not required by the Charter. The Court's minority also accepted this position but argued, among other considerations, that the Saskatchewan legislation itself was not justified in creating two classes of constituencies and in reverting to a more generous deviation from the electoral quotient. The provincial election of 21 October 1991 was then conducted using the boundaries drawn by the commission in 1988.

Reacting to this decision, the press created the impression that the Supreme Court had backed away from the fundamental principle of voter equality. This was not the case. The Court reaffirmed that "relative parity of voting power" is the first condition of "effective representation". This reaffirmation of the equality of the vote must also be read in the context of earlier court decisions. In *Dixon* (1989), Justice McLachlin had stated that a 25 per cent allowable deviation, the deviation recommended by the 1988 Fisher Commission on Electoral Boundaries for British Columbia, constituted "a tolerable limit". Given that the provincial boundaries at issue in the Saskatchewan case were drawn so that all constituencies, except for the two northern constituencies, were within a 25 per cent deviation, it is understandable that, in writing the majority opinion in the *Carter* case, she would not revisit the question of the allowable deviation. Second, the decision clearly stated that any departures from this first condition must be "justified on the ground that they contribute to better government of the populace as a whole". (quoted in *Carter* 1991, 35, 36)

Voter equality need not imply that other representational objectives cannot be realized even where a substantial equality of the vote among constituencies is achieved. Support for this approach is evident in the decisions of electoral boundaries commissions over the past 25 years. (Courtney 1988) Not all commissions have achieved comparable results, however, demonstrating that legislative reform is needed to advance the equality of the vote. This is especially the case for Canada's federal constituencies compared with provincial constituencies. Because Canada's federal constituencies are larger than the provincial ones, it is relatively easy for the former to accommodate communities of interest while adhering closely to the equality of the vote. U.S. courts have accepted that the equality of population criterion need not be applied as stringently at the state level as at the federal level, a lesson that should not be lost on Canadians.

Community of Interest

The concept of community of interest is subtler and more complex than the apparently straightforward concept of voter equality; it lacks the clarity and political appeal of "one person, one vote". The concept also carries the legacy of the political compromises and accommodations, if not outright gerrymandering, that accounted for many of the past inequalities among constituencies – inequalities that could not be justified with reference to any sound principle of representation. The recent Saskatchewan provincial experience has resurrected this concern. Removing partisanship from constituency design may eliminate gerrymandering, but it does not eliminate the need for compromise.

In the current statutory framework for drawing electoral boundaries, community of interest incorporates the several objectives that are linked to it – community of identity, the historical pattern of a constituency, and manageable geographic size in sparsely populated, rural or remote regions. Along with other socio-economic factors, these indices of community of interest constitute legitimate criteria for purposes of representation and thus constituency design.

An important assumption is implicit in the design of constituencies on a territorial basis – that the efficacy of the vote is enhanced to the degree that constituencies represent the shared interests of local communities. This assumption does not presuppose that all communities of interest are geographically concentrated. Some interests are dispersed, and electoral boundaries drawn on a territorial basis cannot recognize them. But many others are concentrated, and boundaries commissions must determine which should be the basis for the boundaries they draw.

The rational approach is to draw boundaries that correspond as closely as possible to the boundaries of communities of interest. To the degree that MPs seek to represent the shared interests of their constituents (and not just the interests of those who voted for them), constituencies should be designed to incorporate the communities of interest in the general region to be represented. In this way the representation of interests is advanced, particularly in areas where communities possess clearly identifiable interests.

Similarly, the efficacy of the vote of members of these communities is enhanced because they have a greater chance of collectively influencing the choice of a representative. This promotes political participation: individuals are more likely to vote when they believe their vote may influence the outcome of an election. When a community of interest is dispersed across two or more constituencies, its voters' capacity to promote their collective interest is diminished accordingly. Their incentive to participate is likewise reduced because the outcome has a lesser relevance to their community of interest. When this occurs, especially if it could have been avoided, the legitimacy of the electoral system is undermined.

The recent experience in the United States with court-mandated redistricting to accommodate communities of interest is testimony to this. After community of interest objectives were ignored by earlier efforts to secure near-equality of the vote, the Americans had to adjust their approach to redistricting to acknowledge the importance attached to community of interest, especially by members of minority groups – whose interests had never been recognized, except in negative ways, in the design of electoral districts. This practice, referred to as the "affirmative action gerrymandering", has grown in the United States. In recent years, redistricting legislation has evolved from "passive protection" to "active encouragement" of minority group representation. (Cain 1984, 66)

In the United States, Congress has built upon the non-discrimination principles of its *Voting Rights Act of 1965* to ensure that district boundaries are drawn on the basis of voter equality and do not disperse the votes of minority groups. The U.S. Supreme Court has used this Act and the amendments of 1982 to protect collective, as opposed to individual, voting rights. This U.S. experience illustrates that it is possible to design electoral districts in ways that promote the equality of the vote on the one hand and community of interest on the other.

In the United States, wherever possible, it is now considered necessary that a racial or ethnic minority group constitute a majority within an electoral district in order that it be able to determine the outcome of an election and thus be able to elect a candidate from its community. The assumption here, of course, is that serious candidates, representing one of the two major political parties, will be forthcoming from such a community. Even where such a community cannot constitute a majority, the intention is to create electoral districts within which such communities may constitute a significant minority and thus influence the outcome of elections. In each case, the purpose of such "affirmative action gerrymandering" is to ensure that these communities of interest do not have their vote diluted by their dispersal over two or more adjacent electoral districts.

Although community of interest has remained an important consideration in the drawing of federal electoral boundaries in Canada, this should not be taken to mean that the issue of representation of minority groups has always been adequately addressed. As we discuss in the final section of this chapter, Aboriginal peoples, for example, have generally been less than satisfied with the decisions of Canada's boundaries commissions in this respect.

While independent boundaries commissions are clearly the most effective mechanism to eliminate partisanship in the design of constituencies, political independence does not guarantee that the rights of minority groups will be secured. Greater sensitivity to the full range of communities of interest is necessary to accomplish this goal.

The right to an equally weighted vote – as expressed in "one person, one vote" – is an individual right. But citizens, especially those who belong to minority groups, also have a constitutional right to equal protection and benefit of the law. When constituencies do not divide these communities, this objective is enhanced. Indeed, given the demographic weight of members of minority groups in certain areas, it is possible to maximize their electoral influence by ensuring that their community of interest is respected in drawing constituency boundaries.

In terms of their demographic profile, most ethno-cultural groups, including visible minorities, are concentrated in Ontario. In fact, almost half of those belonging to a visible minority group in Canada are concentrated in Ontario, and over three-quarters are located in seven cities across Canada (see Table 4.11).

Table 4.11
Visible minority group members by metropolitan census region, Canada, 1986

Region	Number	Percentage of total population
Montreal	204 740	7.0
Winnipeg	49 530	7.9
Vancouver	230 840	16.7
Toronto	586 495	17.1
Halifax	15 025	5.1
Calgary	72 600	10.8
Edmonton	72 560	9.2
Total	1 231 790	5.0

Source: A. Pelletier 1991 RC, adapted from Statistics Canada data.

In terms of their demographic profile within constituencies, ethno-cultural communities are significant in several federal constituencies. Ethno-cultural communities constitute a majority in 11 constituencies; seven of these are in Ontario. Statistics Canada's 1986 census also indicates ethno-cultural communities constitute 21–50 per cent of the total population in 125 constituencies; 54 of these are in Ontario. Indeed, in fully half of Ontario's federal constituencies these communities account for more than 21 per cent of the total constituency population. In none of these cases, however, does a single ethno-cultural group constitute more than 40 per cent of the population. Table 4.12 details the profile of the 11 constituencies where these ethno-cultural communities are in a majority.

The ability of such groups to elect representatives from their own communities often depends on there being enough voters who have the same ethno-cultural origin as the candidate. The point is not that individual community members always vote the same way – indeed, the candidate's characteristics and party affiliation are important considerations – but that they have an opportunity to collectively influence the outcome. Candidates must also have a political incentive to acknowledge and, once elected, to represent the interests of such communities. At the very least, the ability of ethno-cultural communities to influence the outcome of an election should not be damaged by artificial boundaries.

The drawing of electoral boundaries in Vancouver in 1988, which decreased the Chinese Canadian population's representation, illustrates how ignoring communities of interest substantially minimizes the weight of certain groups and the efficacy of the vote of members of such communities. In 1988, the constituency of Vancouver East (25.4 per cent Chinese) was the only one that had a Chinese population exceeding 20 per cent, whereas in 1984 there had been two: Vancouver Kingsway (24.6 per cent) and Vancouver East (23.9 per cent). Yet by rearranging the 1984 boundaries of Vancouver South and Vancouver Quadra alone, it would have been possible to obtain a third constituency with more than 20 per cent Chinese, namely Vancouver South. (A. Pelletier 1991 RC)

Table 4.12
Constituencies where ethno-cultural groups (single origin) constitute more than 50 per cent of the population, Canada, 1986
(per cent)

Constituency	Total ethno-cultural representation	Predominant ethno-cultural group	Second predominant ethno-cultural group
Mount-Royal	62.2	Jewish (37.7)	Black (2.6)
York South	52.8	Italian (17.7)	Black (6.8)
Don Valley North	53.0	Jewish (10.9)	Chinese (9.8)
Trinity–Spadina	62.7	Chinese (13.1)	Italian (7.9)
Eglinton–Lawrence	63.3	Italian (23.7)	Jewish (11.3)
York West	63.6	Italian (28.3)	Black (7.9)
York Centre	66.1	Italian (31.0)	Jewish (13.6)
Davenport	73.1	Italian (21.4)	Chinese (3.0)
Winnipeg North	71.9	Ukrainian (13.3)	Jewish (7.1)
Regina–Qu'Appelle	64.5	German (16.8)	Ukrainian (5.2)
Vancouver East	56.1	Chinese (25.4)	Italian (7.6)

Source: A. Pelletier 1991 RC, adapted from Statistics Canada data.

This understanding of an equally effective vote for members of a community of interest is not new to our political tradition; it did not arise from the adoption of the Charter, although the Charter does reinforce it, as clearly stated in the *Carter* decision in 1991. This tradition recognizes that neither the franchise nor representation is merely an individualistic phenomenon; both also take expression through collective or community functions. The individualistic perspective is based upon a partial and incomplete understanding of the electoral process and representation. In advancing the ideal of equally weighted votes, it does promote a critical constitutional right. But in ignoring the community dimension, this perspective is unrealistic at best; at worst it ignores the legitimate claims of minority groups.

It is unrealistic because it assumes that voters do not vote as members of communities of interest or expect to be represented on this basis – and therefore that it does not matter to them how boundaries are drawn so long as constituencies are equal in size. This is not the reality of voting and representation in Canada – or elsewhere for that matter. Many voters do expect to be represented, at least in part, on this community of interest basis. And they therefore care about the way constituency boundaries are drawn.

At worst, the individualistic perspective assumes that electoral majorities or pluralities constitute the exclusive basis for representation, with communities of interest accorded no recognition. This perpetuates the underrepresentation of certain minority groups in the House of Commons by denying the legitimacy of their communities of interest in the drawing of electoral boundaries. It also prevents them from influencing the selection of candidates as well as the outcome of elections as members of a community.

An Approach to Reform

Our approach to electoral reform posits that relative equality of the vote must be the primary objective in drawing electoral boundaries. Having constituencies with relatively equal numbers of voters will promote the equal value of each citizen's vote. It will also result in a House of Commons whose membership on average more accurately reflects the actual distribution of the national vote than would be the case if constituencies were allowed to vary significantly in their populations. This desired outcome will enhance the legitimacy of the House of Commons. At the same time, there is more than sufficient evidence from the Canadian federal experience, the experience in certain provinces, and comparative experience, especially in the United States and Australia, to indicate that this objective can be achieved while giving due regard to communities of interest. Given the number and size of Canada's federal constituencies, the electoral quotient in each province is sufficiently large to allow ample room for consideration of community of interest while adhering to relative equality of the vote. In short, greater adherence to equality of the vote can be realized, while adhering to community of interest, if the law requires commissions to respect a lower deviation from their province's quotient.

Proposals for Reform

The process of designing constituencies by independent boundaries commissions for each province has worked well. The use of such non-partisan commissions has made it possible to give consideration to community of interest criteria without partisanship being a factor. In the United States, in contrast, the courts have had to insist on strict equality of the vote because there, federal redistricting is carried out by state legislatures. We, on the other hand, have been able to allow for variations from electoral quotients on the ground that independent commissions will use this allowance for non-partisan purposes. At the same time, we have noted progress by electoral boundaries commissions toward the objectives that should govern their drawing of constituencies, namely, equality of the vote and increased efforts to justify variations from electoral quotients.

Recommendation 1.4.2

We recommend that the use of independent electoral boundaries commissions for each province and the Northwest Territories, as well as the composition and manner of their appointment, be maintained.

Recommendation 1.4.3

We recommend that the boundaries commission for each province establish the boundaries of the constituencies in its province according to the principles that the vote of each voter is of equal weight and that each constituency reflects communities of interest.

To achieve representation by population and at the same time draw electoral boundaries so that constituencies effectively represent communities of interest, several improvements are necessary. They include changes to:

- the permitted deviation from electoral quotients;
- the power of boundaries commissions to ignore the quotient altogether;
- the definition of community of interest as a basis for constituency design;
- the basis for determining the quotient;
- the frequency of boundaries readjustment; and
- the process of securing public response to the proposals of boundaries commissions.

Deviations from the Quotient

The provision allowing boundaries commissions to deviate by ±25 per cent of the provincial electoral quotient was generous at the outset. The Australian law on which the 1964 *Electoral Boundaries Readjustment Act* was based provided at that time for a 20 per cent deviation. This deviation has since been reduced there to 10 per cent. Given that the Australian case has been singled out in this regard as the best example of the tradition of other Commonwealth countries (*Carter* 1991, 37–38), that country's experience is germane to our discussions.

The experience of Canadian electoral boundaries commissions since 1964 demonstrates that greater equality in representation can be achieved while still reflecting community of interest. Determining what the deviation should be entails an element of judgement, but we note progress toward population equality over the past three decades. Following the 1987 boundaries readjustment, 81 per cent of the constituencies were within 15 per cent of the provincial quotient. This was an increase from 67 per cent in 1976, 72 per cent in 1966, and 43 per cent in 1952. Given this progress, and given Canada's constituency design, geography and population dispersal, the figure of 15 per cent is both reasonable and realistic. It remains larger than the 10 per cent allowed in Australia, a country that shares many common geographic and demographic characteristics with Canada. A 15 per cent deviation above and below is sufficient allowance for the accommodation of communities of interest within the Canadian context; the population of a constituency at the lower limit would be approximately 75 per cent of that of a constituency at the upper limit.

Lowering the permitted deviation to ±15 per cent would, in fact, enhance the equality of the vote in each province. Since voters cast their votes for candidates in single-member constituencies, lowering the permitted deviation will result in constituencies being closer to the provincial quotient. The closer constituencies are to the provincial quotient, the closer the total membership of the House of Commons will be, proportionately, to the voting preferences of Canadians. Greater adherence to the equality of the vote, in short, both secures the individual's right to a vote of equal value and enhances the efficacy of the vote of communities, at the constituency, provincial and national levels. This result will thereby serve to enhance public confidence in the federal electoral process by increasing the degree to which the membership of the House of Commons reflects the national vote.

Recommendation 1.4.4

We recommend that

(a) **electoral boundaries commissions be permitted to deviate from their provincial electoral quotient by no more than 15 per cent; and**
(b) **the rules for dividing the two constituencies of the Northwest Territories remain different with respect to the population criterion.**

Extraordinary Circumstances
The discretion to depart altogether from the quotient in "extraordinary" circumstances is, in our view, an unjustified departure from the principles that should govern the process. Commissions are not required to justify such departures, and no legislative guidance is provided on either principles or criteria. As John Courtney explained at our hearings:

> [It] places unrealistic burdens on the Election Boundary Commissions....
> They don't have any definition of the Act to refer back to; and therefore

it places them in a very awkward position.... And it's difficult, I think, for commissions to withstand the special pleading that will undoubtedly be brought before them by interested groups. (Saskatoon, 17 April 1990)

The integrity of the law has been severely undermined by this provision. There may be sound reasons for using the maximum variation to create some constituencies where communities are dispersed over an extremely large area. This is recognized in the present law, which allows boundaries commissions to depart from the electoral quotient to the limit of the permitted variation "to maintain a manageable geographic size for constituencies in sparsely populated, rural or northern regions of the province". The traditional argument for the overrepresentation of these areas is based on the obstacles to personal contact – for campaigning and constituency service – that these constituencies present. The evidence does not lend it much support. In fact, the population in most northern constituencies is concentrated in relatively few centres, albeit widely dispersed. And, increasingly, the population is moving to these centres.

More significant is that only one of the five constituencies created under the "extraordinary" clause is among the 10 largest constituencies in geographic size, excluding the constituencies of the Yukon and Northwest Territories. This constituency is Labrador, the largest constituency in Newfoundland by geographic size. By contrast, Ontario has five constituencies larger in geographic size than the single Ontario constituency created under this provision, while in Quebec, where two such constituencies were created, one is the tenth largest and the other the thirteenth largest in geographic size (Appendix B).

We conclude that the "extraordinary" clause has been used mainly for reasons other than to create constituencies of manageable size. Neither Australia nor the United States has considered it necessary to have a special provision for large constituencies. The geographic size of their largest constituencies is comparable to our largest constituencies, yet they adhere much more closely to their electoral quotients than do our largest constituencies (Appendix C).

Advances in travel and communications technology, combined with the administrative and technical resources available to MPs, particularly those from the constituencies in question, mean that geographic size is no longer the obstacle to constituency service it once was. In our view, concerns about manageable size in sparsely populated regions can be accommodated within the population variation we recommend.

Recommendation 1.4.5

We recommend that the provision be removed whereby boundaries commissions may exceed the permitted variation from their provincial electoral quotient under circumstances they deem extraordinary.

Parliament might wish to allow one or more constituencies to surpass the permitted variation for reasons of geography or sparsity of population. In this case, Parliament should provide for this in the *Canada Elections Act* itself, although we do not believe surpassing the maximum deviation is necessary or desirable. The integrity of the electoral system requires that the boundaries created by electoral boundaries commissions conform in every instance to provisions respecting the electoral quotient.

Community of Interest

Recognizing community of interest as a general objective in constituency design presupposes the existence of more than one expression of such interests. The law, for example, identifies not only "community of interest", but also "community of identity" and "the historical pattern of constituency". Provincial laws vary in their statement and treatment of this objective. Quebec's electoral law is perhaps the most comprehensive, for it begins by defining what an electoral constituency "represents". It states:

> An electoral division represents a natural community established on the basis of demographical, geographical and sociological considerations, such as the population density, the relative growth rate of the population, the accessibility, area and shape of the region, the natural local boundaries and the limits of local municipalities.

Provincial electoral laws recognize that factors other than population equality should be considered in designing constituencies. They also recognize that attempts to accommodate factors other than population invariably require decisions on the merits of competing claims. Existing municipal boundaries, for example, may compete with the boundaries of ethnocultural or linguistic communities. As Alan Stewart concludes:

> If conflicts between these factors are to be resolved, there must be some ultimate standard by which the competing claims can be compared. That standard must be community of interest, which requires the weighing of the subjective salience and objective importance of the various shared allegiances and values supporting competing boundary proposals. (Stewart 1991 RC)

Community of interest cannot be interpreted other than on a case-by-case basis. This is acknowledged implicitly in the use of a boundaries commission for each province and by the requirement that commissions conduct public hearings. Although commissions are to be independent of partisan politics, the fact that there are 11 separate commissions assumes that decisions are based on judgement, not merely technical considerations. Public hearings are the mechanism whereby claims can be articulated by those who wish to see a community of interest recognized in electoral boundaries.

In our view, it is the responsibility of electoral boundaries commissions to interpret how the various claims should be assessed and to determine which claims should be accommodated.

At the same time, we consider it essential that commissions not only consider communities of interest but also justify their boundary proposals with reference to community of interest objectives. This can be accomplished if commissions are directed to consider constituencies as representing communities established on the basis of demographic, sociological and geographic considerations and if they take into account the accessibility, area and shape of a region, its natural local boundaries and ecology, and the boundaries of local government and administrative units, as well as treaty areas.

By approaching the design of electoral constituencies in this manner, boundaries legislation and boundaries commissions need not give preference to any one factor. Changes in boundaries ought to accommodate changing patterns of community formation and reflect what is paramount at any point in time. Justice McLachlin made this point clearly in the *Carter* case when she stated that "inequities in our voting system [ought not] to be accepted merely because they have historical precedent". (1991, 38) The same can be said for past preferences in the design of constituencies. This is especially the case with any statutory provision to systematically overrepresent certain areas or to insist on particular boundaries being used, such as the use of municipal boundaries for urban constituencies as legislated in some provinces.

Recommendation 1.4.6

We recommend that

(a) **electoral boundaries be drawn to represent communities of interest formed on the basis of demographic, sociological and geographic considerations, taking into account the accessibility, shape and ecology of a region, the boundaries of local government and administrative units, as well as treaty areas; and**

(b) **electoral boundaries commissions justify their proposals and final decisions with reference to these community of interest considerations and contextual factors.**

Ecological Factors

Among the factors that should be considered in designing constituencies is the ecology of a region. At our public hearings, as well as at the most recent hearings of the commissions for Ontario and British Columbia, interveners urged that boundaries be drawn in ways that reflect the need to define communities in terms of local ecosystems.

This concern has emerged over the past decade, reflecting a new environmental consciousness. In addition, the science of ecological land classification has advanced to the point where ecosystem boundaries can be identified with some precision. Several government agencies, such as the Ontario conservation authorities established to co-ordinate water management, have administrative boundaries established on the basis of ecosystems.

Natural borders, such as rivers and mountains, have been used to define electoral boundaries in the past. But an ecosystem embraces what some natural borders have been used to separate; a watershed ecosystem, for example, encompasses both sides of a river. Using ecological considerations to define communities would obviously call for a new approach.

Our research does not support the claim that drawing boundaries in a manner more sensitive to ecological considerations would facilitate environmental protection. (Macdonald 1991 RC) Neither electoral nor jurisdictional boundaries are major factors in formulating and implementing environmental law. On the other hand, communities are beginning to express their interests and identities in a new way. This development should be recognized in constituency design; hence our recommendation that the ecology of a region be taken into account in drawing electoral boundaries. We urge the Canada Elections Commission to make every effort to ensure that staff support to boundaries commissions includes ecologists.

The Basis and Timing of Constituency Design

Efforts to achieve equality of the vote are also affected by the process for designing constituencies. Under the present law, boundaries are redrawn only every 10 years, following the decennial census. Since the 1964 reforms, boundaries have remained in place longer between each redrawing of the electoral map. (Courtney 1988, 688) With continuing change in population distribution and community size, designs intended to achieve population equality inevitably deteriorate over each 10-year period. In addition, the boundaries commission process takes time, and the new boundaries do not come into effect until one year after the commissions complete their work. As Munroe Eagles notes:

> At the time of the last election held on 1966 boundaries (1974), for example, virtually four in every 10 ridings exceeded 25 percent of their respective provincial electoral quotients. Similarly, the last election held on 1976 boundaries (1984) saw more than one in five ridings exceed the 25 percent threshold of tolerable deviations. Even though the current boundaries have only been used once, projected population figures calculated for 1991 suggest just under a fifth (17.4 percent) of all districts would exceed the 25 percent tolerance if an election were to be called this year. (1991a RC)

The 1988 election, for example, was conducted on boundaries established after the 1981 census. By 1988, comparability of population among constituencies had already been seriously eroded, particularly in Ontario, as shown by the results of Statistics Canada's mid-term population projections in 1986.

In the redrawing of the electoral map following the 1981 census, only 8 per cent of Ontario constituencies exceeded the quotient by ±15 per cent. All were on the low side – that is, less than the quotient – and all but one were in sparsely populated northern Ontario. By 1986, however, two years before the first election conducted on these boundaries, it is estimated that more than 25 per cent of Ontario constituencies deviated from the quotient by more than 15 per cent – more than a threefold increase. The greatest increase was in southern Ontario.

After the 1981 census, no southern Ontario constituency had a population more than 15 per cent over the quotient; by 1986, it is estimated that 11 constituencies had populations that exceeded the quotient by 15 per cent, with six of them exceeding it by 25 per cent. In the province as a whole, constituencies with populations more than 15 per cent under the quotient rose from eight to 14 between 1981 and 1986, with five falling short by 25 per cent or more. With one more federal election to be conducted on the basis of the present boundaries, it is estimated that close to 50 per cent of constituencies in Ontario will likely deviate from the quotient by more than 15 per cent.

Common sense and evidence from other jurisdictions show that maintaining comparability between constituencies requires the most current data available. The most current, complete and accurate, of course, would be the actual number of voters on the final voters lists for the most recent election. This approach is used in Alberta, Quebec and Saskatchewan, as well as Great Britain and Australia. Australia provides an interesting model: boundaries must be redrawn every seven years but also must be redrawn more often should population shifts warrant. This occurs whenever more than one third of the constituencies within a state exceed the 10 per cent variation on the quotient for more than three consecutive months or where population shifts among states require a redistribution of seats among two or more states during the seven-year cycle for both boundaries readjustment and redistribution.

Because we use total population as the basis for drawing electoral boundaries, readjustment cannot occur more than once every 10 years, given that Statistics Canada's mid-term projections are not sufficiently precise for this purpose. The result is a deterioration in population comparability over time. There are several powerful reasons for Canada to use the number of voters, not total population, as the basis for boundaries readjustment.

First, equality of the vote constitutes a compelling reason for drawing boundaries on this basis. Only citizens who have reached the age of 18 have the right to vote. As Justice McLachlin stated in the *Dixon* case, "relative equality of voting power is fundamental to the right to vote enshrined in s. 3 of the Charter". (1989, 293) Although Justice McLachlin was not discussing the drawing of electoral boundaries on the basis of total population versus the number of voters in this instance, the concept of equality of voting power clearly relates to the numbers of voters in constituencies, not the total numbers of persons.

Second, using number of voters instead of total population would maintain better comparability across constituencies in a highly mobile society because it could be done more frequently (after every election).

Third, it would enhance the equality of the vote, because only voters would be counted. As Munroe Eagles put it, "it would allow a purer measure of relative vote equality to be achieved". (1991a RC)

At the same time, our research confirmed that there is a close relationship between the number of voters and the total population of a constituency. (Eagles 1991a RC)

Areas with the greatest differences between population and voters are in Canada's three largest metropolitan centres, because of their relatively large numbers of recent immigrants. But even in these instances major disruptions would not occur. What would result is greater equality of the vote when the boundaries are drawn and less deterioration in this equality over time relative to the present system. At the same time, given that MPs must serve all residents, not just voters, the data show that drawing boundaries based on the number of voters constitutes an excellent proxy for total population.

In a very few constituencies, MPs would have to provide service to a larger number of non-voters, especially non-citizens. Instead of drawing electoral boundaries in ways to acknowledge this fact, these few MPs should have additional staff and facilities, similar to those provided to MPs from remote or sparsely populated regions. These service functions relate primarily to tasks performed by the staff of MPs in any event; they are not matters of representation with respect to an MP's functions within the House, where constituencies are to be represented according to the equality of the vote.

A system based on the number of voters would also reduce disruption for participants in the electoral system. If relatively minor changes took place more frequently, the system would avoid the highly disruptive changes that often result from boundaries readjustments after the decennial census. This has been the experience in Australia, and our research suggests that this would hold true for Canada as well. More frequent but smaller adjustments to boundaries would contribute to greater stability in boundaries readjustment. In the last exercise of redrawing the electoral map, for example, the boundaries of all but 13 constituencies were changed. More frequent adjustments, even with greater adherence to voter equality, as Munroe Eagles concludes, "would ameliorate the disruptive aspects of necessary boundary revisions by spreading them over a longer period of time than is currently the case". (1991a RC)

Disruption can also be minimized by adjusting boundaries more frequently only where the deterioration of voter equality has passed a certain threshold. The Australian approach is helpful here: a formula triggers adjustments when the number of voters in a certain percentage of constituencies exceeds the permitted deviation. We consider it reasonable that the number of constituencies in a province exceeding the deviation after a general election should be no higher than 25 per cent of the total number of constituencies in that province.

Recommendation 1.4.7

We recommend that

(a) **electoral boundaries be redrawn in all provinces after each redistribution on the basis of the number of voters registered for the most recent federal election;**

(b) **after each general election the Canada Elections Commission determine the electoral quotient for each province and recommend whether adjustments to boundaries should be undertaken;**

(c) **electoral boundaries be redrawn after each general election in any province where 25 per cent or more of the constituencies contain a number of voters deviating from the provincial quotient by more than 15 per cent;**

(d) **no boundaries commission be established according to (a) for any province if there was no change to the number of members of the House of Commons assigned to the province and a boundaries commission had been established for the province after the most recent general election according to (b) and (c); and**

(e) **no boundaries commission be established for any province after a general election according to (c) during the period commencing on the first day of the year before the year of a decennial census and ending on the day the final report is completed by the boundaries commission established after the census.**

After each redistribution, then, and whenever the Canada Elections Commission determined that a province's electoral boundaries should be redrawn after a general election, it would establish electoral quotients for all provinces, or at least the provinces where boundaries are to be redrawn, and electoral boundaries commissions would be appointed. In cases where the Canada Elections Commission determined, following a general election, that less than 25 per cent of a province's constituencies deviated from the electoral quotient by 15 per cent, no boundary adjustments would occur.

Processes and Procedures

Under the *Electoral Boundaries Readjustment Act*, electoral boundaries commissions must be established by the Governor in Council within 60 days of the time that the chief statistician of Canada presents a certified return of the census data to the designated minister and the chief electoral officer. This is usually nine to 10 months after the decennial census in June. The chief electoral officer must then transmit to the commissions detailed statistics and related maps to allow them to begin their work. The commissions must transmit their descriptions and boundaries of constituencies to the chief electoral officer, for transmittal to the Speaker of the House of Commons, within one year of the time when the chief electoral officer has sent them the electoral maps and statistics.

Traditionally, however, the commissions have been established at the end of the 60-day period. Furthermore, the commissions have been required to use part of their one-year mandate to hire staff, arrange office space and set up logistical support. To put it differently, the commissions are usually not fully operational before July or August of the year following a census year.

In order to avoid these unnecessary delays, the electoral boundaries commissions should be established and appointed no later than the end of September of the year a decennial census has been conducted. This would give the commissions six to seven months to hire administrative support staff, arrange office space and logistical support, recruit and appoint specialists in co-operation with the Canada Elections Commission, and begin work on the boundaries of constituencies based on the voters lists from the previous general election and the preliminary census data, which will be used to assign seats to provinces. The commissions could be fully operational by the time the official census data are available. Given that the preliminary data do not vary greatly from final data on the certified return of the chief statistician, commissions could use with confidence the preliminary number of seats for their province.

With this approach, the reports of the commissions would then be due eight months after the Canada Elections Commission, on the basis of the certified census return of the chief statistician, has transmitted its report to each boundaries commission. If a commission decided or was required to conduct a second round of public hearings, as we will discuss, the deadline would be one year. Where a second round of hearings was not conducted, six months would be cut off the current time limit.

Recommendation 1.4.8

We recommend that

(a) **electoral boundaries commissions be established and appointed by the end of September in the year that a decennial census is conducted or within 60 days of the Canada Elections Commission determining that a boundaries adjustment is required in one or more provinces following a general election; and**

(b) electoral boundaries commissions report to the Canada Elections Commission within eight months after they have received from the Canada Elections Commission the official census data or within eight months after the date of establishment of an electoral boundaries commission in a province following a general election, unless a second round of hearings is held, in which case the reporting date shall be extended a further four months.

Under the *Electoral Boundaries Readjustment Act* the boundaries that are subsequently brought into force by a "representation order" cannot come into effect for at least one year. This is to permit the necessary changes associated with a modification of the boundaries to be effected. Among other things, this allows for the appointment of returning officers. In Volume 2, Chapter 3, we make recommendations that would ensure returning officers would be in place earlier than has often been the case. This would allow the time until new constituency boundaries come into effect to be reduced from one year to six months following a redistribution of seats. Combined with our above recommendation, this would shorten the time for new boundaries to come into effect by as much as eight months. A further two months could be cut from the overall process if Parliament is not involved, as recommended hereafter. And furthermore, when a boundaries readjustment is required following a general election in one or more provinces, a separate representation order should be made for each province as soon as the report of each boundaries commission is complete. This would mean boundaries readjustment could take effect in one or more provinces without having to wait for the reports of all boundaries commissions, given that the number of seats for each province would not be altered.

Recommendation 1.4.9

We recommend that

(a) the representation order issued after a redistribution of seats following a decennial census be effective on the first dissolution of Parliament that occurs at least six months after the day on which the order was issued; and

(b) a representation order be issued for each province, when following a boundaries readjustment as required after a general election, to be effective on the first dissolution of Parliament that occurs at least six months after the day on which the order was issued.

Each electoral boundaries commission is required to conduct at least one public hearing after making public its initial proposals for constituency boundaries. Hearings are conducted throughout the province if warranted by the public response. At these hearings, interested individuals and groups may suggest changes to the preliminary map.

Public hearings are essential if the design of constituencies is to respect and reflect community of interest objectives. Through them, citizens can participate in determining a critical dimension of representative government. During the last round of boundary changes, for example, the 11 commissions received over 800 representations from individuals, groups and municipalities. Thus the process is not only independent and impartial but also organized to allow those who will be represented to express their preferences about the geographical structure of political representation. We consider this approach preferable to that taken in Australia – where hearings are conducted prior to, instead of after, the publication of an electoral map – because Canadians can make their representations based on a proposed preliminary map. This is useful especially where major changes must be made. The analogous experiences of municipal zoning and development processes and numerous regulatory processes indicate the effectiveness of this approach to promoting public participation.

After the public hearings, the electoral boundaries commissions consider the suggestions and objections raised and make revisions as appropriate. The commissions then submit their reports on the proposed boundaries to Parliament through the chief electoral officer. The process does not require or permit another round of public hearings by the commissions, even where a commission's new proposals contain revisions not contemplated during the public hearings.

If more than 10 Members of Parliament object to any of the commission reports, however, the objections are heard by a committee of the House of Commons. Parliament has no authority to approve, amend or reject commission reports. Thus this procedure lengthens the process by at least two months while contributing only marginally.

This was illustrated by the experience with the 1987 reports. The Commons committee held public hearings in British Columbia on the report of the commission for that province. It also submitted a report to the commission, rather than simply recording MPs concerns. Finally, it went so far as to request the members of the Saskatchewan commission to appear before it. The commission chair declined, stating that "such an appearance would compromise the independence of the Commission." (quoted in Sancton 1990, 448)

These provisions of the Act and their use by Members of Parliament raise questions about the independence of the process. In Australia, which served as a model for our boundaries readjustment process, parliamentary involvement ceased a decade ago. Clearly, further discussion remains necessary before commissions submit their final reports because they may make substantial and unanticipated changes to their preliminary maps following their public hearings. The most recent British Columbia commission, for example, removed one seat from Vancouver following objections to its first proposals. When substantial and unanticipated changes are made, a second round of hearings should be held.

But hearings by a Commons committee remove the process from the authority and independence of the boundaries commissions. If each commission were required to conduct a second round of hearings when its second set of proposals departed significantly from its preliminary map, the parliamentary stage could be eliminated. Individual MPs would retain the right to appear before a commission at both rounds of hearings.

Second-round submissions would be restricted to addressing changes in a commission's original report. The second round could not be used to repeat submissions made at the first hearings; the second round would examine boundaries changed in response to interventions in the first round and resulting changes in other parts of the province.

Electoral boundaries commissions should be permitted to conduct a second round of hearings when they deem their revisions to be substantial. To secure the right of citizens to be heard when significant and unforeseen revisions have been proposed, this decision should not rest solely with a commission, nor should the boundaries readjustment process be prolonged unduly. A standard mechanism is therefore required to ensure that significant revisions are considered at a public hearing if citizens wish to be heard.

This mechanism would involve a threshold for measuring significant revisions. The threshold must not be so high that citizens are denied the right to a second hearing; nor should it be so low that matters raised in the first round can be repeated or commissions tempted to draw boundaries in ways intended to avoid a second round of hearings. Based on our estimate of the impact of revisions, we propose that the threshold provide for a second round of hearings when the gross number of voters added to or removed from a constituency as a result of a revision exceeds 25 per cent of the total number of voters in the constituency.

The second round of hearings would work in the following manner:

1. After the first round of hearings on the preliminary map, new boundaries would be drawn and a new electoral map published.
2. If the new map contained changes in the boundaries set out on the preliminary map, the commission could invite submissions on these changes.
3. Where revisions to the preliminary map resulted in the addition to or removal from a constituency of a total number of voters representing 25 per cent or more of the number of voters in any constituency, the commission must invite submissions on these revisions. If submissions are received, the commission must hold public hearings.
4. Following consideration of submissions, the commission would prepare its final map and report.

5. The final report would be submitted to the Canada Elections Commission, which would transmit it, along with the draft representation order, to the minister responsible for proclamation of the order by the Governor in Council.

Recommendation 1.4.10

We recommend that

(a) the present procedure for parliamentary committee hearings on electoral boundaries be discontinued; and

(b) where revisions to the preliminary report of an electoral boundaries commission are made, the commission invite submissions and hold public hearings on these changes; and that where, in the aggregate, revisions involve the addition to or removal from a constituency of 25 per cent or more of the number of voters in any constituency, the commission invite submissions on these revisions and hold public hearings to consider the submissions.

The Names of Constituencies

Since 1964, electoral boundaries commissions have been responsible for naming the constituencies they design. Names as well as boundaries are thus subjects for their consideration and for comments at public hearings. The Act is explicit in assigning this responsibility, and the minister who introduced the bill was equally explicit that boundaries commissions, not MPs, were to have the final say. As Allan MacEachen stated:

> The task of assigning names to the constituencies is for the provincial commissions.... It is possible [for MPs] to make representations to the commissions at hearings [but] government members will have to take their chances along with opposition members as to the names of their constituencies. (Canada, House of Commons, *Debates*, 20 October 1964, 9263–64)

The 1964 legislation contained no guidelines on naming, and at the time there was no intention to depart from the tradition of using geographically specific names. The reports of the first electoral boundaries commissions in 1966 maintained this tradition. The potential for dispute was quickly revealed, however. Of the first 10 objections to these reports, four concerned constituency names.

Since then, MPs have successfully asserted their right to change the names of their constituencies through the mechanism of the private member's bill. Since 1967, passing bills changing constituency names has been a formality: all such bills have been passed unanimously and without debate. Since the 1987 redistribution 18 names have been changed in this manner, but the process affords no opportunity for public participation.

Every name changed in this way since 1967 has involved a change in geographical designation. And in all cases, names have been lengthened by what Norman Ruff referred to in our public hearings as "galloping hyphenation". (Victoria, 26 March 1990) Forty per cent of the constituency names currently used contain either double (36 per cent) or multiple (4 per cent) hyphenation.

Changing constituency names using private member's bills involves costs to the public treasury and to local constituency associations. In addition, boundary adjustments are affected in at least two ways. First, from the perspective of local representation, it is often impossible to choose a name that fully captures the constituency's geographic areas and communities of interest, no matter how many hyphenated words are strung together. As Ruff noted:

> Two names or directional qualifications [east, west, north or south] are perhaps justifiable.... But three and certainly four name combinations are surely overly cumbersome if not absurdities. (Brief 1990, 11)

Second, and more important, is the effect on the willingness and flexibility of commissions to change boundaries to enhance the equality and efficacy of the vote. So long as geographic names are the only means of designating constituencies, controversy can be anticipated whenever names must be altered to reflect boundary changes. Commissions may be pressured to draw boundaries simply to avoid offending a community's pride in its name being used in the name of a constituency.

Other jurisdictions avoid this problem by not using geographically specific names or by using other designations. Numbers, for example, designate U.S. congressional constituencies. In Quebec, the Commission de la représentation électorale, advised by the Commission de toponymie, has the authority to name provincial electoral constituencies after notable persons. The same approach is used in Australia; Aboriginal names and geographical names are also permitted. In Australia, the use of names other than geographic gives electoral boundaries commissions the flexibility to enhance the equality of the vote. In both Australia and Quebec, naming a constituency after a renowned person normally assumes there is some identification of the person with the local community.

To remove obstacles to independent boundary design, two conditions concerning names must be met. First, electoral boundaries commissions should use other than geographically specific names where necessary or appropriate. This would remove obstacles to changing electoral boundaries on the grounds that names would be affected.

Second, the authority to name constituencies should rest solely with electoral boundaries commissions, as originally intended in 1964. This would ensure that names other than geographically specific names would be used where necessary or appropriate. MPs would retain the right to present their views with respect to constituency names before the commissions.

At the same time, the Canadian Permanent Committee on Geographical Names should be requested to assist boundaries commissions with constituency names, including names with local historical significance. This federal-provincial-territorial committee maintains the National Toponymic Data Base.

Commissions should retain existing geographic names wherever possible, provided they contain no more than a single hyphenation. Names of persons or historic locations should be preferred whenever the constituency cannot be designated adequately by reference to a single locality, including a qualifying direction (e.g., East). Where the name of a person is used, the person should have some historic connection to the local community or area in question.

Recommendation 1.4.11

We recommend that

(a) **electoral boundaries commissions be encouraged to use other than geographic names to designate constituencies, particularly where this would avoid the use of multiple hyphenation;**

(b) **the legislation specify that the name of a constituency not be changed other than during the boundaries readjustment process; and**

(c) **the commissions ask the Canadian Permanent Committee on Geographical Names to suggest names for constituencies where changes are required or contemplated and that the designations of these constituencies and the rationale for the choice be presented in the commissions' preliminary reports.**

ABORIGINAL PEOPLES AND ELECTORAL REFORM

Introduction

One of the most significant challenges to our electoral democracy concerns the representation of Aboriginal peoples in the House of Commons. Aboriginal peoples – Indian, Inuit and Métis – are almost 3.5 per cent of the Canadian population.[2] The total Aboriginal population of Canada is thus greater than that of any of the four Atlantic provinces. Since Confederation, however, only 12 self-identified Aboriginal persons have been elected to the House of Commons: three from Manitoba in the 1870s, when the Métis constituted a majority in that province, and nine since 1960, when Indians living on reserves were granted the right to vote and thus to be candidates. Six of those nine have been elected from the Northwest Territories, where Aboriginal peoples constitute a majority in the Territories' two constituencies.

Canada's Aboriginal people are widely dispersed across the constituencies south of the 60th parallel. Including constituencies that encompass the northern areas of provinces where a significant proportion of Aboriginal people reside, there are only three constituencies where they constitute more than 25 per cent of the population, namely, Churchill in Manitoba, Prince Albert–Churchill River in Saskatchewan and Kenora–Rainy River in Ontario, with 53.9, 29.1 and 25.6 per cent respectively.[3] It should be noted that these population figures include those under the age of 18, the number of which is proportionately higher for Aboriginal peoples – of the order of 50 per cent more.[4]

Many Aboriginal people see this situation as a major factor militating against significant electoral participation. They feel their votes are ineffective in asserting their identity and interests. Partly as a consequence of this, voter participation among Aboriginal peoples has been lower than the national average except in those few cases where there has been a self-identified Aboriginal candidate. (Eagles 1991b RC; Gibbins 1991 RC)

Several factors, in addition to geographical dispersal, can account for the current level of voter participation by Aboriginal people and thus their capacity to have their representational needs met through the electoral process. First, Aboriginal peoples, with the exception of the Métis, did not have the right to participate in the electoral process until fairly recently. The Inuit were denied the vote from 1934 to 1950, and Indians on reserves did not receive the vote until 1960. Traditions of political participation, accordingly, did not develop in these communities in parallel with the rest of Canadian society. On the contrary, the denial of the vote to Indians until 1960 reinforced the idea that they were "distinct" from other Canadians at both the practical and the symbolic level. Political participation is unlikely to be enhanced if changes are not made to secure effective representation for Aboriginal people. Our past is replete with symbols of their exclusion from the Canadian polity. Elimination of discrimination based on law is not sufficient; symbols of inclusion are also needed.

Second, in addition to the fact that Aboriginal people number disproportionately among the poor, the homeless, the transient and the poorly educated, their traditional pursuits of hunting and trapping in hinterland and remote areas have made it difficult, if not impossible, to enumerate or register many of these Canadians within the current framework.

Third, less than adequate communications media are responsible for diminishing the awareness and interest of Aboriginal people in the electoral process. The Aboriginal press and the CBC Northern Services for the eastern Arctic lack the resources necessary to overcome these obstacles. (Alia 1991 RC) Moreover, there is insufficient information available from Elections Canada in the indigenous languages of Aboriginal peoples.

Fourth, officials from Elections Canada are not conversant in local Aboriginal languages, nor are there many Aboriginal people employed as elections officials. Since 1960, for example, only one returning officer has been identified as being of Aboriginal descent, even though 253 out of 295 return-ing officers in the last general election assumed their position for the first time. Similarly, only a few Aboriginal people have ever been assigned the position of deputy returning officer.

Fifth, the voting process itself has been, as we have noted, less than welcoming to those voters who find themselves, for one reason or another, in special circumstances or with special needs. Aboriginal people find them-selves disproportionately among those who have been negatively affected by the requirements and regulations of the present voting process, espe-cially given their geographic locations and their languages.

Finally, our largest political parties have only recently acknowledged the need to address the issue of Aboriginal representation and political participation. Both the Progressive Conservative Party and the Liberal Party have created an Aboriginal structure to represent Aboriginal peoples within their party organizations. An Aboriginal "caucus" was created within the Progressive Conservative Party in 1985, and an Aboriginal peoples' "com-mission" was created as part of the Liberal Party of Canada in 1990. The New Democratic Party has recently adopted measures to ensure the participation of Aboriginal people within its governing structures.

Elsewhere in our report, in Volume 2, Chapter 5, for example, we make recommendations that address the concerns noted above. Aboriginal peoples, nonetheless, consider that their distinct status and particular inter-ests require something more than these kinds of changes, however impor-tant they may be in increasing their electoral participation. Working within the basic features of the current constitutional framework, two options are available to enhance the effective representation of Aboriginal peoples. The first would require electoral boundaries commissions to give the effective representation of Aboriginal people much greater weight in the drawing of electoral boundaries than has been the case. The second would enshrine in law a process whereby Aboriginal people would have the right to choose to be represented by Members of the House of Commons elected in "Aborig-inal constituencies". The number of Aboriginal constituencies would be a function of the number of Aboriginal voters that choose to vote in Aboriginal constituencies in proportion to the size of the other constituencies in a province.

Drawing Electoral Boundaries to Enhance the Efficacy of Aboriginal Peoples' Votes

Requiring that electoral boundaries be drawn in a manner that enhances the efficacy of the vote of Aboriginal peoples can hardly qualify as a novel concept. The very concept of community of interest is a cornerstone of our tradition in the design of constituencies. The legislation governing the pro-cess constitutes an explicit attempt to ensure that, as much as possible, the boundaries of constituencies are drawn in ways that pay particular atten-tion to the special interests and identities of segments of the population. The use of geographically based constituencies, especially in areas where there is significant diversity of communities, has obvious limitations as a mechanism for ensuring the election of persons from particular communities of interest or identity. However, our tradition is one where we have sought to promote a measure of "representativeness" in those elected. Throughout our history, for example, we have often kept rural constituencies smaller in population to preserve their integrity as agricultural constituencies and to enable them to be represented by persons from these communities. In recent years, we have recognized, in drawing electoral boundaries in urban constituencies, the desires of various ethno-cultural communities to be represented by someone with their ethno-cultural identity. In all of these cases, we have implicitly attempted to have MPs elected who belong to the ethno-cultural communities of the constituencies they represent.

One approach to improving Aboriginal electoral representation and participation within our existing system would thus be to give priority to Aboriginal communities in the drawing of electoral boundaries. Recognizing that due consideration has not always been given to Aboriginal communities, this approach would make it an explicit responsibility of electoral commissions. Boundaries of treaty areas should not be overlooked.

This approach would be comparable to the recent experience in the United States, where Congress, supported by executive action and judicial decisions, has sought to enhance the elected representation of minority groups, especially Blacks and Hispanics. This approach, notwithstanding some considerable controversy, has been successful in many areas precisely because of the concentration of racial and ethno-cultural communities there as well as the public recognition of the degree to which the groups affected have been subject to long-standing discrimination in electoral representation and participation. In the Canadian context, however, the legacy of contentious discrimination has been less manifest, especially since electoral boundaries have been drawn by independent boundaries commissions for over a quarter of a century. In the case of Canada's Aboriginal peoples, nonetheless, there has been criticism that the existing process has been less than receptive to their communities in the drawing of constituency boundaries by these commissions. (Committee for Aboriginal Electoral Reform, in Canada, Royal Commission 1991, Vol. 4) The major criticism is that several commissions have ignored the need to draw boundaries in ways that might enhance the influence of Aboriginal votes, such as by drawing boundaries on an east-west, rather than north-south, axis.

In response to these criticisms, we commissioned research to determine if boundaries could be drawn so as to create Aboriginal majorities or significant minorities wherever possible. The research focused on the possible redesign of constituency boundaries in British Columbia, Alberta, Saskatchewan, Manitoba, northern Ontario and northern Quebec, that is, in those provinces or areas of provinces where there are significant numbers of Aboriginal people.

By giving due consideration to Aboriginal communities while adhering to the ±15 per cent variation from provincial electoral quotients that we recommend, the research demonstrated that in addition to the three seats in the Yukon and Northwest Territories where Aboriginal people already constitute a significant minority or a majority, seven constituencies could be created with an Aboriginal population constituting more than 20 per cent of the total electorate. Of these seven, one constituency would have an Aboriginal population of nearly 60 per cent, one would have more than 40 per cent, two would have more than 30 per cent, two would have more than 25 per cent and one would have more than 20 per cent. In total, then, 10 constituencies would have a significant Aboriginal population. An additional eight constituencies would have an Aboriginal population of over 10 per cent. (Small 1991 RC)

Although this approach would undoubtedly enhance the electoral significance of the Aboriginal vote, it would not ensure the selection or election of Aboriginal candidates in significantly greater numbers than the three Aboriginal MPs elected in 1988. As a result, the Aboriginal peoples of Canada would remain systematically underrepresented in the House of Commons. Consequently, the measures would fall short of what is required to overcome the symbols of exclusion of the past and restore the legitimacy of the House of Commons in the eyes of Aboriginal people. Moreover, this approach assumes that Aboriginal people form simply one among many communities of interest; it does not recognize their unique and special status. A more direct relationship between Aboriginal voters and constituency design is preferable.

Aboriginal Constituencies

A precedent for the direct representation of Aboriginal peoples has long existed in the state of Maine, which adopted guaranteed Aboriginal representation in its state legislature in 1820. Maine's two main Indian communities, the Penobscot and the Passamaquoddy tribes, each have the right to elect a single representative to the state legislature. This system guarantees that the perspectives of both tribes are heard on all issues. Because those electing these representatives are also eligible to vote for a representative from the constituency in which they reside, these two Aboriginal representatives do not have a vote in the state legislature, although they possess all other rights as members, including that of voting in legislative committees. The New Brunswick government has recently indicated its interest in adopting this approach for its provincial legislature.

In 1867, the same year as Canadian Confederation, the New Zealand Parliament dedicated four seats to its Maori Aboriginal peoples from which they elect members to the national Parliament. These seats overlay other constituencies and are geographically designed so that Maori voters belong to one of these Maori constituencies and elect one member under the plurality voting system. Since 1975, each Maori voter has had the option of registering the Maori roll for their region or on the electoral list for the constituency in which they reside. Unlike Aboriginal representatives in the

Maine legislature, these representatives are full members of the New Zealand Parliament. While many Maori voters now opt to vote in the "general" constituencies, thereby increasing their overall political influence, the four guaranteed seats assure Maori from all regions of New Zealand a voice in Parliament. This explains why this guaranteed Aboriginal representation continues to this day. As Gary P. Gould, President of the New Brunswick Aboriginal Peoples' Council, stated at our public hearings, "Through guaranteed representation, guaranteed participation, the Maoris have become New Zealanders." (Sydney, 5 June 1990)

As demonstrated by the representations to our public hearings, Canadian Aboriginal peoples are aware of, and impressed by, this New Zealand precedent. Indeed, proposals drawing on this experience have been made on numerous occasions in the past, one recent example being that of the Native Council of Canada in the early 1980s. (Committee for Aboriginal Electoral Reform, in Canada, Royal Commission 1991, Vol. 4) Earlier calls for guaranteed representation included those made by Louis Riel in 1870 and by the Malecite Nations in 1946.

Assessments of the New Zealand model and experience vary in the conclusions they reach. (Gibbins 1991 RC; Fleras 1991 RC; New Zealand, Royal Commission 1986) The New Zealand system of four guaranteed seats, it should be emphasized, underrepresents the Maori in proportion to their share of the total population; Maori people constitute approximately 13 per cent of the population, but their four guaranteed seats represent only 4 per cent of the seats in the national Parliament. (Fleras 1991 RC) At the same time, however, the Maori themselves strongly defend this system as giving them a greater say in the governance of New Zealand than they think would otherwise be the case. (New Zealand, Royal Commission 1986)

A recent royal commission on electoral reform in New Zealand concluded that as long as the single-member plurality voting system was retained there, separate Maori seats should be continued. It also recommended that the number of Maori seats be proportionate to the population on the Maori roll, that is, there would no longer be four seats or some such fixed number.

The Case for Aboriginal Constituencies

Canada's electoral system is based upon a consent of citizens to be governed. The design of the electoral system must always respect the fact that Parliament is the central institution of governance in the country. Its legitimacy will be strengthened if, over time, its composition reflects the importance of the various communities in the polity. In this regard, three useful lessons can be drawn from the New Zealand experience.

First, any system of direct Aboriginal representation should provide a process for the creation of Aboriginal constituencies so that Aboriginal voters might exercise their right to direct representation if they so wished. It should not establish or guarantee a fixed number of seats.

Second, the opportunity to directly elect MPs from Aboriginal constituencies by registering as an Aboriginal voter should be a matter of choice and not imposed on individuals.

Third, Aboriginal constituencies should be created according to a formula that enables Aboriginal voters to be represented proportionately to their population in their province. When Aboriginal constituencies are established, their MPs would thus possess the same degree of legitimacy as other MPs from territorially based constituencies, and other Canadians would not have their right to effective representation jeopardized.

A Canadian system based on the lessons drawn from the New Zealand experience, as the Committee for Aboriginal Electoral Reform recommended to us, could constitute a major step toward greater participation of Aboriginal people in the governance of Canada. It certainly would not constitute a form of electoral 'apartheid'. Its purpose and effect would be to include Aboriginal people more effectively in the democratic process and to enhance their sense of political efficacy, rather than to exclude them as is the intent under an apartheid regime. To those who believe in according people the freedom to be themselves, careful implementation of the concept would be counted a gain in civilization. As the Committee for Aboriginal Electoral Reform stated:

> There has been a general feeling among Aboriginal people that the electoral system is so stacked against them that [Aboriginal constituencies] are the only way they can gain representation in Parliament in proportion to their numbers. Direct representation of Aboriginal people would help to overcome long-standing concerns that the electoral process has not accommodated the Aboriginal community of interest and identity. Aboriginal [voters] would elect Members of Parliament who would represent them and be directly accountable to them at regular intervals. MPs from [Aboriginal constituencies] would understand their Aboriginal constituents, their rights, interests, and perspectives on the full range of national public policy issues. (Committee for Aboriginal Electoral Reform, in Canada, Royal Commission 1991, Vol. 4)

For the concept of Aboriginal constituencies to be acceptable, three conditions must be fulfilled. First, there must exist a consensus among Aboriginal peoples in favour of the measure. Second, the practical form the concept will take must be compatible with Canadian traditions and parliamentary system, conform to our constitutional framework and be workable. Third, there must exist compelling reasons for non-Aboriginal Canadians to adopt legislation giving Aboriginal peoples the right to a guaranteed process to choose to create Aboriginal constituencies. These conditions are examined below.

Consultations with Aboriginal Peoples

During the course of our public hearings and our initial research on the electoral participation of Aboriginal peoples, the idea of Aboriginal constituencies quickly came to the forefront of reform proposals. The general concept of Aboriginal constituencies was raised by or discussed with the many Aboriginal spokespeople who appeared at our hearings. In every case, these spokespeople stressed the need for a thorough consultation process with Aboriginal peoples before the Commission made any proposals to enhance Aboriginal representation in Parliament.

In March 1990, Senator Len Marchand appeared before us with a detailed proposal for the establishment of Aboriginal constituencies.

To ascertain Aboriginal views on Aboriginal representation in the House of Commons, we asked Senator Marchand, who in 1968 was the first Indian person elected to the House of Commons, to lead a series of preliminary consultations with Aboriginal leaders on the concept of Aboriginal constituencies as described in his comprehensive brief to the Commission. These consultations with national and regional leaders found general support for the basic concept of Aboriginal constituencies. Nonetheless, there was a perceived need for more extensive consultation to consider the proposal in greater detail and to assess the degree of support throughout Aboriginal communities across Canada. Accordingly, the above-mentioned Committee for Aboriginal Electoral Reform, chaired by Senator Marchand and composed of three MPs and one former MP, was created to conduct a more comprehensive round of consultations across Canada.

This second round of consultations was based on a position paper, published in the Aboriginal press, that outlined the general principles for the creation of Aboriginal constituencies in a manner that would enable Parliament to implement such a system by acting alone under section 44 of the *Constitution Act, 1982* and that, except for the territorial dimension of electoral boundaries, would be consistent with the basic principles used in drawing the electoral map. On this basis, the Committee's proposal applied the following principles.

First, as seats in the House of Commons are assigned by the constitution to provinces, Aboriginal constituencies would be contained within provincial boundaries, although they would overlay geographically other constituencies within a province or even cover an entire province. Aboriginal constituencies would thus be part of a province's total number of seats; they would not be seats separate from a province's total. Where one or more Aboriginal constituencies were created in a province, the boundaries of the province's other constituencies may have to be redrawn to reflect this fact.

Second, Aboriginal constituencies would be created only when the number of people registered as Aboriginal voters in a province met the minimum number required for a constituency in accordance with the principle of representation by population. In this way, Aboriginal constituencies would satisfy the general criterion of equality of the vote. They would not be given special treatment with respect to a province's electoral quotient. For this reason, the committee noted that an Aboriginal constituency could not be created in any of the four Atlantic provinces without a constitutional amendment.

Third, Aboriginal voters would have the choice of registering as Aboriginal voters or on the general voters lists in the regular constituency in which they reside. They could not be on both lists and thus could not vote more than once. Such voters would not be forced by this system to register as Aboriginal voters. This choice would have to be made, however, before the boundaries of constituencies were drawn. This would occur at least every 10 years following a redistribution of seats, subsequent to the decennial census. It could also occur after an election, on a province by province basis, whenever a redrawing of constituency boundaries became necessary. Once this decision on registration was made, any Aboriginal voter who wished to switch from one list to the other could not do so until the time of the next election, at which time those who had reached the voting age since the last registration could also be registered.

Fourth, the criterion for registration as an Aboriginal voter would be Aboriginal self-identification. This would require, only when an objection is raised, proof of Aboriginal ancestry or community acceptance, the increasingly recognized practice in Canada and internationally. Decisions on objections to any self-identified Aboriginal voters on the voters register for the Aboriginal constituency would be made by a panel of Aboriginal voters. This would be similar to the processes now found in the *Canada Elections Act* for objections to the names on preliminary voters lists, objections that are decided upon by revising officers at formal sittings to hear objections.

Fifth, where the number of Aboriginal voters enrolled on the Aboriginal register in a province required the creation of more than one Aboriginal constituency for a province, the constituencies would be designed on the basis of the comparable population and community of interest criteria used by the electoral boundaries commission for the province. This would allow a commission to create two or more Aboriginal constituencies on a geographical basis or on the basis of distinct Aboriginal peoples within the province. In either case, the commission would make its decisions following discussions and public hearings involving Aboriginal people.

The Committee found general support for its proposal for Aboriginal constituencies, including a majority view that this would not detract from, but rather complement, the objective of self-government and other Aboriginal political objectives. In commenting at our public hearings on Aboriginal participation generally in the Canadian political process, Ovide Mercredi, then Vice-Chief, Manitoba Region, of the Assembly of First Nations, expressed the view that "there is no inconsistency in Canada recognizing our collective rights of self-government and us still getting involved and maintaining our involvement in the political life of the state, which means getting involved in federal elections". (Winnipeg, 19 April 1990)

At the same time, there was support for the creation of a sufficient number of constituencies to reflect the diversity of Aboriginal peoples. The Committee recognized in its report that a number of constituencies proportionate to the population of Aboriginal people could not accommodate this diversity in its entirety. It did recommend, however, that the permitted variation from electoral quotients be as large as possible to accommodate different Aboriginal communities. It also recommended that if two or more Aboriginal constituencies were to be created in a single province the distinct communities of different Aboriginal peoples be the basis for drawing Aboriginal electoral boundaries.

The Committee found general acceptance of the need for Aboriginal voters to be enrolled on Aboriginal registers to give effect to this proposal. The criterion of self-identification was also accepted. A specific recommendation was that any objection to the Aboriginal identity or ancestry of an individual voter place the onus on those who objected rather than on the voter.

Finally, the Committee found majority support for having the question of Aboriginal constituencies in the Atlantic provinces considered in separate discussions between Aboriginal peoples and the federal and provincial governments concerned.

Our assessment of these consultations and the Committee's report is that there is sufficient support for the basic concept of providing, in the law, a process allowing for the establishment of Aboriginal constituencies among Aboriginal people. As the Committee concluded:

> Increasing the number of Aboriginal people in Parliament is not the full answer to all Aboriginal issues, but it can be an effective means to promote many Aboriginal aspirations.... Aboriginal views will continue to be expressed by Aboriginal leaders and their organizations and through Aboriginal governments. But Aboriginal people are also citizens of Canada and have as much right as any other citizen to participate freely in the parliamentary process on an equal footing with other Canadians. (Committee for Aboriginal Electoral Reform, in Canada, Royal Commission 1991, Vol. 4)

Aboriginal Constituencies in the Canadian Context

The creation of Aboriginal constituencies would build upon the Canadian tradition of accommodating both individual and collective rights. The Canadian political system has always recognized that there must be a reconciliation of individual rights and membership in the national political community on the one hand and the legitimate interests of citizens for the preservation and promotion of diverse and separate communities within Canada on the other. As Charles Taylor has succinctly put it, "Accommodating difference is what Canada is all about." (C. Taylor 1991, 75)

An explicit acknowledgement of the distinct status of Aboriginal peoples would not constitute a departure from the Canadian tradition. The concept of a community's right to elected representation is not foreign to Canada. Section 80 of the *Constitution Act, 1867*, for example, entrenched special rights in the drawing of electoral boundaries for the Quebec legislative assembly for a number of English-speaking communities. The second schedule to that act entrenched the boundaries of 12 constituencies with English-speaking majorities. These boundaries could not be changed without the concurrence of the majority of members representing these constituencies. This provision remained in effect until 1970. Similarly, since Confederation, Quebec's 24 senators have each represented an "electoral division" within that province – an arrangement that was intended to ensure Senate representation for Quebec's English-speaking minorities and that remains in force.

On a less explicit, but equally effective, basis, "dual-member" constituencies at both the federal and provincial levels, wherein each voter has two votes and elects two members for a constituency (a constituency with roughly double the population of a single-member constituency), have been used in a number of areas to encourage the election of representatives from specific groups. The former federal constituency of Halifax, for example, was a dual-member constituency until 1966 so that the Liberal and Progressive Conservative parties could each nominate a Roman Catholic as one of its two candidates and thus virtually ensure that whichever party's candidates won, there would be a Roman Catholic MP for Halifax. A similar use was made of dual-member constituencies in the Nova Scotia provincial assembly to ensure the election of Acadian Members of the Legislative Assembly.

The adoption of the Charter has not altered this tradition; indeed, the Charter has actually enhanced the claims of various collectivities to constitutional and political recognition. (Cairns 1990) The Charter is not an exclusively individualistic document; rather, it contains both a symbolic and a juridical recognition of the collectivist dimension of Canadian diversity.

Aboriginal Constituencies and the Best Interests of All Canadians

From a non-Aboriginal Canadian perspective, there exist four compelling reasons to enact legislation on Aboriginal constituencies at the federal level. Each flows from the unique status of Aboriginal peoples and the concepts of fairness and respect for one's contractual obligations, which are the cornerstones of liberal societies.

The Unique Constitutional Status of Aboriginal Peoples   Beginning with the *Royal Proclamation of 1763* protecting the Indian peoples' interests in the land of what was then British North America, the British Crown declared its recognition of Indian peoples as constituting Indian nations separate from the European settlers in the territory under the Crown. At Confederation, this responsibility was assumed by the government of Canada, and Parliament was granted powers by the *Constitution Act, 1867* to make law for "Indians, and Lands reserved for the Indians". In each of these ways, including the various treaties between the Crown and Indian nations, the separate status of Indians was recognized. Treaties, in particular, confirmed this status; by definition, treaties between the Crown and other peoples recognize that such peoples have separate status. There were further expressions of constitutional

Indian rights when the prairie provinces received ownership and control of natural resources in 1930. These transfers were made part of the Canadian constitution and protected hunting, fishing and trapping rights for Treaty Indians, as well as protecting unfulfilled land rights arising out of the treaties. In 1939, the Supreme Court of Canada declared that Parliament also had responsibility for the Inuit people. While no judicial decision has been rendered concerning responsibility for Métis people, the *Manitoba Act, 1870* recognized the land rights of the Métis within the boundaries of Manitoba as then constituted and this was constitutionally entrenched by the *Constitution Act, 1871*.

Existing Aboriginal and treaty rights are protected under section 35 of the *Constitution Act, 1982*. This section identifies the Aboriginal peoples of Canada as the Indian, Inuit and Métis peoples. Section 25 of the *Constitution Act, 1982* provides constitutional protection of Aboriginal and treaty rights from legislative impairment by the *Canadian Charter of Rights and Freedoms*. This provision referentially incorporates in the Canadian constitution rights and freedoms pertaining to Aboriginal peoples that existed before Canada was created – an explicit reference is made to the *Royal Proclamation of 1763*. Additionally, rights protected in this section are not qualified by the word "existing". This protection is given further weight by section 35.1, which requires the government of Canada and the provincial governments to consult the Aboriginal peoples at a constitutional conference before any amendments are made to clause 24 of section 91 of the *Constitution Act, 1867* and to sections 25 and 35 of the *Constitution Act, 1982*, the constitutional provisions that affect Aboriginal rights.

The Expressed Desire of Aboriginal Peoples to Preserve Their Separate Identity   From the Aboriginal peoples' perspective, they entered into treaties to protect their traditional lifestyle against the influx of immigration. Their leaders were reserving not only the living space for their respective people, but the means to establish and maintain their way of life in the new economic order that was emerging.

The maintenance of their distinct identity has been a major concern of Aboriginal peoples since Confederation. For example, this was clearly expressed on each occasion when the issue arose of giving the vote to Indians. Indians feared that the extension of the vote to them could threaten their relation to the Crown and Parliament's responsibilities for them. Indian populations living on reserves have always been subject to a complex array of legislation that treated Indians and non-Indians differentially. The reserve system also restricted the mobility and residence of non-Indians. When an Indian woman on reserve married a non-Indian, the latter could not become a member of the reserve. When a non-Indian woman married an Indian on reserve, she acquired Indian status and, prior to 1960, thereby lost her right to vote. Whereas the government of Canada sought to pursue a policy on integrating Indians into the general society and polity with the publication of a white paper in 1969 (Canada, Department of Indian Affairs 1969), there was vehement opposition to the proposal. The explicit rejection of this integrationist policy on the part of Indians at a critical juncture of Canadian and U.S. political history, when it was the conventional wisdom that racial integration was preferable to separate status, reaffirmed their choice of separate identity. Finally, the very concept of self-government as applied to Aboriginal peoples is predicated upon a claim to separate identity within the Canadian polity and a rejection of assimilation.

Hence, contrary to other minorities in North America, Aboriginal peoples have always viewed segregation as an essential means of defending their cultural heritage. In his submission to our Commission, Ovide Mercredi stated that he welcomed "the opportunity to tell another commission of our strong commitment for our right to maintain our distinct identity and of our right to live and survive as distinct peoples in Canada". (Brief 1990, 6) The unique status of Aboriginal peoples in constitutional law protects and gives substance to this fundamental choice. Legislation concerning Aboriginal constituencies would simply extend this historical acceptance of their will to the electoral process, without imposing any burden on non-Aboriginal Canadians.

The Special Responsibilities of Parliament   Under section 91(24) of the *Constitution Act, 1867*, Parliament has exclusive power to legislate in relation to "Indians, and Lands reserved for the Indians". The power is exclusive. Consequently, the federal government provides Aboriginal peoples with services that other Canadians receive from provincial and local governments. Although the constitution does not prevent provincial governments from extending any services to Aboriginal peoples, they have generally not been forthcoming in assuming these responsibilities. This unique situation is of particular importance in the design of our electoral system.

To the extent that non-Aboriginal Canadians are represented in the legislatures of the provinces, they have a voice in the formulation of those policies that fall within provincial jurisdiction. In contrast, for Indian and Inuit peoples it is the Parliament of Canada that has jurisdiction in these matters. It is especially critical that they be present in Parliament, given that their particular interests and general welfare are largely determined by the extent to which they are effectively represented there. An example of the need for such direct representation was provided by Ovide Mercredi and by Phil Fontaine, Grand Chief of the Assembly of Manitoba Chiefs, in their separate accounts of Parliament's inattention to the treaty rights of Indian people to hunt migratory birds when Canada entered into the *Migratory Birds Convention* with the United States and Mexico. (Winnipeg, 19 April 1990; Winnipeg, 29 May 1990) Effective representation is best achieved by direct representation, where MPs who are and who are elected by Aboriginal people speak directly on behalf of their Aboriginal constituents. Given that the constitution requires that the Aboriginal peoples be consulted on any matters affecting them before any constitutional amendments are made and that they must be invited to participate in constitutional conferences, it logically follows that they should also be directly represented in Parliament in order to participate in statutory changes that affect them.

Equality and Effective Representation   Direct Aboriginal representation promotes political equality by ensuring that the right of Aboriginal peoples to "effective representation", as articulated by the Supreme Court of Canada in the *Carter* (1991) decision, is placed on an equal footing with that of other Canadians. Other Canadians have chosen to live in the territorial communities where they vote and are represented. Aboriginal peoples, however, should not be denied the right to effective representation simply by virtue of the fact that non-Aboriginal Canadians have settled in Canada in areas adjacent to their communities and thereby have diminished the efficacy of the vote of Aboriginal communities by their greater numbers.

We recommend the continuation of the Canadian system of single-member constituencies defined in a geographic manner because we consider it the best way to achieve the desired equality and efficacy of the vote within the Canadian system of responsible parliamentary government generally. We recognize, nonetheless, that there is nothing "natural" or sacrosanct about this approach.

In accepting an exception to the drawing of electoral boundaries for the creation of Aboriginal constituencies, non-Aboriginal Canadians merely would be acknowledging that they have adopted an electoral system that reflects the unique status and the geographically dispersed character of Aboriginal communities across Canada. It would also acknowledge the crucial fact that although Aboriginal people constitute a minority of the population in every province, the total number of Aboriginal people in Canada, as we noted at the outset, is larger than the total population of each of the four Atlantic provinces.

Summarizing the Case for Aboriginal Constituencies

As noted above, there exist enough precedents in Canada and abroad to support the proposition that the concept of Aboriginal constituencies is not at odds with our tradition and that it is compatible with a parliamentary democracy. Given Canadian traditions respecting collective rights and other efforts to secure the effective representation of various groups in Parliament, the cabinet and government generally, the idea of Aboriginal constituencies, although an innovation in direct representation, would not be contrary to the basic spirit of the federal political process. It is significant that the Monarchist League of Canada, an organization especially concerned with preserving our constitutional heritage, recommended to the Citizens' Forum on Canada's Future the creation of Aboriginal constituencies in order to ensure the effective representation of Aboriginal peoples while maintaining the federal system of single-member constituencies. (Monarchist League of Canada 1991)

As evidenced by the proposal submitted by the Committee for Aboriginal Electoral Reform, such a concept can be implemented within our present constitutional framework. Since section 25 of the Charter places Aboriginal peoples in a special constitutional position, there is no valid reason to believe the establishment of a right to direct representation through a well-crafted process whereby they could vote in Aboriginal constituencies would not survive any challenge in the courts that sought to demonstrate that this right has a negative impact on the equality rights of other Canadians. Under our proposal, such a claim would be without grounds.

Moreover, the direct representation of Aboriginal peoples would not constitute a legal precedent for extending such a right to ethno-cultural communities. Only the Aboriginal peoples have a historical and constitutional basis for a claim to direct representation. Only the Aboriginal peoples have a pressing political claim to such representation. Only Aboriginal peoples can make the claim that they are the First Peoples with an unbroken and continuous link to this land.

In sharp contrast, Canada's ethno-cultural communities have immigrated to Canada and, in so doing, have exercised free choice to accept the electoral system here. The Charter's recognition of the multicultural heritage of Canada does not alter this fact. Furthermore, the stated position of ethno-cultural community representatives at our public hearings, as well as our research on ethno-cultural communities, indicates that members of ethno-cultural communities wish to enhance their participation in Canadian electoral politics by gaining greater access to the existing avenues of elected office and by having their communities more effectively recognized in the drawing of boundaries for general constituencies.

The extensive consultations have elicited a broad consensus in favour of the Committee for Aboriginal Electoral Reform's detailed proposal. We acknowledge that certain Aboriginal leaders may hold a different point of view; however, we never have unanimous agreement in Canadian society, and there is no reason to expect a different situation among Aboriginal peoples. Given that the seats are allocated to each province and that registration would be voluntary, it is quite possible that Aboriginal leaders in one or more provinces will oppose the concept. Even if, at the outset, Aboriginal people in only one or two provinces took advantage of the choice to create an Aboriginal constituency, this would constitute sufficient endorsement for the concept. Profound social innovations take time to mature, and this one should be no exception.

It must be recognized that Aboriginal people are taking significant risks by accepting an approach that guarantees them a process to create Aboriginal constituencies rather than a guaranteed number of seats and by accepting that each of them should have the right to choose whether to register as an Aboriginal voter. The number of Aboriginal voters required to create an Aboriginal constituency in any one province may not be sufficient at the time when electoral boundaries are drawn because a number of Aboriginal voters in a province may have exercised their right not to register. This fundamental element of choice also means that Aboriginal people may exercise their choice differently at different points in time. The process that we recommend gives them this option; it does not guarantee Aboriginal constituencies in any province.

Contrary to some opinion, Aboriginal constituencies would not "ghettoize" Aboriginal peoples or isolate their representatives in Parliament. These constituencies and their MPs would be different but fully a part of the Canadian electorate and its representation in the House of Commons. Aboriginal voters who choose to vote in Aboriginal constituencies would cast their ballots for candidates who spoke not only to their specific representational objectives but also to the broader issues of national politics from an Aboriginal perspective. In this way, Aboriginal peoples could participate in Canadian politics without being assimilated. Aboriginal MPs would participate in the full range of deliberations and decisions before the House of Commons.

MPs representing other constituencies would be required to consider Aboriginal views and interests as articulated and advanced by the MPs representing Aboriginal constituencies, by members of Aboriginal communities outside Parliament and by Aboriginal voters who chose to remain on the general list. These interests could no more be 'hived off' to MPs from Aboriginal constituencies than the particular communities of interest of MPs representing other constituencies can be ignored. Parliamentary government presupposes that matters of legislation and legislative scrutiny affecting the national interest are debated and undertaken by Parliament as an institution.

The fact that MPs from Aboriginal constituencies would represent less than 4 per cent of the Canadian electorate and would still be relatively few in number does not detract from this reality. MPs from the smaller provinces recognize that the particular provincial interests their constituents share must compete with the interests of larger provinces in a context where majority rule prevails. However, it is also the case that interests of minority groups, however defined, are best protected and secured when they have representatives who can speak directly and explicitly on their behalf. As the Métis Society of Saskatchewan succinctly put it: "How better can the Aboriginal peoples ... contribute to [the] continuing evolution of Canada, than by direct participation in the House of Commons?" (Saskatoon, 17 April 1990)

Any suggestion to the effect that MPs from Aboriginal constituencies would be something less than 'real MPs' ignores the fact that their constituents are no less entitled to be represented in the House of Commons by virtue of the fact that they have constituencies established on a slightly different criterion. Even in constituencies where there are clearly defined communities of interest, such as in agricultural or fishing areas, constituents are also interested in or concerned about the effects of the full range of public policy issues on the political agenda.

Similarly, there is nothing in the basic idea of Aboriginal constituencies to detract from the fundamental roles performed by political parties in our national institutions of government. Although Aboriginal citizens have the same rights as other Canadians to form their own political parties or to nominate independent candidates, the national political parties would have every incentive to practise a policy of inclusion with respect to these voters and those who seek to represent them. The risk of a politics of fragmentation in this respect is not any greater than in other communities of interest, especially since the Aboriginal communities of Canada are already well organized for the purposes of non-partisan political involvement. Our national political parties would undoubtedly have to make efforts to accommodate these new constituencies, but this has been the challenge that parties wishing to govern have always had to meet. Diversity, and not uniformity, has been the fundamental characteristic of the Canadian polity, and the larger national parties have always sought, however imperfectly, to reflect this in their structures and policies.

Finally, the creation of Aboriginal constituencies should not be considered an alternative to, or substitute for, other Aboriginal political objectives, such as Aboriginal self-government. Whatever final form it might take, self-government is not inconsistent with Aboriginal participation in the House of Commons, nor do we see any contradiction between the goal of Aboriginal self-government and the objective of a more effective say for Aboriginal peoples in Canada's central political institution. On the contrary, a cogent and persuasive case can be made that both processes are complementary and mutually reinforcing.

Moreover, it should be noted that most discussions on self-government assume the existence of a land base or a territorially defined jurisdiction. Such an approach would exclude a large, heterogeneous segment of the Aboriginal population: most non-status Indians, those Métis living outside communities where they form a majority, and the approximately one in four status Indians who do not live on reserves or in settlements on Crown land. Although we recognize that some efforts have been made not to overlook the interests of these Aboriginal peoples in the pursuit of the goal of self-government, the establishment of Aboriginal constituencies would give them additional guarantees that their voice would be heard in Parliament. Finally, the creation of Aboriginal constituencies would not abrogate or derogate from any Aboriginal treaty or other rights and freedoms that pertain to Aboriginal peoples. However, the establishment of a process whereby Aboriginal constituencies could be created would require the explicit and substantial support of Aboriginal people.

Establishing Aboriginal Constituencies
The model of Aboriginal constituencies that we recommend, unlike the New Zealand model, does not guarantee Aboriginal peoples a specific number of constituencies, either nationally or by province. Rather, it is the process

for creating such constituencies in one or more provinces that is guaranteed. Constituencies would be created whenever sufficient numbers registered as Aboriginal voters in a province within the 15 per cent variation we recommend for the drawing of electoral boundaries. In this way, Aboriginal constituencies would be created in response to the number of registered Aboriginal voters in a province.

We acknowledge that three different peoples – Indian, Inuit and Métis – are recognized as Aboriginal peoples and that furthermore there are several distinct peoples encompassed therein. We also acknowledge that there will not be a sufficient number of Aboriginal constituencies created in any province to fully reflect this diversity. At the same time, Aboriginal peoples are recognized constitutionally as a distinct group of Canadians, and Aboriginal constituencies would reflect what they have in common. All general constituencies reflect a diversity of communities with different interests and concerns. Finally, it is a fundamental objective of democracy to reconcile, as much as possible, differences among communities within constituencies and to represent the interests and concerns of communities within each constituency. In each of these respects, Aboriginal constituencies will be no different from general constituencies.

This system would apply only to Aboriginal peoples within the provinces. Based on our estimates of Aboriginal voters by province, up to eight Aboriginal constituencies could be created at the next readjustment of constituency boundaries: one in each of Quebec, Manitoba, Saskatchewan and Alberta; two in Ontario; and one or two in British Columbia. Aboriginal constituencies would not be required in the Northwest Territories, given that its two assigned seats already contain Aboriginal majorities. The Aboriginal population in the Yukon is too small to justify an Aboriginal constituency there. The Yukon currently is assigned one seat, and its total population is well below the national quotient.

The total Aboriginal population of Quebec means that the Inuit proposal for an Aboriginal constituency in northern Quebec could not be met: the population of all Aboriginal people in this area is too small to justify an Aboriginal constituency. In the case of the three prairie provinces, where the Indians and Métis desire the creation of an Aboriginal constituency for each of their two communities, the numbers do not indicate that this would be possible at the outset.

The present and projected populations of Aboriginal people in the Atlantic provinces would not justify the creation of an Aboriginal seat in any of these four provinces. The combined populations of Aboriginal people in all four provinces would justify a single seat only if the provincial quotient of Prince Edward Island were used. The creation of an Aboriginal constituency for Atlantic Canada, cutting across provincial boundaries, would thus require a constitutional amendment by Parliament analogous to its creation of seats in the two federal territories. Given that Atlantic Canada is already overrepresented as a region, we support the Committee for Aboriginal Electoral Reform proposal that the *federal and provincial* governments concerned meet with Aboriginal leaders in the area to determine how a seat could be allocated through a constitutional amendment for the purpose of creating an Aboriginal constituency.

In view of the facts, therefore, that Aboriginal peoples constitute distinct peoples in Canada and desire to be directly represented in Parliament by MPs elected by them, that their interests as distinct communities and the First Nations of Canada cannot be adequately recognized within the existing system of drawing constituency boundaries, that Aboriginal constituencies could be created while respecting the equality of the vote of all Canadians, and that consultations with Aboriginal people indicate solid support for the establishment of Aboriginal constituencies, we recommend a process whereby Aboriginal constituencies could be created.

Recommendation 1.4.12

We recommend that

(a) the *Canadian Elections Act* provide for the creation of Aboriginal constituencies by electoral boundaries commissions in any province where the number of self-identified Aboriginal voters enrolled on an Aboriginal voters register warrants the establishment of one or more such constituencies in relation to a province's electoral quotient;

(b) where two or more such constituencies are to be established within a province, the distinct Aboriginal representational needs within that province be the primary basis for drawing the boundaries of these Aboriginal constituencies, on either a province-wide or geographical basis, provided that the province's electoral quotient is respected; and

(c) the name of Aboriginal constituencies be in an Aboriginal language, reflect the historical link of the community to the land or a historic Aboriginal name or event, and be determined in consultation with the Aboriginal people concerned.

Our recommendation that constituencies not be permitted to vary by more than 15 per cent of a province's electoral quotient should determine the minimum number of registered self-identified Aboriginal voters necessary for the creation of an Aboriginal constituency. Electoral equality for Aboriginal peoples requires Aboriginal constituencies; in this respect Aboriginal people are treated differently from non-Aboriginal people in order to ensure equality. At the same time, however, the equality of the vote of non-Aboriginal voters should not, and need not, be undermined in order to secure the equality of the vote for Aboriginal peoples. A variation greater than 15 per cent as the *minimum* number required to create

Aboriginal constituencies would diminish the efficacy of the vote of non-Aboriginal communities of interest, especially ethno-cultural communities in urban areas, by requiring that general constituencies in a province contain a proportionately greater number of voters. It is also the case that Aboriginal constituencies would be created whenever the number of Aboriginal voters reached the threshold of the electoral quotient minus 15 per cent; non-Aboriginal communities of interest, on the other hand, cannot be assured that electoral boundaries commissions will use this minimum to enhance their efficacy of the vote. For every constituency with a voter population at or close to this lower limit of minus 15 per cent, there is another one with a voter population at or close to the upper limit of plus 15 per cent.

It must be recognized that the process of creating Aboriginal constituencies presents the possibility that, in one or more provinces, an Aboriginal constituency could exceed the province's electoral quotient by more than 15 per cent. This could occur because Aboriginal constituencies would come from the fixed number of seats assigned to a province on the basis of the number of registered Aboriginal voters in the province in relation to the electoral quotient for that province. The electoral quotient for a province is established by dividing the total number of voters registered in the province for the last general election, including Aboriginal voters, by the number of seats assigned that province.

If, for instance, the total number of registered voters in a province was 700 000 and the province was assigned 10 seats, the electoral quotient would be 70 000. The permitted variation of 15 per cent would set the minimum number of voters in a constituency at 59 500 and the maximum at 80 500. If the number of registered Aboriginal voters at the time when an Aboriginal constituency could be created was below 59 500, no Aboriginal constituencies would be created at that time. If the number of Aboriginal voters was within this range of 59 500 to 80 500, there would be one Aboriginal constituency and it would be within the permitted variation from the electoral quotient as all general constituencies must be. If the number of registered Aboriginal voters was greater than 80 500 but less than 119 000 – the number required to create a second Aboriginal constituency – the voter population of the single Aboriginal constituency would exceed the 15 per cent variation. In this case, however, there is no alternative but to allow such a constituency to exceed the maximum variation. This is not an ideal situation, but it is an inherent characteristic of any process that governs the creation of constituencies on other than a formula that divides the total electoral population of a province by the number of seats assigned to it. This is a logical outcome of the process regardless of the size of the permitted variation from the electoral quotient; increasing the permitted variation would not remove this possibility.

Simulations of the impact of a variance of 15 and 25 per cent were made with projections of the electorate for 1991, 2001 and 2011, respectively. The most significant conclusion to be drawn from these simulations is that the extent to which Aboriginal voters enrol on the Aboriginal voters register will be the determining factor because, under most scenarios, the Aboriginal electorate is very close to the number of voters required to create one or more constituencies in the provinces where this will apply.

Given the importance of the direct representation of Aboriginal peoples and thus the enhancement of their political participation in the process of electoral democracy, this possibility does not detract from the fact that the effective representation of Aboriginal peoples would still be greater than under the current system. Counterbalancing the possibility of such an under-representation of Aboriginal voters in any Aboriginal constituency that exceeded the permitted deviation is the fact that Aboriginal constituencies would be created whenever the *minimum* number of Aboriginal voters is registered. Although this would not give Aboriginal voters any special rights, it is the case that general constituencies cannot expect as a matter of course to be at the low side of the permitted variation. It is also the case that Aboriginal peoples generally are advantaged by the fact that the two seats in the Northwest Territories, where they form majorities, are over-represented in relation to the electoral quotients for every province, including Prince Edward Island. As a practical matter it is further the case that Canadians have accepted that provincial electoral quotients may vary considerably across the provinces, from a current high of just over 87 000 in Ontario to a low of just over 30 000 in Prince Edward Island. Finally, it must be noted that the system we are recommending for the creation of Aboriginal constituencies, when taken together with our recommendation to allow constituency boundaries to be drawn more frequently than only once every 10 years as is now the case, makes the complete process more responsive to changes in the number of voters registered in a province, including of course the number of Aboriginal voters registered in a province.

Recommendation 1.4.13

We recommend that the number of Aboriginal constituencies in a province be equal to such integer as is obtained by dividing the number of voters on the Aboriginal voters register by a number equal to 85 per cent of the electoral quotient for the province.

Finally, given the formula that we recommend for the assignment of seats to provinces in conjunction with population projections for the next redistribution of seats following the 1991 census, we consider it necessary to ensure that a transitional provision be introduced whereby a province would not lose a seat at a redistribution if one or more Aboriginal constituencies had been created in that province. Population projections indicate that this provision, if necessary, would apply only to Manitoba or Saskatchewan. This small adjustment would not unduly affect the proportionate representation of provinces in the House of Commons and can be constitutionally justified to allow for the introduction of this model of Aboriginal constituencies with the least amount of contention over its effects on provincial representation in the House of Commons.

Recommendation 1.4.14

We recommend that section 51 of the *Constitution Act, 1867* provide that any province, where the redistribution of seats in the House of Commons calls for the reduction of one seat and the boundaries readjustment for the creation of an Aboriginal constituency, be assigned this additional seat for as long as the province has one or more Aboriginal constituencies.

The creation of Aboriginal constituencies should not be considered as affecting any other Aboriginal rights or claims. Aboriginal constituencies acknowledge Aboriginal peoples' desire to be directly represented in the House of Commons. Such representation is not a substitute for Aboriginal self-government or other freedoms.

Recommendation 1.4.15

We recommend that the *Canada Elections Act* state that the creation of Aboriginal constituencies not be construed so as to abrogate or derogate from any Aboriginal, treaty or other rights or freedoms that pertain to Aboriginal peoples.

To create Aboriginal constituencies, Aboriginal voters would be required to register in the provinces where such constituencies could be created. Those who wish to vote in an Aboriginal constituency, moreover, would have to be enrolled on the province's Aboriginal voters register. To register as an Aboriginal voter, an individual would have to identify herself or himself as an Aboriginal person and, only if challenged, may have to provide evidence of Aboriginal ancestry or community acceptance. The burden of proof when an objection is raised should, however, rest with those who are objecting.

Recommendation 1.4.16

We recommend that

(a) **Aboriginal voters have the right to enrol on the Aboriginal voters register in their province; and**
(b) **an Aboriginal voter be defined as a voter who self-identifies as an Aboriginal person, but if an objection is raised, he or she may be required to provide evidence of Aboriginal**

ancestry or community acceptance, although the burden of proof should rest with those making the challenge.

Although the mechanics and provisions required to implement Aboriginal voter registration are outlined in greater detail in Volume 2, Chapter 5, it needs to be emphasized here that Aboriginal voters would not be required to compile these lists either for determining whether Aboriginal constituencies would be created in a province or for electoral administration. Rather, as is the case with voter registration generally, responsibility will continue to be a function of the federal machinery of election administration under the general supervision of the Canada Elections Commission.

For the initial registration of Aboriginal voters, and on every occasion when a registration is undertaken to determine whether an Aboriginal constituency is to be created, the chief electoral officer of Canada, assisted by a provincial election office headed and staffed by Aboriginal voters, would be required to undertake a concerted Aboriginal registration drive, making full use of Aboriginal media and Aboriginal organizations. Such a concerted approach is necessary not only to overcome traditional obstacles to enumeration and other forms of registration among Aboriginal voters but also to recognize the significant risks that Aboriginal voters will have assumed by accepting this process for creating Aboriginal constituencies. Aboriginal voters should be assured that the voter registration system will be as complete and accurate as possible.

Recommendation 1.4.17

We recommend that

(a) **the registration of Aboriginal voters in each province to determine whether the number of Aboriginal voters warrants the creation of one or more Aboriginal constituencies be undertaken under the general supervision of the Canada Elections Commission;**

(b) **the registration process be administered by persons qualified to be registered as Aboriginal voters; and**

(c) **the Commission be required to seek the co-operation of Aboriginal organizations and media in conducting Aboriginal voter registration drives.**

Following the 1991 census and the redistribution of seats to provinces to be undertaken subsequent to this census, the chief electoral officer will be able to indicate the potential number of Aboriginal constituencies that could be established in each of the six provinces in question. Given that the next federal general election will be held in 1992 or 1993, the new distribution of seats will not take place until after this election, as the law requires a period of one year between the redrawing of constituency boundaries following a redistribution and the use of the new boundaries for a general election. The first opportunity to create an Aboriginal constituency in any province, therefore, cannot occur until after the next election. Given our recommendation on when electoral boundaries should be readjusted, however, opportunities for creating Aboriginal constituencies could occur more frequently than every 10 years.

Finally, as we outline in Volume 2, Chapter 5 the ongoing process of voter registration for each election, the voting process and the organization, staffing and responsibilities for electoral administration will be virtually the same for Aboriginal constituencies as for general constituencies. In order to deal with the geographic size and dispersed voter population in Aboriginal constituencies, these constituencies will be included among the new category of "remote constituencies" that we recommend for all similarly characterized general constituencies. Only with respect to a few matters will there be differences, and these are described in Volume 2, Chapter 5.

NOTES

1. The commission for the Northwest Territories was subject to different requirements. This commission, in dividing the Northwest Territories into constituencies, was required to give "special consideration to the following factors: (i) ease of transportation and communication within the electoral districts, (ii) geographical size and shape of the electoral districts relative to one another, and (iii) any community or diversity of interests of the inhabitants of various regions of the Northwest Territories". (*Electoral Boundaries Readjustment Act*, s. 15(3))

2. Estimates of the Aboriginal population

	Population	
	1986	1991
Aboriginal people[a]	851 517	933 395
Canada	25 353 000	26 807 500
Aboriginal population as.a percentage of the Canadian population	3.36	3.48

[a]The definition of the Aboriginal population here follows that used by such agencies as Statistics Canada and is the aggregate of the following: registered Indians, Inuit and Métis plus non-registered Indians and Canadians of multiple ethnic origins who also list themselves as North American Indian, Inuit or Métis. (Canada, Statistics Canada 1989). Data on these categories using the 1986 census and for 1991 projections were provided by the Secretary of State as based on the 1986 census. Since 1986 census enumerators were not permitted to enumerate on some reserves, the estimates here take those census data for all but registered Indians (i.e., Inuit, Métis and

multiple ethnic origin Aboriginal people) and add to them the data on Registered Indians provided by the Department of Indian and Northern Affairs for both the 1986 figures and the 1991 projection estimates. (Loh 1990) The population data for Canada are from Canada, Statistics Canada (1990b, 1990c).

3. These estimates are not based only on the underreporting of the Aboriginal population in the 1986 census by constituency (for Canada, a total of 373 265 Aboriginals of single ethnic origin; the total including multiple Aboriginal origins and non-enumerated reserves is 851 517), but also include the apportioning of the extra amount relative to the total estimated Aboriginal population for 1986 among the constituencies. Apportioning the additional amount of the total estimate of Aboriginal people was undertaken on a probability basis such that constituencies that already contained a large number of Aboriginal people were assigned a smaller portion of the additional amount to bring the constituency populations up to estimated provincial totals of the Aboriginal population. (Canada, Statistics Canada 1988) Probability estimates are based on the data from Loh (1990); and estimates by province of the Aboriginal population were provided by the Secretary of State.

4. The percentage of the population aged 17 and under, based on 1986 data, is:

Aboriginals	42.9%
Canada	25.9%

Expressed as a percentage of their relevant total populations, the number of those aged 17 and under is two-thirds larger among Aboriginal peoples than among the total Canadian population. (Canada, Statistics Canada 1988; Loh 1990; and 1986 census data provided by the Secretary of State)

APPENDICES

Appendix A

Allocation of seats in Canada, Australia, United States
(lower chambers)

Canada

Province / territory	Number of seats 1987	Population 1981	Quotient	Percentage difference from the national quotient
Ontario	99	8 625 107	87 122	0.13
Quebec	75	6 438 403	85 845	-1.33
Nova Scotia	11	847 442	77 040	-11.45
New Brunswick	10	696 403	69 640	-19.96
Manitoba	14	1 026 241	73 303	-15.75
British Columbia	32	2 744 467	85 765	-1.43
Prince Edward Island	4	122 506	30 627	-64.80
Saskatchewan	14	968 313	69 165	-20.50
Alberta	26	2 237 724	86 066	-1.08
Newfoundland	7	567 681	81 097	-6.79
Northwest Territories	2	45 741		
Yukon	1	23 153		
Total	295	24 343 181		
(w/o the territories)	292	24 274 287	87 005	
Average deviation (%) from the national quotient				14.32

Source: Adapted from Canada, Elections Canada 1986, 17.

Note: The national quotient is determined by dividing the total population, excluding the territories, by 292 seats.

Appendix A (cont'd)

Australia

State	Number of seats 1988	Population 1988	Quotient	Percentage difference from the national quotient
New South Wales	51	5 660 475	110 990	0.08
Victoria	38	4 233 557	111 409	0.46
Queensland	24	2 706 170	112 757	1.68
Western Australia	14	1 519 918	108 566	-2.10
South Australia	13	1 401 221	107 786	-2.81
Tasmania	5	447 842	89 568	-19.23
Total (w/o the territories)	145	15 969 183	110 897	
Average deviation (%) from the national quotient				4.39

Source: Adapted from Australia, Australian Electoral Commission 1989.

Note: The national quotient is determined by dividing the total population, excluding the territories, by 144 seats (Tasmania has one extra seat protected under the Constitution).

Appendix A (cont'd)

United States

State	Number of districts 1981	Population 1980	Quotient	Percentage difference from the national quotient
Alabama	7	3 893 888	556 270	7.11
Alaska	1	401 851	401 851	-22.62
Arizona	5	2 718 215	543 643	4.68
Arkansas	4	2 286 435	571 609	10.07
California	45	23 667 902	525 953	1.28
Colorado	6	2 889 964	481 661	-7.25
Connecticut	6	3 107 576	517 929	-0.27
Delaware	1	594 338	594 338	14.44
Florida	19	9 746 324	512 964	-1.23
Georgia	10	5 463 105	546 311	5.20
Hawaii	2	964 691	482 346	-7.12
Idaho	2	943 935	471 968	-9.12
Illinois	22	11 426 518	519 387	0.01
Indiana	10	5 490 224	549 022	5.72
Iowa	6	2 913 808	485 635	-6.49
Kansas	5	2 363 679	472 736	-8.97
Kentucky	7	3 660 777	522 968	0.70
Louisiana	8	4 205 900	525 738	1.23
Maine	2	1 124 660	562 330	8.28
Maryland	8	4 216 975	527 122	1.50
Massachusetts	11	5 737 037	521 549	0.43
Michigan	18	9 262 078	514 560	-0.92
Minnesota	8	4 075 970	509 496	-1.89
Mississippi	5	2 520 638	504 128	-2.93
Missouri	9	4 916 686	546 298	5.19
Montana	2	786 690	393 345	-24.26
Nebraska	3	1 569 825	523 275	0.76
Nevada	2	800 493	400 247	-22.93
New Hampshire	2	920 610	460 305	-11.37
New Jersey	14	7 364 823	526 059	1.30
New Mexico	3	1 302 894	434 298	-16.37

Appendix A (cont'd)

United States

State	Number of districts 1981	Population 1980	Quotient	Percentage difference from the national quotient
New York	34	17 558 072	516 414	-0.56
North Carolina	11	5 881 766	534 706	2.96
North Dakota	1	652 717	652 717	25.68
Ohio	21	10 797 630	514 173	-0.99
Oklahoma	6	3 025 290	504 215	-2.91
Oregon	5	2 633 105	526 621	1.40
Pennsylvania	23	11 863 895	515 822	-0.68
Rhode Island	2	947 154	473 577	-8.81
South Carolina	6	3 121 820	520 303	0.19
South Dakota	1	690 768	690 768	33.01
Tennessee	9	4 591 120	510 124	-1.77
Texas	27	14 229 191	527 007	1.48
Utah	3	1 461 037	487 012	-6.22
Vermont	1	511 456	511 456	-1.52
Virginia	10	5 346 818	534 682	2.96
Washington	8	4 132 156	516 520	-0.54
West Virginia	4	1 949 644	487 411	-6.15
Wisconsin	9	4 705 767	522 863	0.68
Wyoming	1	469 557	469 557	-9.58
U.S. total	435	225 907 472	519 328	
Average deviation (%) from the national quotient				6.39

Source: Adapted from United States, Department of Commerce 1983.

Note: The national quotient is determined by dividing the total population by 435 seats.

Appendix B

Canada: exceptional circumstances in 1986–87 boundaries readjustment

Constituency (province)	1981 population	Percentage deviation from quotient	Percentage province average deviation	Percentage average deviation without exceptions	Area km^2	Larger/ smaller constituencies in the province
Timiskaming (Ont.)	60 523	-30.5	7.4	7.2	32 466	5 larger
Bonaventure– Îles-de-la-Madeleine (Que.)	52 046	-39.4	10.1	9.4	8 155	12 larger
Gaspé (Que.)	62 986	-26.6	10.1	9.4	12 268	9 larger
Labrador (Nfld.)	31 318	-61.4	17.5	6.5	310 155	Largest
St. John's East (Nfld.)	104 416	28.8	17.5	6.5	1 148	Smallest

Source: Canada 1987; Canada, Elections Canada 1988.

Appendix C

Canada: the 10 largest provincial (in geographic size) readjusted constituencies
(1986–87 readjustment)

Constituency (province)	Area (km^2)	1981 population	Percentage deviation from prov. quotient
Abitibi (Que.)	554 837	86 312	0.5
Churchill (Man.)	480 460	65 254	-10.9
Manicouagan (Que.)	465 680	69 488	-19.1
Cochrane–Superior (Ont.)	351 240	65 927	-24.3
Prince Albert–Churchill River (Sask.)	312 980	69 352	0.3
Labrador (Nfld.)	310 155	31 318	-61.4
Kenora–Rainy River (Ont.)	307 560	74 612	-14.4
Skeena (BC)	242 846	77 697	-9.4
Prince George–Peace River (BC)	215 213	85 626	-0.1
Athabaska (Alta.)	196 260	72 501	-15.8

Source: Canada 1987; Canada, Elections Canada 1988.

Note: In comparison, the area (km^2) of the territorial constituencies are: Nunatsiaq (NWT) – 3 433 165, Western Arctic (NWT) – 1 138 844 and the Yukon – 455 400.

Australia: the 10 largest (in geographic size) redistricted districts
(1984 redistricting)

District (state)	Area (km^2)	Electors 1984 redist.	Percentage deviation from state quotient
Kalgoorlie (W. Australia)	2 308 320	63 299	-0.2
Grey (S. Australia)	848 561	68 241	0.7
Kennedy (Queensland)	772 000	65 747	5.0
Maranoa (Queensland)	625 200	65 909	5.3
Riverina–Darling (NSW)	280 071	66 779	1.4
O'Connor (W. Australia)	168 001	67 236	6.0
Leichhardt (Queensland)	141 300	61 614	-1.6
Parkes (NSW)	124 514	66 749	1.3
Gwydir (NSW)	105 764	67 172	2.0
Farrer (NSW)	67 809	66 772	1.4

Source: Australia 1984.

Note: In comparison, the area (km^2) of the Northern Territory is 1 347 525.

NSW: New South Wales

Appendix C (cont'd)

United States: the 10 largest (in geographic size) redistricted districts
(post-1980 census state redistrictings)

State	Area (km²)	1980 population	Percentage deviation from state quotient
Nevada (District 1)	274 176	399 857	-0.1
Montana (District 2)	231 928	376 619	-4.3
Oregon (District 2)	182 614	526 968	-0.0
Nebraska (District 3)	154 975	523 827	0.1
New Mexico (District 3)	146 174	432 492	-0.4
Montana (District 1)	144 627	410 071	4.3
New Mexico (District 2)	142 549	436 261	0.5
Arizona (District 3)	141 739	544 870	0.2
Colorado (District 3)	137 165	481 854	0.0
Kansas (District 1)	127 942	472 139	-0.1

Source: United States, Department of Commerce 1983.

Note: In comparison, the area (km²) of the largest single-member states are: Alaska – 1 478 457, Wyoming – 251 202, South Dakota – 196 715 and North Dakota 179 486.

Appendix D

Prospective allocation of House of Commons seats: formula using Alberta as the base, with 26 seats, 1991, 2001, 2011

Province/territory	Percentage of population[a]			Seats by population			Adjustment[b]			Total seats			Percentage of seats[c]		
	1991	2001	2011	1991	2001	2011	1991	2001	2011	1991	2001	2011	1991	2001	2011
Newfoundland	2.2	2.0	1.8	6	5	5	—	1	1	6	6	6	2.1	2.1	2.1
Prince Edward Island	0.5	0.5	0.4	1	1	1	3	3	3	4	4	4	1.4	1.4	1.4
Nova Scotia	3.4	3.2	3.1	9	8	8	1	2	2	10	10	10	3.4	3.5	3.5
New Brunswick	2.7	2.5	2.4	8	7	6	2	3	4	10	10	10	3.4	3.5	3.5
Quebec	25.4	24.8	24.4	71	65	61	3	8	11	74	73	72	25.4	25.5	25.5
Ontario	36.8	37.2	37.5	102	97	94	—	4	6	102	101	100	35.1	35.3	35.5
Manitoba	4.1	3.9	3.9	11	10	10	2	2	1	13	12	11	4.5	4.2	3.9
Saskatchewan	3.7	3.6	3.6	10	9	9	3	3	2	13	12	11	4.5	4.2	3.9
Alberta	9.4	10.0	10.4	26	26	26	—	—	—	26	26	26	8.9	9.1	9.2
British Columbia	11.9	12.4	12.6	33	32	32	—	—	—	33	32	32	11.3	11.2	11.3
Northwest Territories										2	2	2			
Yukon										1	1	1			
Total				277	260	252	14	26	30	294	289	285			

Source: Canada, Statistics Canada 1990b.

[a]Population percentage of the total population of 10 provinces; excludes the Yukon and NWT.
[b]Seats added to bring provincial number to Senate floor or last distribution less one.
[c]Percentage of seats of 10 provinces, excludes three for the Yukon and NWT.

Appendix D (cont'd)

Prospective allocation of House of Commons seats: formula using British Columbia as the base, with 33 seats, 1991, 2001, 2011

Province/ territory	Percentage of population[a]			Seats by population			Adjustment[b]			Total seats			Percentage of seats[c]		
	1991	2001	2011	1991	2001	2011	1991	2001	2011	1991	2001	2011	1991	2001	2011
Newfoundland	2.2	2.0	1.8	6	5	5	—	1	1	6	6	6	2.1	2.1	2.1
Prince Edward Island	0.5	0.5	0.4	1	1	1	3	3	3	4	4	4	1.4	1.4	1.4
Nova Scotia	3.4	3.2	3.1	9	9	8	1	1	2	10	10	10	3.4	3.5	3.5
New Brunswick	2.7	2.5	2.4	8	7	6	2	3	4	10	10	10	3.4	3.5	3.5
Quebec	25.4	24.8	24.4	70	66	64	4	7	8	74	73	72	25.4	25.3	25.4
Ontario	36.8	37.2	37.5	102	99	98	—	2	2	102	101	100	35.1	35.1	35.2
Manitoba	4.1	3.9	3.9	11	10	10	2	2	1	13	12	11	4.5	4.2	3.9
Saskatchewan	3.7	3.6	3.6	10	10	10	3	2	2	13	12	11	4.5	4.2	3.9
Alberta	9.4	10.0	10.4	26	27	27	—	—	—	26	27	27	8.9	9.4	9.5
British Columbia	11.9	12.4	12.6	33	33	33	—	—	—	33	33	33	11.3	11.5	11.6
Northwest Territories										2	2	2			
Yukon										1	1	1			
Total				276	267	261	15	21	23	294	291	287			

Source: Canada, Statistics Canada 1990b.

[a]Population percentage of the total population of 10 provinces; excludes the Yukon and NWT.
[b]Seats added to bring provincial number to Senate floor or last distribution less one.
[c]Percentage of seats of 10 provinces, excludes three for the Yukon and NWT.

Appendix D (cont'd)

Prospective allocation of House of Commons seats: formula using Ontario as the base, with 103 seats, 1991, 2001, 2011

Province/ territory	Percentage of population[a]			Seats by population			Adjustment[b]			Total seats			Percentage of seats[c]		
	1991	2001	2011	1991	2001	2011	1991	2001	2011	1991	2001	2011	1991	2001	2011
Newfoundland	2.2	2.0	1.8	6	5	5	—	1	1	6	6	6	2.1	2.1	2.1
Prince Edward Island	0.5	0.5	0.4	1	1	1	3	3	3	4	4	4	1.4	1.4	1.4
Nova Scotia	3.4	3.2	3.1	9	9	8	1	1	2	10	10	10	3.4	3.4	3.4
New Brunswick	2.7	2.5	2.4	8	7	6	2	3	4	10	10	10	3.4	3.4	3.4
Quebec	25.4	24.8	24.4	71	69	67	3	4	5	74	73	72	25.3	25.0	24.7
Ontario	36.8	37.2	37.5	103	103	103	—	—	—	103	103	103	35.3	35.3	35.4
Manitoba	4.1	3.9	3.9	11	11	11	2	1	—	13	12	11	4.5	4.1	3.8
Saskatchewan	3.7	3.6	3.6	10	10	10	3	2	1	13	12	11	4.5	4.1	3.8
Alberta	9.4	10.0	10.4	26	28	29	—	—	—	26	28	29	8.9	9.6	10.0
British Columbia	11.9	12.4	12.6	33	34	35	—	—	—	33	34	35	11.3	11.6	12.0
Northwest Territories										2	2	2			
Yukon										1	1	1			
Total				278	277	275	14	15	16	295	295	294			

Source: Canada, Statistics Canada 1990b.

[a]Population percentage of the total population of 10 provinces; excludes the Yukon and NWT.
[b]Seats added to bring provincial number to Senate floor or last distribution less one.
[c]Percentage of seats of 10 provinces, excludes three for the Yukon and NWT.

Appendix D (cont'd)

Prospective allocation of House of Commons seats: formula using Quebec as the base, with 71 seats, 1991, 2001, 2011

Province/ territory	Percentage of population[a]			Seats by population			Adjustment[b]			Total seats			Percentage of seats[c]		
	1991	2001	2011	1991	2001	2011	1991	2001	2011	1991	2001	2011	1991	2001	2011
Newfoundland	2.2	2.0	1.8	6	6	5	—	—	1	6	6	6	2.1	2.0	2.0
Prince Edward Island	0.5	0.5	0.4	1	1	1	3	3	3	4	4	4	1.4	1.3	1.3
Nova Scotia	3.4	3.2	3.1	9	9	9	1	1	1	10	10	10	3.4	3.3	3.3
New Brunswick	2.7	2.5	2.4	8	7	7	2	3	3	10	10	10	3.4	3.3	3.3
Quebec	25.4	24.8	24.4	71	71	71	3	2	1	74	73	72	25.3	24.4	24.0
Ontario	36.8	37.2	37.5	103	107	109	—	—	—	103	107	109	35.3	35.8	36.3
Manitoba	4.1	3.9	3.9	11	11	11	2	1	—	13	12	11	4.5	4.0	3.7
Saskatchewan	3.7	3.6	3.6	10	10	10	3	2	1	13	12	11	4.5	4.0	3.7
Alberta	9.4	10.0	10.4	26	29	30	—	—	—	26	29	30	8.9	9.7	10.0
British Columbia	11.9	12.4	12.6	33	36	37	—	—	—	33	36	37	11.3	12.0	12.3
Northwest Territories										2	2	2			
Yukon										1	1	1			
Total				278	287	290	14	12	10	295	302	303			

Source: Canada, Statistics Canada 1990b.

[a]Population percentage of the total population of 10 provinces; excludes the Yukon and NWT.
[b]Seats added to bring provincial number to Senate floor or last distribution less one.
[c]Percentage of seats of 10 provinces, excludes three for the Yukon and NWT.

Appendix E

Redistribution comparisons of various formulas, 1991, 2001, 2011

Province (method)	Seats by population			Adjustment			Total seats		
	1991	2001	2011	1991	2001	2011	1991	2001	2011
Newfoundland (current)	6	5	5	1	2	2	7	7	7
(Que. – 75)	6	6	6	—	—	—	6	6	6
(Que. – 71)	6	6	5	—	—	1	6	6	6
(Ont. – 103)	6	5	5	—	1	1	6	6	6
(Ont. – 105)	6	6	5	—	—	1	6	6	6
(Alta. – 26)	6	5	5	—	1	1	6	6	6
(BC – 33)	6	5	5	—	1	1	6	6	6
Prince Edward Island (current)	1	1	1	3	3	3	4	4	4
(Que. – 75)	1	1	1	3	3	3	4	4	4
(Que. – 71)	1	1	1	3	3	3	4	4	4
(Ont. – 103)	1	1	1	3	3	3	4	4	4
(Ont. – 105)	1	1	1	3	3	3	4	4	4
(Alta. – 26)	1	1	1	3	3	3	4	4	4
(BC – 33)	1	1	1	3	3	3	4	4	4
Nova Scotia (current)	9	9	9	2	2	2	11	11	11
(Que. – 75)	10	10	9	—	—	1	10	10	10
(Que. – 71)	9	9	9	1	1	1	10	10	10
(Ont. – 103)	9	9	8	1	1	2	10	10	10
(Ont. – 105)	10	9	9	—	1	1	10	10	10
(Alta. – 26)	9	8	8	1	2	2	10	10	10
(BC – 33)	9	9	8	1	1	2	10	10	10
New Brunswick (current)	8	7	7	2	3	3	10	10	10
(Que. – 75)	8	8	7	2	2	3	10	10	10
(Que. – 71)	8	7	7	2	3	3	10	10	10
(Ont. – 103)	8	7	6	2	3	4	10	10	10
(Ont. – 105)	8	7	7	2	3	3	10	10	10
(Alta. – 26)	8	7	6	2	3	4	10	10	10
(BC – 33)	8	7	6	2	3	4	10	10	10
Quebec (current)	71	69	68	4	6	7	75	75	75
(Que. – 75)	75	75	75	—	—	—	75	75	75
(Que. – 71)	71	71	71	3	2	1	74	73	72
(Ont. – 103)	71	69	67	3	4	5	74	73	72
(Ont. – 105)	73	70	68	1	3	4	74	73	72
(Alta. – 26)	71	65	61	3	8	11	74	73	72
(BC – 33)	70	66	64	4	7	8	74	73	72
Ontario (current)	103	104	105	—	—	—	103	104	105
(Que. – 75)	109	113	115	—	—	—	109	113	115
(Que. – 71)	103	107	109	—	—	—	103	107	109
(Ont. – 103)	103	103	103	—	—	—	103	103	103
(Ont. – 105)	105	105	105	—	—	—	105	105	105
(Alta. – 26)	102	97	94	—	4	6	102	101	100
(BC – 33)	102	99	98	—	2	2	102	101	100

Appendix E (cont'd)

Redistribution comparisons of various formulas, 1991, 2001, 2011

Province (method)	Seats by population			Adjustment			Total seats		
	1991	2001	2011	1991	2001	2011	1991	2001	2011
Manitoba (current)	11	11	11	3	3	3	14	14	14
(Que. – 75)	12	12	12	1	—	—	13	12	12
(Que. – 71)	11	11	11	2	1	—	13	12	11
(Ont. – 103)	11	11	11	2	1	—	13	12	11
(Ont. – 105)	12	11	11	1	1	—	13	12	11
(Alta. – 26)	11	10	10	2	2	1	13	12	11
(BC – 33)	11	10	10	2	2	1	13	12	11
Saskatchewan (current)	10	10	10	4	4	4	14	14	14
(Que. – 75)	11	11	11	2	1	—	13	12	11
(Que. – 71)	10	10	10	3	2	1	13	12	11
(Ont. – 103)	10	10	10	3	2	1	13	12	11
(Ont. – 105)	11	10	10	2	2	1	13	12	11
(Alta. – 26)	10	9	9	3	3	2	13	12	11
(BC – 33)	10	10	9	3	2	2	13	12	11
Alberta (current)	26	28	29	—	—	—	26	28	29
(Que. – 75)	28	30	32	—	—	—	28	30	32
(Que. – 71)	26	29	30	—	—	—	26	29	30
(Ont. – 103)	26	28	29	—	—	—	26	28	29
(Ont. – 105)	27	28	29	—	—	—	27	28	29
(Alta. – 26)	26	26	26	—	—	—	26	26	26
(BC – 33)	26	27	27	—	—	—	26	27	27
British Columbia (current)	33	35	35	—	—	—	33	35	35
(Que. – 75)	35	38	39	—	—	—	35	38	39
(Que. – 71)	33	36	37	—	—	—	33	36	37
(Ont. – 103)	33	34	35	—	—	—	33	34	35
(Ont. – 105)	34	35	35	—	—	—	34	35	35
(Alta. – 26)	33	32	32	—	—	—	33	32	32
(BC – 33)	33	33	33	—	—	—	33	33	33
Territories (All methods)							3	3	3
Totals (Current)	278	279	280	19	23	24	300	305	307
(Que. – 75)	295	304	307	8	6	7	306	313	317
(Que.– 71)	278	287	290	14	12	10	295	302	303
(Ont.– 103)	278	277	275	14	15	16	295	295	294
(Ont.– 105)	287	282	280	9	13	13	299	298	296
(Alta.– 26)	277	260	252	14	26	30	294	289	285
(BC– 33)	276	267	261	15	21	23	294	291	287

Source: Royal Commission Research Branch.

5

POLITICAL PARTIES AS PRIMARY POLITICAL ORGANIZATIONS

INTRODUCTION

"Without political parties, there can't be true democracy."

THREE-QUARTERS OF THE Canadians participating in our attitudinal survey agreed with this statement on the need for political parties. (Blais and Gidengil 1991 RC) At election time, votes are cast almost exclusively for candidates of political parties rather than for independent candidates. In the past two decades, more than 94 per cent of the votes were for candidates of the three largest parties. These facts indicate that Canadians appreciate the important role that political parties play in our electoral democracy.

Political parties give voters meaningful choices, both in the direct election of their individual Members of Parliament and in the indirect election of a government. As MP Chris Axworthy stated before our Commission, "The clash of ideas and personalities, the freedom to help determine the future of one's country, the precious liberty to vote for or against a platform or a person, all of these are unthinkable without the assistance of political parties." (Saskatoon, 17 April 1990)

Comparative and historical experience demonstrates that parties, as primary political organizations, are best suited to performing a host of activities essential to representative democracy. Among the fundamental activities performed by parties are the selection and recruitment of candidates for elected office, the selection of political leaders and the organization of electoral competition. The electoral and institutional successes of parties depend, in part, on their ability to establish meaningful linkages with citizens by articulating policy alternatives and ideas, and by establishing themselves as vehicles for political participation and education. Together, these many activities aim to provide parties with a capacity to represent different and sometimes competing interests in society, and to structure and order choices for the purpose of governing. These objectives are especially challenging in Canada, given our pronounced regional, linguistic and cultural diversity.

Canadian parties have evolved from relatively elite institutions dedicated, for the most part, to controlling and distributing patronage. They are now more sensitive and appreciative of their role and responsibilities as primary political organizations. Parties have abandoned many of the questionable practices and traditions that once characterized their competitive pursuit of political power. In recent years, however, the parties have employed strategies and techniques that are at times inconsistent with public expectations of what values should guide the political and electoral processes in Canada. More and more Canadians, including party members, are critical of the way parties select their candidates and leaders, the control party leaders appear to exercise over their supporters in Parliament, the behaviour of the parties during elections, their failure to change party organization and membership to reflect Canadian society, and their shortcomings in providing significant opportunities for political participation.

Canadians are questioning the ability of political parties to accommodate diverse and sometimes competing regional interests within federal institutions. There is concern that parties are not responding to individuals and groups that have representational needs different from those traditionally fulfilled by parties. This critical assessment of political parties has discouraged interests not traditionally represented by them from now turning to the parties. Further, the preoccupation with trying to win elections has restricted the importance the parties give to affirming political values and fostering political participation by individual citizens.

Despite these criticisms, Canadians also expect parties, as primary political organizations, to continue to perform their essential functions in representative democracy. In criticizing the representational and electoral profile of political parties, Canadians are in some ways indicating they want parties to do more, not less. They want parties to be more responsive, more representative and more attentive to public attitudes. There are opportunities, then, to affirm and broaden the role of parties as the pre-eminent political institutions that contribute to a vibrant representative citizen democracy. These opportunities exist at three levels.

First, parties can adjust their processes and procedures for selecting candidates and political leaders to promote rather than undermine public trust in the way elected representatives are recruited and selected. Second, parties can strengthen their institutional and organizational capacity to communicate with and involve individuals who are sympathetic to their core ideas, values and traditions. Third, political parties and leaders can adopt new instruments and resources to help them accommodate and integrate diverse interests. Reform, then, should aim to move from cynicism and apathy toward dignified, intelligent political participation of individual citizens.

Reconciling the regional, economic and cultural differences in Canada is a complex and continual task. In accepting this responsibility, parties are being asked to both embrace and confront the varied and sometimes tumultuous features of Canada's political landscape. Expectations that parties can effortlessly or continually mediate conflicting interests, however, are misplaced. In affirming the role of political parties, parties should not be assigned with unattainable goals or objectives. (Elkins 1991 RC)

Since Confederation, the party system has seen many changes in the number of parties presenting alternative programs, their socio-economic and regional bases of electoral support, and the opportunities for political participation. Canadian parties could now be undergoing another critical period of transformation, a metamorphosis that would not be surprising, given the major changes that have occurred in the Canadian polity over the past decade. These include the emergence of new parties and the increasing attractiveness of interest groups as an alternative to political parties for political participation.

We are not concerned with how these changes affect the fortunes of individual parties. Rather, our objectives focus on the health and vitality of political parties as the primary political organizations that:

1. structure electoral choice and thus make the vote meaningful;
2. provide mechanisms for political participation and thus enhance democratic self-government; and
3. organize elected representation in Parliament and thus contribute to the effective operation of responsible government.

Canadians at present may be critical of their parties' performance in all these respects. Nonetheless, they recognize the essential role of parties in securing democratic government. If electoral law reform can strengthen political parties as primary political organizations in the service of democratic government, such reform should be identified and implemented.

THE ROLE OF POLITICAL PARTIES

The role of political parties in Canada must be understood in the context of how our system of parliamentary government has evolved. The system has fundamental constitutional characteristics that not only assume a structure of political representation in Parliament that makes it possible to form a government and hold it responsible to elected members, but also structure electoral choice, making it possible for voters to determine who forms the government. In addition, our political values ascribe a high priority to the right – even the obligation – of citizens to be self-governing. Our tradition has assigned an important role to parties. They provide opportunities for citizens to exercise their rights and to perform their civic obligations through volunteer participation in political activities and public discourse. We also recognize, of course, that geographical, social and economic factors influence the forms and functions of political parties at different times.

Parliamentary Government

The Canadian constitutional system of parliamentary government predates the founding of the Canadian federation in 1867. All the British colonies in North America benefited to varying degrees from English laws and liberties, including the right to 'representative government'. This right, first realized in Nova Scotia in 1758, did not entail 'responsible government' at the outset. It was achieved much later, and only after long and often acrimonious debate between governors and elected assemblies over who should determine the composition of and exercise control over the executive council – the body that came to be known as the cabinet. While Great Britain had adopted the principle that the executive, the Crown's "cabinet council" (Mackintosh 1977), must enjoy the confidence of the House of Commons, in the British North American colonies the governor retained exclusive control over the membership and management of the executive council. (Dawson 1970)

In Upper and Lower Canada the struggle for responsible government led to armed rebellion in 1837. In Nova Scotia, the forces for responsible government led by the articulate Joseph Howe used less violent but no less effective means. In each case, the struggle was complicated by British imperial authority. The local governor was caught in a web of conflicting instructions and demands from the British government, from his executive council (which was dominated by a very narrow stratum of society), and from the elected legislature (which was increasingly composed of representatives who insisted on constitutional reform). The legislature, moreover, had begun the process of organizing into legislative parties; candidates increasingly contested elections under the banner of a party.

In Great Britain and the United States in the late eighteenth century, the debate over the formation and legitimacy of political parties revolved around the question of the harm parties might afflict on the body politic. Parties were depicted as odious factions or cabals, whose behaviour, in pursuing narrow self-interest, would undermine established authority. In Canada, there were echoes of this debate. Joseph Howe, for example, initially argued the need for a "single party for Nova Scotia" that would represent the interests of the whole colony. Later, at the time of Confederation, Sir John A. Macdonald spoke of the need for a broadly based Liberal-Conservative coalition to ensure the future strength of the newly founded nation. Because the issue of factions had been settled earlier in Great Britain and the United States, and the battle for responsible government gave a common ground for competing reformers, the issue of factionalism never really took hold in Canada.

Because of the continuing reluctance of the governors to pay heed to their legislatures, even after armed rebellion, the executive branch of government became increasingly ineffective and illegitimate. As a result, Lord Durham was sent to North America as governor-in-chief of all five provinces, with the mandate both to restore order and to enquire into the origins of the 1837 rebellions. His 1840 report advocated the adoption of responsible government, but not through formal legislation. Instead, he recommended using a dispatch from the British government instructing each colonial governor "to secure the co-operation of the Assembly in his policy, by entrusting its administration to such men as could command a majority". (Durham 1839 [1912, 279–80])

British authorities and the governors they appointed implemented the recommendation only half-heartedly. Ironically, the result was that governors became even more enmeshed in the politics of the colonies, frequently seeing themselves not only as the representative of the Crown but also as their own 'prime minister', supported by the party of their executive council. A change in government in Great Britain in 1846 led to serious efforts at reform, primarily by appointing as governors individuals likely to be responsive to the wishes of the elected assemblies. Thus on 25 January 1848, following a general election in Nova Scotia and a vote of non-confidence, the executive council resigned and a new council was formed.

This change marked the constitutional transformation to responsible government. Most important, it was an event that signalled the first significant acknowledgement of political parties as an integral part of parliamentary government. It did so precisely because the governor was able to identify a legislative party that commanded the confidence of a majority in the elected legislature. The leader of this party asked the governor to form a new government. Very quickly, similar changes in government occurred in the other colonies.

Those who demanded constitutional reform did not seek to undermine the role of the executive within parliamentary government. On the contrary, they sought to strengthen the effectiveness and legitimacy of the executive by ensuring that it had the support of a majority in the elected legislature. Their principal demand, therefore, was that the executive be made directly responsible to the legislature and that both the raising of revenue and the expenditure of public monies be subject to the approval of the legislature.

British political parties in the form of factions and 'connexions' had existed since the Revolution Settlement of 1688, primarily as parliamentary organizations. (Mansfield 1965) Parties and party government, as well as the notion of organized opposition, came to be accepted as fully legitimate by the nineteenth century. Yet British parties failed to extend significantly their organizational network beyond Parliament, even after the *Reform Act* of 1832. Parties were seen primarily as instruments of parliamentary management, for constructing majorities in the House to allow ministers of the Crown to govern. (Stewart 1986)

By contrast, Canadian political parties extended much further into, and as a result became more deeply rooted in, Canadian society, largely because of the battles over responsible government. It quickly became evident to political practitioners that "systematic and comprehensive party organization had become part of the Canadian political game". (Stewart 1986, 55) By Confederation, political parties were considered an essential component of the effective operation of responsible government and the central focus for the mobilization and participation of citizens in political life.

The Building of National Political Parties

In the immediate post-Confederation period, Sir John A. Macdonald hoped to maintain a broadly based Liberal-Conservative party consisting of

Conservatives and moderate reformers. The base of his new party became more restricted, however. Soon two parties, the Conservatives and Liberals, emerged as the contending organizations in the new federal electoral process and in Parliament. To build a working majority in Parliament, these coalitions of the former colonial political parties – initially the Conservatives and later the Liberals – still had to court "loose fish" and "waiters on Providence", as Members of Parliament without a clearly identified party allegiance were then labelled. (Reid 1932, 12) By 1878 the secret ballot had been introduced and elections were held simultaneously in the five eastern provinces, rather than over several days. At this time elections became contests between the candidates identified with the two political parties.

Thus political parties had undergone the transformation from essentially legislative coalitions into disciplined legislative parties and electoral organizations that became the defining characteristic of the Canadian party system for the next four decades. Diverse factions within the parties in the early post-Confederation period were kept together through the exceptional leadership skills of the two dominant leaders of the first several decades of Canadian party politics: Sir John A. Macdonald and Sir Wilfrid Laurier. The party leaders used the federal cabinet to provide representation for the significant regional, religious and ethno-cultural groups that constituted the local bases of national party support. Conflicts between regions and classes were accommodated within the two parties as both attempted to appeal to a cross-section of interests broad enough to secure electoral victory.

The Conservative and Liberal parties emerged as national institutions through the adroit use of patronage at the local level and the recruitment of dedicated local party workers. These party workers were prepared to serve as standard bearers, whether the party was in government or in opposition. Both parties built up extensive extra-parliamentary networks of local notables, as well as "cold water men" who were willing to put in long hours whether or not their party was in power. (Stewart 1986, 78) The national party structures, anchored in local party networks, served to bind supporters to their party's values and policies.

The local partisan press cultivated loyalty to the party and its ideas: to give but a few examples, the Conservative *Free Press* and Liberal *Advertiser* in London, the Conservative *Empire* and the Liberal *Globe* in Toronto, the Conservative *La Minerve* and the Liberal *La Presse* in Montreal, and the Conservative *Herald* and the Liberal *Chronicle* in Halifax. Rival newspapers in these communities were the declared supporters of the two parties. The newspapers disseminated their parties' platforms, provided editorial support, and educated their readers on the strengths of its party and the foibles of the opposition.[1]

Overall, the press of Canada's early years served as primary vehicles of political education and socialization. Often the party itself was a critical source of funds for a partisan newspaper, especially when the party formed the government. Sometimes important political figures owned or controlled newspapers outright; Clifford Sifton, for example, a prominent minister in the cabinet of Sir Wilfrid Laurier, acquired a controlling interest in the *Manitoba Free Press* and the Brandon *Sun* in 1898. When a party won office, as Sir John Willison, a well-known journalist of the post-Confederation years, recalled in his memoirs, "all appointments and statements of policy were reserved for the party organs". (Willison 1919, 121)

Canada was not alone in having a partisan press. In both the United States and Great Britain, commitment of a newspaper to a political party was more than rhetorical declarations of unconditional support. Politicians of the late nineteenth-century in Canada "saw newspapers as essential vehicles of publicity, indeed a surrogate for organization, which could confound foes, strengthen party discipline and morale, and educate electors". (Rutherford 1982, 212) The partisan press assisted parties by weaving them into the fabric of daily life. Party supporters identified with their party by reading the appropriate paper. The partisan press in turn served to support the extra-parliamentary role of parties; they gave party supporters political information about local and national debates, education on public and party policy, and a means for expressing political opinions.

By the end of the nineteenth century, Canada had a competitive two-party system. The two parties had risen above the parochialism of provincial politics and pursued a national agenda accommodating a wide array of interests. At the same time, each party in power had unabashedly cultivated local partisan ties through federal government patronage. As communication and educational vehicles for the two parties, the partisan press fostered party allegiance. Partisanship so thoroughly penetrated Canadian political life, especially in the four original provinces with their relatively stable social structures, that it contended with religion and language as a decisive cleavage in communities.

The Emergence of the Multi-Party System

The competitive two-party system in Canada lasted for five decades following Confederation. Profound economic and social dislocations contributed to substantial political change during and following the First World War. These changes revealed the shortcomings of the two traditional parties in accommodating significant interests in Canadian society. Canadians were also becoming dissatisfied with the principal features of the national party system: disciplined parliamentary representation, compliant extra-parliamentary organizations, extensive patronage by the governing party and the close alliance of both national parties with eastern financial interests.

During the First World War, the conscription issue split the Liberal Party and resulted in a wartime Unionist government: a coalition of Conservatives and Liberals with virtually no MPs or electoral support from Quebec. At the same time, Canadians began to question the patronage system because of dubious procurement practices for military supplies during the war. In addition, western Canada's population, and therefore its weight in the House of Commons, had increased dramatically since the turn of the century.

In 1900, western Canada had 17 seats or 8 per cent of the total number of seats in the House of Commons; by 1917, its number of seats had increased to 57 or 24 per cent of the total. Moreover, since the late nineteenth century, western Canada had been settled primarily by immigrants from the United States, Great Britain and central Europe. These immigrants had no connections with, or interest in, the political mores and values of eastern Canada. Their society and economy, based on the large-scale production of agricultural commodities, did not lend itself to the same organizational tactics that the two parties had used so successfully in the east during the time of Macdonald and Laurier.

An equally important factor was the National Policy. This policy had three major dimensions: a transcontinental railway, settlement of the West through immigration and tariff protection against U.S. imports. The Conservatives adopted the National Policy and the Liberals retained it when they came to power. By 1917, however, western Canadians had come to view the National Policy as an instrument that worked to their disadvantage while favouring eastern Canadian economic interests. The Unionist government formed in 1917 further loosened partisan ties in the West, in that Unionists portrayed themselves as a non-partisan coalition government encompassing all political persuasions supporting the war effort. (Morton 1967)

In the 1920s, Canadian agrarian interests, inspired by the populist and progressive movements in the United States, organized into political groups to challenge the two traditional parties federally and provincially. These farmers' groups campaigned on platforms that were opposed to political parties as the primary agents of representation in a system of parliamentary government. The farmers argued that the tradition of party discipline in particular impeded the ability of elected representatives to represent adequately the interests of their constituents. Federally, the Progressive Party won 65 seats in the 1921 general election, displacing the Conservatives as the second largest party in Parliament. The 1921 election was also a watershed in that no party had a clear parliamentary majority; the Liberals fell one seat short. In the immediate post-war era, United Farmer parties won elections in Alberta, formed a short-lived coalition government with labour interests in Ontario and, on their own or in coalition with labour, constituted the official opposition in several provinces. In Quebec, the weakened provincial wing of the Conservative Party joined forces with a number of disaffected Quebec Liberals to form the Union nationale in 1935. It won its first electoral victory in 1936.

With the urbanization, industrialization and social dislocation after the First World War came outbursts of civil strife, such as the Winnipeg General Strike of 1919. These factors also led to the proliferation of labour movements and parties, including the Federated Labour Party, the Independent Labour Party and the Socialist Party of North America. Two labour candidates were elected in the 1921 election. Factions on the left were centred around either the British Fabian model or the Bolshevik model of the Soviet Union. Their feuding prevented the formation of a single, cohesive party of the left. Out of the various splits, the Co-operative Commonwealth Federation (CCF) emerged in the 1930s as a broadly based movement that incorporated most left-wing groups and many Progressives. The more radical elements that favoured the Soviet socialist model coalesced around the Communist Party of Canada, originally created in 1921. (Avakumovic 1975)

The entry of additional parties into Parliament following the 1921 election was not an entirely new phenomenon. In 1896, the year that saw the Liberals come to power under Sir Wilfrid Laurier also saw the election of four McCarthyites, a group of dissident Conservatives, and two Patrons of Industry. But this was seen as temporary, a consequence of the Manitoba schools crisis and the shift of electoral support to the Liberals after several years of Conservative rule. These small parties disappeared in subsequent elections.[2] It was the size of the Progressive contingent in the House in 1921, displacing the Conservatives as the second largest party, that marked the beginning of a new era.

The 1921 election also brought home some of the unique attributes of the single-member plurality electoral system. Combined with Canadian political geography, the system worked to the advantage of smaller parties that enjoyed a regionally concentrated electoral base, but to the disadvantage of parties of similar size with a geographically dispersed base. In 1921, for example, the Progressives actually received fewer votes than the Conservatives – 23 per cent versus 30 per cent – yet received more seats than the Conservatives – 65 versus 50. In subsequent years, small parties lacking a regional base fared poorly. Thus, in 1935 the Reconstruction Party under H.H. Stevens garnered 9 per cent of the total vote, dispersed mainly across the five eastern provinces, and was able to send only one candidate to Parliament.[3] In contrast, the Social Credit Party, with only slightly more than 4 per cent of the vote in 1935, won 17 seats, because its support was concentrated in Alberta and a small part of Saskatchewan.

The federal Progressives failed to establish themselves as a credible political organization, and by the end of the 1920s were a spent political force. Their credibility was undermined in part by their own anti-party philosophy, which led them to reject the opportunity to become the official opposition, even though they constituted the second largest party in the House of Commons. (Covell 1991 RC) Although remnants of the Progressive movement reappeared in other forms, 1921 marked the end of Canada's two-party system. In the 1930s, the Social Credit Party emerged on the national scene, although its electoral support and nearly all its seats came from Alberta. At the other end of the political spectrum, the CCF coalition of western farmer groups and eastern trade unions emerged to champion the socialist ideal. In a bid to capture more support from western Canada and in response to increased public support for the CCF in the early 1940s, the name of the Conservative Party was changed to Progressive Conservative. The change of name was a condition of John Bracken, the Progressive Premier of Manitoba, accepting the leadership of the Conservative Party in 1945.

The possibility of new parties and movements entering the political arena, and enjoying success when their support is geographically concentrated, remains a hallmark of the Canadian party system. In the 1940s, partly because of conscription, the Bloc populaire came to the fore in Quebec. Although it obtained only two seats in the federal election of 1945, a few years before it had more than 33 per cent of the popular support in public opinion polls in Quebec, thereby threatening both Liberal hegemony in that province and its overall majority in Parliament. (Gallup 1943) In the 1960s, the Créditistes in Quebec overshadowed their Social Credit counterparts in the rest of the country, taking 26 seats in Quebec in the 1962 election.

Institutional Responses

The "profound shifts in the political culture" of Canada during the First World War and throughout the 1920s led to three important institutional changes. First, the introduction of the merit principle in the public service and the resultant decline of patronage "deprived the party organizations of the glue that held them together, and which had tightly bound federal and provincial partisan interests. The [governing party] lost the power to dominate the administrative machinery of the state. This major institutional change ended party life as Canadians had known it for 50 years." (Carty 1988b, 20) Second, near-universal suffrage was adopted in 1919 with the extension of the franchise to women. Third, the practice of gerrymandering became discredited, and electoral administration was placed under the authority of the independent office of the chief electoral officer.

The 1921 federal election saw both the fracture of the two-party system in Canada, and the election of the Liberal leader, Mackenzie King, as prime minister. King's response to the social and political changes of the 1920s was to adopt a new style of brokerage politics. Under his leadership, localism declined as the primary focus of national party politics and organization. In its place, regional and national party organizations became key instruments in the politics of representation and accommodation.

King also responded to the sharp differences arising from the tumultuous period between 1911 and 1921 by emphasizing political accommodation and consensus. During the 1920s and 1930s, he disarmed the Progressives by adopting a number of their populist policies and by gradually bringing many of their caucus members into the Liberal Party. Throughout his long tenure as prime minister, he was also able to recruit prominent provincial politicians into his government. Regional interests were thus represented in the federal cabinet by strong ministers who were responsible for the extra-parliamentary organizations and political networks in their regions. (Bakvis 1991)

In addition to using the cabinet for the strategic accommodation of regional interests, King strengthened the financial and organizational resources of the Liberal Party. The National Liberal Federation (NLF) was created in 1932, in part to lessen the national party's dependence on its provincial organizations and to strengthen the party's fund-raising capabilities. The NLF gave the Liberals a permanent extra-parliamentary organization. Such an organization was increasingly necessary because of the decline of the partisan press and the emergence of radio not only as an important political medium but also as one that was primarily non-partisan almost from the outset. The NLF also allowed Mackenzie King to distance himself from the provincial Liberal parties. Some provincial parties, such as the Ontario party under Mitchell Hepburn, were becoming increasingly troublesome to their federal counterparts. (Whitaker 1977)

As the dominant party in a multi-party system, in many ways the Liberal Party was in an enviable position. But several developments reduced the importance of the party not only as a grassroots organization but also as an instrument of governance.

The first was the development of a larger and more competent public service. By the late 1920s, Mackenzie King had begun recruiting academics from Queen's, McGill and the University of Toronto to fill the most senior positions of the public service. This was the beginning of the Ottawa mandarinate, a group of well-educated and highly skilled men who brought to their jobs a pronounced national and international orientation. (Granatstein 1982) Significantly, their work included advising ministers on policy.

The influence of this mandarinate increased partly in response to the need to manage larger government departments and more complex tasks, as well as to maintain the links to the specialized interests served and affected by these departments. Many of the policies adopted by government were therefore initiated, accordingly, not by ministers or their party but by federal bureaucrats. The party was no longer solely responsible for generating ideas and initiatives and developing them into coherent policies.

This trend extended well into the post-war period, as the mandarinate became largely responsible for formulating the policies of post-war recovery and implementing new social welfare programs. A few of these senior civil servants also moved into elected politics, including John W. (Jack) Pickersgill, Mitchell Sharp, Charles M. (Bud) Drury and Lester B. Pearson. The last was recruited directly into cabinet as minister of external affairs by King's Liberal successor as prime minister, Louis St. Laurent. The actual number of mandarins moving into the Liberal Party was limited, nonetheless, this development contributed to the perception that the top levels of the Liberal Party and the federal bureaucracy had become thoroughly intertwined. Not surprisingly, the party was seen as increasingly remote from its roots, and its organization at the local level atrophied: the Liberal Party had become the "Government party". (Whitaker 1977, 87)

John Diefenbaker, the leader of the Progressive Conservative Party, exploited these perceptions during the infamous pipeline debate of 1956, when the Liberal government used closure to force legislation through Parliament. Capitalizing on these sentiments in the 1957 election campaign, Diefenbaker succeeded in forming a minority government, ending 22 years of Liberal rule. In the 1958 election Diefenbaker won one of the largest parliamentary majorities ever, drawing significantly on populist sentiments, particularly in western Canada.

During the long period of Liberal Party rule, from 1921 to 1957, interrupted only by the short-lived Meighen Conservative government in 1926 and the Bennett Conservative government of 1930–35, party politics was characterized by one-party dominance in an increasingly multi-party system. The dominance of the Liberal Party was founded on Mackenzie King's skilful stewardship and fostered by the weakness of the other parties. Particularly when there were so many parties, the Liberals could often win seats with pluralities that were far less than a majority of the votes cast. For example, in the 1945 federal election there were on average 4.5 candidates per constituency in Quebec, including Liberals, Conservatives, Independent Liberals, Communists and members of the Bloc populaire. The Liberals won 81 per cent of the seats (53 of 65) with 51 per cent of the vote.

Liberal dominance notwithstanding, both the Liberal and Conservative parties had become essentially parliamentary parties and political organizations concerned with winning elections. Local party organizations continued to have primary responsibility for recruiting, selecting and nominating candidates. Local Liberal organizations in many provinces, however, were dominated by regional ministers, party notables in the provincial wings of the party or, in the case of Newfoundland, by the Liberal Premier, Joseph Smallwood.

The national extra-parliamentary organizations of both parties became more important when they adopted national conventions to select party leaders. But the long tenure of King as Liberal leader throughout this period offered little opportunity for this new procedure to enhance the participation of Liberal Party members in national party affairs. For the Progressive Conservatives, the selection of John Diefenbaker in 1956 demonstrated the capacity of party members to exercise their authority independent of the parliamentary party.

The relatively infrequent use of this new opportunity for involvement, however, meant the minimal role of members in party affairs beyond elections did not substantially change. Moreover, patronage at the local level was becoming less effective in mobilizing and maintaining strong links between the national party leadership and local activists. Urbanization had eroded the rural character of political society in the 1900s, and the decline of the partisan press further diminished party attachments. Finally, the accelerating influence of the federal bureaucracy on policy formation and administration attenuated the influence of local and regional party notables on national policy and the management of public affairs.

For the CCF, and to a much lesser extent the Social Credit Party, the concept of party as a political movement meant something different for the role of its members. In the CCF, for example, party members were involved in determining party policy. This implied an obligation for the party to mobilize and educate its membership on public affairs, and a responsibility for members to participate in other than electoral activities. The success of the CCF in these regards was attributable largely to the capacity of the party to build on farmers' co-operatives in the west and trade unions in the east. Given the relatively limited attachment of Canadians generally to these two parties, however, the influence of this model of a political party was marginal in overall Canadian political life.

Pan-Canadianism and Participatory Democracy

A new era in party politics was introduced with the election of the Diefenbaker Progressive Conservatives in 1957. During Diefenbaker's tenure the role of the federal bureaucracy was challenged, most notably by the extensive use of royal commissions for policy ideas and advice. The New Democratic Party (NDP) was formed in the early 1960s to strengthen the connection between Canada's labour unions and the socialist movement. The Liberal Party, under Lester B. Pearson, began rebuilding, focusing primarily on the revival of grassroots participation in policy development.

The use of royal commissions to address several major policy issues illustrated that the Progressive Conservatives' populist electoral appeal was not grounded in a comprehensive package of alternative public policies. The party had focused almost exclusively on parliamentary and electoral activities during its period in opposition. It had no organized capacity to address public policies, and was therefore not prepared for governance. Once in office, the Progressive Conservatives paid a heavy price for this shortcoming.

As the Liberals overhauled party structures, they rejected the tradition of regional notables dominating the extra-parliamentary party. The Liberals placed new emphasis on eliciting grassroots participation to revitalize the party's policy development. These efforts were exemplified by the much-heralded Kingston Conference of 1960, which set the policy agenda for the first Pearson government, elected in 1963. Moreover, once in office, Pearson brought with him the chief architect of party policy, Tom Kent, to ensure a party policy presence in the inner circles of the cabinet, the caucus and the central bureaucratic structures that served the prime minister in his role as head of cabinet. (Doern 1971)

Several developments hampered the revitalization promised by this new phase in Liberal party affairs. First, the fate of the national parties was tied increasingly to the ability of the leaders to connect directly with the electorate. This meant that party apparatuses were centralized for electoral campaigns. Second, the new means of advertising during elections – television – required nationally directed campaign advertising. Third, the parties began to use opinion polls to gauge public response to policy issues and to determine public views on the relative importance of items on the national agenda. As a consequence, policy development was increasingly influenced by party pollsters and became geared to electioneering. These developments widened the gulf between the extra-parliamentary party membership and the central party strategists. (Carty 1991a RC)

Both the Progressive Conservative and Liberal parties failed to obtain a majority in the 1962, 1963 and 1965 elections. In 1962, the Social Credit Party captured 30 federal seats, most of them in Quebec, with only 12 per cent of the popular vote. This demonstrated not only the inability of the larger parties to generate a majority, but also the ease with which a smaller party with regionally concentrated voter support could gain entry to Parliament. In 1965, the Quebec wing of the Social Credit Party broke with the national party, forming the Ralliement créditiste under the leadership of Réal Caouette. The NDP was also building its electoral support steadily during this period, after CCF support declined to a post-war low in 1958.

Leadership Politics, Executive Federalism and Interest Groups

Beginning with the Liberal government of Pierre Elliott Trudeau in 1968, a deliberate effort was made to enhance the capacity of the central political apparatus – the prime minister and the cabinet – to monitor developments in and proposals from government departments and agencies. The federal government was looking for alternative sources of policy advice for the executive. These alternatives came from newly expanded bureaucratic agencies such as the Privy Council Office and the Treasury Board Secretariat, as well as from a partisan agency, the Prime Minister's Office. The Liberal Party as such had little involvement in offering policy advice or direction. More important, there was a perception that MPs, constituted as the caucuses of the parliamentary parties, had little influence, despite their impact on many public policies. This perception was reinforced by the fact that the activities of MPs frequently took place in caucus or in other arenas out of the limelight. (Thomas 1991 RC)

The emergence of a new mandarinate in Ottawa was a much publicized feature of the Liberal government of Pierre Elliott Trudeau. Neither the Progressive Conservative government of Joe Clark nor the current government of Brian Mulroney, however, significantly altered the basic features of the central machinery of government as it relates to the role of the parliamentary party and the extra-parliamentary party. Prime Minister Mulroney has been more sensitive to the claim of the Progressive Conservatives that government policy should reflect the stated values and policy preferences of the party; in this respect, there is a new balance within the central executive machinery that mixes technical and partisan input. (Aucoin 1986; 1988)

The role of the party in parliamentary government remains contentious. Despite the reforms of parliamentary committees under the Trudeau and Mulroney governments, the perception persists that MPs who are not in the cabinet have little collective or individual capacity to influence public policy.

Since the 1960s, a second arena labelled executive federalism has evolved; under executive federalism, national agreements are reached by political executives from federal and provincial governments. This arena has been essentially closed to elected legislatures and extra-parliamentary party organizations. Only ministers and their advisers participate in these deliberations and decision-making forums.

The origins of executive federalism lie in the dramatic transformation of federal-provincial relations during the 1960s and 1970s, stimulated partly by the Quiet Revolution in Quebec and partly by the growing importance of provincial governments in delivering social and economic programs. It soon became evident that few national decisions of any significance could be made without the direct participation of provincial governments.

As a result, federal-provincial conferences of ministers, including conferences restricted to first ministers (the prime minister and premiers), began to displace the federal cabinet, and especially Parliament, as the arenas for reaching national decisions and representing regional interests. These conferences also offered a mechanism for regional accommodation that cut across party lines. The increasing separation of the federal and provincial wings of the national parties meant that provincial interests were more likely to be represented through federal-provincial relations than through political parties, even when the same party was in power at both levels.

The exclusive nature of federal-provincial summits has attracted criticism. Political scientists began commenting many years ago on the consequences of these intergovernmental processes, including processes at the bureaucratic level, on relations between the executive and legislative branches. These commentators also noted the effects on the access interest groups have to decision makers. (Smiley 1980; Simeon 1972) Public and media attention to this phenomenon is more recent, stemming largely from the use of these processes for the constitutional changes that resulted in the Meech Lake Accord of 1987. Despite the perception that these processes were closed, the Meech Lake Accord was subject to the approval of Parliament and all ten provincial legislatures. The requirement for unanimity ultimately defeated the accord when it did not receive approval in two provincial legislatures. As Alan Cairns (1990) has noted, the perceived exclusionary qualities of executive federalism are now especially problematic with the *Canadian Charter of Rights and Freedoms*. Along with other factors, the presence of the Charter has prompted women's, ethno-cultural and Aboriginal groups to seek greater participation in the major decision-making processes and institutions that affect their interests.

The continued presence of many parties and the difficulties of the two largest in accommodating demands for participation coincided with the rapid rise of organized interest group politics during the 1970s and 1980s. This development further undermined the credibility of political parties as primary vehicles for articulating and promoting political ideas and interests. In addition to a proliferation of groups representing specific economic interests, a variety of new groups sprang up promoting various 'public interest' objectives. Although pressure groups were traditionally seen as mainly representing established economic interests, by the early 1970s the notion of interest group politics had taken on a different meaning as advocacy groups became increasingly important and effective. The increasing prominence of these new groups was stimulated in part by direct financial support from various government agencies; sometimes cabinet ministers encouraged this support as a means of cultivating backing for their policies and political support in their constituencies or regions. (Pross 1986)

These developments also emerged from and reflected broader social changes. There was a generational change in attitudes about politics and the most effective means of political participation. There was a generational revolt against the 'end of ideology' ethos that pervaded North American political and intellectual life in the early and mid-1960s. Furthermore, younger generations in Canada and abroad were less enamoured with established political parties of all persuasions. They preferred to pursue their particular political interests, ranging from environmental causes to the rights of women and minority groups, through single-issue organizations with the sole purpose of promoting a specific cause.

The growth of the administrative state in response to the expansion of government's role in society and the economy had the effect of diffusing power throughout the federal bureaucracy. This, coupled with the limited capacity of governing parties, and even opposition parties, to respond quickly and decisively to new policy issues, created an incentive for interest groups to bypass the traditional avenues of access to political power. Instead, groups often found it more effective to put their demands to particular government departments and agencies and to marshal their energies behind their specific issue.

Interest groups have also been evolving. Some groups have been able to show that using highly public tactics can indeed result in changes in government policies. This has had a demonstration effect among interest groups. As a further consequence, many citizens have found that pursuing a single issue through a single-purpose organization is much more satisfying than participating in a political party, where they would have to accommodate their goals with competing interests.

As a result, many citizens, especially large numbers of well-educated activists, have eschewed partisan politics, and thus political parties, as mechanisms of democratic political participation. (Nevitte 1991 RC)

This affects parties across the political spectrum. Three dimensions of this phenomenon are critical.

First, many of these activists express, explicitly or implicitly, strong anti-party attitudes. The legitimacy of political parties as primary political organizations is questioned in ways reminiscent of earlier populist movements such as the Progressives. (Covell 1991 RC) Political parties are painted either as organizations unwilling to adopt wholeheartedly the particular goal espoused by activists or as obstacles thwarting the direct expression of popular sentiments.

Second, many interest groups are using sophisticated tactics that allow them to shape the political agenda, especially as interpreted by the mass media. These groups are no longer willing to work within political parties or to confine themselves to the executive-bureaucratic arena.

Third, many groups have begun to involve themselves in elections by supporting or opposing parties, their candidates or both. Sometimes, this involvement has benefited particular parties or candidates; in other cases the involvement has been non-partisan, at least in directing support to any single party. Although some environmentalists have become involved in electoral politics through the Green Party, in general the new advocacy groups have not attempted to form distinctive political parties of their own. They are more likely to pursue their objectives through other means.

The Public Image of Political Parties

In many ways we seem to be in an era of anti-politics, although the rapid emergence of new parties points to the need to exercise caution in drawing conclusions. Canadians appear to distrust their political leaders, the political process and political institutions. Parties themselves may be contributing to the malaise of voters. In submissions and at Commission hearings, Canadians complained about perceived abuses at the constituency level in nomination contests and delegate selection for leadership conventions. Media reports of these types of complaints tarnish perceptions of the parties.

Whatever the cause, there is little doubt that Canadian political parties are held in low public esteem, and that their standing has declined steadily over the past decade. They are under attack from citizens for failing to achieve a variety of goals deemed important by significant groups within society. Table 5.1 shows that compared with other important social and political institutions in Canada, public confidence and respect for political parties is modest and has been declining over time.

Governments, and the parties forming them, are blamed for failing to deliver on many if not all these goals. Yet achieving these goals requires trade-offs in a parliamentary context, and political parties remain the only organizations capable of reconciling conflicting interests and generating consensus on the fairest way of doing so.

Table 5.1
Public respect and confidence in Canadian institutions
(per cent)

Institutions	Year	A great deal or quite a lot	Some	Very little	No opinion
Churches, organized religion	1979	60	27	12	2
	1984	54	30	15	1
	1989	55	29	15	1
Public schools	1979	54	29	12	4
	1984	56	30	11	4
	1989	62	30	6	2
Supreme Court	1979	57	21	8	14
	1984	55	26	10	9
	1989	59	24	11	5
Newspapers	1979	37	38	22	3
	1984	37	42	20	2
	1989	36	44	19	2
House of Commons	1979	38	36	15	11
	1984	29	41	20	10
	1989	30	43	21	6
Large corporations	1979	34	35	24	8
	1984	28	43	22	6
	1989	33	43	20	5
Political parties	1979	30	43	22	5
	1984	22	43	30	5
	1989	18	46	33	3
Labour unions	1979	23	34	36	7
	1984	21	36	39	4
	1989	28	37	31	5

Source: Gallup Report, 9 February 1989.

Note: Wording of question: "I'm going to read a list of institutions in Canadian society. Would you tell me how much respect and confidence you, yourself have in each one – a great deal, quite a lot, some or very little?"

Worldwide, respect for politicians has fallen, but this drop may be more pronounced in Canada. Table 5.2[4] depicts changes over a quarter of a century in responses to standard questions measuring political cynicism. It shows a steady rise in the proportion of Canadians agreeing with statements such as "government does not care about people like me" and "those elected soon lose touch with the people". Table 5.3 displays data for similar questions asked in the United States over a roughly comparable time period. Not all the questions are identical, but it appears that in the United States the rise in cynicism is not as pronounced as in Canada.

At the same time, Canadians still seem to have a great deal of respect for their MPs. Paralleling U.S. survey findings, more than 60 per cent of Canadian voters who had an opinion felt that their MP did a good to very good job of keeping in touch with people in the constituency. (Blais and Gidengil 1991 RC) Of those who had had contact with their MP, 65 per cent indicated being "somewhat satisfied" to "very satisfied" with the result. (Blais and Gidengil 1991 RC)

Table 5.2
Evolution of political cynicism in Canada
(per cent cynical)*

	1965	1968	1974	1979	1984	1988	1990
1. Government does not care	49	45	59	53	63	—	70
2. Government crooked	27	27	—	—	—	52	—
3. Government wastes	38	46	—	—	—	66	—
4. Distrust government	39	39	—	—	—	49	—
5. Those elected lose touch	60	61	65	65	78	—	79
6. Government not smart	56	49	—	—	—	63	—

Source: Blais and Gidengil 1991 RC.

*Indicates response category presented in the table. Percentages exclude don't know category and missing values.

Wording of questions:
1. I don't think governments care much what people like me think.
   *1. Basically agree.
   2. Basically disagree.
2. Do you think that:
   *1. Quite a few of the people running the government are a little bit crooked?
   2. Not very many are crooked?
   3. Hardly any of them are crooked?
3. Do you think that people in the government:
   *1. Waste a lot of the money we pay in taxes?
   2. Waste some of it?
   3. Don't waste very much of it?
4. How much of the time do you think you can trust the government in Ottawa to do what is right?
   1. Just about always.
   2. Most of the time.
   *3. Only some of the time.
5. Generally, those elected to Parliament seem to lose touch with the people.
   *1. Basically agree.
   2. Basically disagree.
6. Do you feel that:
   1. Almost all of the people running the government are smart people who usually know what they are doing?
   *2. Quite a few of them don't seem to know what they are doing?

Table 5.3
Evolution of political cynicism in the United States
(per cent cynical)*

	1968	1972	1976	1980	1982	1984	1986
1. Government does not care	44	50	54	55	49	44	55
2. Government crooked	26	38	42	49	—	33	—
3. Government wastes	61	68	77	80	68	66	—
4. Distrust government	38	46	66	74	67	55	62

Source: Adapted from Blais and Gidengil 1991 RC.

*The wording of the questions was similar to that in Table 5.2. Note, however, that in item 1 the word 'government' is replaced with 'public officials'.

What do Canadians dislike about their political parties? Table 5.4 presents the percentage of agreement with four propositions about parties. Respondents clearly believe that parties confuse rather than clarify issues and that they 'squabble' too much. At the same time, there is much less agreement on whether all parties are the same; about half of respondents perceive some meaningful choice between parties. Feelings about confusing issues and squabbling may, however, partly reflect the limited efforts by parties to engage in political education and discussion of policy issues.

Table 5.4
Attitudes about parties in Canada
(per cent)

	Basically agree
1. Parties are the same	47
2. Too much party squabbling	81
3. Parties confuse the issues	87
4. MPs should vote freely	78
5. Without political parties, there can't be true democracy	74

Source: Blais and Gidengil 1991 RC.

Note: Wording of the questions:

1. All federal parties are basically the same; there isn't really a choice.
   1. Basically agree.
   2. Basically disagree.
2. Our system of government would work a lot better if the parties weren't squabbling so much of the time.
   1. Basically agree.
   2. Basically disagree.
3. The parties confuse the issues rather than provide a clear choice on them.
   1. Basically agree.
   2. Basically disagree.
4. We would have better laws if Members of Parliament were allowed to vote freely rather than having to follow party lines.
   1. Basically agree.
   2. Basically disagree.
5. Without political parties, there can't be true democracy.
   1. Basically agree.
   2. Basically disagree.

The strong agreement with the statement that MPs should "vote freely rather than having to follow party lines" when voting on controversial issues reflects not only on parties but also on the parliamentary system within which parties operate. Survey evidence over the years clearly indicates that most Canadians resent the norms of party discipline as they operate in Parliament, and that these views are not a recent phenomenon. (Johnston 1986; Blais and Gidengil 1991 RC)

It is generally agreed that in responsible government, cohesive parliamentary parties are an essential link between the position and policies of the parties in Parliament and the actions pursued by the cabinet. Parties become meaningful only to the extent that party members in Parliament hold to a common position. Without cohesive parties it would be difficult for voters to vote for or against a party or a party policy. Even so, Canadian parliamentary parties have traditionally been much more exacting when it comes to enforcing party discipline than parties in Great Britain, for example. MPs, therefore, could be given greater scope and freedom on certain kinds of votes – as long as these votes were not treated as confidence motions – without necessarily undermining the theory and practice of responsible government.

The norms for party discipline in the Canadian House of Commons seem to be changing. The May 1991 Speech from the Throne promised new House procedures to "enhance the role of individual members and afford them greater independence". (Canada, House of Commons, *Debates*, 13 May 1991, 5) In September 1991, the federal government announced as part of its constitutional reform proposals that "the Government of Canada, in cooperation with all parties in the House of Commons, will explore ways and means to strengthen the representational and legislative capacities of individual members of Parliament". (Canada 1991, 15) Possible reforms included more free votes in the House of Commons, giving more attention and priority to private members' bills and an expanded role for parliamentary committees in reviewing government legislation.

At the same time, Canadians understand that the role of cohesive political parties in organizing the vote in the House of Commons is important. This is reflected in the response to the fifth item in Table 5.4. Nearly three-quarters of respondents indicated agreement with the statement: "Without political parties, there can't be true democracy." (Blais and Gidengil 1991 RC) The paradox in the responses to items 4 and 5 no doubt reflects the fact that Canadians do indeed wish to vote based on the party and its leadership. This interpretation is corroborated by the fact that independent candidates do poorly. (Bertram 1991 RC) Even incumbents who leave their party on a point of principle to sit as independents seldom fare well at election time – whether or not they were well regarded in the constituency. The quality of the local candidate is still important; it can make the difference in tight constituency races. The evidence overall, however, indicates that voters tend to vote primarily on the basis of party and party leadership.

Canadians would like greater control over their representatives and over public policies, especially between elections. This impulse is reflected in public opinion data and in several proposals received by the Commission calling for the use of referendums and the introduction of procedures for constituents to recall their MPs. These suggestions are discussed in Volume 2, Chapter 9.

Canada's political geography complicates the situation. The national swing in electoral results has never been unusually strong, but regional swings have been quite pronounced, often as strong and sometimes stronger than the national swing. (Jackman 1972; Ferejohn and Gaines 1991 RC) In the 1988 election, for example, the Atlantic region tended to vote in one direction, Quebec in another direction and Ontario somewhat evenly among the three largest parties. This likely indicated, in part, different responses to the free trade issue.

Despite high turnover at the level of individual MPs, elections do not necessarily spell significant change. (Blake 1991 RC) Even when the governing party changes, as in 1984, the basic regional characteristics underpinning the winning party may remain in place, with most MPs in the governing party still from Ontario and Quebec. This is a complaint heard frequently in western Canada. Here, unfortunately, the party system reflects the facts of Canada's large size and regional diversity. The majority of voters live in central Canada. To enhance the influence of the less populous provinces would depart significantly from the principle of representation on the basis of population, a cornerstone of our democratic system. There are other means available to remedy some of the problems arising from our political geography, including a reformed Senate.

Nonetheless, concerns about our political parties as primary political organizations are significant and legitimate. Except at election time, political parties appear to provide only very limited opportunities for participation by ordinary citizens. At the level of the constituency association, which is virtually the only avenue for obtaining membership in one of the larger parties, participation in party affairs between elections is very limited. Evidence indicates that on average a core of only 19 party members in each constituency association meets regularly. (Carty 1991a RC)

In recent years, the parties have been outflanked by public interest groups as a channel for political participation by ordinary citizens. Political parties are at a disadvantage in this respect; interest groups frequently focus on single issues and are largely unconcerned with balancing competing objectives within the organization. Parties must reconcile often sharply conflicting interests, for example, bridging the needs between environmentalists and forestry workers or business owners. Furthermore, although they are often highly visible, interest groups represent at best only a limited spectrum of public opinion. It falls to the political parties to represent those whose interests are not articulated by organized groups.

The Diversity of the Party System in Canada

Although the historical treatment of political parties in Canada has focused mostly on the traditions and records of the three largest parties, the landscape of the Canadian party system is much more rich and varied. Many smaller parties have developed partisan constituencies of loyal and committed supporters. And while these parties normally have nominal electoral success in federal elections, their presence suggests a party system that is more complex than generally assumed. Further, electoral support for these parties indicates that, despite the increased activism of interest groups, Canadians are hesitant to abandon the institution of party and embrace excessive factionalism. Our attitudinal survey showed that many Canadians want the electoral process to be made more accessible to the non-traditional parties so that voters have a broader choice in the selection of their elected representatives. The presence of a large number of distinct parties indicates that many Canadians want their representational needs affirmed through the electoral process rather than through the specific agendas of interest groups. A brief review of several of these parties follows.

The Communist Party of Canada (CPC) was founded in 1921 in a political climate that was hostile to communist ideology. The structure of the CPC was modelled on guidelines established by the 1919 Communist International for all communist parties. Unlike most other Canadian political parties, the CPC was not organized on territorially defined units but around small cells of workers and supporters. The cells were part of an overall hierarchical structure that was highly centralized and dominated by the party leadership.

Although the electoral success of the CPC was modest in the Great Depression, it was banned in 1931 by the Conservative government of R.B. Bennett. The ban was lifted in 1934. From 1943 to 1959, the CPC reorganized itself as the Labour Progressive Party. In the early 1940s the Communist Party enjoyed a small measure of electoral success. Communist members were elected to the provincial legislatures of Ontario and Manitoba, and Fred Rose, a Communist MP, was elected to the House of Commons in a 1943 by-election. (Whitehorn 1991)

The party was subjected to public hostility and state scrutiny during the McCarthyite period of the 1950s. It was also affected by internal party struggles following the destalinization movement in the Soviet Union. In the 1960s the Communist Party fractured into rival pro-Maoist and pro-Marxist-Leninist factions, reflecting international divisions within the communist movement, as represented by the Sino-Soviet disputes.

The contemporary communist movement in Canada continues to be fractured among rival ideological groups. The CPC itself, however, "continues to adhere to democratic centralism and a Moscow-directed policy orientation". (Whitehorn 1991, 355) In the 1980, 1984 and 1988 federal elections, the faction bearing the name the Communist Party of Canada "ran 52 candidates and received 6022, 7609 and 7180 votes respectively for an average of less than 150 votes per candidate". (Whitehorn 1991, 359)

The Libertarian Party of Canada was founded in 1973 by Bruce Evoy and a small group of Canadians who espoused a free-enterprise ideology. The creation of the party was partly a response to a perception that the federal Progressive Conservative Party was not sufficiently receptive to market-oriented economic policies. Many of the Libertarian Party's founding members had been involved in fledgling Libertarian groups during the 1950s and 1960s. The founding of the American Libertarian party in 1972 provided a catalyst for the emerging Canadian movement. American free-enterprise writers and academics who were especially prolific during this time served as the intellectual inspiration for Libertarian Party members in Canada. The party ran 24 candidates as 'independents' in the 1974 federal election and first achieved registered party status in the 1979 federal election.

The Green Party of Canada was founded in 1983 largely through the efforts of environmental activist Paul George. In the early 1980s, the membership base of the party was restricted mostly to British Columbia and Ontario. When it was founded, the party was concerned primarily with peace activism and halting the proliferation of nuclear weapons. In more recent years, the party has stressed environmental protection issues.

The 1983 founding convention of the Greens was marked by internal conflict over the organizational structure of the party. Delegates attending the convention were divided on whether decision making inside the party should be based on consensual or majority-rule principles. The issue went unresolved until the party adopted a national constitution in 1988 that established a highly decentralized party structure. Provincial divisions of the party were given rotating responsibility for maintaining the party at the federal level.

From its inception, the Green Party has promoted values that reflect some of the traditions of the European Green parties, but it is also infused with a North American concern about wilderness preservation. (Bakvis and Nevitte 1990) These values include non-violence, sustainable economic development, the preservation and restoration of ecosystem diversity, eco-feminism, cultural and multi-racial diversity, and consensual and decentralized decision making. Because the Greens are adverse to the notion of a hierarchical structure, they respond to the legal requirement in the *Canada Elections Act* that they have a leader by appointing a nominal leader who has very restricted formal authority within the party. The role of official spokesperson has been divided among members representing the party's five regions.

The Christian Heritage Party (CHP) was founded in the lower mainland of British Columbia in 1986 by a group of people concerned with issues of fiscal responsibility and traditional family lifestyles. Its first president was Bill Stilwell. Many of the party's members were former Progressive Conservative supporters who believed that the party had become inattentive to a number of issues critical to preserving traditional family values and structures in Canada. Many CHP members are dedicated pro-life supporters who are critical of the positions maintained by the three largest parties on this issue.

The CHP held its founding national convention in November 1987 in Hamilton, Ontario. At the convention, more than 500 delegates endorsed the party's guiding principles, policies and constitution. The party's fundamental principles include civil government in accordance with biblical principles, and the promotion of fiscally and socially conservative policies. By 1988 the party had constituency associations in most provinces. In the 1988 federal election the CHP was registered as a political party and nominated 63 candidates.

The populist-based Reform Party can be traced back to discontent in the western provinces with the policies of the federal Progressive Conservative government in the late 1980s. In the spring of 1987, Preston Manning, John

Muir and Stan Roberts founded a non-partisan western-rights movement called the Western Reform Association (WRA). The association focused on several federal government policies that many western Canadians had criticized, and on the influence western Canadians had in the central institutions of the federal government. At an assembly in May 1987, 76 per cent of WRA delegates voted in favour of forming a new party that would present its concerns to western voters through electoral competition. In November 1987, the Reform Party of Canada held its founding meeting in Winnipeg. At the convention, Preston Manning was acclaimed as party leader.

Following the issue of the writs for the 1988 federal general election, the Reform Party was officially registered as a political party. It nominated candidates in 72 constituencies. In 1989 the Reform Party elected its first MP, Deborah Gray, to the House of Commons in an Alberta by-election. A Reform Party candidate received the largest number of votes in a special election held in Alberta in 1989 to determine what name the provincial government would present to the federal government to fill a Senate vacancy, as provided for in the 1987 Meech Lake Accord. (McCormick 1991, 345)

In 1990 a group of MPs dedicated to promoting Quebec sovereignty in the House of Commons organized themselves into the Bloc québécois. The MPs were formerly members of the Progressive Conservative or Liberal parliamentary caucuses. A candidate of the Bloc québécois ran successfully as an 'independent' in a federal by-election in August 1990. Party registration rules did not allow the Bloc québécois to become registered without nominating candidates in at least 50 constituencies during a federal general election; the Bloc québécois was therefore unable to have its name placed on the ballot during the by-election.

The views and values of the Bloc québécois MPs are based on a formal party mission statement or manifesto. The party sees its mandate as "[to] contribute to the achievement of Quebec sovereignty and the negotiation of relevant agreements".

The Bloc québécois' founding convention, attended by 400 delegates, was held in June 1991 to draft a party constitution. The constitution was finalized in August 1991. The constitution gives members an active role in developing party policies. The general policies of the Bloc québécois are determined by delegates attending biennial conventions. Party leaders are elected by a majority of delegates from constituency associations and have considerable authority over the organizational structure of the party. Members of the Bloc québécois must be residents of Quebec, be at least 16 years of age and adhere to the objectives of the party.

THE PUBLIC AND PRIVATE DIMENSIONS OF POLITICAL PARTIES

Canadian political parties are essentially private organizations. They always have been, and should remain so for very good reasons. Citizens have the right to associate freely for political purposes. Legislation concerning parties, therefore, must be careful not to invade their internal affairs or jeopardize the right of individuals to associate freely. At the same time, political parties are responsible for a number of critical functions in the electoral process and, as most democracies take for granted, constitute an integral component of democratic governance. For certain purposes, then, parties deserve special acknowledgement in law and must be subject to some public regulations.

The Constitution and Organization of Parties

The structure of the large national parties reflects our parliamentary heritage and the federal nature of the country. Their structure also reflects various tensions within the parties as they try to reconcile the conflicting demands of the parliamentary party, the electoral campaign team and the party associations nationally, provincially and locally.

Party Structure and Organization

The basic organizational structure of the parties represents their efforts to manage and direct their activities toward achieving their objectives. Their structure is also affected by low levels of political participation, which limits the number of volunteers available. Parties must assign most organizational tasks to party officials and paid staff. For the larger parties, their goals are primarily electoral – winning office. For others, such as the Christian Heritage Party and the Greens, their goals lie much more in promoting certain values, and in the long run, raising the consciousness of the Canadian public. In these respects, these new parties are much like the CCF in its early days.

Key structural dimensions of the largest parties encompass the distinctions between the party leadership – including party professionals responsible for the national election campaign – and the parliamentary party and the extra-parliamentary party, including local associations and rank-and-file members. These distinctions underscore a central tension in the Progressive Conservative, Liberal and New Democratic parties, namely calls for openness, mass debate and autonomy of local associations on the one hand, and pressures for legislative flexibility and executive action on the other. In keeping with the role of these parties as primarily electoral machines, the forces for executive action have come to predominate in key areas related to running national election campaigns. Furthermore, it is the party leader who has tended to dominate not only the extra-parliamentary party but also the parliamentary party. Particularly now, with the personalities of party leaders dominating election campaigns, party structures have come to revolve in large measure around the party leader in the House of Commons. (R. Pelletier 1991 RC)

The three largest parties have roughly similar organizational formats. In all three, the biennial convention is considered the party's supreme authority. Between conventions, the party's national executive, or the federal council in the case of the NDP, renders decisions. The real power, however, tends to reside in the executive or steering committees and in the national party offices. At election time, the national campaign committees predominate, as they draw on key party personnel and prominent figures and, in the case of the governing party, cabinet ministers.

Yet for all the influence enjoyed by party leaders and a party structure operating apparently to their advantage, a central management team does not control all party activities. Party leadership has surprisingly little control over important areas of party activity, especially candidate selection.

Furthermore, the three largest parties must deal with the provincial wings of their parties, that is, the wing of the party organized to compete for power at the provincial level. The need to develop appropriate organizational structures in this respect is complicated by the nature of Canadian federalism. Party structures must take into account that both voters and members may have different party preferences at the federal and provincial levels. There is also often considerable tension between the federal government and provincial governments, even when the same party is in power at both levels.

The need to reconcile these federal-provincial considerations has important implications for the way in which party members participate in party affairs and the manner in which functions such as candidate selection are handled. Although these parties face a similar dilemma in dealing with their provincial wings, each has found a different structural solution to the problem.

The Progressive Conservative Party operates with separate federal and provincial parties although all their provincial legislative members have automatic convention delegate status in the federal party. While it normally employs a field organizer in each province, the provincial parties have no role in the federal party. In the Atlantic provinces, the field organizer shares office space and support staff with the provincial party. In the other six provinces, the party maintains separate offices. The federal party has direct links with grassroots federal constituency associations, bypassing the provincial level.

Each province is represented by a vice president on the national executive committee, but such members are not necessarily linked with the provincial party. Although provincial party leaders, the president, women's president, youth president and vice presidents of each provincial association sit on the national executive, this body rarely meets. (Dyck 1991 RC) The more critical decisions are made in the executive committee of the national executive, which meets more frequently, and in particular, in the steering committee. The steering committee can act in the name of the executive committee between meetings of the latter, and thus holds de facto authority for most decisions affecting party operations. The relative absence of formal structural links with provincial parties gives the Progressive Conservative Party flexibility in cultivating a national orientation and at the same time maintaining informal links with parties at the provincial level that are not Progressive Conservative.

Between 1932 and 1968, the Liberal Party of Canada was called the National Liberal Federation of Canada; and in some important respects it is still a federation of 10 provincial and two territorial units. In four provinces known as the 'split' provinces – Quebec, Ontario, Alberta and, most recently, British Columbia – the federal Liberal Party exists alongside the provincial Liberal Party. In these provinces, the Liberal Party of Canada is represented through provincial associations; for example, by the Liberal Party of Canada (Ontario) in Ontario and by the Parti libéral du Canada (Québec) in Quebec. These associations have separate or concurrent responsibilities with the national party for fund raising, for setting rules for the candidate selection process, for policy development and the adoption of resolutions for national policy conventions, and for the maintenance of membership lists. These provincial associations are governed by separate constitutions. However, if a conflict arises between the constitution of the national party and the provincial association, the national policy of the party takes precedence.

In the remaining provinces and territories the structure of the Liberal Party is integrated – they are called 'unitary' or 'joint' parties – and the provincial organization functions as a branch of the federal party. In most of the western provinces the provincial half of the joint party is weak or virtually non-existent, which means that the integrated party really has meaning only in the four Atlantic provinces. The Liberal Party of Canada, however, does keep separate offices in Quebec, Ontario and Alberta, and fund-raising offices in Newfoundland and British Columbia. (Wearing 1988, 183) Further, there are 12 regional presidents that sit on the national executive.

Before 1990, one could become a member of the national Liberal Party in the provinces with joint parties only by joining both federal and provincial parties. After constitutional amendments passed in 1990, it became possible to take direct membership in the federal party in all provinces and territories through local constituency associations. Finally, even in the integrated provinces, few joint federal-provincial constituency associations remain. Where they exist, one association tends to be a shell for the other – in New Brunswick and Nova Scotia, for example, the provincial constituency associations are the real engines of activity. (Dyck 1991 RC)

The NDP has by far the most integrated structure of the three largest parties, having joint organizations in all provinces and territories except Quebec. Although its constitution does not use the term confederation, it does provide for an autonomous provincial party in each province. There is no provincial party representation on the federal executive, but the federal council comprises the leader, president, several Members of Parliament, representatives from various trade unions, the secretary and treasurer of each provincial party, as well as three additional representatives from each provincial section. In recent years, the size of the council has increased from approximately 110 to 175 members to accommodate expanded representation for women, Aboriginal persons and ethno-cultural groups. Membership in the provincial party brings with it automatic membership in the federal party. Provincial offices, executives and conventions serve both levels. In recent years there has been concern in the NDP that provincial associations occupy most of the attention and energies of the membership. As a consequence, a Council of Federal Ridings was established recently in most provinces "to combat the dormancy of the federal party at the provincial and constituency levels between federal elections". (Dyck 1991 RC)

In a break with party tradition, constitutional amendments were passed in 1989 recognizing the NDP of Canada (Québec) as a separate entity from the Nouveau parti démocratique du Québec. In that province it then became possible to belong to a provincial party other than the NDP and still belong to the federal party, something that is not permitted in other provinces. In August 1990, when the Quebec provincial party refused to support the federal candidate in a federal by-election, the federal party severed all links with the provincial association.

When the two parties with integrated or partially integrated federal-provincial structures collect funds under the rubric of federal income tax credits, the provincial wing can use these funds in the provincial, and possibly even the municipal, electoral arena. The law is not explicit on this issue, but those responsible for handling party finances in at least two parties expressed concern about potential abuses from the lack of clear legislation or guidelines. (Dyck 1991 RC)

In contrast with the Progressive Conservative, Liberal and New Democratic parties, the Reform Party of Canada is unencumbered by provincial wings; it has decided not to compete for power at the provincial level. Central to the party's decision-making process are the party assemblies, which meet at least every two years, and the executive council. While in theory the assemblies can decide most matters, most power resides in the party's executive council. It is composed of the party leader, the provincial or territorial directors, the chief executive officer of the party fund and provincial or territorial representatives where they have constituency associations.

The Reform Party constitution has a unique provision for referendums: party members "may initiate a formal referendum of the Party membership by submitting a petition to the Secretary of the Party requesting such a referendum and signed by not less than 5% of the Party membership". (Article 8 (b)) Referendums can relate to "any important constitutional, social, economic, or political issue". (Article 8 (a)) Significantly, however, the results of such referendums are merely advisory; they are not binding on the leader or the executive council. Overall, the Reform Party's constitution gives more power to the party leader than those of most other parties. "Between Assemblies, interim policies and objectives of the Party shall be those determined by the Leader in consultation with and approved by the Executive Council", provided party principles are maintained. (Article 1(d))

The constitutions of the Liberals and the NDP, because these parties have federal organizational forms, leave the local nomination process to be specified in their provincial associations' constitutions. This decentralization leads to varying practices within the same party and hampers efforts by the leadership to encourage local associations to accept changes in the nomination process. For example, the British Columbia NDP has a series of provisions governing appeals of nomination contests, while the Manitoba NDP has none; the constitution of the federal Ontario Liberals has rules governing nomination finances, but there are none in the New Brunswick party. (Carty and Erickson 1991 RC)

Although the Progressive Conservative and Reform parties' constitutions tie their constituency associations directly to the national party, neither is significantly more centralized than the Liberals or the NDP for nomination practices. Essentially, the rules are left to be specified in local associations' constitutions, subject only to age provisions for party membership, a local resident qualification for constituency association membership and a minimum notice requirement for a nomination meeting. The Reform Party's national constitution requires that local party members "shall conduct a thorough search ... to find the best possible candidate". (Article 4(a)) This suggests greater central control than the other parties, yet it still indicates that the traditional right to choose the local candidate remains with the constituency association. Among the other parties, the Christian Heritage Party's constitution has by far the most extensive rules governing the nomination process in constituency associations and the operation of provincial and territorial councils and the party youth caucus. For example, the constitution requires members to reside in the constituency of the local association, and it specifies the term of office of executive members of associations and councils and the frequency of meetings of the executive and membership of constituency associations.

The organization of the three largest parties also takes into account non-territorial characteristics. In 1973, the Liberal Party set up a Women's Commission and a National Youth Commission. The Progressive Conservative Party operates a PC Youth Federation and a PC Women's Federation, while the NDP has Young New Democrats and a Participation of Women Committee to promote the involvement of women throughout the party. The creation of special committees and commissions for multiculturalism and Aboriginal people in the Liberal, Progressive Conservative and New Democratic parties indicates how current issues and concerns are handled organizationally by the parties. It was not until the 1960s that these special party groupings were actively included. These organizations have become more prominent in the management of the parties' processes and activities.

These sectoral constituencies are within each party, but the NDP also has to accommodate organized labour. The party was formed as a grouping of social and economic interests. From the outset, organized labour was a special player in NDP ranks, providing financial support, volunteer labour, meeting halls and public expressions of support. The integral link between the NDP and the labour movement is recognized in the party's national constitution. Article VIII (1)(f) of the constitution states that the membership of the council shall include "one member representing each of the fifteen affiliated organizations with the largest number of affiliated members". This clause effectively guarantees the trade unions 15 members on the council, given that they are the largest organizations affiliated with the NDP. Keith Archer observes that labour leaders typically "occupy approximately 20 to 25 per cent of the executive and officer positions" in the party. (1990, 30) Yet overall, according to Archer: "Only a small, and declining, proportion of union members in Canada belong to locals affiliated with the NDP." (1990, 71)

One of the most important management tools available in any large public organization is its constitution. Typically, it provides a formal guide to the structure and the distribution of power within the organization, articulates the organization's values and goals, and specifies the rights, obligations and duties of its members and officers. A constitution is especially important for the leadership, giving it authority for its actions, for managing the activities of the organization, and in particular, for creating an organizational culture and mobilizing the membership to achieve the organization's goals.

If the constitution is to serve its purpose, there must be a reasonably good fit between the constitution's provisions and the organization's practices. Too large a contrast between formal constitutional provisions and party activities can lead to cynicism and a crisis of authority at critical moments.

To varying degrees the three largest parties suffer in that their formal constitutions only partially approximate the reality of their organizational structures. At the same time, they give party leaders only limited means to mobilize party members. There are areas where party constitutions provide no rules or guidelines about appropriate behaviour. In other areas, practices or local norms clearly contravene the constitution, yet little or no effort seems to be made to enforce party regulations. Finally, given the formal autonomy assigned to local associations, party leaders are actually constrained from intervening in most aspects of candidate selection.

Indeed, the only real authority party leaders have over candidate selection is that provided by law – the requirement that party leaders concur with the nomination of the party's candidate in each constituency. If the leader withholds approval, this action is seen as interventionist. Unfortunately, party constitutions offer little in the way of intermediary steps that could more effectively support party goals for candidate selection and the like.

The Liberals and Progressive Conservatives have both been concerned with what are seen as abuses in candidate and leadership delegate selection and with the need generally to update their constitutions in changing circumstances. The Liberal Party, for example, struck the Liberal Reform Commission in June 1990, charging it with reviewing a variety of key party organizational matters. Yet doubts remain about whether the three largest parties have the organizational capacity to address the issues now confronting them.

The federal nature of the Canadian political system has influenced the rules and procedures of all the parties, resulting in considerable variation in the rules that exist and the way in which they are applied. Several questions are pertinent. Are these differences appropriate in national parties competing for national office? Do the party constitutions contribute to public confidence in our electoral system and in the parties when they regulate only to a very limited extent such important activities as candidate selection? Finally, do the structure and constitutional framework of the parties really serve the objective of building a broader and more active membership and of mobilizing that membership behind goals deemed important by the national party?

Registration of Parties

Recognition of Parties in Law

Full legal recognition of political parties in their electoral capacity did not occur until the 1970 *Canada Elections Act*. Before this, legislation applied solely to individual candidates, not to parties. In 1874, when the *Dominion Elections Act* brought in the doctrine of agency (first introduced in Great Britain in 1854), the individual candidate and the candidate's official agent were made responsible for reporting election expenditures. The doctrine of agency was not extended to political parties.

Beginning in the 1920s, procedural changes in the House of Commons, stimulated in part by the presence of more than one opposition party, implicitly noted the existence of parties. (Courtney 1978) The *Canadian Broadcasting Act, 1936* recognized the existence of political parties explicitly by giving the Canadian Broadcasting Corporation full powers to assign broadcasting time "on an equitable basis to all parties and rival candidates". In the 1950s *Hansard* began including a separate appendix listing the party affiliation of MPs. In 1963, an amendment to the *Senate and House of Commons Act* acknowledged the existence of parties, in that leaders of parliamentary parties other than the prime minister and leader of the official opposition could receive a special stipend. Further procedural changes followed, giving speaking privileges to spokespeople for each opposition party in the House of Commons. In its 1966 report, the Committee on Election Expenses recommended the registration of political parties and that the principle of agency apply not only to candidates but also to political parties. These changes were adopted by amendment to the *Canada Elections Act* in 1970 and 1974.

Essentially unchanged since then, the *Canada Elections Act* provides a regulatory mechanism, in the form of a registration procedure, through which parties gain access to public funding in the form of income tax credits, partial reimbursement of election expenses and free broadcasting time. Through the same mechanism they become accountable for reporting on their financial activities annually and after each election. The present registration procedure also provides a means of identifying the parties on the ballot, for protecting the names and acronyms used by the parties, and for implementing each party leader's obligation to confirm the party's official candidate in each constituency.

Under the *Canada Elections Act* parties are generally treated as organizations whose exclusive function is electoral competition. Except for tax credits, registered parties receive public funding for election-related activities only. It is important to emphasize that the activities of parties between elections are not addressed in the current registration process; nor are the constituency associations of parties and the crucial functions they perform.

Political parties are legally recognized also under the *Parliament of Canada Act*. Parliamentary parties in the House of Commons with "a recognized membership of twelve or more persons in the House [of Commons]" are acknowledged as organizations with continuing roles and responsibilities, and they receive money for their leaders' offices. Parties also receive annual grants for research activities and research staff under rules established by the House of Commons Board of Internal Economy. Research money was first given to opposition parties in 1968; it was extended to the government party in 1979. The research budgets and criteria for funding are determined by the Board. The size of the annual grant is based on the number of MPs elected. The Board has discretion as to whether parties with fewer than 12 members should receive money. For the 1991 fiscal year, the budget for the research office of the Liberal Party was $926 700, the NDP received $647 000 and the Progressive Conservative Party received $1 085 800. This means that parties receive public funding in addition to reimbursements for election expenses.

Parties in Parliament thus have the resources to engage in continuous policy research and development. In contrast to their position under the *Canada Elections Act*, the parliamentary parties are treated as organizations with roles extending beyond periods of electoral competition. The annual research grants are given to parties, not to individual MPs. This approach to allocating research money implicitly if not explicitly recognizes the role of parties in structuring policy ideas and choices. In practice, however, the research done by the parliamentary parties is essentially geared to the short-term needs of parliamentary debate or Question Period; rarely do the parliamentary parties engage in policy development. Nor do they use these resources to promote political education or party discourse on matters of broad public policy.

Comparative Experience

The extent to which parties are legally recognized and regulated in other jurisdictions varies considerably, but two essential points can be made.

First, in many countries including the United States, regulation of the internal affairs of political parties is more extensive and detailed than it is in Canada. Second, even where the legal recognition of parties is limited, there is often legislation to protect the unique place that political parties occupy in the democratic affairs of the nation.

In Great Britain, parties are not registered and do not receive public funding except for free broadcast time. However, the special position of British parties is recognized by measures such as a complete ban on election advertising in the broadcast media during the election period, which is applied to everyone including candidates and interest groups.

In Australia, the legal procedure for registering parties distinguishes between parliamentary and non-parliamentary parties. A non-parliamentary party may be registered if it has at least 500 members and a written constitution; at least 10 party members and the party secretary must make the application. A parliamentary party must meet the additional qualification of having one or more elected members in the national or a state legislature. If minimum thresholds are met, registered parties are eligible for limited election expense reimbursements. The main intent of the Australian legislation, therefore, is to provide a mechanism for public funding of political parties.

In the United States, the *Federal Election Campaign Act* of 1971 (s. 431(16)) defines a political party as "an association, committee, or organization which nominates a candidate for election to any Federal office whose name appears on the election ballot as the candidate of such association, committee, or organization". Any organization satisfying this definition is subject to federal election disclosure rules. Varying from state to state, detailed rules govern access to and the operation of primaries for federal parties. In the United States, therefore, although there is only limited recognition of political parties in federal law, many of the activities of parties, such as candidate selection, are extensively regulated.

Whether a party's name appears on the ballot is also determined by individual states in the United States. With one exception, all states require small parties and independent candidates to go through an onerous petition process to have their names and party affiliations placed on the ballot. Democratic and Republican candidates are for the most part exempt from petition requirements. This can be seen as an implicit means of protecting the primacy of the two main parties.

In Germany the legal framework governing political parties is more fully developed. The *Basic Law* (Germany's constitution, enacted in 1949) recognizes the crucial role of parties in democratic governance and establishes the primary ground rules for parties. "They can be freely formed. Their internal organization must conform to democratic principles. They must publicly account for the sources of their funds." (Article 21(1)) The *Basic Law* also specifies that "details [rules applying to parties] shall be regulated by federal legislation". (Article 21(3)) Many of these "details" were subsequently consolidated and enacted in the *Law on Political Parties* in 1967. The

Federal Electoral Law, enacted in 1956, also contains provisions applying to political parties. The *Law on Political Parties* (s. I(2)) defines political parties as "associations of citizens who set out to influence either permanently or for a long period of time the formation of political opinions ... and to participate in the representation of the people ... provided that they offer sufficient guarantee of the seriousness of their aims" as demonstrated by the scale of their organization, the number of members and the extent of their public support.

In practical terms, participation in elections to the federal and *Länder* legislatures and maintenance of a permanent administrative organization are the prerequisites for a political party in Germany. Any organization with these two characteristics becomes subject to the *Party Law*, which endows parties with a legal capacity that includes the right to sue and be sued. The *Party Law* also details the requirements of parties for their internal organization, the holding of meetings, internal voting procedures (e.g., use of the secret ballot), the rights of members and party arbitration courts. Under the *Party Law*, however, German parties are essentially self-regulating. Only if it can be demonstrated that a party's internal workings or constitution are undemocratic can that party be brought before the Federal Constitutional Court and be declared unconstitutional. The role of federal returning officers and the sanctions available to them are restricted to enforcing the rule requiring parties to inform them of the party's statutes and the names of members of the executive committee. The *Party Law* also specifies and regulates the principles and scale of reimbursement of election expenses.

The French constitution and specific legislation establish the right of citizens to organize for political action and recognize the special position of political parties. Article 4 of the constitution states: "political parties and groups shall be instrumental in the expression of the suffrage. They shall be formed freely and shall carry on their activities freely. They must respect the principles of national sovereignty and democracy." No advertising is permitted during election campaigns, other than advertising by political parties at locations designated for election posters and on state-allocated broadcasting time. This ban comes into effect three months before the first day of the month in which the election is held. To collect tax-deductible donations, parties must appoint an official agent and make regular financial reports to the appropriate authorities. Direct funding from the state is also available, but only to parties with at least one seat in the National Assembly, or more specifically, to parliamentarians who declare themselves to be a member of a political party. In 1990, 830 of 896 members of the National Assembly and the Senate declared themselves to be members of one of the 29 parties. The position and the obligations of political parties are enshrined in the constitution; their role is protected and fairness is ensured by restrictions on political advertising during election campaigns, restrictions that include banning all non-party advertising.

In several countries there is special recognition of the role political parties play in promoting democratic governance. Particularly in countries that have suffered political upheaval or dictatorship there is explicit constitutional recognition of political parties and the role they are expected to play. This is true not only of Germany, but also of Italy and Greece. Elsewhere, legal recognition, usually in the form of registration procedures, is related to the public funding of parties. In the United States, although there is only limited acknowledgement of parties in federal law, there is nonetheless detailed regulation of federal party activities by state law. All these countries recognize that parties play an important public role in ensuring the continuing viability of the democratic system.

Provincial Comparisons

The *Canada Elections Act* represented a milestone in introducing a registration procedure for political parties. Since that time, most provincial governments have followed with similar legislation. The federal law restricts the registration of parties to the electoral period and does not require registration of local constituency associations. Over time, provincial authorities have refined the federal model, taking into account the federal example and local circumstances. It is therefore useful to examine the provincial experience, because it reflects the evolution of Canadian values and expectations on these matters.

In seven of the 10 provinces – Alberta, British Columbia, Manitoba, New Brunswick, Ontario, Quebec and Saskatchewan – parties may register between elections. The conditions are highlighted in Table 5.5. Two other provinces, Nova Scotia and Prince Edward Island, have registration procedures for parties; in Nova Scotia, registration, or official recognition, can take place only during the election period. In Newfoundland, political parties are not recognized explicitly in the provincial *Election Act*, nor does Newfoundland provide any public funding, directly or indirectly, for political parties.

Five provinces provide for the registration of constituency associations. This was first introduced in Ontario in 1975 by the *Election Finances Reform Act*. Quebec adopted the principle in its 1977 legislation; Alberta also adopted requirements similar to Ontario's in 1977. New Brunswick's 1978 *Political Process Financing Act* provides for disclosure of the finances of registered constituency associations. In British Columbia, constituency associations of recognized political parties wishing to issue tax credit receipts must register with the Commissioner of Income Tax. Our research indicates these requirements are an established part of the regulatory system in these provinces, that they work well and that they do not impose a heavy burden on local associations. (Barrie 1991 RC; Johnson 1991 RC; Massicotte 1991 RC; Mellon 1991 RC)

Table 5.5
Political party registration requirements: provincial comparisons

Jurisdiction	Registration requirement	Inter-election registration	Constituency association registration
Canada	X		
British Columbia[a]	X	X	X
Alberta	X	X	X
Saskatchewan	X	X	
Manitoba	X	X	
Ontario	X	X	X
Quebec	X	X	X
Nova Scotia[b]	X		
New Brunswick	X	X	X
Prince Edward Island	X		
Newfoundland			

Source: Royal Commission Research Branch.

[a]Political parties, candidates and constituency associations wanting to issue tax receipts are required to register with the Commissioner of Income Tax at the Income Taxation Branch in Victoria.

[b]Political parties may register between elections, however "recognized political parties" can only register when an election is called. Recognition is necessary for political parties to issue tax credit receipts.

Registration of constituency associations is intended to serve broader purposes than simply offering an accountability mechanism relating to financial reporting and the right to issue income tax receipts. In this connection the Ontario experience is instructive. In its 1975 report, the Ontario Commission on the Legislature (the Camp Commission) criticized constituency associations for being weak and poorly organized, and suggested political life at that level would be revitalized by giving associations the right to use the income tax credit, thereby strengthening their fund-raising capacity. David Johnson reports that, "party officials are uniformly pleased with the enhanced financial and organizational health of constituency associations [in Ontario] and the increased role these bodies can play in the political process". (1991 RC)

On the whole, the provinces provide greater flexibility in the registration of political parties, in particular by providing opportunities for new parties to become registered during the inter-election period (Table 5.6). The provincial registration regimes also tend to be more extensive by virtue of the fact that four provinces have mandatory registration of local associations.

Table 5.6
Inter-election political party registration requirements: provincial comparisons

Jurisdiction	Requirements
British Columbia	Registration with the provincial Income Taxation Branch to receive authorization to issue tax receipts for contributions.
Alberta	Registration under one of three conditions: (1) minimum of three seats in legislature after most recent election; (2) nominated candidates in at least 50 per cent of constituencies during a previous or current election period; and (3) demonstrate support by supplying names, addresses and signatures of at least 0.3 per cent of eligible voters.
Saskatchewan	Parties must register with the chief electoral officer (CEO) before they can solicit or receive contributions or spend on behalf of the party or candidate. CEO may de-register party if at close of nominations for general election it has failed to nominate at least 10 candidates.
Manitoba	Registration with CEO under one of three conditions: (1) party has four or more seats in legislature; (2) party must endorse five or more candidates in general election; and (3) party supported by a petition signed by 2500 voters or more. CEO may de-register automatically if party does not field at least five candidates in election.
Ontario	Registration under one of two conditions: (1) parties must nominate candidates in at least 50 per cent of constituencies following the issue of the writs for general election before being eligible to register; and (2) a party can apply to the Ontario Elections Finance Commission by providing names, addresses and signatures of 10 000 qualified voters who support the party.
Quebec	Parties must agree to nominate candidates in at least 10 constituencies. Application must include the names, addresses and signatures of 1000 voters declaring support.
New Brunswick	Registration with CEO if party leader was elected by convention, party has constituency associations in at least 10 constituencies and undertakes to present candidates in at least 10 constituencies at the next election.

Source: Royal Commission Research Branch.

Improving the Registration Process

There are a number of deficiencies in the current practices for recognizing parties:

- There is a gap between the *Canada Elections Act* and the *Parliament of Canada Act*. The former treats parties as electoral machines, while the latter provides for public funding of parliamentary parties for inter-election activities.
- The registration procedure provides only a single definition, which makes no distinctions between small parties that are unlikely to reach the threshold for obtaining reimbursement and the larger parties seriously seeking to form the government.
- There is no provision for registering the constituency associations of political parties.
- There is a gap between what the law considers a legally registered party and the criteria used by broadcasters to allocate broadcasting time among the parties.
- Even though election finances are regulated, the law provides no framework to govern internal party processes. For instance, the critical issue

of membership – who can and cannot participate in the affairs of the party and in opportunities for potential education and discourse – is not addressed.

There are two broad reasons why the conduct of parties generates legitimate public concern. First, the state subsidizes parties and candidates through tax credits and provides reimbursements for election expenses. Many interveners at our public hearings argued that given the significant public subsidy of parties and their candidates, there is a public interest in ensuring that parties conduct their nomination and leadership processes in ways that meet norms and expectations concerning the use of public monies.

Second, public concern arises because party activities have a significant impact on our electoral democracy, and there exists, therefore, a legitimate public interest. Parties have a critical public role: they provide the vehicle for nominating candidates and for choosing leaders, even prime ministers. These activities are understandably scrutinized in terms of public norms and values. Because parties serve as the principal gatekeepers in determining which candidates and leaders are selected, there is a legitimate public interest in ensuring that fair and equitable procedures apply to candidate and leadership selection processes.

> In the Canadian political system, the leadership selection process that goes on in the political parties is a critical part of our whole democratic process.... And so, that process becomes very much a public process.... As a member of a political party who becomes a voting delegate at a convention, I have pre-selected for all Canadians who may become Prime Minister of this country. (R. McCarney, Symposium on the Active Participation of Women in Politics, 1 November 1990)

Given that the public has a definite stake in the way the parties fulfil their public responsibility, it is reasonable and justified that parties adhere to standards for constitutional practices, membership requirements and full financial disclosure and transparency.

Party Constitutions

In the discussion of party structures, practices and constitutions, several problems became evident: party constitutions are often silent on important issues relating to candidate selection and the like; there is considerable variation in rules and procedures from one constituency association to another; and constitutional provisions relating to membership requirements can be ignored or overridden at the constituency level. The registration requirements in the *Canada Elections Act* are silent on these fundamental questions. Nor does the Act provide a definition of the purposes of a registered party.

The adoption of the *Canadian Charter of Rights and Freedoms* has heightened awareness among Canadians of the primacy of certain democratic values and ideas. The Charter is now the foremost constitutional document in the country; it articulates the democratic principles that bind Canadians together as members of the same political society. An opportunity exists for political parties to embody some of these principles through the development of constitutions that seek to be both inspirational and functional. Currently, the constitutions are mostly a collection of rules and procedures that establish the organizational structures of the parties and identify the different responsibilities of the parties' constituent parts. This is not to deny that the constitutions affirm certain principles, but only to suggest the constitutions have not fully captured the spirit and intent of the Charter as these constitutions relate to the internal dynamics of parties and their election and inter-election activities.

Recommendation 1.5.1

We recommend that registered political parties, as the primary political organizations formed on the basis of a shared set of ideas and principles for the purposes of:
> **nominating candidates for election to Parliament; mobilizing electoral support for their candidates; engaging their members in discussion of democratic governance; providing forums for the development of alternative policies and programs; preparing their elected members for their parliamentary responsibilities; and organizing the processes of representative and responsible government,**

have constitutions that promote democratic values and practices in their internal affairs and that are consistent with the spirit and intent of the *Canadian Charter of Rights and Freedoms*.

The treatment of political parties in electoral law should recognize their organizational diversity. At the same time, the full range of operational and financial activities of all parties should be reflected in the legal provisions for registration and in democratic constitutions. These requirements should extend not only to the national party and local constituency associations, but also to provincial associations of federal registered parties that represent the interests of the party in specific provinces by organizing election and inter-election activities. This would ensure that, notwithstanding the differences among the parties, all parties were subject to the same general procedural and administrative requirements.

A democratic constitution must adhere to minimum standards. The complaints we have heard include: inconsistency in rules and in applying them; the inability of national parties to rectify abuses when they do occur; variations in, or the absence of, appeal procedures and means to adjudicate disputes; and the practice of according disproportionate weight to certain categories of members in the selection of leadership convention delegates.

Recommendation 1.5.2

We recommend that

(a) the democratic constitution of a party and of its registered constituency associations be submitted as part of the registration application to the Canada Elections Commission, and contain the following:
(1) provisions that those members who nominate a candidate for election to the House of Commons, select delegates to a leadership convention, or elect the party leader, be voters;
(2) clear and consistent rules applying to all aspects of the selection process for candidates, leaders, delegates and party officers, as well as membership requirements;
(3) rules and procedures for meetings and proceedings;
(4) a rule that a person may vote only once at a meeting and may vote only at one meeting to select a constituency candidate, delegates for a leadership convention, or a leader or to conduct the affairs of a constituency association;
(5) provisions for remedies and processes to fairly resolve disputes between party members and the constituent parts of the party; and
(6) specific sanctions that would be applied in cases of violation of its constitutions and rules; and
(b) nothing in the above requirements be construed to imply that a registered political party cannot have provincial associations that may exercise all or part of the responsibilities of the national party; and in such cases, the powers of the provincial associations be delineated in the constitution and by-laws of the party, and the constitution and the by-laws of the provincial associations be consistent with the requirements of the *Canada Elections Act* and filed with the Canada Elections Commission.

Registration of Political Parties
At present, a political party seeking registration under the *Canada Elections Act* must nominate candidates in 50 constituencies during a federal election. An application to be registered must be received by the CEO 60 days before the writs for a general election are issued. If the application is not received 60 days before the election is called, the party can be registered only for the subsequent federal election. Once the writs have been issued, any

party that has met the application deadline and has nominated candidates in 50 constituencies can be registered. Registered parties that do not nominate candidates in at least 50 constituencies 30 days before election day and that did not have at least 12 MPs in the House of Commons when the writs were issued, may be de-registered at the discretion of the chief electoral officer. In 1988, for example, the Social Credit Party continued to be registered by the CEO, although it did not nominate 50 candidates. The registration of the party was permitted by the CEO, in part, to recognize its historical participation in the Canadian electoral process.

In the 1988 federal election, there were 12 registered political parties. Table 5.7 lists these parties, as well as the number of candidates nominated by each.

Table 5.7
Number of registered political parties and number of candidates nominated, 1988 federal election

Registered political party	Number of candidates
Progressive Conservative	295
Liberal	295[a]
NDP	295
Social Credit	9
Communist Party of Canada	52
Libertarian	88
Parti Rhinocéros	74
Green Party	68
Confederation of Regions	52[b]
Party for Commonwealth of Canada	61[c]
Reform Party	72
Christian Heritage Party of Canada	63

Source: Canada, Chief Electoral Officer 1989, 59.
[a]The Liberal Party of Canada nominated 295 candidates, but one candidate withdrew before polling day.
[b]One candidate withdrew before polling day.
[c]Two candidates withdrew before polling day.

The current registration process is essentially tied to the electoral cycle. The process does not allow the registration of emerging parties that acquire substantial public support between elections. This denies them access to the tax credit and to other public benefits available to registered parties.

Allowing new parties to register between elections would promote fairness and accessibility. Inter-election registration would demonstrate that the electoral process and the political process are open to new parties that are committed to promoting the interests and ideas of citizens in ways different from the existing parties. The proposal is feasible, because new political parties can register between elections in several provinces. However, the criteria for inter-election registration would have to be sufficiently rigorous to ensure that the process was not misused by groups not fully committed to participating in the electoral process as political parties. The substantial benefits attached to registration must not be allowed to be diverted for other purposes.

The Canada Elections Commission would maintain a registry for qualified political parties. When applying for registration, in addition to meeting the requirements set out above, a party would need to provide (as with the current regulations) the full name and abbreviation of the party; name and address of the party leader (or the person designated by the governing body), party officers, chief agent and auditor; the address of party headquarters; and the names and addresses of financial institutions where the party's accounts are located.

The Canada Elections Commission would not register a political party if all requirements were not met, or, if in the opinion of the Commission, the name or the abbreviation of the name closely resembled the name or abbreviation of the name of a registered party, another political party for which an application had already been made, contained the word 'independent' or would create confusion with a formerly registered party or with a party that was represented in the House of Commons.

We propose that inter-election registration be achieved through the use of a petition procedure. A party wanting to register would have to document that it had the support of a sufficient number of voters who are members in good standing of the party. This would require a petition to test the new party's ability to mobilize public support through the establishment of a broad membership base during the inter-election period. A party that could document support from at least 5000 members who are voters would meet such a test.

There is currently an inconsistency between the registration process in the *Canada Elections Act* and the treatment of parliamentary parties in the *Parliament of Canada Act* and in the internal operations of the House of Commons. Parliamentary parties with 12 or more MPs receive public funding for research and additional stipends for party leaders. These parties are recognized as having important contributions to make to public debate and discourse. This recognition should be reflected in the registration process found in the *Canada Elections Act*.

A political party that nominates candidates in 50 constituencies would demonstrate serious intent to engage in the rigours of electoral competition at a level that indicates relatively broad appeal for its program and ideas. Moreover, experience since 1974 shows that this level is neither unduly onerous nor too lenient for registration. We believe that this threshold should continue to serve as a benchmark in determining which parties may be registered under the *Canada Elections Act*.

Recommendation 1.5.3

We recommend that

(a) all registered parties, as a condition of registration provide:
(1) the full name of the party;
(2) the party name or the abbreviated identification and logo, if any, of the party to be shown in any election documents, and that these be distinct from any other party currently or formerly registered or that was represented in the House of Commons;
(3) the address of the office where party records are maintained and to which communications may be addressed;
(4) the names and addresses of financial institutions where the party's accounts are kept;
(5) the name and address of the party leader or designated head, who must be a voter;
(6) the names and addresses of the officers of the party, who must be voters;
(7) the name and address of the person who has been appointed auditor of the party;
(8) the name and address of the chief agent of the party;
(9) a statement in writing signed by the persons who are identified as the chief agent and auditor of the party stating that each has accepted the appointment; and
(10) a recent audited financial statement;
(b) a political party be allowed to register at any time before the issue of the writs by:
(1) satisfying the administrative requirements for registration;
(2) submitting its constitution and by-laws, which must be in accordance with the requirements of the *Canada Elections Act* and duly adopted by a general meeting of members;
(3) undertaking to nominate candidates in at least 50 constituencies for the subsequent federal election; and
(4) submitting the declared support of 5000 voters who are members in good standing of the party;
(c) a political party that has nominated candidates in at least 50 constituencies in the most recent federal election or that is recognized as a parliamentary party under the *Parliament of Canada Act*, qualify automatically as a registered party by:
(1) filing for registration;
(2) satisfying the above administrative requirements for registration; and

(3) submitting its constitution and by-laws which must be in accordance with the requirements of the *Canada Elections Act* and duly adopted by a general meeting of members; and

(d) the Canada Elections Commission not accept the application for registration nor register a political party during the period from the close of nominations to election day.

Under the current legislation, political parties can be deleted from the registry maintained by the chief electoral officer. The Act gives the chief electoral officer little discretion other than complete deregistration when enforcing or interpreting the Act for minor infractions of the Act or of electoral regulations. In some instances, deregistration may be a response that is either too sweeping or too impractical. Therefore, it would be appropriate for the Canada Elections Commission to have intermediate sanctions available that fall short of deletion as well as the authority to de-register political parties when warranted.

Recommendation 1.5.4

We recommend that

(a) the Canada Elections Commission have the power to suspend the registration of a political party for any period;

(b) a registered party be subject to suspension when it is determined that it has violated conditions of its registration;

(c) a registered party be subject to deregistration if the Commission deems the party has violated terms of its constitution or failed to comply with the requirements of the Act;

(d) a registered party be automatically suspended if it nominates candidates in fewer than 50 constituencies; and

(e) a registered party, including a parliamentary party recognized under the *Parliament of Canada Act*, be allowed to have its party name placed on the ballot if the party fails to nominate candidates in at least 50 constituencies, but nominates candidates in at least 15 constituencies.

As under the present legislation, deregistration could take place at the written request of the leader and official agent of the party. In all cases of deregistration, monies remaining in the party's accounts after payment of all outstanding liabilities would revert to the public treasury. In Volume 2, Chapter 6 we outline in detail the deregistration procedures that should apply to political parties.

Registration of Constituency Associations
The registration of constituency associations was among the issues addressed by the Accounting Profession Working Group on Election/Party Finance

Reporting at the Local Level (the mandate and composition of the Working Group are described in Volume 2, Chapter 6). We agree with the Working Group's recommendation that, once the relevant legislation comes into effect, every constituency association of a registered political party be obliged to register. Without such a requirement, major gaps would remain in public accountability for financial activities, including accountability for funds that may have benefited from public subsidy, notably surpluses from candidates. Of course, the opportunity to issue tax receipts for contributions would provide an incentive for associations to register. This is not sufficient, however. Mandatory registration is necessary to ensure complete disclosure and to eliminate doubts that this has been done.

Once registered, constituency associations should be allowed to issue income tax receipts. Constituency associations of unregistered parties, however, should not be allowed to register. Registration requirements are intended in part to ensure that parties meet certain standards before they benefit from public funding and the right to issue income tax receipts. To allow constituency associations of unregistered parties access to that benefit would be inconsistent with both the principles underlying registration and the responsibilities entrusted to the registered parties; moreover, it would enable such associations to act as a conduit for funds destined for an unregistered national party. However, an exception should be provided for the constituency association of an independent Member of Parliament. This is discussed in Chapter 6 of this volume.

Recommendation 1.5.5

We recommend that

(a) **all constituency associations of registered parties be required to register with the Canada Elections Commission;**
(b) **the Commission register only constituency associations of registered parties;**
(c) **constituency associations be allowed to issue income tax receipts as long as their registration remains valid and they are in compliance with the requirements of the Act; and**
(d) **the Canada Elections Commission register only one association of a registered party in each constituency.**

Application for Registration
Like political parties, constituency associations wanting to register should file an application with sufficient information to allow an accurate registry to be maintained and to ensure ongoing enforcement of the reporting requirements. The Accounting Profession Working Group recommended a list of items to be included in a constituency association's application for registration. (Canada, Royal Commission 1991a) The four provinces that

provide for the mandatory registration of constituency associations also have requirements for applications. A summary of these requirements is found in the appendix to this chapter.

Recommendation 1.5.6

We recommend that

(a) **the application for registration of a constituency associa-**
    tion include the following information:
    (1) the name of the constituency association and the written
    endorsement of the registered party;
    (2) the constitution of the constituency association, which
    must be in accordance with the requirements of the Act and
    have been adopted by a general meeting of members;
    (3) the name and address of the president of the constituency
    association;
    (4) the name and address of the constituency agent and the
    auditor of the association;
    (5) the address where the association's accounting records
    are kept;
    (6) the name and address of financial institutions where
    the association's accounts are kept;
    (7) a written statement from the constituency agent and
    auditor stating that each agrees to act; and
    (8) a statement of the assets, liabilities and any surplus of
    the constituency association;
(b) **if an application is satisfactory, the information be entered**
    in a registry of constituency associations maintained by the
    Canada Elections Commission, and both the association and
    endorsing party be informed that it has been registered; and
(c) **constituency associations be obliged to notify the Canada**
    Elections Commission promptly of any changes to their
    registration information.

The endorsement of the registered party would be essential for the registration of constituency associations, because there might be cases when two or more groups of party members in a constituency organize associations and apply for registration. In such circumstances, it should be up to the registered party, not the Canada Elections Commission, to determine which association should be registered in that constituency.

Requiring the association to submit its constitution would provide evidence that the association is a validly formed organization. Items 3, 4, 5 and 6 in recommendation 1.5.6 are straightforward and similar to the requirements under the Ontario and Alberta legislation. This information is important for officials of the Canada Elections Commission to answer any questions about the regular reports that the constituency association would be required to file. Like a candidate's official agent, the constituency agent would be the linchpin of the association's financial activities, and with the auditor, would ensure accountability. Under the *Canada Elections Act*, official agents and auditors are required to provide a written statement indicating they have agreed to act; the same requirement (item 7) should apply to the agents and auditors of constituency associations. Finally, as part of its registration application, the association should report its assets, liabilities and any surplus as of the date the application is prepared. These represent the financial resources of the association, some of which may be made available to a candidate during elections, and thus must be accounted for appropriately. The legislation in Ontario and Alberta has similar requirements.

The Canada Elections Commission should have 60 days to review applications for completeness. If there were problems with an application, an official of the Commission would notify the association and the registered party. Notifying the latter is consistent with the party's role in recommending registration and deregistration. If the association could not remedy the problem, it should not be registered. Once the application is judged complete, the association's registration would take effect.

Deregistration of Constituency Associations

The law must provide for the deregistration of constituency associations in certain circumstances. First, associations should not remain registered if the party itself has been de-registered. If they did, they could continue to issue tax receipts, which would be inconsistent and unacceptable. Second, the national party should be allowed to request the deregistration of any of its associations. This could be important, for example, if the executive of an association lost the confidence of local party members and the national party supported the formation of a new association. Because the law would allow only one association of each party to register in a given constituency, parties would need a way of having the former association de-registered, otherwise it would not be possible to register a new one. Third, constituency boundary readjustments could eliminate or combine constituency party organizations, which would require the registry to be adjusted accordingly. Fourth, to ensure registered constituency associations fully respect the constitution they submit as a condition of registration, the sanction of deregistration should be available to the Commission to respond to serious breaches of its terms.

Finally, we propose that deregistration be used if the association violates the Act. For example, if the association's agent fails to submit any of the financial returns required by law, the Commission could suspend its registration for not less than 30 days up to an indefinite period. If the error is not corrected, the association would be de-registered.

As we discuss in Volume 2, Chapter 6, if a constituency association were de-registered at the request of the endorsing party, any association funds would be held in trust by the party until a new constituency association is registered. Similarly, if an association is de-registered as a result of a political party losing its registered status, any funds of the association not required to pay any outstanding liabilities would be paid to the Canada Elections Commission and held in trust.

Recommendation 1.5.7

We recommend that a constituency association be de-registered when:
(1) the national party is de-registered;
(2) the registered party asks for an association to be de-registered;
(3) the boundaries of the constituency are adjusted so that the association disappears or is merged with one or more other constituency associations; or
(4) the constituency association violates the terms of its constitution or fails to comply with the requirements of the *Canada Elections Act*.

Political Parties and Ballot Identification
In recent federal elections, a small number of parties have been unable to meet the registration requirement of nominating candidates in 50 constituencies. These parties have nominated candidates for federal elections in the past, but their inability to nominate at least 50 has denied them the opportunity to have the party name on the ballot beside their candidates' name. Some of these parties have been committed to electoral competition over several elections. In the 1988 election, about half the 154 candidates without their party affiliation specified on the ballot were actually candidates for unregistered parties. These candidates were not permitted to have their party name placed on the ballot. Candidates may be identified on the ballot as independent, but if they are candidates of an unregistered political party, no identification is provided and they are considered 'non-affiliated'.

The absence of unregistered parties' names from the ballot has two consequences. First, these parties lose the opportunity to present clear choices to voters, because the public is unaware that the parties have nominated candidates to act as standard bearers for their ideas and policies. Second, voters are deprived of the opportunity to make a full assessment of the choices they are offered. If the smaller parties had their names on the ballot, voters would be better informed about candidates' ideas and policies, as expressed through their parties. The electoral law can be amended to allow the smaller parties to have their names on the ballot, while retaining procedures to ensure that parties applying for this privilege have some measure of public support and are committed to electoral competition. These parties would not be able to issue tax receipts for financial contributions, nor would they qualify for reimbursement of election expenses; however, during the election period, their candidates would. In sum, the electoral law should be amended to recognize the legitimacy of these smaller parties in the electoral process.

Recommendation 1.5.8

We recommend that a political party be entitled to be identified on a ballot beside the name of its candidates in a general election and any election that follows until the next general election if:
(1) it satisfies the administrative requirements identified in recommendation 1.5.3;
(2) the leader of the party is a voter;
(3) the name of the political party is distinct from any other party currently or formerly registered or represented in the House of Commons; and
(4) it endorses candidates in at least 15 constituencies in the general election by the close of nominations.

THE SELECTION OF CANDIDATES AND LEADERS BY POLITICAL PARTIES

Our system of government requires that the prime minister and the cabinet have the support of a majority of members in the House of Commons. In practice, this means that party government is the operative dynamic. Under party government, members of the House of Commons organize themselves as members of parliamentary parties that support or oppose the prime minister and cabinet. This has had a profound influence on the procedures adopted by parties to nominate candidates and select leaders.

Candidate Selection

Elections to the House of Commons are essentially contests among the candidates of competing political parties. This is recognized in our electoral law, which allows candidates of registered political parties to be identified on the ballot. This recognition is reinforced by the requirement that all such candidates be confirmed officially by the party leader.

The selection of candidates by political parties is one of the most fundamental functions that parties perform. It distinguishes them from all other types of organizations that bring individuals together to promote common political ideas, interests and values. As R.K. Carty and Lynda Erickson put it, "It is through this process of labelling candidates that parties ... make their principal contribution to the conduct of electoral democracy and responsible government as it is practised in Canada." (1991 RC)

As a result of the parties' constitutional arrangements, the candidate selection process is primarily a function of the local constituency associations. Each constituency association decides not only who will be its candidate, but also when and by what procedures candidates will be selected. In performing this function, local associations are primarily responsible for the degree to which citizens can exercise their constitutional right to be a candidate. Although candidates of smaller or new political parties – and even independent candidates – are occasionally elected to the House of Commons, the vast majority of elections are contests between the candidates of the largest parties. Securing nomination by one of these parties is thus the normal access to electoral politics and membership in the House of Commons.

During our public hearings, we heard from a large number of interveners who were critical of the candidate selection process in the large national political parties. They argued that the democratic qualities of the process have been undermined by recent practices. Individuals and groups from many backgrounds and experiences claimed that selection processes have become too exclusionary, too expensive and too open to abuse by local party elites or narrowly defined interest groups. For these interveners, the practices used by local party organizations to select candidates do not advance, and may even violate, the principle of fairness that is crucial to the integrity of the electoral process. Many concluded that these objectives could be realized only by extending federal electoral law to include the candidate selection processes.

Historical Development

The development of national political parties in the decades immediately following Confederation stands as one of the most significant accomplishments of Canada's first political leaders.

The success of Sir John A. Macdonald and Sir Wilfrid Laurier was due to their recognition of the need to build their parties both inside and outside Parliament. This was no mean feat; as David Smith has noted, "the centre of gravity of the post-Confederation parties was located in the constituencies". (1985, 10) The single-member constituency basis of the electoral system, which predated the emergence of national political parties, combined with what Smith describes as the "intense localism" that characterized political life, required these leaders to build from the ground up.

During the first half-century after Confederation, party adherents met to select their party's candidates whenever this was necessary, but formal party membership did not exist. The formulation of party policy and the selection of the party leader were the prerogatives of the parliamentary party, that is, the caucus of Members of Parliament in each party.

The informal character of the extra-parliamentary party led to candidate selection being remarkably open to local party supporters. In contrast to the practices of their British counterparts, the two national parties did not recruit candidates on a national basis, or exercise national party control over the local nomination of candidates. (Carty and Erickson 1991 RC) As a consequence, these two parties also differed from the British parties in that candidates were selected almost exclusively from among local party adherents.

These features of candidate selection were gradually altered in the second decade of this century. Several factors promoted this development. First, the two largest national parties increasingly sought to have candidates in all constituencies. This meant that efforts had to be made in areas where the party was electorally weak, or where the local party was unable or even unwilling to field a candidate. These efforts obviously required a greater role by the national party in recruiting, if not formally selecting candidates. These efforts were further stimulated by the advent of radio broadcasting as an election campaign instrument, especially as regulated access to this new medium included incentives for parties to nominate as many candidates as possible.

Second, the Liberal Party developed the practice of regional ministers assuming an increasingly interventionist role in recruiting and selecting candidates in the local areas within their informal, but nevertheless real, spheres of influence. (Whitaker 1977; Meisel 1962) Third, the emergence of a third national party, the Co-operative Commonwealth Federation, brought with it centralized control in the candidate selection process, exercised by the provincial councils of this national party over local party associations. This was deemed necessary to prevent "infiltration [by] Communists".(Carty and Erickson 1991 RC)

Developments in the national parties themselves were even more significant. In the 1960s, the increasingly active role of national party associations in leadership selection and review, as well as in party policy discussions, resulted in increased competition for appointment as delegates to national party conventions within local party associations. These changes coincided with a greater recognition of political parties in the electoral law. For instance, reforms to federal electoral law in the 1970s allowed registered national political parties to be identified on the ballot next to the names of candidates. This required the national leader of a registered party to endorse the nomination of a local association as the party's official candidate. In addition, reforms to election finance law concerning reimbursement of election expenses further increased the advantages of running complete slates of candidates across the country.

As a consequence, the candidate selection process of the national parties has become more formalized and thus more restricted. As late as 1962, Howard Scarrow could still report that open nomination conventions, in which all interested voters could participate, were still common. However, the practice of open conventions to select candidates was gradually abandoned with the adoption of formal membership requirements. (Scarrow 1964) By the 1988 election, almost all local constituency associations of the Progressive Conservative, Liberal and New Democratic parties stipulated that only individuals who held valid party memberships, as defined and prescribed by the local association, could participate in selecting the local party candidate. (Carty and Erickson 1991 RC)

This evolution of candidate selection was characterized by increasingly formalized and structured processes at the local level. In part, this was the result of similar developments in national party associations. There is competition within local constituency associations over candidate selection and the selection of delegates to national leadership and policy conventions. This has meant a tightening of the rules of membership and the procedures governing decision making by the membership to ensure that factions or advocacy groups do not control the process, and that a certain degree of fairness prevails.

Local constituency associations in the large national parties have not generally become centres of great activity, however, let alone of intense intra-party competition. In many cases, the local association still finds itself in the position of having to search for a prospective candidate for nomination. And in many local associations, the executive can still exert considerable influence, if not dominance, over the candidate recruitment and selection process without much reaction from the party membership. Finally, incumbent MPs are infrequently challenged for their party's nomination. Thus the local autonomy that has characterized candidate selection has in some large measure been the result of the low degree of competition for party nominations.

International Comparisons

Candidate selection is the key stage in the political recruitment process. The rules and procedures used by political parties to select candidates indicate the priority they attach to democratic and representational values. The degree to which national parties are able to apply national objectives and standards also indicates the commitment of parties to recruiting and selecting candidates who represent different segments of society. Canada's experience contrasts sharply with that of most comparable political systems where national parties have a much stronger role.

In many countries, the selection of party candidates is either regulated extensively by law, as in the United States and Germany, or more centrally controlled by the parties, as in Great Britain. The United States and Germany, for different reasons, have intervened to ensure that the procedures for selecting candidates adhere to democratic principles. In the United States, this regulatory approach was imposed on political parties by judicial decisions that incorporated candidate selection into the electoral process. In Germany, the *Basic Law* adopted after the Second World War requires political parties to be democratic in their processes and procedures, and the electoral law spells out what this means for parties when they select candidates.

The imposition of democratic procedures on U.S. political parties resulted, in the first decades of the present century, from reactions to widespread political corruption, and more particularly, to the manipulation of the candidate selection process by both Republican and Democratic party bosses.

Public demands for reform resulted in state legislatures enacting detailed regulations for candidate nomination. Public regulation was seen as the only defensible response to the failure of the political parties to ensure that nominations were managed democratically.

As a result of a series of court decisions known as the *White Primary Cases* made between 1927 and 1953, parties in the United States were prevented from restricting access to the primaries. Following the *White Primary Cases*, most commentators and lower courts have concluded that any party limitation on participation involving the candidate selection process can be subject to constitutional restraints. In *Storer* (1974, 735) the U.S. Supreme Court termed primary elections "not merely an exercise or warm-up for the general election but an integral part of the electoral process". Various court rulings, on the other hand, have prevented state legislatures from regulating the internal processes of party conventions in the absence of a compelling state interest. (Feigenbaum and Palmer 1988, 15–16)

Candidates in 44 U.S. states are now selected through open or closed primaries. (Feigenbaum and Palmer 1988, 15) In open primaries, registered voters can select candidates for the Republican or Democratic party without formally declaring their party preference. In closed primaries, voters must state whether they will vote for Democratic or Republican candidates. Thirty-eight states use closed primaries, six use open primaries, and the remaining six use party conventions or caucuses. All states using primaries also have laws regulating their timing and administration. In every case, only registered voters may participate. As a consequence, national and state party organizations have a nominal role in candidate selection. Those seeking nomination, therefore, must establish their own campaign organizations to mobilize support and raise money.

In Germany, candidates can be elected to the federal Bundestag in one of two ways. Of the 496 seats in the Bundestag, half (248) are filled from single-member constituencies, using a plurality voting system, just as in Canada. The other half are filled from candidates on party lists, using a system of proportional representation.

Germany's *Party Law* requires parties to nominate candidates by secret ballot, specific details of which are found in the *Electoral Law*. Constituency candidates must be nominated by a meeting of the general membership of the local constituency association or by delegates elected by the membership.

Although the individual parties can implement specific nomination rules and procedures, they are required to submit a complete account of the nomination convention to the constituency returning officer. The returning officer must review the nomination process to ensure that administrative and procedural rules have been respected. Parties have access to an extensive appeal process if they believe a returning officer has made an unwarranted ruling. (Roberts 1988)

In most other countries, the state does not impose a regulatory framework on candidate selection. However, with only a few exceptions, national or central party organizations have a major role in the selection process. The exceptions include Belgium and, to a lesser extent, Australia where the candidate selection process is managed at the state level.

In Great Britain, the recruitment process is administered by the national parties. Although nominations are the prerogative of local constituency associations, candidates must be endorsed by the national parties, which maintain lists of eligible candidates who may apply to local constituency associations if they want to seek election. All applicants are first screened by the national parties. Those who pass the initial stage are subject to extensive scrutiny by local party representatives.

A local selection committee decides which contestant will be nominated in a specific constituency. As in Canada, there is a strong tradition of local autonomy in the selection process, to the point where "local party activists tend to be suspicious of their national organizations and jealously guard their right of selection". (Denver 1988, 58) Membership on the local selection committees varies from 20 to 25 members and includes the executive of the local constituency association. In the case of the Labour Party, it also includes representatives from the constituent parts of the party (for example, women, youth and trade union organizations).

Candidates seeking nomination must submit a formal application to the selection committee. The number of applicants depends on whether the constituency is considered a safe party seat, a marginal seat or a hopeless seat. When a nomination in a Conservative Party safe seat becomes available, the number of applicants may be 200 to 300; for marginal seats between 50 and 100 candidates usually apply; and even for hopeless seats, there are often 15 to 30 applicants. A similar number apply for Labour Party nominations. Once applications are received, the local selection committee screens the applicants until 20 or so remain. The 20 are interviewed by the committee, which selects a short list of three or four. Committee members hold a secret ballot, and the applicant who receives the most votes becomes the constituency association's candidate. National and regional party representatives frequently monitor the selection process to ensure that the party's rules and procedures are respected. An applicant can appeal the choice of the local selection committee if the rules are violated. Candidates selected by local committees must then be approved by the national party organization.

Unlike Canada, where candidates are selected through party conventions, most political parties in western democracies such as Great Britain and Germany, restrict the selection process to a small group of constituency members – either a delegate convention or a local constituency committee. (Gallagher 1988, 240) The national organization in most parties must also give formal approval to a nominated candidate. In Italy and Ireland, the national executive of a political party often adds the names of candidates to the lists selected by local associations. (Gallagher 1988, 240–42) In New Zealand, the national party holds half the positions on local selection committees.

Candidate Selection Process in the 1988 Federal General Election

Decentralized candidate selection processes in Canada have resulted in a wide array of procedures and practices. Moreover, less is known about this aspect of party politics than about any other similarly significant dimension of national politics. The tradition of local autonomy has also meant that, in the absence of national objectives, the national parties have no central reporting requirements on local candidate recruitment and selection procedures or practices. On the basis of a survey of the official agents of candidates in the 1988 general election for the three large national parties, we can identify a number of salient features of candidate selection. The representative sample included just under a third of all associations for the three parties. (Carty and Erickson 1991 RC)

The survey revealed that just over 80 per cent of the nomination contests for all three parties were completed before the writs were issued. Moreover, constituency associations with incumbent MPs seeking re-election were far more likely to hold early nomination conventions. Post-writ nominations were usually held in constituencies where the political parties were electorally weak. In approximately two-thirds of the constituency associations, the timing of nomination conventions was decided by the local party executive; in one-fifth of the associations the full membership selected the date; and in the remaining cases, party officials other than local executives had to convene a nomination convention because in these constituencies, the party was weak or badly organized.

For the 1988 federal election, each of the three large national parties held 295 nomination meetings, for a total of 885. The level of competition varied considerably within each party, and from province to province. Any measurement of the competitiveness of nomination contests must be assessed against the presence of a large number of uncompetitive contests where the parties were either electorally weak or where incumbent MPs were not challenged for the nomination. Almost two-thirds of the nomination races surveyed were uncontested, including 90 per cent of incumbents. Two contestants sought the nomination in 20 per cent of the constituency associations, and three or more contestants competed in almost 15 per cent of constituencies. In constituency associations where there was no incumbent, almost 60 per cent of the party nominations were uncontested.

Although the mobilization of party members is essential to a contestant seeking a nomination, the data indicate that, even in competitive nomination races where there were significant increases in paid membership, the turnout rate for new members attending candidate selection meetings averaged less than 50 per cent. "The simple truth is that, in most cases, the majority of party members do not bother to turn out to vote at nomination meetings, even when they are contested."(Carty and Erickson 1991 RC)

Local membership expanded most rapidly where an incumbent was challenged for the nomination. Even where membership increased for these races, the number of members who actually attended nomination conventions averaged less than a third of the total.

Membership requirements varied considerably among constituencies and parties. Just over half the associations of the three large national parties allowed non-residents of the constituency to vote at nomination conventions. This included a large proportion of Progressive Conservative associations, which in theory were precluded from doing so by the party's national constitution.

Few associations required lengthy membership periods. The majority allowed individuals to vote during the nomination convention if they had held a party membership for between one week and one month. Membership fees varied within and among parties. These minimal membership requirements made it easy for individuals to join the party in order to participate in the candidate selection process.

Half the local constituency associations had formal search committees, including 15 per cent of the associations where an incumbent was seeking re-election. Most associations, however, did not actively seek assistance from national party organizations in recruiting potential nomination contestants. (Carty and Erickson 1991 RC)

Less than 15 per cent of local constituency associations in the three large national parties had guidelines on nomination spending limits. Neither the development nor the enforcement of the spending guidelines were initiated by the central party organizations. Rather, various constituency associations used guidelines at their own discretion. Spending in the constituencies with guidelines, however, was not significantly lower than in constituencies without them.

The mobilization of new party members and the high cost of the small number of competitive nomination races received extensive media scrutiny and coverage in the 1988 federal election. As a result, the candidate selection process acquired a high public profile. Newspaper readers and television viewers were left with the impression that the candidate selection process as a whole was subject to widespread abuse and that large amounts of money were being spent by numerous contestants seeking party nomination.

Carty and Erickson suggest that media coverage of the candidate selection process in the 1988 federal election focused mostly on a small number of competitive nomination races where large amounts of money were spent and controversial practices were used by candidates to mobilize support. The narrow scope of this coverage contributed to public perceptions that the candidate selection process was marked mostly by high spending and abuse of party membership rules. Carty and Erickson (1991 RC) conducted a content analysis of the treatment of candidate selection by *The Globe and Mail*; it is reasonable to suggest that this newspaper's coverage was representative of the other media. The survey of *The Globe and Mail* coverage of the selection process for the four months before the 1988 election was called suggests that its readers were not necessarily given a representative picture of the way in which candidates were nominated (see Table 5.8). Approximately 66 per cent of the stories carried by *The Globe and Mail* about the candidate selection process concerned contested nominations. This figure contrasts with data from the survey of official agents, which indicates that just over 34 per cent of nominations were contested by two or more candidates (Table 5.9). A third of *The Globe and Mail* stories reported on internal party conflicts concerning the accreditation and mobilization of new party members; however, the recruitment of new members led to internal party conflicts in only 9 per cent of nomination contests. Further, approximately 20 per cent of *The Globe and Mail*'s news articles concerned the use of internal party appeal mechanisms to challenge membership rules or nomination results. In reality, less than 6 per cent of the nomination contests involved internal party appeals.

Table 5.8
Media images of party nominations, 1988
(per cent)

The Globe and Mail stories reporting	
Contested nominations	66
Conflicts over mobilization	28
Appeals	19
Local-national conflict	10
Ethnic mobilization	5
Nomination expenses	4
Local issue	0
Total stories	93

Source: Carty and Erickson 1991 RC.

Note: All stories in *The Globe and Mail*, 1 June–30 October 1988, that reported nominations.

Table 5.9
Image v. reality, 1988
(per cent)

Nomination meetings	Press image[a]	Constituency reports[b]
Contested	66	35
Conflicts over recruitment	28	9
Appeals	19	6
Local-national conflict	10	4
Specific issue	0	21

Source: Carty and Erickson 1991 RC.

[a]Press image refers to *The Globe and Mail* reports.
[b]Constituency association survey done by the authors.

This limited but telling examination of *The Globe and Mail* coverage suggests a considerable gap between perceptions of how the candidate selection process functioned in 1988 and actual practices. For example, survey data indicate that only in a small number of highly competitive constituencies was a large amount of money spent by candidates seeking nominations. When supporters were mobilized to become members of a candidate's campaign organization, the average cost was nine times the cost for constituencies where new members were not recruited. An assessment of the candidate selection process must be based on a full understanding of the dynamics and factors shaping the nomination of party candidates, not on inaccurate perceptions of experience. *The Globe and Mail*'s coverage misses an essential point: many of the problems associated with the nomination process – the low proportion of women recruited, for example – stem not from the high level of competition in a limited number of constituency associations, but from the large number of uncompetitive, relatively closed nomination contests conducted by local party insiders.

Canadian political parties stand at one end of the continuum between local responsibility and autonomy for candidate selection on the one hand, and party member participation in candidate selection, on the other. There is no public regulation of these processes, and with the exception of the NDP, there is little in the way of national or provincial party control or influence over the procedures used by local party associations. In comparative terms, Canadian parties are highly decentralized and open, with relatively little direction and control from the national level. While this decentralization stems from a longstanding tradition of localism in party affairs and is frequently praised in those terms, the present structure and its results have raised a number of concerns, particularly regarding the competitiveness and openness of the system.

Close to two-thirds of constituency nomination contests are uncompetitive – that is, the nomination is by acclamation. This contributes to what is perceived to be the closed nature of nominations, because it is often assumed that this outcome is the result of decisions by local executives. Opportunities exist to introduce changes to the candidate selection process that will make it more open, more amenable to grassroots participation and more consistent with democratic principles and processes.

Improving Candidate Selection Rules and Practices

In competitive nomination races, the processes and rules used by local party associations to nominate candidates provide frequent opportunities for abuse. In particular, the membership rules of many constituency associations have allowed campaign organizations for nomination contestants to enlist people for the sole purpose of voting on the day of the nomination convention. In theory, recruiting new members provides the opportunity to rejuvenate the local association by involving new people. It is normal for this process to accelerate around the time of candidate selection and this should be encouraged. However, the practice of these campaign organizations paying the membership fees of 'new members' with no expectation whatsoever that they will remain members afterward raises legitimate questions.

Such enthusiastic mobilization techniques are not new. In a Liberal Party nomination contest in the 1962 federal election, an estimated three-quarters of the 1200 persons attending and voting in the convention to select the association's candidate had no previous party involvement. (Scarrow 1964, 57) In the 1968 election, membership in the Liberal constituency association for Davenport (in the Toronto area) increased "from 150 to 5,445 in a few weeks". As was later observed, "Here, as elsewhere, the outcome [of the nomination] may have been determined by non-residents and ten-year-olds who, under the rules, could not be debarred from voting." (Beck 1968, 401) However, as our hearings indicated, public tolerance for such practices and the rules that allow such behaviour has diminished significantly. Expectations as to proper behaviour are much higher today; parties cannot ignore these new ethical standards. To the degree that abuses related to membership are found in candidate selection contests, the integrity of political parties as primary political organizations are undermined, as is the electoral process itself.

Constituency associations have to adhere to democratic constitutions and procedures for selecting candidates, delegates to national party conventions and their own executive officers. Our recommendation will reinforce this practice now that open party conventions are the norm. At the same time, it will ensure that party members who wish to be nominees for candidacy have their rights protected by the constitutions of constituency associations, including provisions for complaints within the party locally, provincially and nationally, and, where necessary, to the Canada Elections Commission. The critical relationship between open party conventions and our objective of enhancing access to elected office requires that this approach be strengthened.

Recommendation 1.5.9

We recommend that the candidate nominated by a registered constituency association be selected by an open convention of members held for this express purpose.

The second matter that needs to be considered in regard to these conventions concerns the right of party members at the local association level to participate in the selection and therefore the nomination of candidates. At present, rules governing who may participate in this crucial function vary within and among the large national parties. Practices also may vary from the formal constitutions of the national party or local associations. At the same time, under the *Canada Elections Act*, a candidate must be nominated by at least 25 persons who are "qualified as electors in an electoral district in which an election is to be held". (s. 80) This occurs after the local association has made its choice at a convention.

The import of this section of the Act lies in its recognition that candidates, who must be voters, should be nominated by their peers, that is, by other voters. In other words, those who wish to nominate a candidate in a constituency must be qualified as voters in the constituency wherein the candidate is nominated. This is consistent with the principles embodied in the electoral process, given its basis in territorially defined electoral constituencies. It restricts the capacity to nominate a candidate to those who will be affected by the local election. It also is fair to those who wish to be candidates, because it means that only voters of a nomination contestant's constituency would be involved in nomination.

This traditional approach to nomination, as found in the *Canada Elections Act* and the political principles underlying it, has not informed the practices of the local associations of our larger parties. It is not surprising that many have questioned the integrity and fairness of these practices. Integrity is questioned whenever the responsibilities of party associations are not taken seriously. Fairness is undermined whenever it is possible to manipulate rules to serve the interests of some at the expense of others.

At the local and national level, parties have every right to be as inclusive as they wish in their general membership. Thus they can allow non-citizens, those under the voting age and, at the constituency level, people who do not reside in the constituency to be members and to participate in the affairs of the association. Local associations also have every right to promote competition for party candidacy to ensure that the eventual candidate has the broadest possible base of support within the party. At the same time, certain basic norms of democratic citizenship, as exercised through political parties, must be protected and enhanced. The right to select candidates for federal elections should therefore be reserved for those members of an association who are voters, as we recommend in recommendation 1.5.2.

In chapters 6 and 7 of this volume, we recommend changes to the candidate selection process and to election finance laws affecting candidates for the House of Commons. These changes are designed to affirm the principle of fairness in electoral competition and to promote the integrity of the electoral process. Among the most salient recommendations are: full disclosure requirements, spending limits for the candidate selection process and more timely and comprehensive reporting on the size, source and use of political contributions for candidates seeking election to the House of Commons. The recommendations are guided by the central assumption that election finance laws are a critical determinant in the degree to which the candidate selection process is both accessible and founded on democratic principles and processes.

Endorsement of Candidates by Political Parties

Section 81(1)(*h*) of the *Canada Elections Act* requires candidates wanting to use the name and logo of a specific party on election documents to have the official endorsement of that registered party through a statement signed by either the party leader or by a designate. The primary purpose of this requirement is to ensure that party names and logos are not abused by candidates not associated with the registered political party they may claim to represent. This measure contributes to the integrity of the electoral process by ensuring that party names and logos are used to affirm the distinct ideas and values of individual parties, and that the names and logos are not used to mislead voters in their electoral choices. Consequently, this requirement should remain; however, the endorsement of the candidates by the registered party need not be restricted to the party leader or the leader's designate. The party may choose to assign this function to a person designated by its governing body.

These concerns extend beyond registered political parties. We recommend that political parties that are not registered but that nominate candidates in at least 15 constituencies have their name placed on the election ballot. As noted, a number of candidates representing small political parties in recent elections were not identified as such, since their parties were not officially registered because they did not nominate candidates in at least 50 constituencies. By having the name of these parties on the election ballot, voters would be able to assess more precisely the partisan affiliation of candidates. In short, the name of the party should be used at the exclusive discretion of the party. Consequently, the requirement that candidates representing political parties be endorsed by that party should also be extended to parties qualifying for ballot identification only.

Recommendation 1.5.10

We recommend that candidates of a registered political party or of a party that has qualified for ballot identification who want to use the party name, logo or abbreviated identification on election documents have the written endorsement of either the party leader, his or her designate or a person designated by the governing body of the party.

Reducing Representational Deficits

As discussed in Chapter 3 of this volume, important segments of our society are underrepresented in the House of Commons. A measure of underrepresentation, as defined by the percentage of MPs from different groups relative to their demographic weight, is presented in Table 5.10. According to this measure, women have an electoral representation ratio of 26 per cent: they constitute a majority of the population but only 13.2 per cent of the sitting MPs in 1988 were women.

Table 5.10
Representational deficit of certain groups of Canadians in the House of Commons
(per cent)

Groups of Canadians	Percentage of total population[a]	1984	1988
Women	51.0	19.4	25.9
Ethno-cultural groups (visible minorities excluded)	15.4	94.2	92.2
Visible minorities only	6.3	17.5	31.7
Aboriginal peoples	3.0[b]	21.1	28.6

Source: Young 1991a RC; A. Pelletier 1991 RC; and Royal Commission Research Branch.

Note: Representational deficits are calculated as the ratio of the percentage of MPs from each of the groups identified above relative to their percentage of the Canadian population.

[a]Based on the 1986 census.
[b]Includes single and multiple origins for Métis, Indian and Inuit.

These data underscore the fact that the representational deficit for women is the most extreme. The representation of women shows not only a significant deficit, but also that this deficit has persisted over the seven decades since they first received the franchise. Furthermore, their underrepresentation cuts across all other segments of society. Among ethno-cultural groups, only six of 121 (5 per cent) ethno-cultural MPs elected since 1965 were women. In 1988, only two of 48 women candidates from ethno-cultural groups were elected. As discussed previously, this serious underrepresentation of a significant portion of society has important implications. The legitimacy of our democratic institutions suffers as a consequence. As well, there is a legitimate public interest in having equitable representation so that public policy is sensitive to the concerns and interests of various segments of society. It is generally accepted, for instance, that women have different policy perspectives that are not sufficiently reflected in legislatures and parliaments.

The failure to achieve greater representativeness within the House of Commons, particularly for women, is an index of the pervasiveness of systemic discrimination within our society. Even though they may not be overtly or intentionally discriminatory, political parties, particularly at the local level, contribute to this inequity through their attitudes, behaviour and organizational practices. Not surprisingly, throughout our public hearings, symposiums, consultations and research, we have been urged to address the problem of underrepresentation through reforms relating to access to elected office. These demands have centred on two major aspects of the electoral process: the barriers that individuals face in seeking elected office, and the rules and practices of constituency associations.

Our recommendations respond to these demands for more equitable representation with measures described in detail in Chapter 3 and in this chapter. In particular, we target the nomination stage, which interveners and research identified as the most significant barrier to entry to the House of Commons. Inspired by the 1974 electoral reform, which established limits on election expenditures and clearly secured greater fairness in the electoral process, we recommend parallel measures for the candidate selection process (see Volume 1, Chapter 6). Specifically, for the nomination stage we recommend the adoption of spending limits as well as income tax credits to remove or ease the financial barriers that may be faced by persons seeking nomination. Given that women continue to remain, for the most part, the primary caretakers for children, we also recommend that child care expenses be deductible for those seeking candidacy during the nomination period, and for candidates during the writ period. Finally, we propose that the right to candidacy be protected by establishing in law the right of employees to obtain a leave of absence to seek nomination and be a candidate.

The above measures are aimed at individuals seeking nomination. In addition, constituency association rules and processes to enhance the inclusion of women in the electoral process must also be reformed. Given the central role of constituency associations in identifying and recruiting prospective candidates, we recommend that local constituency associations be required to commit themselves to recruitment processes that demonstrably promote the identification and nomination of candidates from a broad cross-section of Canadians. The evidence is compelling: rigorous and systematic search procedures generally lead to the identification of more qualified and more representative candidates. Further, these procedures do not compromise the openness or competitiveness of the selection process; on the contrary, they ensure a broader choice of potential candidates.

In addition, we recommend rules to govern the eligibility of those voting in nomination meetings, that is, residency, citizenship and age requirements. The absence of such rules or their inconsistent application has, in some instances, led to abuses that have tended to disproportionately affect candidates from underrepresented groups, and thus to dissuade potential candidates from these groups from seeking nomination.

We also recommend measures to increase the presence in the House of Commons of the two other underrepresented groups: visible minorities and Aboriginal peoples. These measures include the criteria and processes of developing constituency boundaries, which emphasize the recognition of communities of interest, and the guarantee of a process for the creation of Aboriginal constituencies, as outlined in Chapter 4 of this volume.

Our recommendations to enhance the representational profile of the House of Commons respond to the concerns and suggestions advanced in our public hearings, seminars and discussions with representatives of the above groups and practitioners. The consensus is that these reforms in themselves should operate to redress representational deficits, particularly those of women, by reducing the barriers that lead to systemic discrimination.

The effects of the 1974 reforms were immediate and conclusive. Limits on election expenditures and the ability to issue tax receipts for political contributions promoted greater fairness and encouraged more vigorous competition. No candidate could win simply by overpowering his or her rivals financially. There are good reasons to expect our proposed changes to have a similar impact on the nomination process by the next election. Further, political parties have become increasingly active in increasing the representation of women. The large national parties offer training sessions as well as other types of assistance to potential candidates. Parties' continued efforts in this direction will accelerate the impact of our recommendations by increasing the presence of women in the House of Commons. Some additional measures that parties could adopt include: greater training for candidates in public speaking; greater information on policy issues, particularly for those from underrepresented groups; training in fund-raising techniques and computer-related technology; training in cross-cultural understanding for all elected members; and outreach programs for underrepresented groups, notably for women from visible minority communities.

Our philosophy in addressing the underrepresentation of women in the House of Commons has been guided by a desire to respond to the practical suggestions proposed both by women's groups at our public hearings and political practitioners at our symposium on the active participation of women in politics. Our proposals are not unduly intrusive in the affairs of political parties, and they strengthen open competition and equality in both the nomination and election processes. They are also expected to be effective in increasing the number of women MPs.

It is possible, nonetheless, that the potential effects of our proposed framework are overestimated. Systemic discrimination may be so engrained in the attitudes and practices of our political parties that it requires a more determined approach by the leadership of the parties. The political leadership of a party can shape party attitudes and organizational behaviour and thus influence the representational profile of its caucus in the House of Commons. Should the significant underrepresentation of women persist following the next election, it will be necessary to revisit the measures required to correct the historical inequities resulting from systemic discrimination.

International experience shows that the most powerful tools for increasing the representation of women involve mandatory measures, especially quotas. It is the prerogative of each political party to impose such a system internally, but the electoral law should avoid such an approach. However, approaches used in other organizations can be instructive in suggesting measures that would encourage the adoption of behaviour that promotes greater representational equity. They generally enhance rather than diminish the quality of candidates selected.

For example, universities now identify applicants on entrance exams by number only; similarly, symphony orchestras carry out blind auditions with the musicians concealed from the judges. These procedures, which ensure that the evaluation of candidates is solely based on the quality of the performance and not influenced by sex, have resulted almost immediately in the selection of a greater number of women. Hence, such procedures have not only eliminated systemic discrimination, but also have improved the overall quality of the successful candidates.

At the federal level and in several provinces, government contracts are subject to employment equity provisions. For example, since 1986, the federal government has had a policy on employment equity for suppliers to Supply and Services Canada: with some exceptions, contracts of a certain size must be awarded to suppliers who meet prescribed employment equity requirements. (Canada, Supply and Services Canada 1990) Another example of policy that helps bring about change is in workers' compensation. Many provinces determine workers' compensation premiums similarly to the way in which the insurance industry calculates premiums. Employers having a history of accidents below the industry average benefit from lower premiums, whereas those who do not conform to certain minimum standards of health and safety for their employees are penalized. The evidence shows that even in highly decentralized situations, organizations are able to engineer a change in attitudes and a new awareness of safer conduct which result in a lower incidence of accidents. Such approaches have proved to be highly effective in achieving desired outcomes in a variety of organizations. There is no reason to assume that parties would not respond to similar incentives, if analogous measures were adopted.

Therefore, should the overall percentage of women in the House of Commons be below 20 per cent following the next federal election, we propose that an incentive be adopted whereby registered political parties would receive an additional reimbursement based on the proportion of female MPs in their House of Commons caucus. The Canadian Advisory Council on the Status of Women offered a similar proposal to encourage greater participation of women in the electoral process: to increase the reimbursement of election expenses of registered political parties fielding a certain percentage of women candidates. (Brief, June 1990)

This provision would be applied as follows: if at either of the next two elections the percentage of women in the House of Commons has not reached 20 per cent, any party with at least 20 per cent of its House of Commons caucus consisting of women MPs would be eligible for a higher rate of election reimbursement. This increased level of reimbursement would be equal to the percentage of that party's representation of women. For example, a party with 25 per cent women MPs would receive an election reimbursement equal to 125 per cent of the reimbursement to which it would otherwise have been entitled. The bonus would be capped for each party at 150 per cent. The measure would be dropped when the overall percentage of women in the House of Commons reached 40 per cent. It would be valid only for the two elections following the next general election. How the parties pursued the objective of increasing the representation of women in the House of Commons would be up to them; the law would not impose mandatory requirements on political parties. In other words, the focus of this approach would be on outcome, not on process. It recognizes that the parties face different issues, and that their constitutions, organizations, structures, traditions and practices vary. Finally, given that the dynamics of such a system are difficult to predict precisely, we recommend that the Canada Elections Commission review this measure after the third election, if still in place, and the Commission recommend to Parliament whether it should be retained or adjusted.

Recommendation 1.5.11

We recommend that should the overall percentage of women in the House of Commons be below 20 per cent following either of the next two elections, then:
(1) at the two elections following the next election, the reimbursement of each registered political party with at least 20 per cent female MPs be increased by an amount equivalent to the percentage of its women MPs up to a maximum of 150 per cent;
(2) this measure be automatically eliminated once the overall percentage of women in the House of Commons has attained 40 per cent; and
(3) following the third election, if this measure is still in place, the Canada Elections Commission review it and recommend to Parliament whether it should be retained or adjusted.

Leadership Selection

Historical Background
The evolution of the leadership selection processes can be divided into three phases. The first phase was in the early post-Confederation period, when the selection of national party leaders was modelled on British practices. National leaders from Sir John A. Macdonald to Arthur Meighen in the Conservative Party, and from Alexander Mackenzie to Sir Wilfrid Laurier in the Liberal Party, were selected by the retiring party leader in consultation with senior party notables, caucus members and, most crucially, with the Governor General.

The formal selection of the prime minister, and consequently the leader of the governing party, was seen as the prerogative of the Governor General. In 1896, for example, the Governor General Lord Aberdeen resisted pressures from the Conservative Party to have Sir Charles Tupper replace Mackenzie Bowell as leader. Although Bowell had been discredited within his own party, the Governor General was "determined not to see Tupper as the first minister". (Courtney 1973, 37) The Conservative Party caucus persisted in its support for Tupper and Aberdeen agreed to appoint him prime minister. John Courtney suggests (1973, 39), "1896 was, for good reason, a key year in Canadian party politics, in so far as the governing party asserted with some success a claim to choose its own leader ... independent of vice-regal wishes".

The role of the parliamentary caucus in leadership selection increased significantly when the Liberal Party was in opposition. Following the party's defeat in the 1878 election, Liberal MPs pressured Alexander Mackenzie to resign. Mackenzie did so, and the caucus voted in Edward Blake as his successor. Laurier was selected Liberal leader in a similar fashion in 1887.

The second phase of the leadership selection process began with the election of Mackenzie King as Liberal leader at a national party convention in 1919. For the first time, the extra-parliamentary wing of a national party played a pivotal role in the selection of a leader. The move to a national leadership convention was partly a response by the party establishment to the deep divisions that had developed within the Liberal Party following the conscription crisis of the First World War. The party's parliamentary caucus was dominated by MPs from Quebec; Laurier felt it important that his successor should come from English Canada so that the Liberals would not be reduced to a regional party from Quebec in the next federal election. This objective could not be met if the parliamentary caucus selected an MP from Quebec as Laurier's successor. Laurier's experience with the Liberals' national policy convention of 1893 had "convinced him of its worth as a vehicle for uniting and strengthening the party". (Courtney 1973, 60) With support from key members of the parliamentary caucus, Laurier was able to convince the Liberal Party that a national leadership convention attended by delegates from across the country would be the best forum for selecting a new leader who would keep the party united.

In 1927, the Conservative Party held a national delegate convention to elect Robert Bennett as leader. Since then, except when Arthur Meighen took over the party leadership briefly in 1940, national conventions have been used to select national party leaders. The national convention was adopted to ensure the parties' extra-parliamentary wings had greater participation in important party activities, to make the internal party organization more democratic and to offset the regional weaknesses of party caucuses. (Perlin 1991 RC) These objectives remain valid today.

The adoption of national conventions also altered the relationship between the party leader and the parliamentary caucus. As a result of being elected by a large number of party delegates representing the various constituent parts of the party and regions of the country, the leader was elevated to a status shared by no other member of the party. Members of Parliament were elected from single-member constituencies, but only the national party leader could claim to have been selected by a national constituency. Mackenzie King made frequent use of this fact when dealing with recalcitrant ministers who were excessively protective of their regional interests. (Bakvis 1991)

The move to national leadership conventions as television events represented a third phase in the evolution of leadership politics. The 1967 Progressive Conservative convention, which saw the election of Robert Stanfield as leader, was the first to be nationally televised. As a result of changes in modern communication techniques, party leaders became the medium through which party policies and ideas were conveyed to the electorate. Leaders became public persuaders and assumed greater responsibility for mobilizing support for their parties.

Stanfield's selection as leader was preceded by an intense struggle within the Progressive Conservative Party over whether the extra-parliamentary wing of the party could force a formal review of Diefenbaker's leadership. Senior party strategists saw a leadership review mechanism as the only means available to remove Diefenbaker. Following the 1967 convention, the party amended its constitution to include a formal leadership review. This mechanism was used by some party members to challenge Joe Clark's leadership in 1983. Although he won endorsement from 67 per cent of the delegates attending the 1983 national convention, Clark felt his support within the party was insufficient. He called a leadership convention, and was subsequently defeated by Brian Mulroney. The Liberal leadership review mechanism, first introduced in 1966, was used most recently by Liberal Party members who challenged John Turner's leadership following the party's defeat in the 1984 election.

The constitution of the Progressive Conservative Party now provides for a formal leadership review following the party's defeat at a federal general election. The Liberal Party's constitution provides for an optional leadership review after every election, regardless of whether the party is defeated. While a successful leadership review normally requires extraordinary organizational effort by those wanting to replace the party leader, the presence of the device serves to hold national party leaders formally accountable to their members.

The leadership selection process in the New Democratic Party is unique among the three largest parties. Unlike the other two large parties, the NDP does not have the equivalent of a formal leadership review mechanism. However, at each biennial convention, the national NDP leader is elected as an officer of the party. A leadership vote, then, "is a regular and mandatory part of the convention agenda". (Archer 1991a RC) No incumbent leader has been seriously challenged at a convention.

The Reform Party of Canada has also adopted a formal review mechanism in its national constitution. The party is required to hold a national assembly of its members every two years. At every assembly, delegates are asked whether they want a leadership vote to be called. If a majority of delegates support a leadership review, the executive council of the party is required to hold a leadership vote "not sooner than 3 months and not later than 6 months from the date of the vote held at the Assembly".

With the increased prominence of leadership conventions in Canadian politics, the third phase in the evolution of the leadership selection process has been accompanied by changes in the competitive nature of leadership campaigns. "The critical factor in this change has been the growth in the size of conventions and the broadening of the base of participation in delegate selection." (Perlin 1991 RC) More than 2000 party delegates attended the

1967 Progressive Conservative leadership convention, and the same number of Liberal delegates attended the convention that elected Pierre Elliott Trudeau in 1968. The number of delegates increased to 3000 at both the 1983 Progressive Conservative and 1984 Liberal conventions. Approximately 2500 delegates attended the 1989 NDP leadership convention and there were 4600 delegates at the 1990 Liberal convention. In addition, the number of individuals participating in the selection of delegates for the 1990 Liberal convention has been estimated at between 75 000 and 100 000. (Perlin 1991 RC)

The role of national delegate conventions in selecting national party leaders in Canada contrasts sharply with British practices. British party leaders are selected by parliamentary caucuses. There are significant differences in the selection processes used by the Conservative and Labour parties, but in neither case is leadership selection seen as the responsibility or prerogative of the general party membership.

U.S. presidential candidates are selected at national conventions, although the delegates do not cast ballots as individuals but as representatives of their states. Unlike the Canadian practice, presidential candidates are not elected through a secret ballot, nor is the candidate with the lowest vote count on each ballot required to withdraw.

Delegate Selection and Representativeness
The increase in the number of delegates attending national leadership conventions has not necessarily been accompanied by a balanced representation from the different socio-demographic groups. Considerable progress has been made, but gender parity in the composition of delegates attending national leadership conventions has not yet been achieved. At the 1983 Progressive Conservative convention, 37 per cent of the voting delegates were women; the comparable number for the 1989 NDP convention was 37 per cent, while 45 per cent of delegates attending the 1990 Liberal convention were women. Youth delegates have had disproportionate representation at recent leadership conventions. In 1983, 40 per cent of voting delegates at the Progressive Conservative convention were youth; of the Liberal delegates in 1984, 31 per cent were under 30. (Wearing 1988, 204) The large number of youth delegates reflects the relative ease with which Liberal and Progressive Conservative campus clubs at universities and other educational institutions are accredited by the national parties. (Perlin 1991 RC) On the other hand, delegates from the New Democratic Youth organization attending the NDP convention in 1989 represented only 2 per cent of convention delegates, although the actual proportion of those under 30 was higher.

The NDP's formula for sending constituency delegates to national leadership conventions also distinguishes the party from the Liberal and Progressive Conservative parties. The NDP permits "one delegate for every 50 constituency members for the first 200 members, and one delegate for every 100 thereafter". (Archer 1991a RC) The delegate selection process in the NDP skews the regional representativeness of the leadership convention.

During the 1989 leadership convention, more than half the voting delegates were from the western provinces, and a further 27.5 per cent came from
Ontario. Delegates from Quebec made up 9.2 per cent and the four Atlantic
provinces combined accounted for only 5.4 per cent of all delegates.
Delegates from trade unions formally affiliated with the NDP represented
18.4 per cent of the total number of delegates attending the leadership convention, while 4.6 per cent were from central labour organizations such as
the Canadian Labour Congress.

Concomitant with the rapid growth in the number of delegates attending
national leadership conventions, there has been a dramatic increase in the
categories used by the Liberal and Progressive Conservative parties to classify delegates. There are as many as 18 separate categories. They can be
grouped under three general headings: (1) ex-officio delegates, including
members of the House of Commons, the Senate and provincial legislatures,
elected officers of the national and provincial executives, and defeated candidates for the House of Commons; (2) delegates from the constituent parts of the
national parties, such as women's and youth organizations; and (3) delegates-
at-large elected from local constituency associations. The proliferation of delegate categories has raised the issue of multiple voting. (Perlin 1991 RC) An
individual could conceivably cast several votes, depending on the number
of categories into which he or she fits. The number of instances of multiple
voting has not been documented, and the practice is likely not widespread.
Yet the possibility of it occurring does not enhance the legitimacy of the
delegate selection process.

Local constituency association delegates constituted 53 per cent of the
delegates attending the 1983 Progressive Conservative convention, and 54 per
cent of voting delegates for the 1984 Liberal leadership contest. (Carty 1988a,
84) Each constituency association of the Progressive Conservative Party could
send six delegates to the national convention, while the comparable number
for the Liberals was seven in 1984 and 12 in 1990. The NDP has six categories
of delegates: constituency, affiliated union, central labour, youth, caucus and
federal council. Two-thirds of the delegates attending the NDP leadership convention in 1989 were from the constituencies; one-fifth represented unions.

Elected delegates play a far more crucial role in the selection of party
leaders at leadership conventions than they did previously. As R.K. Carty
notes, "traditionally ... leadership conventions appear to have been dominated
by members of the party establishment". (1988a, 85) The pre-eminent role
of the party establishment has been replaced by campaign organizations
dedicated to the leadership ambitions of single contestants. Increasingly, constituency delegates are elected as slates committed to a single leadership
contestant.

Assessing the Leadership Selection Process

Elaborate constituency mobilization and organization techniques are critical
to effective leadership campaigns. Leadership campaign organizations have

become highly professional. They maintain computerized data banks on the strength of delegates' commitment to various contestants, and they conduct opinion polls to test the credibility of contestants and policies. Potential delegates are contacted and tracked using direct mail and telemarketing. Leadership contestants are now obliged to establish local organizations in as many constituencies as possible to influence delegate selection, and national campaign tours have become indispensable to the serious contestant. Lengthy leadership campaigns culminate in convention-week events modelled on the U.S. presidential nomination conventions. This sophisticated approach to leader selection has been accompanied by intense media scrutiny and coverage. For a short period, major leadership aspirants receive considerable prime-time broadcast coverage, and their leadership qualities and policy ideas are assessed in detail by the print media.

The media also give equal attention to the tactics and methods of leadership contestants. Recent leadership conventions have become highly controversial on two fronts. First, the practice by campaign organizations or special-interest groups of paying party membership fees to recruit instant party members who help elect sympathetic delegates or slates of delegates has undermined the integrity of the leadership selection process. These activities have often occurred close to the delegate selection meeting because the parties do not have standardized or consistent membership requirement rules in place. The fluidity of membership requirements in most parties creates unnecessary opportunities for the use of questionable strategies in the leadership selection process. For example, individuals residing in one constituency can be provided with party memberships and transported to a delegate selection meeting in another constituency where they then vote to select delegates. During recent Liberal and Progressive Conservative leadership conventions, there were frequent media reports of delegate selection meetings being packed with minors, non-voters and instant partisans. These members were mobilized for the specific purpose of supporting the leadership aspirations of individual contestants. They had no previous history of party activism, and they were not encouraged to participate in further party activities following the delegate meeting. Abuses of party membership rules and controversial mobilization techniques first became part of the public image of the leadership selection process because of media scrutiny of the competition between the campaign organizations of Joe Clark and Brian Mulroney during the 1983 Progressive Conservative race. (Carty 1988a; Martin et al. 1983) Among the new members recruited were minors and individuals from community shelters who had no previous or lasting commitment to the party. (Graham 1986, 157–58)

This is not to suggest that there are no merits to the 'transformation of constituency politics' as a result of changing recruitment techniques. The competitive pursuit of delegates by various campaign organizations across the country during the 1983 Progressive Conservative leadership race helped give the party an organizational presence in many constituencies where it had been relatively weak. Moreover, competition to mobilize support for the election of loyal delegates has in many cases increased the participatory base of local constituency politics. (Carty 1988a)

The highly competitive and open nature of delegate selection that characterizes leadership campaigns in the Liberal and Progressive Conservative parties is less prominent in the NDP. Only half the constituency delegate positions were contested during the 1989 NDP leadership campaign, and seldom did leadership contestants run a slate of delegates. Further, the delegate positions given to the trade unions were not contested publicly.

The second controversial dimension of the selection process is the cost and financing of recent leadership campaigns. Large sums of money and resources are now needed by the campaign organizations of leadership contestants to mobilize support and ensure the selection of delegates. It has been estimated that the top two contestants during the 1990 Liberal leadership contest raised approximately $2 million each. Reliable estimates for the amount of money spent by the leading contenders for the 1983 Progressive Conservative leadership convention are difficult to obtain, because contestants were not required to disclose what they spent or how much they raised. Neither of these national parties has required leadership contenders to provide full public disclosure of who contributed to their campaigns or in what amounts.

The concern that the leadership campaign organizations are raising and spending excessive amounts of money must be weighed against contending and concurrent pressures from party members, and at times the public at large, that leadership aspirants engage in contestants' debates across the country and provide frequent opportunities for the critical assessment of their views and policies. In response to these expectations, leadership contestants are often required to establish large organizations to ensure that they can accommodate the pressures for an open, accessible campaign.

Both the NDP and the Liberal Party have moved toward partial public funding of leadership contests by channelling contributions to leadership campaigns through the parties, thereby making them eligible for a tax receipt. Receipted contributions to contestants for the Liberal leadership race in 1990, for example, totalled $1 954 958; contestants who channelled contributions to their campaigns through the party paid a total of $608 151 in "candidate levies". (Reform Commission of the Liberal Party 1991, 16)

The use of public funding for leadership conventions has become a source of controversy. First, legislation does not specifically provide for the use of the tax credit for such purposes. In a brief to our Commission, the Minister of National Revenue noted,

> while it cannot be doubted that expenses incurred by leadership candidates are expenses within the purposes for which the party has been established, the need for the channelling of the funds through the party in order to qualify for tax assistance gives the transaction an air of artificiality.

> If it is Parliament's intent to allow tax-assisted contributions to be uti-
> lized in party leadership campaigns, consideration should be given to
> having the legislation clearly and directly reflect this intent. (Brief 1990, 7–8)

Second, concern has been expressed that it is inappropriate for public
funding to be used for leadership campaigns without implementing financial disclosure and accountability rules that match those in the *Canada
Elections Act* on election campaigns and party financing.

The use of the tax credit system to help finance party leadership campaigns introduces a clear public dimension to the process. The tax credit helps
leadership contestants raise funds from a broader base of party members than
might otherwise be the case. This in turn may lower barriers for those who
do not have access to substantial donors.

Party Responses to Public Criticisms

Political parties have made tentative efforts to respond to public criticism
of the leadership selection process. Active party members appear to share
the views of the electorate. A survey of Liberal delegates attending the 1990
leadership convention showed a significant measure of support for either
party or public regulation of the leadership selection process. Approximately
half the delegates surveyed supported public regulation of the selection
process. Just over two-thirds agreed that there should be at least partial
public regulation of leadership selection, given parties' important public
responsibilities. Ninety per cent supported spending limits for leadership
campaigns, a majority supported limits on the size of financial contributions
to leadership campaigns and about 90 per cent wanted full public disclosure
of contributions and expenditures. (Perlin 1991 RC)

Several provincial parties have responded to public criticism by selecting their leaders through direct election by all party members in good
standing, although the new-found virtue of this approach may not be totally
unrelated to the tight financial position of the parties at the time. Leaders
of the Parti québécois were elected through direct election in 1985 and 1987,
as were leaders of the provincial Progressive Conservatives in Prince Edward
Island in 1987 and in Ontario in 1990. At its 1990 national convention, the
Liberal Party of Canada adopted a policy resolution that supported the direct
election of its next leader. The feasibility of the resolution is being examined
by the party's internal reform commission. Advocates of direct election
argue this approach is more democratic, because it limits the influence of
the party establishment over the selection of the leader and gives more influence to rank-and-file members. Direct election of party leaders may also
reduce the opportunities for abuse of membership rules. It is seen as a credible mechanism for rebuilding public confidence in the leadership selection process. At the same time, this process may dampen the considerable
publicity and interest that typically surrounds a leadership convention. As
well, direct election does not necessarily guarantee broader participation.

Lower-than-expected participation has been experienced in several provincial leadership conventions that used the direct election method.

The parties have recently made efforts to regulate spending during leadership conventions. The NDP established internal spending limits of $150 000 per candidate for its 1989 leadership campaign. Contestants were required to submit a full account of expenditures and fund-raising activities before ballots were cast at the convention. None of the seven contestants exceeded the spending limit, but it is not clear that the expenses subject to the limit covered all the contestants' major costs. (Archer 1991a RC) For example, several campaign organizations made extensive use of volunteer labour from trade unions, thereby reducing the need for paid professional staff. In addition, the party subsidized leadership aspirants, for example, by paying their travel costs. In short, the accounts of expenses submitted by the contestants did not show the total costs involved in the exercise.

Spending limits of $1.7 million were set by the Liberal Party for its 1990 leadership campaign. Other campaign rules prohibited the contestants' campaign organizations from purchasing party memberships in federal constituencies, student clubs or women's associations; nor were the organizations allowed to incur expenses to help delegates attend constituency selection meetings or the national convention. The Liberal Party also established financial disclosure and transparency rules, but contestants were not required to indicate the specific source or size of contributions.

These efforts at self-regulation have not assuaged concerns that the role of money in the selection of national leaders has the potential to undermine the integrity and fairness of the process. At the same time, it remains difficult for party officials to enforce the rules that do exist. Once the campaign begins, control of the process and of the party is essentially in the hands of the leadership contestants. Unless one of the contestants launches a complaint before the party's rules committee, the party has little direct authority to ensure that the rules are followed.

Reforming the Leadership Selection Process

The selection of national leaders is a central responsibility of our political parties. Current practices used to select national party leaders suggest three concerns: legitimacy, fairness and public confidence. The legitimacy of the leadership selection process is undermined when constituency delegates and supporters are recruited indiscriminately and without due regard to the dignity of individual citizens. The principle of fairness is undermined in leadership selection by the absence of credible or enforceable spending limits. Spending limits for parties and candidates are an integral part of electoral law in Canada. They ensure that the dynamics of electoral competition are not determined exclusively by the ability to raise and spend large sums of money. Public confidence is undermined by the absence of full and complete disclosure, particularly when public monies are used and when there is doubt that the rules are enforced. Full public disclosure must mean more than the leadership contestants tabling general financial accounts to their parties after the leadership convention. Information is needed on the number and identification of individual contributors. Both delegates and the public should have the opportunity to fully assess the sources and sizes of the financial contributions that a leadership contestant receives.

None of the large parties, provincially or federally, has a permanent set of rules and guidelines in place to govern their leadership selection processes. While the party constitutions may include some general provisions on the management of leadership conventions and campaigns, specific rules directed at the conduct of leadership campaigns such as delegate selection rules, spending limits and disclosure rules are not established until the party leadership becomes vacant. Even then, there is no requirement that the parties put in place rules that set the parameters within which leadership campaigns raise and spend money and mobilize support during the selection of delegates. The absence of permanent or well-developed rules for leadership campaigns can mean that the drafting of temporary rules becomes the source of internal party conflict, whereby leadership campaign organizations lobby to have rules established which favour their interests.

Several parties have set internal spending limits for recent leadership campaigns. Limits were issued as internal guidelines to be followed by contestants' campaign organizations. While the national parties may want to see credible spending limits set and enforced, their ability and resources to meet this objective are modest. The value and intent of spending limits can be realized only if they have the sanction of law. This has been confirmed to the Commission by many experienced party officials. The presence of legal sanctions that enforce spending limits for leadership campaigns would be an effective deterrent to campaign organization excesses, in much the same way as spending limits in the electoral law have required parties and candidates to adjust the way they plan and implement campaign strategies based on their ability to spend a set amount of money.

During our public hearings, representatives from the political parties stated that the leadership selection process must remain within the purview of political parties. They noted that parties are essentially private, self-regulating organizations made up of volunteers. Many interveners, however, submitted proposals for public regulation of the leadership selection process. Among the proposals were recommendations on campaign spending limits, spending disclosure requirements, contribution limits, contribution disclosures, restrictions on sources of contributions and public subsidization of certain campaign expenses.

The party processes and practices used to select leaders should reflect, and in fact affirm, the separate and distinct histories, traditions and cultures of each party. Accordingly, each party should be able to establish rules that are consistent with its structure, internal processes, membership base and revenue base. However, the leadership selection processes should not undermine the principles of fairness and equity that are fundamental to our electoral process, particularly since public funding is involved.

These considerations lead us to conclude that changes to the financing of leadership campaigns must be guided by two general objectives. First, minimum requirements should be set out in electoral law to ensure that leadership selection in all registered parties is guided by common values and principles that promote the integrity of the electoral process and that affirm the principle of fairness in electoral competition. To this end, requirements for spending limits, financial disclosure rules and the use of the tax credit should be included in electoral law.

In Chapter 6 of this volume, we recommend that spending limits for registered political parties be based on $0.70 per registered voter. Based on the potential number of registered voters in 1990, parties nominating candidates in all constituencies would have spending limits of $12.63 million for the next federal election. Consequently, a spending limit that restricted each leadership contestant to 15 per cent of the party's election expense limit would be approximately $1.89 million. This limit is consistent with the expenditures of leadership contestants for recent leadership campaigns by the large national parties and would be sufficient to allow leadership contestants to engage in competitive, national campaigns.

Leadership contestants would acquire access to the tax credit as a result of being accredited bona fide contestants by their parties. Further, the tax receipts would be issued by the party, rather than by representatives of the leadership contestants. Consequently, any financial surpluses accumulated by leadership contestants that represent any portion of the amount of political contributions that would have benefited from the tax credit, based on the spending limit established by electoral law or by the party, are essentially public funds. Consequently, such surpluses should revert either to the party, the party foundation or to a registered constituency association. The leadership contestant would decide where to assign her or his financial surplus. For example, if spending limits for leadership contestants were $1.8 million and the contestant raised $2.1 million and spent $1.5 million, $300 000 of the $500 000 surplus would have benefited from tax credits. This amount would revert back to the party or any of its constituent elements. The objective here would be to affirm that the use of the tax credit for the leadership selection process is very much the prerogative, privilege and responsibility of the registered party as a collectivity.

Ensuring adherence to these rules, given that they are founded on ideas and values central to our system of representative democracy, should be the responsibility of the Canada Elections Commission. In meeting this objective, leadership contestants should be required to designate agents with responsibilities that are similar to those assumed by official agents for candidates during general elections. The appointment of such agents would ensure that the financial records of leadership contestants are maintained in accordance with generally accepted accounting procedures and principles and the requirements of the Act. As a consequence, the financial activities of the leadership campaign organizations could be readily compared and assessed by party members.

Second, the treatment of the leadership selection process in electoral law should be neither so restrictive nor so intrusive as to impair the capacity of individual parties to establish rules and processes that reflect their own distinct traditions and character. Consequently, parties must be provided with the opportunity to establish internal rules governing their leadership selection process. Some parties may choose to adopt rules that impose stricter financial disclosure requirements and spending limits for leadership contestants, for example less than 15 per cent of the party's election expenses. Such rules could provide party members with further opportunities to assess the patterns of political contributions used by leadership contestants to finance their campaign organizations. Our recommendations are designed to meet each of these objectives.

Recommendation 1.5.12

We recommend that, as a condition of registration, the constitution of a party be filed with the Canada Elections Commission and include the following provisions:
(1) only members residing in the constituency who are in good standing for 30 days before the date set for a meeting to select delegates for a leadership convention be able to vote for delegates;
(2) for members who reside outside a constituency that is selecting delegates for a leadership convention, only members who are in good standing at least six months before the date set for the meeting be able to vote for the election of delegates;
(3) only members who are in good standing at least 30 days before the date set for the election of the leader through universal suffrage of party members be able to vote for the election of the party leader; and
(4) immediately on determination that the process for the selection of a leader will be initiated, specific rules to govern the process be adopted by the relevant party authorities, including
    (i) obligations for leadership contestants to provide full disclosure of financial activities, including size and source of financial contributions of $250 or more in the aggregate;
    (ii) spending limits, which may be less than the 15 per cent of the election expenses permitted the party under the *Canada Elections Act* for the most recent federal general election; and
    (iii) requirements for a preliminary report by leadership contestants on their expenses and revenues on the day preceding the election of the leader.

Recommendation 1.5.13

We recommend that the *Canada Elections Act* be amended to include the following provisions:

(1) leadership contestants be required to file a report on expenses and revenues to the Canada Elections Commission within three months of the day the vote is held to select the leader;

(2) spending by individual leadership contestants of registered parties not exceed 15 per cent of the election expenses permitted the party under the *Canada Elections Act* for the most recent federal general election;

(3) each contestant for the leadership of the party be required to appoint an agent with responsibilities similar to those of the official agent of a candidate;

(4) the spending limits for leadership campaigns take effect from the time the party sets and announces a date for the election of its leader, and apply to the date when the party leader is elected;

(5) bona fide contestants for a registered party's leadership, as determined by the party, be eligible to use the tax credit system in fund-raising activities, through a mechanism established by the registered party;

(6) tax credits for leadership campaigns be issued only by the party, and the total amount of contributions to a leadership contestant for which tax credits are attributed not exceed the total spending limit established by the party for each leadership contestant; and

(7) any portion of financial surpluses accumulated by leadership contestants that would have qualified for tax credits revert, at the discretion of the leadership contestant, to the registered political party, to the party's registered party foundation or to one of the party's registered constituency associations.

STRENGTHENING THE ROLE OF POLITICAL PARTIES

Codes of Ethics

Political parties are subject to criticism for failing to correct behaviour that undermines confidence in the integrity of parties and the political process. A complaint that frequently arose in our hearings is that political parties are either unwilling or incapable of monitoring and enforcing fair procedures in party activities. The concern is that where incidents or allegations of misbehaviour arise, parties have been reluctant to assume responsibility for reviewing and revising the practices that gave rise to the allegations.

Perceptions that parties may not accept the seriousness or immediacy of public concerns encourage suggestions that an increasing range of party activities should be regulated. Public expectations of parties are more extensive and demanding than ever before, and the public's judgements of party behaviour are no longer confined to the election period. Canadians increasingly perceive a public interest in how parties nominate candidates and select leaders, and also in the outcomes of these processes in terms of fair representation. Broadened public expectations challenge the parties to ensure that they address values that cut across party lines by conducting themselves in ways that instil confidence in the integrity and fairness of the political process.

In responding to these increased demands for regulating internal party activities, the experiences of other kinds of organizations that face similar challenges are relevant. Many have responded by implementing codes of ethics, which are written statements of an organization's basic values and principles of behaviour. Codes of ethics provide individual members of these organizations with a framework for evaluating daily practices and decisions. Although there is considerable variation in the scope and structure of ethical codes and in the specific values they articulate, they all share two essential elements: an explicit statement of the organization's values and principles, which are grounded in its philosophy, objectives and traditions; and an explicit statement that commits all members of the organization to these values and principles.

While codes of ethics are increasingly commonplace for corporations, professional associations and public servants, there is little practical experience of political parties adopting them. Nevertheless, there is much to commend a code of ethics to political parties.

A code of ethics would establish an important organizational instrument of party governance, giving party executives and leadership a tool to manage and give coherence to the behaviour, practices and standards of the party. A code of ethics would help foster and reinforce agreement with the fundamental values that underpin and distinguish a political party. Acceptance of and commitment to the basic party principles and values are essential if the leaders of these large and decentralized organizations are to exercise effective direction and ensure that members' activities reflect their basic precepts and values. By specifically articulating these values in a code of ethics, and stating how they should inform the conduct of all members, parties could facilitate and promote the shared culture that binds members to a party.

A code of ethics would motivate appropriate behaviour and help peer pressure enforce an articulated and generally recognized set of behavioural expectations. In so doing, a code would enhance the ability of party leaders to promote compliance with and conformity to the party's principles and standards. The codification of these standards and expectations would make it easier and more justifiable to impose sanctions for those who fail to uphold the code.

With the adoption of a code of ethics would come the responsibility that party members conduct themselves in ways that reflect and reinforce the basic philosophy and values of the party. This would facilitate evaluation of the party practices and rules and address any disparities between desirable standards and current practices. By establishing a framework for members to assess and re-evaluate their own and others' conduct that might undermine confidence and respect for their political party, a code of ethics would provide not only the rationale, but also the justification for insisting that the party membership reform its procedures and seek affirmative and innovative ways of correcting problems.

For example, a party might be committed to enhancing its representational base to include more women and members of underrepresented groups, but its internal practices and procedures might pose unintended or unrecognized barriers to full participation. Setting out greater representativeness as a basic value or principle in a code of ethics would enable members to identify barriers and to challenge those who maintain them. A commitment to fair representation, for instance, could be the basis for insisting that the party strengthen search committees or other mechanisms that enhance the party's representative nature.

Crystallizing the party's basic values and principles in a code of ethics would be particularly valuable to party members who make difficult decisions in the competitive environment of electoral campaigns. It would enhance the incentive and inclination of party members to put the party's long-term interest in protecting its integrity and public respect ahead of potential and illusive short-term gains.

A code of ethics would also be a vehicle to promote internal discussion and debate about political practices in the light of the standards and principles the party has articulated. The very act of consulting other party members and discussing the activities with reference to a code of ethics would foster reflection on members' and parties' practices. Members who have ethical concerns about the practices of others within the party would also have a basis for criticizing and resisting these practices. These steps are crucial for modifying behaviour within parties and for altering perceptions about the appropriate criteria for making decisions.

The affirmation of a party's basic principles and values in a code of ethics would help bind members to the common purpose of strengthening the party and affirming its integrity. A willingness to uphold its basic standards would be seen as a strong commitment to the party.

Another important contribution of a code of ethics would be to infuse the value of party membership with greater importance. Unlike western European party systems, which encourage and promote meaningful membership in all party activities, Canadian parties are criticized for placing too great an emphasis on the voting capacity of members in leadership and nomination activities, at the expense of their contribution to the more general objectives and functions of the party. A code would encourage parties to evaluate the importance of membership by determining what guidelines and principles should govern it, including the role of members in leadership and candidate selection processes. The requirement that the executive enforce the code's principles and establish sanctions for violations would encourage more serious consideration of members' responsibilities and obligations. Furthermore, the responsibility of each member to evaluate his or her own practices in relation to the code would contribute to the significance of membership by making each member a vital part of the organization in all aspects of the party's operations.

Separate codes for each of the political parties would seem preferable. A code of ethics should affirm rather than impair the distinct political histories and cultures of the parties. The very existence of a large number of registered political parties in Canada is indicative of the diversity of ideas and values they represent. Each party has established its own organizational and structural traditions to accommodate the representational objectives of its members, candidates and leaders. Further, separate codes that are more reflective of the parties' own unique histories would engender more sympathetic support from party members to their code's ideals and values.

Nonetheless, codes for different parties would likely include a number of common themes. For example, ethical codes might provide statements about the rights and obligations of membership, establish standards for recruiting candidates and leaders, outline the norms that should govern these processes, establish guidelines for soliciting contributions, articulate principles to assess election advertising campaigns and establish guidelines for mobilizing the vote on election day.

A code of ethics would help reconcile public demands for greater regulation with the legitimate desire of parties to manage their internal affairs. It would allow the parties to respond to the concerns underlying demands for regulation in a way that does not undermine their capacity to organize their internal operations. Implementing a code of ethics would represent a more assertive and deliberate response to the perceived problems than promising internal reforms that may or may not take place.

Public confidence requires that the basic election rules be clearly articulated in a fair and transparent regulatory framework. Normative expectations, however, may not be satisfied simply by conforming with established laws. Legal requirements represent the minimum standards that have to be obeyed without penalty. Although obeying the law is a requisite for appropriate conduct, it does not in itself exhaust obligations. Consequently, political parties will always be subject to demands that activities be regulated when these activities appear to depart significantly from public expectations of appropriate conduct, or when parties are perceived as being incapable of or unwilling to modify the offending practices.

For example, serious concerns were raised about the way party members conduct themselves during elections. These criticisms cannot be addressed easily by regulations. Elections are activities in which parties should be given as broad a margin as possible to promote policies and platforms and to distinguish themselves from their partisan rivals; it would therefore be difficult, and arguably ill-advised, to regulate party election strategies and tactics. Nevertheless, the integrity of the electoral process is threatened by public concerns that election advertising is deceptive, that it cheapens the electoral system and alienates voters, or that suspect election practices are used to manipulate and exploit certain groups of voters.

A critical factor in determining the effectiveness of codes of ethics is enforcement. If codes are to constitute a meaningful and useful organizational tool for party leaders, exhortations to engage in appropriate behaviour are insufficient. Parties face a challenge in enforcing their codes, particularly in light of the parties' dispersed nature and their essentially volunteer character. Enforcement must reflect the objectives, structure and culture of the political party adopting a code of ethics, but certain steps could maximize the effectiveness of a code in encouraging ethical reflection in decision making.

For example, constituency associations could establish procedures to review complaints from members that other members or party officers have not acted in accordance with the code. Mechanisms should also be established to interpret the code and its application in particular circumstances. Parties may wish to introduce a division of labour between local associations and the national executive in making recommendations and imposing sanctions or penalties. For example, parties might require that the local constituency association assume responsibility for making immediate recommendations on whether a nomination convention was conducted fairly, but allow the national executive, through an appeal mechanism, to make the final determination and decide on appropriate penalties or sanctions. The penalties parties could establish for non-compliance might include, for example, reprimand, disqualifying membership, suspending membership or revoking membership. When party officers or candidates violate the code, penalties could include reprimand, disqualifying candidates from nomination or leadership, prohibiting members from serving in an official party capacity, disqualifying elected delegates, revoking membership or nullifying the result of a selection process.

Both the development and the implementation of a code of ethics within a party could be made the primary responsibility of an ethics committee. Representation on the committee would come from the party's national executive and the constituencies. The ethics committee would consult extensively with party members and officials on the contents and purposes of the party's code, and assist in publicizing the code throughout the membership. In this way, the participatory qualities and mobilization attributes of the code could be enhanced. The presence of an active, credible ethics committee within the party would increase the prominence and meaning of the code as a determinant in how party members and officials participate in electoral and political activities. The ethics committee could be used as a forum to promote the code as an instrument for attracting new members to the ideas and values represented by the party.

Parties might also require an ethics committee to submit annual reports to either the leadership or the general membership of the party. These reports would provide valuable information on common problems and concerns that the party might wish to redress by internal reforms or amendments to the code. In addition, this information would be valuable if the national party wished to hold advisory or educational meetings on the state of compliance with the code.

Satisfying public and party expectations requires effective leadership capable of frank appraisals of whether party conduct and members' activities satisfy expectations. Although legislative reforms should accompany changing ethical expectations, electoral law can and should go only so far in encouraging certain kinds of behaviour. A code of ethics would give leadership the tools for promoting and enforcing – and members a clearer sense of obligation to – the principles of the party. Whether motivated by a new sense of public and party responsibility or by enlightened self-interest to reform activities before public confidence declines further, the articulation of acceptable standards of behaviour for members, parties and local associations would go a long way toward instilling public and member confidence in the integrity of political parties. In short, it would give parties an effective way to manage their own conduct and forestall increased demands for regulation.

Recommendation 1.5.14

We recommend that

(a) **each registered party adopt a code of ethics; and**
(b) **each party set up an ethics committee to help ensure adherence to and promotion of the code.**

The Policy Development and Education Roles of Parties

Since Confederation, the meaning and substance of party membership have changed considerably. In the early years, and indeed well into this century, membership in a political party was not determined by fees or formal membership requirements. Yet from the 1870s onward, the partisanship of individuals was easily defined. Party membership served political, economic and social functions. Members from competing parties engaged in frequent and open debate. Dedicated members gave parties a permanent and meaningful presence in community life.

With the decline of broadly based parties enjoying a strong organizational base in local constituencies came a decline in partisan identification. In more recent decades, the value and meaning of party membership have changed further as many citizens have found other ways of engaging in political action through interest groups, which have redirected their volunteer energies away from parties and toward other private organizations.

Based on the recent history of the leadership and candidate selection processes, party membership is seen less as an integral facet of partisan politics and more as a useful instrument for mobilizing support for an individual wanting to become a party candidate, leader or officer. New members are recruited for the specific purpose of providing votes for an individual. In such cases, membership recruitment is not designed to bind new members to the ideas of the party, but to advance the electoral aspirations of individuals. To this extent, membership recruitment is not primarily a function performed by parties in a collective sense. Parties benefit, of course, but the benefits may be only short-term.

For the Liberals, Progressive Conservatives and the NDP, recruitment of members and administration of membership lists are handled at the local or provincial level. None of the three national party organizations has a single centralized membership list. Membership fees and formal requirements in the Progressive Conservative Party are established by local constituency associations. The Liberal Party's approach to membership rules varies from province to province: "some provincial organizations, such as the Liberal Party of Canada (Québec) and the four western provinces, have centralized membership lists and fees; others, such as Ontario, traditionally have not, although all the provincial parties are supposedly moving to centralized memberships". (Wearing 1988, 193) Membership fees and requirements in the NDP are determined by the provincial organizations.

The absence of centralized party lists limits the ability of national party organizations to provide services to or communicate directly with their members. In fact, the national parties do not possess precise estimates of the number of party members whose membership fees are paid up. None of the three largest parties have a regular means of communicating directly with their members or of informing them about the activities and objectives of the national party organizations. The national executive of the Progressive Conservative Party uses a number of informal devices to communicate with some members. For example, the minutes of the national executive meetings are frequently distributed to all constituency presidents and secretaries, and regional vice presidents have been given some responsibility to report to members on the activities of the national party. The NDP national executive restricts communications with the general party membership to financial reports and policy statements made by party executives at biennial party conventions. The national president of the Liberal Party makes an oral report on party activities at biennial policy conventions. These weak linkages among the national party organizations, the constituency associations and the party members impede the ability of individual parties to instil the distinct party culture, ideas and values that attract committed, dedicated members. On too many occasions, individuals joining political parties are given responsibilities only during the relatively short periods of electoral competition. As noted by one party official in 1989, "if everyone who works on an election arrived on our doorstep tomorrow morning, three years away from an election ... we wouldn't know what to do with them" (quoted in R. Pelletier 1991 RC). After the election has been called, fought and concluded, party members become isolated from the day-to-day activities of the party organization, and they are provided with few incentives to be active participants in party affairs.

Levels of political voluntarism and activism remain relatively high in Canada, but the number of individuals joining parties and committing themselves to partisan politics is declining. (Nevitte 1991 RC) This stands in contrast to developments in some other countries, where membership in both small and large parties has actually increased. (Selle and Svåsand 1991) For many Canadians, political parties are not seen as plausible institutions for organizing and managing collective political action.

As Jane Jenson argued, during the debate leading to adoption of the 1974 reforms, "the idea that parties might serve as a bridge between individual citizens and the state remained a somewhat foreign concept in federal politics". (1991b RC) The main concerns at the time were controlling the costs of election campaigns and ensuring that the parties had adequate revenue for that purpose. Party registration had been introduced in 1970, and political parties were implicitly recognized in the regulations for election broadcast advertising and the tax credit. Nevertheless, "this recognition of parties did not necessarily emerge from any philosophy that the parties were important national institutions nor pay any systematic attention to them as actors with responsibilities for the health of the Canadian polity". (Jenson 1991b RC)

The dilemma is that the core of the party organization is concerned primarily with elections; it is much less interested in discussing and analysing political issues that are not connected directly to winning the next election, or in attempting to articulate the broader values of the party.

An important step in strengthening parties as primary political organizations is for parties to reaffirm the value and dignity of membership as an integral part of partisan politics. The parties need to recapture their position and reassert their role in the realm of political education, policy development and value articulation, including the creation of broader partisan networks. An element of current popular sentiment would like to see politics and political parties removed as much as possible from the making of public policy; the continued health of our democracy, however, requires that people in Canada become more involved in political life through political parties. One means of doing so would be to encourage political parties to develop an institutional base for engaging individuals in activities less clearly linked to short-term electoral considerations.

In most western democracies, political parties do not limit their activities to electoral contests. They educate and mobilize core supporters and party members through conferences, seminars and specialized publications, they prepare for the logistics of governance and, in the case of parties in power, they go beyond the bureaucracy to tap into networks of knowledgeable supporters on specific policy matters.

Fulfilling these needs is generally recognized as important for the well-being of both parties and democratic governance. For this reason, political parties in most democracies have the capacity to draw on well-developed networks of expertise, and to engage in the political education of their own members and party sympathizers on major issues. This capacity for distilling and disseminating knowledge often has an institutional base, either formally within the party as in many European countries, or in one or more centres outside but still closely allied to the party or to key figures in it, as in the United States and Great Britain. That these activities are deemed important by governments and the public is shown by the fact that a number of jurisdictions fund parties directly through grants or allowances in non-election years.

The Federal Republic of Germany introduced annual funding in 1959. Although the Constitutional Court ruled in 1966 that public funding for activities other than election campaigns was unconstitutional, the following year the *Party Law* was adopted providing reimbursements to parties that resemble annual funding: 40 per cent is paid immediately after the election, 10 per cent the second year, 15 per cent the third year, and the remaining 35 per cent in the last year before the next election. The *Party Law* also provided for annual block grants to the foundations associated with parties that gained at least 5 per cent of the vote in an election. (Pinto-Duschinsky 1991 RC)

Annual funding of political parties was introduced in France in 1988. The fund is distributed in two parts. The first is allocated to parties represented in the National Assembly and the Senate on the basis of the number of seats they hold. The remainder is assigned to parties that had at least 75 candidates in the last National Assembly elections, and is allocated on the basis of their results in the first round of those elections. Italy, Sweden and Austria also fund political parties through annual payments. In the Netherlands, annual payments are made only to support party foundations rather than the parties. (Wolinetz 1991)

Three Canadian provinces, Quebec, New Brunswick and Prince Edward Island, provide annual funding to political parties. Quebec introduced its system in 1975. All "authorized parties" receive a monthly "allowance", and section 83 of the Quebec *Election Act* states,

> The allowance shall be used to reimburse the expenses incurred by the parties for their current administration, the propagation of their political programs and the coordination of the political activities of their members; it shall be paid only if the expenses are actually incurred and paid.[5]

New Brunswick has provided annual funding to parties since 1978. Parties qualify if they are represented in the Legislative Assembly or have had at least 10 candidates at the last election (the province has 58 constituencies). The amount of the annual grant is determined by multiplying the number of votes cast for the party's candidates at the last election by an amount stipulated in the *Political Process Financing Act* (the amount is adjusted annually to the consumer price index).[6] In Prince Edward Island, parties qualify for annual grants only if they hold at least two seats in the 32-member Legislative Assembly.[7]

Political parties at the federal level in Canada have generally been able to raise much larger amounts of money than in the past. Their capacity to do so has varied over time, and at the end of 1989 two of the larger parties had an accumulated deficit. In these circumstances, there is little reason to believe that parties will shift resources to the kind of activities that would strengthen their role as primary political organizations – activities such as promoting political participation, education and policy development. As Michael Robinson, Chief Financial Officer of the Liberal Party, stated with regret at our seminar on election and party financing: "Political parties in their current structure, faced with competing demands for funds, will always put them to electoral purposes as opposed to long-term policy development or value articulation."

Institutions for such long-term policy development in other democracies are important in several respects. Their advice to party leaders on alternative policies is not dictated by short-term electoral considerations. They provide the space to re-examine policy directions in a manner that does not imply that a change is necessarily forthcoming and does not elicit or require an immediate response by groups or competing parties. They give party leaders important connections to wider networks of people in universities and the private and non-profit sectors, individuals who are not necessarily party members but who are part of a broader constituency sympathetic to the general aims and values espoused by the party. These institutions engage in political education by holding seminars and conferences on significant policy problems, publishing periodicals dealing with party philosophy and policy issues and by regularly bringing core party members, including cabinet members and MPs, into contact with experts from outside the party. These institutions also help newly elected governments with the transition period by preparing the party leadership for the logistics of implementing the party's policies and programs. They play the critical role of recruiting and developing individuals who are skilled, sympathetic and familiar with the problems of democratic governance, and who can be placed in key positions within the government.

These institutions therefore supply the capacity both to help develop the party's philosophy and to help implement it. They also help strengthen the presence of the party in those sectors of society where the political party may not find ready acceptance as a strictly electoral machine. In short, these organizations provide a buffer in which the party leadership, legislators, the extra-parliamentary party and citizens can interact and communicate with each other.

In most democracies, political parties have the capacity to engage in these activities either through formal institutes or through less formal means – that is, informal but fairly direct alliances between an outside institute and the party. For the most part, however, Canadian political parties lack this capacity for political education and policy interpretation. This includes the NDP – the party that usually prides itself on its stance on issues. Overall, Canadian political parties have a reputation for being weak other than in the performance of electoral functions.

The reasons for this situation are many and complex. The Liberals and Progressive Conservatives, and to a degree the NDP as well, in seeking to bridge disparate interests and social cleavages, have not always developed firm positions on issues. The free trade issue in the 1988 election, however, shows that parties are certainly capable of doing so under the right circumstances. In Canada, moreover, the lower levels of party identification and the higher levels of volatility and turnover, especially at the constituency level, make parties and individual MPs even more sensitive to short-term factors than legislators in Great Britain or the United States need to be. (Blake 1991 RC) The levels of electoral volatility for these countries are contrasted in Figure 5.1. There is also Canada's geography: like the population, parties are physically dispersed, making it difficult to find the time and resources to engage in political dialogue.

Canada does have a number of institutes and foundations with mandates to undertake public policy research, including the C.D. Howe Institute, the Institute for Research on Public Policy (IRPP), and the Fraser Institute.

Figure 5.1
Legislative turnover in Canada, the United States and United Kingdom: percentage of seats changing party, 1950–1990

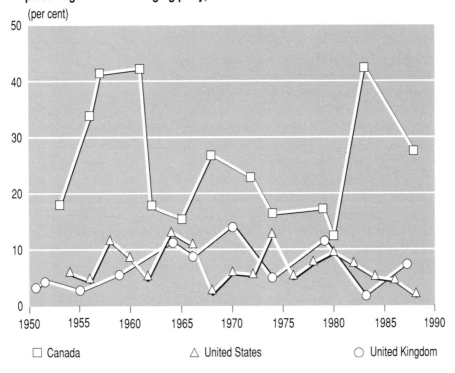

Source: Adapted from Blake 1991 RC.

However, these organizations have generally attempted to depict them-selves as non-partisan. Furthermore, except at the most senior level, they have few direct or even indirect links with political parties. In part this relates to the development of a political culture in which it is not consid-ered good form to be linked explicitly with a specific party or movement. Some institutes, such as the IRPP, were created in the early 1970s when many people felt distinct political beliefs were no longer important. "The end of ideology", as one analyst put it, (Bell 1960) led to a commitment to non-partisan, technocratic solutions to social and political problems.

The absence of party links also relates in good part to the institutes' status as charitable organizations for tax purposes. Under Revenue Canada rules (Canada, Revenue Canada, Taxation 1987), any educational activities engaged in by a charitable organization must not "include the dissemina-tion of information directed toward achieving a political purpose". The effect has generally been to make boards of directors of research institutes wary of taking what could be interpreted as a political stance. In contrast, in the United States, foundations formed under section 501(c)(3) of the *Internal Revenue Code*, can accept unlimited tax-deductible contributions, yet still engage in political education, as long as they do not participate directly in election campaigns. (Lindquist 1989)

It could be argued that no matter how compelling the case for parties to have their own foundations, the exigencies of day-to-day electoral poli-tics override any interest Canadian political parties might have in creating them, and further, that it would be unwise to force parties to accept some-thing they do not want. This conclusion is open to question. Indeed, the best evidence of the need for party-based institutes is that all the large national parties have made efforts to create such organizations in the past, and have expressed interest in continuing such efforts.

The Liberal Party in the late 1960s and again in the 1980s launched a program of political education revolving around seminars and after their defeat in 1984, published a periodical entitled *De Novo*, drawing on contrib-utors from within and outside the party and the academic community.

In the early 1980s, following the defeat of the Progressive Conservative government under Joe Clark and stimulated by the view that neither the parliamentary research office nor any of the institutes had been of any help in preparing the party for the transition from opposition to government, a group of Progressive Conservatives headed by Frank Oberle launched the National Foundation for Public Policy Development. It received letters patent and held its first official meeting on 14 May 1982. A conference was held in the fall of that year and a newsletter begun, but the foundation received an apparently fatal blow when its application for charitable tax status was rejected by Revenue Canada. At about the same time, the party was beginning to mobilize for the next election and funding for the foun-dation became a low priority, with the result that it disappeared soon after. (Lindquist 1989)

The NDP has an affiliated institute, the Douglas-Coldwell Foundation. However, the links between the foundation and the party are weak, in part because the Douglas-Coldwell Foundation does not wish to compromise its charitable tax status, and in part because the Foundation undertakes only limited activities. In addition, the leadership of the NDP has not been able to develop a strategy that would make effective use of the research and policy resources of the Foundation. Instead, the approach used by the party has tended to see policy development as one dimension of the short-term focus of adversarial politics. Policy research and development are the basic responsibilities of senior party officials who either report to the party leader or members of the parliamentary caucus. Despite the ideological cohesiveness between the Foundation and the NDP, there has been no cred-ible bridging of the two separate organizational traditions and interests. The presence of the Douglas-Coldwell Foundation and the limited use the NDP has made of it show the inability of the Canadian party system to establish a strong institutional basis that develops and presents cogent, long-term and well-developed policy alternatives to Canadian voters. Encouragingly, there are discussions on revitalizing the Douglas-Coldwell Foundation and giving it a more meaningful role.

In sum, the failure of the large national parties to engage in political education has limited their opportunities to accommodate and mediate conflicting representational needs. They lack well-established networks of knowledgeable supporters who can provide advice on policy problems and policy implementation, or promote and defend the trade-offs that con-stitute an inherent part of sound public policies. In the absence of such opportunities to participate in the political process, many individuals have pursued their particular visions through specialized interest groups.

The experience of several other countries serves as a useful guide to strengthening political parties as primary political organizations. The links between parties and their members need to be revitalized and broadened, and the capacities of parties to develop public policies must be enhanced. From an institutional point of view, this is best accomplished under the auspices of a party institute or foundation that would be separate from the party's day-to-day and short-term electoral activities. The creation of party foundations by large registered parties would make a valuable contribution to our society.

Party foundations would have a mandate to engage in political edu-cation and to develop and articulate alternative policy responses to public issues. They would be linked to their parties, but would nonetheless operate under separate boards of directors. The party itself would determine the pro-cess for selecting and appointing board members. For example, the party leader or any party officer could be appointed to the board of directors. The boards would be responsible for appointing the directors, approving the program of activities of the organizations and, with the directors, have control over and responsibility for the budgets. The directors, in consultation with the boards, would be responsible for developing and implementing programs of activities consistent with the mission and goals outlined in their constitutions and for maintaining liaison with their party leaders, the parliamentary parties and the constituent parts of the parties. To ensure a consistent and credible organizational presence, the constitutions of the foundations would have to meet the corporate requirements established for non-profit organizations as identified in the *Canada Corporations Act*.

Paradoxically, the contribution of foundations to parties will be enhanced if a certain space is provided between these organizations and the parties. On the one hand, this is imperative to give the flexibility, credibility and autonomy of action necessary to engage in meaningful policy development and education, and to attract sympathetic but non-partisan talents. On the other hand, parties and their leaders must be protected from attacks and criticism if and when alternative public policies are explored and discussed within their respective foundations.

In recommending that political parties establish party foundations or strengthen their existing foundations, we envisage a mission that would include the following kinds of activities:

- acting as a critical institutional base for a series of networks extending into different policy fields, and drawing on specialists from various sectors to provide sources of advice for the party executives and leadership to generate new ideas, and to examine the feasibility of implementing the party's policies;
- acting as a base for identifying and recruiting knowledgeable individuals with expertise in specific policy fields, in the programs and operations of government, and with the skills needed to support government leaders and to assist a party in the transition from opposition to government; and
- acting as a forum in which the party leadership can interact with various constituents of the party to help chart policy initiatives and to mobilize support in a manner that would not be possible in formal policy conventions or in government.

Recommendation 1.5.15

We recommend that

(a) registered parties be encouraged to create party foundations;
(b) the purpose of the party foundations be:
   (1) to provide registered parties with a permanent institutional base for the development and promotion of policy alternatives;
   (2) to bring together party members to participate in seminars and conferences on public policy issues;

(3) to maintain a publication program to promote the education of party members;

(4) to serve as a source of policy and research advice to registered parties in their roles as opposition and government parties; and

(5) to assist registered parties during transitions from opposition to government, and from government to opposition; and

(c) to be eligible for direct and/or indirect funding, party foundations be required:

(1) to meet the requirements for a non-profit organization established under the *Canada Corporations Act*;

(2) to have a constitution separate from their party's, explicitly stating the mission and goals of the organization, outlining procedures for selecting board members and the director, and providing a reasonable degree of autonomy to allow for and encourage the free flow of ideas and debate on important issues;

(3) to have a board of directors that represents the constituent parts of the party including, if the party so decides, the party leader or any party officer;

(4) to have specific provisions prohibiting the director and other full-time personnel from participating directly in the preparation of election-related material or in the conduct of election campaigns, unless they take unpaid leave from their positions;

(5) to present annual reports to the Canada Elections Commission on their activities and programs, including full disclosure of all revenues, expenditures and contributions, consistent with the financial disclosure requirements for political parties; and

(6) to prohibit any transfers of funds from the foundation to the political party other than for specific administrative services provided by the party.

Each foundation's constitution would be submitted to the Canada Elections Commission. In addition, audited financial statements and an annual report detailing the foundation's activities would be published and submitted to the Canada Elections Commission.

Funding would be in part through a system of annual payments from public funds to each party's foundation. The threshold for such funding would be a requirement that a registered party receive at least 5 per cent of the popular vote in the preceding election. The annual payments to foundations would be equal to $0.25 times the number of votes a qualifying registered party received at the previous general election. If such a system were now in place, the annual payments would total $3.04 million and would be allocated to the parties as follows: Progressive Conservative Party, $1 569 674; Liberal Party, $879 122; and New Democratic Party, $589 979.

Party foundations should be encouraged to solicit funds from private sources, whether they are individuals, businesses, unions or private foundations. The foundations could also benefit from existing trusts and endowments held by registered parties where limited use has been made of such funds. To this end, it would be necessary to amend the *Income Tax Act* to provide that registered party foundations are eligible for the tax credit allowed for donations to charitable organizations. This tax incentive could well be useful in encouraging contributions from those who might be more inclined to support a party foundation than to donate to a party. Under this scheme, political parties and party foundations would be encouraged to solicit contributions from different sources.

However, in receiving this special status the foundations should meet the conditions required of charitable organizations registered under the *Income Tax Act* to ensure that the annual grants received by the foundations are used to fulfil their purpose and mission. A circular on the role and responsibilities of charitable organizations issued by Revenue Canada states that:

> to ensure that most of a charity's funds are used for charitable purposes, to discourage inappropriate accumulations of capital, and to keep administrative expenses to a reasonable level, the Act requires all charities to satisfy an annual minimum expenditure test which is based on what happened in the prior year. Every "registered charity" is required, each year, to have expended its "disbursement quotas". (Canada, Revenue Canada, Taxation 1985, 10)

The term "disbursement quotas" is defined in paragraph 149.1 (1)(e) of the Act. The quotas are used, in part, to calculate the dollar value of donation receipts in the preceding year, subject to certain exclusions. Specifically, charitable organizations are required "in any taxation year, [to] expend amounts that are equal to at least 80% of the aggregate of amounts for which it issued donation receipts in its immediately preceding taxation year". (Canada, Revenue Canada, Taxation 1985, 3) Further, to ensure they have credible administrative structures in place that can co-ordinate and implement their diverse responsibilities, the organization and composition of the board of directors of the foundations should be consistent with the registration requirements for charitable organizations.

Recommendation 1.5.16

We recommend that

(a) public funding be provided for registered party foundations, subject to the threshold of a registered party having

at least 5 per cent of the national vote in the preceding election, in the form of an annual grant of $0.25 for each vote received by the registered party in the preceding election;

(b) the application for the creation of a party foundation be presented to the Canada Elections Commission by the registered party;

(c) a registered party that has not set up a foundation be ineligible for the annual grants;

(d) if the foundation is set up in any calendar year following a general election, the foundation be entitled to the total annual grant for that year;

(e) the *Income Tax Act* be amended to provide that contributions to registered party foundations be eligible for a tax credit on the same scale as the credit that now applies to donations to charitable organizations;

(f) foundations be obliged to comply with the requirements for charitable organizations under the *Income Tax Act*; and

(g) the composition of the board of directors for the foundations be consistent with the requirements for charitable organizations registered under the *Income Tax Act*.

Requiring registered parties to receive at least 5 per cent of the national vote in the preceding federal election as a condition of receiving annual grants for foundations would make funding available to those parties that have a credible and visible presence in the legislative and electoral processes. Party foundations should be structured to assist parties in organizing the processes of parliamentary opposition and government. The foundations would provide research and advice to parties that make periodic transitions between opposition and government. In the past, parties have had difficulties in making such transitions. Parties newly elected to government often do not have experienced officials or representatives who are well briefed on the exigencies of governance and on the complexities of the policy process. Only a small number of parties would be involved in such transitions. Further, the 5 per cent threshold would mean that annual funding for party foundations would be directed to those parties that have the organizational and political resources to engage effectively in legislative representation and accommodation of conflicting interests. Since 1945, no political party has won at least 5 per cent of the national vote in a federal election without electing at least six MPs.

Some registered parties that satisfy the electoral threshold for one election and set up party foundations may in fact fall below the threshold in a subsequent election. These parties, based on their ability to nominate candidates in 50 constituencies, would still be registered parties. While these parties would retain the right to have their foundation registered and accredited by the Canada Elections Commission, the level of public support they received would be sufficiently modest to justify disqualifying them from annual public funding. Finally, as is the case with any institutional innovation, there is no guarantee that foundations will yield the expected benefits. We propose a comprehensive review after seven years to ensure that both the parties and the foundations take the mandate of the foundations seriously.

Recommendation 1.5.17

We recommend that

(a) a registered party that has established a foundation but does not receive 5 per cent of the national vote in the following election be permitted to continue to have its foundation accredited by the Canada Elections Commission;

(b) any registered party that has been de-registered have its foundation de-registered by the Canada Elections Commission; and

(c) public funding provisions for party foundations be reviewed after seven years by the Canada Elections Commission and that the Commission report to Parliament on the results of its review.

The creation of party foundations supported by public funding would greatly promote and enhance activities that Canadian political parties have attempted in only a limited fashion in recent years. The institutionalization and extension of these activities would help to open new avenues for political participation, provide new opportunities for the exercise of political leadership, and ultimately strengthen the representational capacity of the parties.

THE FINANCING OF REGISTERED POLITICAL PARTIES

The Pattern of Party Financing, 1974–1990

The capacity of federal political parties to perform their roles as primary political organizations is also related to the state of their finances. Before 1974, the Liberal and Progressive Conservative parties were in most cases able to collect fairly substantial sums to run election campaigns. During non-election years, however, their spending and revenue declined dramatically. For example, the Liberal Party spent $5.5 million on the 1974 election campaign; the Progressive Conservatives spent $4.5 million. During calendar year 1973, however, the Liberals had spent $407 130 and the Progressive Conservatives had spent $900 195. The contrast was less marked in the case of the NDP, which spent only a small fraction of what the two older parties were spending on election campaigns: the NDP spent $353 852 during the 1974 election; its regular budget in 1973 had been around $250 000. (Paltiel 1975, 196–97)

Reviewing the overall impact of the 1974 legislation, which introduced an income tax credit for political contributions, W.T. Stanbury has stated that it "transformed the financing of federal political parties in Canada. Its most important consequence has been to provide all the main parties with vastly larger sums to spend in the years *between* elections." (1991 RC) Table 5.11 provides an overview of the revenue (contributions and other sources of income) and expenditures of the Progressive Conservative, Liberal and New Democratic parties from 1 August 1974 to the end of 1990.

Immediately after the 1974 legislation came into effect, the Liberal Party's revenue exceeded that of the Progressive Conservative Party. The latter benefited from its early move to solicit funds by direct mail, and by 1978 its revenue had risen to $5.5 million (compared with just over $5 million for the Liberal Party). (Seidle and Paltiel 1981, 242–43) The financing of the NDP improved considerably during the post-1974 period, and by 1978 the NDP's federally receipted revenues totalled $3.4 million.

As Table 5.11 indicates, although revenue for these three parties increased during the period up to and including 1983, a different pattern subsequently emerged: revenue for the Progressive Conservatives and NDP continued to rise most years, but the Liberal Party was able to better its 1983 revenue in only two of the four subsequent non-election years.

A further contrast between the pre- and post-1974 periods lies in the sources of these parties' funding. Before adoption of the *Election Expenses Act*, the Liberal and Progressive Conservative parties were financed by contributions from at most a few hundred corporations, primarily to finance election campaigns. The NDP relied on union contributions and relatively small donations.

Tables 5.12, 5.13 and 5.14 report the proportion of these three parties' total contributions since 1 August 1974 by source. The NDP has consistently obtained the greatest share of federally receipted contributions from individuals: in non-election years (excluding the first five months the legislation was in effect), the proportion averaged 80 per cent; in election years, when the party usually receives a number of large union donations, the share from individuals has averaged 63 per cent.

The Progressive Conservative Party initially obtained less than half the value of its total contributions from individuals, but by 1981 donations from individuals accounted for 62 per cent of the total. Except for the 1984 election year, the proportion remained above 50 per cent until 1987, when it dropped to 47.5 per cent. In 1990, the party received 42.4 per cent of the value of its contributions from individuals.

The proportion of the Liberal Party's total contributions from individuals has been greater than 50 per cent during four of the eight non-election years since 1980. In 1989, the proportion was 37.7 per cent (lower than any non-election year since 1974). In 1990, 61.8 per cent of the total value of contributions to the Liberal Party were from individuals; however, this includes contributions to candidates and fees paid to the party by delegates who attended the June 1990 leadership convention.

Table 5.11
Revenue and expenditures of the Progressive Conservative, Liberal and New Democratic parties, 1974–1990
(thousands of dollars)

| Period | Progressive Conservative Party | | Liberal Party | | New Democratic Party | | |
	Revenue	Expenditure	Revenue	Expenditure	Total revenue[a]	Federal revenue[b]	Expenditure[c]
1974	1 721[d]	1 597[d]	2 217[d]	1 936[d]	1 437[e]	N.A.	1 270[e]
1975	1 203[f]	889[f]			2 580	N.A.	2 570
1976	4 084	3 497	5 823[g]	4 707[g]	2 925	2 281	2 381
1977	3 774	4 233	4 587	4 187	3 525	3 006	3 105
1978	5 465	5 470	5 018	5 283	4 184	3 400	3 514
1979E	8 376	5 184	6 302	2 771	6 020	4 741	4 678
EE		3 845		3 913			2 190
R	794		718		496		
1980E	7 564	4 923	7 457	3 702	6 101	4 921	5 992
EE		4 407		3 846			3 086
R	978		910		677		
1981	6 950	7 542	5 592	5 116	6 003	3 856	6 491
1982	8 521	8 521	6 746	6 781	7 108	4 766	4 871
1983	14 767	13 199	7 736	6 277	8 669	5 972	8 009
1984E	21 979	20 777	11 598	11 999	10 513	7 357	7 407
EE		6 389		6 293			4 731
R	1 438		1 416		1 064		
1985	15 073	11 654	6 163	8 149	10 152	6 464	11 071
1986	15 639	14 141	10 719	11 166	14 639	6 984	15 188
1987	13 058	13 490	8 882	9 274	12 608	6 833	14 012
1988E	25 231	21 124	16 358	10 176	18 754	12 162	14 933
EE		7 922		6 840			7 061
R	1 782		1 539		1 589		
1989	14 521	12 824	6 397	7 115	13 865	7 746	12 507
1990	11 298	10 635	13 778	13 327	15 439	9 043	14 262

Source: Adapted from Stanbury 1991 RC, Tables 3.1 and 3.2.

E = Election year; EE = 'Election expenses' for the party; R = Reimbursement of election expenses by federal government, that is, one-half permitted spending on the electronic media for advertising in 1979 and 1980 and 22.5 per cent of total allowable expenditures in 1984 and 1988.

[a]Before 1980, the chief electoral officer did *not* include provincially receipted revenue in the NDP revenue figure. As of 1976, this revenue has been included here. After 1980, the chief electoral officer's report included as revenue provincially receipted revenue, as well as provincial rebates and subsidies.
[b]Federally receipted contributions plus other income and reimbursement of party 'election expenses'.
[c]Total expenditure for the party including most of its provincial sections (does not include Ontario).
[d]From 1 August 1974 to 31 July 1975.   [f]From 1 August 1975 to 31 December 1975.
[e]From 1 August 1974 to 31 December 1974.   [g]From 1 August 1975 to 31 December 1976.

Table 5.12
Value of contributions to the Progressive Conservative Party, by source, 1974–1990
(per cent)

Year	Individuals	Business and commercial organizations	Trade unions	Other[a]
1974–75[b]	45.84	51.83	0.0	2.33
1976	48.89	49.32	0.0	1.80
1977	49.16	48.62	0.01	2.20
1978	49.62	48.95	0.0	1.44
1979E	38.00	59.94	0.01	2.05
1980E	40.24	57.75	0.0	2.01
1981	62.15	37.03	0.0	0.82
1982	63.23	35.67	0.0	1.10
1983	64.54	34.16	0.0	1.29
1984E	47.96	52.04	0.0	0.0
1985	54.05	45.95	0.0	0.0
1986	51.88	48.10	0.01	0.0
1987	47.53	52.47	0.0	0.0
1988E	41.49	58.51	0.01	0.0
1989	49.63	50.30	0.01	0.06
1990	42.42	57.48	0.0	0.09

Source: Calculated from data reported in Stanbury 1991 RC, Table 4.1 and fiscal period returns for 1990.

E = Election year

[a]Includes other organizations and governments.
[b]1974–75 figures combine 1 August 1974 to 31 July 1975 and 1 August 1975 to 31 December 1975.

While year-to-year comparisons are useful, a better index of the parties' ongoing financial health is their accumulated surplus or deficit. Stanbury's analysis is reported in Table 5.15. During the 1980–1990 period, the Liberal Party ran an accumulated deficit of $4.77 million, while the Progressive Conservatives had an accumulated surplus of $1.25 million. The NDP as a whole ran an accumulated deficit of $2.44 million during the 1980–1990 period. This contrasts with the period between the coming into force of the election expenses legislation and the end of 1979, when all three parties ran a surplus. On this basis, there is room to question how successful one if not two of the largest parties have been in meeting the spending pressures they have faced in recent years – pressures that are particularly strong in the context of running competitive election campaigns. (The Liberal Party's deficit is rooted in the 1984 campaign, when it spent almost $6 million, virtually half its total revenue, including the post-election reimbursement for that year.)

Table 5.13
Value of contributions to the Liberal Party, by source, 1974–1990
(per cent)

Year	Individuals	Business and commercial organizations	Trade unions	Other[a]
1974–75[b]	51.40	46.22	0.03	2.35
1975–76[c]	52.79	45.98	0.01	1.22
1977	44.84	51.80	0.03	3.33
1978	43.97	52.05	0.01	3.97
1979E	22.69	74.24	0.03	3.04
1980E	36.63	60.00	0.03	3.34
1981	41.24	53.10	0.03	5.63
1982	52.34	41.31	0.04	6.30
1983	44.78	48.63	0.04	6.55
1984E	49.09	50.60	0.02	0.28
1985	56.17	43.66	0.02	0.15
1986	54.18	45.63	0.05	0.14
1987	39.31	60.50	0.10	0.09
1988E	35.94	63.96	0.04	0.06
1989	37.72	62.16	0.05	0.07
1990	61.81	37.94	0.03	0.22

Source: Calculated from data reported in Stanbury 1991 RC, Table 5.1 and fiscal period returns for 1990.

E = Election year

[a]Includes other organizations and governments.
[b]From 1 August 1974 to 31 July 1975.
[c]From 1 August 1975 to 31 December 1976.

The financing of candidates' campaigns reveals a different situation. Following the 1984 general election, the combined surplus of all candidates was more than $8 million. (Canada, Chief Electoral Officer 1989, 47) The comparable figure for the 1988 election was $9.6 million. (Canada, Chief Electoral Officer 1991, 10) The Liberal Party has been able to benefit somewhat from the healthy state of most candidates' election finances. Since the 1979 election, the party has regularly 'taxed' a proportion of candidates' reimbursements. Following the 1988 election, the party collected $2.27 million by obliging the majority of its candidates to pass on 50 per cent of their reimbursements to the federal party. (Stanbury 1991 RC) In 1988, the British Columbia section of the NDP required all candidates in the province to remit 100 per cent of their reimbursements to help meet its quota for the federal party. Candidates submitted a total of $558 127. (Stanbury 1991 RC) Party representatives indicate that through various other arrangements, candidates have shared some of the funds received through reimbursements.

Table 5.14
Value of contributions to the New Democratic Party, by source, 1974–1990
(per cent)

Year	Individuals	Business and commercial organizations	Trade unions	Other[a]
1974[b]	89.47	0.99	9.30	0.24
1975	80.14	5.56	14.20	0.09
1976	80.33	4.17	15.33	0.16
1977	77.23	6.64	15.25	0.88
1978	78.32	6.34	15.04	0.29
1979E	55.36	3.85	38.47	2.31
1980E	60.64	2.08	36.65	0.63
1981	81.15	3.09	14.57	1.19
1982	83.20	3.18	10.43	3.19
1983	86.99	0.72	11.08	1.21
1984E	63.45	0.79	32.96	2.79
1985	81.71	1.04	15.40	1.85
1986	77.89	2.75	18.14	1.23
1987	77.05	0.76	21.67	0.51
1988E	71.46	2.39	24.76	1.39
1989	83.12	0.75	13.99	2.14
1990	72.60	1.70	14.08	11.62

Source: Calculated from data reported in Stanbury 1991 RC, Table 6.3 and fiscal period returns for 1990.

E = Election Year

[a]Includes other organizations and governments.
[b]From 1 August 1974 to 31 December 1974.

Table 5.15
Accumulated surplus (or deficit) of the three largest federal parties, 1974–78, 1979, 1980–84, 1985–1990
(thousands of dollars)[a]

Party	1974–78	1979	1980–84	1985–1990
Progressive Conservative	561	241	(3 560)	4 811
Liberal	1 505	336	(2 558)	(2 211)
New Democratic[b]	1 811	(350)	(453)	(1 988)

Source: Adapted from Stanbury 1991 RC.

[a]Nominal dollars.
[b]New Democratic Party as a whole as reported to the CEO after a few minor adjustments.

Another perspective on the state of the national parties' finances can be gained by examining the number and average size of individual contributions. Table 5.16 indicates that excluding election years, the number of individuals donating to the three largest parties has declined in recent years. For the Progressive Conservative Party, the peak was in 1983, when a leadership convention was held, with 99 264 contributions from individuals. (The number for 1990 – 27 702 – was less than one-third that number.) Except for 1990, when the party held a leadership convention, the largest number of individuals contributing to the Liberal Party was in 1986 – 35 369; in 1989, the number was 19 970. The number of individual contributions to the NDP

Table 5.16
Number and average size of contributions by individuals to the Progressive Conservative, Liberal and New Democratic parties, 1974–1990[a]

Year	Progressive Conservative Party[b]		Liberal Party[c]		New Democratic Party	
	Number	Average ($)	Number	Average ($)	Number	Average ($)
1974 (5 mos)	6 423	284	4 117	321	27 910	132
1975	10 341	253	13 373	292	58 889	90
1976	23 409	197	18 261	274	56 142	77
1977	20 339	192	21 063	209	60 169	82
1978	35 615	153	22 350	192	67 133	78
1979E	34 952	170	13 025	170	63 655	80
1980E	32 720	167	17 670	240	62 428	88
1981	48 125	136	24 735	128	56 545	77
1982	52 694	134	27 968	156	66 665	58
1983	99 264	119	33 649	125	65 624	98
1984E	93 199	135	29 056	220	80 027	64
1985	75 117	125	28 545	131	97 364	56
1986	52 786	170	35 369	186	90 487	64
1987	39 320	168	28 972	131	87 927	59
1988E	53 893	199	30 642	163	118 390	69
1989	40 191	170	19 970	119	89 290	67
1990	27 702	161	36 361	196	116 448	50

Source: Adapted from Stanbury 1991 RC, tables 8.2 and 8.3.

E = Election year

[a]In 1989 dollars. The table does not include contributions by individuals to *candidates* in election years.
[b]The original figures for the Progressive Conservative Party were for 1 August 1974 to 31 July 1975 and 1 August 1975 to 31 December 1975. They were recomputed on a pro rata basis to fit the calendar years.
[c]The original figures for the Liberal Party were for 1 August 1974 to 31 July 1975 and 1 August 1975 to 31 December 1976. They were recomputed on a pro rata basis to fit the calendar years.

in non-election years was the greatest in 1990 – 116 448. The number of donations from individuals to other registered parties was much higher in 1989 – 17 232 – than in any other year since the 1974 legislation came into effect; in 1990, that number rose to 37 837. The number of contributions to the Reform Party from individuals was 7630 in 1989 (its first full year as a registered party) and 23 462 in 1990. The Christian Heritage Party received 7541 contributions from individuals in 1989 and 9226 in 1990. Further details on the financing of parties other than the Progressive Conservative, Liberal and New Democratic parties in 1990 are found in Table 5.17.

As indicated in Table 5.18, the number of individual contributions to candidates has increased at each election since 1979. Table 5.18 also shows that, when adjusted for inflation, the average size of donations from individuals in recent non-election years has been considerably smaller than during the initial period after the legislation came into effect.

Although the number of individuals making political contributions to federal parties and candidates rose after 1974 (and has certainly been much higher than before adoption of the *Election Expenses Act*), the proportion of Canadians who participate in this way is low. In both the 1984 and 1988 election years, less than 2 per cent of Canadians made a political contribution to a party or candidate, and the rate was no higher in any other year since 1974. (Stanbury 1991 RC) Thus, while the base of federal party finance has broadened, only a small fraction of Canadians financially support the federal political process.

Table 5.17
Other registered parties: financial activities, 1990

Party	Revenue ($)	Expenses ($)	Number of contributions (N)	Average contribution ($)
Christian Heritage Party	497 956	376 665	9 268	54
Party for Commonwealth of Canada	350 038	406 402	431	108
Communist Party	487 805	471 994	710	465
Confederation of Regions Western Party	159 841	196 057	2 962	54
Green Party	52 928	56 337	389	136
Libertarian Party	57 152	57 530	476	120
Reform Party	2 213 762	1 721 468	23 736	93
Parti Rhinocéros	400	230	2	200
Social Credit Party	22 853	15 466	212	108

Source: Adapted from Canada, Elections Canada 1990.

Note: Total revenue for the Communist, Confederation of Regions Western and Commonwealth of Canada parties consists of total contributions and other revenue, while the other parties listed contributions as their sole source of revenue.

Table 5.18
Number of contributions from individuals to parties and candidates, 1974–1990

Year	PC, Liberal and NDP	Other parties	All parties	All candidates	Total
1974 (5 mos)	34 703	7 796[a]	42 499		42 499
1975	82 603	2 007[b]	84 610		84 610
1976	97 812	11 432	109 244		109 244
1977	101 571	2 754	104 325		104 325
1978	125 098	5 040	130 138		130 138
1979E	111 632	7 701	119 333	67 323	186 656
1980E	112 908	3 865	116 773	70 528	187 301
1981	129 405	1 600	131 005		131 005
1982	147 327	1 538	148 865		148 865
1983	198 537	6 556	205 093		205 093
1984E	202 282	8 700	210 982	87 456	298 438
1985	201 026	1 622	202 648		202 648
1986	178 642	2 442	181 084		181 084
1987	156 219	2 603	158 822		158 822
1988E	202 925	5 410	208 335	104 807	313 142
1989	149 451	17 232[c]	166 683		166 683
1990	180 511	37 837[d]	218 348		218 348

Source: Stanbury 1991 RC, Table 8.1.

E = Election year.

[a]From 1 August 1974 to 31 July 1975.

[b]From 1 August 1975 to 31 December 1975.

[c]Includes 7 541 for the Christian Heritage Party (22 October 1988 to 31 December 1989) and 7 630 for the Reform Party. The total number of contributions from individuals to the Confederation of Regions Western Party was not disclosed; the number included here, 265, is based on those contributing $100 or more and so is understated.

[d]Includes 23 462 contributions to the Reform Party and 9 226 to the Christian Heritage Party.

Public Funding and the Political Contribution Tax Credit

As indicated in Table 5.19, seven provinces provide direct public funding to parties and/or candidates. All provide election reimbursements to candidates, three provide election reimbursements to parties, and three fund political parties through annual allowances. Reimbursements for federal registered parties and candidates are discussed in Chapter 6 of this volume. All provinces except Saskatchewan and Newfoundland provide indirect public funding through a provincial tax credit for political contributions.

The total and per-voter cost of public funding at the federal and provincial levels is presented in Table 5.20. At the federal level, the cost per voter ($1.03 a year in 1989 dollars) is higher than in four provinces, but is considerably lower than in the three maritime provinces and Manitoba, and somewhat below the cost in Ontario ($1.29) and British Columbia ($1.20).

Table 5.19
Public funding programs of political parties and candidates in Canada

Jurisdictions	Candidates: election reimbursements	Parties: election reimbursements	Parties: annual funding	Tax credits
Canada	X	X		X
British Columbia				X
Alberta				X
Saskatchewan	X	X		
Manitoba	X	X		X
Ontario	X	X		X
Quebec	X		X	X
Nova Scotia	X			X
New Brunswick	X		X	X
Prince Edward Island	X		X	X
Newfoundland				

Source: Constantinou 1991 RC, tables 6.1, 6.3 and 6.5–6.8.

Table 5.20
Public funding of political parties and candidates in Canada: cost
(1989 dollars)

Jurisdictions	Total	Total cost per voter per year
Prince Edward Island	682 038	2.55
New Brunswick	6 195 949	2.47
Manitoba	3 031 310	2.08
Nova Scotia	3 541 638	1.42
Ontario	10 747 033	1.29
British Columbia	2 126 069	1.20
Canada	**72 662 758**	**1.03**
Saskatchewan	2 406 893	0.90
Quebec	14 125 769	0.76
Alberta	1 393 351	0.47
Newfoundland	None	None

Source: Constantinou 1991 RC, Table 6.12.

Note: Cost is calculated based on most recent election cycle for which complete data were available.

The political contribution tax credit is an incentive to donors rather than a direct grant of public monies. Therefore, it is also essential to measure its costs to the public treasury to assess the behaviour of contributors and to determine how, and if, any modifications should be enacted to improve its effect on the finances of registered parties.

Table 5.21 reports the number and cost of federal tax credits claimed since 1974. The data indicate that, for the most part, the number of individuals claiming tax credits and the cost of those credits (in foregone revenue) have risen in successive non-election years. Between 1975 (the first full year when the tax credit was in effect) and 1978, the number of individuals claiming the credit nearly doubled (64 547 individuals claimed the credit in the latter year). The number and amount of credits claimed peaked in 1986, when 117 566 individual taxpayers claimed credits worth $9.93 million; including credits claimed by corporations, the total was $10.77 million. In 1987, the number of individuals claiming credits dropped to 102 824 and the total amount to $8.47 million. Based on preliminary statistics, the number of individuals claiming the credit rose somewhat in 1989, to 108 740, as did the total cost ($10.21 million).

A similar pattern has developed in election years. The number of individuals claiming the credit has risen at each election, and the number claiming the credit in 1988 (184 410) was nearly double the number in 1979 (92 353). The total cost of credits claimed rose from $7.63 million in 1979 to $18.85 million in 1988.

The tax credit has been successful in broadening the base of party finance, but the number of individuals making political contributions dropped in the late 1980s, and even at the peak, it represented only a small fraction of Canadians. This implies that the tax credit may not be as strong an incentive as some have suggested. In fact, as Table 5.22 indicates, a significant proportion of individuals do not claim the tax credit for their political contributions, although the percentage of those who do has risen in recent years. Until 1980, less than 50 per cent of those making contributions claimed the credit. The claim rate subsequently rose, and in 1986, 1987 and 1989 almost two-thirds of those who made contributions claimed the credit. The 1989 claim rate (based on preliminary statistics) was the highest since the tax credit was initiated.

Indirect public funding through the tax credit represents a significant share of federal party finances: the value of tax credits claimed was equal to 29 per cent of the parties' total revenue during the 1985–88 cycle and 30.7 per cent of their total revenue during the 1981–84 cycle. (Michaud and Laferrière 1991 RC)

During our public hearings there were comments that the political contribution tax credit is more generous than the tax credit for donations to charitable organizations. This is true only for political contributions up to $1150; at that point, the tax credit for charitable donations provides greater benefit to the taxpayer. If the scale for the charitable donation credit were applied to political contributions, the result would be a greater tax benefit (and increased cost to the treasury) for larger contributions, many of which come from corporations, and less benefit for smaller contributions, most of which come from individuals. This would not be desirable.

Table 5.21
Federal income tax credits for political contributions, 1974–1989

Year	Individuals (N)	Tax credits: individuals ($)	Corporations (N)	Tax credits: corporations ($)	Tax credits: totals ($)
1974	19 584	1 273 000	N.A.	N.A.	1 273 000
1975	36 227	2 394 000	N.A.	N.A.	2 394 000
1976	48 313	2 800 000	N.A.	465 000	3 265 000
1977	48 027	3 114 000	N.A.	500 000	3 614 000
1978	64 547	3 973 000	N.A.	634 000	4 607 000
1979	92 353	6 111 000	N.A.	1 233 000	7 344 000
1980	95 547	6 378 000	N.A.	1 247 000	7 625 000
1981	77 114	4 910 000	N.A.	538 000	5 448 000
1982	85 941	6 268 000	3 507	567 000	6 835 000
1983	104 599	8 237 000	4 178	762 000	8 999 000
1984	151 308	13 588 000	7 561	1 595 000	15 183 000
1985	109 310	8 624 000	5 995	1 254 000	9 878 000
1986	117 566	9 934 000	3 979	836 000	10 770 000
1987	102 824	7 660 000	3 647	808 000	8 468 000
1988	184 410	17 515 000	5 471	1 333 000	18 848 000
1989	108 740	8 874 000	5 744	1 333 000*	10 207 000
Total	1 446 410	111 653 000	40 082	13 105 000	124 758 000

Source: Data provided by Revenue Canada, Taxation.
N.A. = Data not available.
*Preliminary statistics.

A number of interveners called for changes in the federal political contribution tax credit to provide a greater benefit to taxpayers making such contributions. They pointed out that the scale of the tax credit has not been adjusted since it was adopted in 1974, and that its value to the taxpayer has declined as a result of inflation. Some claimed the present cut-off of $100 discourages contributions greater than that amount, and proposed that the cut-off be raised. Other interveners suggested simplifying the scale while increasing the total allowable credit.

Table 5.22

Number of individuals making political contributions and number claiming the federal income tax credit for political contributions, 1974–1989

Year	Number of individual donors to parties and candidates	Number of individuals claiming tax credits	Number claiming tax credit as a percentage of total donors	Average individual credit*
1974	42 499	19 584	46.1	65
1975	84 610	36 227	42.8	66
1976	109 244	48 313	44.2	58
1977	104 325	48 027	46.0	65
1978	130 138	64 547	49.6	60
1979E	186 656	92 353	49.6	66
1980E	187 301	95 547	51.0	67
1981	131 005	77 114	58.9	64
1982	148 865	85 941	57.7	73
1983	205 093	104 599	51.0	79
1984E	298 438	151 308	50.7	90
1985	202 648	109 310	53.9	79
1986	181 084	117 566	64.9	85
1987	158 822	102 824	64.7	75
1988E	313 142	184 410	58.9	95
1989	166 683	108 740	65.2	82

Source: Stanbury 1991 RC, Table 8.4; 1989 tax credit statistics provided by Revenue Canada, Taxation.

E = Election year

*Nominal dollars.

In research for the Commission, Michaud and Laferrière examined the possible impact of raising the cut-off to $125 for the 75 per cent rate. The researchers estimated that, at the very least, the average donation would increase from $118 to $123 and the claim rate for the tax credit would rise from 59 to 61 per cent. At the most, the average donation would rise to $132 and the claim rate to 65 per cent. According to their projections, the cost of the tax credit in 1988 would have increased to $21.7 million under the first scenario, and to $24.8 million under the second. This would represent increases of 15 and 31 per cent respectively over the actual cost of the tax credit that year, whereas revenues to parties would have risen by a mere 7 per cent. This research illustrates that the cost to the treasury of the tax credit is sensitive to changes in the rules: even a modest increase can be expected to lead to a considerably greater cost to the public treasury.

Quebec and Ontario changed the scale of their tax credits several years after they were introduced. Quebec increased the maximum credit from $75 to $140, effective 21 December 1983 (compared with $500 at the federal level); the maximum for Ontario's tax credit was increased from $500 to $750 effective 1 January 1986. Total contributions to the Parti libéral du Québec and the Parti québécois rose from $4.3 million in 1983 to $6.4 million in 1984 (the latter was a pre-election year, which may account for some of the increase). In Ontario, contributions to the three largest provincial parties in 1986 totalled $6.3 million, which was considerably lower than in 1984, the previous pre-election year, when the corresponding total was $12.6 million. (Constantinou 1991 RC)

The decline in political contributions from individuals in recent years and the variable claim rate for the tax credit lead us to ask whether the incentive provided by the credit is as strong as has sometimes been thought. Our research indicates that any change in the scale would cost significantly more to the public treasury than the amount of additional revenues that would accrue to parties. Hence, the cost-benefit analysis does not support a change. Moreover, Quebec is the province where contributions from individuals are the most numerous in relative terms; yet, it is the province with by far the least generous tax credit. Finally, Ontario's experience of a change in the scale of the tax credit did not lead to more or higher contributions. Clearly, from a public finance policy point of view, it is difficult to justify a more generous tax credit. If there is to be additional public funding of political parties, we are more inclined to support measures that give the parties greater assurance that they will receive adequate funding for activities that would strengthen them as primary political organizations.

Recommendation 1.5.18

We recommend that the scale of the federal political contribution tax credit not be changed.

A further issue concerns the use of the federal political contribution tax credit. Two questions must be addressed: (1) Which contributions should qualify for federal income tax receipts? (2) What activities ought to benefit from federally receipted funds?

We have concluded that registered parties should be allowed to issue tax receipts for contributions to leadership campaigns, and that those seeking nomination as candidates should have the same right in relation to contributions to their campaigns. In both cases, we propose that there be spending limits and that candidates be obliged to disclose the sources of contributions over $250 (the threshold we recommend for all political contributions in Chapter 7 of this volume).

Some political parties have been issuing tax credit receipts for delegate fees to party conventions. This may not have been anticipated when the 1974 legislation was adopted. The *Income Tax Act* refers to "an amount contributed" by a taxpayer to a registered party or officially nominated candidate, but does not specify the nature of contribution. This being said, attendance at party conventions is a form of political participation that should be encouraged. Giving a tax receipt for delegate fees may lower barriers to participation for party members, and in turn encourage a wider range of members to be active. This could help to strengthen political parties as primary political organizations. We therefore conclude that parties should continue to be permitted to issue tax receipts for convention fees, and that the *Income Tax Act* need not be amended in this regard.

As noted earlier, in certain cases national party funds, including contributions for which federal income tax credits are issued, are being used to finance political activity at the provincial and possibly the municipal levels. We recognize that this issue is related to party structure. According to W.T. Stanbury, "several millions of dollars each year raised by the NDP using the federal income tax credit for political contributions [are] spent on provincial political activities". (1991 RC, chapter 13)

The *Income Tax Act* is silent about the legitimate uses of contributions to federal parties for which tax credits have been issued, but it does not disallow intra-party transfers of funds that have benefited from the federal tax credit. Provincial party organizations can issue receipts to enable contributors to claim provincial tax credits in eight provinces, which is the proper course. Moreover, political finance legislation in a number of provinces (Ontario, Quebec, New Brunswick and Alberta) disallows transfers to parties outside the province (in some cases, with minor exceptions during elections), thus preventing provincially receipted funds from being used for federal political activities. In Saskatchewan and Newfoundland, the two provinces that do not have such a tax credit, relying on the federal tax credit to fund provincial parties raises serious questions. We acknowledge that party structures may differ significantly, but it is not acceptable for a federal tax incentive to be used to assist provincial or municipal political activities unless this is specifically determined by Parliament.

Recommendation 1.5.19

We recommend that the *Income Tax Act* be amended to specify that receipts allowing taxpayers to claim the political contribution tax credit be issued only for contributions intended to support the activities of a federally registered party, including its registered constituency associations, a candidate during a federal election or a person seeking the nomination as the candidate of a federally registered constituency association or the leadership of a federally registered party.

NOTES

1. The relationship between the press and political parties was not hard and fast, nor were individual newspapers always unwavering in their support. *La Presse* in Montreal, for example, initially radical Liberal in orientation, favoured the Conservatives from 1887 to 1896, then moved to the Liberal camp. The *Globe* in Toronto, while primarily a Liberal party organ, did not always toe the party line. (Rutherford 1982)

2. These two small parties, in attracting 9 per cent of the vote, effectively contributed to the defeat of the Conservatives. After 1896 no candidates from smaller parties or independent candidates were elected until 1921, except for a single candidate in 1908, and voting support for such candidates remained at between 1 and 2 per cent.

3. H.H. Stevens was Minister of Trade and Commerce in the 1930–35 Conservative government before splitting with Prime Minister R.B. Bennett over economic policy.

4. The data in the following tables are taken from the Survey of Attitudes about Electoral Reform, which was conducted at the Institute for Social Research at York University. The survey was conducted under the direction of André Blais and Elizabeth Gidengil and was based on about 2950 30-minute interviews of a random sample of Canadians between 13 September and 4 November 1991. The questionnaire included about 130 items on the electoral process. For details, see Blais and Gidengil (1991 RC).

5. In Quebec, payments are determined as follows: the total amount of funding each year is equal to $0.25 multiplied by the number of voters at the last general election; each party receives a payment in proportion to its share of the popular vote at that election. During the 1986–89 period, total payments were $4.5 million.

6. In New Brunswick, during the 1983–87 period, payments totalled $3 365 361. At $1.59 per voter per year, New Brunswick's program is the most generous of the three provinces with annual funding.

7. In Prince Edward Island, grants are determined by multiplying an amount (not to exceed $1.00) determined by the cabinet (after consultation with the leader of the opposition) by the number of votes the party received at the last general election. During the 1986–89 period, payments totalled $257 847 ($1.04 per voter per year) (all data in Notes 5, 6 and 7 from Constantinou 1991 RC).

APPENDIX: APPLICATION REQUIREMENTS FOR REGISTRATION OF CONSTITUENCY ASSOCIATIONS

Accounting Profession Working Group

Proposed registration of constituency associations of registered parties. Application requires:

- a letter of endorsement from the chief agent of the registered party;
- the name of the constituency association and the registered party that endorses it;
- the names of the principal officers;
- the name and address of the constituency agent and auditor;
- the address where accounting records are kept;
- the name and address of the financial institutions where accounts are kept;
- the names of signing officers for each account;
- a statement of assets, liabilities and surplus of the constituency association; and
- a written statement from the constituency agent and auditor stating that each agrees to act.

Ontario

Provides for registration of constituency associations of registered parties (if not registered, associations cannot accept contributions). Application requires:

- the name of the association and of the registered party endorsing it;
- the address(es) where records are kept and where communications are to be sent;
- the names of principal officers, the chief financial officer, all persons authorized to accept contributions and signing officers;
- the name and address of all financial institutions where accounts are kept; and
- a statement of assets and liabilities as of not earlier than 90 days before application.

Quebec

"Party authorities" (may be at level of constituency, region or province as a whole) registered on application of authorized party's leader. Application requires:

- the name and address of the party authority;
- the address where books and accounts are kept; and
- the name, address and telephone number of the "official representative" of the party authority.

Alberta

Associations of registered parties and of independent Members of the Legislative Assembly may register (if not registered, associations cannot accept contributions). Application requires:

- the name of the association and of the registered party or independent member endorsing the association;
- the address(es) where records are kept and where communications are to be sent;
- the names of principal officers, the chief financial officer and signing officers;
- the name and address of all financial institutions where accounts are kept; and
- a statement of assets and liabilities as of not earlier than 90 days before application.

New Brunswick

District associations of registered parties may register (if not registered, associations cannot accept contributions). Application, to be signed by party leader, requires:

- the name of the association;
- the names and addresses of officers; and
- the address(es) to which communications are to be sent and where books and accounts are kept.

British Columbia

There are no provisions for the registration of political parties or constituency associations under the *Election Act*. Pursuant to section 8.1 (1) of the British Columbia *Income Tax Act*, a " 'recognized political party' means a bona fide affiliation of electors comprised in a political organization that has as a prime purpose the fielding of candidates for election to the Legislative Assembly".

Under the Political Contributions Program, constituency associations of recognized political parties wishing to issue political contribution tax credit receipts are required to apply in writing to the Commissioner of Income Tax, Income Taxation Branch, Revenue Division of the Ministry of Finance and Corporate Relations. Under guidelines issued by the ministry, associations "must register individuals authorized to issue receipts on their behalf with the Commissioner of Income Tax". (British Columbia, Elections BC 1991)

6

Fairness in the Electoral Process

FAIRNESS AS THE PRE-EMINENT VALUE IN THE ELECTORAL PROCESS

OUR CANADIAN POLITICAL tradition has long recognized the freedoms of expression and association for election debate and competition among political parties. Even before Confederation, these features of electoral democracy were well established for essentially two reasons. First, they were implicit in the right of British subjects to representative government. Representative government implied elections with freedom of political expression about issues and candidates; it also implied freedom to organize political factions or parties. Second, the competing forces from the earliest days of representative government in the British North American colonies represented powerful and influential interests. The struggles for responsible government before Confederation were not contests between a cohesive political establishment and the masses but rather competitions between opposing political elites. Freedom of expression and freedom of association thus reflected both the constitutional principles of parliamentary government and the fragmentation of political power and influence.

At the outset, the competing elites who organized and dominated the institutions of parliamentary government did not consider universal suffrage and full access to elected office necessary to representative and responsible government. As a consequence, acceptance of these fundamental rights grew incrementally. First came the elimination of 'plural voting' – which had given those possessing property in more than one constituency more than one vote – so that each voter would have only one vote at any election. Second, the franchise was gradually extended to eliminate discrimination on the basis of property, race or sex.

With successive developments, our political system has matured to the point where the fundamental equality of citizens has been acknowledged. The adoption of the *Canadian Charter of Rights and Freedoms* was clearly our most explicit effort in this regard. The Charter did not establish new democratic rights and freedoms, since these were in accord with contemporary values, norms and practices. The right of every citizen to vote and to be qualified for membership in the House of Commons was considered so fundamental a characteristic of our democracy that the relevant section of the

Charter was explicitly protected from the notwithstanding clause. (s. 33 of the Charter)

Central to the recognition of these rights and freedoms is the principle of equality. Canadians are to be treated equally in their claim to these freedoms and rights; each possesses the same status. This equality of status is not meant to be a mere formality. Rather, the purpose of the Charter recognition of these rights and freedoms is that they be secured equally by all citizens. This purpose cannot be realized simply by a declaration of formal equality.

Laws are required to give meaningful expression to the equality principle implicit in these Charter rights and freedoms. The constitutional recognition of these rights and freedoms constitutes a necessary but insufficient condition if citizens are to have an equal opportunity to exercise meaningful influence over the outcome of elections. For this fundamental equality of opportunity to be realized in the electoral process, our electoral laws must also be fair. In other words, the Charter establishes the equality of citizens; only if electoral processes themselves have the property of fairness, however, can this outcome be achieved in practice. This accords with the predominant view of Canadians that the federal electoral process must first and foremost reflect and promote fairness. (Fortin 1991 RC)

Fairness is thus the central value that must inform electoral laws if they are to promote the desired outcome of the equality of citizens in the exercise of their democratic rights and freedoms. In this sense, fairness gives meaningful effect to rights and freedoms by setting a standard that the law must meet in regulating behaviour or providing benefits. Electoral laws are fair only to the degree that they promote the meaningful exercise of the rights and freedoms essential to a healthy electoral democracy.

In the case of the democratic right to vote, as discussed elsewhere in this report, this means a number of conditions beyond the constitutional provision of the universal franchise. Canadian election law, accordingly, provides that each voter may vote only once. Furthermore, the law governing the drawing of constituency boundaries states that constituencies must have reasonably equal populations. Election laws governing the registration of voters and access to the voting process are also meant to facilitate the exercise of the franchise. It has long been unacceptable, for instance, to have only one polling station in a constituency; closing the list of voters at the issuance of the election writ is equally unacceptable. The successive reforms that have occurred over the course of our history clearly demonstrate that the meaningful exercise of the right to vote demands fair election laws and administrative mechanisms.

The meaningful exercise of the right to be a candidate for election demands that access to candidacy not be restricted by unreasonable laws or practices. Canadian election law and administrative procedures in this regard have long been relatively open, at least for qualified voters. Gone, for instance, are the days when constituency returning officers could rig elections by failing to notify a party when nominations were to be made or by holding a meeting for the official nomination of candidates at remote places. Property qualifications were also removed in the last century, as was the practice of taxing candidates to finance the election. The deposit required of candidates, furthermore, has not been increased since 1882. The number of signatures required for a nomination has never been excessive.

Canadian election law has generally had little effect on freedom of association. Indeed, only in the last two decades has the law formally acknowledged that Canadian elections involve political parties. Previously, the law applied essentially to voters and candidates. Since Canadian election law has generally been silent on parties or other political groups, its effect on freedom of association with regard to the electoral process has been minimal. There are two exceptions: a 1919 law that was used to prosecute members of the Communist Party in the 1930s until its repeal in 1936 and the order to disband the Fascist Party of Canada during the Second World War under the *War Measures Act*. The advent in 1970 of formally registered parties under the *Canada Elections Act* did not fundamentally alter this state of affairs, as the registration criteria and procedures, with some exceptions, have not been onerous.

Finally, in the case of freedom of expression, it is worthy of note that 40 years before freedom of expression was entrenched in the Charter in 1982, the Supreme Court of Canada recognized that it was one of the most fundamental rights in a liberal democracy. In the Court's view, the importance of free debate to representative government was undeniable. (*Reference re Alberta Statutes* 1938) The entrenchment of freedom of expression in the Charter recognized and reaffirmed the importance of free speech to the Canadian polity. However, free speech, like all other protected rights, is subject to reasonable limitations that can be imposed when rights conflict with competing fundamental values and other protected rights.

Canadian law has long regulated the role and use of the broadcasting media through both election and broadcasting laws. The justification for such regulation has been based on the particular characteristics of radio and television media, for which, because airtime is by definition finite, rules relating to access and broadcast time are required. From the outset, the regulation of radio and television access and time had to recognize that the freedom of expression of parties had to be limited in some respects to secure the meaningful exercise of this freedom by parties and the right of voters to hear a reasonable representation of the points of view of all parties. This required an explicit 'fairness doctrine' to provide access to and to allocate time on these media. (Courtney 1978, 41, 43)

Since 1974, freedom of expression has been further affected by the spending limits imposed on candidates and registered parties and by the restrictions on independent election spending by other individuals and groups under the *Canada Elections Act*. The adoption of these limits and restrictions sought to ensure the equal opportunity of each candidate and party to exercise freedom of expression in the electoral process in a meaningful manner. This was achieved by limiting the capacity of one or more candidates or parties, or others who might directly promote or oppose them, to dominate election discourse simply because they could afford to buy more media time or space. The 1974 law also sought to enhance fairness in the opportunities of candidates and parties to attain meaningful freedom of expression by providing partial reimbursements for candidate and party election expenses and income tax credits for political contributions. In addition to supporting the right of individuals to candidacy and the right of individuals to participate through political parties, these provisions recognized that public funding was important to allow candidates and parties a fair opportunity to mount effective campaigns through the mass media.

Electoral laws promote fairness in the exercise of freedom of expression only to the extent that there are reasonable opportunities for citizens, particularly candidates, as well as political parties to present their case to other voters. Freedom of expression in this respect is crucial to the realization of the fundamental objectives of our electoral democracy. In addition to a meaningful right to vote, to be a candidate and to join with others through political parties to promote shared political aims, voters must be able to influence the outcome of an election by communicating freely to other voters their own views about candidates and parties. Freedom of expression in this sense is both a democratic right in itself and a means to the realization of other democratic rights. Free and democratic elections are not possible without freedom of expression.

Freedom of expression in the electoral process, however, cannot be meaningfully achieved unless the laws that govern this process explicitly seek to promote fairness in the exercise of this freedom. In this critical respect, the electoral law should not presume that all participants will have equal resources to communicate with the electorate. To do so would be to ignore the fact that different participants draw on different bases of political support to finance their electoral campaigns. Nor should electoral law assume that inequalities among participants are irrelevant to the outcome of elections. To do so would be to ignore the known effects of political communication: the capacity to communicate often, to use different media and to develop messages with the assistance of marketing and advertising experts is a significant factor in the political persuasion of voters.

In these respects, the electoral process must not be equated with the economic marketplace. A fundamental and inherent feature of democratic rights is that, unlike economic assets, they are universally distributed. They are acquired and exercised freely without any monetary charge, and they cannot be bought and sold. For instance, electoral laws explicitly state that a voter may not 'sell' her or his vote in exchange for any benefit. The marketplace prescribes an equality of opportunity to participate but allows relatively free rein for individuals and groups to advance their economic self-interests by accumulating unequal amounts of resources. In direct contrast, at the heart of the electoral process lies the principle of the equality of voters. The importance of this principle has been captured by the eminent political scientist, Robert Dahl: "If income, wealth, and economic position are ... political resources, and if they are distributed unequally, then how can citizens be political equals? And if citizens cannot be political equals, how is democracy to exist?" (1989, 326)

How and where a democratic society draws the line between the domain of democratic rights and that of the marketplace are matters of continuing debate. There is an inherent tension between the freedom to do fully as one wishes to advance one's political interests or political cause, with whatever resources one has at one's disposal, and the rights of others to participate equally in the governance of their political society. This tension has long been recognized by political philosophers and jurists alike, and exists in theory as well as in the making and adjudication of laws. (Jenson 1991a RC) Decisions in this regard will always be subject to controversy and debate because "human goals are many, not all of them commensurable, and in perpetual rivalry with one another". (Berlin 1969, 171) Some will dispute the decision about which value deserves primacy, while others will challenge where the line has been drawn.

It is remarkable how the evolution of both democratic theory and institutions is testimony to the degree to which fairness, as equality of opportunity, has increasingly come to be regarded as fundamental. The principle of fairness does not override basic rights and freedoms, for that would imply the rights and freedoms are not themselves contained within the basic notion of justice. But, in certain circumstances, fairness may justifiably restrict the exercise of certain freedoms in the pursuit of justice itself.

The principal means whereby Canadians actively participate in elections is as supporters of candidates and members of political parties. Political parties provide opportunities for individuals who share similar values to promote their common objectives. Although political parties co-ordinate and channel individual expression and participation in the electoral process, individuals and groups other than candidates and parties can also express their views independently. The expression of such views is important during elections when assessments of issues, candidates, parties and governments are most likely to evoke response and provide the basis for voters to judge those who seek to represent them and to govern. Freedom of expression is essential if there is to be meaningful debate on important and contentious issues.

There is, therefore, no question of the importance and justification of freedom of expression. At the same time, the capacity to spend money on advertising campaigns to publicize an individual's or group's views on election issues, parties or candidates is not an appropriate measure of whether individuals or groups have sufficient opportunities to exercise their right to freedom of expression. The ability to spend significant amounts of money to promote one's view is not, in itself, a requisite for freedom of expression.

Because discrepancies in resources directly affect the ability to acquire media time or space to communicate a message, unrestricted freedom to express political views during an election cannot prevent some electoral communications from overwhelming the communications of others, thereby advantaging one political point of view. As Robert Mutch has written, "Limits cannot increase the speech opportunities of the nonwealthy majority, but they do reduce the degree to which the debate is dominated by wealth." (1988, 64)

The objective of fairness in the regulation of election spending, therefore, is neither to control the costs of elections for the principal 'players', namely candidates, parties and their partisan supporters, nor to advantage them over other independent individuals or groups. Rather, it is to ensure that some are not able to dominate election discourse because of their financial resources. In the words of the noted political theorist, John Rawls:

> Those similarly endowed and motivated should have roughly the same chance of attaining positions of political authority irrespective of their economic and social classes.... The liberties protected by the principle of participation lose much of their value whenever those who have greater means are permitted to use their advantage to control the course of public debate. (1972, 225)

In the 1960s, Canadian legislators recognized the need to limit election expenditures. While the rising costs of election campaigns were a major concern, the 1966 report of the Committee on Election Expenses (the Barbeau Committee) and the subsequent reform legislation of 1974 testified to the increasing awareness that fairness in the electoral process could not be realized without a new regulatory framework. The framework that emerged from legislative changes in the 1970s, along with subsequent amendments to it, contained three principal elements: (1) limits on the election expenses of candidates and registered political parties; (2) restrictions on the independent election spending of all other individuals and groups; and (3) broadcasting regulations on when, how and to what extent political parties and candidates could advertise on television and radio. This regulatory framework applied only during the election period.

The need to promote fairness in the electoral process to give full meaning to democratic rights and freedoms was regarded as a legitimate and pressing concern; the means chosen were judged the most appropriate and effective, as well as the least restrictive of freedom of expression and association. Canadian political parties, unlike those in countries such as Great Britain and France, were not barred from purchasing time on the electronic media; rather, to allow a reasonable opportunity for the various parties to be heard, limits were placed on the amount of advertising time any one party could buy. Moreover, each of the three elements of the 1974 reforms was considered an essential pillar of the framework. Although not without shortcomings in promoting fairness, this framework placed Canada at the leading edge of western democratic political systems in securing the rights and freedoms of Canadians as they applied to electoral democracy.

Restrictions on the election expenditures of individuals or groups other than candidates or parties were central to the attempt to ensure that the financial capacities of some did not unduly distort the election process by unfairly disadvantaging others. The objective of these restrictions on independent expenditures was to ensure that money was not spent in ways that would nullify the effectiveness of spending limits on candidates and political parties. If individuals or groups were permitted to run parallel campaigns augmenting the spending of certain candidates or parties, those candidates or parties would have an unfair advantage over others not similarly supported. At the same time, candidates or parties who were the target of spending by individuals or groups opposed to their election would be put at a disadvantage compared with those who were not targeted. Should such activity become widespread, the purpose of the legislation would be destroyed, the reasonably equal opportunity the legislation seeks to establish would vanish, and the overall goal of restricting the role of money in unfairly influencing election outcomes would be defeated. At issue was not the protection of candidates or parties from critical assessments by individuals or groups but rather limits on the ability of individuals or groups to incur election expenses to directly or indirectly influence the outcome of elections.

To avoid unfair outcomes, it was considered imperative that there be limits on the spending of individuals and groups who might directly or indirectly support the election of one or more candidates or a party. The need for such restrictions was recognized by the Barbeau Committee in 1966, which recommended that all groups other than registered parties and candidates be prevented from using paid advertisements that directly promoted or opposed a candidate or party during the election:

> The Committee has no desire to stifle the actions of such groups in their day-to-day activities. However, the Committee has learned from other jurisdictions that if these groups are allowed to participate actively in an election campaign any limitations or controls on the political parties or candidates become meaningless. In the United States, for example, *ad hoc* committees such as "Friends of John Smith" or "Supporters of John Doe" commonly spring up to support a candidate or party. Such committees make limitation on expenditures an exercise in futility, and render meaningless the reporting of election expenses by parties and candidates. (Canada, Committee on Election Expenses 1966, 50)

The Barbeau Committee's reference to the "day-to-day activities" of groups remains relevant. Where it has been enacted, the regulation of independent expenditures has not been intended to silence debate. Rather, the regulation is intended to restrict the ability of an individual or an advocacy group to launch an advertising campaign on an issue that is central to the campaign, independently of a candidate or a party. Even if the advertising campaign avoided directly endorsing or opposing a particular candidate or party, it could help the chances of one side and hinder the chances of another. In these direct and indirect ways, such spending on an issue central to the campaign would in effect augment the spending of one or more candidates or parties. While all candidates and parties would be subject to the election spending limits, those who did not benefit from groups making independent expenditures on behalf of the issues the candidates or parties support might well be put at a disadvantage; the same would apply to candidates and parties whose policies became the target of negative advertising by individuals or advocacy groups.

In 1984, Judge Medhurst of the Alberta Court of Queen's Bench ruled that the particular provisions of the 1974 law, as amended in 1983 to prohibit *all* independent election spending to directly promote or oppose a particular candidate or party, was an unjustified restriction on freedom of expression. (*National Citizens' Coalition Inc.* 1984) The federal government decided not to appeal the judgement or to amend the law in a manner consistent with the Charter. Elections Canada decided not to enforce the law outside Alberta during the 1984 and 1988 general elections, even though the judgement was not binding on courts outside Alberta. These decisions destroyed the overall effectiveness of the legislative framework for promoting fairness in the exercise of freedom of expression and of democratic rights during Canadian elections. The experience of the 1988 general election clearly demonstrates this. The gaping hole in our existing framework in relation to independent expenditures is patently unfair. The conundrum that this development presents for electoral reform is now widely acknowledged. Without fairness, we may continue to have a 'free' society, but we would certainly diminish the 'democratic' character of our society. The Charter couples these two dimensions. It is essential that both Parliament and the courts acknowledge this fundamental fact.

Given the centrality of fairness as a fundamental condition of equality of opportunity in the electoral process, the electoral regulatory framework must be rebuilt. This requires a law with provisions that promote fairness by limiting the election expenses of candidates and parties, by securing access to the broadcast media, and by also limiting, but not ruling out, the opportunity for other individuals and groups to spend independently of candidates and parties during the election period in ways that may directly or indirectly affect the election outcome for at least one candidate or party.

LIMITING ELECTION EXPENSES

Background to the 1974 Legislation
The issue of limiting spending in federal elections was not seriously considered until the 1960s. The 1874 *Dominion Elections Act*, which was modelled fairly closely on the British *Corrupt Practices Act* of 1854, introduced requirements for candidates to appoint an agent and to report on their election expenditures. In 1883, Great Britain introduced statutory spending limits

for candidates as part of the *Corrupt and Illegal Practices Prevention Act*. In this case, as Leslie Seidle has noted, Canada did not follow the British example: "Canadian elections in the nineteenth century were often associated with extravagant expenditure, but no single election approached the excesses of the 1880 British contest. There was some awareness of the principles which had been introduced in the 1883 Act, but no one campaigned for a drastic rewriting of the Canadian law along British lines." (1980, 286–87)

The cost of Canadian elections began to stimulate debate in the 1930s. Some complained that candidates' campaigns were unnecessarily costly because there were too many paid workers. At the national level, spending increased as the parties began to rely on the services of advertising agencies. (Seidle 1980, 170) In 1938, C.G. Power introduced a private member's bill that proposed limitations on candidates' expenditures and annual reporting of political parties' spending and contributions. Power reintroduced his bill in the following session; it was studied by a special committee but not adopted. In 1949, he tabled a similar bill, which received second reading but went no further.

In the absence of support from the national parties, isolated efforts such as Power's had no impact. The situation began to change in the late 1950s. From 1957 to 1963, four general federal elections were held. Although in each case the large national political parties were able to obtain significant amounts of money to conduct their campaigns, each election was successively more costly, in large part because of increased spending on television advertising, first used in the 1957 general election. The widespread concern about the rising cost of elections, particularly for the national political parties, led to the establishment in 1964 of the Committee on Election Expenses. The Chair of the Committee was Alphonse Barbeau, who had helped develop the 1963 reforms to Quebec's electoral law, which introduced election spending limits for the first time in Canada. The Committee comprised persons who had been active in the Liberal, Progressive Conservative and New Democratic parties, as well as a prominent political scientist.

In its report, the Committee stated that "a body of evidence presented to [the Committee] supports the need ... for some form of control of, and limitation on, election expenditure". (Canada, Committee on Election Expenses 1966, 49) The Committee's approach to the issue was threefold.

First, as a way of limiting election costs, the Committee recommended parties and candidates be prohibited from advertising on television or radio and from using paid print media except during the four weeks immediately preceding election day. Political parties were also to be barred from purchasing any paid advertising time on television or radio that was additional to their share of six hours of subsidized paid time each broadcaster would be obliged to provide during that period.

Second, the Committee recommended a limit of $0.10 per voter on candidates' spending on broadcast and print advertising. The Committee rejected a "total dollar limitation" for candidates because it assumed that "any attempt to place such a limitation could be easily circumvented". (Canada, Committee on Election Expenses 1966, 49) It did not favour any form of statutory spending limits for political parties, preferring to rely on disclosure as a form of discipline: "The Committee suggests that as a first step reports on expenditures, and the attendant publicity, (provided the system adopted is rigorous enough), would oblige parties to put wise limits on their expenditures." (Canada, Committee on Election Expenses 1966, 32) A related recommendation was that the doctrine of agency be extended to political parties.

Third, the Barbeau Committee recognized that the restrictions on the purchase of broadcast time by parties and the advertising spending limits for candidates it proposed would be effective only if accompanied by regulations on the expenditures of other individuals and groups. The Committee recommended that all groups other than registered parties and candidates be prevented from using paid advertisements that directly promoted or opposed a candidate or party during the election.

Parliament did not begin to consider the issues addressed by the Barbeau Committee until October 1970, when a special committee of the House of Commons, known as the Chappell Committee after its chair, Hyliard Chappell, was appointed to consider amendments to the *Canada Elections Act*. In its report, the Chappell Committee adopted a much more comprehensive approach to spending limits: it proposed limits on the 'election expenses' (not just the advertising expenses) of candidates *and* of parties. (Canada, House of Commons 1971) In May 1972, just before Parliament was dissolved, Bill C-211 was introduced but not adopted. The bill included advertising spending limits for candidates only and a maximum of six and one-half hours of broadcast advertising time for purchase by the parties. Clearly, Members of Parliament saw the need for more comprehensive reform than the senior organizers and executives of the national parties.

The 1972 election returned a minority Liberal government. Calls for reform came from the New Democratic Party, which held the balance of power in the House of Commons, and, increasingly, from Canadians whose concern about party finance and election spending was stimulated by the Watergate revelations in the United States.[1] (Mutch 1991 RC) This led to the introduction of legislation, adopted as the *Election Expenses Act*, which came into effect on 1 August 1974.

The Act provided for overall limits on the election expenses of both candidates and parties. A candidate's election expenses could not exceed the aggregate of: $1.00 for each of the first 15 000 voters on the preliminary list for the constituency; $0.50 for each voter between 15 001 and 25 000; and $0.25 for each additional voter. Amendments adopted in 1977 and 1983 permit additional spending in constituencies where the number of voters is less than the average in all constituencies and in geographically large constituencies.

The limit for a registered political party's election expenses was determined by multiplying $0.30 by the number of voters on the preliminary lists in constituencies where the party had officially nominated candidates. In the 1979 election, the average spending limit for candidates was $27 744; the spending limit for a registered party with candidates in all constituencies was $4 459 249. Since amendments adopted in 1983 the candidate and party limits have been adjusted on 1 April each year to reflect the change in the consumer price index during the previous 12 months.

The Act also explicitly recognized that limiting spending by candidates and parties would require the regulation of spending by other individuals and groups. Consequently, under what was then section 70.1 of the *Canada Elections Act* (now section 259), individuals or groups were prohibited from incurring expenses during elections to directly promote or oppose candidates or parties, except if authorized by the official agent of a candidate or party (in which case the spending had to be counted against the election expenses limit of the candidate or party concerned). At the same time, the legislation (s. 70.1(4)) attempted to strike a balance between the integrity of spending limits generally and the ability of non-registered participants to spend money to promote 'policy issues' by establishing a 'good faith' defence from prosecution. Individuals and groups were allowed to incur expenses to promote or oppose a registered party or candidate if they could establish that the expenditures were incurred for the purpose of gaining support for their views on policy issues or for advancing the aims of a non-partisan organization.

It soon became apparent that enforcing this good faith defence was problematic. Not only was there uncertainty about what kinds of activities were entitled to the defence, but court decisions extended it to explicitly partisan messages that included no articulated policy position. For example, an advertising banner flown from an airplane during a by-election with the message "O.H.C. Employees 767 C.U.P.E. vote but not Liberal" was interpreted by the court as a legitimate attempt to oppose the government's anti-inflation program, even though it did not specify any policy position.[2] (*R. v. Roach* 1978) Within five years, the chief electoral officer had good reason to warn Parliament that the law on independent spending was inadequate and had the potential to undermine the effectiveness of the spending limits for candidates and parties.

In 1983, Parliament responded to these concerns and amended the *Canada Elections Act* by removing the good faith defence. As a result, section 70.1 effectively prohibited individuals or groups from incurring independent expenditures to directly promote or oppose candidates or parties during elections. However, the legislation did not prohibit groups or individuals from incurring expenses to promote 'issues' as long as their messages did not directly promote or oppose a party or candidate. Members from the three parliamentary parties recognized during the debate in the House of Commons that the amendments might conflict with a strict interpretation of freedom of expression but justified them as necessary to preserve the principles of fairness and equity in elections. (Canada, House of Commons, *Debates*, 25 October 1983, 28295–99)

The amended legislation was challenged by the National Citizens' Coalition. The decision, rendered in 1984 by a lower Alberta court, held that the government had not demonstrated the justification for limiting the freedom of expression of individuals or groups during elections to the degree provided by the amended section 70.1. This decision was handed down before the Supreme Court of Canada had articulated a set of rules for determining the reasonableness of legislation that conflicts with a protected right. (*R. v. Oakes* 1986) The judgement in the *National Citizens' Coalition* case, which held that limits could be justified only where "a real likelihood of harm to a society value" would occur without the impugned legislation (1984, 264), set a far more stringent test than the one subsequently relied on by the Supreme Court. However, the 1984 decision, handed down on the eve of an election, was not appealed by the federal government; nor was alternative legislation enacted. Moreover, although the decision was binding only in Alberta, Elections Canada decided not to enforce the law elsewhere in the country.

Comparative Experience

The comparative experience of major western democracies in limiting election spending illustrates a variety of approaches. In Great Britain, for instance, candidate spending limits have been in effect since 1883. Party spending is not subject to statutory limits, but there is a ban on purchasing time on television and radio for election advertising; this constitutes an indirect, yet no less effective, limit on spending by political parties. The *Representation of the People Act* also prohibits individuals or groups from spending money at the constituency level "with a view to promoting or procuring the election of a candidate" or "disparaging another candidate" unless authorized in writing by the candidate's agent (in which case the spending counts against the candidate's limit). Moreover, groups participating in national campaigns may not advertise on radio or television; like parties, they may advertise only in newspapers.

In France, there are candidate spending limits for National Assembly and presidential elections, but no limits on political party spending. However, there is a ban on all paid political advertising during the election period on radio and television and in newspapers. This ban encompasses paid political advertising by individuals or groups.

In Germany, there are no spending limits on candidates or parties, but there are low limits on the amount of paid political advertising that political parties may purchase. Although the German law contains no specific prohibitions on independent advertising expenditures, such advertising has not been evident to any great extent in German elections. It may be that broadcasters and publishers consider it would be inconsistent to allow a significant amount of independent advertising expenditures when they must respect restrictions on advertising by political parties.

In the United States, congressional and presidential spending limits, enacted by the *Federal Election Campaign Act* of 1971, as amended in 1974, were struck down by the U.S. Supreme Court in 1976. In *Buckley* (1976), the Court declared that spending limits were a violation of First Amendment guarantees of free speech, except when such limits were linked to the acceptance of public funding, which was then and remains part of the framework for presidential elections. (Given this exception, the Canadian law limiting the election expenses of candidates and parties would be valid in the U.S. context, since these limits are linked to a system of public funding.) The Court referred to the expenditure limits as "substantial rather than merely theoretical restraints on the quantity and diversity of political speech" (*Buckley* 1976, 19) and concluded that:

> The First Amendment denies government the power to determine that spending to promote one's political views is wasteful, excessive, or unwise. In the free society ordained by our Constitution it is not the government, but the people – individually as citizens and candidates and collectively as associations and political committees – who must retain control over the quantity and range of debate on public issues in a political campaign. (*Buckley* 1976, 57)

At the same time, the U.S. Supreme Court did not question contribution limits, expressing the view that the "major evil" associated with rapidly increasing campaign expenditures was the danger of candidates becoming dependent on large contributions. (*Buckley* 1976, 55) This emphasis was also reflected in a 1980 decision of the District Court for the District of Columbia on independent expenditures. The judges considered the prevention of corruption "the singular interest justifying" campaign finance regulations and that "spending money can just not be equated with *giving* money as a source of possible corruption". (*FEC* v. *AFC* 1980, 494, 498, emphasis in original)

As a consequence, independent expenditures in the United States may be made for or against candidates, and there are no limits on the amount of independent expenditures political action committees (PACs) or any other group or organization may incur. In the 1987–88 election cycle, PACs alone spent U.S. $20.3 million on independent expenditures, about U.S. $16.0 million of which was spent by 'non-connected' (most often single-issue) PACs; there were U.S. $13.6 million and U.S. $6.7 million in independent expenditures in relation to the presidential and congressional races, respectively. In 1990, total independent expenditures in relation to candidates seeking election amounted to U.S. $4.1 million. The vast majority of this spending came from non-connected PACs (U.S. $1.9 million) and trade, membership and health organizations ($1.8 million). In addition, PACs play a major role in funding the campaigns of congressional candidates, who are not subject to spending limits.

The issue of independent expenditures has raised several concerns in the United States. Although such expenditures have not consistently influenced election outcomes (Magleby and Nelson 1990, 58), they have had some impact as a result of the targeting of candidates. Independent expenditures since 1982 have been primarily in support of candidates, although there have been prominent examples of independent expenditures being the source of negative advertising against candidates. Herbert Alexander (1991 RC) brings to light one such example:

> Michael Dukakis' campaign was hurt by explosive ads highlighting a felon named Willie Horton, who, while on a prison furlough program in Massachusetts, had escaped and brutally raped a Maryland woman. These commercials, designed to question Dukakis' record on crime, were produced and aired not by the Bush campaign, but by two independent expenditure groups [PACs], and were widely shown on television news programs.

The issue of independent expenditures raises further questions because it is often not clear that the PAC is separate from the candidate's campaign. For example, most voters did not know that the PAC 'Americans for Bush' had no connection with George Bush's campaign for the presidency in 1988. In fact, there have been many allegations that these expenditures are not truly independent of the candidate's campaign; however, only a few such expenditures have been judged illegal by the Federal Election Commission. Furthermore, this form of spending reinforces the incumbency bias of PAC contributions. In congressional elections since 1984, independent expenditures, as well as PAC contributions to candidates, have greatly favoured incumbents over challengers. (Magleby and Nelson 1990, 55)

The Canadian Experience

Candidates and Parties

During our public hearings, over four-fifths of the interveners who addressed the issue of spending limits spoke in favour of the general principles enshrined in the present federal electoral law. This mirrored the results of our major attitudinal study, in which 93 per cent of respondents supported spending controls on political parties; this level of support did not vary significantly by region. (Blais and Gidengil 1991 RC) Among practitioners, support for spending limits is also strong: 79 per cent of respondents to our survey of constituency association presidents said they found the rules for limiting the election spending of federal candidates and parties "very satisfactory" or "satisfactory". (Carty 1991a RC) While opinion surveys indicated Canadians were strongly in favour of spending limits even before they were adopted at the federal level,[3] the effects of spending limits on the dynamics of subsequent election campaigns have illustrated that greater fairness was not an abstract goal. This experience has reinforced public support for spending limits and helps explain why Canadians believe limits must remain a cornerstone of federal electoral law.

We were also told that another objective of democratic government – namely, accessibility to the electoral process – is enhanced by diminishing the significance of financial resources for those who are considering running for office. Spending limits lower barriers to participation faced by those who do not have generous financial backing or personal wealth. Limits also provide a form of 'insurance policy': if a campaign becomes heated, they allow the candidate to resist pressure to spend ever greater amounts (a problem frequently faced in the United States, where, except for presidential elections, there are no election spending limits). Our research indicates that candidates in the 1988 Canadian election spent a higher proportion of their limit in the more competitive races. (Heintzman 1991 RC) Candidates who come close to spending their limit are obliged to rely on other means, such as more effective mobilization of volunteers and voters – a sound and constructive outcome. In the absence of limits, spending in the most competitive contests would likely escalate significantly. Because spending limits prevent such escalation, those with fewer resources are not put at a direct disadvantage relative to those with better-financed campaigns. This, in turn, can encourage a greater number and variety of people to become candidates, leading to increased representation from the diversity of groups that constitute the body politic.

A number of interveners commented, during our hearings, on this relationship between spending limits and accessibility to elected office. Harry Katz, representing five Metropolitan Toronto Progressive Conservative associations, said:

> It seems some people have, let's say, more access to funds than others.... And that maybe in the interest of having a good cross-section of representation in our parliament, that money should not be as big a barrier.... There shouldn't be a barrier at all, hopefully, to people running for election. (Toronto, 30 May 1990)

In a similar vein, Judy Erola told our symposium on the active participation of women in politics that the 1974 legislation "has led to the growth of [the number of] women in the House of Commons". (Montreal, 1 November 1990)

Our research confirmed that the financial situation of women is a major barrier to their seeking election. In her survey of a sample of women candidates in the 1988 election, Janine Brodie found that lack of funding ranked as the most significant obstacle faced by women candidates. (1991 RC) Not surprisingly, many advocates of spending limits link this issue of accessibility to the democratic rights protected by the *Canadian Charter of Rights and Freedoms.* By mitigating financial barriers, limits encourage more people to seek elected office, thus adding meaning to the right to stand as a candidate guaranteed by section 3 of the Charter. This reflects the strong support of Canadians for measures to ensure their constitutional rights are fully protected and can be effectively exercised. The increased number of women candidates and elected Members of Parliament since 1974, while the result of numerous factors, has obviously been enhanced by the presence of spending limits.

A telling point in the Canadian experience is the empirical evidence of the effects of spending limits on electoral competition. Contrary to the argument often heard in the United States that spending limits diminish electoral competition, the evidence since the introduction of spending limits in Canada in 1974 is that there has *not* been a decline in electoral competitiveness. During the 1974–1988 period, 6.0 per cent of the members of the U.S. House of Representatives were defeated. Moreover, the rate of defeat for members of the House of Representatives has actually been dropping and has been below 5 per cent since 1982. In Canada, however, the average rate of defeat during the four general elections since the spending limits came into effect was 24.9 per cent; the average defeat rate for the last three elections to which spending limits did not apply (1968, 1972, 1974) was 20.3 per cent (adapted from Atkinson and Docherty 1991, Table 1). Although a number of factors affect electoral competition, it is evident that Canadian federal elections since the introduction of spending limits have become more, not less, competitive, and incumbency rates for the House of Commons during that period have been markedly lower than for the U.S. House of Representatives.

The conclusion that must be drawn from all of the above considerations is that spending limits during election campaigns constitute a significant instrument for promoting fairness in the electoral process. They reduce the potential advantage of those with access to significant financial resources and thus help foster a reasonable balance in debate during elections. They also encourage access to the election process. This adds meaning to the fundamental right of candidacy by enhancing the opportunity for a more representative House of Commons. Finally, spending limits (as designed in our electoral law) help achieve these democratic objectives without diminishing electoral competition.

The evidence from the Canadian experience also supports spending limits for both candidates and political parties. A few interveners at our hearings suggested retaining spending limits for candidates but abolishing them for parties. Such an arrangement, it was suggested, would result in a regulatory scheme similar to that of Great Britain, where candidate spending is limited by law but party spending is not subject to statutory limit. This proposal ignores the fact that in Great Britain there is a ban on purchasing time on television and radio for election advertising. Limiting only candidate spending while preserving the right of parties to purchase

broadcasting time for election advertisements would leave a very important part of the election contest unregulated. The objective of fairness in
the electoral process would thus be diminished greatly. Furthermore, if the
parties had free rein and candidates did not, there could be potential for abuse.
For example, a party could concentrate its advertising spending in ways that
benefited certain candidates – perhaps those in a particular region – while stop-
ping short of direct advocacy of those candidates. As a result, the integrity
and purpose of candidate spending limits would be compromised.

Independent Expenditures by Individuals and Groups

At our public hearings, more than 150 interveners argued that to protect the
integrity of candidate and party spending limits, some form of regulation
for individual or group election activity was necessary. Regulation could
be through financial limits on spending, restrictions on the nature of advertisements or rules concerning the timing of advertisements. Only 33 interveners said no restrictions should be imposed on the independent spending
of groups or individuals. An attitudinal survey conducted in 1991 reflected
what interveners told us at our hearings: 75 per cent of those interviewed
support spending limits for those who "represent specific group interests".
(Frizzell 1991)

The issue of spending limits for individuals and groups other than candidates and political parties became a salient one in the 1988 election. In that
general election, individuals and groups, for the first time since their activities were restricted in 1974, incurred significant independent expenditures
during a campaign. Individuals, corporations, labour unions and other groups
spent more than $4.7 million on advertising. (Hiebert 1991b RC, Table 1.1)

The vast proportion of independent expenditures was directed at the
issue of free trade. Moreover, four times as much money was spent to promote free trade as was spent to oppose it. (Hiebert 1991b RC) Most of the
advertisements paid for by individuals and groups, particularly those promoting free trade, were confined to advocacy and information about this
issue, without direct partisan reference. Most of the 1988 independent
advertisements thus would have been within the bounds of the legislation
as amended in 1983. Nevertheless, the lopsided nature of the independent
campaign on free trade raised a new question about the relationship between
independent expenditures on issues and candidate and party spending
limits.

Until the 1988 election, the underlying assumption of regulatory attempts
to limit the election advertising of individuals and groups was that it was
necessary to prohibit only directly partisan advertisements. It was assumed
that the advocacy of issues did not represent a threat to the integrity of
candidate and party spending limits. The 1988 election experience clearly
demonstrated that advertisements promoting an issue but not explicitly
exhorting voters to vote for a particular candidate or party could themselves
be grossly unfair because they can constitute an endorsement of a particular

party, if one party can be clearly distinguished from others on the basis of its stand on a central election issue.

It cannot be expected that roughly equal amounts of money will be spent to promote both sides of an issue. The free trade issue in 1988 was a clear example of how one side of a debate can spend considerably more money than the other. Only one of the three largest parties, the Progressive Conservative Party, supported free trade. This meant that the benefits of money spent by individuals and groups accrued mainly to that party. Groups and individuals promoting free trade spent $0.77 on advertisements for every $1.00 of the entire advertising budget of the Progressive Conservative Party, whereas independent expenditures on advertisements against free trade accounted for only $0.13 for each $1.00 of the total advertising budgets of the two large parties opposing free trade. (Hiebert 1991b RC) Richard Johnston, using data from the 1988 Canadian National Election Survey, has shown that independent interest group advertising may have affected the outcome to the advantage of the Progressive Conservative Party. (Johnston et al. 1991)

Although most of the advertising supporting free trade sponsored by individuals and groups focused on the issue without referring explicitly to a candidate or party, there were some examples of partisan advocacy. Because partisan advocacy conveys an explicit exhortation to action, it represents a direct assault on the fairness principle. An advertisement that targets a candidate for assuming the 'wrong' position on an issue conveys a corollary message to vote against that candidate. Conversely, an advertisement that promotes a particular issue and clearly identifies the candidate most sympathetic to that issue carries an equally direct message that the best way to promote the issue is to elect that particular candidate.

In the 1988 election, advertisements against free trade attempted to convince voters that the proposed agreement was not good for Canada. Among these advertisements was a comic book entitled "What's The Big Deal?", which was distributed in 24 daily newspapers. The comic book combined messages about the dangers of free trade with unflattering caricatures of members of the governing party, framed to instil doubt that voters could take at face value these leaders' words about the benefits of the agreement for Canada. (Pro-Canada Network 1988) The National Citizens' Coalition, on the other hand, sought to convince voters to vote for free trade by giving critical assessments of the leaders of the Liberals and NDP, who opposed free trade.

There were also examples of partisan advocacy at the constituency level, primarily by groups that waged a personal and direct attack on candidates. For example, Campaign Life Coalition, the political wing of the pro-life movement in Canada, targeted candidates in more than 30 constituencies and mailed materials or canvassed against candidates who were perceived to be pro-choice. A considerable amount of Campaign Life political campaigning was low budget – pamphlets and canvassing. (Hiebert 1991b RC)

However, there were also examples of broadly directed advertising on the issue of abortion. In the November 1988 edition of its publication *Vitality*, the Coalition for the Protection of Human Life identified 125 candidates from the Progressive Conservative, Liberal and New Democratic parties who supported the position of Campaign Life on abortion (the candidates' position was based on the response to a questionnaire); the publication was distributed beyond the Coalition's membership. (Tanguay and Kay 1991 RC) In addition, the Saskatchewan Pro-Life Association reportedly spent $40 000 on a province-wide advertising campaign in addition to publishing a special issue of its newsletter. (Spencer 1988)

Based on an assessment of 14 major Canadian daily newspapers and information provided by the newspapers or advertisers, it is evident that during the 1988 election more than $100 000 was spent on newspaper advertisements on issues other than free trade and abortion. A number of the campaigns were oriented mainly toward issues, but some also criticized parties or party leaders. The Friends of Portage Program for Drug Dependence spent more than $45 000 in major Montreal and Toronto dailies on advertisements calling for drug abuse to be made a key election issue and claiming that the prime minister, party leaders and parties had ignored the problem. The peace movement, under the general rubric of the Canadian Peace Pledge Campaign, accounted for more than $28 000 of the total advertising expenditure in the newspapers surveyed. The campaign's most expensive advertisement, which appeared in the Toronto *Globe and Mail* (15 November 1988, A-11), reported the positions of the three largest parties on arms control and disarmament, denounced the government's policies in this area and urged voters to "vote for peace-supporting candidates". In our survey of constituency association presidents, half the respondents indicated that in the 1988 election single-issue groups had actively supported or opposed candidates. (Carty 1991a RC)

Defining Election Expenses

Limits on the election expenses of candidates and parties and of other individuals and groups are necessary to promote the meaningful realization of democratic rights and freedoms in the electoral process. Spending limits on candidates and parties have clearly enhanced fairness by reducing the likelihood that candidates and parties with access to significant financial resources are unduly advantaged over those with less access. The result is a more reasonable balance in the election discourse. In addition, spending limits for candidates enhance fairness by promoting access to candidacy and thus elected office. Moreover, spending limits do not discourage electoral competition; rather, if both reasonable and effective, they encourage competition.

Spending limits on individuals and groups are also essential if election outcomes are not to be unduly influenced by independent advertising campaigns. Since the purpose of all election spending, including independent election spending, is to influence the outcome of elections, that is, the election of candidates and indirectly the formation of the government, independent spending must be subject to some limit. However, it would be unfair, as well as unconstitutional, to ban all independent election spending. Some independent participants consider it essential to meaningful election expression that their messages refer explicitly to candidates or parties and that they be able to identify candidates and parties in their advocacy of particular issues. Moreover, independent groups can enrich the election debate by bringing their issues into the election discourse.

Nonetheless, Canadian experience, especially the 1988 general election, as well as U.S. experience demonstrates clearly that independent election spending can influence the outcome of elections by subjecting voters to election advertising skewed to one point of view. Canadian and comparative experience also demonstrate that any attempt to distinguish between partisan advocacy and issue advocacy – to prohibit spending on the former and to allow unregulated spending on the latter – cannot be sustained. At elections, the advocacy of issue positions inevitably has consequences for election discourse and thus has partisan implications, either direct or indirect: voters cast their ballots for candidates and not for issues.

For the definition of election expenses to be effective in limiting such expenses, it must encompass all the election-related expenditures of candidates, parties, other individuals and groups to directly or indirectly influence the outcome of an election. First, the definition of election expenses must obviously include spending that seeks to promote or oppose, directly or indirectly, the election of a candidate, since it is candidates who are seeking elected office.

Second, the definition of election expenses must include spending to promote or oppose a registered party or the program or policies of a candidate or registered political party. The central role political parties play in election campaigns means that spending to promote or oppose a registered party must be counted as an election expense. At the same time, candidates offer themselves as individuals and, in the vast majority of cases, as standard bearers of a registered party with programs and policies that indicate to the electorate what they represent. The vitality of electoral democracy is dependent on candidates and parties with clearly defined programs and policies. The greater the degree to which elections are characterized by competing programs and policies, the greater the extent to which individuals and groups are likely to incur election expenses on the issues raised, thereby promoting or opposing particular candidates and parties.

Third, the definition of election expenses must encompass spending to approve or disapprove a course of action advocated or opposed by a candidate, registered party or leader of a registered party, since candidates, parties and their leaders are expected to take public positions on salient issues of public policy. The approval or disapproval of a course of action by a candidate, party or party leader will normally be explicitly or implicitly encompassed within a candidate's or party's program or policies. However, during elections issues may emerge or be reformulated in ways not fully treated by a program or policy platform. It is thus essential that the definition of election expenses encompass spending to approve or disapprove the positions taken in response to the events of an election campaign.

Recommendation 1.6.1

We recommend that 'election expenses' be defined to include "the cost of any goods or services used during an election:
(1) to promote or oppose, directly or indirectly, the election of a candidate;
(2) to promote or oppose a registered party or the program or policies of a candidate or registered party; or
(3) to approve or disapprove a course of action advocated or opposed by a candidate, registered party or leader of a registered party;
and include an amount equal to any contribution of goods or services used during the election."

The scope of election expenses, as defined above, is discussed in Volume 2, Chapter 6.

The Level of Spending Limits

Spending Limits for Candidates
Under the *Canada Elections Act*, as we have noted, the spending limits for candidates are based on a formula that is tied to the number of voters on the preliminary voters list in each constituency. Since the 1983 amendments, this maximum is adjusted on 1 April each year to reflect the change in the consumer price index during the previous 12 months. The Act allows additional spending in sparsely populated constituencies (those with fewer than 10 voters per square kilometre) and those where the number of voters is less than the average of all constituencies. In the 1988 election, this meant that the average maximum allowable election expense for a candidate was $46 887. Based on indexation since then and Elections Canada estimates of the increase in the electorate since the 1988 election, if a general election were held before 1 April 1992, the average spending limit would be $55 155. To assess the adequacy of the present limits, we must consider three issues.

The first issue is whether the limits are now too restrictive, as shown by the degree to which candidates have been spending near the limit. Since 1979, the reported spending of candidates of the Progressive Conservative, Liberal and New Democratic parties has fluctuated, as indicated in Table 6.1. However, the proportion of these three parties' candidates who spent more than 90 per cent of the limit rose from 20.7 per cent in 1979 to 31.5 per cent in 1988. In the case of Progressive Conservative candidates, 30.5 per cent spent more than 90 per cent of the limit in 1979, whereas 50.2 per cent did so in 1988. The proportion of NDP candidates spending more than 90 per cent of the limit rose from 3.2 per cent in 1979 to 19.1 per cent in 1988. For the Liberals, the proportion remained about the same: 28.4 per cent in 1979 and 25.1 per cent in 1988.

In comparison, in the 1989 Quebec provincial election, 84 per cent of the candidates of the Parti libéral du Québec spent more than 90 per cent of the limit, as did 90 per cent of Parti québécois candidates. In Ontario, which has higher limits than the federal and Quebec limits (see Table 6.7), 12 per cent of the candidates of the three largest parties spent more than 90 per cent of the limit in the 1990 provincial election.

Table 6.1
Average spending by candidates as a percentage of the 'election expenses' limit

	1979	1980	1984	1988
Progressive Conservative Party	77.6	72.4	89.0	85.8
Liberal Party	79.8	77.5	79.0	70.0
New Democratic Party	34.4	38.4	37.8	52.8

Source: Stanbury 1991 RC, Table 12.19.

The largest component of candidates' election spending is print advertising, which includes newspaper advertising, brochures, flyers and other printed publicity. For Progressive Conservative and Liberal candidates, the percentage spent on print advertising has risen since 1980 (see Table 6.2). Office expenses are the second largest component of candidates' election expenses, averaging 23 per cent of candidates' spending for the three largest parties in 1988. Radio and television advertising account for a small share of candidates' election expenses and this has been declining for candidates from all three of these parties.

The second issue in assessing the level of candidates' spending limits is the degree to which they would have to be adjusted to cover spending that is not now subject to the limits but would be if the definition of election expenses we recommend is adopted in legislation. At present, 'other expenses', as defined in Volume 2, Chapter 6, are not subject to the limits. As indicated in Table 6.3, most candidates in the 1988 election for whom data are available reported 'other expenses' that were not very large. In some cases, however, the amounts were significant. For example, 48 per cent of Progressive Conservative candidates reported spending more than $5000 on 'other expenses', as did 29 per cent of the Liberal candidates and 11 per cent of NDP candidates. Further, 9 per cent of Progressive Conservative candidates, 3 per cent of Liberal candidates and 0.6 per cent of NDP candidates reported spending more than $20 000 on 'other expenses'.

Table 6.2
Candidates' advertising spending as percentage of total 'election expenses', 1980–88

Category	Party	1980	1984	1988
Print advertising	Progressive Conservative Party	48.7	50.7	55.0
	Liberal Party	43.0	47.5	53.2
	New Democratic Party	43.7	42.5	41.4
Radio and TV advertising	Progressive Conservative Party	13.3	8.7	7.9
	Liberal Party	13.1	10.7	7.3
	New Democratic Party	12.5	8.4	5.3
Total advertising	Progressive Conservative Party	62.0	59.1	62.9
	Liberal Party	56.1	58.2	60.5
	New Democratic Party	56.2	50.9	46.7

Source: Stanbury 1991 RC, Table 12.16.

Table 6.3
Other expenses of candidates, 1988 election

Amount of other expenses ($)	Progressive Conservative Party (N)	Liberal Party (N)	New Democratic Party (N)	Others (N)	Total (N)
Less than 1 000	48	69	69	73	259
1 001– 3 000	38	61	53	13	165
3 001– 5 000	36	35	25	2	98
5 001– 7 000	21	25	10	1	57
7 001–10 000	28	14	4	1	47
10 001–15 000	30	12	3	0	45
15 001–20 000	11	8	0	1	20
20 001–25 000	8	3	1	0	12
25 001–40 000	11	3	0	0	14
More than $40 000	2	2	0	0	4
Number of candidates*	233	232	165	91	721
Average other expenses	$7 496	$4 486	$1 946	$939	$4 430

Source: Stanbury 1991 RC, Table 12.22.

*Information available only for candidates who had a surplus.

The third issue is the degree to which annual indexation of the spending limits may have fallen behind price increases of major components of candidates' campaigns. During our hearings, a number of party representatives addressed this issue. Most agreed that the annual indexation based on the

consumer price index had not kept pace with certain key costs. Our research
has confirmed this. As shown in Tables 6.4, 6.5 and 6.6, the increases in
costs of advertising on television and in daily and weekly newspapers have
been about double the rise in the consumer price index since 1980 (the appropriate comparison date: the spending limits were indexed retroactively to
1980 as a result of amendments in 1983).

Table 6.4

Increase in the cost of television advertising and consumer price index, 1980–88
(per cent)

Period	Change in consumer price index	Change in television advertising costs local / national	Differential rate of increase
1980–84	37.5	59	+21.5
1984–88	17.5	60	+42.5
1980–88	61.6	119	+57.4

Source: Royal Commission Research Branch.

Table 6.5

Increase in cost of advertising in major daily newspapers and consumer price index, 1980–88
(per cent)

Period	Change in consumer price index	Change in daily (Mon.–Fri.) advertising costs	Differential rate of increase
1980–84	37.5	73.50	+36.0
1984–88	17.5	40.00	+22.5
1980–88	61.6	143.72	+82.1

Source: Royal Commission Research Branch.

Note: Based on transient cost per line (black and white). Sample includes *Toronto Star, Ottawa Citizen, Le Devoir,* Halifax *Chronicle-Herald, Vancouver Sun* and *Winnipeg Free Press.*

Table 6.6

Increase in cost of local weekly newspaper advertising and consumer price index, 1980–88
(per cent)

Period	Change in consumer price index	Change in local weekly advertising costs	Differential rate of increase
1980–84	37.5	41.1	+3.6
1984–88	17.5	70.3	+52.8
1980–88	61.6	124.5	+62.9

Source: Royal Commission Research Branch.

Note: Based on cost per line (black and white). Sample includes *Assiniboia Times,* Saskatchewan; *Altona Red River Valley Echo,* Manitoba; *Kingston This Week,* Ontario; *Le Réveil à Chicoutimi,* Quebec; and *Scotia Sun,* Nova Scotia.

Together, these points lead to a number of conclusions. A significant and increasing number of candidates are spending close to the limit: nearly one-third of the candidates of the three largest parties spent more than 90 per cent of their limit in the 1988 election. This may well indicate the limits need to be raised to ensure candidates are able to put forward their program effectively. Second, spending on 'other expenses' must be considered in light of our recommendation for a more inclusive definition of election expenses. Some allowance should be made for candidates' campaign costs that are now classified as 'other expenses' but would become subject to limitation – for example, the remuneration of poll agents and the costs of public opinion polling and research. The former is significant in some campaigns, and the latter, while not now a major item for most candidates, could become so with changes in campaign techniques and technological developments (see Volume 2, Chapter 6).

In addition, it is necessary to address the failure of the present indexation rule to keep up with the increase in major campaign costs. Raising the present average candidate limit of $55 155 by 25 to 30 per cent would help redress this situation and allow room for 'other expenses' that would be brought within the spending limits. In many respects, this higher limit would not mean the actual spending allowed would be much greater, only that additional elements of spending in recent campaigns would fall under the more encompassing definition and be fully reported.

Two other matters must be addressed: the scale of the spending limits and the amount allowed per voter at the intervals on the scale. At present the intervals on the scale are from 0 to 15 000 voters, 15 001 to 25 000 voters, and more than 25 000 voters. In the 1974 base formula the amount per voter was $1.00 for the first interval, $0.50 for the second and $0.25 for the third.

While the *amount allowed per voter* must be adjusted to raise the limit to the new average level, the *scale* itself must also be adjusted. The total electorate grew by nearly 30 per cent between 1974 and 1988; the average number of voters per constituency rose from 51 398 to 59 793, an increase of 16 per cent. If each cut-off point on the scale were raised by 5000 voters, that is from 15 000 to 20 000 and from 25 000 to 30 000, these changes would capture the growth in the number of voters.

Using this scale, and doubling the rates of the 1974 base formula, we would raise the present average limit to $69 197, an increase of 25.5 per cent. Doubling the amounts per voter stipulated under the 1974 legislation has the advantage of being straightforward, even with future indexation. The allowable spending per voter would rise to $1.16, which is still lower per voter than in all provinces that have limits except for Quebec and Ontario (see Table 6.7).

A related issue is the allowance for additional spending in geographically large constituencies. At present, the Act allows candidates in constituencies with, on average, fewer than 10 voters per square kilometre to incur additional election expenses of $0.15 cents for each square kilometre;

the maximum by which the spending limit can be increased is 25 per cent (the amount of additional spending allowed for each square kilometre has been indexed since the 1983 amendments). In the last election, this provision affected 91 constituencies, including those that are the largest and most remote.

Table 6.7
Candidate election expense limits per voter (for an election held before 1 April 1992)
(dollars)

Jurisdiction	Allowable spending per voter
Nova Scotia	3.53
Saskatchewan	3.41
New Brunswick	2.04
Manitoba	2.00
Prince Edward Island	1.51
Canada (recommendation)	**1.16**
Ontario	1.00
Canada (present limits)	**0.93**
Quebec	0.90

Source: Royal Commission Research Branch.

During our hearings, we were told that candidates in northern and remote constituencies face particular difficulties. In many cases, more than one campaign office is needed, which is not usually so in smaller, particularly urban, constituencies. However, our research indicates that even with the additional spending allowed, candidates in the sparsely populated constituencies do not spend a much greater share of the limit than elsewhere: the average proportion of the limit spent by all candidates in the sparsely populated constituencies in the 1988 election was 46.4 per cent, compared with 41.0 for the remaining constituencies. At the same time, an examination of candidates' post-election returns indicated that travel expenses in the 91 constituencies that fall under the sparsely populated rule are on average almost twice what they are in the other constituencies. Even though a candidate's travel expenses are exempted from the limits (and will continue to be under our recommendations), provision must be made to accommodate the travel costs of key campaign staff.

It is important that the spending limits reflect the diversity of conditions across the country so that candidates can run competitive campaigns and reach as many voters as possible. Accordingly, we propose that in these sparsely populated constituencies, the additional allowable spending per square kilometre be raised to $0.30 and that the maximum upward adjustment be doubled from 25 to 50 per cent. Based on Elections Canada estimates of the electorate, the average limit in these 91 constituencies would rise to $71 280 – an increase of 26.2 per cent (compared with 25.5 per cent for the other constituencies) over the average limit in these sparsely populated constituencies if an election were held before 1 April 1992.

At present, the *Canada Elections Act* also allows additional spending in constituencies where the number of voters is less than the average in all constituencies. In such cases, for the purpose of calculating the spending limit, the number of voters for the constituency is increased by one-half the difference between the number of voters on the preliminary list in that constituency and the average number of voters in all constituencies. The new formula for calculating candidates' maximum election expenses will largely eliminate the need to retain an additional upward adjustment, except in the case of constituencies with fewer than 30 000 voters. Based on current estimates of the size of the electorate, there are eight such constituencies, and their average spending limit for an election held before 1 April 1992 would be $47 687. Under the proposed formula, the average allowable spending in those constituencies would rise to $55 716 – an increase of only 16.8 per cent relative to the 1988 election. This difficulty could be resolved by stipulating in the legislation that any constituency with fewer than 30 000 voters be 'deemed' to have 30 000 voters.

One final matter must be considered for calculating the spending limit. The *Canada Elections Act* now stipulates that the limits, subject to the two exceptions already discussed, are determined by the number of names on the preliminary lists of voters. In the 1988 election, for the country as a whole, the number of names on the final lists was 2.9 per cent greater than the number of names on the preliminary lists; in certain constituencies, the difference was considerably greater. If the spending limits were based on the final number of registered voters, they would take into account the actual electorate. Candidates and parties would still plan their campaign budgets largely on the basis of the preliminary lists but could expect to be able to spend somewhat more. This is also relevant to the nomination spending limits discussed later, as they will be set as a proportion of the candidate's election spending limits in the constituency.

Recommendation 1.6.2

We recommend that a candidate's 'election expenses' not exceed the aggregate of:
- **$2.00 for each of the first 20 000 registered voters for the constituency;**
- **$1.00 for each registered voter between 20 001 and 30 000; and**
- **$0.50 for each additional registered voter.**

Recommendation 1.6.3

We recommend that

(a) for calculating a candidate's election expenses limit, any constituency where the number of voters is less than 30 000 be deemed to have 30 000 voters; and

(b) candidates in constituencies with, on average, fewer than 10 voters per square kilometre be allowed to incur additional election expenses of $0.30 for each square kilometre, but that the additional permitted spending not exceed 50 per cent of the election expenses limit that would otherwise apply.

Spending Limits for Political Parties

The present legislation stipulates that a registered political party's maximum 'election expenses' are not to exceed $0.30 per voter in the constituencies where the party has candidates; this is indexed to changes in the consumer price index. Based on this formula, in the 1988 election registered political parties could spend $0.47 per voter. The limit for the Progressive Conservative and New Democratic parties was $8 005 799 each, as they nominated candidates in all constituencies. The limit for the Liberal Party was $7 977 679 because it did not have a candidate in one constituency. If a general election were held before 1 April 1992, the spending limit for a registered party with candidates in all constituencies would be $0.54 per voter; based on Elections Canada estimates of the increase in the electorate since 1988, the limit would be approximately $10 044 000.

Since the 1979 election, the reported election expenses of the three largest parties have risen significantly. The Progressive Conservative Party's spending rose from 87.7 per cent of the limit in 1979 to 99.96 per cent in 1984, then dropped slightly to 98.95 per cent in 1988. Spending by the Liberal Party rose from 86.2 per cent of the limit in 1979 to 98.5 per cent in 1984, then dropped to 85.7 per cent in 1988. The New Democratic Party's reported election expenses rose the most and at every election: from 49.1 per cent in 1979 to 88.2 per cent in 1988. On four occasions a party reported spending more than 95 per cent of the limit: the Progressive Conservatives in 1980, 1984 and 1988, and the Liberals in 1984.

Advertising counts for the greatest share of these parties' reported election expenses. In the 1988 election, the three parties' spending on television, radio and print advertising averaged 53.4 per cent of their total election expenses; television advertising alone accounted for an average of 30 per cent of their election expenses (Table 6.8).

Given our recommendation that all major items specifically related to a party's election campaign be covered by the definition of 'election expenses' and, with a few specific exceptions, be subject to limitation, it is necessary to consider to what degree the limits for parties would have to be raised to cover those items now excluded from the limits. Unfortunately, there are no publicly reported data on the extent to which the annual operating expenses of these political parties include spending during the writ period on items excluded from the definition of 'election expenses'. The parties do report their spending on various items, but, on the basis of these reports, it is not possible to determine when such spending occurred. However, our research and consultations with the representatives of the parties have provided us with estimates of the scale and timing of spending on excluded items.

Table 6.8
Parties' spending on advertising as a percentage of total election expenses, 1980–88

Category of spending	Party	1980	1984	1988
Television advertising	Progressive Conservative Party	42.6	27.5	30.8
	Liberal Party	41.9	26.9	29.6
	New Democratic Party	37.8	24.5	35.3
Radio advertising	Progressive Conservative Party	14.8	19.3	19.6
	Liberal Party	15.1	17.0	15.0
	New Democratic Party	7.6	10.4	6.8
Print advertising	Progressive Conservative Party	13.1	3.2	10.2
	Liberal Party	10.4	12.1	11.9
	New Democratic Party	13.8	3.3	2.2
Total advertising	Progressive Conservative Party	70.5	50.1	59.5
	Liberal Party	67.5	56.0	56.5
	New Democratic Party	59.2	38.2	44.3

Source: Royal Commission Research Branch.

Under our recommendations, for example, the parties' spending on public opinion polling during the campaign would be counted as an election expense and encompassed by their spending limits. Based on interviews with party officials, we estimate that the largest federal parties each spent up to $750 000 on polling during the 1988 election. Our recommendations would also encompass what the current guidelines refer to as "research and analysis" conducted during the election period, as well as "direct mail" to all but party members. Each of these activities is clearly related to the election, and the costs of both should be counted as election expenses. We estimate the three largest parties each spent up to $500 000 on these two activities during the 1988 election.

The preferable course is to have the limits cover all the major aspects of election spending – including activities that flow from our recommendations, such as communicating with voters abroad – and to ensure full reporting. Based on the above estimates, the spending limits for registered parties must be adjusted upward. If spending on the major items referred to in our discussion had not been excluded, our assessment is that the party spending limit for the 1988 election would have been about 10 to 15 per cent higher.

As with candidates, revised spending limits for parties should reflect that the costs of major components of campaigns, particularly advertising, have risen more rapidly than the consumer price index (see Tables 6.5 and 6.6). The present party election expense limit would have to be raised by about 20 per cent to capture the major part of the lag of advertising costs behind the consumer price index.

Table 6.9
Party election expense limits per voter (for an election held before 1 April 1992)
(dollars)

Jurisdiction	Allowable spending per voter
Prince Edward Island	5.48
Nova Scotia	1.61
New Brunswick	1.25
Saskatchewan	0.87
Manitoba	0.87
Canada (recommendation)	**0.70**
Canada (present limits)	**0.54**
Ontario	0.42
Quebec	0.26

Source: Royal Commission Research Branch.

We must also consider the growth of the electorate. If the amount per registered voter stipulated in the legislation were set at $0.70, the spending limit for a registered party with candidates in all constituencies would be $12.63 million, compared with the present estimated limit of $10.044 million. This represents an increase of 26 per cent (based on an Elections Canada estimate of an electorate of 18.1 million). At this rate, federal limits on party spending per voter would remain lower than the limits of five of the seven provinces, and the ranking in Table 6.9 would not change.

Recommendation 1.6.4

We recommend that a registered party's election expenses not exceed the aggregate of $0.70 for each registered voter in constituencies where the party has candidates.

Limits on Independent Election Expenditures
The current *Canada Elections Act* contains a provision that prohibits independent election spending "for the purpose of promoting or opposing, directly and during an election, a particular registered party, or the election of a particular candidate". This provision was declared unconstitutional by a lower court in Alberta in 1984 and is no longer applied anywhere in

Canada. This provision did not place a limit on independent election spending by individuals and groups other than candidates and parties; it banned independent election spending outright. At the same time, it allowed unlimited independent election spending on issues that were not considered to directly promote or oppose a particular registered party or the election of a particular candidate.

Our approach in limiting independent election spending proceeds from two fundamental assumptions. First, any regime that seeks to limit election spending by individuals and groups other than candidates and parties must allow for meaningful freedom of expression. A fair law could not ban such expenses outright. Second, individuals and groups that seek to advocate a position on an issue must also be able to link candidates and parties with the issue. Since voters do not vote directly for issues but rather for candidates, it is essential that messages be permitted to refer explicitly or implicitly to candidates' or parties' positions or views on the issues being promoted. Any law that sought to confine independent spending on advertising or other communications only to messages about an issue, with no reference to candidates or parties and their positions on the issue, would be an unfair restriction on meaningful freedom of expression during an election.

At the same time, any regime based on the premise that individuals and groups can be equated with candidates and registered political parties and thus be subject to a uniform election finance regime would be defective. At a minimum, such an approach would require a comprehensive, intrusive and expensive registration, disclosure and regulatory structure. The lesson from the United States, where such regulation is in place, is that a significant administrative burden would be imposed on individuals and groups, at considerable cost to taxpayers, because an elaborate enforcement machinery is required.

Equally significant, such a regime would not secure fairness in the realization of rights and freedoms because no distinction would be made between the roles in the electoral process of candidates and parties, on the one hand, and individuals and groups, on the other. If the limits imposed on individuals and candidates and on groups and parties were comparable, participants could pool their resources, up to their limits, to support or oppose the election of one or more candidates or parties. Since it cannot be expected that all political interests would have the same ability to gain access to resources, the likely consequence is that the election outcome would be influenced by those with greater access to funding. One set of participants would thus have an unfair advantage over other sets of participants.

Such a regime, even if it banned the pooling of resources by participants and subjected groups to a spending limit comparable to that of registered political parties, could not eliminate the possibility of a group subdividing into smaller groups, thereby multiplying, to increase the amount that could be legally spent in support of a shared election objective. By definition, however, neither candidates nor political parties could adopt this tactic to augment their spending limits. Since voters cast their ballot for only one candidate in each constituency, a single candidate obviously cannot 'multiply' to augment her or his spending limit. For the same reason, a registered political party cannot subdivide to augment its spending limit.

At best, then, such a regime would simply secure transparency in contributions and expenditures. In this respect, it is important to recall that the U.S. regime does not include spending limits for congressional elections; rather the regime seeks to control undue influence and thus relies on limiting the size and source of contributions. For reasons outlined in the following chapter, we do not recommend that there be limits on the size or source of contributions from Canadian voters or groups.

Considering these difficulties, a regulatory approach that seeks to promote the fundamental value of fairness in securing the right of individuals and groups to participate in an election campaign by incurring election expenses must acknowledge that individuals and groups cannot be equated with candidates and political parties in the design of spending limits. The regulatory treatment of independent expenditures must respect the essential and primary role of candidates and political parties in elections by recognizing the nature and potential impact of independent expenditures.

The recognition of the primary role performed by political parties and candidates does not mean that the regulatory regime cannot accommodate independent expenditures. Given the capacity for groups to subdivide into smaller groups, however, any limit on independent election expenses must be the same for individuals and groups. Different spending limits for individuals and groups would merely invite groups to 'multiply', thereby defeating the purpose of spending limits.

We recognize that without precedents to inform a recommended spending limit for independent election expenditures, any recommendation on the spending level can only be an 'educated guess'. In reaching a decision on this limit, we considered three factors. First, we examined the pattern of political contributions to candidates and political parties by individuals and groups. Second, we examined the costs of various forms of election advertising. Third, we considered the likely effects of various levels of spending limits in relation to the limits we are recommending for candidates and political parties. On the basis of these considerations, we propose that each individual or group other than registered parties and candidates be permitted to spend up to $1000 on 'election expenses' during the election period.

Within the Canadian context and experience, $1000 represents a significant political commitment on the part of individuals wishing to spend money independently of the official campaigns of registered participants. The average size of contributions from individuals to the three largest political parties in 1988 was $112; the average donation to the candidates of these parties in the election that year was $135. Indeed, 98 per cent of contributions from individuals to candidates in the 1988 election were less than

$1000; and 92 per cent of contributions from business and 71 per cent of contributions from trade unions were below $1000. (Padget 1991 RC)

The $1000 limit for independent expenditures would permit an individual or group to engage in a significant amount of election activity – for example, by issuing pamphlets and other promotional materials, placing signs, producing and distributing election materials and advertising on local radio, newspapers and, in some places, television. Examination of the evidence brought forward in the *Roach* (1977), *Risdon* (1980) and *Publicis communicateur conseil* (1981) cases – the only cases in which alleged violations of the independent expenditures provisions were brought to court – indicates that the spending in these cases would likely have been within or close to this limit.[4]

A spending limit of $1000 for independent expenditures would also permit individuals and groups to engage in *meaningful* freedom of expression, denied by the 1983 legislation, by allowing them to promote or oppose candidates and parties either directly or indirectly when advocating election positions, as long as their election expenses did not exceed $1000. As noted in Volume 2, Chapter 6, this limit would not apply to free broadcasting time, time on a public affairs program or space in the print media for similar purposes.

The effect of this limit would most likely be to restrict the amount of money spent on media advertising. Although this amount is insufficient for those who wish to mount national media campaigns to promote issues or to assess the positions of political parties, the centrality of fairness in the electoral process justifies this limit. If individuals or groups wished to conduct broader campaigns they could do so by supporting existing parties and candidates (including independent candidates) or by forming a political party and fielding candidates. Moreover, federal election campaigns are relatively short and would be shorter still under our recommendations (less than 50 days). Outside this period, individuals and groups would face no restrictions on the type or amount of spending they wished to incur to promote issues or to criticize parties or elected members.

Restrictions on independent expenditures should in no way impair the right of corporations, unions and other groups to exhort their shareholders, members or employees to act in particular ways during elections. This kind of activity is not, and should not be seen as, a violation of the fairness principle as long as the communications are exclusively with members of the organization. Although groups could not spend more than their legal limit to communicate with persons *outside* their organizations, the right of employers and union leaders to discuss election issues with their shareholders, employees or members must be clearly recognized. There is no reason to presume that a limit on this form of communication is necessary to ensure fairness. Furthermore, labour laws that put restrictions on these rights are clearly in violation of both the spirit and letter of the Charter and should be amended accordingly, since the experience in jurisdictions that do not impose such severe constraints clearly demonstrates they are not essential.

The scope and level of spending we recommend for independent partisan advocacy during elections would be acceptable under the *Canadian Charter of Rights and Freedoms*, which guarantees rights and freedoms and yet establishes principles for imposing limits on them. Limits on these rights and freedoms must meet certain fundamental tests, as established in the *Oakes* case.

First, legislation that limits a right or freedom can be justified only if its objective is related to concerns that are, in the words of the *Oakes* case, "substantial and pressing" in a free and democratic society. (1986, 140) In legislation that limits freedom of expression through measures that impose limits on election expenses by candidates, parties, individuals and groups, the pressing and substantial concerns relate to realizing an equality of opportunity for citizens to exercise their rights to freedom of expression, as well as their democratic rights to vote and to stand as a candidate, in a meaningful way during the election. The standard that must be applied in relation to the limits on the freedom of expression of individuals and groups is the probability that independent expenditures will have an unfair influence on the outcome of the election by advantaging one or more candidates or parties over other candidates or parties. Spending limits for candidates and parties, which have as their objective the promotion of the central value of fairness, cannot achieve this effect by themselves if others face no restrictions at all on their spending during the election period. The experience of the 1988 general election clearly demonstrates this.

Second, a spending limit on independent expenditures is rationally connected to the objective of promoting fairness in the exercise of rights and freedoms during an election and does not place an arbitrary or unfair burden on any particular individual or group. It would apply to all those who wish to engage in any activity covered by our proposed definition of 'election expenses'. At the same time, an expenditure limit on all forms of electoral communication with the public is necessary. Any measures to restrict only certain forms of communications would simply result in other forms of communications being used. For instance, if there were restrictions on advertising in the broadcasting media, advertising could be shifted to the print media; if restrictions applied to all mass or public media, communications could be shifted to direct mail; or, if restrictions included direct mail, individuals or groups could shift to advertising campaigns by way of picketing, posters or campaign leaflets. Alternative means of communications can always be found, as the evolving techniques of electoral campaigning demonstrate. Similarly, the expenditure limit must extend to both direct and indirect messages. Experience, especially that of the 1988 general election, conclusively demonstrates that any attempt to differentiate or distinguish between direct and indirect or partisan and issue advocacy cannot be sustained.

Third, given the seriousness of the objective of promoting fairness in the electoral process generally, the proposed spending limit on independent expenditures also passes the proportionality test set in the *Oakes* (1986) case. It would be impossible to increase substantially the spending limit for independent expenditures and, at the same time, to secure the objective of fairness that candidate and party spending limits are meant to realize. For example, if the limit were twice as high, 35 individuals or groups could spend an amount that would rival what a candidate would be legally entitled to spend under the revised limits we are proposing. If the limit were five times as high, a coalition of 10 interest groups could co-ordinate spending and launch an advertising campaign in a major national newspaper. Moreover, in either case, the individual or group might well spend the money on only one issue. In contrast, in their campaigns, candidates and parties have higher limits but must take positions on and promote or oppose a range of issues of interest to the entire electorate. In addition, under our recommendations, access to candidacy and access to registered political party status are enhanced considerably beyond what are already extremely accessible requirements. In comparative terms, there would be greater opportunities for access to the electoral process than in most, if not all, other western democracies.

Fourth, our proposals also meet the criterion in the *Oakes* (1986) case that the means should impair freedom of expression "as little as possible". A $1000 spending limit, coupled with the freedom of corporations, employers, unions and groups to communicate directly with their shareholders, employees or members on election issues, represents the least restrictive way of limiting freedom of expression while promoting the objective of fairness in electoral competition process. Unlike the 1983 legislation challenged in court, our recommendation allows explicit partisan advocacy and thus does not restrict either the intent or the nature of expression. Although our recommendation imposes a limit on the amount of election expenses individuals or groups may incur, this limit is justified because any greater ability to incur independent expenditures would irreparably weaken the effectiveness of the spending limits for candidates and parties, and thus undermine the central objective of fairness these limits are meant to achieve.

While it is possible that, in certain circumstances, a $1000 spending limit might jeopardize the effectiveness of candidate and party spending limits, the risk that fairness would be compromised by spending at this level would not be so significant as to justify a lower limit, provided that individuals or groups not be permitted to combine resources to augment the spending limit. The regulation of independent expenditure thus must include an explicit restriction against individuals or groups pooling their financial resources to overcome the spending limit. Without such a restriction, the effectiveness of spending limits on individuals and groups could easily be destroyed.

Consistent with our recommendations for sponsor identification of print and broadcast advertising by candidates and registered parties, found in Volume 2, Chapter 6, there should be a requirement that all other distributed advertisements identify the name of the sponsor. This would mean that major violations of the spending limit – for instance, significant spending on commercial television advertising, direct mail, or newspaper, radio or magazine advertisements – would be readily apparent to election participants and election officials. Enforcement of regulations would rely on complaints from participants or voters or the initiative of officials charged with enforcing the election law. In either case, the Canada Elections Commission would have the power to issue a 'mandatory injunction' or 'cease and desist' order instructing the individual or group to comply with the law.

Finally, it is necessary to regulate the timing of any advertisements sponsored by those incurring independent expenditures within the limit we recommend to ensure conformity with the blackout period that applies to candidates and parties. In 1988, some groups advertised on the eve of the election, when candidates and parties are legally incapable of responding. To ensure fairness, it is essential that groups or individuals who seek to assess or criticize candidates and parties do so only when candidates and parties are legally capable of responding. The reasons that justify the blackout period are sufficiently compelling that they must apply to everyone.

Recommendation 1.6.5

We recommend that there be no statutory restrictions on the ability of groups, associations, unions and employers to communicate directly and exclusively with their bona fide members, employees or shareholders on election issues.

Recommendation 1.6.6

We recommend that

(a) election expenses incurred by any group or individual independently from registered parties and candidates not exceed $1000;

(b) the sponsor be identified on all advertising or distributed promotional material; and

(c) there be no pooling of funds.

Recommendation 1.6.7

We recommend that the blackout period for election advertising at the end of the election period include advertising by groups and individuals.

Indexation of Spending Limits

The increases in the spending limits we are recommending are intended to reflect increases in major campaign costs and, more important, to ensure the limits are comprehensive. The limits must remain realistic, however, so that they do not become artificially low and thus tempt participants to seek ways around them. Indexation is therefore required.

As discussed, several interveners at our hearings argued that the consumer price index is not the best measure of changes to the key costs of campaigns. In their submission to the Commission, representatives of the Progressive Conservative Party and the New Democratic Party noted that increases in their parties' major campaign costs – for example, travel and accommodation – had exceeded the increase in the consumer price index. They recommended that the limits be indexed annually based on the cost increases for the component expenditures.

Proposals for an alternative index based on the relevant cost increases raise a number of issues. First, there is no objective and reliable measure of the increase in costs of major campaign activities such as advertising. Second, political parties allocate their expenditures in different ways, and thus a single index might not be appropriate to all parties. Third, our research revealed considerable variations in cost increases across the country; too rigid an index could work to the disadvantage of some candidates while advantaging others.

An alternative would be to provide for indexation of spending limits but not according to a set formula. The Canada Elections Commission would be given responsibility for determining adjustments to the limits. This could be done according to the following procedure:

- during the first three months of each year, the Commission would determine what adjustments were required to reflect changes in the prices of key goods and services used in campaigns;
- a notice of the adjustments would be published in *The Canada Gazette*, and interested parties could then make submissions to the Commission, including at public hearings if the Commission so decided; and
- the revised limits would come into effect on 1 May and apply to any election for which the writ was issued during the following 12 months.

This procedure has a number of advantages. The Commission could survey the most relevant cost increases and variations across the country. Its recommended increases in the limits would probably reflect the increased cost of campaigns more accurately than the consumer price index. This approach would also mean that the spending limits would not lag behind key costs and thus invite evasion.

Recommendation 1.6.8

We recommend that

(a) **the Canada Elections Commission annually determine adjustments to the spending limits for candidates, registered parties, individuals and groups;**
(b) **the adjustments reflect changes in the costs of major goods and services used in election campaigns; and**
(c) **the adjustments be in effect from 1 May each year and apply to any election for which the writ was issued during the following 12 months.**

Spending Limits for Nomination Contests and Leadership Selection

Nomination Contests

At present, the *Canada Elections Act* does not limit spending by those seeking nomination as a candidate (nomination contestants), with one exception: under section 214, "the amount that may be spent for notices of meetings to be held for the principal purpose of nominating a candidate" is limited to 1 per cent of the limit for a candidate's election expenses in that constituency for the previous general election. This section applies to notices sponsored by a person seeking the nomination during the writ period.

This limit in section 214 applies to only a small part of the potential spending of nomination contestants. Moreover, a recent court decision suggests the provision may not be effective in controlling spending even on such advertising.[5] But a more fundamental issue is at stake here. Because nomination spending during the election period can promote a person who subsequently becomes a candidate, there is a serious gap in the regulation of election spending. Substantial nomination spending calls into question the election expense limits: although such spending is possibly directly related to the election, it falls outside the limits. This can allow evasion of the limits and runs counter to the objective of fairness on which the election spending limits are based. The Accounting Profession Working Group proposed a way of limiting nomination spending during the writ period: if, in seeking a nomination, a person who subsequently became a candidate spent more than 10 per cent of the amount a candidate was entitled to spend in that constituency in the previous general election, the excess would have to be reported as an election expense of the candidate and be deducted from the candidate's election spending limit. (Canada, Royal Commission 1991a, Part 2)

The question of nomination spending must, however, be seen in a broader context. In Volume 1, Chapter 3, we recommend that there be nomination spending limits no matter when the nomination contest takes place, to encourage fairness in the electoral process and encourage access for those seeking nomination as a candidate. Constituency associations can take further steps to promote fairness. For example, they can hold meetings where all nomination contestants may present their positions, or they can encourage community newspapers and cable television channels to provide such exposure.

We suggest in Volume 1, Chapter 5 that political parties should take greater responsibility for regulating party activities linked to the election process. For example, the constitution of a party could include rules for regulating the financial activities of the nomination process throughout the party. Alternatively, the constituency associations might choose to develop rules that would be tailored to their particular situation. In either case, there should be requirements that each nomination contestant not spend more than a defined amount and submit a preliminary report on his or her spending and contributions no later than the day of the nomination meeting. This would provide important information to the party members choosing a candidate.

For the reasons outlined in Volume 1, Chapter 3, and because public funding will be involved, the *Canada Elections Act* should contain a minimum set of rules in relation to the nomination process, namely, spending limits, disclosure procedures and a requirement that each nomination contestant appoint an agent.

The present spending limits for candidates apply during a set period, that of the election. For limits on nomination spending to be equitable and practicable, they, too, must apply to a set period. Some constituency associations now require that members be notified at least 30 days before a nomination meeting is to be held. A nomination period of a maximum of 30 days, during which the limits would be in effect, is reasonable.

The statutory limits should be high enough to allow competitive campaigns but low enough to ensure that those with access to greater resources do not have an unfair advantage. Because nomination costs can vary from constituency to constituency, it would be preferable to set nomination limits as a percentage of candidates' spending limits rather than at a set amount. This would allow additional spending in, for example, geographically large constituencies. In addition, because election spending limits would be indexed, nomination limits set as a percentage of those limits would be adjusted correspondingly without requiring an amendment to the legislation.

The possible level of nomination spending limits was addressed in our survey of constituency association presidents. Those who favoured statutory spending limits for nomination contests were asked what would be a reasonable limit; the median response was $5000. (Carty 1991a RC) In Janine Brodie's survey of women candidates from the 1988 election, 79 per cent of respondents suggested the limit be below $5000. (Brodie 1991 RC, Table 2.15) Based on our recommendations and if nomination spending limits were set at 10 per cent of the election expense limits for candidates, the average nomination spending limit would be $6920. As noted in Volume 1, Chapter 5, we propose that, as a condition of registration, parties be required to submit financial rules for nomination campaigns. Although any party could choose to set a lower spending limit, the *Canada Elections Act* should provide that in no case would a nomination contestant be allowed to spend more than 10 per cent of the election expenses limit in effect for a candidate in that constituency at the time of the nomination meeting. As with candidates, there should be specific legal penalties for persons exceeding the nomination spending limit.

A related issue is spending for nomination meetings held during the election period. In sponsoring such meetings, constituency associations may spend a significant amount of money. Even if the expenses are not directed toward supporting a particular nomination contestant, they may provide publicity and exposure for the contestants, including the one who is chosen and becomes the candidate. During an election, excessive spending on nomination meetings could run counter to the intent of the election spending limits and diminish fairness. We therefore propose that, in sponsoring a nomination meeting during the writ period, a constituency association be prohibited from spending more than 10 per cent of the election spending limit for candidates in that constituency.

Consistent with our recommendation that the definition of candidates' election expenses be comprehensive, the nomination spending limit should fully cover relevant spending on goods and services during the nomination period. For this purpose, the legislation should stipulate that 'nomination expenses' have the same meaning as 'election expenses'.

Recommendation 1.6.9

We recommend that

(a) **spending by those seeking the nomination of a registered constituency association not exceed 10 per cent of the limit for a candidate's election expenses in that constituency in effect at the time of the nomination meeting, except if the rules of the registered party provide for a lower limit;**
(b) **this limit apply during a nomination period of a maximum of 30 days; and**
(c) **during an election period, the expenses incurred by the constituency association or registered party for the nomination of a candidate not exceed 10 per cent of a candidate's allowable election expenses in that constituency.**

A number of other issues are related to our recommendation to regulate spending during the nomination process. Among these are the reporting rules for the financial activities of those seeking nominations and the issuing of tax receipts for contributions to nomination campaigns. Proper accountability must be achieved without creating additional administrative structures.

Our recommendations for the registration of constituency associations provide the basis for such accountability.

We propose that, as a condition of registration, each constituency association be required to appoint a constituency agent. As the linchpin of the reporting procedures for constituency associations, this person should also play a role in the framework for the nomination process. Once the association announced the date of a nomination meeting, the nomination period would begin. Nomination contestants would indicate to the constituency agent their intention to run, in accordance with the rules in the constitution of the party or association.

To ensure financial control and accountability, nomination contestants, like candidates, would be required to appoint an agent. This agent would have responsibilities similar to those of the official agent of a candidate. He or she would be required to authorize all spending on behalf of the nomination contestant. Any unauthorized spending to promote the contestant should be counted against the nomination contestant's limit. The nomination agent would receive a form (approved by the Canada Elections Commission) for recording nomination spending and contributions.

Contributions to a nomination contestant's campaign would be eligible for income tax credits. However, only the constituency agent would be allowed to issue receipts to that effect. It is essential that a limit be placed on the amount of tax credits that could be claimed by those donating to nomination campaigns; otherwise, nomination contestants might be able to solicit contributions well in excess of what they were allowed to spend, which would represent an undue drain on public funds. We therefore propose that, for each nomination contestant, no further tax receipts be issued once the value of contributions for which the constituency agent issues income tax receipts has reached the nomination spending limit.

The agent of the nomination contestant would be required to submit a final financial report to the Canada Elections Commission within a month of the nomination meeting. However, if the nomination takes place during the writ period, it may not be reasonable to require the contestant who is nominated as the candidate, who will be in the midst of an election campaign, to submit his or her nomination financial report within a month. In such cases, the latter report could be filed with the candidate's post-election return. Further details relating to the reporting requirements of nomination contestants are discussed in Volume 1, Chapter 7.

These procedures would require the co-operation of political parties and local associations. Their introduction would oblige those involved to adapt – just as was the case when election spending limits were introduced in the 1970s – and the initial experience with nomination limits may point out the need for some adjustments. In this regard, we propose that the Canada Elections Commission report to Parliament after the first election to which nomination spending limits apply.

Recommendation 1.6.10

We recommend that

(a) those seeking the nomination of a registered constituency association be required to notify the constituency association agent of their intention to do so, in accordance with the rules in the constitution of the registered party or association;

(b) each nomination contestant be required to appoint an agent, with responsibilities similar to those of the official agent of a candidate;

(c) contributions to a nomination contestant's campaign be eligible for income tax receipts issued by the constituency agent, but that once the value of contributions to any contestant for which receipts are issued reaches the amount of the nomination spending limit, no further receipts be issued with respect to this nomination contestant;

(d) as a condition of registration, a party or constituency association submit to the Canada Elections Commission its by-laws or rules concerning the financial activities of nomination contestants, including an obligation to disclose contributions, spending limits and a requirement that, no later than the day of the nomination meeting, each nomination contestant submit to the association a preliminary report on his or her nomination expenses and contributions;

(e) no later than a month after the nomination meeting, nomination contestants be required to submit to the Canada Elections Commission a report on their spending and contributions during the nomination period, except if the nomination takes place during the election period, in which case the contestant nominated as the candidate be required to submit the report no later than the date for submission of his or her post-election return; and

(f) after the first election to which nomination spending limits apply, the Canada Elections Commission report to Parliament on the initial experience with the limits.

Leadership Selection
In Volume 1, Chapter 5, we recommend spending limits for leadership selection based on similar principles. The limits would be set at 15 per cent of the registered party's limit at the previous election and would be in effect during the period from the announcement of the date of the election of a new leader and the day of the vote. Each leadership contestant would be required to appoint an agent, who would be responsible for ensuring financial control and preparing the necessary financial reports – an interim report

(required by party rules) by the day before the vote for the leader is held and a final return (required by law) within three months of the vote. Again, there would be a limit on tax credits issued: once the value of contributions for which income tax receipts were issued equalled the leadership contestant's spending limit, no further receipts could be issued. In addition, if tax receipts were issued for contributions up to the limit but the leadership contestant spent less than the limit, he or she would have to transfer to the party, its foundation or a registered constituency association, the difference between the spending limit and the amount spent.

The procedures outlined above are intended to secure fairer processes for the selection of candidates and party leaders. Spending limits and tax credits for donations to their campaigns would provide greater access, and disclosure requirements would ensure accountability to party members and the public. We are confident these measures will broaden access and thus enhance the representativeness of political parties and of the House of Commons.

PUBLIC FUNDING OF ELECTION PARTICIPANTS

Reimbursements to Parties and Candidates

At present, public funding of federal political parties and candidates is provided indirectly through income tax credits and directly through election reimbursements. Both forms of public funding were introduced in 1974, although the rules relating to reimbursements were subsequently amended.

Under the 1974 legislation, registered political parties were reimbursed for 50 per cent of their election expenses on television and radio advertising. In 1983, the rules were changed; since then, all registered parties have been reimbursed 22.5 per cent of their total election expenses provided they have spent at least 10 per cent of their limit. Candidates qualify for reimbursement by meeting the following requirements: they must have been elected or have obtained at least 15 per cent of the valid votes in the constituency; they must also have submitted their post-election report on spending and contributions and the accompanying auditor's report.

The original legislation provided for a reimbursement of the lesser of the candidate's election expenses and the aggregate of the following: the cost of one first-class mailing to each person on the preliminary list of voters, $0.08 for each of the first 25 000 voters on the list, and $0.06 for each additional voter. In 1983 the formula was amended, and qualifying candidates now receive a reimbursement equal to 50 per cent of the sum of their election expenses and personal expenses up to 50 per cent of the spending limit.

At the heart of this reimbursement system lies the belief that candidates and parties perform important and necessary functions during elections in a democratic system; it is therefore in the public interest for the state to provide public funds to support these functions. Reimbursement also lessens candidates' and parties' reliance on large donations from a few donors and helps ensure that candidates and parties are able to conduct effective campaigns. Finally, reimbursement lowers the cost of running for office, thereby facilitating access to the system.

Although the value of candidate and party reimbursements to our electoral democracy has been clearly established in principle, there remains the question of whether the current system fulfils its purpose. The way in which public money is spent in elections should instil confidence in the electorate. For such confidence to exist, the public must perceive that the candidate and party reimbursement system distributes public funds fairly and equitably. In evaluating the current reimbursement system, we thus must determine whether the current reimbursement system meets the goal of fairness in the electoral process.

Those who favour maintaining the present system claim it has achieved its stated goals and that it exhibits a certain fairness in the way it distributes public funds. The system, they argue, enables candidates with sufficient popular support to spend enough money to run a competitive campaign, secure in the knowledge that they will be reimbursed 50 per cent of their expenses. In the same way, parties able to spend 10 per cent of their limit can be similarly secure in spending more, because they can count on a 22.5 per cent reimbursement. As for fairness, some argue that the 15 per cent popular support threshold for candidates and the 10 per cent spending threshold for parties ensure that frivolous candidates and parties are not given public money for their efforts.

We do not accept these arguments. Fairness in elections requires that the present system be reassessed on two grounds. First, the thresholds candidates and parties now face represent a significant hurdle for election participants and exclude a number of legitimate parties and candidates from access to a reasonable share of public funding. Second, the present reimbursement system for both candidates and parties is based on the amount they spend, rather than on their level of popular support.

During our hearings, we were told that the 15 per cent vote threshold for candidate reimbursement is too high. In an electoral system where the winning candidate may need less than 40 per cent of the vote, a rule that defines 10 or even 14 per cent of the vote as insignificant is difficult to defend. The 15 per cent candidate threshold is also an all-or-nothing rule that fails to reflect the relative popular support of candidates. In its brief to the Commission, the Ontario New Democratic Party pointed out that the present system can lead to "the situation of one candidate with 15.1% of the vote receiving a reimbursement of approximately $20–$25,000, while another candidate with 14.9% [does not receive] any public support." (Brief, 1990)

The requirement in the party reimbursement provisions that parties must spend 10 per cent of their spending limit ignores a party's level of popular support entirely. It rewards only the well-financed parties. This has implications for the legitimacy of the public funding rules:

There is no doubt that the current Canadian election-finance legislation based on the registration of political parties and reimbursement for campaign and media expenses strengthens the position of those already "on the inside" and creates severe hindrances to the introduction of new parties or the expansion of small ones. (Jenson 1991b RC)

The two thresholds send a clear message to smaller parties and their candidates as well as to independent candidates: their participation is not welcome. This may also contribute to unwarranted rigidity in the Canadian party system, an effect that should not be underestimated. According to Joseph Wearing,

The discrimination against smaller Canadian parties appears to ignore the contribution made by such parties through much of our political history. Independent Labour parties, the Progressives, Social Credit, the CCF, the Reconstruction Party, the Bloc populaire, and others would have been at a severe disadvantage if they had entered the electoral scene under the present law. (Wearing 1991, 333)

The record shows that candidate reimbursement has been almost strictly the privilege of candidates for the Progressive Conservative, Liberal and New Democratic parties, leaving virtually all other party and independent candidates with no public funding at elections (see Table 6.10). In the four elections since the legislation came into effect, 2404 candidates from the three largest parties were reimbursed, compared with only 51 candidates from other parties and four independent candidates. On no occasion have the candidates of more than one party other than the three largest parties been reimbursed; in 1988, for instance, 11 of the Reform Party's candidates qualified, but not one of the candidates of any other smaller party did so. In the four elections in question, the proportion of candidates not receiving reimbursements has ranged between 53 per cent in 1979 and 57 per cent in 1980. Among those candidates not reimbursed under the present system were several whose electoral support approached, but fell short of, the 15 per cent threshold. In the 1984 and 1988 elections, for example, 226 candidates received more than 10 per cent of the vote but were not reimbursed.

This pattern can also be seen in the distribution of the money allocated through reimbursement over the past four elections. Of the $41 946 841 allocated to candidate reimbursement since 1979, only $736 449 (1.76 per cent of the total reimbursed) has gone to candidates from other than the three largest parties.

The reimbursements to registered parties tell a similar but more striking story. Since the introduction of the 10 per cent threshold in 1983, only one party other than the three largest parties has qualified for reimbursement: the Christian Heritage Party, in 1988. Under the previous rules, in the 1979 and 1980 elections, the Social Credit Party was the only small party

Table 6.10
Reimbursements to candidates, federal general elections, 1979–88

Party	1979		1980		1984		1988	
	(N)	Cost ($)	(N)	Cost ($)	(N)	Cost ($)	(N)	Cost ($)
Progressive Conservative Party	219	2 867 691	215	2 871 029	282	5 117 066	293	6 055 597
Liberal Party	273	3 594 244	275	3 656 074	238	4 081 353	264	4 655 526
New Democratic Party	147	1 670 601	152	1 884 863	140	1 917 095	170	2 839 253
Social Credit Party	29	359 273	8	111 802	—	—	—	—
Reform Party	N.A.	N.A.	N.A.	N.A.	N.A.	N.A.	11	162 122
Christian Heritage Party	N.A.	N.A.	N.A.	N.A.	N.A.	N.A.	—	—
Parti Rhinocéros	—	—	—	—	—	—	—	—
Union populaire	—	—	—	—	N.A.	N.A.	N.A.	N.A.
Libertarian Party	—	—	—	—	—	—	—	—
Marxist-Leninist Party	—	—	—	—	N.A.	N.A.	N.A.	N.A.
Confederation of Regions Western Party	N.A.	N.A.	N.A.	N.A.	3	28 870	—	—
Communist Party	—	—	—	—	—	—	—	—
Green Party	N.A.	N.A.	N.A.	N.A.	—	—	—	—
Party for the Commonwealth of Canada	N.A.	N.A.	N.A.	N.A.	—	—	—	—
Parti nationaliste	N.A.	N.A.	N.A.	N.A.	—	—	N.A.	N.A.
Independent	2	25 972	—	—	1	26 340	1	22 070
Total	670	8 517 781	650	8 523 768	664	11 170 724	739	13 734 568

Source: Canada, Chief Electoral Officer 1979a, 1979b, 1980a, 1980b, 1984a, 1984b, 1988, 1989.

Note: N.A., not applicable – party did not run candidates in year indicated.

to receive more than $270 in reimbursement payments. Moreover, the Social Credit Party was reimbursed only a total of $9518 following these two elections, compared with the average amount of $762 263 paid out to each of the three largest parties in the same two elections. Over the past four elections, parties other than the Progressive Conservative, Liberal and New Democratic parties together received a total of $58 835 (0.44 per cent of the $13 460 246 paid out) even though they won 3 to 6 per cent of the vote in every election (see Table 6.11).

Table 6.11
Reimbursements to political parties, federal general elections, 1979–88
(dollars)

Party	1979	1980	1984	1988
Progressive Conservative Party	793 967	977 835	1 437 512	1 782 391
Liberal Party	718 020	909 923	1 415 921	1 538 972
New Democratic Party	496 350	677 481	1 064 413	1 588 627
Social Credit Party	7 769	1 749	—	—
Christian Heritage Party	N.A.	N.A.	N.A.	48 906
All others	143	268	—	—
Total	2 016 248	2 567 256	3 917 846	4 958 896

Source: Canada, Chief Electoral Officer 1979b, 1980b, 1984b, 1988.

Note: N.A., not applicable – party was not registered in year indicated.

The case of the Christian Heritage Party in 1988 clearly illustrates this shortcoming of the present party reimbursement system. In that year, the Christian Heritage Party was reimbursed $48,906, having spent more than 10 per cent of its spending limit. But the Reform Party, which won almost three times as many votes as the Christian Heritage Party and had 11 candidates qualify for reimbursement, received no reimbursement whatsoever because it did not spend more than 10 per cent of its limit. The 10 per cent spending threshold therefore makes the system of public funding of election participants inaccessible to emerging parties, except those able to spend enough money to reach that threshold.

In short, the present reimbursement system has disproportionately overcompensated the three largest parties and their candidates and undercompensated the smaller parties, their candidates and independent candidates. This is in large part the result of the thresholds, although the fact that reimbursements are based on amounts spent rather than on popular support is also a factor.

In contrast, many western European countries have vote-based funding systems in which public financial support of election participants depends on the level of electoral support. In Germany, for example, all political parties winning more than 0.5 per cent of the vote are reimbursed through a system of annual payments at a rate of DM 5 per vote received. Italy's system of party funding, instituted in 1974, provides public funds according to votes won. In elections for the National Chamber, parties must run candidates in two-thirds of the ridings, and win either at least one seat or at least 2 per cent of the popular vote to receive public funding. Austria provides public funding to any party receiving more than 2.5 per cent of the vote.

In European countries such as these, vote-based public funding and low thresholds have contributed to a greater flexibility within the electoral system. In these cases, Jenson notes, "the existing parties have not used their positions of strength to block innovators. Instead, the parties have ensured that equality of opportunity is part of the regulatory package." (Jenson 1991b RC)

A reimbursement system based on electoral support, and not the ability to spend money, would lead to a fairer distribution of public funding to election participants by introducing greater equity. At the same time it would recognize the relative differences in popular support. The electoral system would be more responsive, giving emerging parties a fair opportunity to grow and lowering the obstacles many candidates now face. For these reasons, we support changing the present reimbursement system to a vote-based reimbursement system for both parties and candidates.

The issue of the proportion of election public funding provided to parties on the one hand and to candidates on the other must also be addressed. Over the post-1974 period as a whole, average proportions were 76.3 per cent for candidates and 23.7 per cent for parties. As Table 6.12 indicates, reimbursements to parties, although the amounts are significant, account for a relatively small share of total direct public funding.

Table 6.12
Federal election reimbursements to parties and candidates, federal general elections, 1979–88
(dollars)

Election	Total reimbursements	Total reimbursements to parties	Total reimbursements to candidates
1979	10 534 029	2 016 248 (19.1%)	8 517 781 (80.9%)
1980	11 091 024	2 567 256 (23.1%)	8 523 768 (76.9%)
1984	15 088 570	3 917 846 (26.0%)	11 170 724 (74.0%)
1988	18 693 464	4 958 896 (26.5%)	13 734 568 (73.5%)

Source: Canada, Chief Electoral Officer 1979b, 1980b, 1984b, 1988.

Payments under the present reimbursement system do not reflect the needs of candidates and parties. This is indicated by surpluses from candidates' election campaigns. Following the 1988 election, for instance, the total surpluses of candidates, including reimbursements received, amounted to $9.6 million. (Canada, Chief Electoral Officer 1991, 10) More than 75 per cent of Progressive Conservative and Liberal candidates had surpluses after the 1988 election, as did more than half the New Democratic Party candidates (see Table 6.13). The surpluses averaged $20 080 for Progressive Conservative candidates, $12 727 for Liberal candidates and $10 421 for New Democratic Party candidates. For the 11 candidates who raised more than $100 000 in that election, the surpluses ranged from $38 236 to $96 284. (Stanbury 1991 RC, chapter 12)

In this context, it is not surprising that transfers from national parties to candidates' campaigns declined after adoption of the 1974 reforms. The

Liberal Party, for example, transferred $2.6 million to its candidates in 1974, but only about $300 000 in the 1979 election and $485 000 in 1988. (Stanbury 1991 RC, chapter 5) The Progressive Conservative Party transferred about $1.7 million to candidates in the 1974 election; this dropped to $450 000 in 1979 (Seidle and Paltiel 1981, 257) and totalled $232 000 in the 1988 election. (Stanbury 1991 RC, Table 4.7) The national parties recognize that candidates generally, given the benefit of the tax credit and the likelihood of reimbursement, have needed less financial assistance since the 1974 legislation. As noted in Volume 1, Chapter 5, the New Democratic and Liberal parties have 'taxed' some of the surplus funds from candidates' campaigns by requiring that a certain proportion be paid to the federal level, a practice that is bound to accelerate unless a better balance is found in the allocation of public funding through reimbursements.

Table 6.13
Analysis of surpluses reported by candidates, 1988 federal general election

Party	Number of candidates	Number reporting a surplus	Number receiving reimbursement[a]	Candidates reporting a surplus (%)	Total surplus reported[b] ($)	Average surplus reported[c] ($)
Progressive Conservative Party	295	231	230	78	4 639 000	20 080
Liberal Party	294	234	220	80	2 978 000	12 727
New Democratic Party	295	167	143	57	1 740 000	10 421
Reform Party	72	21	11	29	140 000	6 650
Christian Heritage Party	63	31	0	49	104 000	3 368
Confederation of Regions Western Party	52	9	0	17	2 400	262
Communist Party	52	8	0	15	1 800	223
Green Party	68	9	0	13	1 300	143
Libertarian Party	88	8	0	9	1 900	242
Social Credit Party	9	1	0	11	N.A.[d]	81
Parti Rhinocéros	74	0	0	0	—	—
Party for the Commonwealth of Canada	61	0	0	0	—	—
Independent	154	4	0	3	N.A.	63

Source: Stanbury 1991 RC, Table 12.33.

[a]Number of candidates reporting a surplus who *also* received reimbursement.
[b]Surplus = contributions – election expenses – personal expenses – campaign expenses + reimbursement.
[c]Only for those candidates reporting a surplus. Amounts may vary slightly because of rounding.
[d]N.A.: not available.

To ensure that candidates and parties are able to fulfil their functions within the electoral process, we need to consider both the criteria by which election participants qualify for reimbursement and the level at which each should be so funded. The system of public funding should ensure that the reimbursement of candidates and parties applies only to those who receive a minimum level of electoral support. Based on our review of the practice in other jurisdictions and our commitment to fairness in electoral competition, we propose that the threshold for registered parties be 1 per cent of the valid votes cast nationally (in 1988, this would have been 131 756 votes) and that any candidate who receives 1 per cent of the valid votes cast in a constituency qualify for reimbursement.

We propose that registered parties that receive at least 1 per cent of the valid national vote be reimbursed $0.60 for each vote and that candidates who receive at least 1 per cent of the valid votes in a constituency be reimbursed $1.00 for each vote received. In all cases, qualifying parties or candidates would not receive a reimbursement greater than 50 per cent of their election expenses.

To ensure the new reimbursement formula is equitable, adjustments are required (as is the case for spending limits) for candidates in geographically large constituencies and constituencies with a small electorate. Candidates' 1988 post-election returns indicated that candidates in the 91 sparsely populated constituencies spent twice as much on 'personal expenses' as other candidates, largely as a result of travel costs. Candidates in the 25 sparsely populated constituencies that would be designated as 'remote' under our proposals (see Volume 2, Chapter 2) spent almost twice as much on 'personal expenses' as the candidates in the remaining 66 constituencies, and their 'personal expenses' were about 18.4 per cent of their 'election expenses'.

The additional costs these candidates face should be reflected in the reimbursement formula. We therefore propose that qualifying candidates in sparsely populated constituencies receive $1.25 for each vote received and those in remote constituencies receive $1.50 for each vote received. Finally, to allow a reasonable level of reimbursement, we propose that qualifying candidates in constituencies with fewer than 30 000 voters receive a reimbursement equal to the amount obtained by multiplying their share of the vote by 30 000 times the amount per vote that would otherwise apply. (Based on the 1990 estimated electorate, there are eight such constituencies; four of these fall in the 'remote' category and one other is sparsely populated.)

Table 6.14 illustrates the pattern of reimbursements that would have been obtained if our recommended system had been in place for the 1988 election. The total reimbursements to parties would have risen by 53 per cent (from $4.96 million to $7.59 million). Unlike under the present rules, the Reform Party would have qualified for reimbursement, but the Christian Heritage Party (which received less than 1 per cent of the national vote) would not have qualified. Based on our recommendation, the candidates' total reimbursements would have been 90.5 per cent of the total reimbursements to candidates in 1988. However, 1157 candidates would have qualified for reimbursement, an increase of 57 per cent. All candidates of the Progressive Conservative, Liberal and New Democratic parties would have received a reimbursement, as would all but one of the candidates for the Reform Party. In addition, 202 other candidates would have qualified, including 20 independent candidates; in 1988, only one candidate not affiliated with a registered party (an independent) was reimbursed.

Table 6.14
Reimbursements under present rules and under recommendations

Party	Number of candidates reimbursed (1988)	Total reimbursements to candidates (1988) ($)	Number of candidates reimbursed (recom-mendation)	Total reimbursements to candidates (recom-mendation) ($)	Reimburse-ments to parties (1988) ($)	Reimburse-ments to parties (recom-mendation) ($)
Progressive Conservative Party	293	6 055 597	295	5 243 445	1 782 391	3 400 538
Liberal Party	264	4 655 526	294	4 046 048	1 538 972	2 523 043
New Democratic Party	170	2 839 253	295	2 659 943	1 588 627	1 611 185
Reform Party	11	162 122	71	301 434	0	56 184
Other	1	22 070	202	179 227	48 906*	0
Total	739	13 734 568	1 157	12 430 097	4 958 896	7 590 949

Source: Royal Commission Research Branch.

*Christian Heritage Party.

Based on Elections Canada estimates, the electorate would be 5 per cent greater if an election were held in late 1992. If turnout were the same as in 1988, we estimate the total cost of reimbursements under our recommendations would be about $20 021 046, which represents a moderate increase over the total cost in 1988 ($18 693 494). Although it is impossible to predict accurately the pattern of reimbursements in a future election, these proposed changes would ensure that national parties receive increased reimbursements and that a considerably greater number of candidates would qualify for reimbursement.

The total reimbursements assigned to candidates would be lower than in the past. This is a function of the amount per voter we propose, not of the basis of the formula. The tax credit, paired with spending limits, has strengthened the capacity of candidates to finance their campaigns. In the future, constituency associations would be able to issue tax receipts on an ongoing basis, and their healthier finances would further benefit candidates, which is the justification for the proposed amount per voter. What is most important is that our proposed system is much fairer because the benefits of public funding for candidates as well as for registered parties would be distributed based on their electoral support.

Recommendation 1.6.11

We recommend that

(a) registered political parties that receive at least 1 per cent of all the valid votes cast be reimbursed $0.60 for each vote received but that no party be reimbursed an amount greater than 50 per cent of its election expenses;

(b) candidates who receive 1 per cent of the valid votes in a constituency be reimbursed $1.00 for each vote received, except that

(1) candidates in constituencies with, on average, fewer than 10 voters per square kilometre be reimbursed $1.25 for each vote received;

(2) candidates in 'remote' constituencies be reimbursed $1.50 for each vote received; and

(3) candidates in constituencies with fewer than 30 000 voters be reimbursed the amount obtained by multiplying their share of the vote by 30 000 times the amount per vote that would otherwise apply;

but that no candidate be reimbursed an amount greater than 50 per cent of his or her election expenses;

(c) after each election, the Canada Elections Commission review the scale of the reimbursements; and

(d) any adjustments to the scale of the reimbursements be made through a regulation of the Commission.

Independent Candidates and Independent Members of Parliament

Our recommendations for changing the system of public funding for elections would give independent candidates a greater chance to qualify for reimbursement. There are two additional issues of fairness that relate to the situation of independent candidates and independent Members of Parliament.

The *Canada Elections Act* now obliges candidates of registered parties to transfer any surplus after an election to the registered party or a local association; any other candidate must transfer a surplus to the Receiver General for Canada. This means that a candidate of a registered party, including a Member of Parliament, who runs in a subsequent election may be able to benefit from a surplus through a transfer from the registered party or constituency association. However, this opportunity is not open to independent candidates.

This anomaly should be corrected to ensure greater fairness in electoral competition. This can be done by having the surplus funds of any candidate not nominated by a registered constituency association kept in trust by the Canada Elections Commission. If the person contested the next election or a by-election during the period leading to that election, the surplus would be remitted to the financial agent of the candidate; if a constituency association was registered in the former candidate's constituency before the next election, the surplus could be remitted to it upon the request of the former candidate; otherwise, the funds would revert to the federal Receiver General. A candidate nominated by a registered constituency association should be obliged to transfer any surplus after an election to that association.

Recommendation 1.6.12

We recommend that

(a) **following an election, the surplus of any candidate other than those nominated by a registered constituency association be held in trust by the Canada Elections Commission; and**
(b) **if she or he is a candidate in the subsequent general election or a by-election during the intervening period, the funds be transferred to the financial agent of the candidate; if a constituency association is registered in her or his constituency, the funds be transferred to that constituency association upon the request of the former candidate; and, if not, the funds be transferred to the Receiver General for Canada.**

A final question is whether associations to support independent Members of Parliament should be allowed to register. Funds raised by the constituency party association of a Member of Parliament may benefit the Member at the time of re-election – for example, through a transfer or loan from the association to the candidate's campaign organization. However, our recommendation that the associations of registered parties acquire the right to issue tax receipts between elections would put independent Members of Parliament at a disadvantage in running against other candidates because they could not benefit from the incentive to fund raising that this right would provide. This would be unfair and could be resolved by following the example of Alberta, where an association of an independent member of the Legislative Assembly is allowed to register.

The association of an independent Member of Parliament should retain its registration only as long as the Member remains in office. Otherwise, there would be potential for abuse through the issuing of tax credits. We therefore propose that the association of an independent Member of Parliament be de-registered if the Member retires, does not stand for re-election or is defeated. It would be consistent with our above recommendation to allow the funds of the association, once de-registered, to be held in trust.

If the former independent Member of Parliament was a candidate at the following general election or at a by-election during that period, the funds held in trust would be transferred to the candidate's financial agent; otherwise, the funds would revert to the Receiver General for Canada.

Recommendation 1.6.13

We recommend that

(a) **constituency associations of independent Members of Parliament be eligible to register as local associations and be authorized to issue income tax receipts for political contributions;**

(b) **any such association be de-registered as soon as the Member of Parliament retires, indicates she or he will not stand for re-election or is defeated, and its funds be held in trust by the Canada Elections Commission; and**

(c) **if the former independent Member of Parliament is a candidate at the following general election or at a by-election during that period, the funds held in trust be transferred to the financial agent of the candidate and, if not, the funds be transferred to the Receiver General for Canada.**

ACCESS TO BROADCASTING

Introduction

The issue of equitable access to broadcast time for parties and candidates has been controversial in Canada since the 1930s. Indeed, it was evident to the Barbeau Committee (Canada, Committee on Election Expenses 1966, 331) that questions of election spending were in large part questions about access to media. Any examination of fairness in electoral competition, of campaign costs or of public confidence in the electoral process must come to terms with the central role of the modern mass media. As David Taras has put it, "Virtually every aspect of the election campaign will involve the media; in fact, to a large degree the media are the stage on which the election is fought." (Taras 1990, 152) Indeed, the 1988 Canadian Election Study refers to the most recent Canadian federal election as "a media event *par excellence*". (Johnston et al. 1991, 1:17)

In addition to spending limits and public subsidies, our tradition of electoral democracy includes limits on the use of certain expensive campaign activities, such as paid advertising, and on access to free-time political broadcasts. These measures help to ensure fairness in the system. In comparing western democracies, Goldenberg and Traugott concluded that the closer broadcast regulations are to creating a free market, the greater the likely imbalance in media access among opposing candidates. (1987, 454)

Fairness in electoral competition requires that the contenders be given reasonable access to those media channels that are likely to be most effective in carrying their arguments to voters. Since the emergence of political broadcasting, there have been numerous investigations and discussions about which contenders should have access to the air waves and how the available time should be divided among them. Over the years there has emerged a system of 'regulated competition' in which 'recognized political parties' are allocated broadcast time.

Forms of campaign communication

Unmediated	Partially mediated	Mediated
Paid time	Leaders debates	News coverage
Free time	Interview shows	Public affairs
Direct mail		
Telemarketing		

In examining these issues, distinctions must be made among the various media. It is important to distinguish between the broadcast media, which have been regulated almost since their inception, and the print media, which have not (though they are subject to some legal restrictions of general application, such as the laws of libel and slander). It is also essential to distinguish between those forms of campaign communication that allow the parties relatively direct access to voters and those that are filtered through journalists and commentators. There is considerable demand from both parties and voters for more unmediated communication. As Table 6.15 shows, there is also considerable support for increased programming that permits direct access.

The emergence of party politics in the nineteenth century was accomplished in part through the efforts of the partisan press. In Canada, the partisan press was a major feature of the political landscape until well into the second half of this century. From 1867 until the 1950s, voters could for the most part be divided into partisan groupings. They looked to the newspaper aligned with the party for the positions they should take and the candidates for whom they should vote. Press coverage thus tended to reinforce existing loyalties. Changes in the newspaper industry and the advent of the broadcast media, with their regulated impartiality, helped to erode these party ties. By 1960, the overtly partisan press was on its way out in Canada, though some newspapers still have partisan leanings. (Desbarats 1990a, 83–85; Charron 1991 RC; Rutherford 1978, 38–76) With a few exceptions, Canadian newspapers strive for non-partisan news coverage, though many respond to political events from an ideological perspective that sometimes makes them closer to one party than to others.

Table 6.15
Public assessment of voter information sources during election campaigns
(per cent)

	Very useful/ somewhat useful	Not very useful/ not at all useful	Don't know
Debates on specific issues on the Parliamentary Channel	74.9	21.6	3.5
More free-time broadcasts for political parties	61.5	36.0	2.5
More broadcasting advertising for political parties	40.0	57.5	2.5
More televised leaders debates	78.4	19.8	1.9
More phone-in shows with party spokesperson on radio and television	75.7	21.2	3.2
Party policy position papers mailed to all voters	64.8	32.0	3.3

Source: Frizzell 1991.

Note: N = 1 743.

Percentages may not add to 100 due to rounding.
Wording of the question:
"How useful would you say the following would be in providing voters information during election campaigns?
Would you say they were very useful, somewhat useful, not very useful or not at all useful?"

The decline of the overtly partisan press, accompanied by increased geographical mobility after 1950, created a problem for political parties. The party newspaper and interpersonal networks in the community had always been enough to mobilize their core supporters. With those channels declining in effectiveness, the party strategists had to seek out other means. Paid advertising, especially broadcast advertising and party political broadcasts, was the obvious alternative. The parties looked first to radio and later to television to meet these needs. Advertising and free-time broadcasts had several advantages for the parties: (1) they were under direct party control; (2) they reached beyond the core vote and could be used to recruit new supporters and mobilize old ones; and (3) they were not immediately counteracted by another party's competing message. (Smith 1981, 182–83) While effective, broadcast advertising is costly; professional assistance is required for optimal effectiveness.

Despite the increased reliance on advertising, the parties continue to rely on news coverage as the major means for reaching voters, especially where opportunities for advertising are restricted. Political parties in the industrial democracies have increasingly found it necessary to court "media exposure by doing and saying what the media will deem worth covering". This development, accompanied by the increasingly commercial nature of the broadcast media, has led to a situation in which "the politician's right to state [a] case in the media is more circumscribed than it once was". (Smith 1981, 183) The loss of these partisan channels, combined with the increasing brevity of broadcast news reports, encouraged the parties to look for alternative means to reach both core voters and possible converts or recruits.

Broadcasters have traditionally accepted considerable responsibility for educating their audiences on the issues of the day. Indeed, one of the major reasons for the creation of public broadcasting in the 1930s was to take advantage of the educational potential of radio. The obligation to present diverse perspectives on public questions was written into the 1936 *Broadcasting Act* and has been retained in subsequent versions (1991 *Broadcasting Act*, s. 3). (Peers 1969, 44–47) The obligation to inform voters about important issues is accepted by serious journalists, and the CBC acknowledges its special responsibilities in this regard. (Canada, Task Force on Broadcasting Policy 1986, 107) The emergence in recent decades of a common set of journalistic practices that transcend public-private distinctions (Gilsdorf and Bernier 1991 RC) and the increasing dependence of the CBC on advertising (Canada, Task Force on the Economic Status of Canadian Television 1991, 102) have eroded this commitment somewhat. The central tension of political journalism – between its obligation to provide the public with a continuing education in public affairs and the need of the news media to perform their 'merchandising function' to survive – has become an important fact of life for public as well as private broadcasters. Even in Quebec, where the Société Radio-Canada has been "at the heart of all the debates ... that have stirred Quebec society over the past 30 years" (Canada, Task Force on Broadcasting Policy 1986, 209), the commitment to traditional election coverage appears to have declined. (Desbarats 1990a, 24; Frizzell and Westell 1989, 86; Charron 1991 RC)

In the early days of political television, candidates were given considerable broadcast time to communicate their messages to the public. Political leaders were able to talk directly to voters through party broadcasts on radio and television and to appear on interview shows. On the television news shows, with their larger audiences, campaign reports routinely ran longer than two minutes. More important, segments of uninterrupted speech from a party leader – 'sound bites' in broadcast jargon – were much longer than they are today. For example, in the 1968 U.S. presidential campaign, the average sound bite was 42.3 seconds; in 1988, it had shrunk to 9.8 seconds. (Adatto 1990, 20) "By 1988," Kiku Adatto concludes, "television's tolerance for the languid pace of political discourse, never great, had all but vanished." In the absence of a comprehensive Canadian television archive, comparable research in this country has not yet been done. However, one 1984 study found that of almost six hours of broadcast time on CBC's *The National*, only 12 per cent – a little over 42 minutes – was devoted to the party leaders speaking. (Comber and Mayne 1986, 92)

CBC figures indicate that Canadian party leaders were allocated somewhat longer clips on *The National* during the 1988 campaign. *The National* carried 8696 words spoken by the leaders during the seven weeks of leaders tour coverage. The average number of words spoken by each leader per newscast was about 60, but they were not evenly distributed over the seven weeks. In response to criticism, the CBC monitored the word count closely and increased the length of the clips over the campaign. The average was only about 38 words during the first week, when public interest is thought to be less, but rose to 92 words for each leader in the final week. A sound bite of 60 words is the equivalent of about 20 seconds, with 92 words closer to 30 seconds.[6]

Data from the National Media Archive indicate that during the 1988 federal election campaign party leaders were, however, given considerably less opportunity to speak than journalists. The number of 'statements' attributed to journalists on the two English-language television newscasts outnumbered those from the Progressive Conservative, Liberal and New Democratic party leaders combined by more than two to one (see Table 6.16). These data illustrate clearly that television reporters spend more time commenting on the words and actions of candidates than reporting them. A recent study on U.S. electoral coverage revealed that the amount of time journalists spent in assessing the performance of politicians jumped dramatically from 6 per cent in 1968 to 52 per cent in 1988. (Adatto 1990, 21)

Table 6.16
Source of statement by program, 1988 federal election campaign

Source of statement	CBC – The National		CTV National News	
	N	(%)	N	(%)
Party leaders*	186	(19.7)	121	(19.1)
Local candidates	56	(5.9)	43	(6.8)
Party spokesperson	67	(7.1)	47	(7.4)
Journalists	378	(40.1)	290	(45.7)
Other	256	(27.1)	134	(21.1)
Total	943	(100.0)	635	(100.0)

Source: Based on data reported in National Media Archive 1991.

*The sum of all statements by the leaders of the Progressive Conservatives, Liberals and NDP.

Although party leaders have considerable capacity to influence the agenda of political coverage, they have little control over the tone. When they do have an opportunity to put their appeals directly to the electorate, the leaders tend to get a generally positive response, as our research on the leaders debates shows. (Barr 1991 RC)

Surveys show that Canadians are reasonably satisfied with the political news coverage available to them, despite some misgivings. (Canada, Royal Commission 1981, 33–38) Table 6.17 indicates that, for coverage of federal election campaigns, most Canadians believe the media are generally accurate and fair in their campaign coverage. As in the 1981 survey, however, there were doubts. For example, many respondents felt that the smaller parties did not receive sufficient coverage, as shown in Table 6.18. This view was held not only by supporters of smaller parties but also by substantial numbers of respondents who regarded themselves as supporters of one of the three largest parties. (Blais and Gidengil 1991 RC) A separate survey of local constituency activists found them to be generally less satisfied with the coverage. Although most were "somewhat satisfied" with the coverage of the campaigns they were involved in, the overall response was unenthusiastic, with supporters of the smaller parties most dissatisfied. (Carty 1991a RC)

Table 6.17
Assessment of media coverage: fairness and accuracy
(per cent)

	Very good	Good	Poor	Very poor	Don't know
Accuracy[1]	11.6	61.1	17.9	4.9	4.5
Fairness[2]	6.9	53.3	28.6	6.3	4.9

Source: Blais and Gidengil 1991 RC.

Note: N = 2 947.

Wording of the questions:
"1. How good a job do you feel the media does in accurately reporting on federal election campaigns? Do they do a very good job, a good job, a poor job, or a very poor job?
2. How good a job do you feel the media does in treating all the federal political parties fairly? Do they do a very good job, a good job, a poor job, or a very poor job?"

Table 6.18
Mention of political parties in news coverage, by medium, 1988 federal election
(per cent)

Parties mentioned	Television N=78	Daily newspapers N=205	Community newspapers N=242
No party mentioned	—	.5	2.5
Three largest parties only*	85.9	79.5	51.7
Smaller parties only	2.6	6.8	13.2
Both types	11.5	13.2	32.6
Total	100	100	100

Source: Hackett 1991 RC.

*Progressive Conservative, Liberal and New Democratic parties.

The relative lack of coverage of smaller parties during the 1988 campaign, especially in the broadcast media, is shown in Table 6.19. These data illustrate a gap between journalistic practices and public demand. The media have been slow to adapt to the increase in the number of registered parties since 1974 and, in particular, to the increased public interest in what they have to say. The public demand for greater attention to smaller parties, though fuelled by short-term concerns regarding specific issues, is also part of a general process of expanding participation. Many voters wish to hear views not encompassed by the largest parties. (Blais and Gidengil 1991 RC)

Analyses of voter attitudes suggest that a sense of involvement in the electoral process and participation are likely to be enhanced by a greater diversity of communication channels and perspectives. (MacDermid 1991 RC)

Table 6.19
Assessment of media coverage: attention to small parties
(per cent)

Too much	2.8
Too little	53.7
About the right amount	38.3
Don't know	5.2

Source: Blais and Gidengil 1991 RC.

Note: N = 2 947.

Wording of the question:
"What about small parties that don't win many votes? Does the media pay them too much, too little, or about the right amount of attention?"

As a result of commercial pressures and changes in journalistic practices, the commitment of the Canadian media to political education has diminished. As we were told at our media seminar, media values are not driven by political education; instead, they respond to the expressed wants and needs of the audience. We were also told that the media do not share a commitment to an election as a process. Indeed, although they take special care to provide balanced coverage of the three largest parties, they maintain that normal news values should apply to election coverage. News coverage based on criteria of human interest and convenience is unlikely to meet the information needs of some significant groups of voters. Although the French-language media continue to provide more political analysis than their English-language counterparts, there are still important gaps in the coverage. (Charron 1991 RC) Thus, while the news media continue to play a vital role in disseminating campaign information, this analysis makes clear the need to supplement news media coverage with campaign information from other sources.

Political broadcasting in Canada has been formally regulated since the establishment in 1932 of the forerunner of the CBC, the Canadian Radio Broadcasting Commission (CRBC). From 1932 to 1936, the CRBC provided its own national radio service and also supervised the broadcasting activities of others. Its successor, the CBC, then performed these same functions from 1936 to 1958, at which time a policy decision was made that a broadcaster should not also be the regulator of other broadcasters. In 1958, an independent regulatory authority separate from the CBC, namely, the Board of Broadcast Governors (BBG), was established. When Canadian broadcasting experienced expansion with the advent of cable, there was a perceived need to create a regulatory authority with a wider mandate and responsibility. Consequently, the Canadian Radio-Television Commission was created in

1968. This evolved into the Canadian Radio-television and Telecommunications Commission (CRTC) in 1975 to accommodate still further changes in the communication industry.

These regulatory bodies have developed in tandem with legislation concerning political broadcasting and broadcasting policy in general. The main principles have been set out in the *Canadian Broadcasting Act 1936* (and subsequent versions), the 1958, 1968 and 1991 *Broadcasting Act* and the *Canada Elections Act*. The primary principle underlying political broadcasting is contained in the *Broadcasting Act* (1991, subsection 3(1)(*i*)(iv)): the programming by the Canadian broadcasting system should "provide a reasonable opportunity for the public to be exposed to the expression of differing views on matters of public concern". This provision expresses clearly the expectation that the broadcast media will play an important role in educating voters on public issues.

The 1988 Public Notice issued by the CRTC summarizes the main principles governing the need for balance in controversial broadcasting, of which political broadcasting has been described as an "offshoot". (Boyer 1983, 437) The principles are:

(a) CRTC regulation, as a general rule, should not constrain or inhibit the ways and means of presenting controversial issues.

(b) Broadcasters have a responsibility to become involved in controversial issues of public concern.

(c) Broadcasters should devote a reasonable amount of air time to the coverage of controversial public issues and should provide an opportunity for the presentation of differing points of view.

(d) The public, through the presentation by broadcasters of the various points of view in a fair and objective way, should be placed in a position to make its own informed judgement on controversial issues.

(e) It is for the broadcaster in the first instance to determine what is a reasonable, balanced opportunity for the expression of differing views, subject to review by the Commission....

Once a licensee chooses to give free time, it must allocate some time to all political parties duly registered under the applicable legislation. (CRTC 1988)

The right of the public to be informed in a "fair and objective way" has been a constant theme throughout the evolution of political broadcasting in Canada. The regulatory authorities periodically remind broadcasters of their obligation to provide equitable treatment. Equitable, however, does not mean equal. It pertains to the fact that "all candidates and parties are entitled to some coverage that will give them the opportunity to expose their ideas to the public". (CRTC 1988)

The "equitable principle" applies within each of what the CRTC considers the four categories of political campaign broadcasts: paid-time, free-time, news and public affairs programs (at least to the extent that the last two categories broadcast campaign debates and constituency profiles). Although the CRTC does not provide any fixed rule on defining equity, it suggests there are signposts to help broadcasters determine whether they are indeed providing equitable election coverage. These signposts are found in the *Canada Elections Act* regarding factors to be considered by the broadcasting arbitrator in the allocation of paid and free time. The factors involve the percentage of seats and popular vote received by the political parties at the last general election and the number of candidates each party ran at that time.

During the election period, compliance with the rules on equitable coverage has depended largely on the broadcasters themselves, since the CRTC lacked suitable sanctions under the 1968 *Broadcasting Act*. Threats of problems with licence renewal or of prosecution are generally out of proportion to the complaints received about election broadcasting. However, broadcasters do not want to alienate the regulator and are concerned with their public image. Therefore, a complaint forwarded to a broadcaster by the CRTC is usually acted on.

At each federal general election, the CRTC is required, no later than three days after the issue of the writs, to prepare and send to the broadcasting arbitrator a set of guidelines regarding the applicability of the *Broadcasting Act* and its regulations concerning the conduct of broadcasters and network operators during a general election. Within the next two days the broadcasting arbitrator is to issue to broadcasters and network operators guidelines on time allocation under the *Canada Elections Act*, booking procedures for broadcast time, the aforementioned CRTC guidelines and any other pertinent matters. The information is published according to the requirements of the *Canada Elections Act*. The amount of time is determined by the broadcasting arbitrator under rules set out in this Act. The guidelines issued by the arbitrator apply only to political parties; the CRTC retains authority over the rules governing individual candidates and other kinds of political broadcasting.

For complaints during election campaigns, the CRTC has relied primarily on mediating between complainants and broadcasters. Its normal procedures, geared to public hearings, are not well suited to the pace of election campaigns. A concern that CRTC procedures were too slow caused the parties to seek the creation of the post of broadcasting arbitrator (established in 1983), but this perception resulted primarily from problems with the allocation of paid and free time among the parties. The CRTC generally deals quickly with complaints and, with the co-operation of broadcasters, is usually able to bring about a resolution. It is a complaint-driven process. The guidelines the CRTC circulates to Members of Parliament, all broadcasters and the registered parties include the names and phone numbers of the officials designated to deal with interpretations of the guidelines. These officials respond to complaints by contacting the broadcaster, usually within 30 minutes of receiving the complaint, and seeking a resolution.

The problems arise in those very few cases where agreement cannot be reached. The 1991 *Broadcasting Act* gives the CRTC the power to issue mandatory orders but only after a public hearing, with due notice to all interested parties. This procedure will assist the CRTC to deal with general issues after the campaign and to prepare for the next election but provides no direct redress during campaigns.[7]

It became clear from our public hearings that parties and broadcasters are generally aware of the regulations and procedures governing election broadcasting, but many candidates are not. The Canada Elections Commission and the CRTC should work together to refine the guidelines and ensure that all candidates receive them. It should be made clear to all candidates that they have the right to complain to the CRTC when they feel they have not been treated equitably (as defined in the guidelines). Complaint procedures should be explicit.

The CRTC has spent many years refining the regulations for political broadcasting under the *Broadcasting Act*. These regulations apply at all times, not just during the federal elections, and it would not be efficient to involve the Canada Elections Commission in their administration. There are, however, particular issues of free and paid time that arise only during elections. These matters have previously been handled by the broadcasting arbitrator. The Canada Elections Commission should take on these responsibilities and make whatever arrangements it deems appropriate to deal with them. Moreover, it will be necessary for the Commission and the CRTC to work together to refine the guidelines, make the rights and obligations of registered parties and candidates clear to them, and ensure that the guidelines are distributed in good time, preferably on a regular basis as well as after the writs are issued.

Paid Time

Concern with political broadcasting dates to 1928 when the Royal Commission on Radio Broadcasting (the Aird Commission) recommended that it be "very carefully restricted". (Canada, Royal Commission 1929, 13) Problems with paid time moved to the forefront during the 1935 election, with the violation of Canadian Radio Broadcasting Commission rules requiring parties to pay in advance for airtime. (Canada, Committee on Election Expenses 1966, 363)

Over time, regulatory responsibility for political broadcasting has been vested with different bodies. Since 1958, public and private stations alike have been required to provide time for the transmission of political messages in election campaigns. A key principle has always been fairness in the allocation of time so that all main points of view may be heard. The CBC had a policy of offering free, but not paid, time for political parties until directed by the 1974 and 1977 changes to the *Canada Elections Act* to make paid time available. (Boyer 1983, 427) Now all broadcasters, including the CBC, must make a total of six and one-half hours available for purchase by parties during election campaigns. The aim of these provisions was to ensure that parties had access to the broadcasting system for unfiltered messages.

Paid time is important in federal elections, given the high level of volatility in the Canadian electorate and the effectiveness of paid time in reaching undecided voters. Over the last five elections, an average of approximately 43 per cent of Canadian voters made their vote decisions during the campaign, responding mainly to the issues of that campaign rather than to longer term ideological or partisan commitments. (Clarke et al. 1991, 110) Volatility was particularly high in 1988. For example, one survey indicated that in the 1988 election more than 60 per cent of voters reported making their vote decisions during the campaign itself. (*Maclean's*/Decima 1988, 19) Further, more than 25 per cent of voters stated that they had changed their voting intentions at least once during the campaign. The 1988 Canadian Election Study concluded after examining opinion poll data that there were significant shifts in vote intention during the campaign period in eight of the last 10 federal elections. (Johnston et al. 1991, chapter 2)

Paid time has become increasingly important to parties not only because it mobilizes supporters and converts undecided voters, but also because it avoids the filtering process of the news media. The decreasing opportunities for parties to reach voters with their own messages through news coverage have increased the importance of paid time not only for the parties but also for the electorate. Despite the brevity and the nature of the messages, the advertisements reflect the party's own views of what they have to offer voters and are, therefore, useful information for the electorate (see Table 6.20).

Table 6.20
Public assessment of paid election advertising
(per cent)

Do without advertising	31.3
Need advertising	66.1
Don't know	2.6

Source: Blais and Gidengil 1991 RC.

Note: N = 2 947.

Wording of the question:
"Which of the following statements comes closer to your opinion?
We could do without party advertising, because it doesn't really inform us about what the parties stand for.
We need party advertising because it is the only way that parties can get their message directly to the voter."

Research in the 1970s in the United States indicated that many voters learned more about policy issues from the party advertisements than from news coverage. (Patterson and McClure 1976, 3–24) This finding has been confirmed in more recent studies. (*The Economist* 1991, 21) Recent studies in Canada suggest that many voters, especially those who do not follow politics closely, become aware of issues and party positions and form impressions of the leaders from party advertisements. (Johnston et al. 1991, chapters 1, 4, 6 and 8) The attention-grabbing and repetitive nature of advertising promotes learning. Most of the 1988 party advertisements, for example, had at least some policy content, and the most effective of them distilled a central policy argument.[8] Although the points were made dramatically and not argued in detail, the outlines of the debate were presented in the paid time. Interested voters, having learned of the competing positions, could turn to other sources for further information.

Comparative Perspectives on Paid Time

Several western democracies have a system of paid time operating along with a free-time system. France, Great Britain and Sweden provide free time only. (Gerstlé 1991 RC; Semetko 1991 RC; Siune 1991 RC) Almost all the jurisdictions with paid time have wrestled with the question of the amount of time each political party would be permitted to purchase. The exception is the United States, which places no limits on the time that can be bought. (Graber 1991 RC) In the most recent German election, parties were permitted to buy time on the commercial television and radio stations at cost price (i.e., the labour, quality control and production costs incurred by the broadcaster in the scheduling and transmitting of party advertisements). The two parties with the most seats in the Bundestag were allocated up to 25 minutes each; the smaller parties were given a maximum of 12.5 minutes. (Schoenbach 1991 RC) The Australian Parliament is currently addressing a proposal to ban paid time altogether. In a two-year trial period there, paid-time purchases were de-regulated, resulting in soaring advertising costs and a demand for bringing back regulation. Before deregulation, broadcasters were permitted an extra minute per hour of advertising where full broadcasting schedules would not otherwise permit reasonable opportunities to all political parties to present their messages before polling day. (Warhurst 1991 RC) In many democracies, the issues of controlling election advertising costs and of appropriate rules for access to paid time for political parties have been matters of concern in recent years.

The Current Paid-Time System

The present paid-time system in Canada is complex and cumbersome, prompting many complaints. The system contains many restrictions that arose from a desire for fairness among all parties, a fear that wealth would otherwise dominate the air waves, and the expressed need of the parties for some control on increasingly expensive advertising costs, especially television advertising. The desire to control Canadian electoral broadcasting and election spending led to a prohibition on using broadcasting stations outside Canada for political advertising.

As already mentioned, the current system outlined in the *Canada Elections Act* is overseen by the broadcasting arbitrator. The arbitrator is either unanimously selected by the registered political parties or, failing unanimity, chosen by the chief electoral officer. The arbitrator plays a key decision-making role, overseeing the allotment of time to each party and, if necessary, any negotiations with the broadcasters. The position was established to help speed the process of dealing with these matters.

The Act stipulates that political parties entitled to purchase paid time are permitted to broadcast such material only within a defined period during the general election campaign. This period of advertising is restricted to 28 days, beginning Sunday the 29th day before polling day and ending at midnight on the second day before election day. During the permitted paid-time advertising period, every broadcaster must, subject to *Broadcasting Act* regulations and its own conditions of licence, make available for purchase by all registered political parties a total of six and one-half hours (390 minutes) of prime-time broadcasting. In addition, every broadcaster must make available for purchase by unregistered political parties a total of up to 39 minutes: each such party is entitled to an amount equal to the lesser of six minutes or the smallest portion of broadcasting time made available to any of the registered political parties under the paid-time allocation formula. Broadcasters are expected to pre-empt previously scheduled commercials to provide this time to the parties.

The allocation of the paid time is determined by the application of four rules. If the parties themselves can agree on a division of time, that becomes the governing allocation. In the absence of agreement, three other rules come into play: (1) the formula set out in the Act; (2) the prohibition on any one registered party receiving more than 195 minutes, which represents 50 per cent of the total broadcasting time; and, (3) the discretion of the arbitrator to change the allocation if the arbitrator considers the time allotted to be unfair to any of the registered parties or contrary to the public interest.

A party's allocation under the paid-time formula for each election campaign is based on that particular party's activities in the *last* election. Under the formula, equal weight is given to (1) the percentage of seats in the House of Commons held by each of the registered parties and (2) the percentage of the popular vote at the previous election of each registered party; half of the weight given to these two factors is given to a third factor – the number of candidates endorsed by each of the registered parties at the previous general election expressed as a percentage of all candidates endorsed by all registered parties at that election. The entitlements under the formula for the 1984 and 1988 elections and the allocation established by the broadcasting arbitrator for an election held before 1992 are shown in Table 6.21.

The effect of this allocation, should an election be called under the existing rules, is to place an upper limit of seven minutes on the amount of time that can be bought from any broadcaster by any party other than the three largest parties. Since broadcasters are forbidden to sell more than the amount allocated, this allocation would not allow any smaller party to run an effective advertising campaign on the broadcast media, regardless of its capacity to raise funds. Although such a party could buy as much print advertising as it could afford, it would not be able to compete on television or radio, the most potent instruments of modern election campaigns. The unfairness of the existing system lies not only in the imbalance shown in Table 6.21, but also in its clear bias against emerging parties, regardless of popular support and resources.

Table 6.21
Allocation of paid broadcast time by party, 1984, 1988 and 1991
(minutes)

Party	1984	1988	1991
Progressive Conservative Party	129.0	195.0	178.0
Liberal Party	173.0	89.0	113.0
New Democratic Party	69.0	67.0	73.0
Parti Rhinocéros	8.0	7.0	5.0
Communist Party	5.5	3.0	—
Libertarian Party	5.5	5.0	—
Pro-Life Party	5.5	—	—
Green Party	5.5	4.0	5.0
Confederation of Regions Western Party	5.5	4.0	—
United Canada Concept Party	5.5	—	—
L'Action des hommes d'affaires	5.5	—	—
Parti nationaliste	—	6.0	—
Party for the Commonwealth of Canada	—	4.0	4.0
Social Credit Party	—	3.0	—
Christian Heritage Party	—	3.0	5.0
Canada Party	—	3.0	—
Reform Party	—	3.0	7.0
Student Party	—	3.0	—
The Western Canada Concept Party	—	3.0	—
Western Independence Party	—	3.0	—
Total	417.5	405.0	390.0

Source: Report of the Broadcasting Arbitrator 1984 and 1989 (see Canada, Chief Electoral Officer 1984a, 1989) and Royal Commission Research Branch.

Note: The 1991 figures are those announced by the broadcasting arbitrator at the annual meeting of the registered parties held in Ottawa, 3 May 1991. The meeting is required by the *Canada Elections Act*, section 314. Since the parties could not agree on an alternative allocation, the entitlements established by the broadcasting arbitrator are binding for any election held before the next annual meeting. Under the current rules, they could change slightly to accommodate new parties.

To control campaign costs and to alleviate concerns that some broadcasters would charge high rates for party advertising, the paid-time system also contains a stipulation requiring broadcasters not to charge political parties more than their most favoured rate. This rate is defined as the lowest rate charged by that broadcaster for an equal amount of equivalent time on the same facilities at any time during the period. (*Canada Elections Act*, s. 321)

Finally, the present paid-time system has a 10-day booking period. Not later than 10 days following the issuance of the writs, political parties entitled to time must notify in writing each broadcaster and network operator from whom it intends to purchase broadcasting time of its daily and hourly preferences, along with its preferences on the proportion of commercial and program time to be made available to it. The provisions of the *Canada Elections Act* are generally interpreted according to the rule that broadcast messages of two minutes or less are considered commercial time (paid time), whereas those longer than two minutes are deemed to be program time (usually free time, although parties and candidates may purchase program time). In recent elections, however, the regulators have classified free time allocated to the parties as program time, regardless of length.

Reforming Paid Time

Although there was criticism of the paid-time system during the public hearings, few interveners called for its abolition. In fact, there exists considerable public support for the retention of paid time. Two-thirds (66.1 per cent) of respondents to our attitudinal survey agreed with the following statement: "We need party advertising because it is the only way that parties can get their message directly to the voter." (Blais and Gidengil 1991 RC) Less than a third (31.3 per cent) agreed with the following statement: "We could do without party advertising because it doesn't really inform us about what the parties stand for" (see Table 6.20). Canadians also strongly support restrictions on the amount of money political parties can spend on advertising: 74.8 per cent agreed with the view that "We should limit spending on party advertising, otherwise parties with more money will have an unfair advantage." In contrast, only 22.6 per cent of respondents favoured the statement that "Freedom of speech is such a fundamental right that parties should be allowed to advertise as much as they wish" (Table 6.22).

Table 6.22
Paid advertising: limits
(per cent)

Freedom	22.6
Limits	74.8
Don't know	2.6

Source: Blais and Gidengil 1991 RC.

Note: N = 2 947.

Wording of the question:
"Which of the following two statements comes closer to your own opinion?
Freedom of speech is such a fundamental right that parties should be allowed to advertise as much as they wish.
We should limit spending on party advertising, otherwise parties with more money will have an unfair advantage."

Research, numerous submissions and our Toronto symposium on media and elections have convinced us that the current paid-time broadcasting system must be changed to accommodate the needs of the electorate, the political parties and the broadcasters. We consider the ability of political parties to communicate with the electorate too important to be left entirely to the discretion of the broadcasting industry. We agree with the general statement by the CRTC in 1987 that the "broadcaster does not enjoy the position of a benevolent censor who is able to give the public only what it 'should' know. Nor is it the broadcaster's role to decide in advance which candidates are 'worthy' of broadcast time." (CRTC 1987) It is, in our view, reasonable to require licensed broadcasters, as part of their public-service obligations, to make time available to the parties. This obligation arises only every four years or so, under normal circumstances, and lasts only about four weeks. At the same time, a less complex and more easily administered system would help alleviate many genuine concerns and actual problems.

Advertising Period   To adapt the system to the shorter campaign we propose, we recommend that the advertising period begin 11 days after the election is officially called and end at midnight on the second day before election day. To ensure an orderly process, the registered parties would be required to book their paid time as soon as possible after the writs are issued. The advertising period would remain approximately four weeks. If the registered parties and the broadcasters could not agree on bookings within 10 days after the writs are issued, the Canada Elections Commission would be given the mandate to resolve any disputes immediately.

Delaying the start of advertising in this way would serve three important purposes. First, it would place all parties on a level playing field for the broadcasting of election advertising. In other words, a party in power would not have an unfair advantage over the other parties as a result of knowing the date the election would be called. Second, the proposed advertising period would allow sufficient time for the parties to plan their media campaign and produce a first series of broadcast messages; this would minimize the disruption that the broadcasters face in having to reschedule up to 360 minutes of advertising time. Third, the ban would encourage parties to begin their campaigns through other avenues. The same rules should apply to by-elections.

Recommendation 1.6.14

We recommend that

(a) an advertising period be designated to begin 11 days after the day the writs are issued and to end at midnight on the second day before election day;

(b) the registered parties and broadcasters seek agreement on the scheduling of paid campaign advertising time by the end of the tenth day after the writs are issued; and

(c) failing agreement, the Canada Elections Commission establish a schedule.

Eligibility   As is currently the case, every broadcaster should be obligated to make paid time available for the parties, subject to regulations set out in the *Broadcasting Act* and to the broadcaster's own licensing conditions. We recognize and adopt the expanded scope given to the definition of "broadcaster" in the *Canada Elections Act* as a result of the passage of the new *Broadcasting Act*. The new definition is broadened to include the pay and specialty channels in the obligation to make paid time available for purchase.

The current provision in the *Canada Elections Act* that each broadcaster must make a set amount of time available to the parties should also be retained. We propose that only registered parties be entitled to purchase the paid time made available by these provisions. The current Act allows unregistered parties to exercise an entitlement to broadcasting time. We believe this should be eliminated, not only because it is unfair to those parties meeting registration requirements but also because, as observed by the former broadcasting arbitrator, it gives "groups of all kinds [the ability] to organize themselves ... as 'parties' in order to obtain both paid and free broadcasting time during an election". (Canada, Chief Electoral Officer 1984a, 83)

Recommendation 1.6.15

We recommend that only registered parties be eligible to purchase the paid time broadcasters are obliged to make available under the *Canada Elections Act*.

Broadcasting Time for Advertising by Registered Parties   Since the 1974 reforms, the *Canada Elections Act* has in effect expropriated (at the most favoured rate) 390 minutes of paid time from each broadcaster to be allocated among the political parties for partisan advertising during the final four weeks of the campaign. To determine the amount of time that broadcasters should be required to make available to registered political parties during the advertising period, we examined both the purchases made by the parties in 1988 and the time required by a political party to mount an effective broadcast advertising campaign.

The total party allocation per broadcaster is divided by agreement between each network and its individual affiliates based on requests from the registered parties. (s. 307(2), *Canada Elections Act*) Based on data from the parties, it appears that no party purchased its maximum allocation on any television station. The maximum was reached on a small number of radio stations. However, the NDP approached its limit on the CBC Windsor television station, the only television outlet in a hotly contested area. This occurred because the party made a major network purchase and therefore had only limited time available for local advertising on that station. The Liberal Party also approached its limit on that television station, buying mainly local time; the time purchased by the Progressive Conservatives was somewhat less. The Liberal Party was allocated 89 minutes of paid time in 1988, and its purchases approached the upper limit for only two television outlets (of 59 from which it purchased time) and only 14 radio stations (of 212). Data for the Progressive Conservative Party were available only for the CBC and selected CBC affiliates, but it appears likely that with 195 minutes per broadcaster available to it, the party did not approach its upper limit in many cases, if at all. It did not do so on any CBC television station. The limits on campaign spending precluded any of these parties that aspired to run a national campaign from buying anything approaching its paid-time upper limit on more than a handful of stations.

Table 6.23
Estimated paid television time needed for effective campaigning, one political party

City	GRP objectives[a]			Average GRPs per spot (30 seconds)[b]	Number of spots (30 seconds)	Number of minutes[c]
	Network	Non-network	Total			
Vancouver	824	576	1 400	5.5	255	127.5
Calgary	816	184	1 000	8.1	123	61.5
Winnipeg	896	104	1 000	7.1	141	70.5
Toronto	800	600	1 400	3.3	424	212.0
Montreal (English)	1 136	64	1 200	10.0	120	60.0
Montreal (French)	784	616	1 400	11.6	121	60.5
Halifax	752	248	1 000	6.9	145	72.5

Source: Cossette 1991.

[a]Gross rating point (GRP) is a measure of advertising effectiveness. The GRP figure is calculated by multiplying the estimated audience reach of an advertisement (expressed in rating points, that is, the percentage of potential audience reached) by the frequency of appearance of the advertisement (or spot). The GRP objective is the number of GRPs required to run an effective advertising campaign.

[b]Expected number of GRPs per 30-second spot, based on audience data for each area.

[c]Number of minutes required in each metropolitan area on all available stations. In practice, a party would allocate this total among several stations.

To assess the viability of the allocation, projections were made of the amount of broadcast time a political party needs to make its case effectively to the voters. (Cossette 1991) These projections were based on the amount of broadcast time needed in major markets, where time required is likely to be highest because of competing messages. That analysis was based on the assumptions that the party would already be known and that its strategy would be similar to recent practices (using television as the major medium, radio as a supplement, and a mix of network and local station time that would vary by market).

This study established the number of minutes of paid advertising such a hypothetical party would require to reach the maximum number of voters during the four-week advertising period in any given market. It was calculated that the largest amount of time purchased by a party on any station in the markets studied would be 85 minutes (the share of the 212 minutes in Toronto that would go to the most popular station). The purchase of additional time beyond that level would be very unlikely because it would produce diminishing returns for the party.

On the assumption that in any given federal election there would be no more than the equivalent of four competitive parties seeking advertising time in a particular market, the analysis indicated that the maximum time required would be 340 minutes. Because parties need flexibility to adjust to changing conditions, the broadcasters should be required to provide 360 minutes of paid-time, to be allocated among the parties.

We have already noted the unfairness of the current allocation formula. The current formula draws distinctions among the parties that are clearly inequitable. Equity and cost control can be ensured by the spending limits as long as any party is prohibited from purchasing more than a fixed proportion of the total time made available. As a consequence, there will no longer be any need for the complex allocation formula that now exists in the Act; each party would be at liberty to determine how much it wants to spend on television and radio advertising, subject only to the spending limits and the cap on the amount of time it can purchase from any one broadcaster.

A cap on the amount of time that any one party can purchase is necessary for several reasons. Without such a limit, some form of allocation mechanism would be needed to deal with situations where the parties taken together wished to purchase more time from a particular station than it was required (and willing) to provide. Otherwise the complications and inequities of the existing system would remain. The cap will also prevent a party from saturating one area of the country to the point where national parties would be placed at a distinct disadvantage. If no restriction is placed on the ability of a party to buy as much of the available time in a particular region as it wished, the national parties would not be able to compete because of the overall spending limit and the imperative that they campaign across the country. The dynamics that such behaviour would set in motion are clearly not in the long-term interest of the nation.

We propose that the cap be 100 minutes, which is about 30 per cent of the time required to be made available by broadcasters. No party would be permitted to purchase more than that amount of time on any broadcasting outlet. Should the total time requested by the registered parties from any broadcaster exceed the amount required to be made available, the broadcaster would have the option of selling more time than required (as long as no party exceeded the cap) or not exceeding the required amount and negotiating an equitable allocation with the parties concerned. If the parties failed to reach an agreement, the Canada Elections Commission would determine the time for each party.

In estimating the paid broadcast advertising time needed by a party for effective campaigning, our consultants also projected the likely costs of the time for the next election. (Cossette 1991) These projections reflect fairly accurately the costs incurred for broadcast advertising by the registered parties in 1988, adjusted for increased rates. This means that the time made available corresponds with the proposed spending limits and gives us added confidence in the projections. The time required and the party cap for any broadcasting outlet meet the cost-control objectives of the 1974 reforms, greatly simplify the process and provide fair access to paid time for all parties. The time available to each party will meet the needs of the parties in both crowded major markets and smaller markets with limited broadcast outlets and will encourage a national focus for Canadian federal election campaigns.

Radio is still used to a significant degree during election campaigns. Our projections indicate that the paid time on radio to run an effective campaign should be considerably more than for television. There are, however, many more radio than television outlets, and radio is, according to party strategists, used more selectively. (Cossette 1991) The 1988 party purchases indicated only a few instances where time purchased on radio approached the maximum. There is, therefore, no compelling reason to make a distinction between radio and television broadcasters. The required paid time provision should, therefore, remain the same for radio and television.

In the opinion of the broadcasting arbitrator, it is a technical violation of the *Canada Elections Act* (s. 307(1)) for party advertisements to be broadcast outside of prime time during the advertising period. (Canada, Chief Electoral Officer 1984a, 83–84) Under a ruling by the Commissioner of Elections, however, the parties were permitted, with the agreement of the broadcasters involved, to schedule advertising at other times in both 1984 and 1988. With the increasing fragmentation of broadcasting audiences and the growing capacity of party strategists to target party advertising to specific groups of voters, it is likely that parties will continue to request that some of the advertising time they are permitted to purchase be scheduled outside of prime time. There is no reason to deny the parties this flexibility. We recommend that parties be permitted to request and broadcasters to schedule party advertising outside of prime time during the election period. (Canada, Chief Electoral Officer 1984a, 83–84, 91–92)

Recommendation 1.6.16

We recommend that each broadcaster be required to make 360 minutes available in prime time (or such other time

as mutually agreed on) for purchase by registered parties during the advertising period, subject to a maximum of 100 minutes for purchase by any registered party from any broadcaster.

Broadcasting From Outside Canada   Since the *Canada Elections Act* applies only to Canadian broadcasters, the upper limit of advertising any broadcaster may allow each party to purchase would remain effective only if parties are restricted to purchasing advertising time from broadcasters within Canada. Otherwise, a party, provided it had the funds and would not exceed its spending limit, could purchase a significant amount of time from a U.S. border station and defeat the purpose of the cap. This would run counter to the fairness principle. Therefore, it is necessary to retain the existing prohibition against the purchase of paid time from broadcasters operating outside Canada.

Recommendation 1.6.17

We recommend retaining the prohibition in the *Canada Elections Act* against the purchase of time from broadcasting stations outside Canada during an election.

Advertising Rates   Advertising costs remain a major element in campaign spending and a barrier to entry for new parties. To assist in controlling these costs, as well as to make it easier for emerging parties to participate in the paid-time campaign, we recommend that broadcasters be required to make paid time available at 50 per cent of the lowest commercial rate. Such a discounted rate recognizes that paid time serves an important function not only for parties but also for voters. Given its genuinely valuable role in providing information to voters, it is in the public interest to facilitate party access to this means of communication.

So that this requirement does not constitute an excessive burden on broadcasters, we recommend that half of the paid time carried by any broadcaster whose commercial sales time is limited by regulation be considered as program time and not counted against the commercial time limit as established by the CRTC for that broadcaster. The maximum commercial time permitted for most television broadcasters is 12 minutes per hour. (CRTC 1986, s. 11) Specialty programming undertakings and FM radio stations have individual limitations as part of their conditions of licence. This recommendation reflects the 1988 practice in which the one- and two-minute free-time party television spots, though presented in the style of advertising, were considered program time.

This recommendation has several advantages. It recognizes that parties currently do not receive the discounts available to most commercial advertisers. It also recognizes the public interest in having effective party advertising at reasonable cost. In addition, it maintains a uniform rate for all registered parties, an important goal of previous reforms. For the broadcasters, it reduces the need to pre-empt commercial advertisers and provides more flexibility in scheduling. The inconvenience of rescheduling advertising already booked is therefore reduced. This will be particularly important for the specialty services, many of which are permitted fewer advertising minutes per hour than other broadcasters. For the past two years, AM radio operators have had no limits on their commercial time and therefore do not face problems of pre-emption or opportunity costs when they carry party advertising. Finally, the financial impact on broadcasters is negligible.

Individual candidates also make use of broadcast advertising, albeit not to the same extent as the largest parties. It is important, therefore, to ensure that candidates who choose to purchase paid time have fair access. Under current rules, broadcasters are not required to make time available. If, however, a broadcaster chooses to sell time to any candidate, it must provide equitable access to all candidates and must sell the time at the most favoured rate. That is, broadcasters must charge for paid time sold to candidates for election advertising the lowest rate that they would charge to any other person for equivalent time on the same facilities. (*Canada Elections Act*, s. 321) This regulation is essential to ensure that all candidates are treated fairly.

Recommendation 1.6.18

We recommend that

(a) **each broadcaster be required to provide time to registered parties at 50 per cent of the most favoured rate at which comparable time is sold to other advertisers;**
(b) **notwithstanding any provision in the *Broadcasting Act*, CRTC regulations or conditions of licence, each broadcaster be permitted to classify one-half of the paid political advertising sold during the advertising period as program time, not to be counted against its maximum permitted advertising time; and**
(c) **each broadcaster that makes available paid time to individual candidates must do so on an equitable basis and at a rate that does not exceed the lowest rate charged for an equal amount of time on the same facilities to any person at any time in the same period.**

Role of Canada Elections Commission   To deal effectively with the administrative matters arising from these recommendations, it will be necessary for the Canada Elections Commission to undertake the functions currently performed by the broadcasting arbitrator, which include dealing with issues arising from paid-time scheduling. To this end, we recommend that the

Commission issue election broadcasting directives and guidelines annually, informing the registered parties and the broadcasters of their rights and obligations. This should include informing the parties of normal broadcasting booking and cancellation procedures. For political parties to have the best opportunity to communicate their messages to voters, it is essential that the parties continue to be able to place their advertising at preferred times. Parties will be required to meet the booking deadline already noted – the end of the tenth day after the writs are issued – and to provide appropriate notice for cancellations. To simplify matters in the shorter period recommended, parties should book network time first to allow affiliates to respond effectively to requests for the remaining time on local stations. These proposals were made in the reports of the broadcasting arbitrator (see Canada, Chief Electoral Officer 1984a, 1989).

Recommendation 1.6.19

We recommend that

(a) the Canada Elections Commission issue directives and guidelines regarding the booking and cancellation of paid time and its fair distribution among parties; these should reflect normal commercial practices, with due regard for the urgent needs of election campaigns and the need to make every effort to accommodate the scheduling requests of parties; and

(b) the Commission assume the functions currently performed by the broadcasting arbitrator.

Educational and Community Broadcasters   Under current rules, provincial educational broadcasters and community radio stations are not required to make paid time available to the parties. This exemption is based on their educational role and non-commercial status. To the extent that educational broadcasters do not sell advertising to political parties, federal regulations should not apply. In other words, so long as these broadcasters stick to their mission and do not voluntarily become enmeshed in the electoral campaign by selling time for election advertising, the rules would not apply to them. However, if these broadcasters sell advertising to political parties during the election period, then they will become subject to the same rules that apply to commercial broadcasters. Educational broadcasters are subject to provincial control as well as federal regulation. However, the federal provision pertains to a central objective of the *Canada Elections Act*, it is limited to the election period, and it applies only when such a broadcaster has sold time to political parties and thus does not constitute an invasion of provincial jurisdiction.

Recommendation 1.6.20

We recommend that any community broadcaster or provincially operated educational broadcaster that sells advertising time to any registered party or candidate during the election period be automatically subject to the requirements of the *Canada Elections Act*.

Liability Broadcasters have often expressed concern about litigation that might result from bumping scheduled advertisements of commercial clientele as a result of the requirements of the *Canada Elections Act*. To alleviate their concerns, we recommend that the Act specifically protect them from liability. Broadcasters would, of course, have additional protection against lawsuits if they included a clause in their standard commercial contracts with advertisers protecting themselves against such a possibility. Further, we concur with the CBC that party paid-time advertisements should be in the language of the network or station.

Recommendation 1.6.21

We recommend that

(a) broadcasters be explicitly protected from liability for the bumping of commercial advertisements by party advertisements if such occurrence arises from the requirements of the *Canada Elections Act*; and

(b) broadcasters not be required to accept advertisements from parties in languages other than the language in which they normally broadcast.

Free Time

As early as 1934, the question of political parties being given free radio time was raised by William Lyon Mackenzie King in the House of Commons:

> Radio ... plays such an important part in all matters affecting public opinion that it would be quite proper that some provision should be made whereby, for example, each political party which has a representative following should be entitled to have broadcast at the expense of the state one or two addresses which would set forth its platform or policies before the people. (Canada, House of Commons, *Debates* 30 June 1934, 4511)

With the decision of the CBC in 1944 to allocate one half-hour (later extended to one hour) of free time monthly on its national networks to all parties represented in the House of Commons, guidelines were first established regarding the distribution of this time. If there were only two parties represented in the House of Commons, the time was divided between the two parties equally. If the House included representation from more than two parties, the 40/60 rule came into play, namely, that two-fifths of the time was given to the governing party and the remaining three-fifths divided up among the opposition parties. (CBC 1944; Peers 1969, 342)

The 1958 *Broadcasting Act* gave the Board of Broadcast Governors the power to require licensees to broadcast public-interest programs and to make regulations regarding the equitable allocation of time for partisan political messages, although the Board did not have the power to actually require public or private network operators to allocate free time. The CBC, as part of its mandate, made free time available to what it considered bona fide national parties – those that not only had representation in the House of Commons but also reflected a substantial body of opinion in the country, had policies on a wide range of issues, had a recognized national leader, had a nationwide organization, sought the election of candidates in a minimum of three provinces, and fielded a minimum of one candidate for every four constituencies. (CBC 1944) The criteria for access to free broadcast time varied over time, until they were superseded by the definition of a registered party in the 1974 revisions to the *Canada Elections Act*, but they always represented an attempt to identify the "serious" parties.

Free-time political broadcasts in Canada have had a number of objectives. In particular, the CBC offered the time in lieu of paid time, which it did not wish to provide. The CBC wished to ensure that all parties had a reasonable opportunity to explain their positions on the issues and that no one, because of position or wealth, was in a position to dominate the air waves. (Soderlund et al. 1984, 118–19; LaCalamita 1984) These rationales also applied to political party broadcasts between elections. To this day, the CBC refuses advocacy and controversial advertising, preferring to offer free time and news coverage, and makes paid time available to political parties during the advertising period of campaigns only because it is required to do so by law. Private broadcasters, obligated to provide time for public-service programming, often chose to provide free time to parties and candidates while also selling them other time.

With the advent of television, free time was offered on that medium also. On radio the broadcasts had attracted reasonable audiences, so the transition from radio to television was a concern for party strategists. Parties at first rejected the time and then presented themselves as if on radio (the infamous "talking heads"). This format did not attract substantial audiences, especially in light of the rapid proliferation of alternative program choices. As Dalton Camp put it, "if the format was right for politics [in that it promoted issue-oriented presentations], it was wrong for television" and it soon became clear that "if the parties were to use television, it would have to be on television's terms." (Camp 1981, xv)

Although longer free-time broadcasts had reasonable audiences in the 1970s, the parties opted in 1988 for shorter items, almost indistinguishable from spot advertisements. The items were two minutes in length for the three largest parties and one minute for the smaller parties. They could be inserted easily into ongoing programming, much like paid time, and therefore were likely to be viewed by a greater number of uncommitted voters than more traditional free-time formats. In fact, because the networks controlled the scheduling, they attempted as a courtesy to place them like spot advertisements in isolation from competing partisan political messages. In content, for the largest parties at least, they tended to be extended versions or clusters of the paid advertisements.

Indeed, CTV noted in its report to the CRTC on its coverage of the 1988 election that "while designated in the Act as a form of 'free' program time ... this amount of time ... is in fact unpaid commercial time [for] the registered parties". (CTV 1989, 9) The original intention, as the CTV report noted, was to "ensure that all parties contesting an election, regardless of their economic capacities, would be entitled to time [on] licensed conventional networks". In this spirit, CTV through its own facilities and those of its affiliates provided production assistance to smaller parties without compensation. The CBC provided a similar courtesy. The CBC recommended a minimum length of three to four minutes for free-time blocks, noting that "the original intent of free time was to ensure that the parties would have access to the airwaves for discussing, in a more profound way than is possible in a 30 or 60 second 'commercial', the major issues of the campaign". (Brief 1990, 15)

Critics have argued that brief broadcasts do not serve the purpose of promoting issue-oriented discussion as the more traditional free-time formats were intended to do. They have also argued that free-time segments should have a minimum length. Longer segments, especially when clustered into free-time programs, do not have the most attractive feature of paid time, namely, unintended viewing by possibly uncommitted voters. The two-minute segments could be considered more successful to the extent that they were more like spot advertisements. Because they are less easily aimed at specific voter types and are scheduled by the networks, however, they are still regarded by party strategists as at best a supplement to paid time.

There is a clear need for direct communication between politicians and voters. This appears to be a major consideration in the public support for mandatory leaders debates and in the general support for other unmediated sources. In addition, as Blais and Gidengil put it, "there is ... widespread sentiment that the system should be more open to small parties". (1991 RC) A free-time system that provides meaningful access for smaller parties appears to us to be the best alternative to intrusive regulations. The provision of alternative forms of direct access to national audiences promotes fairness and diversity in electoral communication without raising concerns about traditional media freedoms.

In the course of our discussions on this issue, it became clear that the whole concept of free-time broadcasts required reconsideration. If the free-time segments continue to shrink in size and to be placed in ongoing programming, the only thing distinguishing them from paid advertisements, apart from production costs, would be the fact that they are free. If a minimum length were required, on the other hand, they would have to be clustered to avoid excessive disruption of broadcast schedules, would generally attract relatively small audiences, and would not be regarded as a priority for the parties, other than smaller parties lacking the resources to purchase time. The central question, therefore, is whether they have outlived their usefulness or could be reformed to serve their original purposes.

Essential Features of the Current Free-Time System

As with paid time, free time is to occur within the legislated advertising window, namely, from the 29th day before election day to the second day before election day. Free time is not considered an election expense incurred by political parties. Unlike paid time, free time need not be broadcast in prime time. While all broadcasters in Canada must make paid time available to registered parties, the provision of free time is required only of those network operators that (1) reach a majority of Canadians whose mother tongue is the same as that in which the network broadcasts; (2) are licensed for more than the carriage of a particular series of programs or type of programming; and (3) are not involved in distribution undertakings such as cable. Because of ambiguous wording in the *Canada Elections Act* (s. 316), there is arguably a fourth criterion: only those network operators who offered free time in the last election are required to offer it in subsequent elections. This question arose in the 1988 election when a network operator not in existence in the previous election wondered whether it was obligated to provide free time. The Quatre Saisons network decided to comply with the spirit of the legislation and provide the time, but the incident did prompt the broadcasting arbitrator to suggest the Act be changed to stipulate an express minimum free-time requirement not based on the previous election. (Report of the Broadcasting Arbitrator 1989; see Canada, Chief Electoral Officer 1989, 64) To date, the radio networks offering free time have been CBC-AM English, CBC-AM French, Radiomutuel and Télémédia; the television networks have been CBC English, CBC French, CTV, TVA and Quatre Saisons.

Free time is allocated according to a formula stipulated in the Act (s. 316(2)): two minutes is to be given to every registered party and to every political party that waives its right to paid time. The rest goes to all registered parties that have been allocated paid time in the same proportion established under the paid-time allocation. There is also the additional proviso that no network operator can make available less free time than it did in the previous election. In the 1988 election, CBC English, CBC French and CTV offered a total of 214 minutes of free-time broadcasting; TVA and Quatre Saisons networks allocated 62 minutes each. The English and French CBC-AM networks offered 120 minutes; Radiomutuel and Télémédia offered 62 minutes each. Table 6.24 indicates how the free time was allocated on the CBC television network in the 1984 and 1988 elections. Allocations on other networks were similar.

Table 6.24
Allocation of free broadcast time by party, 1984–88
(minutes per station on CBC-TV [English], Radio-Canada TV [French] and CTV)

Party	1984	1988
Progressive Conservative Party	64.9	101
Liberal Party	87.0	46
New Democratic Party	34.7	35
Parti Rhinocéros	4.9	4
Communist Party	2.75	2
Libertarian Party	2.75	3
Pro-Life Party	2.75	—
Green Party	2.75	2
Confederation of Regions Western Party	2.75	2
United Canada Concept Party	2.75	—
L'Action des hommes d'affaires	2.75	—
Parti nationaliste	—	3
Party for the Commonwealth of Canada	—	2
Social Credit Party	—	2
Christian Heritage Party	—	2
Canada Party	—	2
Reform Party	—	2
Student Party	—	2
The Western Canada Concept Party	—	2
Western Independence Party	—	2
Total	210	214

Source: Reports of the Broadcasting Arbitrator (see Canada, Chief Electoral Officer 1984a, 1989).

Comparative Experience

Free time is widely used in democratic societies and is often seen as a way to provide fair access to minority points of view. Of the nine democracies we examined most closely, only one, the United States, does not provide free time for the broadcasting of messages by political parties during election campaigns. (Graber 1991 RC) Australia, Denmark, France, Germany, Great Britain, Israel, Norway and Sweden all have free-time systems, with each country having its own unique time allocation formula.

Australia allocates time to those parties that contest at least 10 seats and show evidence of popular support. A party demonstrates popular support by either electing a member to the Commonwealth Parliament at the previous election or polling at least 5 per cent of the valid votes for either federal or lower state house in the preceding general or state election. These free-time broadcasts usually consist of two-minute slots plus the policy speeches of the leaders at the launching of the election campaign. (Warhurst 1991 RC)

Denmark gives equal access to all parties that have collected signatures amounting to 1/175 of the valid votes cast in the previous election. The equal-treatment principle relates to specific prime-time election programs broadcast on radio and television, such as panel debates with representatives from all parties. (Siune 1991 RC)

France allocates equal and comparable access during presidential and legislative elections. The formula for legislative elections allocates equal amounts of free time to the leaders of the governing party and to all the opposition parties taken together, with the latter time being allocated among them according to the number of members each has in the National Assembly. Parties with no Assembly members are entitled to a few short broadcasts. In the most recent presidential run-offs, the two presidential candidates received two hours each on television and radio, spread over four programs. (Gerstlé 1991 RC)

The free-time ratio in Great Britain for parties represented in Parliament is based on the proportion of votes cast in the previous general election. Any party not represented in the House of Commons is eligible to receive one five-minute segment if it contests 50 or more seats. (Semetko 1991 RC)

Norway gives equal time if the party has been represented in the Parliament during one of the last two election periods, has a current national organization and runs candidates in a majority of the districts. Parties not qualified for equal treatment will be given time in short programs combining statements by party representatives and questioning by journalists. (Siune 1991 RC)

The Swedish free-time rule is to give equal access to parties represented in the Parliament. Small parties not represented in the Parliament have only limited access to national broadcasting. (Siune 1991 RC)

In the German system, each party running in the election is granted at least one free commercial on public radio and television stations. Extra free-time spots are determined by a party's level of representation in the *Bundestag*, being roughly proportional to the number of seats that party holds. The segments are usually broadcast immediately before or after prime-time news shows and must not exceed two and a half minutes. (Schoenbach 1991 RC)

In Israel, the public broadcaster provides one half hour of television each night, prior to the national news at 9 p.m., for the last 30 days of the campaign (one hour of radio time), allocated among the parties according to seats held in the previous House. (Elizur and Katz 1979, 230) The parties receive time slots up to 10 minutes long, allocated by an impartial committee. (Elizur 1986, 186; Arian 1985, 258) The two largest parties have in recent elections interspersed light entertainment and policy documentaries with clips from speeches and other material. As in most other jurisdictions, the broadcast time is free to the parties, but they must pay for production. (Elizur 1986, 190)

Even in the one country that does not provide for free time, the United States, proposals have recently emerged for some form of free-time broadcasting during presidential campaigns. For example, *Washington Post* political reporter Paul Taylor has proposed that the presidential candidates of the Democratic and Republican parties be given five minutes of free time on all networks on alternative nights during the last month of the campaign. (Taylor 1990, 267–84) More recently, the Joan Shorenstein Barone Center on the Press, Politics and Public Policy, Harvard University, put forward a proposal for a series of 90-minute programs on all major television channels ("Nine Sundays") that would combine candidate debates and exploration of issues. (*New York Times* 1991, A-19) In each case, the proposals are designed to provide more substantive information to citizens and thus counter growing cynicism about electoral politics.

Reforming Free-Time Broadcasts

In response to the need expressed by voters and the parties for more unmediated communication and to ensure that greater direct access be given to all political parties, we conclude that the present free-time system needs to be changed. Our objective is a free-time structure that would provide both enhanced access to national broadcast media for the parties and better campaign information for voters. Further, if the free time were required to be scheduled in prime time, there would likely be greater efforts by the parties to ensure that their segments were informative and appealing.[9] A new free-time structure should provide an alternative to news and public affairs coverage, as well as party paid-time broadcasts and additional leaders debates. It should duplicate neither the efforts of the news media nor the existing communications channels available to parties. Rather, it should supplement other sources of campaign information and other means of campaigning for parties.

In examining such programming in other countries, we were impressed by the lively debate in the British party election broadcasts and the Israeli free-time programs. Some Canadian programming from past elections, when segments were longer, also showed considerable creativity and popular appeal. For example, in 1984, the NDP presented a four-minute segment entitled "Mouseland", an animated version of a speech by the late Tommy Douglas, long-time leader of the party. The segment, though inexpensively produced, received a positive public response, according to party officials.

Although Canadian campaigns and the broadcasting environment are quite different from those in most European countries, given our vast program choice and the availability of paid time, extended free-time broadcasts would broaden public debate in Canada. This appears to be the view of the networks, as already noted. At its best, a new free-time system could provide a forum for extended debate and controversy over the future directions of the country and attract a new generation of interested voters to such interchanges. Much would depend on the willingness of the parties to make creative use of such extended segments.

One option would be providing 5- or 10-minute segments each night, perhaps restricted to a "talking heads" format.[10] Although this model would probably enhance the issue content of presentations, it is unlikely to attract significant audiences or promote lively interchange. Neither would it fit easily into network schedules. In the highly competitive North American media, regularly scheduled longer programs are more likely to attract a politically attentive audience. Other audiences would be reached by the paid time.

The benefits of a reformed free-time system are significant. To explain policy proposals and, in the case of the governing party, to defend its record, the largest parties require access in longer segments than are suitable for paid time or permitted by current journalistic practices. The smaller parties, lacking the resources for extensive paid time and generally receiving little news coverage, need such direct access to a national audience. In addition, free-time broadcasts provide an alternative to requiring access for the leaders of the smaller parties to televised leaders debates or to news coverage, with all the difficulties that would accompany those options. Free time is needed, in summation, as a supplement to paid time, news and public affairs coverage to provide at least some access to national broadcasting for all registered parties.

Recommendation 1.6.22

We recommend that

(a) **the current provision on the free-time political broadcasting system set out in the *Canada Elections Act* be abolished; and**

(b) **a free-time broadcasting regime be established, with programs to begin on a date after the writs to be set by the Canada Elections Commission and to end on the second day before election day, with the following characteristics:**
(1) television and radio network operators, as well as specialty broadcast undertakings presenting primarily general news and public affairs programs, be required to provide to the Canada Elections Commission ten 30-minute free-time broadcasts in prime time (at least 24 minutes of which would be available to parties);
(2) networks broadcasting in French whose primary audience is in Quebec and those networks reaching a majority of Canadians outside Quebec whose primary language is French be required to provide to the Canada Elections Commission five 30-minute free-time broadcasts in prime

time (at least 24 minutes of which would be available to parties); and

(3) the specific days and times of these broadcasts be mutually agreed upon by the networks and registered parties, and in the event there is no agreement by the first day of the free-time broadcasting period established by the Canada Elections Commission, the Commission be mandated to establish forthwith the specific days and times for the programs.

Under the current rules, the three major television networks, CBC English, CBC French and CTV, provide 214 minutes of free time. Under the proposal, each would be required to provide ten 30-minute programs (or 300 minutes) to the Canada Elections Commission which, in turn, would be required to give 24 minutes of this time to registered parties. The total time turned over to the parties would thus be 240 minutes, or slightly more than is provided by CBC and CTV now, but in a form less disruptive to network scheduling. The two French-language private networks currently provide 62 minutes and would be required to provide five 30-minute programs, or 150 minutes. The parties would receive 120 minutes. It is reasonable to require broadcast networks to contribute to voter information in this way. The time would, of course, be considered program time and Canadian content, with the networks being permitted to sell advertising time before and after the program.

It is our intention that the format of these programs be as innovative as possible. We suggest only a framework. At the latest, on the 11th day after the writs are issued, all network operators (and specialty broadcast undertakings presenting primarily news and public affairs programs) would provide two 30-minute free-time broadcasts per week in prime time, to be broadcast simultaneously by all participating broadcasters. The times should be negotiated with the registered parties. The Parliamentary Channels would be required to repeat the French and English programs at other times, and others would be invited to do so.

Recommendation 1.6.23

We recommend that

(a) participants in the broadcasts include all registered parties;
(b) the broadcasts be a magazine show format made up of party segments of approximately four minutes each; and
(c) the Parliamentary Channels be required to repeat each of the French and English broadcasts a minimum of three times, and broadcasters have the option of repeating these broadcasts except during the blackout period at the end of the election period.

To grasp the possible benefits of the free-time proposal, it is helpful to imagine what the political parties might do with their segments. The early broadcasts might feature the leaders of the largest parties, as is done in Great Britain and Australia. The leaders of the smaller parties could respond or use their segments to focus on a competing set of issues. Standard features, like profiles of party leaders and other prominent candidates, could be supplemented by other, perhaps creative, materials that high-lighted differences among the parties or drew attention to particular strengths and weaknesses. More simply, parties could present highlights of their leaders' campaign speeches, providing the substance and detail that they often complain is lacking in news coverage. It would also be pos-sible to prepare 'documentaries' on particular problems they wish to address, using visuals, graphics, 'experts' and other forms of argument or endorse-ment. As a supplement to paid-time programs and campaign news, these programs have the potential to provide a new linkage between parties and voters.

Allocating Free Time

In devising an allocation formula for the free-time broadcasts, we need to balance the claims of fairness and equity and those of the voters' need for information. We propose the registered parties each receive an allocation of one or more four-minute segments. These segments could be combined but not divided to ensure a minimum length per segment and to encourage a clear differentiation from paid time. No party would be able to program more than 12 minutes in any 30-minute show, ensuring that the programs would be in a 'magazine' format, with messages from at least two parties appearing on each program. This would provide the opportunity for comparison, which voters have identified as a priority.

Our proposed formula would provide emerging and smaller parties greater access than they have had in the past and also would provide more time to those parties that achieved significant levels of popular support in the previous election. By providing a minimum amount of time for all parties, our proposal ensures that all registered parties have a guaranteed minimum of national exposure, regardless of their capacity to purchase paid time. The time to be made available to the smaller parties would be significantly greater than under the current formula and would be in prime time. This increased access responds to the concerns of these parties that they are not likely to be represented in televised leaders debates or to be given much news coverage. By providing additional time based on the popular vote in the previous election, we also have provided a platform for the parties with established voter support. Parties with the organizational capacity to contest at least half the seats are given additional time, as are parties with representation in the House of Commons when the writs are issued. To recognize the claims of emerging parties that have gained rep-resentation in the House of Commons, the allocation formula provides for additional time for any party that did not contest the previous election or did not receive more than 5 per cent of the popular vote but has at least one member in the House of Commons.

These provisions are based on a realistic assessment of electoral competition. Parties that are serious participants in the electoral process will, under the procedures we have proposed, be registered before an election is called. The use of the popular vote in the previous election to determine the allocations, as is done in Great Britain, ensures that parties with a representative following are given ample opportunity to put their messages before the voters. By providing additional time to registered parties with candidates nominated in more than half the constituencies, the formula provides some scope for emerging national parties.

Moreover, the formula would ensure that the truly competitive parties have sufficient broadcast time to promote themselves to the Canadian electorate by allocating at least 40 per cent of the total time made available to those registered parties that received more than 5 per cent of the popular vote in the last general election. Where such an adjustment results in an allocation that is less than two full four-minute segments, those parties that did not receive more than 5 per cent of the popular vote in the last general election should have the option of presenting one four-minute segment and a shorter segment or one longer segment. The 5 per cent threshold effectively distinguishes those parties that have established a core of popular support among voters from those that have not.

The French networks, with smaller potential audiences, are required to provide only five programs. Although some networks, perhaps especially the CBC (Société Radio-Canada), might well choose to offer more, the smaller number of programs necessitates flexibility in the allocation of time among the registered parties. We recommend, therefore, that the same basic formula apply to all networks but that the Canada Elections Commission be empowered to modify the allocation for the French programs in the interests of fairness, taking into account the number of constituencies contested by each party in the coverage area of each network or specialty service.

Table 6.25 shows the free-time allocation that the parties received in 1988 under the current formula, the time they would have been given in 1988 (on the basis of the 1984 popular vote) and a hypothetical allocation for the next election (based on the 1988 vote). The CBC allocation for 1988 is used as an example (the proportions were the same on all networks). It is, of course, difficult to predict how many registered parties there will be for the next election.

To understand the formula, it is helpful to consider a hypothetical example. The formula provides each new party with a basic allocation, one four-minute segment. If the party has candidates in half the constituencies, it receives an additional segment. If it has achieved representation in the House of Commons before the writs for the general election have been issued, another segment is allocated. Thus, the maximum allocation for a new party is three segments. Had the party been registered for the previous election, it would have gained a further segment, for a total of four. Thus, a party that failed to gain 5 per cent of the popular vote can, under the formula, qualify for additional segments through organizational activity between general elections.

Table 6.25
Free time allocation to federal political parties: 1988 actual and proposed formula

Party	Actual 1988 allocation	Proposed formula based on 1984 vote		Proposed formula based on 1988 vote	
	CBC minutes	minutes[a]	(segments)[b]	minutes	(segments)
Progressive Conservative Party	101	72	(18)	63	(15)
Liberal Party	46	42	(10)	49.5	(12)
New Democratic Party	35	30	(7)	31.5	(7)
Canada Party	2	7	(2)	7	(2)
Christian Heritage Party	2	7	(2)	7	(2)
Party for the Commonwealth of Canada	2	7	(2)	7	(2)
Communist Party	2	7	(2)	7	(2)
Confederation of Regions Western Party	2	7	(2)	7	(2)
Green Party	2	7	(2)	7	(2)
Libertarian Party	3	7	(2)	7	(2)
Parti nationaliste	3	7	(2)	7	(2)
Reform Party	2	7	(2)	7	(2)
Parti Rhinocéros	4	7	(2)	7	(2)
Social Credit Party	2	7	(2)	7	(2)
Student Party	2	7	(2)	7	(2)
Western Canada Concept Party	2	7	(2)	7	(2)
Western Independence Party	2	7	(2)	7	(2)
Total	214	240	(59)	242	(60)

Source: Canada, Chief Electoral Officer 1989; Royal Commission Research Branch.

[a]The allocations have been adjusted to comply with the rule that the total free time to be allocated among parties that failed to receive more than 5 per cent of the popular vote in the previous election does not exceed 96 minutes (40 per cent of the total). In the example shown here, one minute was taken from the allocation for each smaller party and added to the time available for allocation among those parties that did achieve the 5 per cent threshold (divided in proportion to their share of the popular vote). The objective of this rule is to ensure that an increase in the number of registered parties would not result in an allocation of time to those parties that had established themselves as contenders in the previous election that was too small to permit them to communicate their positions effectively to the electorate.

A party that had achieved representation in the House of Commons at dissolution would be allocated additional time. In addition, any party that nominated candidates in at least half the constituencies for an upcoming election would receive more time.

[b]In many cases, the time allocated to a registered party cannot be divided evenly into four-minute segments. Parties may add the remaining time to another segment or present one shorter segment.

Recommendation 1.6.24

We recommend that

(a) broadcast time on the free-time programs be allocated as follows:
(1) one program segment to all registered parties;
(2) one additional segment to all parties registered by the issue of the writs that were registered at the previous general election but received less than 5 per cent of the vote;
(3) one additional segment to all registered parties with candidates nominated in more than half the constituencies;
(4) one additional segment to any registered party represented in the House of Commons (that is, at least one Member of Parliament) when the writs are issued, if the party was not registered or did not receive more than 5 per cent of the vote in the previous general election; and
(5) the remaining segments to be allocated among those registered parties that received more than 5 per cent of the vote in the previous general election, in proportion to the votes each received;
(b) if the total time allocated to those parties that did not reach the 5 per cent threshold in the previous election exceeds 40 per cent of the total time made available, individual party allocations be reduced proportionately to remain within that cap; and
(c) for the French networks, the time be allocated to each registered party on a similar basis as for other networks, with due consideration for fairness and the number of candidates endorsed by each party in the area these networks are licensed to serve.

To ensure smooth administration and encourage high production values, a producer for each official language is required. These producers would administer the programs, prepare opening and closing announcements and promotional materials, and be available to work with the parties and networks to produce the most effective broadcasting possible. Neither the Canada Elections Commission nor the producers would be responsible for the content of the party segments, but the producers would be available to assist and advise parties on request. Given the partisan nature of the program, the Canada Elections Commission should seek the advice of the registered parties before appointing producers. It would be helpful if the producers were selected before the writs are issued.

Recommendation 1.6.25

We recommend that

(a) **to ensure high production values for free-time broadcasts, the Canada Elections Commission appoint a producer for each official language, after consulting with the registered parties; and**

(b) **the producers oversee the programs and assist the parties on request.**

The programs that we envision would involve a wide variety of styles. The parties should be encouraged to be innovative and to enter into the debate as fully as possible. The Israeli programs involve charge and counter-charge, as well as issue discussions. The twice-weekly frequency that we propose permits such interchanges. As the Barbeau Committee put it,

> Effective political programming will be controversial, almost by defini-
> tion. It must arouse public interest and discussion in order to justify its
> necessarily high costs. If it fails to do this, then it is useless to politicians
> and burdensome to broadcasters and the public. (Canada, Committee on
> Election Expenses 1966, 375)

It is our hope that these programs become major events in Canadian federal election campaigns.

The time when party segments are broadcast will be important to the participants. However, it would be undesirable to establish rules in the abstract. Given that parties may well have differing tactical preferences, the parties and the producers should negotiate the schedule. It would be desirable for the segments presented by any given party to be spread throughout the campaign. If there is no agreement, the Canada Elections Commission should decide the schedule. It would not be unreasonable to allocate the segments by lot, as is normally done for speaking order in the televised leaders debates. For the programs to be effective, the schedule must be established as soon as possible after the writs are issued.

Recommendation 1.6.26

We recommend that

(a) **the schedule of broadcast for party segments in the free-time broadcasts be decided by negotiation among those parties participating and the producers; and**

(b) **if there is no agreement, the schedule be decided forthwith by the Canada Elections Commission.**

The free-time broadcasts of 30 minutes each would offer a real alternative to other forms of campaign communications, such as the increasingly expensive paid-time commercials. They would also meet the expressed needs of the parties and voters for direct and unmediated access to voters and provide a real opportunity for the parties to communicate their policies. Simultaneous carriage on the major networks would build audiences; repeats on the Parliamentary Channels, and possibly by other broadcasters, would allow the registered political parties to reach more of the Canadian electorate.

Leaders Debates

Although televised leaders debates began with the Kennedy–Nixon debates in 1960 and first appeared in Canada soon after (in the Quebec provincial election of 1962 and in the federal election of 1968), they did not become a common feature of election campaigns in industrial democracies until the late 1970s. By 1980, such debates had been held in national elections in at least 10 countries. (Smith 1981, 174–75) They became even more common over the next decade. Televised leaders debates were staged in the last four U.S. presidential elections and in three of the last four Canadian federal elections.

Canada's first televised leaders debate was held in Quebec in November 1962, after long and difficult negotiations that almost did not succeed. The debate aroused considerable interest in other provinces and at the federal level, but emulation was slow, and in Quebec itself there was a long hiatus, despite the central role of television in subsequent Quebec politics. (Charron 1991 RC) Nevertheless, there was a televised debate in the 1968 federal election and the 1971 Ontario election, and by the 1980s such debates were common. With the debates in Saskatchewan and British Columbia in 1991, it is now possible to report that at least one televised leaders debate has been held in every province. Although debates have not been held in every recent provincial election, they are now a regular feature of most provincial elections, and party leaders risk popular disapproval if they refuse to participate. (Bernier and Monière 1991 RC)

Well on their way to becoming institutionalized, debates are by no means codified. The experience in Canada and elsewhere has been that, at every election, agreement among parties and broadcasters on such matters as timing, format and rules of participation has been difficult to achieve. Although past agreements undoubtedly shape future ones, each negotiation seems to produce variations. Indeed, the negotiations do not always succeed. When debates are not held, it is usually because parties and broadcasters cannot agree on some aspect of format or timing, or because participation is perceived by one of the large parties as too risky. In some cases, broadcasters are concerned about costs. It is not surprising, therefore, that the debates have been the subject of considerable discussion and controversy here and abroad.

As Anthony Smith put it a decade ago, "The television age has introduced the notion that direct debate ... is the natural climax of an election
campaign and that without it the electorate has been denied some essential
proving of the candidates." (1981, 185) In all the countries we examined,
debates attract large audiences. They stimulate interest in politics, help voters determine the basic issues of the campaign, increase awareness of parties and leaders, and help to legitimize political institutions. (Bernier and
Monière 1991 RC) Our research indicates that the 1984 and 1988 Canadian
debates increased voter information, especially among less-informed voters,
and stimulated voter interest. (Barr 1991 RC) The potential of debates to have
significant effects on voter preferences was clearly shown by the post-debate
polls in 1984 and 1988, though their capacity to produce significant change
in the longer term distribution of voter preferences depends on many other
factors. (Barr 1991 RC; Clarke et al. 1991, 101–4) In addition, it appears that
televised debates have an overall positive influence on voters' evaluations
of all participating leaders. (Barr 1991 RC) Such direct leader-to-voter communication is, therefore, beneficial.

Often promoted as political spectacles, debates draw large audiences in
all of the democracies, far larger than any other campaign event. Our research
confirms previous studies: about two-thirds of adult Canadians watched
at least one debate in 1984 and 1988 (Table 6.26). Voters not only watch
them, they also regard them as important and useful. (Bernier and Monière
1991 RC) Indeed, asked to indicate what innovations would be useful in providing voter information, 78 per cent of a national sample supported additional leaders debates and 75 per cent favoured debates on specific issues on
the Parliamentary Channels (Table 6.15).

Table 6.26
Audience for leaders debates
(per cent)

Yes	64.4
No	34.2
Don't know	1.4

Source: Blais and Gidengil 1991 RC.

Note: N = 2 947.

Wording of the question:
"In the last two federal election campaigns, in 1984 and 1988, there were leaders debates on TV. Did you
happen to watch any of them?"

Public Concerns and Proposals

A lack of consensus characterizes the central issues. For instance, interveners from different parties called for the inclusion in the *Canada Elections Act*
of a requirement that one or more televised leaders debates take place at
every election. Others, especially from the media, said debates are information programming and should not be regulated but rather left up to the
networks and the parties. Experienced politicians were to be found on both

sides of the issue. The capacity of a party with a substantial lead in the polls, usually the incumbent, effectively to veto the holding of debates was held to be unfair by Peter Desbarats, Dean of Journalism at the University of Western Ontario, and others. Representatives of the three large parties argued that the process was working well and should be left as open as possible.

Media representatives were unanimous in the view that journalists are best suited to ensure impartiality and fairness and to determine the scope and nature of debates. As the CBC put it in its submission,

> Leaders' debates have traditionally been initiated by the broadcast networks and the formats negotiated with the participants well in advance. Particular attention has been paid to the need for both apparent and real equity, as well as to the fact that circumstances dictate a need for flexibility, for a dynamic approach designed to recognize the public's right to assess both the parties' platforms and their leaders' abilities to explain and defend those platforms in a scrupulously fair context. (Brief 1990, 12)

The brief argues that the networks must be free to invite leaders to take part whenever their parties have "gained an appreciable level of public approval and support" (1990, 13), as has been done at both federal and provincial levels in the past.

The appropriate role for emerging parties was a major point of discussion. A number of interveners called for participation by the leaders of all registered parties; others, concerned that too many participants would reduce the utility and appeal of the debates, called for some other form of access to broadcast time for leaders of smaller parties. The most common suggestion was for a separate debate for these party leaders, perhaps a round-table discussion with simultaneous translation, or for some form of compensatory free time. Several interveners suggested that parties not included in televised debates should receive additional free time. Preston Manning, leader of the Reform Party, noted that a debate involving 10 or 12 party leaders would be impractical and suggested that provision should be made for some other form of national exposure for other party leaders. (Calgary, 22 May 1990) This position had broad support in the hearings. Questions of format and timing were also raised in the public hearings, but there was no consensus. The format that has emerged in Canada, however, is highly regarded elsewhere. (Bernier and Monière 1991 RC)

Public Support for Leaders Debates

Our national attitudinal survey indicated there is considerable public support for mandated debates with broad participation. As shown in Tables 6.27 and 6.28, more than half of respondents favoured a legal requirement that televised leaders debates be held and half wanted all registered parties to participate. André Blais and Elisabeth Gidengil found 40 per cent of their respondents to be consistently positive toward debates and 23 per cent consistently negative. (1991 RC) Those respondents most likely to approve of mandatory debates are the less well informed – for whom debates are a convenient source of information – and those who are less trusting of politicians. The demand for direct access to the views of all parties is notable. Studies in several countries indicate that debates increase the public's knowledge of politics and politicians. (Bernier and Monière 1991 RC)

The popular appeal of televised leaders debates derives not only from the dramatic confrontation they provide but also from the fact that they allow voters to compare leaders directly, unmediated by journalists. As Bernier and Monière put it, "the unique characteristic of televised debates is that they offer citizens an inexpensive, first-hand source of comparative information". (1991 RC) The debates provide direct and convenient access to information about the priorities of the major contending parties and the personalities of the leaders. Other campaign activities do not provide such quick and easy access to such rich, comparative information.

Table 6.27
Public assessment of whether debates should be mandatory
(per cent)

Yes	56.5
No	40.5
Don't know	3.0

Source: Blais and Gidengil 1991 RC.

Note: N = 2 947.

Wording of the question:
"Do you think the law should require party leaders to participate in a televised debate at each election?"

Table 6.28
Leaders debates: public assessment of who should participate
(per cent)

Leaders of three major parties	23.3
Leaders of all parties in Parliament	19.8
Leaders of all ten registered parties	50.0
Some other combination	1.8
Don't know	5.1

Source: Blais and Gidengil 1991 RC.

Note: N = 2 947.

Wording of the question:
"As you may know, in federal elections there are usually about ten registered parties. Who do you think should participate in the debate: the leaders of the THREE MAJOR parties, the leaders of all parties WITH MEMBERS IN PARLIAMENT, or the leaders of ALL TEN REGISTERED PARTIES?"

Conclusions

In light of the obvious usefulness of televised leaders debates, we considered a range of questions. Should broadcasters be required to carry debates?

Should party leaders be required to participate? Should there be regulations or guidelines regarding who should be invited, and how often and when debates should be held?

In answering these questions, we must balance the claims of fairness with the practicalities of organizing effective, appealing and informative debates, as well as the right of voters to have the information to make a clear choice among those who have a chance of forming the government.

In our examination of the practices of other democracies, we found that debates are now an accepted part of campaigns but direct regulation is rare. In no countries are broadcasters required to carry leaders debates. Nor are there any instances of required participation by party leaders, except for the state of New Jersey, which requires candidates to participate in a series of debates if they accept any of the public funds available to subsidize campaign costs. (New Jersey Statutes, Title 19, Elections)

The Quebec *Election Act* of 1984 was interpreted in 1985 as requiring a televised leaders debate to include "all the leaders of the parties represented in the National Assembly or which have obtained at least 3% of the valid votes at the last general election". (1984, c. 51, s. 427) The networks proposed various formats that they believed would not dampen audience interest, but none was acceptable to all the party leaders and no debate was held. After careful consideration, the Quebec *Election Act* was amended in 1989 to exclude from its provisions debates between party leaders. (1989, c. 1, s. 88) In short, after a limited attempt at regulating this area, the National Assembly decided to leave organization of the debate to the networks and the political parties. (Bernier and Monière 1991 RC)

The debates have evolved without direct regulation and are now deemed to be an important part of the campaign process. Regulation of the debates might ensure their utility to voters in the short term but at the expense of the capacity to adapt them to changing technologies and the specific circumstances of particular campaigns. The capacity to adjust to the emergence of a new national party or an influential regional party is part of daily journalism but is not easily incorporated into a regulatory structure.

We support the general principles expressed in the CRTC guidelines (CRTC 1988 13):

> In the case of so-called 'debates,' it may be impractical to include all rival parties or candidates in one program. However, if this type of broadcast takes place, all parties and candidates should be accommodated, even if doing so requires that more than one program be broadcast.

Bernier and Monière suggest that the leaders of parties not invited to participate in the primary debates be offered the opportunity to participate in a program focused on these parties, perhaps in the form of a round-table discussion with questions from journalists. (1991 RC) This option should be considered by the networks in the interests of fairness and as a way to broaden the range of issues discussed in campaigns.

Despite the undoubted value of televised leaders debates in modern democracies, there are good reasons why direct regulation remains rare. Once begun, regulation would require the development of a detailed legal framework or delegation of authority to a regulatory body. Such a legal framework, with requirements for network broadcast, rules for selecting participants and guidelines on format, would inhibit flexibility and the evolution of the process. Debates have become institutionalized without regulation, and it is our expectation that they will continue to evolve as a result of the interests and concerns of the networks, political parties and voters. The risk exists that no debate will be held in any particular campaign or that emerging parties will feel themselves unfairly excluded. At the same time, however, leaving the matter to the networks and the parties will allow for the most rapid adjustment to changing political realities.

Negotiations leading up to leaders debates are difficult and politically sensitive and carry a substantial risk of failure. The competing interests of the political parties and the networks make for complex discussions. Negotiations among the parties and the networks are often long and arduous and sometimes fail to produce agreement. Protracted negotiations in many countries and the risk of failure have led many commentators to call for established procedures. (Bernier and Monière 1991 RC) Several interveners, some of whom had participated in such negotiations, indicated that having a neutral person preside over the discussions would be beneficial. The parties participating in the debates and networks should agree on the selection of a chairperson in the first five days after the issuance of the writs.

We believe in the value of televised leaders debates and we strongly urge the networks and the political parties to do all they can to ensure that they are held. Further, they should be accessible to the maximum number of Canadians, including those with hearing disabilities. For this reason, all televised leaders debates should be closed-captioned, and sign language should also be provided. In the interests of fairness, the leaders of *all* registered parties should have an opportunity to express their views through the broadcast media. The new free-time provisions recommended above would help restore equity in this regard.

Recommendation 1.6.27

We recommend that

(a) televised leaders debates not be required by law;
(b) all matters of organization continue to be negotiated among the networks and the parties, subject to the appropriate CRTC regulations and guidelines;
(c) parties participating in the debates and networks select a chairperson by the fifth day following the issue of the writs; and

(d) televised leaders debates be closed-captioned, and sign language also be provided.

Government Advertising during Election Campaigns

The ability of the governing party to direct government advertising is perceived as giving that party an unfair competitive advantage. Concern has already been expressed at the federal level. For example, the 1986 federal *White Paper on Election Law Reform* recommended new provisions to restrict government advertising during an election. (Canada, Privy Council Office 1986, 18)

The only provision contained in the present *Canada Elections Act* concerning government advertising is that contained in section 48(1), which makes it an offence for persons acting on behalf of registered political parties to procure or acquiesce in the publication in a government publication of material promoting or opposing a particular party or candidate.

Two provinces, Saskatchewan and Manitoba, have much broader prohibitions on government advertising during election campaigns. Saskatchewan prohibits all government boards, departments, commissions, agencies and Crown corporations from publishing in any manner "any information or particulars of the activities of the department, board, commission, Crown corporation or agency except in the case of an emergency where public interest requires the publication of any such information or particulars". (*Election Act*, s. 229) The measure was introduced in the 1970s and has not met with controversy or caused administrative difficulties. The Saskatchewan government issues internal guidelines outlining examples of ongoing activities exempt from the prohibition and reminds the civil service that the phrase "in case of an emergency" in the Act is to be interpreted rigidly.

A similar measure exists in the Manitoba *Elections Finances Act*, which reads,

> **56(1)** No department of the government of Manitoba and no Crown agency shall
>
> (a) during an election period for a general election, publish or advertise in any manner; or
>
> (b) during an election period for a by-election in an electoral division, publish or advertise in any manner in the electoral division;
>
> any information concerning the programs or activities of the department or Crown agency, except
>
> (c) in continuation of earlier publications or advertisements concerning ongoing programs of the department or Crown agency; or
>
> (d) to solicit applications for employment with the department or Crown agency; or

(e) where the publication or advertisement is required by law; or
(f) where the publication or advertisement is deemed necessary
by the Chief Electoral Officer for the administration of an
election.

The Manitoba Act also provides the opportunity for anyone to file a complaint with the chief electoral officer if that person believes the prohibition on government advertising has been violated. The Manitoba chief electoral officer is to provide details of all justified complaints in the annual report to the Speaker of the Assembly.

Because governing parties may be perceived to have an unfair advantage because of their access to public funds, it is important that measures to ensure fairness in electoral competition address this perception.

Recommendation 1.6.28

We recommend that all federal government advertising during the election period be governed by the following rules:

(a) no department of the government of Canada and no Crown agency or corporation shall during an election period publish or advertise in any manner in the area where the election is held any information concerning the programs or activities of the department or Crown agency or corporation except
(1) in continuation of earlier publications or advertisements concerning ongoing programs; or
(2) to solicit applications for employment or to solicit tenders for goods and services; or
(3) where the publication or advertisement is required by law; or
(4) where the publication or advertisement is deemed necessary by the Canada Elections Commission for the administration of an election; and
(b) on receipt of a complaint, the Canada Elections Commission shall consider the alleged violation of these prohibitions, investigate the matter if it is deemed necessary, and, if it so judges, issue a cease-and-desist order.

NOTES

1. In June 1972, members of the campaign committee to re-elect Richard Nixon were caught burgling the offices of the Democratic National Committee. Subsequent investigations revealed major violations of election law, notably illegal contributions from corporations and foreign nationals, cash contributions and reporting irregularities. Media revelations and congressional

investigations eventually resulted in President Nixon's resignation. (Mutch 1991 RC)

2. The accused, D.V. Roach, was president of the Ontario Housing Corporation Employees' Union, affiliated as Local 767, Canadian Union of Public Employees.

3. In a 1949 Gallup poll, 78 per cent of respondents who had an opinion agreed "there should be a limit on the amount each party can spend in an election campaign"; in 1972, the corresponding level of support was 84 per cent. (Gallup Report 1972)

4. Brian Risdon had issued leaflets during a by-election denouncing David Crombie, a candidate, for alleged dishonesty as mayor of Toronto in firing Risdon from his position as the city's chief plumbing inspector in 1977. The leaflet read, "Crombie Lied ... Is this the kind of man you want in Ottawa??" Risdon was found guilty of incurring an unauthorized election expense and fined $50. In 1981, Publicis communicateur conseil was found guilty of sponsoring six billboards during the 1980 general election in the constituency of Langelier. The billboards read, "Oui à Trudeau". The firm pleaded guilty and was fined $600. On the *Roach* case, see note 2.

5. Grant MacLaren sought a party nomination in the constituency of Vancouver South after the writs were issued for the 1988 election. MacLaren spent $4477 on advertisements in five community newspapers distributed free of charge. The Supreme Court of British Columbia determined that MacLaren was not guilty of an offence against section 214 for the following reasons: according to Elections Canada guidelines, the limit in that section applies only to notices in the electronic or print media; on the basis of section 213 of the Act, the print media (not defined in the Act) are considered "periodical publications"; however, because the definition of "periodical publication" in the Act stipulates that the latter is "printed for sale" and the community newspaper was distributed free of charge, section 214 did not apply. (*R. v. MacLaren* 1991)

6. The word counts reported here were generously provided by the CBC. They are used for illustrative purposes, in the absence of comparable data for other networks. The estimates for the length of sound bites are based on a consensus that the average number of words per second in a news clip is approximately three. The CBC radio show "Commentary" has estimated that its speakers average about 2.2 spoken words per second. However, the program's lecture style presentations are slower than normal television discourse, as in interviews, scrums and press conferences. These bring the average to about three words per second.

7. The CRTC does not keep a record of complaints, most of which are received by telephone, or of their resolution. The experience of the Legal Division is that there have been one or two complaints a day during recent campaigns, down from 15 to 20 in the 1970s. The decline appears to be a result of broadcasters and candidates becoming more aware of the regulations. Nearly all complaints are from candidates and involve allegations of inequitable treatment.

8. The Canadian Election Study 1988 reported that the television advertisements placed by the three largest parties had considerable issue content, focusing mainly on the free trade agreement, but raising other issues as well. Although there was emphasis on the party leaders and a tendency for the spots to become more negative as the campaign progressed, the advertisements provided a clear sense of the priorities of the parties. (Johnston et al. 1991, 4: 14–17)

9. Some recent trends in broadcasting indicate that the free-time broadcasts might well have a reasonable degree of audience appeal. At a time when North American network audience shares have been declining, Canadian news and current affairs programs have recorded significant increases in viewing. The audience share for Canadian programming increased by nearly 30 per cent from 1984–85 to 1988–89. Information programming, mostly news and public affairs, constituted 41 per cent of prime-time Canadian viewing in 1988–89. (Ellis 1991, 26–33) The recent Environics Media Study survey data indicate that this trend is likely to continue. (Adams 1991) If the parties make effective use of the time, it seems likely that significant numbers of voters who want to discover the priorities of the parties will tune in.

10. Television is the dominant medium not only because of its audience appeal but also because of its structure. As Johnston and his colleagues note, "If a party's objective is to direct – or redirect – a national campaign then it has little choice but to work through television. Of the mass media, only television is sufficiently centralized to have a unidirectional effect on the whole electorate." (1991, 4:4)

7

STRENGTHENING PUBLIC CONFIDENCE IN THE INTEGRITY OF THE ELECTORAL PROCESS

INTRODUCTION

PUBLIC CONFIDENCE IN the integrity of the electoral process is essential if citizens are to believe that their democratic rights are secured. Their confidence is affected by many factors. Chief among these is the extent to which the public perceives: (1) that the electoral process does not allow undue influence through financial contributions to candidates or political parties; (2) that the policies and practices of the media in election coverage and political advertising curtail undue manipulation of voters; and (3) that elections are administered independently and impartially, and the election law is enforced effectively and reasonably.

Electoral law and electoral practices must be responsive to public concerns, especially for those matters that have given rise to doubts about the effectiveness of the current system. Securing public confidence in the integrity of the electoral process demands a certain degree of state involvement and regulation. At the same time, this does not necessarily imply that all activities be subject to regulation, that on certain matters there are not alternative ways to ensure the integrity of the electoral system, or that existing processes are inadequate.

In some cases, public confidence in the integrity of the electoral process must be balanced by an equally legitimate public interest in democratic rights, which may preclude extensive, or indeed any, state regulation. Consequently, public confidence may be best enhanced through a combination of regulation in one area and no regulation in another. In seeking to advance this objective of strengthening public confidence in the integrity of the electoral process, it is necessary to adopt regulations or new procedures only where these are needed and only to the degree required to ensure objectives are met.

DISCLOSURE

The Need for Disclosure

Full disclosure of information on financial contributions and expenditures is an integral component of an electoral system that inspires public confidence. Essential to enhancing the integrity of the political system are the principles of transparency and public accountability. Full and timely disclosure requirements help remove suspicion about the financial activities of candidates and parties by opening the process to public scrutiny. As a spokesperson for the Fédération professionnelle des journalistes du Québec said during our hearings, "It is essential for the public to know what are the influences behind the parties that direct the destiny of the country." [tr] (Quebec, 30 April 1990)

Full disclosure is also essential to the enforcement of laws regulating political finance. Without full disclosure of candidates' and parties' campaign expenditures, spending limits could not be enforced effectively. Similarly, disclosure of expenditure information provides accountability for the public funds that parties and candidates receive directly through reimbursement of election expenses and indirectly through the tax credit for political contributions.

Disclosure of the size and source of contributions to parties and candidates decreases the likelihood that contributors of large amounts will try to exercise undue influence over elected officials, or that candidates and parties will accept contributions that might suggest undue influence. In effect, there is much validity to the assertion that "sunshine is the best medicine".

Current Disclosure Provisions

The principle of disclosure was first reflected in federal electoral law in 1874. The *Dominion Elections Act* of that year required a candidate's official agent to submit a statement of election expenses to the returning officer within two months after an election. Those who did not file could be fined $20 for every day of default. That Act was amended in 1908 by adding a requirement that the official agent also submit a "detailed statement of all contributions, payments, loans, advances, deposits or promises of money ... made to" the agent for election purposes. The 1920 *Dominion Elections Act* required that the agent also report the names of all persons from whom contributions were received. However, these statements did not have to be audited and no official was responsible for verifying them. It was thus not certain that they represented an accurate record of candidates' spending and contributions to their campaigns. Furthermore, no one had the duty of ensuring they were filed, although a Member of Parliament could not take his or her seat until the statement was submitted. On average, 48 per cent of non-elected candidates did not submit their statements following the six elections from 1962 to 1974 inclusive (adapted from Seidle 1980, 149).

The 1974 *Election Expenses Act* extended disclosure to registered parties and strengthened the reporting requirements then in effect for candidates. Registered political parties must submit an audited annual return of the party's receipts and expenses (other than election expenses) to the chief electoral officer within six months of the end of the year. The return must include the names of all individuals, businesses, trade unions and other organizations that contributed more than $100 to the party that year and the total amount of contributions from each source during the year. In addition, the report must include the amounts of money spent on the operating expenses of the party during the year.

After a general election, registered parties and candidates must file audited post-election returns. Parties' returns are due six months after the election and must detail the parties' election expenses during the writ period. This includes only spending that falls under the statutory definition of 'election expenses'; contributions and other expenses are reported in the parties' annual returns. Candidates' returns are due four months after the election and must include all candidates' election, personal and other campaign expenses, as well as the total amount of money and commercial value of goods and services contributed to candidates' campaigns. These returns must provide the source and amount of all contributions more than $100 in total received by candidates during the writ period.

Summaries of candidates' election and personal expenses are published in local newspapers after they have been received by the returning officer. The returning officer makes the full reports available for public inspection for six months after their receipt. After every general election, the chief electoral officer has published a summary of the parties' and candidates' returns (although this is not required by law). In addition, the chief electoral officer annually distributes a compilation of the registered parties' yearly returns, including the lists of the names of all contributors who gave more than $100 in the aggregate to each party and the amount of the contributions.

Disclosure is thus a cardinal principle of the present federal regulatory framework for party and election finance. This principle remains fundamental, but steps need to be taken to ensure that it is applied more effectively.

Broadening Disclosure

Currently, constituency party associations are virtually unrecognized by the *Canada Elections Act*. Section 232 of the Act requires a candidate of a registered party to transfer any surplus after an election "to any local organization or association of members of the party in the electoral district of the candidate or to the registered agent of the party"; all other candidates must transfer any surplus to the Receiver General. The expression "local organization or association" is not defined in the Act, however, and there is no disclosure of these funds once they have been transferred.[1]

Nonetheless, in other respects the financial activities of constituency party associations are linked to major elements of the current federal framework. First, the candidates' surplus that associations receive may reflect the benefit of public funding for candidates – either directly through the post-election reimbursement or indirectly through the political contribution tax credit. Second, constituency associations often finance campaigns for those seeking a nomination as candidate as well as the pre-writ activities of persons chosen as candidates. Transfers of funds from an association to the official agent of a candidate, once an election has been called, must be reported, along with the original source of any contribution exceeding $100.

However, it is often difficult, if not impossible, to conform to this latter requirement; full disclosure is thus not achieved. Third, the associations play a role in fund raising between elections. If the donor wishes a tax receipt, this is provided by the registered party, and the source and amount of any such contribution exceeding $100 must be disclosed in the registered party's annual return. If the donor does not wish a receipt, however, the contribution goes to the association without any public disclosure, even for contributions exceeding $100.

A survey of constituency association presidents (Carty 1991a RC) indicated that candidates' post-election surpluses are generally transferred to constituency associations: 67 per cent of respondents indicated the surplus went to the association's general accounts while 28 per cent reported that the surplus went to the association's trust account.[2] The same survey included the following question: "What is the value of the funds your association currently has available to it?" Sixteen per cent of respondents indicated the value was between $10 000 and $24 999, 8 per cent between $25 000 and $49 999, and 1 per cent more than $50 000. Hence, there is little doubt that some associations have accumulated substantial financial reserves.

Precisely because constituency associations are outside the ambit of the present legislation, it is not possible to have an accurate picture of the value of the funds they have at their disposal or of the associations' ongoing financial activities. This shortcoming in the current federal framework should be corrected. Leaving it as is will undermine public confidence in the elements of the regulatory system that have generally functioned well and have helped strengthen the integrity of electoral democracy in Canada.

Improving Disclosure of Financial Information

Given the limitations of the existing provisions for disclosure of financial information, a number of measures would enhance the utility and accessibility of the system. An effective disclosure system takes into account both the potential level of interest in the disclosed information and the way it is presented. To achieve openness, adequate information must not only be disclosed but also be arranged meaningfully and in a format that is accessible to potential users.

An important element of an effective disclosure system is timeliness in reporting. Currently, it is possible for a contribution to a political party to remain publicly unreported for up to 18 months; for example, a contribution made in January 1990 need not have been disclosed until early July 1991. There are two reasons for this lengthy delay: (1) the 12-month period covered by the report; and (2) the six months between the end of the reporting period and the latest date the party can submit a report to the chief electoral officer which, in effect, is the earliest date that all the parties' reports can be released to the public.

One way of reducing the time between the date a contribution is made and the date it becomes public knowledge is to decrease the length of the reporting period. A number of other jurisdictions require more frequent reporting. In the United States, parties and candidates must report twice during non-election years, four times during election years and even more frequently just before and after the election. In New Brunswick, registered parties and constituency associations must submit full financial reports every six months. The administrative and financial burden that frequent reporting could entail must also be considered, however. A reasonable balance should be struck between the need for a shorter reporting period and the burden being imposed on those reporting. This can be achieved by requiring more frequent reporting of contributions, while retaining the present requirement for a full audited return covering all financial activities during the year.

Recommendation 1.7.1

We recommend that registered parties and registered constituency associations file an unaudited report of contributions for the first six months of the year and a full audited return on their financial activities for the entire year.

As shown in figures 7.1 and 7.2, several Canadian provinces require that reports be submitted three or four months after the end of the reporting period. Candidates in Canadian federal elections are now required to file their post-election returns four months after the election. Considering the provincial experience and the extensive computerization that has occurred since the requirements were adopted in 1974, the maximum of six months between the end of the fiscal year or the end of an election campaign and the date when registered parties' returns must be reported is excessive. A three-month deadline is practical and, combined with the recommendation that contributions be reported twice a year, would provide considerably more timely disclosure.

As for reporting requirements for the nomination process, we propose that, in addition to the obligation under the party's rules that each nomination contestant submit a preliminary report on his or her spending and contributions no later than the day of the nomination meeting, each nomination contestant be required to file a final report with the Canada Elections Commission within a month of the nomination meeting. The source of contributions $250 or more in total would have to be identified. If the nomination takes place during the writ period, however, it may be burdensome to require that, in the heat of an election campaign, an officially nominated candidate be required to submit his or her nomination financial report within a month. The same holds true if the reporting deadline were to fall during the writ period. In such cases, the latter report could be filed concurrently with the candidate's post-election report.

Figure 7.1
Comparisons of time between election and when report submitted

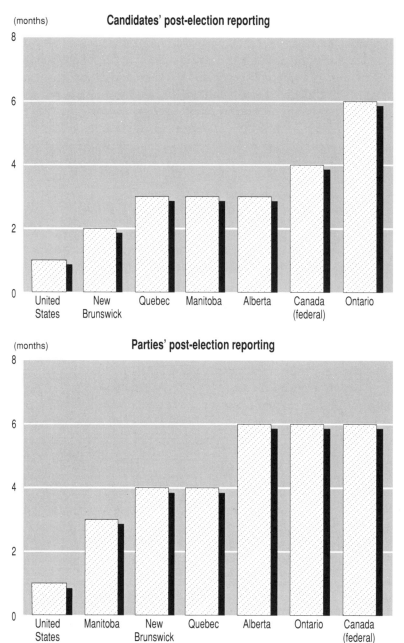

Source: Alberta *Election Finances and Contributions Disclosure Act* (1978); *Canada Elections Act* (1970); Manitoba *Elections Finances Act* (1985); New Brunswick *Political Process Financing Act* (1978); Ontario *Election Finances Act, 1986*; Quebec *Election Act* (1989); United States *Federal Election Campaign Act* (1971).

Figure 7.2
Comparisons of time between end of reporting period and when report submitted

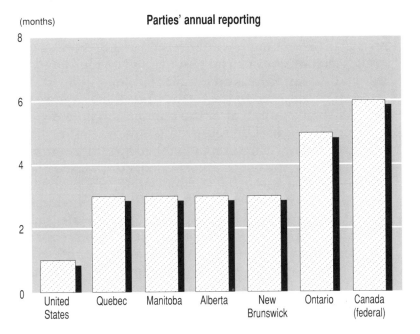

Source: Alberta *Election Finances and Contributions Disclosure Act* (1978); *Canada Elections Act* (1970); Manitoba *Elections Finances Act* (1985); New Brunswick *Political Process Financing Act* (1978); Ontario *Election Finances Act, 1986*; Quebec *Election Act* (1989); United States *Federal Election Campaign Act* (1971).

Figure 7.3
Comparisons of amount of information reported

Jurisdiction	Name	Amount	Address	Date	Employer	Occupation
Canada (federal)	X	X				
Alberta	X	X	X			
Manitoba	X	X	X			
Quebec	X	X	X			
New Brunswick	X	X	X	X		
Ontario	X	X	X	X		
United States	X	X	X	X	X	X

Source: Alberta, *Election Finances and Contributions Disclosure Act* (1978); *Canada Elections Act* (1970); Manitoba *Elections Finances Act* (1985); New Brunswick *Political Process Financing Act* (1978); Ontario *Election Finances Act, 1986*; Quebec *Election Act* (1989); United States *Federal Election Campaign Act* (1971).

Similar provisions should apply to leadership contestants. In addition to the requirement under the party's rules that each leadership contestant submit a preliminary financial report by the day before the vote to select the leader of a registered party, the contestants would be required to submit a final report to the Canada Elections Commission within three months of the leadership vote.

Recommendation 1.7.2

We recommend that

(a) no later than three months after the end of the reporting period or the election, all financial reports filed by registered political parties, candidates and registered constituency associations be submitted to the Canada Elections Commission;

(b) no later than a month after the nomination meeting, nomination contestants be required to submit to the Canada Elections Commission a report on their spending and contributions during the nomination period, except if the nomination takes place during the election period, or if the reporting deadline falls during the election period, in which case the candidate be required to submit the report no later than the date for submission of his or her post-election report; and

(c) no later than three months after the day of the vote to select the leader of a registered party, leadership contestants be required to submit to the Canada Elections Commission a final return on their spending and revenue.

For disclosure to be effective in ensuring openness and discouraging undue influence, sufficient information must be included to identify contributors, whether they are individuals, businesses, unions or other organizations. In cases of individual contributors with the same last name or corporations that give only their corporate registration number, it is impossible to identify the contributor with certainty. Clearly, a balance must be achieved between the public's right to know and the right to privacy. As shown in Figure 7.3, current Canadian federal rules require less information about contributions than many provinces or the United States.

The American *Federal Election Campaign Act* forbids the use of lists of contributors for soliciting contributions or for commercial purposes. To enforce this, 'dummy' (fictitious) entries may be included to help detect illegal use of the lists. If mail that contravenes this provision is received at a 'dummy' address, an investigation into the use of the lists can be launched. (Young 1991b RC) To prevent abuse, the *Canada Elections Act* should include similar rules.

Recommendation 1.7.3

We recommend that

(a) for contributions that must be reported:
(1) the contributor's full address (including street address, city/town/municipality, province and postal code) and the date of the contribution be required;

(2) numbered corporations be required to disclose one of the following: the name under which the corporation is registered provincially, the name that appears on the corporation's letterhead, or the names of the directors of the corporation as registered with Consumer and Corporate Affairs Canada; and

(3) registered parties, registered constituency associations, candidates, nomination contestants and leadership contestants be required to make their best effort to collect this information;

(b) use of disclosed information for non-election purposes be illegal; and

(c) to enforce this provision, 'dummy' entries on lists of contributors be permitted.

The current disclosure provisions of the *Canada Elections Act* require that parties report the source and the total amount of all contributions of more than $100 each year. This threshold has remained the same since 1974, even though a $100 contribution in 1974 would be worth about $300 in 1991 dollars. In two provinces, the threshold for reporting political contributions is higher than the federal requirement: $250 in Manitoba and $375 in Alberta. The federal law should be updated, while preserving the original purpose of the threshold: to strike a balance between confidentiality and the need for sufficient public knowledge to remove suspicion about political finance. Confidentiality has particular consequences for certain ideological parties, whose supporters might be dissuaded from making relatively small contributions if their name were to be disclosed. Raising the threshold for reporting at the federal level would not impair the public's knowledge of contributions that are large enough to be politically significant. The source of smaller donations would remain private.

Recommendation 1.7.4

We recommend that

(a) registered parties and registered constituency associations report all contributions from any one source totalling $250 or more in any year;

(b) candidates, nomination contestants and leadership contestants report all contributions from any one source totalling $250 or more in the reporting period; and

(c) the Canada Elections Commission review this threshold every five years and adjust it accordingly.

Accuracy is obviously an important element of an effective disclosure system. Although the *Canada Elections Act* now requires parties' and candidates' returns be audited, the auditors are not required to certify that the records have been kept according to generally accepted accounting practices. This means that auditors lack the mandate to perform a complete audit of the party's or candidate's financial affairs. We agree with the Canadian Institute of Chartered Accountants that financial statements should be prepared according to generally accepted accounting practices. (See, for example, the Canadian Institute of Chartered Accountants *Handbook* (CICA 1991).) This being said, it would be reasonable to have somewhat less stringent reporting requirements for candidates, associations, nomination contestants, leadership contestants and political parties with fairly little financial activity. Accordingly, we recommend in Volume 2, Chapter 6, and Volume 3 that, when the income and expenses of a candidate, registered constituency association, nomination contestant, leadership contestant or registered party are both less than $5000 during a reporting period, a short-form return may be filed.

To ensure full accountability, the requirement that parties' and candidates' returns be audited should be extended to returns submitted by registered constituency associations and leadership contestants. However, as we recommend in Volume 2, Chapter 6, the returns of registered parties, registered constituency associations, candidates and leadership contestants would not have to be audited if income and expenses during the reporting period were both less than $5000.

Recommendation 1.7.5

We recommend that as part of any returns they are required to file under the *Canada Elections Act*, registered political parties, registered constituency associations, candidates and leadership contestants submit financial statements prepared according to generally accepted accounting principles and audited according to generally accepted auditing standards.

For disclosure to be most effective, information must be presented in a format that makes it easily accessible, understandable and usable. Research on the experiences of the U.S. Federal Election Commission, the New York City Campaign Finance Board, the Canadian Lobbyist Registry and other such bodies suggests that if disclosed information on the financial activities of federal parties and candidates were available in formats that made it more accessible, such as on-line computer information systems and data bases, there would be greater interest in the information and more meaningful analysis would be available to Canadians. (Young 1991b RC) In its report, the Accounting Profession Working Group (Canada, Royal Commission 1991a, Part 5, 9) concluded: "The development of an electronic system to facilitate the reporting and filing of election finance information is entirely feasible and could take many forms." To assist this process, the Canada Elections Commission should develop procedures to computerize filing of ongoing and post-election financial reports.

Recommendation 1.7.6

We recommend that

(a) contribution information be available in computerized format and accessible in machine-readable form, and in its printed form be arranged alphabetically by category of contributor and by province; and

(b) the Canada Elections Commission implement procedures for computerized filing of financial returns.

Elections Canada documents are the primary source of information about political finance. Currently, there is no Elections Canada publication that summarizes disclosed financial information for the layperson. Moreover, existing documents would be more accessible to the public if they included contextual information about the regulation of political finance as well as the meaning and categorization of the information included.

Recommendation 1.7.7

We recommend that the Canada Elections Commission develop and publish, annually and after every general election, an analysis and summary of party and election finance information and include contextual information in publications to enhance their utility to users.

Contributions to Members of Parliament

During our work, some questions were raised about contributions to Members of Parliament between elections. At present, there is no legislation that requires a Member of Parliament to disclose his or her financial interests. However, the *Parliament of Canada Act* and the House of Commons *Standing Orders* contain provisions that relate to compensation received by Members of Parliament in relation to their duties.[3]

We were told that, on occasion, a constituency association may assume certain expenses incurred by a Member of Parliament. Under our recommendations for the registration of constituency associations and disclosure of their financial activities, such a payment from a constituency association to a Member of Parliament would have to be disclosed in the association's annual return; this information would be available for the public to review.

Disclosure of constituency association finances will not, however, cover direct contributions to Members of Parliament. Such contributions should, of course, be declared as taxable income. However, to the extent that our recommendations will broaden disclosure of the sources of party and election finance – including contributions to nomination and leadership contestants – it is inconsistent that Members of Parliament not declare publicly all contributions. In the interest of greater openness in the political process, we propose that Members of Parliament be required to abide by the same standards of disclosure that apply to registered parties and constituency associations.

Recommendation 1.7.8

We recommend that the *Parliament of Canada Act* be amended to require Members of Parliament to disclose any contribution received in a manner and format that conforms to the requirements in the *Canada Elections Act* for contributions to registered parties and registered constituency associations.

POLITICAL CONTRIBUTIONS AND UNDUE INFLUENCE

The Legitimacy of Political Contributions

Political parties require funds – often in significant amounts – to wage competitive election campaigns and to finance their activities as ongoing political organizations. Similarly, candidates must seek adequate funding for their campaigns. Parties and candidates usually rely on contributions from party members, supporters and others – for example, business and unions – who share their values and policy positions. As our research indicated (Michaud and Laferrière 1991 RC), contributors are most often motivated by a commitment to support the democratic process and the political activities that keep this process vibrant. Contributors, through their financial support, may help influence the course of public debate and public policy – but such influence is both indirect and legitimate.

On occasion, however, it is asserted that some contributions were made with an expectation that they would lead to direct material benefit for the donor or that they actually led to such benefit. In these cases, the donor can be said to be exerting undue influence, which Ian Greene has defined as "an attempt, whether actually realized or not, to influence a candidate or party in relation to the electoral process in a way which violates the principle that all citizens have a right to be treated as equals in the design and operation of the administrative and policy processes in government". (1991 RC) To the degree that contributors to parties and candidates are able to exert such undue influence, the integrity of the political and electoral processes is jeopardized. Moveover, if such a perception exists, public confidence will be undermined.

Fraudulent Contributions

In Canada, contributions made in the expectation that special privileges will result are illegal. Section 121 of the *Criminal Code* covers "frauds on the government" and applies in particular to persons who make election contributions with the intention of obtaining government contracts. Section 121(2) states:

> Every one commits an offence who, in order to obtain or retain a contract with the government, or as a term of any such contract, whether express or implied, directly or indirectly subscribes or gives, or agrees to subscribe or give, to any person any valuable consideration
>
> *(a)* for the purpose of promoting the election of a candidate or a class or party of candidates to Parliament or the legislature of a province; or
> *(b)* with intent to influence or affect in any way the result of an election conducted for the purpose of electing persons to serve in Parliament or the legislature of a province.

Section 121(1)*(e)* is broader and applies to "frauds on the government" resulting from illegal contributions or the equivalent made at any time. It stipulates that it is an offence to offer, give or agree to offer or give to "a minister of the government or an official a reward, advantage or benefit of any kind as consideration for cooperation, assistance, exercise of influence or an act or omission" relating to "the transaction of business with or any matter of business relating to the government". An offence against either section 121(2) or 121(1)*(e)* is indictable; in each case the offender is "liable to imprisonment for a term not exceeding five years".

In addition, under section 119 of the *Criminal Code*, which is concerned with bribery, anyone who "gives or offers, corruptly" to a Member of Parliament or of a provincial legislature "any money, valuable consideration, office, place or employment in respect of anything done or omitted or to be done or omitted by him in his official capacity for himself or another person" is guilty of an indictable offence. It is also an offence under section 119 to accept such a bribe: a Member of Parliament or of a provincial legislature commits an indictable offence if he or she "corruptly ... accepts or obtains" or even attempts to obtain "any money, valuable consideration, office, place or employment for himself or another person in respect of anything done or omitted or to be done or omitted by him in his official capacity". In either case, an offender could be imprisoned for up to 14 years.

Based on the 1963 *R. v. Bruneau* decision, it is a corrupt act for a Member of Parliament to accept such a bribe in connection not only with his or her legislative duties but also with his or her participation in an "administrative act of government". In *Bruneau*, the MP had accepted $10 000 from a constituent who wished to sell some land he owned to the federal government for a new post office; it was the practice to consult the local MP as to the best location. The MP was found guilty and given a suspended sentence and probation for two years. On appeal, a sentence of five years imprisonment was substituted. The decision included the following statement: "The responsibility of a member of Parliament to his constituency and to the nation requires a rigorous standard of honesty and behaviour, departure from which should not be tolerated." (*R. v. Bruneau* 1963, 269)

The significance of these sections of the *Criminal Code* has been summarized by Patrick Boyer (1983, 52):

> These provisions of the Criminal Code are widely cast, but the essential point is narrow and obvious: individuals, corporations and others need fear nothing if their contributions are motivated by a desire to support the political processes of the country, but they should be nervous if the motive is, baldly, to support their own interests. Political contributions should be invested with a spirit of altruism. When they originate with a corrupt intent, the Code is offended.

The intent of the *Criminal Code* in relation to political contributions is clear. Even so, the importance of fully respecting these provisions cannot be understated; nor can the importance of ensuring that all those active in political life are fully aware of the intent of the law and the consequences of deviating from it. For although the *Criminal Code* is one of Canada's most fundamental laws, many of those who enter politics are not fully aware of the details of the sections summarized above. Since the *Election Expenses Act* came into effect, political parties have distributed materials and held training sessions with candidates and official agents to explain the law and guidelines on the control and reporting of election expenses. This has helped bring about a common understanding of these matters among the key participants in election campaigns. Bearing in mind the importance of the *Criminal Code* provisions relating to fraudulent political contributions, parties should ensure executive officers, candidates, official agents and, indeed, all their members are fully informed about these provisions.

Recommendation 1.7.9

We recommend that

(a) **in training sessions and guides or manuals for candidates, agents and executive officers, political parties explain sections 119 and 121 (and successor sections) of the *Criminal Code* relating to bribery and fraudulent payments, as well as the relevant penalties for offenders; and**

(b) **sections 119 and 121 of the *Criminal Code* be included in the code of ethics of each political party.**

Contribution Limits

At the federal level in Canada, the regulation of party and election finance is based on spending limits for parties and candidates, augmented by public funding and disclosure. Spending limits are intended to ensure fairness in the electoral process. When paired with public funding, the result is a cap on the amount of money a party or candidate will need to raise from private contributions. For example, in the 1988 general election, candidates' election expenses were limited, on average, to $46 900; a candidate wanting to spend close to the limit and who expected to qualify for reimbursement thus had to secure some $23 000 from various sources. In addition, disclosure of the size and source of political contributions allows the public to decide whether any donation or class of donations might raise concerns of undue influence.

Regulatory systems based on contribution limits, on the other hand, are not primarily concerned with the amount of money spent, but with preventing undue influence by eliminating donations whose size and/or source might make them suspect. In the absence of spending limits, the dynamics of campaigns, particularly competitive ones, inescapably lead to rapid escalation in costs, creating pressure for additional funds. In such situations, the relation between donors and fundraisers may require close scrutiny, and such systems often must rely on disclosure procedures that are considerably more rigorous and timely than systems based on spending limits. For example, at the federal level in the United States, during the period from the twentieth day to 48 hours before an election, contributions of $1000 or more must be reported to the Federal Election Commission within 48 hours.

Given the concerns of some interveners who appeared before us, we examined the necessity and desirability of adopting limits on the size and/or source of contributions to political parties and candidates.

Size of Contributions

The argument for limiting the size of contributions is based on the view that contributors may gain undue influence by contributing to political parties and candidates an amount that is significant in absolute or relative terms. Consistent with this view, a Member of Parliament who raised $50 000 in seeking election would be more susceptible to undue influence if that money came from two sources giving $25 000 each, than if that money came from 50 donors giving $1000 each. Hence, limits on contributions ensure that donations are relatively small, thereby reducing the opportunity for undue influence by one or a few contributors.

A survey of the 1988 Canadian general election indicates that, as a rule, candidates' campaigns did not rely on large contributions: contributions of $1000 or more accounted for less than 20 per cent of the total revenue of candidates of the three largest parties. Such contributions represented 19.4 per cent of the total revenue of Progressive Conservative candidates, 18.4 per cent for New Democratic Party candidates, and 15.0 per cent for Liberal candidates (see Table 7.1). Of all contributions of $1000 or more, almost 60 per cent were exactly $1000 and nearly 80 per cent were less than $2000. Only eight contributions to candidates were greater than $10 000, the largest of which – $29 021 – was contributed by a candidate to his own campaign.

Table 7.1
Value of contributions of $1 000 or more to candidates, as a percentage of total revenue, 1988 federal election

Category of contributor	PC		Liberal		NDP	
	$	%	$	%	$	%
Individual	1 158 810 [3 928]	8.1	558 589 [1 894]	6.3	343 165 [1 163]	6.0
Business	1 779 959 [6 034]	13.3	943 630 [3 199]	8.7	59 176 [201]	1.0
Union	0 [0]	0.0	3 000 [10]	0.0	858 360 [2 910]	11.4
Total	2 938 770 [9 962]	19.4	1 505 219 [5 102]	15.0	1 260 701 [4 274]	18.4

Source: Padget 1991 RC.

Note: Numbers in brackets are the average value per candidate.

Some of the largest contributions to candidates were made by candidates' family members. (Padget 1991 RC)

Bearing in mind the need to run nation-wide campaigns and an ongoing organization, the definition of what constitutes a large contribution has to change when considering the funding of political parties. In 1988, contributions of $10 000 or more from corporations accounted for 26 per cent of total revenues for the Progressive Conservative Party and 22 per cent for the Liberal Party. (Stanbury 1991 RC) Only six corporations gave $100 000 or more in 1988, the largest being a contribution of $136 500 to the Progressive Conservative Party from Agra Industries Limited; the largest donation from a corporation to a political party thus represented about one-half of one per cent of the incumbent party's total revenue that year.

Large contributions from individuals are even less important as a share of total party revenue. In 1988, contributions of $2000 or more from individuals accounted for 11.3 per cent of the total value of contributions to the Progressive Conservative Party and 7.9 per cent of contributions to the Liberal Party; only 14 individuals contributed more than $10 000 to the three largest national parties that year. The largest contribution from an individual – $103 000 – was made to the New Democratic Party by Irene Dyck, and the largest donations to the Progressive Conservative and Liberal parties from individuals were $40 000 each.

The largest single contribution in 1988 was just over $1 million; it was made to the New Democratic Party by the Canadian Labour Congress. Contributions exceeding $10 000 from trade unions accounted for 11 per cent of total contributions to the New Democratic Party in 1988.

Even in an election year, then, donations of $10 000 or more have not accounted for more than a quarter of total party revenues. Largely because of reforms introduced in 1974 and subsequent developments in fund raising, smaller donations, particularly from individuals, represent a much greater share of private party funding. Thus, while some may have a perception to the contrary, there are few instances in Canadian candidate and party financing where a contribution's size relative to total revenue would reasonably give rise to suspicion that a donor may acquire undue influence.

Four Canadian provinces limit the size of contributions to parties and candidates. In two provinces, contribution limits were at the centre of the initial reform legislation. In its report, the Ontario Commission on the Legislature (Camp Commission) recommended contribution limits as a way of ending "the substantial dependence of our political parties upon the substantial contributions of a few". (Ontario Commission on the Legislature 1974, 31) Limits on the size of political contributions were adopted as part of the 1975 *Election Finances Act*; the legislation also included limits on advertising spending during elections by candidates, parties and constituency associations. In 1977, Alberta adopted legislation modelled on the Ontario Act, but without any form of spending limits. (Barrie 1991 RC)

In 1977, Quebec instituted limits on both the size and source of contributions. The maximum annual contribution from any one elector is $3000 for each political party (this is not increased in an election year, so any contributions to candidates count against that limit). Quebec had adopted spending limits in 1963, and these were retained when this reform was introduced in 1977. New Brunswick's 1978 *Political Process Financing Act* was modelled closely on Quebec's 1977 legislation. (Mellon 1991 RC) However, New Brunswick's legislation does not confine the right to make political contributions to electors; the maximum annual contribution from any one source was $9000 but in 1991 was changed to $6000 for each political party.

In both Ontario and Alberta, there are annual limits on contributions to parties and constituency associations in non-election years: in Ontario, $4000 to each registered party and $750 to any constituency association, with an aggregate of $3000 to constituency associations of each registered party; in Alberta, the corresponding limits are $15 000, $750 and $3750. In both provinces, increased contributions are allowed in election years: contributors may double their contributions to each registered party and may contribute additional amounts to candidates. In Ontario, the latter limit is $750 to any candidate, up to an aggregate of $3000 to the candidates of each registered party; in Alberta, contributors may also give $1500 to any candidate, with a maximum of $7500 to the candidates of each registered party. Ontario's regulatory regime was modified in 1986 by the adoption of comprehensive spending limits; Alberta continues to have no spending limits.

The regulation of political finance at the federal level in the United States relies strongly on limits on the size of contributions. There are differing limits on the amounts individuals may contribute to candidates, party committees and political action committees (see Table 7.2). A contribution from an individual to a single candidate, for example, is limited to $1000, although a contribution to a candidate may be made both for the primary and subsequently to his or her election campaign. But the U.S. regulatory system is much more complex than this suggests and sums above $1000 can be channelled in regulated and unregulated ways to assist a candidate.

For example, an individual may donate five times as much money – $5000 – to a political action committee (PAC) as to a candidate's committee, and the PAC in turn may donate up to $5000 to a given candidate (Table 7.2). Moreover, although individuals are limited to $25 000 per year in *total* contributions to candidates, candidate committees, national parties, PACs or other committees, PACs themselves are not subject to any such limit. Thus, while PACs may not contribute over $5000 to any one candidate, many are able to contribute to hundreds of candidates. As a result, PACs have come to provide an increasing share of candidate revenue – approximately 32 per cent of total contributions to Congressional candidates in the last two U.S. federal elections. Of the $150 million PACs provided to Congressional candidates in 1990, more than three-quarters went to incumbents. (Federal Election Commission 1991c)

We noted that many reform proposals in the United States to diminish reliance of Congressional candidates on the PACs often include provisions for increased public financing. Although Congressional campaigns (House and Senate) do not benefit from public funding, presidential campaigns do. Public funding accounted for approximately half the total spending by both Republican and Democratic presidential election campaigns in 1988. Payments from the Presidential Election Campaign Fund to candidates totalled $159.7 million in 1988. (Federal Election Commission 1990, 12) Each of the two major parties has been assigned $10.6 million in public funding for the 1992 presidential nominating conventions; each of the two major party nominees is to receive $53 million in public funds for the general election, and additional public funding will be provided through matching grants during the primaries (these amounts will be adjusted in early 1992 when the 1991 cost-of-living adjustment (COLA) becomes available). (Federal Election Commission 1991a) According to Herbert Alexander, "were that money not available, presidential candidates would likely be forced to do what congressional aspirants already are doing: pursue more PAC money". (1991 RC)

"Soft money" contributions, channelled through state and local party organizations, are not covered by federal limits on the size and source of funds or by reporting requirements. While soft money is not purported to be spent on federal election campaigns, it is spent on activities such as voter registration and 'get out the vote' drives, which can assist federal candidates. In 1988, soft money expenditures on behalf of the Bush and Dukakis campaigns were approximately $22 million and $23 million respectively, and there were nearly 400 contributions of $100 000 or more. (Alexander 1991 RC) According to a recent study by the American Centre for Responsive Politics (Goldstein 1991a), during the 1989–1990 Congressional election cycle, more than $25 million in soft money was collected by the Democratic and Republican national committees, including 40 contributions of $100 000 or more. During the first six months of 1991, the major Democratic and Republican national party committees collected $14.7 million in soft money. (Goldstein 1991b)

Table 7.2
U.S. federal contribution limits

Contributions from	To candidate[1]	To national party committee[2] per calendar year[3]	To any other committee per calendar year	Total contributions per calendar year
Individual	$1 000 per election[4]	$20 000	$5 000	$25 000[5]
Multicandidate committee[6]	$5 000 per election	$15 000	$5 000	No limit
Party committee	$1 000 or $5 000[7] per election	No limit	$5 000	No limit
Republican or Democratic senatorial campaign committee, or the national party committee, or a combination of both	$17 500 to Senate candidate per calendar year in which candidate seeks election	Not applicable	Not applicable	Not applicable
Any other committee or group[8]	$1 000 per election	$20 000	$5 000	No limit

Source: Reproduced from Federal Election Commission 1986.

[1]The candidate limit covers all contributions made by one donor to a *candidate committee* and to an *unauthorized single-candidate committee* supporting the same candidate. This means, for example, that if an individual contributes $500 to a candidate in connection with the primary election, that same contributor may give no more than $500 to an unauthorized single-candidate committee supporting the same candidate in the primary election.

[2]For purposes of this limit, each of the following is considered a national party committee: the party's national committee, its national House campaign committee and its national Senate campaign committee, provided they are not authorized by any candidate.

[3]Calendar year extends from January 1 through December 31.

[4]Each of the following elections is considered a separate election: primary election, general election, runoff election, special election and party caucus or convention which has authority to select the nominee.

[5]Individual contributions intended for specific candidate count against the donor's annual limit for the year in which the election is held. All other individual contributions count against the annual limit for the year in which the contribution is made.

[6]A multicandidate committee is any committee with more than 50 contributors which has been registered for at least 6 months and, with the exception of State party committees, has made contributions to 5 or more Federal candidates. [A political action committee (PAC)] may qualify as a multicandidate committee.

[7]Limit depends on whether party committee is a multicandidate committee.

[8]Other committees may include [a PAC] not qualified as a multicandidate committee; group includes an organization, partnership or group of persons.

The increased importance of soft money is linked to the dynamics of the U.S. political system. In the absence of comprehensive mandatory spending limits, it is difficult to prevent spending from escalating, particularly in highly competitive campaigns. U.S. candidates thus have a greater need for private contributions than their Canadian counterparts. This is reflected in the differences in campaign spending in the two countries. In the 1988 United States Senate elections, the spending of the five candidates who ran the most expensive campaigns averaged US$3.36 for each state resident 18 years of age or over.[4] In contrast, during the 1988 Canadian election, the election expenses of the five candidates who spent the greatest percentage of their spending limit averaged $0.95 per voter. The high cost of campaigns means U.S. Congressional candidates and their staff spend an inordinate amount of time and energy fund raising. Members of the U.S. Congress who participated in our Canada–United States Campaign Reform Symposium at the John F. Kennedy School of Government were explicit on this matter and concurred with the following assessment:

> Except for the exceptionally wealthy, raising political money has become a throbbing headache that drains vital time and energy from the job of governing. This chore leaves many members part-time legislators and full-time fund-raisers. (Smith 1988, 155)

The experience at the federal level in the United States during the past 15 years indicates that, despite extensive regulation, including ongoing disclosure, enforcement remains an onerous task. New channels for money have been found – some of them outside party and candidate organizations. This process has been fed by spending pressures, and in 1988 even the presidential election saw considerable 'soft money' spending outside the statutory spending limit.

Table 7.3
Estimated number of contributions to candidates exceeding provincial contribution limits, 1988 federal election

Maximum allowed*	PC		Liberal		NDP		Total	
$	N	%	N	%	N	%	N	%
1 500 (Ont.)	405	0.75	214	0.61	240	0.98	859	0.75
2 250 (Alta.)	207	0.38	115	0.33	139	0.57	461	0.40
3 000 (Que.)	87	0.16	51	0.14	95	0.39	233	0.20
9 000 (N.B.)	5	0.009	2	0.006	9	0.037	16	0.014
Total number of individual, business and union contributions	54 183	100	35 336	100	24 447	100	113 966	100

Source: These findings are derived from a data base of all contributions of $1 000 or more reported in the election expense returns of all 885 candidates of the Progressive Conservative, Liberal and New Democratic parties.

*Contribution limits at time of 1988 election. A candidate in an Ontario election may receive a maximum of $1 500 from one source: $750 directly from a contributor and $750 indirectly via the constituency association. The aggregate maximum during election years in Alberta is $2 250: $1 500 directly from a contributor and $750 indirectly via the constituency association. In Quebec and New Brunswick, contributors are limited to $3 000 per party and $9 000, respectively, in total contributions each year. In Quebec, only qualified voters may make political contributions; this limit on source was not considered in the above table.

In contrast, comprehensive spending limits, as in the Canadian case, help check the demand for political contributions. While parties and candidates may often have to work hard to finance their campaigns, no one may spend more than the limit; they know therefore that the need for fund raising will not spiral out of control as a result of spending pressures. Thus, while spending limits serve an important purpose in themselves, that of encouraging fairness in the electoral process, they also lessen the need to garner huge financial reserves and – in the heat of the campaign – to call on those whose motives might be questionable. Even so, a regulatory regime may combine spending and contribution limits, as in Quebec, Ontario and New Brunswick. It is important, however, to assess the potential impact and dynamics of such a step at the federal level.

Table 7.4
Estimated value of contributions to candidates affected by provincial contribution limits, 1988 federal election

Maximum allowed*	PC		Liberal		NDP		Total	
$	$	%	$	%	$	%	$	%
1 500 (Ont.)	577 735	5.4	319 884	5.0	484 922	13.4	1 382 541	6.7
2 250 (Alta.)	326 247	3.0	192 730	3.0	334 706	9.3	853 683	4.1
3 000 (Que.)	200 617	1.9	126 633	2.0	243 709	6.8	570 959	2.8
9 000 (N.B.)	41 485	0.4	21 021	0.3	25 364	0.7	87 870	0.4
Total value of individual, business and union contributions	10 778 580	100	6 355 141	100	3 609 986	100	20 743 707	100

Source: These findings are derived from a data base of all contributions of $1 000 or more reported in the election expense returns of all 885 candidates of the Progressive Conservative, Liberal and New Democratic parties.

Note: The amounts shown represent the value of federal contributions that exceeded each of the provincial limits. This is the amount of revenue that would have been lost had the indicated limits been imposed at the federal level.

*Contribution limits at time of 1988 election. A candidate in an Ontario election may receive a maximum of $1 500 from one source: $750 directly from a contributor and $750 indirectly via the constituency association. The aggregate maximum during election years in Alberta is $2 250: $1 500 directly from a contributor and $750 indirectly via the constituency association. In Quebec and New Brunswick, contributors are limited to $3 000 per party and $9 000, respectively, in total contributions each year. In Quebec, only qualified voters may make political contributions; this limit on source was not considered in the above table.

Based on 1988 data, our research estimates that the application of contribution limits at any of the levels that now apply in four provinces would have had a minimal impact on the financing of the campaigns of federal candidates. More than 99 per cent of all contributions to candidates of the three largest parties in 1988 were under the strictest provincial limit (Ontario) of $1500 (Table 7.3). Moreover, such limits would have only slightly diminished the financial base of most candidates because only a small fraction of the total value of contributions exceeded the provincial limits. NDP candidates together would have lost 13.4 per cent of their revenue from these sources if a contribution limit of $1500 had been in place, and candidates of the Progressive Conservative and Liberal parties would have lost an average of 5.4 and 5.0 per cent, respectively (Table 7.4). The higher limits imposed by Alberta, Quebec and New Brunswick would have had even less impact on contributions to candidates.

Table 7.5
Estimated number of contributions affected by provincial contribution limits, largest federal parties, 1988

Maximum allowed*	PC Party		Liberal Party		NDP		Total	
$	N	%	N	%	N	%	N	%
3 000 (Que.)	888	1.31	478	1.26	55	0.05	1 421	0.63
8 000 (Ont.)	336	0.50	207	0.54	21	0.02	564	0.25
9 000 (N.B.)	322	0.47	191	0.50	19	0.02	532	0.23
30 000 (Alta.)	53	0.08	28	0.07	5	0.00	86	0.04
Total number of individual, business and union contributions	67 926	100	37 888	100	120 669	100	226 483	100

Source: This table is derived from a data base of all contributions by individuals, business and trade unions of $2 000 or more to the Progressive Conservative, Liberal and New Democratic parties in 1988.

*Contribution limits at time of 1988 election. In Quebec, electors may contribute up to $3 000 a year to a political party. Contributions to a party in Ontario during any year are limited to $4 000, with an additional $4 000 permitted during a campaign period. In New Brunswick only individuals, corporations and trade unions may contribute up to $9 000 a year. During the campaign period in Alberta the contribution may not exceed $30 000 to each registered party less any amount contributed to the party in that calendar year. In Quebec, only qualified electors may make political contributions; this limit on source was not considered in the above table.

As for the financing of the largest federal parties in 1988, nearly 99 per cent of contributions to the Progressive Conservative and Liberal parties were under the most restrictive provincial limit (Quebec) of $3000; an even greater share of contributions to the NDP was under this limit (Table 7.5). (In Quebec, only qualified voters may make political contributions; this limit on source was not considered in the analysis reported here.) As a proportion of the total value of contributions, provincial limits would have had a much greater effect on party revenue than on candidate revenue. For example, Ontario's election-year limit of $8000 would have diminished each of the largest parties' total contributions by about 20 per cent (Table 7.6).

This research indicates that, unless the limit for contributions to political parties were set at a relatively high level (as in Alberta), a limit would significantly affect the financing of federal parties. As Volume 1, Chapter 5 notes, there are fluctuations in the ability of each of the larger parties to raise funds for competitive election campaigns and its ongoing operations. Although such fluctuations are bound to recur, as the parties' fortunes shift from time to time, we must be attentive to the potential impact of reforms – particularly if they would result in the parties devoting a smaller share of resources to non-election activities. In this context, our conclusion is that limits on the size of contributions to federal political parties would run counter to our objective of strengthening the parties as primary political organizations.

Table 7.6
Estimated value of contributions affected by limits on contributions to the three largest federal parties in 1988

Maximum allowed*	PC Party		Liberal Party		NDP		Total	
$	$	%	$	%	$	%	$	%
3 000 (Que.)	7 465 053	30.42	4 140 937	31.36	1 469 896	13.58	13 075 886	26.92
8 000 (Ont.)	4 660 917	18.99	2 656 579	20.12	1 309 315	12.09	8 626 811	17.76
9 000 (N.B.)	4 329 577	17.64	2 453 593	18.58	1 288 687	11.90	8 071 856	16.62
30 000 (Alta.)	1 274 272	5.19	741 003	5.61	1 104 055	10.20	3 119 330	6.42
Total value of individual, business and union contributions	24 542 036	100	13 203 007	100	10 825 286	100	48 563 279	100

Source: This table is derived from a data base of all contributions by individuals, business and trade unions of $2 000 or more to the Progressive Conservative, Liberal and New Democratic parties in 1988.

The amounts shown represent the value of federal contributions that exceeded each of the provincial limits. This is the amount of revenue that would have been lost had the indicated limits been imposed at the federal level.

*Contribution limits at time of 1988 election. In Quebec, electors may contribute up to $3 000 a year to a political party. Contributions to a party in Ontario during any year are limited to $4 000, with an additional $4 000 permitted during a campaign period. In New Brunswick, only individuals, corporations and trade unions may contribute up to $9 000 a year. During the campaign period in Alberta the contribution may not exceed $30 000 to each registered party less any amount contributed to the party in that calendar year. In Quebec, only qualified electors may make political contributions; this limit on source was not considered in the above table.

However, it might be argued, based on the data reported above, that a limit on the size of contributions to candidates would have little impact on the financing of campaigns but could serve as a form of insurance against attempts to exercise undue influence. A large contribution to a candidate represents a greater share of the latter's revenue than a large contribution to a national party, and a candidate thus might be seen as beholden to the donor. In addition, research on candidate financing in the 1988 election indicates that incumbent Members of Parliament, and ministers in particular, receive a greater number of larger contributions than do other candidates. (Padget 1991 RC) According to this argument, contribution limits would limit the degree to which any candidate would rely on, and perhaps be influenced by, larger donations.

Bearing in mind the parties' structures and sources of finance, it would be very difficult to ensure the intent of such a limit was fully respected unless a similar limit applied at the national party level. For example, political parties routinely fund the campaigns of at least some of their candidates.

Unless transfers from the national level were themselves subject to limit, grants to candidates would be derived at least in part from contributions to the party that were not subject to limit. In addition, large contributions intended for individual candidates could be 'sanitized' by being channelled through the party's coffers. In either case, the original source of candidates' funds would be obscured. In the case of the New Democratic Party, larger donations from the Canadian Labour Congress could be replaced by multiple smaller donations from local branches. The fact that the Canadian Labour Congress makes substantial contributions to the New Democratic Party is public and widely known. The standing of this party as a legitimate participant in our political and electoral process is not questioned by Canadians. Given this situation, it is difficult to understand what would be gained by outlawing such a contribution and forcing it to be subdivided among participating unions. If the public became convinced that the intent of limits on contributions to candidates' campaigns could not be realized, public confidence in the integrity of the electoral process would be weakened, not strengthened.

Our assessment of this issue must also be seen in relation to our recommendations for improved disclosure requirements, which are more timely and complete than those that exist in any province. We recommend that disclosure requirements be broadened to cover registered constituency associations, as well as nomination and leadership campaigns. We also propose that, twice a year, registered parties and constituency associations report on contributions, including the date each was received, and that their reports be filed within three months of the end of the reporting period. This would cut in half the maximum time between the date any contribution above the threshold is made and the date when information about it would be available. These reforms will mean greater transparency and allow the public to have a more complete and timely picture of the sources and pattern of political contributions in Canada.

In light of these recommendations, the problems in adopting limits on the size of contributions and the absence of any compelling evidence (as indicated in tables 7.3 to 7.6) that the number and value of large contributions to federal parties and candidates raise serious concerns about undue influence, we do not recommend introducing statutory limits on the size of political contributions at the federal level.

Recommendation 1.7.10

We recommend that the *Canada Elections Act* not impose limits on the size of contributions to registered political parties, registered constituency associations, candidates, nomination contestants and leadership contestants.

Contribution Sources

Laws governing who may make contributions to political parties and candidates reflect an understanding of who is considered to have a legitimate right to participate in the political process. During our public hearings, some interveners argued that only individuals should be allowed to make political contributions, on the basis that only they have the right to vote. Other interveners argued that business, unions and other organizations have a legitimate role to play in the public arena and therefore should not be prevented from making contributions.

Canada has a long history of collective action. Individuals combine their resources in an array of organizations to achieve goals they share. Among these organizations are business, labour unions and interest groups, all of which have a stake in the political future of the country. Many of these groups have traditionally participated in the political system by providing financial support to parties and candidates.

Their financial participation has sometimes been questioned, however. This was the case early this century: the 1906 and 1907 parliamentary sessions "were among the most scandal-ridden on record" (Canada, Committee on Election Expenses 1966, 18); in addition, Canadians felt the effects of the scandal in the United States concerning secret insurance company financing of the 1904 Republican presidential campaign. (Mutch 1991 RC) In 1908, Parliament passed legislation[5] banning contributions to political parties from corporations. In 1920, this was extended to contributions from any "unincorporated company or association and any incorporated company or association" – the purpose being to exclude union donations. However, in the absence of enforcement or disclosure requirements for parties, neither ban was effective. During the mid-1920s a number of Members of Parliament began a campaign against the provision and in 1930 it was repealed.

The Committee on Election Expenses (Barbeau Committee) considered the possibility of limits on the source of contributions and decided against recommending their adoption. The Committee suggested that public funding, including income tax deductions for political contributions, would lessen "reliance on special interests", and recommended strengthening disclosure requirements, which it considered "indispensable if the electorate is to have confidence in the democratic system". (Canada, Committee on Election Expenses 1966, 34–35)

Since the adoption of the 1974 reforms, individuals have come to play a significant role in the financing of federal political parties. During the 1985–88 election cycle, the Progressive Conservative Party received 47.7 per cent of its total contributions from individuals and 52.3 per cent from business; the corresponding proportions for the Liberal Party were 44.7 and 55.1 per cent respectively. During the same period, contributions to the New Democratic Party from individuals accounted for 74.7 per cent of total contributions, compared with 22.3 per cent from unions. This reflects the degree to which the 1974 *Election Expenses Act* has been successful in changing a system that was once largely funded by corporate and union interests to one that is based on significant financial support from individuals.

As for the participation of business, there has also been a change since adoption of the *Election Expenses Act*. The pattern of party financing prior to those reforms was summarized by K.Z. Paltiel (1977, 6): "The main sources of funds needed to finance the activities of the dominant Liberal and Conservative parties are the centralized corporate industrial and financial firms headquartered in Toronto and Montreal. These business givers may be counted in the hundreds rather than in the thousands, and are identified with the largest firms in the financial and industrial sectors of the country."

W.T. Stanbury has analysed the current pattern of contributions from leading corporations. (1991 RC) He found that, in 1988, contributions from the corporations in the *Financial Post 500* accounted for 14.2 and 18.9 per cent of contributions from business to the Progressive Conservative and Liberal parties, respectively; these contributions represented 7.6 and 8.9 per cent of the total contributions to the two parties. In addition, Revenue Canada data indicate that smaller businesses and corporations are considerably more likely to make a political contribution than are larger corporations; in 1988, 1.2 per cent of smaller businesses (those eligible for the small business income tax deduction) claimed a deduction for political contributions but only 0.3 per cent of larger corporations did so.

Despite the major changes in the sources of party funds since 1974, there are those who argue that only voters should be allowed to contribute financially to parties and candidates. One such advocate of limits on the source of contributions was François Gérin, Member of Parliament, who proposed limiting political contributions to voters:

> "Financement populaire" will reduce the risk of using political activity
> for personal ends and, in particular, will hand back political parties to
> those who are the ultimate source of power: their members and their elec-
> tors. [tr] (Brief, 1990, 3)

The Chairman of the Royal Bank of Canada, Allan Taylor, in a speech given on 26 February 1991, argued that corporate funding of political parties does not contribute to the continuing democratization of and popular participation in politics. While acknowledging that national political parties are "expensive to run", he suggested that limits on both the size and the source of contributions be considered.

As part of its system of *financement populaire*, Quebec limits the source of contributions. Legislation was introduced in 1977 by the Lévesque government, whereby only eligible electors may make political contributions. Some have questioned the degree to which the spirit of Quebec's legislation is fully respected. During our hearings, Raymond Garneau, a former member of the National Assembly and of the House of Commons, made the following observation:

> As for excluding those other than electors, it seems to me – and I have lived in this milieu for quite a while – it is much more a smokescreen than a restraint or true solution to the issue of morality that is so often raised. Everyone knows how easy it is for a political party or anyone else to evade that restriction. [tr] (Montreal, 10 April 1990)

The Chamber of Commerce of Metropolitan Montreal suggested that full disclosure would be preferable to a limit on the source of political contributions:

> We believe the most important element is the fullest possible disclosure of the sources of the funds of candidates and political parties. It is perhaps more important to ensure such transparency than to opt for a limitation on the sources of financing that could risk opening the door to contributions whose origin was obscured in various ways. [tr] (Montreal, 10 April 1990)

The United States, at the federal level, has had extensive experience in restricting the source of political contributions. In fact, the United States is the only democratic country that attempts, at the national level, to confine to individuals the right to make political contributions. Corporations have been prohibited from giving to candidates in the United States since 1907. Contributions from labour unions were banned temporarily in 1943, and the ban was made permanent in 1947.

While corporations and labour unions cannot contribute directly to candidate committees, as noted above many donate soft money to the parties, which can in turn benefit candidates through spending on their behalf in states where there is little regulation of campaign finance. According to Robert Mutch, an authority on campaign finance reform in the United States, soft money is: "Unlimited in amount, unrestricted as to source, and completely untouched by the Act that supposedly regulates federal campaign funding"; and in his view, "soft money is the most effective way yet to evade the FECA [Federal Election Campaign Act]". (1988, 191)

Moreover, the effectiveness of the ban on donations from corporations and unions has been called into question by the activities of political action committees (PACs). There are two principal kinds of PACs. Organizations, including corporations and labour unions, may establish a "connected" PAC, which the law refers to as a "separate segregated fund", and the sponsoring organization is permitted to use its own funds to establish and administer the PAC, and to cover solicitation costs. A corporate PAC may regularly seek voluntary contributions only from its executive and administrative personnel, and shareholders, as well as the families of any of these (together these groups constitute the 'restricted class' of a corporation). The restricted class of a labour organization includes its members, its executive and administrative personnel, and the families of both groups; a labour PAC may solicit this restricted class at any time. However, twice yearly a corporation and its PAC may solicit (in writing) contributions to the PAC from other employees, including members of a labour organization, and their families. Similarly, twice a year the PAC of a labour organization that represents members employed in a corporation may solicit the corporation's employees who are not members of the labour organization (including executive and administrative personnel), shareholders and the families of both groups. (Federal Election Commission 1986, 9–10)

In contrast, a "nonconnected" PAC, referred to as a "political committee" in the law, is not affiliated with any sponsoring organization, and must cover its fund raising and administrative costs from contributions. These groups, which are often focused on a single issue, are not limited to fund raising from a restricted class.

In the 1990 election cycle, PACs contributed a total of $149.9 million to Congressional candidates. Business PACs provided $56.6 million, or 38 per cent of all PAC money, compared with $33.6 million or 22 per cent for labour PACs. Many of these business and labour PACs each gave several million dollars in contributions to various candidates. Nonconnected PACs, which represent one-quarter of the more than 4000 PACs at present, contributed $14.7 million or 10 per cent of all PAC money. (Federal Election Commission 1991c)

While PACs are subject to ongoing disclosure of their finances, their role has been criticized. For some, contrary to the restrictions that remain in the law, PACs have legitimized the involvement of corporations and labour unions in the financing of candidates and parties. Other critics argue that the U.S. regime of contribution limits has not increased the participation of individual contributors but has instead led to greater reliance of Congressional candidates on PACs, particularly those tied to business or labour. According to Herbert Alexander (1991 RC), "PACs have served to increase the role of special interests in the political process".

In Canada, the suggestion to ban political contributions from all sources other than voters raises a number of questions. One of the most fundamental is the compatibility of such a ban with the *Canadian Charter of Rights and Freedoms*. During our hearings (Quebec, 30 April 1990), Patrice Garant of the Faculty of Law, Université Laval, indicated the courts have determined that the Charter right to freedom of expression does not apply only to individuals. Bearing in mind the test of proportionality the Supreme Court of Canada has set, he questioned whether a total ban on contributions from other sources would withstand a challenge under the Charter and suggested the government would have to prove that the objectives of such legislation could be achieved only by such a severe restriction. If the objective of limits on contributions is to eliminate undue influence, how can one contend that $3000 contributed by a qualified voter who is a professional engineer is devoid of any such influence whereas the same amount contributed by his or her firm would represent undue influence? This issue was also addressed by Howard McConnell of the Faculty of Law, University of Saskatchewan, who expressed the view that "corporations and associations are just an aggregate of individuals" and noted that the Supreme Court of Canada has determined "that combinations of individuals could do together whatever an individual could do singly". (Saskatoon, 17 April 1990)

Canadians tend to support the view that business, unions and groups have a legitimate claim to participate in the political process. In our attitudinal survey, 62 per cent of respondents said they thought corporations should have the right to give money to political parties. Support for unions having this right was at 49 per cent, while 62 per cent indicated they thought interest groups should be allowed to make political contributions. (Blais and Gidengil 1991 RC, Table 4.4) A number of witnesses who addressed this question during our hearings shared these views. According to Denise Falardeau, National Vice-President of the Progressive Conservative Party, "the small neighbourhood business also has the right to participate in the democratic process". [tr] (Chicoutimi, 1 May 1990)

In addition, some Canadians who belong to unions choose to participate in the activities of the New Democratic Party in that capacity, and this is reflected in the party's structure. For example, the NDP constitution provides 15 seats on the Federal Council to trade unions affiliated with the party. Delegate positions at leadership conventions are reserved for members representing affiliated unions; these delegates accounted for 18.4 per cent of those who attended the party's 1989 leadership convention. (Archer 1991a RC, Table 1.1) Since the NDP's link with unions is public knowledge and is reflected in the party's structure, it is not inconsistent that unions be allowed to provide financial support to the party.

A further question is whether contributions from individuals, by their nature, are less likely to be associated with undue influence than contributions from other sources. The implicit assumption behind the arguments in favour of limiting the source of contributions is that a larger donation from a businessperson or a professional in his or her personal capacity would not represent potential undue influence, but such a donation from his or her business or firm would. In the case of a small business or a professional firm, the distinction between the owner or partner and the business is a moot point, and an attempt to ban donations from the business or firm itself would not prevent the owner or partner from making political contributions. In either case, the interests in question – whatever their motives – would find expression within the political process. In Quebec, corporate executives and owners of businesses must give in their own name. Even so, they may be inclined to support their preferred party by making contributions at or near the limit. Indeed, in 1989, the year of the last provincial election, more than half of all contributions of $2000 or more to the Parti libéral du Québec were exactly $3000, and contributions of $3000 represented 19.3 per cent of the total value of contributions to the party.

Finally, a ban on political contributions from business and unions might well mean this money would be channelled elsewhere. In the United States, the funding of the political process has been radically altered by the rise of PACs. While the differences between the two countries must be kept in mind, there is a risk that if business and unions were excluded from making political contributions to parties and candidates, they would give greater financial support to interest groups and other organizations. Indeed in the context of the debate on the Canada-U.S. Free Trade Agreement, a number of corporations and unions made significant contributions (some as large as $250 000) to the umbrella organizations on either side. Moreover, some corporations were able to claim their contributions as business expenses and thus as a deduction from income tax. (Canada, Revenue Canada, Taxation 1989) In so doing, the corporation could well have gained a greater tax benefit than if it had made a similar contribution to a registered party or candidate, for which it could claim a tax credit not greater than $500. This may help explain the drop of $262 000 in the total value of tax credits claimed by corporations for 1988 compared with 1984 (see Table 5.21 in Chapter 5).

Canadian organizations with a stake in the political future of the country should not be prevented from supporting parties and candidates who share their policies and values, provided the public has full opportunity to be informed about these financial activities. Nor should an incentive be created to channel funds from these organizations to groups outside the party system.

We reiterate that our recommendations for strengthening disclosure requirements will lead to greater transparency in this area. Based on our assessment of experience in other jurisdictions, our commitment to strengthening parties as primary political organizations and our concern that legitimate contributions not be diverted from political parties, we do not recommend the introduction of statutory limits on Canadian sources of political contributions at the federal level.

Recommendation 1.7.11

We recommend that the *Canada Elections Act* not impose a ban on political contributions from business, trade unions or other organizations, except as noted in recommendation 1.7.12.

We emphasize that our recommendations on the limits and sources of contributions pertain to the advisability of imposing statutory limits. Individual parties, constituency associations, candidates, nomination contestants or leadership contestants may wish to impose restrictions on the size of contributions they will accept or their source, and, in our opinion, it is very much their right to do so. In fact, the credibility of such internal party policies would be strengthened by the implementation of our recommendations on political finance.

Contributions from Foreign Sources

At present, the *Canada Elections Act* does not ban contributions from foreign sources. There is no reason to believe that contributions from foreign sources now pose a problem in Canada. In fact, research has demonstrated that foreign-owned corporations are less likely than Canadian-owned corporations to make political contributions to federal parties in Canada, and that contributions from foreign-owned corporations tend to be smaller than contributions from domestic corporations. (Wearing and Wearing 1990)

However, the challenges Canada faces will increasingly have an international dimension. Issues such as international competitiveness, national sovereignty and the global environment will assume higher priority on the national agenda. The time has come, therefore, to consider whether individuals, corporations and unions who do not belong to the Canadian polity should be allowed to participate in our electoral process through contributions to parties and candidates.

Contributions from foreign sources are banned in many jurisdictions. U.S. electoral law prohibits contributions from "foreign nationals", which includes non-citizens, unless they have permanent residence in the United States, as well as foreign governments, foreign political parties and businesses organized under the laws of or having their principal place of business in a foreign country. Foreign nationals may not establish a political action committee. In France, contributions to legislative candidates from foreign legal entities and foreign states are not allowed. German electoral law forbids any contributions exceeding DM1000 (about $800 Canadian) from foreign sources.

Four Canadian provinces have restrictions on contributions from outside the province. In Quebec, only eligible voters may make contributions, thereby precluding contributions from outside the province, except from those eligible electors living outside Quebec. The Ontario *Election Finances Act, 1986* states that parties and candidates must not "knowingly accept contributions from any person normally resident outside Ontario, from any corporation that does not carry on business in Ontario or from a trade union" that does not hold bargaining rights for employees in Ontario. Similarly, in Alberta, corporate or union contributions from outside the province are prohibited. In New Brunswick, only unions with bargaining rights in the province and corporations that carry on business in the province may donate.

We believe that participation in Canadian elections should be restricted to people and organizations that have a legitimate interest and stake in the future of the country.

Recommendation 1.7.12

We recommend that

(a) political contributions from foreign sources be banned and that foreign sources be defined as:

    (1) any individual who is not a Canadian citizen, permanent resident or landed immigrant;

    (2) any corporation that is foreign controlled, and that a corporation be considered foreign controlled if a majority of its voting shares are held by residents of foreign countries or by corporations that are foreign controlled;

    (3) any trade union that does not hold bargaining rights for employees in Canada; and

    (4) any foreign political party or government;

(b) the law provide that recipients of a contribution must show due diligence in seeking to ensure that a contribution is not from a foreign source; and

(c) if it is determined that a contribution was from a foreign source, the recipient be required to return it; if this is not possible, the contribution be remitted to the Receiver General for Canada.

Income Tax Check-offs

As a result of the reforms introduced in 1974 and changes in the parties' fund-raising methods, contributions from individuals now represent a significant share of their revenue (see tables 5.12 to 5.14). Even so, only a small proportion of Canadians – not more than 2 per cent – make political contributions, and steps should be taken to broaden individual participation in the financing of federal political parties. This could be achieved through an income tax check-off or surcharge. The federal government and some state governments in the United States have used this approach in the past 15 years. An income tax check-off allows taxpayers to assign a small payment from government funds to a party (or candidate) of their choice or to a common fund that is then divided among the parties; this does not increase the amount of taxes owing. With a surcharge, taxpayers indicate that they wish to add a set amount to the total taxes owing; where the revenue from the surcharge is not automatically transferred to a common fund, taxpayers can also indicate which party is to receive the designated amount.

The tax check-off at the federal level in the United States allows each taxpayer to designate $1 of general treasury funds to the Presidential Election Campaign Fund (those filing joint returns may designate $2). Payments from the fund are authorized by the Federal Election Commission and have been used since 1976 to subsidize presidential primary and general election candidates, as well as the parties' nominating conventions. The participation rate (percentage of tax returns indicating $1 or $2 designations) has varied from a high of 28.7 per cent in 1981 to a low of 19.8 per cent in 1989. (Federal Election Commission 1991b) Table 7.7 reports participation rates for various income tax check-off and surcharge programs at the state level. The rates for check-offs have reached 35–40 per cent (in New Jersey and Hawaii, for example), but no state with a surcharge has reported a participation rate higher than 2 per cent (see also Nassmacher 1991).

Table 7.7
Tax check-offs and surcharges in selected U.S. states, approximate participation rates
(per cent)

State	Surcharge	Check-off
Alabama	1–2	—
Arizona	0.50	—
California	0.20	—
Hawaii	—	35–45
Idaho	—	20
Kentucky	—	8.4
Maine	1	—
Massachusetts	1.9	—
Michigan	—	13.1
Minnesota	—	15–17
Montana	1–2	—
New Jersey	—	35–40
North Carolina	0.30	12.5

Source: Royal Commission Research Branch staff collected this information through telephone conversations in May 1991 with representatives of the various agencies responsible for collecting state taxes. The data are approximate because few states maintain detailed breakdowns of the amounts involved. An exception to this is Massachusetts, which publishes a Report on the Limited Public Financing System for Statewide Campaigns in Massachusetts. In addition, some states do not keep separate records of those who use these provisions through joint returns (in most states either one or both spouses may use the funding provisions).

Table 7.8
Projected cost of Canadian income tax check-off
(dollars)

Participation rate[a] %	$1 check-off	$2 check-off	$5 check-off
20	3 307 612	6 615 224	16 538 060
30	4 961 418	9 922 836	24 807 090

Source: Royal Commission Research Branch.
[a]Based on number of Canadian taxpayers for 1988.

Table 7.8 shows the projected total revenue for a Canadian check-off of $1, $2 or $5 at participation rates of 20 per cent and 30 per cent (which approximate the lowest and highest rates for participation in the check-off at the federal level in the United States). With a 20 per cent participation rate, a $2 check-off would cost the treasury $6.6 million annually. If this amount had been divided among the parties represented in Parliament after the 1988 election in proportion to their share of the popular vote, they would have received the following amounts each year: Progressive Conservative Party, $2 976 851; Liberal Party, $2 183 024; and New Democratic Party, $1 455 349.

An alternative would be to follow the U.S. surcharge principle by instituting a voluntary political check-off: taxpayers would have the option of adding a set amount to their income tax payable as a political contribution to a registered party.

In Table 7.9, estimates are provided for such a voluntary check-off based on levels of $1, $2 and $5 and participation rates of 2 and 5 per cent. With a 2 per cent participation rate, a $2 voluntary check-off would provide $1.65 million in annual revenue. If this amount had been divided among the parties represented in Parliament after the 1988 election in proportion to their share of the popular vote, they would have received the following amounts each year: Progressive Conservative Party, $744 212; Liberal Party, $545 756; and New Democratic Party, $363 837.

The revenue from the check-off could be transferred to a single fund and then allocated to the parties according to a statutory formula or the recommendation of the Canada Elections Commission. The former procedure might not be flexible enough to accommodate newly registered parties, particularly if the formula were tied to past election results, while the latter could be criticized for leaving the decision to the Commission's discretion. A preferable option would be to have the names of the registered political parties printed on income tax returns so taxpayers could indicate which party was to receive the specified amount. This would allow any newly registered party to be added to the list on the tax return for the subsequent year.

Table 7.9
Projected revenue from a Canadian voluntary political check-off
(dollars)

Participation rate[a] %	$1 check-off	$2 check-off	$5 check-off
2	330 761	1 653 806	3 307 612
5	826 903	4 134 515	8 269 030

Source: Royal Commission Research Branch.

[a]Based on number of Canadian taxpayers for 1988.

Such a check-off would place no additional burden on the treasury, apart from some administrative costs. With a voluntary political check-off, more Canadians might be encouraged to make a small financial contribution to the political process. While the individual amounts would be small, if 5 per cent of taxpayers participated, the proportion of Canadians making a political contribution of some form would more than double and the additional revenue to the parties would not be insignificant.

An alternative measure to increase the participation of Canadians in financially supporting political parties would be to allow taxpayers to make a political contribution to a registered political party by way of their federal income tax return and to receive the tax credit for the tax year in question. Political parties would have an incentive to contact potential supporters and to inform them of the benefits of the tax credit at the time of year when tax-payers are most likely to be influenced by this information.

We propose that this provision be limited to individual taxpayers and to contributions up to and including $100. Although the degree to which this measure would be used by taxpayers and thus the cost to the federal treasury in tax revenue foregone are difficult to predict, it is reasonable to conclude that it would increase political contributions without significantly increasing the cost to the federal government. Given the Canadian experience with the tax credit for political contributions, this option has the advantage of build-ing on the existing system and encouraging larger contributions than a vol-untary political check-off would provide. The credit claimed for such con-tributions would of course count against the $550 maximum that will continue to apply to tax credits claimed for political contributions in that year, if any.

Contributions made in this way would be transferred to each registered party by the Receiver General. These contributions would be anonymous. Thus, no question of undue influence could arise. The principle of disclo-sure, therefore, would not be undermined by the requirement of confiden-tiality under the *Income Tax Act*.

Recommendation 1.7.13

We recommend that

(a) individual taxpayers be allowed to make a political contri-bution not exceeding $100 to a registered political party when filing their federal income tax returns and to claim the tax credit for that fiscal year; and

(b) the Receiver General forward to each registered political party an amount equal to the political contributions made under this procedure without revealing the names of the individual contributors.

PUBLICATION OF OPINION POLLS DURING ELECTION CAMPAIGNS

Introduction

Because they are presented as 'scientific', published opinion polls raise issues of public confidence in the integrity of the electoral process. Notwith-standing their claims to scientific validity and accuracy in representing the views of all potential voters, opinion polls are susceptible to many forms of error and misrepresentation. The apparent precision of the data they report fails to reflect the fact that they are estimates of the distribution of opinion at a given time. Yet their apparent authority gives them considerable influence over the conduct of campaigns and the choices made by voters.

As our public hearings demonstrated, the publication of opinion polls during election campaigns is controversial.[6] The proponents of regulation

presented three main arguments: that opinion polls, because of their authoritative presentation, have undue influence on election campaigns; that they
can be erroneous or misleading and, indeed, subject to deliberate manipulation; and that they are often presented without proper qualifications and
with insufficient technical information to permit an assessment of their
credibility. The defenders of published campaign polls argued that there is
no evidence of significant influence, that polls are reasonably reliable within
their technical limits, and that they are simply a more systematic form of
opinion-gathering than methods traditionally used by journalists.

Our research demonstrates that polls do have measurable effects on
the conduct of election campaigns and the choices voters make, that there
remain technical and ethical problems in the reporting of polls, despite the
standards of the major polling firms, and that the influence of the scientific polls is distinct from that of other forms of reporting public opinion.

Polls provide useful information to voters, information that is more
reliable than other estimates of public opinion. As sources of information
about the voting preferences and issues that concern other citizens, they
are a great improvement over the guesses of journalists and pundits. Because
Canadians use the information contained in published polls to make their
voting decisions, there is no justification for limiting or impeding their
access to this relevant information. The 1988 Canadian Election Study found
that "polls penetrated deeply into the electorate"; between 70 and 80 per
cent of decided voters reported being aware of poll results. (Johnston et al.
1991, 7–11 and Figure 7–5)[7]

The proliferation of polls, especially if they are published with appropriate technical explanations, has two positive consequences. First, given
their very nature, the only correct method to ascertain whether the results
are accurate is to compare them with other polls taken during the same
period. Hence, the publication of many polls is the best guarantee voters
will ever have that the information published is a true reflection of current
opinions.[8] Second, Canadians will realize that all polls are not equal. A
prohibition on publication would prevent people from learning how to
separate the good from the bad and hence leave them more susceptible to
manipulation over time. There is, therefore, no good reason to prohibit the
publication of polls during election campaigns.

There are, however, good reasons to oblige news organizations that
publish opinion polls during election campaigns to meet certain requirements in order to ensure high standards in the preparation and reporting
of such a powerful information source. To promote high standards and prevent perceptions of undue influence, we suggest a blackout period at the
end of the campaign, timely disclosure and accessibility of methodological
information, and the development of a professional organization of public
opinion pollsters in Canada that has a code of ethics.

Although many estimates of public opinion are described as opinion polls,
most do not qualify in the strict sense of the term. Unrepresentative phone-in

surveys or mail-in questionnaires, haphazard street interviews, or "hamburger polls" obviously do not meet the standards required of a public opinion poll. Their characteristics usually make it easy, however, for voters to assess their credibility. Opinion polls that claim scientific validity must be based on the responses of a representative sample of a defined population. We define an "opinion poll" here as a survey of the public based on a scientific random sample that purports to be representative of a defined population, such as all Canadian residents, eligible voters or voters in a defined region or constituency.

The Effects of Published Opinion Polls

Although the industry in general has become highly professional since public polling was introduced in Canada in 1941, the incidence of technically deficient and poorly reported polls is still substantial. In recent elections, there have been instances of misleading polls, some because of technical errors and others because of partisan misrepresentation. There have even been allegations of fraudulent polls, where the data were said to have been fabricated to counter a poll showing the opposition in the lead. Such "bogus" polls and the more common misrepresented poll have been released to the media in many democracies. (Cantril 1991, 67; Worcester 1991, 199; Hoy 1989, 189–202) It is the willingness of the media to report such polls that makes them significant and troublesome.

An example of an allegedly "phantom" poll was released in Newfoundland four days before the 1989 provincial election. Contrary to two other polls released earlier in the campaign showing the Conservatives with a 6- to 11-point lead, this "poll" indicated that the Liberals had a 3.5-point edge. The poll received front page newspaper coverage, even though the news release about the poll lacked virtually all methodological information and cited unspecified "external data" provided by an unnamed "major national polling organization". (Liberal Party of Newfoundland and Labrador 1989) Given that on election day there was a mere 1 per cent difference in the popular vote between the two parties, the effect of the publication of this poll arguably helped determine the election results. In a subsequently published book, Liberal Party workers are said to have admitted that the poll was fabricated. (Hoy 1989, 202) Phantom polls are detrimental to the integrity of the electoral process and have prompted us to recommend a regulatory framework designed to create deterrents to their publication.

Notwithstanding the frequent assertion of pollsters that their data have minimal influence on voters, recent research provides strong support for the proposition that published opinion polls can significantly influence campaigns and voters. Michael W. Traugott surveyed research in the United States and concluded that, despite the methodological difficulties involved, there is a wide range of documented effects on the public. (1991, 45–46) He cited several studies that demonstrate real but limited effects on voter choice (enough to swing a close election). Albert H. Cantril, in a study for the National Council on Public Polling (NCPP) in the United States, reached a similar conclusion: "Although their impact should not be overestimated, bandwagon effects can no longer be dismissed as unproven." (1991, 216) Traugott (1991) also noted that polls published late in the campaign have the most influence on voting and can depress turnout.

The bandwagon effect refers to the tendency of some voters to back the likely winner, reinforcing the frontrunner's initial advantage. Using a daily tracking survey during the 1988 federal campaign, Richard Johnston and his colleagues found evidence that poll results produced a modest bandwagon effect.[9] (1991, 8:1–4) In a series of quasi-experiments, Edouard Cloutier and his colleagues found clear statistical evidence of a bandwagon effect. (Cloutier et al. 1989)

Recent Canadian research supports the conclusion that published campaign opinion polls create the conditions for a "politics of expectations" that includes both strategic voting and bandwagon effects. (Johnston et al. 1991, 8:8–11; Blais et al. 1990) For individual voters, strategic voting involves considering the prospects of winning when making the voting choice. In making a strategic choice, a voter might cast her or his ballot for a second-choice candidate, either because the preferred candidate was thought not to have a realistic chance to win or because the second-choice candidate might have a better chance to defeat a disliked candidate. Strategic voting is increasing in Canada, as three-party races become more common and poll results more readily available.[10] Voters have every right to expect that the poll results are scientifically valid when they make such choices.

In election campaigns, the indirect effects may be as important as the direct influence on voters. The influence of polls on campaign news coverage is clear. The increase in actual reports on poll results is outstripped by their use to frame coverage of the campaign itself. Party strategists complain that it is difficult to make up ground in a campaign once the media have decided, on the basis of the polls, that a particular party is no longer a viable contender. The polls can sometimes be misleading if there is a lag between the final interviews and the publication of the results, as there often is. (Fletcher 1988, 1990; Traugott 1991) In the United States, Ken Bode of "NBC News" observed that virtually every major election story on the network news in 1988 was influenced by poll results. (Cantril 1991, 4) In Canada, the proportion of television news reports that mentioned polls increased from 16 per cent of all election items in 1980 to 30 per cent in 1988. (Fletcher 1990, 4) In short, the argument that published polls do not influence voter choice or affect the conduct of campaigns is simply untenable.

Reporting of Polls

In addition to problems of misleading or incomplete reporting, many media reports of poll results omit technical information that professionals and academic experts could use to assess their credibility and, hence, alert the public to any serious deficiency.[11] Guy Lachapelle found that although technical information was often missing from news reports on the 22 national polls published during the 1988 campaign, reports of the 37 local and regional polls he examined were even more likely to be deficient in this respect. (1991 RC) It is the latter polls that are likely to increase in number most rapidly in future elections.[12]

Established pollsters such as Burns W. Roper and Robert Worcester worry that the usual emphasis in poll reports on margin of error misleads the public. As Roper put it: "The media have overstressed sampling error and understressed the most important and considerably greater sources of error" (quoted in Cantril 1991, 120). Most media reports state that the poll is "accurate within ±3 per cent, 19 times out of 20". This formula gives the impression that sampling is the primary, if not the only, source of error. Such reporting not only understates the difficulty of achieving a good sample but also underestimates the importance of other sources of error, such as question wording, question order, level of public information, non-response rate and fluidity of opinion.[13]

In Canada, although a number of bills have been introduced to ban or regulate the publication of opinion polls during provincial elections, only British Columbia has had a ban. In 1939, a provision was added to the *Elections Act* (s. 103) banning the taking of "any straw vote" after the issuance of the writ for an election. This provision, which effectively banned polling of all kinds, was repealed without fanfare in 1982. (Lachapelle 1991 RC)

The Comité des sondages of the Regroupement québécois des sciences sociales mounted a campaign for regulation in Quebec in 1977. The group, made up of academics specializing in opinion surveys, was concerned about the possibility that misleading polls would be published during the expected referendum on sovereignty association. They formulated guidelines for public opinion polling and recommended several key regulations. (Comité des sondages 1977) Among the most important was a recommendation that the broadcasting or publication of any poll be accompanied by methodological information that would allow the public to judge its quality and reliability; that technical information about published polls be accessible on request; and that a polling commission be established with a mandate to verify the reliability and validity of polls published or broadcast during election periods. The efforts did not lead to legislation but the academics involved continue from time to time to comment on the methodological soundness of published polls. (Lachapelle 1991 RC)

Comparative Experience

The concerns outlined here are not unique to Canada. Recent studies of polling in the United States (Cantril 1991) and Great Britain (Worcester 1991) have expressed concern about published opinion polls and called for measures of self-regulation and disclosure. Among the 20 countries examined in our research, three ban publication of opinion polls during campaigns and a number of others have blackout periods, ranging from the final 48 hours before the vote to as long as 90 days. Only France has a full-scale regulatory agency, a commission that receives and investigates complaints, requires polling organizations to register and deposit technical information, and enforces a seven-day blackout. Despite this commission, media reporting of polls remains a source of controversy in France. (Lachapelle 1991 RC)

In Great Britain, the polling industry has responded to concerns about polling raised in Parliament and elsewhere by embarking on an ambitious plan to improve the level of professional conduct among pollsters and the media. In 1987, the major pollsters reconfirmed their adherence to the guidelines of the World Association of Public Opinion Research and committed themselves to making public their methodology and publishing a guide for journalists. (Lachapelle 1991 RC) Nevertheless, according to Robert Worcester, technically deficient polls are still published and journalists still frequently misrepresent poll results. (1991, 181–93)

In the United States, the National Council of Public Polls and the American Association of Public Opinion Research (AAPOR) have long-established codes and are considering mechanisms for adjudicating complaints. AAPOR was founded in 1947 in the belief that the marketplace was inadequate to protect the public interest with respect to opinion polls. In Cantril's view, competition and the need for credibility are important incentives for high standards among pollsters but the issues are too complex: "Left to its own devices, the market alone will not sustain attention in the research community and among consumers of research to issues of reliability, validity and responsible reporting." (Cantril 1991, 175) The technical nature of opinion polling makes it too difficult for citizens to make such an assessment. Growth in the number of published opinion polls diminishes the influence of any single poll and promotes professional standards. The best way to check the reliability of a poll is to compare it with others (at least until the election results come in). Competition is a necessary but not sufficient condition for high professional standards.

Some jurisdictions now require that methodological information be disclosed even for private polls once their data enter the public domain. Like those in France, poll results in Belgium and New York state, with specified technical information, must be deposited with a designated agency. The New York regulations require that the methodology of private polls be made public if their results become public. (Lachapelle 1991 RC)

Blackout Provisions

A strong case can be made for prohibiting the publication of polls during the blackout period just before voting day. This is done in many countries and some news organizations voluntarily adhere to a blackout.[14] Such a prohibition reduces the impact of a last-minute poll, to which parties and candidates often cannot respond. Perhaps more important, it combines with the advertising blackout that has been in place since 1936 to provide voters with a period for reflection at the end of the campaign to assess the parties and candidates. Such a prohibition was supported by a number of pollsters and others at the public hearings.

Exit Polls

A blackout provision would also effectively prohibit the publication of the preliminary results of exit polls, a prohibition that received general support at our public hearings, workshops and seminars. Exit polls are surveys taken by asking voters as they leave the polling place how they voted. Polls of this kind provide useful information for journalists and scholars – and for voters themselves – because, if properly conducted, they provide a good basis for assessing the reasons for the election result. With their decisions fresh in their minds, respondents to exit polls are able to provide a good account of the reasons for their voting choice.

There are, however, two primary reasons for prohibiting the publication of exit polls until after the close of voting. In addition to the legitimate concern that the publication of predicted outcomes before the polls close may have bandwagon or depressed turnout effects, the use of such polls before the end of the voting period does not meet the minimum standards of a scientific survey: the sample of the voters cannot be representative. Certain segments of the population tend to vote at specific times; if exit polls do not sample voters throughout the voting period, poll results cannot be representative.

Recommendation 1.7.14

We recommend that the publication or announcement of opinion polls be prohibited from midnight the day preceding election day until the close of all polls on election day.

Disclosure of Technical Information

The central purpose of disclosure requirements is to ensure that the methodological information needed to provide an informed critique of an opinion poll is readily available. Systematic disclosure would provide voters with some measure of the credibility of published opinion polls and would increase the number of voters able to make such assessments. The major benefit of disclosure, however, is that it would contribute to informed debate about poll results and methods. Errors in polls are usually not obvious. With disclosure, those with a stake in the results, as well as other experts, could assess and challenge the validity of survey results. Their assessments and ensuing debate would filter back into the media and thus contribute to a better informed and more aware electorate.[15]

Disclosure in Published Reports

Because methodological information is of interest to a small proportion of citizens, the National Council on Public Polling in the United States has suggested that only a basic minimum of information be provided in news reports themselves. (Cantril 1991, 169) Pollsters believe that such information should be presented not only in primary reports, when a news organization is reporting on its own poll, but also in secondary reports on private polls or polls first published elsewhere. Many pollsters and some journalists argue that ethical journalism requires that a certain minimum of basic information be provided. As Benjamin Bradlee of *The Washington Post* put it: "Just as you attribute to the maximum extent possible in a news story, you should explain the technicalities of your poll. If you are asking people to believe you, you should be able to show them why you should be believed" (quoted in Cantril 1991, 165). If accuracy is a major concern, and it has pride of place in most codes of journalistic ethics, then appropriate reporting of poll results should be considered a high priority. A news story on a poll can only be as accurate as the poll itself.

Figure 7.4
Technical information reported with published opinion polls: *The Globe and Mail*

Question: Now thinking a moment only about the four major parties – the New Democrats, the Liberals, the Progressive Conservatives and the Reform Party – are there any of these parties that you would definitely not vote for?

	July '90	Oct. '90	April '91
Liberal	16	22	20
Progressive Conservative	40	47	37
New Democratic Party	28	20	26
Reform Party	N/A	N/A	17
Bloc québécois	N/A	N/A	6
None of them	4	3	3
No	10	12	12
Not sure/don't know	6	5	5

The Globe and Mail – CBC news poll was designed by journalists from the two sponsoring organizations, with interviews conducted by Canadian Facts, the largest and oldest survey organization in Canada.

The results were obtained from 2 202 telephone interviews with Canadians aged 18 or over (excluding residents of the Northwest Territories and Yukon). Of that total, 1 057 were with residents of Quebec and 1 145 were with residents of the rest of Canada. The poll used a plus-digit sampling method, in which a representative sample of numbers was selected from telephone directories and a constant value added to the numbers. This ensured that both listed and unlisted telephone numbers would be included. Interviews took place between April 4 and April 15, from 10 interviewing centres across Canada.
Data from the interviews were weighted to take account of the fact that one person had been randomly selected from the eligible people in each household, and they were adjusted to reflect the age, sex and regional composition of Canada based on an updated version of the 1986 federal census.

Results obtained from sample surveys may differ from those obtained by questioning all Canadians. The likely deviation can be expressed in probability terms, and is primarily determined by the sample size on which the percentage figure is based.

For results based on the total sample in the poll, the expectation is that in 19 cases out of 20, the results will not differ by more than 2.3 percentage points in either direction from what would have been obtained from a survey of all Canadians.

For results based on smaller subsamples, based on such characteristics as gender or household income, the likely deviation may be larger. The deviation for the regional breakdowns reported in this poll is also higher than for the national results. The probability of deviation in either direction for regional results is 3.0 percentage points for Quebec and 3.3 percentage points for the rest of Canada.

Source: *The Globe and Mail*, 22 April 1991, A5.

Figure 7.5
Technical information reported with published opinion polls: *The New York Times*

Assessing Congress: mixed reviews

Do you approve or disapprove of the way Congress is handling its job?

Approve 27%	Disapprove 60%

Do you think most members of Congress are more interested in serving the people they represent, or more interested in serving special interest groups?

People 20%	Special Interests 71%

Do you think Congress makes the right decisions most of the time, or the wrong decisions most of the time?

Right 51%	Wrong 22%	Both 16%

Over all, who do you think would make better decisions about what to do to reduce the Federal budget deficit. George Bush or Congress?

Bush 24%	Congress 55%

Should the terms of members of Congress be limited to a total of 12 years, or should they be able to serve as long as they are able to get re-elected?

Limited 56%	Unlimited 37%

How the Survey was Conducted

The latest *New York Times* CBS news poll is based on telephone interviews conducted Oct. 8 to 10 with 960 adults around the United States, excluding Alaska and Hawaii. [Those with no opinion were not shown.]

The sample of telephone exchanges called was selected by a computer from a complete list of exchanges in the country. The exchanges were chosen so as to insure that each region of the country was represented in proportion to its population. For each exchange, the telephone numbers were formed by random digits, thus permitting access to both listed and unlisted numbers. The numbers were then screened so that only residences would be called.

The results have been weighted to take account of household size and number of residential telephone lines and to adjust for variations in the sample relating to region, race, sex, age and education.

In theory, in 19 of 20 cases the results based on such samples will differ by no more than three percentage points in either direction from what would have been obtained by seeking out all American adults.

The percentages reported are the particular results most likely to match what would be obtained by seeking out all adult Americans. Other possible percentages are progressively less likely the more they differ from the reported results.

The potential sampling error for smaller subgroups is larger. For example, for registered voters it is plus or minus four percentage points, and for people who are not registered it is seven points.

In addition to sampling error, the practical difficulties of conducting any survey of public opinion may introduce other sources of error into the poll.

Source: The New York Times, 12 October 1990, A21.

Major world newspapers publish technical information routinely. Two excellent examples are shown in figures 7.4 and 7.5. These examples provide the basic information necessary to understand the methodology of the polls. All published polls should be accompanied by this information. In addition, we suggest that the refusal rate (i.e., the number of potential respondents who refused to be interviewed or who did not complete the interview) be included. Refusals are an increasingly important factor in assessing the credibility of a poll. (Cantril 1991, 99–106) These requirements parallel the standards recommended by major international professional polling organizations. It is not unreasonable to expect all news organizations to meet these standards in an election campaign when the published results may affect the outcome. It is a responsibility that Canadian news organizations can no longer eschew.

Recommendation 1.7.15

We recommend that any news organization that sponsors, purchases or acquires any opinion poll and is the first to publish or announce its results in Canada during an election campaign be required to include in that report technical information on the methodology of the poll, including

- **the name of the polling organization,**
- **the sponsor who paid for the poll,**
- **dates of the interviewing period,**
- **the method of collection (for example, telephone, in person, mail questionnaire),**
- **the population from which the sample was drawn,**
- **number of respondents (completed interviews),**
- **the refusal rate (%),**
- **margin of error,**
- **the exact wording of each question for which data are reported, and**
- **the size, description and margin of error for any sub-samples used in the report.**

Accessibility of Technical Reports

In addition to presenting the basic technical information in published reports, news organizations that have sponsored or purchased polls should also make available a more complete report on the polls published. This material should be in the form of a report, perhaps from the polling agency, and made available at the cost of duplication within a reasonable time after publication of the poll results. This requirement should apply not only to primary reports of opinion polls commissioned or purchased by the news organizations but also to any initial news report on a poll that includes tabular material or otherwise purports to be a scientific poll report rather than a news item reporting what someone has said about a poll. This provision is not intended to cover normal news reporting, in which information is attributed to others who make statements about poll results. As noted above, however, ethical journalism requires that journalists verify as far as possible the information they report. When presented with poll results, it is not unreasonable to expect them to endeavour to obtain appropriate technical information.

Opinion polls are presented as scientific. Full disclosure of methodologies is a primary ethical priority of scientific work. Therefore, it is reasonable to require that poll reports include all the technical information identified as significant by the World Association for Public Opinion Research and other such bodies.

Recommendation 1.7.16

We recommend that any news organization that is the first to publish or announce in Canada any opinion poll that it has sponsored, purchased or acquired during a campaign be required to make available to any person, for the cost of duplication and within 24 hours of publication, a full report on the results of questions published, including the results on which the publication or announcement is based and the following technical information:

- **the name and address of the polling organization,**
- **the sponsor who paid for the poll,**
- **dates and times of interviewing,**
- **the method of collection (for example, telephone, in person, mail questionnaire),**
- **the population from which the sample was drawn,**
- **the sampling method,**
- **the size of the initial sample,**
- **the number of ineligible respondents,**
- **number of respondents (completed interviews),**
- **the refusal rate (%),**
- **the response rate (%),**
- **the margin of error,**
- **weighting factors/normalization procedures (if any),**
- **the exact wording of each question for which data are reported,**
- **the size, description and margin of error for any sub-samples used in the report, and**
- **the method used to recalculate percentages when those with no opinion or who did not answer a question are left out.**

Secondary Reporting

Because reports of the results of private polls, unless properly qualified, can be as damaging to public confidence as misleading reports of polls prepared for the media, they should be subject to the disclosure rules whenever they are reported in the media in a manner similar to media polls. This provision, had it been in force in Newfoundland in 1989, would have prevented the publication of the alleged phantom poll.

Recommendation 1.7.17

We recommend that reports in the news media of polls done privately or by other news organizations, when presented for the

first time in Canada in a manner similar to formal reports of media polls, be subject to the same disclosure rules as noted in recommendation 1.7.15.

Professional Standards

There is much that polling organizations themselves can do to promote better reporting of campaign opinion polls. For example, Canadian pollsters could follow the British and U.S. examples and form an organization specifically for those who do public polling. Such an organization could work with the media to promote more informed reporting and could take measures to protect pollsters against leaked polls. Public debate would be enhanced if academic specialists would undertake to monitor and comment on published polls, as has been done in Quebec by those involved with the Comité des sondages. As Cantril notes, most U.S. pollsters stipulate in their contracts that they can release an entire poll if a client leaks partial information that misrepresents the overall findings of the poll. (1991, 170) Such clauses are not the norm in Canada. Indeed, clients usually retain very tight control over the results of polls they commission. This is one of many areas in which an organization of public pollsters in Canada could help to protect the credibility of the industry. In countries where such organizations exist, technical information is exchanged and common problems are more regularly discussed than in Canada.[16]

The influence of published opinion polls is not, of course, confined to election periods. In recent years, published poll results have become an important element in public debate on contentious issues. The increasing frequency of polls has made them a means of communication among regions, communities and social groups, especially on subjects of intense and ongoing public debate. Published opinion polls provide an opportunity for individuals to register their preferences and group loyalties and, more important, to assess those of others. Such assessments can become an important element in opinion formation and can affect policy decisions. For example, in the case of the Meech Lake Accord, the increasing polarization of opinion on the basis of region and language group, as stressed in the media, became an important factor in the public debate and may have limited the options open to negotiators. (Desbarats 1990b) Response to polls may well harden divisions in the society. Advocacy groups, seeking to influence the public agenda, often commission polls for public release, frequently drafting questions to present the best case for their preferences. (Hoy 1989, chapter 14)

In this context of increasing influence for published opinion polls, it is desirable to encourage the highest possible professional standards in the conduct and reporting of polls. It is clear that increased efforts by the polling industry are needed to ensure that poll results are reported accurately and with appropriate qualifications in the news media. In addition, an informed public debate on the strengths and weaknesses of polls would help citizens to understand better this influential information source. Our recommendations for the campaign period will encourage higher professional standards. It is beyond our mandate to propose rules for opinion polls published outside the campaign period but their importance is clear. We hope that the greater access to technical information proposed here will encourage disclosure for all published polls to become the normal course of affairs and result in improved public understanding of polls in general. It is important for the health of our democracy that opinion polls be better understood and reported so that public debate can proceed based on reliable and valid information as to the distribution of opinions on major policy issues.

Recommendation 1.7.18

We recommend that

(a) **polling organizations engaged in election campaign polling for publication develop a professional code of conduct and an association to promote adherence to it; and**

(b) **polling organizations work with the media to improve the standards of poll reporting.**

ELECTORAL COMMUNICATION AND PUBLIC CONFIDENCE

Public confidence in the integrity of the electoral process depends as much on the conduct of the campaign and how it is presented to the public as it does on the credibility of the count. With this in mind, we examine the issue of the traditional blackout period at the end of the campaign, issues related to new campaign technology, concerns about advertising content, criticisms of news coverage, and questions of stereotyping and access to the media for members of minority groups. All of these issues have been raised by concerned citizens and, although many of them are not matters for direct regulation, they clearly deserve attention.

Blackout Period in Election Campaigns

The blackout period before voting day has a long tradition in federal and provincial elections, and is also very much the rule in most democracies. It is intended to protect against last-minute attempts to manipulate voters with misleading information and to provide some insulation between the act of voting and the rhetoric of the campaign.

History of the Blackout Provisions

In response to perceived abuses of political broadcasting in the 1935 election, the Committee on Radio Broadcasting recommended that political broadcasts be prohibited on an election day and the two immediately preceding days. (Canada, House of Commons 1936, 785–86) This recommendation was adopted by Parliament in the *Canadian Broadcasting Act, 1936* and was carried forward into the *Broadcasting Act* of 1958. The prohibition extended to referendums and election campaigns at the federal, provincial and municipal levels. A decade later the length of the blackout period was shortened to one day before polling day and polling day itself by the 1968 *Broadcasting Act*. In 1974, the blackout provisions for federal election campaigns were included in the *Canada Elections Act*.

Current Legislative Blackout Provisions

The present *Canada Elections Act* makes it an offence for registered parties to advertise for the purpose of promoting or opposing a particular party or candidate using the facilities of any broadcasting undertaking, periodical or government publication during three periods. As section 48 states, these three blackout periods are: (1) between the date of the issue of the writs for the election and Sunday, the twenty-ninth day before polling day; (2) on polling day (which includes the prohibition on the premature publication of election results in any manner whatsoever in a constituency before the closing of polls in that district); and (3) on the one day immediately preceding polling day. A similar provision makes it an offence for a candidate to so advertise (section 213). We deal with the blackout period at the beginning of the campaign in Volume 1, Chapter 6, when discussing rules for paid-time advertising.

The end-of-campaign blackout provisions have served a useful purpose in providing the electorate with a brief respite from party advertising just before the vote, during which time they can make their final decision. The blackout has also served parties and candidates well in preventing last-minute advertising blitzes for which there is no chance for rebuttal.[17]

Recommendation 1.7.19

We recommend that the current end-of-campaign blackout provisions in the *Canada Elections Act* remain.

Regulation of Advertising Content

At our public hearings, many interveners expressed concerns about negative or misleading advertising by political parties. There is genuine concern that such advertising will become more common and threaten the relative civility of Canadian campaigns. Some put forth proposals for regulating advertising content. Others proposed increased transparency in party advertising that would require parties to deposit copies of their advertisements, and details of costs of distribution, with the Canada Elections Commission or an election advertising council reporting to the Commission. (Kline et al. 1991 RC) There is a legitimate fear that the negative and misleading advertising that has concerned U.S. observers and, according to some critics, reduced public confidence in the U.S. electoral process, will inevitably come to Canada. (Graber 1991 RC)

The assumption underlying the argument for transparency is that increased media scrutiny would help set limits on party advertising content. Several media representatives have called for greater scrutiny (for example, at our symposium on media and elections in Toronto in February 1991). On the other hand, Graber suggests that one effect of greater media scrutiny of party advertising in the United States has been simply to provide news coverage for ethically questionable advertisements. (1991 RC) In any case, the growth of monitoring services ensures that any advertisement that is published or broadcast is available for journalistic analysis. In short, it seems clear that these proposals would create additional administrative burdens without commensurate benefits for the parties and the Canada Elections Commission.

As in other aspects of the electoral process, however, much can be gained by encouraging consideration of ethical issues and standards of conduct. Those in the advertising industry feel that a double standard exists between political and commercial advertisers. John Coleman, President of the Canadian Advertising Foundation, has remarked how political advertising in Canada is not subject to the monitoring, review and standards provisions faced by commercial advertising, with its self-regulatory code of standards and federal government provisions through Consumer and Corporate Affairs Canada. (Kline et al. 1991 RC) As a result, the constraints faced by commercial advertisers do not apply to election advertising. Coleman argues that "there should be a compliance with basic normal standards for all forms of advertising, including election advertising.... Fair is fair for all within the ambit of existing regulatory provisions ... all advertisers should play by the same rules and with no exceptions" (quoted in Kline et al. 1991 RC).

The Canadian Code of Advertising Standards, which sets out 15 categories for acceptable advertising, has been in place for some 25 years. The provisions apply to all commercial advertising, and advertisers, advertising agencies and the media voluntarily adhere to them. The standards are administered by the Advertising Standards Council (ASC), le Conseil des normes de la publicité and regional councils in major centres. The councils are autonomous bodies and their members are drawn from industry and the public. Complaints from the public or from advertising competitors are heard by the ASC. If an objection is upheld, the advertiser is requested to change the advertisement or withdraw it. Should an advertiser refuse, the media are advised that the advertisement is not acceptable to the ASC and asked not to exhibit it further. Advocacy advertising, including election campaign advertising, is not covered by the code, but there is no compelling reason why standards appropriate to this type of advertising could not be developed.

The problem with campaign advertising is illustrated further through this vivid analogy by U.S. advertising industry executive Malcolm MacDougall:

> Suppose I'm Lipton and I find out that once, way back in 1948, a watch strap got into a can of Campbell's Soup in a factory in the South somewhere.... It was found and no one was hurt and it never happened again. If I ran

an ad that said all that, no one would pay any attention. But suppose I ran an ad with eerie music in the background and I had some poor woman screaming as she discovers the watch strap and I had a grotesque close-up of the Campbell Soup can and my tag line said: 'Do you want a soup like this? Or do you want Lipton? We check every can.' It would be pretty damn effective (quoted in Taylor 1990, 215–16).

In the United States, as in Canada, such a product advertisement would be unacceptable to networks and industry "watchdog" groups. However, a similar political advertisement, drawing on a statement or event from a candidate's past, might well be broadcast. Indeed, 'attack ads', which almost invariably distort an opponent's position or record, have become increasingly common in recent campaigns. In the 1988 United States presidential campaign, nearly half of the 'spots' were negative and a number contained serious distortions. (Taylor 1990, 217) Such advertisements are also becoming more common in Canada. (Romanow et al. 1991 RC; Johnston et al. 1991, chapter 4)

Kline and his colleagues (1991 RC) point to the beneficial effects of the self-regulatory process for commercial advertisements and recommend that an elections advertising commission be established to create a similar process for partisan campaign advertisements. Rather than create a new structure for elections, it would be more effective to integrate this special kind of advertising into the well-established standard-setting process. Therefore, we asked the Canadian Advertising Foundation (CAF) if it would be willing to work with political parties and the media to develop criteria for political party campaign advertising. Clearly, it would be necessary for the criteria to recognize the distinctive functions of election advertising. In addition, the procedures would have to be very rapid for effective action during the campaign advertising period. The CAF responded positively to the proposal and agreed to consider undertaking the task.

Recommendation 1.7.20

We recommend that the Canadian Advertising Foundation establish a working group with the registered political parties and the media to develop standards and compliance procedures for campaign advertising.

Although the paid-time rules require that broadcasters make time available to the parties and attempt to fulfil their scheduling requests, the broadcasters retain some discretion. Canadian broadcasters have the authority to reject political party advertising they believe to be libellous or in violation of their own standards. In practice, they rarely reject party advertising but have occasionally required that an advertisement be modified to meet their standards. Broadcasters should retain this right and legal responsibility, along with the sponsor, for the content of advertisements. This continuing responsibility, accompanied by efforts to develop accepted standards for election advertising, will constrain misleading or scurrilous advertisements without curtailing in any significant way the freedom of the parties to make their arguments.

Recommendation 1.7.21

We recommend that broadcasters retain legal liability for the content of partisan advertising.

Broadcasters should also retain the capacity to refuse to place partisan advertising in the body of their news and public affairs programming. Partisan advertisements sometimes use formats similar to news or public affairs programs. The desire of broadcasters to maintain a clear distinction between advocacy and journalism is well taken.

Recommendation 1.7.22

We recommend that the *Canada Elections Act* not be construed as requiring broadcasters to place partisan advertising sponsored by registered parties in news and public affairs programs.

News Coverage

In modern industrial democracies, the media are major participants in the electoral process. Like political parties, they have a public as well as a private dimension. As Judith Lichtenberg has put it: "The seeming undeniability of the idea that the media are agents in the political process and not simply observers of it provides one important reason for rethinking the traditional responsibilities and prerogatives of the press." (1990, 1) While these prerogatives, a combination of special access and autonomy, are important, the fact that the news media have major effects on public confidence in the electoral process is undeniable. Our commitment to and appreciation of the value of editorial freedom does not relieve us of the duty to examine news and public affairs coverage of campaigns. The coverage is a major element of the electoral process and can have important implications for public confidence in it.

In recent years, there has been considerable criticism of news coverage of election campaigns. In our public hearings, the most common complaints involved limited coverage of smaller parties, and allegations of bias and neglect of minority groups. We also heard concerns regarding the stereotyping of women and visible minorities in the mainstream media.

Concerns about election coverage have also been expressed in the academic literature and various investigations of the media. (See, for example, Charron 1991 RC; Gilsdorf and Bernier 1991 RC; Soderlund 1991;

Soderlund et al. 1984; Wagenberg et al. 1988; Fletcher 1987.) Although observers have noted an increase in attention to campaigns and in issue analysis, they are concerned about the superficiality of most coverage. Coverage in the mainstream media presents a limited range of perspectives, focuses on the leaders of the larger parties at the expense of local candidates and other spokespeople, and often fails to put campaign events in context. (Desbarats 1991 RC; Gilsdorf and Bernier 1991 RC) Peter Desbarats, Dean of the School of Journalism at the University of Western Ontario, told us that the media, especially the broadcast media, lack the space and time to examine the issues thoroughly. He noted that while the news media play an important role in the process, they cannot carry the entire burden of informing voters. (London, 10 May 1990) Although the French-language news media have a tradition of greater commitment to analysis, including attention to historical context, they too have followed these general trends. (Charron 1991 RC)

The general concerns about coverage patterns and their effects on the quality of information made available to voters were noted in earlier investigations.[18] The Royal Commission on Newspapers (1981, 140–42) worried about a decline in the priority newspapers give to political news, the emergence of more cynical, confrontational journalism, and a possible decline in journalistic competition resulting from monopolies in smaller centres and market segmentation – with each news outlet serving a separate readership – in larger cities. An assessment of the 1984 coverage deplored the predominance of "show-business criteria" and called for:

> political reporting that covers ideas, that lets politicians speak for themselves, that places political developments in a historical context, and that discusses politics in terms of the social, economic, and political trends that are shaping our modern world. (Comber and Mayne 1986, 172)

The concern that television had reduced politicians to purveyors of 30-second clips has given way to concern about 12-second sound bites. (Gilsdorf and Bernier 1991 RC) This reduction in the time given to statements by Canadian politicians suggests that our campaign coverage may be moving toward the even more abbreviated U.S. pattern with its 9.8-second sound bites. Even the French-language television services, which have traditionally provided longer items and been less visually oriented than their English-language counterparts, have begun to move in these directions. (Taras 1990, 77; Charron 1991 RC)

This concern over the "shrinking sound bite" reflects the increasing dominance of television in the dissemination of political news. The Environics media study documented this trend, recently reporting that television is both more widely used and more credible as a source of public affairs news and analysis than other media, increasing its lead since 1986. (Adams 1991) Indeed, the study suggests that the future of network television lies in news and public affairs programming. Whether this trend means an increase in entertainment-oriented information programming remains to be seen but many observers have expressed that concern. (Saunders 1991 RC)

Although most Canadian news media accept that they have a social responsibility, they do not regard political education – the provision of a full range of information and perspectives on the issues of the day – as their primary concern. Journalists face a continuing tension stemming from their mandate to provide the public with an education on public affairs, the justification for constitutional protection of press freedom (Canada, Royal Commission 1981, chapter 2), and the commercial interests of their organizations. (Desbarats 1990a, 144) While they continue to provide considerable coverage of elections, many news organizations are increasingly unwilling to devote space to matters they regard as of marginal interest to their audiences, such as the platforms of smaller parties. A similar trend has been evidenced in Quebec. (Desbarats 1990a, 41–42; Charron 1991 RC) The declining commitment to public education in the media, noted by several speakers at our seminar on media and elections, has consequences not only for the flow of campaign information to voters but for news and public affairs information in general.[19]

At the constituency level, for example, our researchers found that reporting on the positions of the candidates declined as the campaign progressed. (Bell et al. 1991 RC) Journalists felt that the main themes had already been reported. This is unfortunate because voters often do not begin to pay attention to such matters until later in the campaign. (Johnston et al. 1991)

This pattern has also been observed at the national level and in other countries. David Broder, the distinguished American political journalist, stated the problem clearly:

> At the very point when the mass audience is probably most eager for basic information on the policies, programs, and personalities of the presidential candidates, the mass media are least likely to deliver those basics, believing – in accordance with our concept of news – that these are old-hat. (1987, 263)

Holli Semetko of the University of Michigan contrasted British and U.S. campaign coverage. (1991 RC) On average, she reported, the British television newscasts devoted nearly twice as much time to issue coverage as did the United States newscasts. The British coverage provided three times as much time to candidates' actual words. In contrast, the United States networks provided five times as much coverage of candidates' personal characteristics. Semetko attributes these and other similar characteristics to the continuing commitment of British broadcasters to public education.

The decline in commitment to public education in Canada, as our news media become less like the British and more like the American (Spencer 1991 RC), underlines the need for alternative campaign communication vehicles and the desirability of reassessing normal news values.[20] Our research found that in Canada normal news values mean that smaller parties will get little coverage. (Hackett 1991 RC) Normal news values also appear to mean that the level of ethnic conflict in nomination contests will be greatly exaggerated, as happened in 1988. (Carty and Erickson 1991 RC) In addition, these values pay little attention to the concerns of groups outside the mainstream of Canadian society, unless they are involved in conflicts. Representatives of ethno-cultural groups and persons with disabilities state they "felt blocked in their attempts to enter their concerns on the media agenda" during the 1988 campaign. (Saunders 1991 RC)

Candidates have expressed concern about campaign coverage that emphasizes national issues at the expense of local concerns. Our research found that, in the press at least, increased attention was given to regional issues in 1988. (Gilsdorf and Bernier 1991 RC) The widening geographical coverage of television and the press has reduced attention to constituency campaigns, however. Our case studies at the constituency level suggest that increased attempts to explore the local and regional implications of national issues would make election campaigns more meaningful to many voters. (Bell et al. 1991 RC)

Our research in Canada and other democratic countries indicates that there are other reforms in news coverage that might lead to a better informed electorate. In most other countries, unlike Canada and the United States, political leaders are given significant opportunities to speak directly to the voters and the newspapers print excerpts from their speeches and summaries of party platforms. (Graber 1991 RC) Doris Graber discovered in her research on U.S. voters that the information that they find most useful is systematic comparison of the records and positions of candidates. The desire of Canadian voters for comparative information is very clear. More work needs to be done on the kind of information and formats for presentation that are most conducive to voter learning. The evidence confirming the potential benefits of systematic comparisons is quite strong. Canada's journalism schools should also be examining formats that foster political learning. (Desbarats 1990a, 191–205)

Regulation of the editorial functions of the media (that is, those aspects dealing with matters other than advertising) would be undesirable. The unfettered editorial judgement of the media makes an important contribution to the campaign process and has the potential to provide an autonomous critique of those seeking power. It is a cornerstone of our political culture and is central to a free and democratic country. Therefore, regulation of the editorial content of any media is not appropriate. This holds true for the broadcast media, though the arm's-length regulation by the CRTC does provide a degree of accountability not present for the print media. The CRTC fields complaints about the coverage and mediates between complainants and broadcasters. Christopher Dornan has noted that "the problem of accountability persists because the press is answerable to no higher authority. But the press cannot be so answerable without compromising its essential freedom. This may be an uncomfortable fact, but it is also a fact of democracy." (1991 RC)

Nevertheless, Dornan argues, the media should provide greater accountability themselves by subjecting their own work to greater scrutiny. He notes that press criticism is increasing in a variety of publications and at the annual conferences of the Canadian Association of Journalists. In addition, our research has found that various news organizations or media associations either have or are working on guidelines or codes of professional conduct. Many journalists agree that the decision-making processes in the media should be more public and responsive.

Accountability has been slow to develop. With the decline of the overtly partisan press, journalists struggled to free themselves from overbearing political constraints and developed a "professional allergy" to any suggestion that they were accountable to anyone. (Desbarats 1990a, 153) In our media practitioners' workshop, journalists debated heatedly whether self-policing should be a collective undertaking and whether a common set of standards could ever be adopted unanimously. The only evidence of unanimity was in the universal antipathy to government regulation of journalists during elections. Since the 1960s this libertarian approach has been challenged by demands for a socially responsible press. Many journalists now accept the general principle that there should be some form of visible public accountability. The Fédération professionnelle des journalistes du Québec has taken the lead in the professional development of journalism and has adopted a charter of journalism. (Desbarats 1990a, 161, 179) The newspaper industry has also seen the creation of voluntary press councils and ombudspersons to improve communications between reporters and editors and their readers, while television networks are exploring the possibility of self-monitoring systems. The CBC has had a code of ethics since 1988 and has recently established the office of 'CBC Ombudsman'. Five Canadian dailies have such offices. (Desbarats 1990a, 170) These recent developments, however, have been initiated with difficulty and the news media often regards them suspiciously.

Several Canadian newspapers have a code of conduct and others are drafting one. The codes of conduct of individual newspapers generally say little or nothing about election coverage, dealing instead with general questions of fairness and balance, or the importance of maintaining a clear division between editorial comment and news. Codes of journalistic practice remain largely unwritten, passed "from one senior editor down to another", as one ombudsperson told us.

Since the early 1970s many provincial and local press councils have been established. Press councils typically are composed of media representatives and members representing the public. The Ontario Press Council was formed in 1972, partly in response to the Special Senate Committee on Mass Media, which proposed the creation of a national press council. After many years of negotiations between unions and management, the Quebec

Press Council was formed in 1973. The Royal Commission on Newspapers also recommended a national press council in 1981 and since then, more reluctant newspapers such as *The Globe and Mail* and other Thomson newspapers have joined the Ontario Press Council. Press councils now meet annually to exchange information and in some cases undertake a limited range of activities as educators of the press and defenders of its interests. They now exist in most provinces and regions across the country, with the Quebec council extending its jurisdiction to radio and television journalism.

As industry watchdogs, press councils do not have powers of enforcement or censorship. However, one example of the usefulness of press councils can be found in their body of "jurisprudence" containing "hundreds of press-council decisions". These decisions constitute "a useful indicator of current journalistic practice in Canada, as well as a practical guide for Canadian journalists". (Desbarats 1990a, 167) According to Desbarats, "the healthy criticism of press councils that is commonly heard in Canada – either that they go too far or not far enough in disciplining the press – illustrates the widespread acceptance of this relatively new institution". (1990a, 166) Nevertheless, in his view, "the whole question of accountability remains one of the great unresolved issues of contemporary journalism" and the development of such professional standards is difficult to nurture in the "harsh world of competitive commercial journalism". (1990a, 172)

As a major arena in election campaigns, the media are subject to considerable pressure from competitors. During the 1988 campaign, the *Toronto Star* was brought before the Ontario Press Council to defend its coverage of the free trade debate on the basis of a citizen complaint. In its defence, the *Toronto Star* acknowledged that it is "a crusading newspaper, with a clear and identifiable point of view" but presented data to show that it provided in its pages a forum for the full range of views on the issue. (Winter 1990, 2, 19–22) Editor John Honderich argued that the *Toronto Star* had a special responsibility to present viewpoints neglected in the generally pro-free trade media. Nevertheless, it took the complaint seriously and offered a detailed response. David Crane, the newspaper's economics editor, claimed that the reader who complained about the coverage had "discussed his strategy with the Conservative party". Complaint mechanisms can become a weapon in competitive battles. As Crane stated: "They tried to have the complaint heard in the middle of the election campaign, to discredit the paper and to influence the campaign." (Winter 1990, 2) It may be that general complaints should not be heard until after the election, but individual complaints about accuracy or misrepresentation that cannot be resolved through the internal mechanisms of the media require more immediate action. Post-election corrections are of little value to the competitors. It is clear that such issues of accountability are thorny ones.

The Canadian Broadcast Standards Council's *Code of Ethics* (1988) comes the closest to being a national code of conduct for broadcast media. Members, which include private radio and television stations across Canada, have agreed to adhere voluntarily to specific codes of broadcasting conduct. The closest resemblance to a national code of conduct for print is the *Statement of Principles for Canadian Daily Newspapers* of the Canadian Daily Newspaper Publishers Association (1977).[21] The statement is intended to complement any existing individual codes of ethics of newspapers. These codes acknowledge the social responsibility of the media.

Brian Brennan of the *Calgary Herald* told us there is a general reluctance in Canada to establish codes of journalistic practice, stemming from the attitude that the media are "free, unfettered and unregulated". According to John Stevens, President of the Canadian Association of Journalists, many oppose codes on the basis that existing practices adequately control journalists and uphold the freedom of the press and that enforcement of such codes is difficult.

Despite this debate, we are encouraged by recent developments among various news organizations in the promotion of a national set of codes. Robert Walker, ombudsperson at the Montreal *Gazette*, suggests that Canada's provincial press councils would be the best body to devise a code. Most Canadian dailies and weeklies are members of press councils, which they finance. Press councils serve as complaint mechanisms for readers who believe newspapers have been unethical, unfair or inaccurate. The code could serve as a set of guidelines in assessing readers' complaints. This would be especially useful during the relatively short period of election campaigns when an existing set of guidelines would allow the councils to deal with complaints more expeditiously.

The *Code of Ethics* of the Radio-Television News Directors Association of Canada (RTNDA) was initially created in 1970 and revised several times, most recently in 1986. Members are encouraged to observe the code, with news directors being requested to publicize its existence where their programming formats permit, and to make available copies of the code to the public. Our research on journalistic codes revealed that the RTNDA was the only organization that publicizes its code and explicitly promotes in writing its observance.

These developments in the print and broadcast media and the new attention to media criticism identified by Dornan (1991 RC) offer hope that the media will be more attentive to professional standards and ethics.

To encourage greater accountability, it would be beneficial if press and broadcasting councils would be more active in providing a forum for complaints about campaign coverage. This would require them to develop more rapid adjudication procedures than they now use. The Canadian Broadcast Standards Council (CBSC), for example, gives a broadcaster 10 working days from receipt of a letter of complaint to take action. If the CBSC is to take on the self-regulatory role envisaged for it when the CRTC agreed to its creation in 1988, it will need to develop faster procedures, at least during election campaigns. The procedures employed by the CRTC itself during election campaigns are much more rapid and the CBSC, which will be in place for the next federal election, will not have an effective role in providing for accountability during election campaigns unless it develops special procedures for campaign periods. The press councils are often even slower. (Desbarats 1990a, 160–68)

With respect to press accountability, our research found that the Canadian press is for the most part free of the abuses that led to the creation of a press complaints council in Great Britain. (Dornan 1991 RC) Our press takes its responsibilities to the democratic process seriously, even though we must not expect it to carry the task of political education nor provide channels for direct party-to-voter communication. The resources devoted to election coverage have increased significantly since the Barbeau Committee examined coverage in the early 1960s. (Canada, Committee on Election Expenses 1966, 331–58) The major newspapers and the television networks have substantially increased the personnel, time and space devoted to campaign coverage. (Fletcher 1988, 167) The advent of CBC Newsworld and services like Vision TV can be expected to add to the depth and diversity of coverage for the coming federal elections. (Hogarth and Gilsdorf 1991 RC)

At the urging of various interveners, we examined the question of a legal right of reply to advertising or editorial content. A British investigation of the issue had concluded that such a right was so open to abuse that it created more problems than it solved. It would require adjudication of the grievance itself and determination of just who should have a right of reply. (Dornan 1991 RC) The proposal was rejected in Great Britain for these reasons and we find no grounds to disagree.

Concerns were also expressed about the stereotyping of women and members of minority groups in the media and their lack of access to participate in the national debate. It was suggested that these problems of access and stereotyping create unfair barriers to effective participation in the electoral process and thus jeopardize confidence in it. Spokespeople for women's groups commented that much reporting still presents the participation of women as candidates or leaders as anomalous and thus discourages the active participation of women. (Symposium on the Active Participation of Women in Politics, Montreal, 31 October to 2 November 1990) Andrew Cardozo, representing the Canadian Ethnocultural Council, commented that issues of concern to ethno-cultural communities often are neglected in campaign coverage, leaving these groups with a sense that they are not part of the campaign debate. Cardozo pointed out that a debate on multiculturalism during the 1988 campaign was ignored by the mainstream media. (Ottawa, 13 June 1990)

Our research found that there was some basis for complaints related to women, persons with disabilities, Aboriginal peoples and ethno-cultural communities, among others. (Saunders 1991 RC; Robinson and Saint-Jean 1991 RC) For example, a study of campaign coverage in 1988 found that reports on the involvement of ethno-cultural groups in nomination contests often implied that their participation was illegitimate. (Saunders 1991 RC) However, remedies for these difficulties are not to be found in regulations, but rather in education to sensitize media personnel and others to the issues, and through assistance to representatives of these groups to help them make their case. Moreover, the 1991 *Broadcasting Act* (section 3(iii)) has widened the scope of Canadian broadcasting policy by including specific reference to the need to serve and reflect, through programming and employment opportunities, the interests and aspirations of Canadian men, women and children, along with the multicultural and multiracial nature of Canada and the special place of Aboriginal peoples within our society. This provision will be reflected in general CRTC guidelines for broadcasters. It should be reflected in the election coverage guidelines as well.

The weaknesses of news coverage of Canadian election campaigns are by no means the responsibility of the news media alone. The issue content of campaigns and the form of presentation are the result of interaction among party strategists, the media and voters (as interpreted by the pollsters). All these participants in the process share the blame for problems such as the lack of issue analysis, excessive focus on party leaders or neglect of local candidates. None can alter these patterns substantially without assistance from the others. One step might be the convening of regular meetings among party personnel, journalists and observers, as was done after the 1988 election by the CBC and Queen's University in Kingston. At the conference, a wide range of issues concerning the relationship between the parties and the news media was discussed. The discussions covered practical concerns and ethical issues. These key participants in the electoral process came to understand one another better and were sensitized to the ethical dimensions of their relationship. The conference was videotaped and subsequently broadcast on CBC Newsworld. A similar seminar was organized in Quebec by the Fédération professionnelle des journalistes du Québec (FPJQ) after the 1989 provincial election. It too resulted in a useful dialogue. (Charron 1991 RC) The Canadian Association of Journalists (CAJ) has organized such discussions at a number of its annual conventions. More frequent and more broadly based meetings that bring together a wider range of participants might be even more beneficial, raising issues such as appropriate rules of access for public debate.

Among the organizations that might take on such a responsibility is the Canadian Journalism Foundation (CJF). The CJF was created in 1990 with the goal of improving Canadian journalism, especially for coverage of politics. One objective of the CJF is to promote interchange between the media and other sectors of society. Regular post-election seminars with party officials, candidates, journalists and others concerned with the electoral process would fit in well with the mission of the CJF. The involvement of journalists through organizations such as the FPJQ and the CAJ would also be beneficial.

News coverage must remain the responsibility of the news media. However, there are areas where they could be more responsive to the complaints we have examined. Campaign coverage would benefit from more widespread use of the kind of post-election analysis undertaken by some of the large news organizations.

Recommendation 1.7.23

We recommend that

(a) press and broadcast councils develop standards for campaign coverage and procedures for dealing with complaints about it;

(b) organizations such as the Canadian Association of Journalists and the Fédération professionnelle des journalistes du Québec continue to hold post-election evaluations of coverage and that other industry organizations institute them; and

(c) organizations such as the Canadian Daily Newspapers Association or the new Canadian Journalism Foundation set up regular seminars on campaign coverage.

New Technologies

The advent of new communication technologies has altered election campaigns in every era. Each major shift, from the party press to the mass press, from print to radio and then to television, has required parties to adapt. Radio created a mass audience and personalized campaigns. Television built on this trend and increased attention to party leaders and their images. The importance of interpersonal networks declined and parties became more professional. With the introduction of new generations of communication technologies, we are on the verge of major changes once again.

New technologies pose major challenges to the established news media. Daily newspapers have suffered a long-term decline in per capita readership and must come to terms with new forms of information delivery. (Desbarats 1990a, 222–23) Because newspapers provide most analytical and investigative reporting, a decline in their willingness or capacity to perform these functions would require adjustments in the system as a whole. (Desbarats 1990a, 22–24) Many voters now make little use of the print media.

Broadcast news organizations have become increasingly important for the dissemination of election information, but they too are facing increased competition for audience attention. The trend toward audience fragmentation is well-established and continuing. (Adams 1991) For example, the number of television services available to Canadians has increased by more than 25 per cent in the last decade. Cable specialty and pay television channels now have, on average, well over 10 per cent of the audience and network audience share has declined by more than one quarter since 1984. (Ellis 1991, 22–24) News and public affairs is the only category of programming to increase audience share. Nevertheless, news organizations also find their budgets squeezed by declining advertising revenues. They are cutting back on news budgets. Despite achieving a greater audience share than their English counterparts, the French-language media are under more serious economic pressure, primarily because they serve a smaller market. Although audiences for news and public affairs programming remain relatively large, budget difficulties may threaten the viability of some of these programs. In recent years, news and public affairs coverage has been expanding but its financial base is shaky. It is for this reason that the industry opposes the creation of a French equivalent of CBC Newsworld, despite its potential benefits for political education and election coverage. (Canada, Task Force on the Economic Status of Canadian Television 1991, 31, 54–55, 63)

As a result of declining audiences for traditional media, advertisers are turning to the "new media" to supplement mass media campaigns and to reach targeted audiences more directly. (Lee 1989, 260–65) In the United States these new media are already heavily used in election campaigns. One impact on campaigns has been the increased volume of campaign information made possible by computers and high speed printers. Direct mail, for example, can be prepared so quickly that a million pieces of mail can be sent out in 12 hours. (Abramson et al. 1988, 93) Also, the greater speed of telecommunications allows for a tighter communications link between headquarters and candidates through satellite linkups, facsimile, electronic mail and computers, potentially centralizing the process.

New technologies such as polling and direct-mail techniques allow for the targeting of voters with special interests or concerns. Targeting is also used on cable television, in "narrowcasting" where candidates can appear only on the television screens they wish to reach. (Abramson et al. 1988, 98–99) The current Canadian regulatory framework does not permit this technology to be used but this might change in the future. These techniques can be used to access an already fragmented electorate and "narrowly defined groups communicating among themselves and not with non-group members". (Abramson et al. 1988, 112)

The process of audience fragmentation began in the 1970s and continued throughout the 1980s as new technologies such as cable, direct broadcast satellite systems and video cassette recorders led the transition from broadcasting to mass audiences to the delivery of specialized programs to target audiences. (Adams 1991) Interactive systems, such as pay-per-view, are continuing the trend in the 1990s. Michael Adams suggests that only news and public affairs programs will continue to reach mass audiences regularly. (Adams 1991) It is probable that even those audiences will diminish as news and public affairs programming is more narrowly targeted. It will take special events to draw the large, undifferentiated audiences of the recent past.

Whereas the broadcast media created a mass audience and nationalized politics, at least within language groups, new technologies individualize political discourse as voters receive customized messages. Unlike the broadcast media, these new media do not present a common agenda of concerns to citizens. They reduce the focus on parties and leaders, and minimize the importance of party networks and volunteers. This could make it increasingly difficult to identify the common good and persuade a majority of citizens to accept that vision. Messages that reach only core supporters of a political party or potential switchers impoverish the debate by keeping counter-arguments out of the public domain, thus weakening public discourse. "This may polarize opinions and exclude part of the electorate from the debate." (SECOR 1990, 63)

The possibility of a direct line between party and voters weakens the processes of discussion and interest aggregation that promote good public policies. To come to a reasoned decision, voters must participate at least as attentive spectators in a public debate. "To the extent that the new media segment the audience geographically and functionally more than it is divided today, that pool of common knowledge and common perspective will be reduced." (Abramson et al. 1988, 113) Narrow special interests stand to benefit most from these technologies.

The underground nature of these emerging communications could reduce constraints against misleading claims and other unethical campaign tactics. There are many examples of this in the United States already as some candidates make allegations about their opponents in forms of communication not easily scrutinized by the mass media, often near the end of campaigns. With no need to concern themselves unduly about "eavesdropping" by other audiences, messages can be tailored to the interests of a narrow segment of the electorate. Indeed, it is possible to disseminate contradictory messages to different groups of voters in this way with little risk of detection. Although direct communications from party to voter are a legitimate campaign tactic, it is important to maintain a significant public forum in election campaigns, as we attempt to do with our paid- and free-time proposals, and to develop deterrents to unethical behaviour.

We have no reason to believe that mass mailing and related techniques have been seriously abused in the past in Canada. However, the use of these new communication techniques is certain to become more widespread in the future and it is prudent to consider the checks and balances necessary to constrain their potential abuse. The most effective check is public scrutiny and we considered proposals to require registered political parties to make public any mass mailings distributed during campaigns.

We rejected these proposals for four reasons. First, the scrutiny of rival parties and an alert media is likely to bring quickly to public attention any misleading or unethical campaign materials during an election campaign. The competitive nature of Canadian campaigns ensures such scrutiny. Media attention will alert the electorate to abuses and also to the nature of the new technologies, which can produce apparently personalized appeals in bulk. In recent years, the news media have been providing increasing coverage of campaign techniques. (Frizzell and Westell 1985, 64)

Second, the code of ethics that we propose for political parties will sensitize party activists to the potential for abuse and the risks involved. This awareness will help the parties to restrain the activities of the occasional overzealous party member. The code will also provide the media and rival parties with guidelines against which they can assess questionable campaign materials. It should deter extreme examples.

Third, disclosure requirements could not cover techniques that do not leave a record, such as telephone canvassing. Any attempt to regulate them would be impossible to enforce.

Fourth, regulation of the registered parties during election campaigns would have limited effectiveness in constraining misuse of these new technologies because advocacy groups would not be covered. Experience in the United States indicates that groups outside the discipline of political parties are most likely to send out unethical mass mailings. Unconstrained by the longer term considerations and direct political competition that parties face, such groups might well circulate materials that raise ethical questions. However, to require such groups to deposit or make public their mass mailings would be intrusive and difficult to enforce.

In summary, disclosure requirements for mass mailings by registered political parties would not deal effectively with the potential for abuse noted in the United States and would constitute a nuisance for the parties. In the absence of serious abuses in Canada, public scrutiny, concern for campaign ethics and an alert media are, for the time being, sufficient checks on the potential for abuse.

ELECTION ADMINISTRATION AND ELECTION LAW ENFORCEMENT

Introduction

A cornerstone of public confidence in any democratic system of representative government is an electoral process that is administered efficiently and an electoral law that is enforced impartially. Securing public trust requires that the election officials responsible for administration and enforcement be independent of the government of the day and not subject to partisan influence. At the same time, the administration of the electoral law must be sensitive and responsive to the participants in the electoral process. This requires that participants receive clear and timely clarifications of the law when needed. Public confidence in the fairness of the electoral process also requires that the administrative processes and operations of the electoral machinery be open to public scrutiny. Finally, the law itself must be seen as credible, with appropriate penalties.

Under the current *Canada Elections Act*, the principal responsibility for the administration of the electoral law is vested in the chief electoral officer (CEO). The CEO is appointed by resolution of the House of Commons and may be removed only for cause by the Governor General and on the approval of the Senate and House of Commons. The Act gives the CEO the general responsibility to direct and supervise the conduct of elections and to issue instructions to all election officers to ensure the law is executed and enforced fairly and impartially. The CEO appoints a Commissioner of Canada Elections who, under the CEO's general supervision, ensures that the Act is complied with and enforced. Prosecutions of election offences under the Act can be instituted only with the Commissioner's consent. Investigations, however, are undertaken by the RCMP and other law enforcement agencies as required. Prosecutions are conducted before the courts because the law treats offences under the Act as if they were criminal offences. Finally, elections are conducted in each constituency by returning officers appointed by the Governor in Council, whose tenure in office is provided for by the Act. The CEO may issue instructions to these officers, as specified in the Act, but they are not members of the staff of the office of the chief electoral officer, or Elections Canada as it is now referred to in practice.

Historical Perspective

Election Administration

The present structure was largely determined by the *Dominion Elections Act* of 1920. Up to that time, elections were administered entirely by the returning officers in each constituency. From 1867 to 1874, these officers were appointed by provincial authorities, as provincial election laws governed federal elections. In 1874, the new federal election law stipulated that these offices be held by the local registrar or sheriff ex officio. Federal control was increased in 1882, when the federal election law gave the power to appoint returning officers to the Governor in Council. Historically, election administration was marked by partisanship by provincial and federal governments not only in the appointment of returning officers, but also in their conduct during elections. The highly decentralized structure of election administration ensured that the intense localism of partisanship affected any efforts by returning officers to conduct themselves fairly and impartially. (Ward 1963, chapter 9)

The 1920 *Dominion Elections Act* established the position of CEO and thus created an independent authority for the conduct of elections. Appointed by resolution of the House of Commons, the CEO was meant to be independent of the government of the day and the tenure of the office was intended to provide impartiality in the administration of elections. Because the government was willing to concede to opposition demands that election administration be impartial, the opposition was willing to allow the government the right to appoint the assistant chief electoral officer. In 1972, the government agreed to a request from the CEO that the CEO be able to advise on the appointment of a new assistant chief electoral officer, assisted by the Public Service Commission. The appointment was based on the ranking of candidates submitted by the CEO. The same procedure was used again in 1981.

The capacity of the CEO to administer elections and direct election officers was strengthened in 1929 when the power to appoint returning officers was vested in the CEO. Unfortunately, the incumbent CEO was partisan in making these appointments, damaging the independence and impartiality of the office itself. As a result, in 1934, the power to appoint returning officers reverted to the Governor in Council, where it remains to this day.

In 1949, the CEO instituted the practice whereby the Civil Service Commission (later to become the Public Service Commission) staffed positions within the office of the CEO. This brought staffing of this office within the merit principle of the federal public service. The permanent and temporary staff of Elections Canada, as the office became called after 1974, are now appointed, except for the position of assistant chief electoral officer, pursuant to the *Public Service Employment Act*. The permanent staff of Elections Canada includes about 55 positions, with approximately the same number of temporary staff for various periods between elections and double that number during elections.

To assist him in the administration of the 1974 *Election Expenses Act*, the CEO invited representatives from each of the parliamentary political parties to serve on an ad hoc committee to ensure that the parties fully understood the new Act and the approach that Elections Canada intended to take in its administration and enforcement. This informal committee, originally meant to be a temporary measure, operated until the 1988 election. It advised the CEO on the guidelines issued to political parties and candidates, and their agents, and on amendments to the Act itself.

Election Law Enforcement

Election law enforcement is one of the more sordid aspects of Canadian electoral history. First, election corruption was widespread for several decades after Confederation, and publicly admitted to be so by all participants. Second, the *Controverted Elections Act* was enforced not by federal electoral machinery, but by citizen petition, initially to the House of Commons and later to the judiciary. The judiciary then reported its findings to the House for a final resolution. This process entailed partisans pursuing petitions to harass elected candidates and parties engaging in trade-offs to influence the outcome. As Norman Ward described it:

> The Controverted Elections Act thus became not so much an instrument for the suppression and punishment of corrupt practices as a means of providing new battlegrounds for party strife and party bargaining. The real purpose of the Act became lost in a maze of circumstances depending primarily on expediency; and corruption, far from being checked by the law, seems actually to have been promoted by its failure. The whole electoral system inevitably acquired a low reputation. (Ward 1963, 251–52)

Technical changes to the Act in 1915 and 1921 made it more difficult for individuals to bring petitions against candidates and the number of controverted elections declined dramatically. Equally important, however, was the expansion of the franchise after the First World War, which reduced substantially the incentive to engage in corrupt practices: there were simply too many voters to bother corrupting the few that could be corrupted. The incidence of prosecutions for corrupt practices also diminished, given the absence of an effective enforcement mechanism. Other than an enforcement responsibility for offences committed by election officers, the CEO had no authority to investigate complaints or to recommend prosecution.

Electoral law first had provisions for the reporting of election expenses in 1874. Yet there was no mechanism for enforcement. As a consequence, candidates continually violated the provisions relating to reporting requirements. Neither the returning officers, to whom reports were to be submitted, nor the CEO after 1920 were given any jurisdiction for enforcing these provisions. (Ward 1963, 263)

Not until the 1974 *Election Expenses Act* was this deficiency in enforcement partly corrected: the position of Commissioner of Election Expenses was created to enforce the election expenses provisions of the Act under the supervision of the CEO. In 1977, this position became the Commissioner of Canada Elections and was assigned responsibility for the enforcement of all provisions of the *Canada Elections Act* under the general supervision of the CEO. Even with this development, the power to investigate remained outside the jurisdiction of the electoral machinery and all prosecutions had to be taken to the courts given the criminal character of offences under the *Canada Elections Act*.

Assessment of the Current Structure

The impartiality and independence of the CEO and Elections Canada are now taken for granted. Even so, government delays in appointing returning officers have made it difficult for the CEO to administer elections. The principal deficiency here, however, is not that these positions are government appointments but that the CEO has a limited capacity to train them, to retain the most competent and to engage them in advance preparations for elections. Our recommendations in Volume 2, Chapter 1 are designed to improve this situation, while maintaining the basic principles of the current system.

At the same time, however, the impartiality and independence of the federal electoral machinery rest entirely on one officer, the CEO. There are no guidelines for the CEO's use of the discretion he or she is given under section 9 of the *Canada Elections Act*. Such discretion must be used frequently during an election to cope with the complex task of administering elections in a highly charged and competitive environment. The use of the above-noted ad hoc committee of party representatives has made administration and compliance with the law easier in some respects, but in general has revealed the serious shortcomings of the overall structure. The CEO, for instance, did not chair this committee during its existence because it had no powers to instruct the CEO on the exercise of discretionary powers. Nor could these representatives commit their parties to whatever the committee might decide to recommend to the CEO. When decisions were called for, the CEO was required to make them alone.

The impartiality and independence of the CEO have not been called into question. From an institutional perspective, however, the need for this officer to exercise individual discretion on controversial issues during the heat of an election campaign, while directing the administration of the election law through an incredibly decentralized system, is imprudent. The CEO has adopted the practice of issuing guidelines for candidates, political parties and agents. The Act does not provide for or require advance rulings or interpretation bulletins to clarify the application of the law, however, even though the principal participants are essentially "registrants" operating under a statutory regulatory regime. Moreover, there is no process to submit proposed guidelines to public scrutiny and consultation. Yet electoral law is fundamental to the democratic rights of citizens and participants in the electoral process. Finally, there is no procedure to ensure that Parliament consider the CEO's proposed amendments to the *Canada Elections Act*, even though the law must keep abreast of changes in election practices and judicial decisions on the constitutional rights of citizens.

Equally important, the effective enforcement of the *Canada Elections Act* is called into question both by the nature of offences under the Act and by the enforcement structure. The Act treats all infractions as though they were criminal offences, despite almost all violations of the Act being now essentially administrative or regulatory in character. For example, of the 862 complaints lodged in the 1988 general election, only 1 per cent dealt with matters of electoral fraud. By treating what are administrative or regulatory infractions as criminal offences, the *Canada Elections Act* unintentionally undermines public confidence in the electoral process. The need to correct this state of affairs was widely supported at our public hearings by numerous interveners, including a former CEO, the current CEO and the Commissioner of the Royal Canadian Mounted Police (RCMP).

Under the present structure the Commissioner of Canada Elections lacks the authority to investigate; all investigations must be carried out by the RCMP. The Act requires, moreover, that all prosecutions must be before the courts. In addition, while the CEO appoints this Commissioner and has the power to instruct him or her to initiate inquiries, only the Commissioner decides whether a case will be brought before the courts. Here too the credibility of the system rests on the decisions of one officer, who receives little guidance as to how to pursue his or her functions.

This enforcement structure has resulted in an unwieldy and unsatisfactory process from many perspectives. Investigations take too long because they are treated as criminal investigations. Candidates are subject to unnecessary embarrassment because they are being investigated by the police. Very few complaints are prosecuted because they require a criminal standard of proof. Because the current elections law is criminal rather than administrative, it is difficult to obtain injunctions. This means there is no efficient legal remedy to stop actions during an election that may affect either the election result or the public's perception of the integrity of the electoral process. Finally, penalties vary greatly without a clear justification for the variations between offences.

The most significant consequence of this situation is that the provisions of the Act are not adequately enforced. Infractions occur. But under the current structure, they cannot be brought to a stop effectively by administrative means. Nor can they be treated as administrative or regulatory infractions in the way they are investigated, adjudicated and punished.

One of the frequent complaints at our hearings concerned the use of the RCMP by Elections Canada to investigate allegations of election offences. The Commissioner can, and does, use other persons as investigators, but must rely on the RCMP, as the federal police force, if powers of search or seizure are needed, since the *Canada Elections Act* does not give these powers directly to the Commissioner except where an election officer may be under investigation. There was widespread support at the hearings for finding alternative means to investigate breaches of election law, most of which are not of a truly criminal nature.

In his testimony, Norman Inkster, the Commissioner of the RCMP, supported the transfer of election investigations to Elections Canada:

> If this investigative function was assumed by a civilian body, it would effectively decriminalize these regulatory or administrative infractions; allow the RCMP to deploy our limited resources to more urgent criminal matters; and reduce the unnecessary embarrassment to individuals who are now the subject of police investigation when in fact their infractions may be of a regulatory nature. (Ottawa, 13 March 1990)

The Commissioner of Canada Elections is expected to act independently of the CEO although the CEO establishes general directives related to enforcement. As Jean-Marc Hamel (then CEO) noted in testimony before the Standing Committee on Elections, Privileges and Procedure (Canada, House of Commons 1988b, 24:83):

> My role is to set the policy and terms of reference. My only interest in individual cases is to make sure that the commissioner follows or respects the policy or guidelines. Under no circumstances do I go to the file or have to give any permission or authority, because the commissioner already has that authority in the legislation.

The policy of Elections Canada is to proceed with the investigation of all legitimate complaints relating to elections, and to prosecute any infraction where this would serve the interests of justice or the public interest and where there is a good chance of success.

Complaint files are kept confidential unless a prosecution is launched. A review of a random selection of 150 of the 1988 cases with the Commissioner of Canada Elections found that 46 per cent of these complaints came from within Elections Canada, 24 per cent from candidates or their campaign workers, 20 per cent from the general public and only 3 per cent from the police. After the 1988 election the Commissioner authorized only 50 prosecutions, the equivalent of 6 per cent of the 862 complaints concerning that election.

There are many reasons for the low proportion of election-related complaints that led to prosecution. Many complaints were not pursued because they were anonymous, considered to be frivolous, did not provide enough information or because the alleged offence was not covered by the law. Some complaints were set aside because they were premature: for example, complaints about excessive election spending that were submitted before the deadline for election returns and not renewed after the return was submitted.

Many complaints, especially from within Elections Canada, were minor. These included election expenses returns that were submitted a short time after the deadline, and minor errors or omissions in returns that were not material or could be easily corrected. In some cases where a candidate had failed to report, there had been no expenses.

In 1988 the Commissioner decided as a matter of policy not to prosecute sales of alcohol on election day if the police had laid a complaint. Some cases of spending over the limit set out in the Act were not prosecuted after the 1988 election either because the amount overspent was too small to justify prosecution or because it was difficult to determine, using the Act's definition of election expenses, whether a candidate had in fact exceeded the limit. Cases of election spending by those other than parties or candidates were not prosecuted anywhere in Canada because of an Alberta court judgement in the National Citizens' Coalition case, even though the Alberta judgement was not binding on the courts of other provinces. The Commissioner also judged that it was not in the public interest to prosecute technical violations of the law: for example, when a candidate reported payments to an election worker as an expense but a union paid the worker directly rather than channelling the payment through the official agent.

The general experience of bodies responsible for election administration is that election offences come to light by means of complaints rather than through active efforts at enforcement. There is really no other alternative, given the numbers of people involved as poll workers and enumerators, as campaign workers for the candidates, and as voters. In addition, some control is built into the system because rival parties and candidates naturally watch each other for irregularities. Hence the complaints filed and prosecutions launched by Elections Canada have some credibility as a means to judge the current extent and nature of election offences.

The record of the past two elections shows that an overwhelming number of complaints are of a financial or administrative nature. As shown in tables 7.10 and 7.11, less than 2 per cent of the complaints arising from those two elections dealt with offences that could be classified as election fraud. This fact, in our view, supports demands to take the enforcement of most election offences out of the courts.

At the provincial level, enforcement of election offences is generally in the hands of the CEO or, in Ontario, shared with a commission responsible for overseeing election financing. As shown in Table 7.12, the number of complaints and prosecutions for election offences at the provincial level is almost nil. Prosecutions are in every case adjudicated by the courts.

Table 7.10
Complaints and prosecutions, 1984 general election

Offences concerning	Complaints		Prosecutions		Prosecutions / complaints %	Prosecutions resulting in convictions %
	N	%	N	%		
Parties, candidates, agents	371	65.4	28	24.3	7.5	50.0
Election officials	14	2.5	0	0.0	0.0	—
Fraudulent vote	7	1.2	0	0.0	0.0	—
Granting 4 hours to vote	54	9.5	1	0.9	1.9	100
Sale of alcohol on election day	82	14.5	82	71.3	100	89.0
Other	39	6.9	4	3.5	10.3	50.0
Total	567	100	115	100	20.3	78.3

Source: Boucher 1991 RC.

Table 7.11
Complaints and prosecutions, 1988 general election

Offences concerning	Complaints		Prosecutions		Prosecutions / complaints %	Prosecutions resulting in convictions %
	N	%	N	%		
Parties, candidates, agents	696	80.7	34	68.0	4.9	70.4
Election officials	21	2.4	1	2.0	4.8	100
Fraudulent vote	8	0.9	3	6.0	37.5	66.7
Granting 4 hours to vote	51	5.9	9	18.0	17.6	66.7
Sale of alcohol on election day	14	1.6	1	2.0	7.1	0.0
Other	72	8.4	2	4.0	2.8	50.0
Total	862	100	50	100	5.8	65.9

Source: Boucher 1991 RC.

Table 7.12
Complaints and prosecutions during the last two elections in Canadian jurisdictions

	Complaints		Prosecutions	
Jurisdictions	Second-last election	Last election	Second-last election	Last election
Canada	567	862	115	50
Newfoundland	0	4	0	4
Nova Scotia	N/A	N/A	0	2
Prince Edward Island	0	0	0	0
New Brunswick	8	4	0	0
Quebec	591	156	49	29
Ontario	20	127[a]	3	20[b]
Manitoba	1	1	1	0
Saskatchewan	0	0	0	0
Alberta	0	1	0	1
British Columbia	0	0	0	0
Yukon	1	0	0	0
Northwest Territories	1	1	0	1

Source: Data compiled from a questionnaire submitted to the chief electoral officers and from annual reports from each jurisdiction. (Boucher 1991 RC)

[a]Includes 77 complaints related to the Patricia Starr case (see Johnson 1991 RC).
[b]All 20 prosecutions were related to the Patricia Starr case.

Since the 1920s the ethical standards of Canadian federal elections, as measured through enforcement activity, have tended to be relatively high. Most election fraud in recent elections has related to padding of the electoral lists. The classic kinds of election fraud and electoral corruption have not emerged in recent elections; perhaps they are a thing of the past. As a consequence, most enforcement activity is now directed to upholding the rules relating to election expenses. While election law should certainly take account of the possibility of election results being affected by corruption, the experience of Canadian elections suggests this is an exception.

There are some serious flaws in the way election laws are enforced that need to be addressed generally, especially if there is to be more comprehensive regulation of election finance. In addition to the problems with relying on the RCMP for investigations, it is often difficult to prosecute offences of an administrative or financial nature through the regular courts. The criminal offence model characterized by the need to prove intent beyond a reasonable doubt is inappropriate for many election offences.

Another difficulty is that measures to enforce election laws are always taken after the fact, because Elections Canada has no legal or practical means to stop actions during a campaign that may affect the election results or the integrity of the electoral system. By contrast, the Directeur général des élections in Quebec can intervene during elections. During the 1989 Quebec election, the Quebec elections office sent 31 warnings to individuals and groups about violations of the independent expenditure provisions of the Act – expenditures that are prohibited during election periods in Quebec. All of these individuals and groups were warned they would be prosecuted if their activity did not cease and all complied. This approach indicates clearly that quick action and certainty of prosecution constitute the best deterrent.

The current penalties for election offences are arbitrary and uneven. For example, a candidate convicted of overspending may be judged to be guilty of a corrupt practice and hence barred from voting or from being a candidate for seven years. A national party that overspends its limit by $1 million can be fined a maximum of $25 000. The agent for a candidate who overspends the limit may lose the right to vote for five years whereas the official agent for a party that exceeds its limit does not. As the above examples suggest, the maximum penalty of $25 000 is much too low for a national party. And the threat of a jail sentence for a minor offence like wearing a party button in the polling station is excessive.

Reforming the Administrative and Enforcement Structure

To improve the administration and enforcement of the *Canada Elections Act* while preserving the independence and impartiality of the federal electoral machinery, there must be fundamental changes that create a new and flexible structure for the administration of elections and the enforcement of electoral law.

Role and Structure of the Canada Elections Commission

An independent multi-member commission rather than a single officer would enhance the capacity of the central electoral machinery to respond effectively and efficiently to the legitimate concerns of citizens and electoral participants in the administration of the election law, to formulate policy, to direct the implementation of policy, to issue clarifications of the law and to propose changes in the law. Multi-member commissions are now used by governments in virtually all cases where a regulatory regime must be administered in an independent and impartial manner. The statutory provisions of the *Canada Elections Act* must be as complete as possible, given that they regulate partisan competition in the most fundamental process of democracy. There must therefore be minimal executive discretion for those administering the Act. No statute, however, can eliminate the need for administrative discretion. This is especially important now that the elections act registers participants and extends the law to their financial and administrative activities. It is further warranted because the operations of Elections Canada during elections are highly decentralized, with more than 200 000 election officials deployed across the country.

A multi-member elections commission to direct election administration on basic policy and policy interpretation is essential to secure the broadest possible compliance with the law by those who are registrants under the law. It is also necessary to give the CEO and the CEO's administrative officers the authoritative policy guidelines necessary to support their administrative decisions, while ensuring the credibility of their actions. A multi-member commission can achieve these fundamental objectives with greater credibility and effectiveness than a single election officer because the commission can be structured to consider several different views in determining what is fair and equitable policy. The shortcomings of the ad hoc committee on the one hand and the legislative process of statutory change on the other prove the need for a more flexible and open structure.

A multi-member elections commission, as a board of directors, would still require a chief executive officer to administer and be responsible for the conduct of elections. The usual practice of such regulatory commissions is to have the chief executive officer also chair its board. This ensures that the commission is advised directly by the officer who is accountable to it for operations, and that the officer responsible for implementing policy is involved in formulating that policy. This enhances accountability because the administrative consequences of proposed policies are addressed by the commission with the chief executive officer participating in commission decision making. The administrative dimensions of policy are thus fully considered before implementation, and the chief executive officer can provide advice in advance. The accountability of the chief executive officer for policy implementation is thus strengthened and clarified.

Those administering elections must be clearly seen as responsible to the House of Commons, separate from the executive branch of government (thus separate from the governing party) and as an independent tribunal for election law enforcement.

Several different administrative bodies in Canada handle both investigations and prosecutions. For our purposes, the structure of provincial securities commissions appears to be the most appropriate on which to model the Canada Elections Commission. Securities commissions generally have two-tiered structures. For example, the first tier of the Ontario Securities Commission is an autonomous statutory tribunal that "formulates policy, sits as an administrative tribunal in hearings, acts as an appeal body from decisions made by the Executive Director and staff, hears appeals from decisions of the Toronto Stock Exchange ('TSE') and the Toronto Futures Exchange ('TFE') and makes recommendations to the government for changes in legislation". (Ontario Securities Commission 1990, 7) The second tier, the Commission's administrative agency, is composed of managers, lawyers, accountants, investigators and support staff. The administrative agency is responsible for the daily operations of the Commission.

There are many instances among securities commissions where a member of the tribunal may become involved in decisions to investigate and prosecute complaints. Such commissions have a built-in safety valve; when a board member is consulted prior to adjudication before the tribunal, the board member is barred from hearing the complaint or from participating in any hearing decision.

The administrative law tradition in the Canadian Bill of Rights and the *Canadian Charter of Rights and Freedoms*, as well as recent jurisprudence, requires that when a federal commission has both adjudicative and prosecuting functions, there must be a clear separation of the two responsible structures to ensure the commission's institutional integrity. (*MacBain* 1985) In short, the institutional design of the commission must be such that the adjudicative and prosecuting functions are not confused, nor should they compromise procedural fairness and natural justice. The commission tier that investigates and prosecutes complaints must be independent of the adjudicative tier.

The institutional integrity of the Canada Elections Commission would be affirmed through a two-tiered structure. There would be no mixing of the Commission's investigative and prosecuting functions on the one hand and the adjudicative functions on the other. In Volume 2, Chapter 8, we outline a scheme whereby the director of enforcement would determine whether to pursue an election law violation before the Commission or before the courts based on the severity of the infraction or offence. Canada Elections commissioners would not hear and assess the investigation of an election law violation or offence before deciding whether it or the courts should adjudicate the matter. Further, the investigations and prosecutions by the office of the director of enforcement would be conducted independently of the Commission tribunal.

This two-tiered structure means that the members of the commission should not only be appointed by the House of Commons, but that the appointment process should be designed to reflect a broad consensus of the elected Members of Parliament and not merely a simple majority of elected MPs. This can be achieved by requiring that all appointments to the commission, including that of chief electoral officer, be made by a two-thirds vote of the House of Commons, a process that will normally require the parliamentary parties to agree on nominations to the commission.

The elections commission should be large enough to reflect a diversity of views and experience and to fulfil its responsibilities as a tribunal. In addition to the CEO, who will chair the commission and be its chief executive officer, it should have two full-time members serving as vice-chairs. Given the nature of the responsibility, the commission chair/CEO should be paid a salary equal to that of the Chief Justice of the Federal Court of Canada and the two vice-chairs should be paid salaries equal to those of the justices of that court. The terms of commission members should be staggered to ensure continuity. Because the formula for appointment requires a two-thirds majority in the House of Commons, the term of a commissioner could be renewed if that is the wish of the House.

If commissioners have had a partisan past, they should be required, on appointment, to sever any formal links with a political party. In addition, their terms should be long enough and the reasons for removal sufficiently restricted so that they can act with independence. This condition is essential if commission members are to adjudicate cases involving election violations. We are confident that persons who have been partisan can act impartially in these cases; their situation will be the same as those with partisan pasts who are expected to act impartially when appointed to the Bench.

If a commissioner is unable to perform his or her duties as identified in the *Canada Elections Act* and is unwilling to resign, the Canada Elections Commission may need to contemplate the removal of the commissioner. The process used to remove a commissioner should be rigorous, credible, non-partisan and established. Since the commissioners would have important adjudicative responsibilities, the process should be similar to the one used to remove federally appointed judges. The procedure for the removal of judges is set out in the *Judges Act*. The Canadian Judicial Council has responsibility for investigating and making recommendations on the possible removal of federally appointed judges. The Council's recommendations must be consistent with the provisions of the Act; section 65 (2) provides the specific reasons for which the Council may recommend removal of a judge. As well, section 69 of the *Judges Act* provides that the Council may be requested to inquire whether certain persons appointed pursuant to an enactment of Parliament to hold office and satisfying the standards of good behaviour should be removed from office for any of the reasons set out in section 65 (2).

The initiation of the process to remove a commissioner should be based on a majority decision of Canada Elections commissioners to request an inquiry by the Canadian Judicial Council. Following its inquiry, the Council would make a recommendation to the Speaker of the House of Commons on whether the commissioner should be removed. The removal of the commissioner would take place only if there was an address based on a two-thirds vote of the House of Commons. As would be the case in the appointment of a commissioner, his or her removal would normally require inter-party agreement.

Recommendation 1.7.24

We recommend that

(a) **a commission be established to be known as the Canada Elections Commission consisting of seven members appointed by a two-thirds vote of the House of Commons;**

(b) **the House of Commons designate a member of the Commission to be the chief electoral officer who will chair the Commission and be its chief executive officer;**

(c) **the House of Commons designate two members of the Commission to be vice-chairs;**

(d) **the chief electoral officer/chair of the Commission be appointed for a seven-year term or until a successor is appointed;**

(e) other members of the Commission be appointed for a five-year term or until a successor is appointed;

(f) when the Commission is established, three of its first six members be appointed for seven years to ensure continuity;

(g) the terms of the chief electoral officer and commissioners be renewable;

(h) (1) a majority of commissioners be permitted to request the Canadian Judicial Council to inquire into whether a commissioner should be removed from office for any of the reasons set out in paragraph 65 (2) (a) to (d) of the *Judges Act*;
(2) the Council's recommendation be made to the Speaker of the House of Commons; and
(3) commissioners be removed only on a two-thirds majority address of the House of Commons;

(i) during their terms in office, the chief electoral officer and commissioners not hold office in or be employed in any capacity by a political party, not be members of a political party and not make political contributions or contributions to a party foundation; and

(j) the chief electoral officer/chair of the Commission be paid a salary equal to that of the Chief Justice of the Federal Court of Canada; the two vice-chairs be paid a salary equal to that of the justices of that court; and the remuneration of the other members of the Commission be fixed by the Governor in Council.

Recommendation 1.7.25

We further recommend that the powers of the Canada Elections Commission include the following:
(1) to formulate policy and direct the chief electoral officer on policy implementation;
(2) to issue policy statements to registered political parties, candidates, agents and other interested individuals or groups;
(3) to review decisions by election officials when requests have been filed by citizens, candidates, parties and their agents;
(4) to conduct public hearings on regulations, policies and guidelines;
(5) to respond to requests for advance rulings or interpretation bulletins from registered political parties, candidates or agents;
(6) to recommend changes to legislation;
(7) to make regulations that are submitted directly to the Speaker of the House of Commons and deemed approved if not referred for debate or to a committee within 15 sitting days after being tabled;

(8) to exercise the functions of the current broadcasting arbitrator;

(9) to submit its annual operating budget to the Treasury Board;

(10) to submit an annual report to Parliament on elections administration and enforcement; and

(11) to maintain a register of political parties, constituency associations and party foundations.

The *Canada Elections Act* must provide rules on how the Commission should be organized to act as a tribunal. The entire Commission should not have to sit on every panel to hear a case. Rather, a panel with at least one commissioner should be designated to adjudicate each case (see Volume 2, Chapter 8). For meetings of the full Commission, a quorum of two members should be sufficient.

Recommendation 1.7.26

We recommend that

(a) when a case is referred to the Commission for adjudication, the chair, or in her or his absence a vice-chair, designate the panel to hear the case;

(b) a panel consist of any number of commissioners; and

(c) the quorum for meetings of the Commission be two members.

Deputy Chief Electoral Officer

If the chief electoral officer (CEO) is absent or unable to act for any reason, the assistant chief electoral officer, who is appointed by the Governor in Council, must assume the CEO's executive duties in regard to the conduct of an election.

We recommend that the title of assistant chief electoral officer be changed to deputy chief electoral officer and that the deputy chief electoral officer normally be present at the meetings of the Canada Elections Commission. This would ensure that he or she would be well informed and prepared to act on behalf of the CEO, in an executive capacity, as required. The deputy chief electoral officer, however, should not be appointed by the Governor in Council. Since this officer would be required to serve in place of the CEO in the CEO's executive capacity under the policy direction of the Commission, this position need not be staffed by resolution of the House of Commons. Appointment by a majority vote of the Commission should be sufficient.

One of the two vice-chairs would be designated acting chair of the committee. The procedure for designating acting chairs would be established by the Commission.

Recommendation 1.7.27

We recommend that

(a) a deputy chief electoral officer be appointed by the Canada Elections Commission;
(b) the deputy chief electoral officer be deemed to be employed in the federal public service; and
(c) a vice-chair be designated to act as chair in the absence of the chair.

Enforcement of the Canada Elections Act

To increase public confidence in the integrity of the electoral process through a more effective and appropriate enforcement mechanism, most violations under the *Canada Elections Act* should be investigated and prosecuted as administrative or regulatory infractions. Given this change in approach to violations under the *Canada Elections Act*, the Canada Elections Commission should be empowered to function as an administrative tribunal to adjudicate alleged infractions of the election law. More serious offences that warrant more severe penalties, such as imprisonment, loss of the right to be a candidate, loss of a seat in the House of Commons and higher fines, should be adjudicated only by a court having criminal jurisdiction. A voluntary compliance procedure should also be instituted to allow a speedy voluntary agreement relating to an infraction without involving the Commission or the courts. *Criminal Code* offences such as breach of trust or influence peddling (sections 122 and 125 of the *Criminal Code*) should continue to be dealt with as criminal offences.

Recommendation 1.7.28

We recommend that election violations be brought before the Commission or prosecuted before provincial criminal courts, depending on the nature and gravity of the alleged violation.

Another shortcoming of the present Act is that enforcement is entirely after the fact. Currently, if Elections Canada becomes aware that an individual or party is committing a violation during a campaign, it has no power to intervene effectively, although in practice, once so informed, most correct their actions. In other regulated areas, the agencies have the power to stop harmful or illegal activities through cease-and-desist orders or mandatory injunctions. The Canada Elections Commission should have similar powers, including the power to intervene unilaterally in emergencies. However, an individual or party affected by such an order should have the right to appear before the Commission and any emergency order should be of short duration.

The Commission should have the powers, rights and privileges vested in a superior court of record for the attendance and examination of witnesses, the production and inspection of documents, the issuance and enforcement of orders, the payment of costs, and all other matters necessary for exercising its powers to compel compliance with the *Canada Elections Act*.

It should also have the power to review, rescind, change, alter or vary any of its decisions or orders on its own initiative or on request. The Commission should be required to provide written reasons for its adjudicative decisions. Finally, any person or party would have the right to seek review of a decision of the Commission to the Federal Court of Canada, within 30 days of the decision being made public, but only on questions involving the Commission's jurisdiction.

Recommendation 1.7.29

We recommend that

(a) **the Canada Elections Commission be constituted as an administrative tribunal to adjudicate infractions under the *Canada Elections Act* with the powers, rights and privileges vested in a superior court of record, but that the Commission not participate in decisions related to investigation and prosecution, which would be the responsibility of the director of enforcement;**

(b) **the Commission be empowered to issue mandatory injunctions and cease-and-desist orders when required to protect the integrity of the electoral process, provided that the person or party affected by such an order has the right to appear before the Commission before the order is handed down, except in cases deemed to be emergencies;**

(c) **the Commission provide written reasons for its decisions;**

(d) **the Commission be empowered to rescind or vary any decision or order it has made at its own initiative or pursuant to a request made before it; and**

(e) **any person or party have the right to seek review of a decision of the Commission to the Federal Court of Canada within 30 days of the decision upon any question involving the jurisdiction of the Commission.**

Director of Enforcement

It is important that Canadians are assured that the Canada Elections Commission will provide a fair and impartial review of matters before it, first, by the person who determines whether an investigation or prosecution should proceed and, second, by the Commission that will either adjudicate the matter or direct the matter to the criminal courts for prosecution.

To ensure the institutional integrity of the Canada Elections Commission, the staff member responsible for investigation and enforcement must be independent of the Commission. A person designated as the director of enforcement will be responsible for decisions relating to investigation of a complaint as well as the initiation and handling of the prosecution. The director of enforcement will have no communication with the commissioners in relation to investigation and prosecution other than when the director appears before an adjudication panel of commissioners to prosecute a case or seek approval for a voluntary compliance agreement.

To ensure the true independence of the director of enforcement from the Commission, the director should be appointed by the Governor in Council. It is also necessary to provide for security for her or his position; therefore the appointment should be for a fixed period. The director of enforcement should have exclusive authority over her or his staff in relation to investigations and prosecutions. Finally, the director of enforcement should be able to make decisions without fear of dismissal unless there is just cause. Removal of the director should only be with the unanimous approval of the Commission.

Recommendation 1.7.30

We recommend that

(a) **the Governor in Council appoint a director of enforcement who will hold office for a five-year term during which she or he may be removed only for cause and with the unanimous approval of the Commission, and the mandate of the director of enforcement be renewable;**
(b) **the office of the director of enforcement be an independent office responsible for investigation and prosecution of offences before the Commission and the courts; and**
(c) **the director of enforcement have exclusive authority over the investigative and prosecutorial staff of her or his office.**

Detailed analysis and recommendations on procedures for the enforcement of the elections act and of the procedure to handle investigations and prosecutions are in Volume 2, Chapter 8.

Regulations Under the Act
Although the current *Canada Elections Act* gives the chief electoral officer powers to exercise some discretion, no provision is made for regulations with the force of law to be made by delegated authority under the Act. As a consequence, matters that in most statutes would be subject to regulations, especially those dealing with the details of enumeration, election finance and the voting process, are contained in the Act itself. For the most part, this approach is justified by the fact that the *Canada Elections Act*

governs the electoral competition between candidates and political parties.

The experience of the past few years, however, demonstrates not only the need for more frequent adjustments in the *Canada Elections Act*, but also the difficulty of making these changes by legislation. Members of Parliament and the political parties have been reluctant to allow changes to be made by other means for fear of giving the government of the day too much influence over the rules governing elections. This is a legitimate and reasonable concern and any revisions to the *Canada Elections Act* must ensure that the basic rules are governed by statutory provisions. The *Canada Elections Act* must remain more comprehensive in its details than normal legislation. Nevertheless, many matters should be governed by regulations. This can be done only if the House of Commons, rather than the government or any other authority, has the final say in changes to such regulations. This is possible if the Canada Elections Commission adopts any new or amended regulations but the power to approve or reject them is reserved for the House of Commons.

Under most statutes, regulations are developed by the responsible minister and the minister's department, or by an independent regulatory board. They do not come into force until they have been approved by the Governor in Council and published in *The Canada Gazette*. Many departments and regulatory agencies publish draft regulations and hold extensive consultations before making their proposals final. Proposed regulations are also reviewed by a special branch of the Privy Council Office for compliance with the Charter and are examined by the joint House of Commons and Senate Standing Committee on Statutory Instruments to ensure that they are within the terms of the powers granted in the enabling statute. This process of making regulations can take up to 16 months from the time the department or agency first submits them in draft form.

Because this delegated regulatory decision making is controlled by the government rather than Parliament, it is not acceptable or appropriate for making regulations dealing with election law. Under normal circumstances, this procedure is also too slow for the needs of the electoral process.

Therefore, a procedure is required that reflects the position of the Canada Elections Commission as an agency of Parliament and ensures the House of Commons deals with proposed regulations expeditiously. The procedure should enable any regulations proposed by the Canada Elections Commission to be deemed to have been adopted 15 sitting days after they have been submitted to the House of Commons, unless they have been referred for debate or to a committee during this period. Any regulations referred for debate or to committee would have to be approved by the House of Commons to take effect. Since in this unique procedure the regulations must be approved by the House of Commons directly rather than by the Governor in Council, there is no need for the Joint Standing Committee on Statutory Instruments to be required to review the regulations (although it could be invited to do so).

Before the Canada Elections Commission proposes any regulations, it should publish them in *The Canada Gazette*, inviting public comment, and conduct hearings on its proposals if deemed appropriate. This means that any proposed regulations would require the Canada Elections Commission, representing a diversity of views, to reach agreement first among its members, then to assess public reaction and response to its proposals, and finally to submit the proposed regulations for scrutiny and approval by the House of Commons. To launch the work of the Commission and allow parties and other registrants to fulfil the various new requirements, the initial set of regulations required to implement the new *Canada Elections Act* should take effect immediately and remain in force for six months. Following that period, the House of Commons would have the opportunity to accept or reject the regulations, along with whatever changes the Canada Elections Commission had proposed.

Recommendation 1.7.31

We recommend that

(a) **where regulations are provided for under the *Canada Elections Act*, they be made by the Canada Elections Commission and submitted directly to the Speaker of the House of Commons, who must table them forthwith;**

(b) **regulations be deemed to be approved if not referred for debate or to a committee within 15 sitting days after they have been submitted to the House;**

(c) **if a regulation made by the Commission has been referred for debate or to a committee of the House of Commons, it require approval by the House of Commons to take effect; and**

(d) **the initial set of regulations required to implement the new *Canada Elections Act* take effect immediately and remain in force for six months, then be approved or rejected by the House of Commons.**

Interpretation Bulletins and Advance Rulings
The Canada Elections Commission would establish policies and direct the chief electoral officer on policy issues. The Commission should also publicize its policies. At the same time, however, participants in the electoral process, particularly those formally registered under the law, need a more formal mechanism to clarify the rules governing them. This can be achieved in two ways: first, the commissioners, acting as a body, can issue policy statements on matters that have caused concern or uncertainty; and, second, Commission staff can issue interpretation bulletins and advance rulings within a defined period at the request of a political party, candidate, agent, constituency association or party foundation. In each case, the necessary

documents would be made public. Both these techniques are commonly used by other government agencies, for example, Revenue Canada, Taxation, various securities commissions, and the Federal Election Commission in Washington.

Recommendation 1.7.32

We recommend that

(a) the Commission be empowered to issue policy statements; and
(b) the chief electoral officer be empowered to issue interpretation bulletins as a guide to the law and be required to respond within a reasonable time to requests for advance rulings on its interpretation of election law and regulations.

Broadcasting Arbitration
The current Act calls for an independent broadcasting arbitrator, appointed by the chief electoral officer, whose function is to allocate free and paid broadcast time at and between elections, and to resolve related disputes. This official acts part-time and has no other responsibilities within Elections Canada. In a dispute over broadcast time, the decisions of this arbitrator are final and not subject to appeal except on points of law.

Given the powers of this function in disputes, which affect the fundamental principle of fairness in electoral competition, the Canada Elections Commission would be a more appropriate authority to exercise this responsibility. Negotiations with political parties could be handled by the Commission's staff, by a single commissioner or by someone appointed by the Commission to perform these specialized tasks. Final decisions on broadcast matters should be made under the authority of the Commission itself. The office of the broadcasting arbitrator should therefore be abolished.

Recommendation 1.7.33

We recommend that the Canada Elections Commission be responsible for all matters relating to broadcasting as found in the *Canada Elections Act*.

Non-Statutory Canada Elections Commission Expenditures
The primary activity of Elections Canada is to carry out elections; its expenditures for this purpose are authorized by statute and not subject to Treasury Board approval, and therefore, government budgetary control.

Both former and the current chief electoral officers have recommended that the financial resources of Elections Canada not be subject to Treasury Board control but instead subject to direct parliamentary authorization, on recommendation of the chief electoral officer, because this office reports directly to Parliament and is not under ministerial authority. In our view, it would be inappropriate to exempt the Canada Elections Commission from federal budgetary policies – for example, a temporary program of expenditure restraint. Although the Commission's non-statutory expenditure estimates should be subject to review by a House of Commons committee, they should continue to be subject to prior approval by the Treasury Board, which is the procedure that applies to other independent agencies, including the Office of the Auditor General of Canada.

Recommendation 1.7.34

We recommend that the Commission's non-statutory budget estimates, as submitted by the Commission, continue to be subject to Treasury Board approval prior to their submission to Parliament.

Reports to Parliament

Although the chief electoral officer reports directly to Parliament, the relationship between Elections Canada and the House of Commons has not been as effective as it could and should be. This has resulted in unnecessary delays in Parliament acting on recommendations for legislative changes made by the chief electoral officer. It has also led to less than satisfactory arrangements between the political parties represented in the House of Commons and Elections Canada.

In future, there should be a much stronger relationship between the House and the Canada Elections Commission. At present, there is no regular schedule for the chief electoral officer to report to Parliament; the statutory report of the chief electoral officer is delivered at the opening of each session of Parliament, but a new session of Parliament is not always held each year. This schedule for reporting may have been appropriate when the chief electoral officer was responsible only for conducting elections, but, as a result of responsibilities added during the past two decades, it is no longer sufficient. Therefore, the Canada Elections Commission should report annually. The House of Commons committee responsible for election matters should be expected not only to respond to this annual report but also to meet with the chief electoral officer and other members of the Commission at least once a year.

Recommendation 1.7.35

We recommend that

(a) the Canada Elections Commission report annually to the House of Commons on its activities and on recommended changes in legislation and election practice; and

(b) the Committee responsible for election matters respond to the Commission's annual report and meet with the chief electoral officer and members of the Commission at least once a year.

Rights of Election Officers and Staff of the Commission
To ensure the independence and impartiality of the federal electoral adminis-tration, we recommend that the chief electoral officer and other members of the Commission, during their term of office, not be permitted to hold office or be employed by a political party, to be a member of a political party or to make political contributions. These prohibitions should apply to election officers, including returning officers, assistant returning officers and the management and professional staff of the Canada Elections Commission.

Recommendation 1.7.36

We recommend that during their terms of office, returning offi-cers, assistant returning officers and the management and pro-fessional staff of the Canada Elections Commission not hold office in or be employed in any capacity by a political party and not be members of a political party or contributors to a political party or candidate.

The public interest demands that an election and its organization not be affected by labour-management disputes. The national interest in holding elections, and having them carried out in an orderly and efficient manner, is paramount and must not be jeopardized or held hostage by any group of persons. Under the *Public Service Staff Relations Act*, which applies to all employees of Elections Canada, the only persons excluded from the right to strike are those employed in a managerial or confidential capacity; some 46 000 public servants were so designated at the time of the federal public service strike in autumn 1991. All others are in a position to strike. In sev-eral provinces, notably Ontario, Manitoba, Quebec and British Columbia, the law does not allow employees of the elections agency to strike.

This issue does not arise only during the writ period. Elections Canada staff are responsible for preparing the vast array of materials required for an election and ensuring these are ready to be shipped across the country when an election is called. The relatively short election period means full preparation is critical: once the writs are issued, there is no time to complete these tasks. Our recommendation to shorten the election period would compound this problem. Given the vital role of all the Commission's staff in carrying out elections and the fact that the date elections are called is not fixed, it is necessary that they be excluded from the right to strike at all times.

Recommendation 1.7.37

We recommend that the *Public Service Staff Relations Act* be amended to allow for the designation of all staff of the Canada Elections Commission as excluded from the right to strike.

The Commission staff should, however, retain the right to union membership and to collective bargaining. We emphasize that our recommendation does not diminish these rights. Rather, we only aim to ensure that the vital processes of preparing for and carrying out elections are not jeopardized by strikes.

International Activities and Responsibilities

In the past, but especially in recent years, Elections Canada has been invited by External Affairs and International Trade Canada, the Canadian International Development Agency, the Speaker of the House of Commons, as well as numerous public and private international agencies, to assist in the promotion of democratic elections around the world. The chief electoral officer indicated during his 4 June 1991 appearance before a House of Commons committee that Elections Canada has devoted about $250 000 in salaries alone to such activities in fiscal year 1990–91. However, neither the *Canada Elections Act* nor the annual budget approved by Parliament gives Elections Canada a specific mandate for these international undertakings.

Aid to democratic electoral development can be grouped under four main headings: evaluation of technical and professional needs; providing technical, professional and materiel needs; overseeing and guiding those responsible for the administration of elections; and, observing the counting of the ballot and evaluating of the process generally. It is clear that for the first three aspects of development aid, the personnel of Elections Canada and the provincial elections offices are the principal, often exclusive, source of expertise. This expertise can be made available without impugning the status of the Canada Elections Commission as an agency of Parliament, not of the executive.

The question acquires a totally different nature, however, if the Canada Elections Commission and its staff were to become involved in areas of political evaluation and supervision of elections abroad or the development of Canadian government foreign policy as a consequence of such evaluation. These decisions reflect the policies, direction and priorities of the government of the day. As such, these matters fall within the authority of External Affairs and International Trade Canada and should remain there.

The mandate of the Canada Elections Commission should be limited to the provision of materiel and of professional and technical assistance. All requests for such assistance, beyond ongoing international activities as approved in the Commission's annual operating budget, should be channelled through External Affairs and International Trade Canada and approved by a House of Commons committee. If the costs of such assistance were not assumed by the sponsoring department or agency of the federal government, the Committee would authorize the amounts to be requested from non-allocated consolidated funds, as is the case for national elections.

Recommendation 1.7.38

We recommend that

(a) the Canada Elections Commission be given a mandate to provide materiel and professional and technical assistance to other countries, provided that all such requests be approved by a House of Commons committee; and
(b) the expenditures required be allocated from the non-allocated consolidated fund or assumed by the sponsoring department or agency.

NOTES

1. Section 33(3) of the *Canada Elections Act* provides that: "An association or organization of the members of a registered party within an electoral district may choose a person or persons to be electoral district agents for the purposes of that registered party in that electoral district...." The name and address of such an agent are to be registered with the chief electoral officer.

2. Two per cent indicated the surplus was turned over to the provincial level of the party and one per cent to the national level. One per cent indicated the surplus was disposed of in other ways, most often to pay off debts or loans (the "other" possible response was open-ended). (Carty 1991a RC)

3. Under section 41 of the *Parliament of Canada Act* a Member is prohibited from receiving "any compensation, directly or indirectly, for services rendered or to be rendered" in relation to any matter before the Senate or House of Commons or a committee of either house. A Member of Parliament who contravenes this provision is liable to a fine of between $500 and $2000 and, for five years after conviction, is disqualified from being a Member of Parliament and from holding any office in the public service of Canada. House of Commons Standing Order 21 provides that: "No Member is entitled to vote upon any question in which he or she has a direct pecuniary interest, and the vote of any Member so interested will be disallowed." (Canada, House of Commons 1990) According to the publication "Conflict of Interest and Members of Parliament" (Canada, House of Commons 1988a, 5), which the Office of the Law Clerk and Parliamentary Counsel distributes to Members of Parliament, "the interest which renders a Member unable to vote must be immediate and personal, and belong specifically to the person whose vote is contested".

4. Each Senate candidate's spending was divided by the voting-age population (VAP) for the state. It should be noted that the VAP includes "aliens,

felons, and others ineligible to vote in most States". (*FEC Journal of Election Administration* 1989, 2) However, the VAP is considered a better measure of the potential electorate in the United States than the number of registered voters (voter registration levels are considerably lower in the United States than in Canada). If the average spending were calculated on the basis of registered U.S. voters, the difference between the United States and Canada would be even greater. Data on Senate candidates' spending are from Federal Election Commission (1991d).

5. The relevant section reads as follows: "No company or association other than one incorporated for political purposes alone shall, directly or indir ctly, contribute, loan, advance, pay or promise or offer to pay any mone ᴣ or its equivalent to, or for, or in aid of, any candidate at an election, or to, or for, or in aid of, any political party, committee, or association, or to, or for, or in aid of, any company incorporated for political purposes, or to, or for, or in furtherance of, any political purpose whatever, or for the indemnification or reimbursement of any person for moneys so used." (*Dominion Elections Act*, 1908, c. 26, s. 36)

6. One measure of the concern of politicians regarding published opinion polls is that at least 22 private members' bills have been introduced on the subject. (Lachapelle 1991 RC)

7. This conclusion is based on daily tracking polls. The study found that awareness peaked during the period when most polls were being published. (Johnston et al. 1991, 7:11)

8. A significant feature of the 1988 campaign was the publication of a Gallup poll on 7 November that appears to have been "a piece of misinformation". (Johnston et al. 1991, 7:13) The poll, which seems to have exaggerated the support for the Liberals, produced an almost immediate bandwagon effect in favour of that party, building on the increased support that followed the televised leaders debates in late October. However, the effect was reversed very quickly by the publication of three other polls that showed a markedly lower level of Liberal support. The distribution of support among the parties returned to the levels established in late October. (Johnston et al. 1991, 7:6–7 and 8:10–12) These data indicate that an incorrect poll can significantly affect voter expectations (and, subsequently, behaviour) but that the publication of competitive polls provides a check on such effects.

9. The 1988 Canadian Election Study (Johnston et al. 1991, 8:10–13) detected a bandwagon effect that accounted in part for a shift of voter support from Progressive Conservatives to Liberals during the second week of November. It attributes the shift among voters neutral on the free trade issue entirely to a bandwagon effect based on poll-generated expectations of which party was ahead. The study detected a similar shift among French-speaking Canadians, which was attributed to the rational desire of voters who are members of a national minority to ensure strong representation in the caucus of the winning party. These effects dissipated when published polls showed that Progressive Conservative support was increasing.

10. The 1988 Canadian Election Study (Johnston et al. 1991, 8:8–10) concluded that there was considerable strategic voting in that election. In particular, the surge in Liberal support after the televised leaders debates consolidated Liberal support among those opposed to the free trade agreement (FTA). The NDP lost support in some regions for that reason. Subsequently, some supporters of the FTA who were considering voting otherwise responded to the increased Liberal support by rallying around the Progressive Conservatives. The expectations that guided these strategic decisions were derived mainly from published opinion polls.

11. Unfortunately, news organizations tend to provide relatively full reports only of the polls they have commissioned. Reporting of others is "quite spotty". (Johnston et al. 1991, 4:11)

12. In his analysis of media reports of 37 local and regional polls, Lachapelle (1991 RC) found that appropriate technical information was often omitted. For example, 19 per cent failed to report the sponsor of the poll, 32 per cent the dates of the interviews, 27 per cent the interview method, 8 per cent the number of respondents, and 30 per cent the margin of error, all considered basic information by pollsters.

13. Such reporting lends a spurious authority to the results. In all polls, there is an inevitable trade-off between cost-effectiveness and speed, on the one hand, and limiting the variance on the other. The inevitable failure to reach some people in the initial sample and the growing incidence of refusal to be interviewed result in problems in the sample. The refusal rates in telephone surveys, by far the most common form of public polling in Canada, are usually more than 25 per cent and often higher. (Cantril 1991, 96) Such high rates cast doubt on the representativeness of samples. The 1988 Canadian Election Study (Johnston et al. 1991, 4:9 and 5:2–10) experimented with varied question wording and found that different wordings tended to result in significantly different distributions of opinion. (See also Blais and Gidengil 1991 RC.)

14. News organizations that do no polling during the final part of the campaign include the CBC (10 days) and the *Los Angeles Times* (two weeks). They may report the polls of others but only with careful qualifications. The 1988 Canadian Election Study found a lag of about two days in the impact of polls and advertising. (Johnston et al. 1991, 8:14) This finding indicates that the blackout period may provide time for rebuttal of erroneous or questionable data.

15. The 1988 Canadian Election Study found that respondents who did not pay much attention to polls tended to be swayed by dramatic or highly visible polls and to retain the effect in the face of new results that contradicted the earlier data. (Johnston et al. 1991, 7:12–13) More attentive voters adjusted their expectations as new poll results were published. "Could it be," the researchers asked, "that the real problem with polls is with citizens who are not routinely aware of them? Such citizens respond to the highest profile polls but seem unable, in contrast to poll *habitués*, to place them in context." (Johnston et al. 1991, 7:13; 9:7) In short, the better educated the public is

regarding polls, the more likely they are to discount erroneous polls, especially when there is ample competition.

16. Most Canadian pollsters are members of the Canadian Association of Marketing Research Organizations, which has a code of professional conduct and holds annual conferences. However, it is not primarily concerned with public polling.

17. The 1988 Canadian Election Study found a lag of about two days in the impact of television advertising. (Johnston et al. 1991, 8:14)

18. Traditionally, criticisms of the French- and English-language media have differed somewhat. Criticisms of French-language journalism have centred on allegations that journalists were too opinionated or ideological and too close to particular political parties or movements, not that they were insufficiently analytical or lacked commitment to political education. (Gagnon 1981; Sauvageau 1981) In recent years, news coverage of election campaigns has become more like that in the English-language media, though a sense of intellectual mission remains. (Charron 1991 RC; Gilsdorf and Bernier 1991 RC)

19. A senior broadcast journalist, speaking at our symposium on political ethics, noted that news organizations are not committed to elections as a process but rather increasingly view them as just another event competing for media attention. He said that media news values are not driven by a commitment to public education but rather by an attempt to meet the apparent wants and needs of audiences. David Taras has commented on this trend: "News organizations ... see elections as an opportunity to celebrate their own interests and credentials, to make headlines, declare winners and losers, and ridicule ... the falseness of politicians. What's lost in the jumble and frenzy of the [campaign] is any sense that elections are meaningful, even sacred events, that must not be taken for granted." (1990, 175–76)

20. Although news organizations often claim that election coverage is determined by "normal news values", there is considerable evidence that election campaigns have been treated differently than other news. For example, a CBC policy since 1979 has stated that elections are to be given "special prominence" in news coverage. Other news organizations have had similar policies. In addition, most major news organizations take special measures to ensure that the leaders of the larger parties are given roughly equal space or airtime. The major criticisms of current news coverage focus not on the amount of attention given to election campaigns but rather on the nature of the coverage. However, even the commitment to "special prominence" for election coverage, which recognizes the importance of elections in a democratic society, are coming under increasing criticism within the media and appear to be eroding. (Taras 1990, 161)

21. In 1991, the CDNPA changed its name to Canadian Daily Newspapers Association (CDNA).

REFERENCES

Abella, Irving, and Harold Troper. 1982. *None Is Too Many: Canada and the Jews of Europe 1933–1948*. Toronto: Lester and Orpen Dennys.

Abramson, Jeffrey B., F. Christopher Arterton and Gary R. Orren. 1988. *The Electronic Commonwealth: The Impact of New Media Technologies on Democratic Politics*. New York: Basic Books.

Action Travail des Femmes v. *Canadian National Railway Co.*, [1987] 1 S.C.R. 1114.

Adams, Michael. 1991. "Big Picture Is Changing on TV News." *Toronto Star*, 30 September.

Adatto, Kiku. 1990. "The Incredible Shrinking Sound Bite." *The New Republic* (28 May): 20–23.

Alexander, Herbert E. 1991 RC. "The Regulation of Election Finance in the United States and Proposals for Reform." In *Comparative Issues in Party and Election Finance*, ed. F. Leslie Seidle. Vol. 4 of the research studies of the Royal Commission on Electoral Reform and Party Financing. Ottawa: RCERPF.

Alia, Valerie. 1991 RC. "Aboriginal Peoples and Campaign Coverage in the North." In *Aboriginal Peoples and Electoral Reform in Canada*, ed. Robert A. Milen. Vol. 9 of the research studies of the Royal Commission on Electoral Reform and Party Financing. Ottawa: RCERPF.

Anwar, Muhammad. 1986. *Race and Politics: Ethnic Minorities and the British Political System*. London: Tavistock.

Archer, Keith A. 1990. *Political Choices and Electoral Consequences: A Study of Organized Labour and the New Democratic Party*. Montreal and Kingston: McGill–Queen's University Press.

Archer, Keith A. 1991a RC. "Leadership Selection in the New Democratic Party." In *Canadian Political Parties: Leaders, Candidates and Organization*, ed. Herman Bakvis. Vol. 13 of the research studies of the Royal Commission on Electoral Reform and Party Financing. Ottawa: RCERPF.

Archer, Keith A. 1991b RC. "The New Democrats, Organized Labour and the Prospects of Electoral Reform." In *Canadian Political Parties: Leaders, Candidates and Organization*, ed. Herman Bakvis. Vol. 13 of the research studies of the Royal Commission on Electoral Reform and Party Financing. Ottawa: RCERPF.

Arian, Asher. 1985. *Politics in Israel: The Second Generation*. Chatham: Chatham House.

Atkinson, Michael M., and David C. Docherty. 1991. "Moving Right Along: The Roots of Amateurism in the Canadian House of Commons." Paper presented at the annual meeting of the Canadian Political Science Association, Kingston.

Aucoin, Peter. 1985. "Regionalism, Party and National Government." In *Party Government and Regional Representation in Canada*, ed. Peter Aucoin. Vol. 36 of the research studies of the Royal Commission on the Economic Union and Development Prospects for Canada. Toronto: University of Toronto Press.

Aucoin, Peter. 1986. "Organizational Change in the Machinery of Canadian Government: From Rational Management to Brokerage Politics." *Canadian Journal of Political Science* 19: 3–27.

Aucoin, Peter. 1988. "The Mulroney Government, 1984–1988: Priorities, Positional Policy and Power." In *Canada under Mulroney: An End-of-Term Report*, ed. Andrew B. Gollner and Daniel Salée. Montreal: Véhicule Press.

Australia. 1984. *Reports of the Electoral Commissions.* Canberra: Commonwealth Government Printer.

Australia. Australian Electoral Commission. Electoral Education Centre. 1989. "Redistributions." Background paper. Canberra: AEC.

Australia. Queensland. Electoral and Administrative Review Commission. 1990. *Report on Queensland Legislative Assembly Electoral System.* Volume 1. Brisbane: Electoral and Administrative Review Commission.

Avakumovic, Ivan. 1975. *The Communist Party in Canada: A History.* Toronto: McClelland and Stewart.

Axworthy, Thomas S. 1991 RC. "Capital-Intensive Politics: Money, Media and Mores in the United States and Canada." In *Issues in Party and Election Finance in Canada*, ed. F. Leslie Seidle. Vol. 5 of the research studies of the Royal Commission on Electoral Reform and Party Financing. Ottawa: RCERPF.

Badger v. *Canada (Attorney General)* (1988), 55 D.L.R. (4th) 177 (C.A.).

Bakvis, Herman. 1991. *Regional Ministers: Power and Influence in the Canadian Cabinet.* Toronto: University of Toronto Press.

Bakvis, Herman, and Neil Nevitte. 1990. "The Greening of the Canadian Electorate: Environmentalism, Ideology and Partisanship." Paper presented at the annual meeting of the Canadian Political Science Association, Victoria.

Balinski, M.L., and H.P. Young. 1981. "Parliamentary Representation and the Amalgam Method." *Canadian Journal of Political Science* 14: 797–812.

Barr, Cathy Widdis. 1991 RC. "The Importance and Potential of Leaders' Debates." In *Media and Voters in Canadian Election Campaigns*, ed. Frederick

J. Fletcher. Vol. 18 of the research studies of the Royal Commission on Electoral Reform and Party Financing. Ottawa: RCERPF.

Barrie, Doreen P. 1991 RC. "Party Financing in Alberta: Low-Impact Legislation." In *Provincial Party and Election Finance in Canada*, ed. F. Leslie Seidle. Vol. 3 of the research studies of the Royal Commission on Electoral Reform and Party Financing. Ottawa: RCERPF.

Bartlett, Richard H. 1980. "Citizens Minus: Indians and the Right to Vote." *Saskatchewan Law Review* 44: 163–94.

Bashevkin, Sylvia. 1991 RC. "Women's Participation in Political Parties." In *Women in Canadian Politics: Towards Equity in Representation*, ed. Kathy Megyery. Vol. 6 of the research studies of the Royal Commission on Electoral Reform and Party Financing. Ottawa: RCERPF.

Beck, J. Murray. 1968. *Pendulum of Power: Canada's Federal Elections*. Scarborough: Prentice-Hall of Canada.

Beh, Andrew, and Roger Gibbins. 1991 RC. "The Campaign–Media Interface in Local Constituencies: Two Alberta Case Studies from the 1988 Federal Election Campaign." In *Reaching the Voter: Constituency Campaigning in Canada*, ed. Frederick J. Fletcher and David V.J. Bell. Vol. 20 of the research studies of the Royal Commission on Electoral Reform and Party Financing. Ottawa: RCERPF.

Belczowski v. *R.*, Fed. T.D., No. T-1182-88, 1991.

Bell, Daniel. 1960. *The End of Ideology: On the Exhaustion of Political Ideas in the Fifties*. New York: Free Press.

Bell, David V.J., and Catherine M. Bolan. 1991 RC. "The Mass Media and Federal Election Campaigning at the Local Level: A Case Study of Two Ontario Constituencies." In *Reaching the Voter: Constituency Campaigning in Canada*, ed. Frederick J. Fletcher and David V.J. Bell. Vol. 20 of the research studies of the Royal Commission on Electoral Reform and Party Financing. Ottawa: RCERPF.

Bell, David V.J., and Frederick J. Fletcher. 1991 RC. "Electoral Communication at the Constituency Level: A Framework for Analysis." In *Reaching the Voter: Constituency Campaigning in Canada*, ed. Frederick J. Fletcher and David V.J. Bell. Vol. 20 of the research studies of the Royal Commission on Electoral Reform and Party Financing. Ottawa: RCERPF.

Bell, David V.J., Frederick J. Fletcher and Catherine M. Bolan. 1991 RC. "Electoral Communication at the Constituency Level: Summary and Conclusion." In *Reaching the Voter: Constituency Campaigning in Canada*, ed. Frederick J. Fletcher and David V.J. Bell. Vol. 20 of the research studies of the Royal Commission on Electoral Reform and Party Financing. Ottawa: RCERPF.

Berlin, Isaiah. 1969. *Four Essays on Liberty*. Oxford: Oxford University Press.

Bernier, Luc. 1991 RC. "Local Campaigns and the Media: The 1988 Election in Outremont and Frontenac." In *Reaching the Voter: Constituency Campaigning in Canada*, ed. Frederick J. Fletcher and David V.J. Bell. Vol. 20 of the research studies of the Royal Commission on Electoral Reform and Party Financing. Ottawa: RCERPF.

Bernier, Robert, and Denis Monière. 1991 RC. "The Organization of Televised Leaders' Debates in the United States, Europe, Australia and Canada." In *Media and Voters in Canadian Election Campaigns*, ed. Frederick J. Fletcher. Vol. 18 of the research studies of the Royal Commission on Electoral Reform and Party Financing. Ottawa: RCERPF.

Bertram, Eric. 1991 RC. "Independent Candidates in Federal General Elections." In *Issues in Party and Election Finance in Canada*, ed. F. Leslie Seidle. Vol. 5 of the research studies of the Royal Commission on Electoral Reform and Party Financing. Ottawa: RCERPF.

Black, Jerome H. 1991 RC. "Reforming the Context of the Voting Process in Canada: Lessons from Other Democracies." In *Voter Turnout in Canada*, ed. Herman Bakvis. Vol. 15 of the research studies of the Royal Commission on Electoral Reform and Party Financing. Ottawa: RCERPF.

Blais, André, and R.K. Carty. 1990. "Does Proportional Representation Foster Voter Turnout?" *European Journal of Political Research* 18: 167–81.

Blais, André, and Elisabeth Gidengil. 1991 RC. *Representative Democracy: The Views of Canadians*. Vol. 17 of the research studies of the Royal Commission on Electoral Reform and Party Financing. Ottawa: RCERPF.

Blais, André, Richard Johnston, Henry E. Brady and Jean Crête. 1990. "The Dynamics of Horse Race Expectations in the 1988 Canadian Election." Paper presented at the annual meeting of the Canadian Political Science Association, Victoria.

Blake, Donald E. 1991 RC. "Party Competition and Electoral Volatility: Canada in Comparative Perspective." In *Representation, Integration and Political Parties in Canada*, ed. Herman Bakvis. Vol. 14 of the research studies of the Royal Commission on Electoral Reform and Party Financing. Ottawa: RCERPF.

Bogdanor, Vernon, ed. 1985. *Representatives of the People? Parliamentarians and Constituents in Western Democracies*. Aldershot: Gower.

Boucher, Cécile. 1991 RC. "Administration and Enforcement of the Elections Act in Canada." In *Democratic Rights and Electoral Reform in Canada*, ed. Michael Cassidy. Vol. 10 of the research studies of the Royal Commission on Electoral Reform and Party Financing. Ottawa: RCERPF.

Boyer, J. Patrick. 1983. *Money and Message: The Law Governing Election Financing, Advertising, Broadcasting and Campaigning in Canada*. Toronto: Butterworths.

Boyer, J. Patrick. 1987. *Election Law in Canada: The Law and Procedure of Federal, Provincial and Territorial Elections*. 2 vols. Toronto: Butterworths.

Breton, Raymond. 1986. "Multiculturalism and Canadian Nation-Building." In *The Politics of Gender, Ethnicity and Language in Canada*, ed. Alan Cairns and Cynthia Williams. Vol. 34 of the research studies of the Royal Commission on the Economic Union and Development Prospects for Canada. Toronto: University of Toronto Press.

British Columbia. Elections BC. 1991. *British Columbia's Political Contributions Program: A Guide to Election Contributions, Valid Receipts, Income Tax Deductions and More*. Victoria: Elections BC.

Brock, Kathy L. 1991 RC. "Fairness, Equity, and Rights." In *Political Ethics: A Canadian Perspective*, ed. Janet Hiebert. Vol. 12 of the research studies of the Royal Commission on Electoral Reform and Party Financing. Ottawa: RCERPF.

Broder, David S. 1987. *Behind the Front Page*. New York: Simon and Schuster.

Brodie, Janine, with the assistance of Celia Chandler. 1991 RC. "Women and the Electoral Process in Canada." In *Women in Canadian Politics: Towards Equity in Representation*, ed. Kathy Megyery. Vol. 6 of the research studies of the Royal Commission on Electoral Reform and Party Financing. Ottawa: RCERPF.

Buckley v. *Valeo* 424 U.S. 1 (1976).

Cain, Bruce E. 1984. *The Reapportionment Puzzle*. Berkeley: University of California Press.

Cairns, Alan C. 1968. "The Electoral System and the Party System in Canada, 1921–1965." *Canadian Journal of Political Science* 1: 55–80.

Cairns, Alan C. 1990. "Constitutional Minoritarianism in Canada." In *Canada: The State of the Federation 1990*, ed. Ronald L. Watts and Douglas M. Brown. Kingston: Queen's University, Institute of Intergovernmental Relations.

Cairns, Alan C. 1991. "Constitutional Change and the Three Equalities." In *Options for a New Canada*, ed. Ronald L. Watts and Douglas M. Brown. Toronto: University of Toronto Press.

Camp, Dalton. 1981. *An Eclectic Eel*. Ottawa: Deneau.

Campbell, Bryan. 1991. "Socio-Demographic Profiles of Women MPs and Candidates in the 1988 Federal Election: A Statistical Note." Paper prepared for the Royal Commission on Electoral Reform and Party Financing. Ottawa.

Canada. 1987. *The Canada Gazette*, Part I, Extra No. 4, Vol. 121 (17 July).

Canada. 1991. *Shaping Canada's Future Together: Proposals*. Ottawa: Minister of Supply and Services Canada.

Canada. Chief Electoral Officer. 1979a. *Report of the Chief Electoral Officer of Canada as per subsection 59(1) of the Canada Elections Act.* Ottawa: Minister of Supply and Services Canada.

Canada. Chief Electoral Officer. 1979b. *Report of the Chief Electoral Officer Respecting Election Expenses.* Ottawa: Minister of Supply and Services Canada.

Canada. Chief Electoral Officer. 1980a. *Report of the Chief Electoral Officer of Canada as per subsection 59(1) of the Canada Elections Act.* Ottawa: Minister of Supply and Services Canada.

Canada. Chief Electoral Officer. 1980b. *Report of the Chief Electoral Officer Respecting Election Expenses.* Ottawa: Minister of Supply and Services Canada.

Canada. Chief Electoral Officer. 1984a. *Report of the Chief Electoral Officer of Canada as per subsection 59(1) of the Canada Elections Act.* Ottawa: Minister of Supply and Services Canada.

Canada. Chief Electoral Officer. 1984b. *Report of the Chief Electoral Officer Respecting Election Expenses.* Ottawa: Minister of Supply and Services Canada.

Canada. Chief Electoral Officer. 1985. *Report of the Chief Electoral Officer of Canada on Proposed Legislative Changes.* Ottawa: Minister of Supply and Services Canada.

Canada. Chief Electoral Officer. 1988. *Report of the Chief Electoral Officer Respecting Election Expenses.* Ottawa: Minister of Supply and Services Canada.

Canada. Chief Electoral Officer. 1989. *Report of the Chief Electoral Officer of Canada as per subsection 195(1) of the Canada Elections Act.* Ottawa: Minister of Supply and Services Canada.

Canada. Chief Electoral Officer. 1991. *Report of the Chief Electoral Officer of Canada as per subsection 195(1) of the Canada Elections Act.* Ottawa: Minister of Supply and Services Canada.

Canada. Chief Electoral Officer. Various. *Report of the Chief Electoral Officer of Canada pursuant to section 193 of the Canada Elections Act.* Ottawa: Minister of Supply and Services Canada.

Canada. Committee on Election Expenses. 1966. *Report.* Ottawa: Queen's Printer.

Canada. Correctional Service Canada. 1985. *Inmate Rights and Responsibilities.* Ottawa: Minister of Supply and Services Canada.

Canada. Correctional Service Canada. Management Information Services. 1990. *Population Profile Report: Population on Register 12/31/90.* Ottawa: Correctional Service Canada.

Canada. Department of Indian Affairs. 1918. *Annual Report for the Year Ended March 31, 1917.* Ottawa: King's Printer.

Canada. Department of Indian Affairs and Northern Development. 1969. *Statement of the Government of Canada on Indian Policy, 1969*. Ottawa: Queen's Printer.

Canada. Elections Canada. 1986. *Representation in the Federal Parliament*. Ottawa: Minister of Supply and Services Canada.

Canada. Elections Canada. 1988. "Federal Electoral District Profiles, 1988." Ottawa: Elections Canada.

Canada. Elections Canada. 1990. "Registered Parties Fiscal Period Returns." Ottawa: Elections Canada.

Canada. Employment and Immigration Canada. 1991. *Employment Equity Act 1990 Annual Report*. Ottawa: Minister of Supply and Services Canada.

Canada. House of Commons. 1988a. *Conflict of Interest and Members of the House of Commons*. Ottawa: Office of the Law Clerk and Parliamentary Counsel.

Canada. House of Commons. 1990. *Standing Orders of the House of Commons*. Ottawa: Speaker of the House of Commons.

Canada. House of Commons. Special Committee on Election Expenses. 1971. *Report*. Ottawa: Queen's Printer.

Canada. House of Commons. Special Committee on Participation of Visible Minorities in Canadian Society. 1984. *Equality Now*. Ottawa: Queen's Printer.

Canada. House of Commons. Special Committee on the Canadian Radio Commission. 1936. *Third and Final Report*. Ottawa: King's Printer.

Canada. House of Commons. Standing Committee on Elections, Privileges and Procedure. 1988b. *Minutes of Proceedings and Evidence*. Issue no. 24 (10 February and 23 February). Ottawa: Queen's Printer.

Canada. Privy Council Office. 1986. *White Paper on Election Law Reform*. Ottawa: Queen's Printer.

Canada. Revenue Canada, Taxation. 1985. "Registered Charities: Operating a Registered Charity." Circular 80–10R, 17 December. Ottawa: Revenue Canada, Taxation.

Canada. Revenue Canada, Taxation. 1987. "Registered Charities: Ancillary and Incidental Political Activities." Circular 87–1, 25 February. Ottawa: Revenue Canada, Taxation.

Canada. Revenue Canada, Taxation. 1989. "Free Trade Business Expenses Deductible if Criteria Met." Press Release, 25 August. Ottawa: Revenue Canada, Taxation.

Canada. Royal Commission on Bilingualism and Biculturalism. 1970a. *Report*. Book 4. Ottawa: Queen's Printer.

Canada. Royal Commission on Electoral Reform and Party Financing. 1991. *Final Report*. Ottawa: RCERPF.

Canada. Royal Commission on Electoral Reform and Party Financing. Accounting Profession Working Group on Election/Party Finance Reporting at the Local Level. 1991a. *Report*. Ottawa.

Canada. Royal Commission on Newspapers. 1981. *Report*. Ottawa: Minister of Supply and Services Canada.

Canada. Royal Commission on Radio Broadcasting. 1929. *Report*. Ottawa: King's Printer.

Canada. Royal Commission on the Economic Union and Development Prospects for Canada. 1985. *Report*. Ottawa: Minister of Supply and Services Canada.

Canada. Royal Commission on the Status of Women. 1970b. *Report*. Ottawa: Queen's Printer.

Canada. Statistics Canada. 1988. *Federal Electoral Districts – 1987 Representation Order: Part 2*. Cat. no. 94–134. Ottawa: Canadian Government Publishing Centre.

Canada. Statistics Canada. 1989. *Ethnicity, Immigration and Citizenship*. Ottawa: Minister of Supply and Services Canada.

Canada. Statistics Canada. 1990a. *Adult Correctional Services in Canada 1989–1990*. Ottawa: Minister of Supply and Services Canada.

Canada. Statistics Canada. 1990b. *Population Projections for Canada, Provinces and Territories 1989–2011*. Cat. no. 91–520. Ottawa: Minister of Supply and Services Canada.

Canada. Statistics Canada. 1990c. *Postcensal Annual Estimates of Population by Marital Status, Age, Sex and Components of Growth for Canada, Provinces and Territories, June 1, 1990*. Cat. no. 91–210. Ottawa: Minister of Supply and Services Canada.

Canada. Statistics Canada. 1990d. *Profile of Visible Minorities and Aboriginal Peoples*. 1986 Census – 20% Sample Data. Ottawa: Statistics Canada.

Canada. Supply and Services Canada. 1990. "Contracts Subject to Employment Equity." Policy Directive 3055 of 31/01/90. Ottawa: Minister of Supply and Services Canada.

Canada. Task Force on Broadcasting Policy. 1986. *Report*. Ottawa: Minister of Supply and Services Canada.

Canada. Task Force on the Economic Status of Canadian Television. 1991. *Report*. Ottawa: Minister of Supply and Services Canada.

Canadian Broadcast Standards Council. 1988. *Code of Ethics*. Ottawa: CBSC.

Canadian Broadcasting Corporation (CBC). 1944. "Political and Controversial Broadcasting: Policies and Rulings, 21 February 1944." Reprinted as Document 23 in *Documents of Canadian Broadcasting*, ed. Roger Bird. Ottawa: Carleton University Press, 1988.

Canadian Daily Newspaper Publishers Association. 1977. *A Statement of Principles for Canadian Daily Newspapers*. Toronto: CDNPA.

Canadian Disability Rights Council v. *Canada*, [1988] 3 F.C. 622 (T.D.).

Canadian Institute of Chartered Accountants. 1991. *CICA Handbook*. Toronto: CICA.

Canadian National Election Study. 1974. Principal investigators: Harold D. Clarke, Jane Jenson, Lawrence LeDuc and Jon H. Pammett. See *Absent Mandate* (Toronto: Gage, 1984) and *Political Choice in Canada* (Toronto: McGraw-Hill Ryerson, 1979).

Canadian National Election Study. 1980. Principal investigators: Harold D. Clarke, Jane Jenson, Lawrence LeDuc and Jon H. Pammett. See *Absent Mandate* (Toronto: Gage, 1984) and *Political Choice in Canada* (Toronto: McGraw-Hill Ryerson, 1979).

Canadian National Election Study. 1984. Institute for Social Research, York University. Principal investigators: Steven Brown, Ronald Lambert, James Curtis, Barry Kay and John Wilson. Funded by the Social Sciences and Humanities Research Council.

Canadian National Election Study. 1988. Institute for Social Research, York University. Principal investigators: Richard Johnston, André Blais, Henry E. Brady and Jean Crête. Funded by the Social Sciences and Humanities Research Council.

Canadian Peace Pledge Campaign. 1988. "Wouldn't You Like to Hand This Down to Your Kids?" *Globe and Mail*, 15 November.

Canadian Radio-television and Telecommunications Commission (CRTC). 1986. "Proposed Regulations Respecting Television Broadcasting." Public Notice CRTC 1986–176. Ottawa: CRTC.

Canadian Radio-television and Telecommunications Commission (CRTC). 1987. "Political Broadcasting – Complaints re: Free Time and Editorial Time Allocations." Circular No. 334. Ottawa: CRTC.

Canadian Radio-television and Telecommunications Commission (CRTC). 1988. "A Policy with Respect to Election Campaign Broadcasting." Public Notice CRTC 1988–142. Ottawa: CRTC.

Cantril, Albert H. 1991. *The Opinion Connection: Polling, Politics, and the Press*. Washington, DC: CQ Press.

Carter v. *Saskatchewan (Attorney General)*. See *Reference re Provincial Electoral Boundaries*.

Carty, R. Kenneth. 1988a. "Campaigning in the Trenches: The Transformation of Constituency Politics." In *Party Democracy in Canada: The Politics of National Party Conventions*, ed. George Perlin. Scarborough: Prentice-Hall Canada.

Carty, R. Kenneth. 1988b. "Three Canadian Party Systems: An Interpretation of the Development of National Politics." In *Party Democracy in Canada: The Politics of National Party Conventions*, ed. George Perlin. Scarborough: Prentice-Hall Canada.

Carty, R. Kenneth. 1991a RC. *Canadian Political Parties in the Constituencies: A Local Perspective*. Vol. 23 of the research studies of the Royal Commission on Electoral Reform and Party Financing. Ottawa: RCERPF.

Carty, R. Kenneth. 1991b RC. "Official Agents in Canadian Elections: The Case of the 1988 General Election." In *Issues in Party and Election Finance in Canada*, ed. F. Leslie Seidle. Vol. 5 of the research studies of the Royal Commission on Electoral Reform and Party Financing. Ottawa: RCERPF.

Carty, R. Kenneth, and Lynda Erickson. 1991 RC. "Candidate Nomination in Canada's National Political Parties." In *Canadian Political Parties: Leaders, Candidates and Organization*, ed. Herman Bakvis. Vol. 13 of the research studies of the Royal Commission on Electoral Reform and Party Financing. Ottawa: RCERPF.

Chandler, William M., and Alan Siaroff. 1991 RC. "Parties and Party Government in Advanced Democracies." In *Canadian Political Parties: Leaders, Candidates and Organization*, ed. Herman Bakvis. Vol. 13 of the research studies of the Royal Commission on Electoral Reform and Party Financing. Ottawa: RCERPF.

Charron, Jean. 1991 RC. "Relations between Political Parties and the Media in Quebec Election Campaigns." In *Reporting the Campaign: Election Coverage in Canada*, ed. Frederick J. Fletcher. Vol. 22 of the research studies of the Royal Commission on Electoral Reform and Party Financing. Ottawa: RCERPF.

Clarke, Harold D., Lawrence LeDuc, Jane Jenson and Jon H. Pammett. 1991. *Absent Mandate: Interpreting Change in Canadian Elections*. 2d ed. Toronto: Gage.

Cleverdon, Catherine L. 1974. *The Woman Suffrage Movement in Canada*. 2d ed. Toronto: University of Toronto Press.

Cloutier, Edouard, Richard Nadeau and Jean Guay. 1989. "Bandwagoning and Underdoging on North-American Free Trade: A Quasi-Experimental Panel Study of Opinion Movement." *International Journal of Public Opinion Research* 1: 206–20.

Cloutier, Richard. 1982. *Psychologie de l'adolescence*. Chicoutimi: Gaëtan Morin.

Comber, Mary Anne, and Robert S. Mayne. 1986. *The Newsmongers: How the Media Distort the Political News*. Toronto: McClelland and Stewart.

Comité des sondages de la Société canadienne de science politique et l'Association canadienne des sociologues et anthropologues de langue française. 1977. *Sondages politiques et politique des sondages au Québec*. [Montreal].

Constantinou, Peter P. 1991 RC. "Public Funding of Political Parties, Candidates and Elections in Canada." In *Issues in Party and Election Finance in Canada*, ed. F. Leslie Seidle. Vol. 5 of the research studies of the Royal Commission on Electoral Reform and Party Financing. Ottawa: RCERPF.

Cooper, J., and I. Christe. 1991. *Voter Participation – A State Report*. Vol. 3, No. 1. Washington, DC: Center for Policy Alternatives.

Cossette. 1991. *Media Recommendations*. Report prepared for the Royal Commission on Electoral Reform and Party Financing. Quebec: Cossette Communication-Marketing.

Courtney, John C. 1973. *The Selection of National Party Leaders in Canada*. Toronto: Macmillan of Canada.

Courtney, John C. 1978. "Recognition of Canadian Political Parties in Parliament and in Law." *Canadian Journal of Political Science* 11: 33–60.

Courtney, John C. 1985. "The Size of Canada's Parliament: An Assessment of the Implications of a Larger House of Commons." In *Institutional Reforms for Representative Government*, ed. Peter Aucoin. Vol. 38 of the research studies of the Royal Commission on the Economic Union and Development Prospects for Canada. Toronto: University of Toronto Press.

Courtney, John C. 1988. "Parliament and Representation: The Unfinished Agenda of Electoral Redistributions." *Canadian Journal of Political Science* 21: 675–90.

Courtney, John C., and David E. Smith. 1991 RC. "Registering Voters: Canada in a Comparative Context." In *Democratic Rights and Electoral Reform in Canada*, ed. Michael Cassidy. Vol. 10 of the research studies of the Royal Commission on Electoral Reform and Party Financing. Ottawa: RCERPF.

Covell, Maureen. 1991 RC. "Parties as Institutions of National Governance." In *Representation, Integration and Political Parties in Canada*, ed. Herman Bakvis. Vol. 14 of the research studies of the Royal Commission on Electoral Reform and Party Financing. Ottawa: RCERPF.

Crepaz, Markus M.L. 1990. "The Impact of Party Polarization and Post-materialism on Voter Turnout." *European Journal of Political Research* 18: 183–205.

Crête, Jean. 1991 RC. "Television, Advertising and Canadian Elections." In *Media and Voters in Canadian Election Campaigns*, ed. Frederick J. Fletcher. Vol. 18 of the research studies of the Royal Commission on Electoral Reform and Party Financing. Ottawa: RCERPF.

Crewe, Ivor. 1981. "Electoral Participation." In *Democracy at the Polls: A Comparative Study of Competitive National Elections*, ed. David Butler, Howard R. Penniman and Austin Ranney. Washington, DC: American Enterprise Institute for Public Policy Research.

CTV Television Network Ltd. 1989. "A Report to the Canadian Radio-television and Telecommunications Commission Regarding Coverage of the 1988 Federal General Election." Ottawa: CTV.

Dahl, Robert A. 1989. *Democracy and Its Critics*. New Haven: Yale University Press.

Dawson, R. MacGregor. 1970. *The Government of Canada*. 5th ed., revised by Norman Ward. Toronto: University of Toronto Press.

Denoncourt, Yves. 1991 RC. "Reflections Concerning Criteria for the Vote for Persons with Mental Disorders." In *Democratic Rights and Electoral Reform in Canada*, ed. Michael Cassidy. Vol. 10 of the research studies of the Royal Commission on Electoral Reform and Party Financing. Ottawa: RCERPF.

Denver, David. 1988. "Britain: Centralized Parties with Decentralized Selection." In *Candidate Selection in Comparative Perspective: The Secret Garden of Politics*, ed. Michael Gallagher and Michael Marsh. London: Sage Publications.

Desbarats, Peter. 1990a. *Guide to Canadian News Media*. Toronto: Harcourt Brace Jovanovich, Canada.

Desbarats, Peter. 1990b. "Television and Surveys Are Playing a New Part in Politics." *Globe and Mail*, 8 June.

Desbarats, Peter. 1991 RC. "Cable Television and Federal Election Campaigns in Canada." In *Election Broadcasting in Canada*, ed. Frederick J. Fletcher. Vol. 21 of the research studies of the Royal Commission on Electoral Reform and Party Financing. Ottawa: RCERPF.

Dixon v. British Columbia (Attorney General) (1989), 35 B.C.L.R. (2d) 273 (B.C.S.C.).

Doern, G. Bruce. 1971. "The Development of Policy Organizations in the Executive Arena." In *The Structures of Policy-Making in Canada*, ed. G. Bruce Doern and Peter Aucoin. Toronto: Macmillan of Canada.

Dornan, Christopher. 1991 RC. "Free to Be Responsible: The Accountability of the Print Media." In *Reporting the Campaign: Election Coverage in Canada*, ed. Frederick J. Fletcher. Vol. 22 of the research studies of the Royal Commission on Electoral Reform and Party Financing. Ottawa: RCERPF.

Durham, John George Lambton, Earl of. 1839. *Lord Durham's Report on the Affairs of British North America*, edited with an introduction by Sir C.P. Lucas. Oxford: Clarendon Press, 1912.

Dyck, Rand. 1991 RC. "Links between Federal and Provincial Parties and Party Systems." In *Representation, Integration and Political Parties in Canada*, ed. Herman Bakvis. Vol. 14 of the research studies of the Royal Commission on Electoral Reform and Party Financing. Ottawa: RCERPF.

Eagles, Munroe. 1991a RC. "Enhancing Relative Vote Equality in Canada: The Role of Electors in Boundary Adjustment." In *Drawing the Map:*

Equality and Efficacy of the Vote in Canadian Electoral Boundary Reform, ed. David Small. Vol. 11 of the research studies of the Royal Commission on Electoral Reform and Party Financing. Ottawa: RCERPF.

Eagles, Munroe. 1991b RC. "Voting and Nonvoting in Canadian Federal Elections: An Ecological Analysis." In *Voter Turnout in Canada*, ed. Herman Bakvis. Vol. 15 of the research studies of the Royal Commission on Electoral Reform and Party Financing. Ottawa: RCERPF.

Economic Council of Canada. 1991. "New Faces in the Crowd." *Au Courant* 11(3): 4–5.

The Economist. 1991. "Morning in America Meets the New World Order." (17 August): 21–22.

Elizur, Judith N. 1986. "The Role of the Media in the 1981 Knesset Elections." In *Israel at the Polls, 1981: A Study of the Knesset Elections*, ed. Howard R. Penniman and Daniel J. Elazar. Washington, DC: American Enterprise Institute for Public Policy Research.

Elizur, Judith, and Elihu Katz. 1979. "The Media in the Israeli Elections of 1977." In *Israel at the Polls: The Knesset Elections of 1977*, ed. Howard R. Penniman. Washington, DC: American Enterprise Institute for Public Policy Research.

Elkins, David J. 1991 RC. "Parties as National Institutions: A Comparative Study." In *Representation, Integration and Political Parties in Canada*, ed. Herman Bakvis. Vol. 14 of the research studies of the Royal Commission on Electoral Reform and Party Financing. Ottawa: RCERPF.

Ellis, David. 1991. *Networking.* Toronto: Friends of Canadian Broadcasting.

Environics Research Group Ltd. 1990. *Youth Attitudes Towards Voting.* Poll prepared for the Royal Commission on Electoral Reform and Party Financing between 28 May and 12 July 1990. Ottawa.

Erickson, Lynda. 1991 RC. "Women and Candidacies for the House of Commons." In *Women in Canadian Politics: Towards Equity in Representation*, ed. Kathy Megyery. Vol. 6 of the research studies of the Royal Commission on Electoral Reform and Party Financing. Ottawa: RCERPF.

Erickson, Lynda, and R.K. Carty. 1991. "Parties and Candidate Selection in the 1988 Canadian General Election." *Canadian Journal of Political Science* 24: 331–49.

FEC v. *Americans for Change*, 312 F. Supp. 489 (1980); affirmed 455 U.S. 129 (1982).

FEC Journal of Election Administration. 1989. "1988 Presidential Election Results." Vol. 16 (Summer): 2.

Federal Election Commission. 1986. *Campaign Guide for Corporations and Labor Organizations.* Washington, DC.

Federal Election Commission, comp. 1988. *Federal Election Campaign Laws.* Washington, DC.

Federal Election Commission. 1990. *Annual Report 1989*. Washington, DC.

Federal Election Commission. 1991a. "FEC Approves Public Funds for 1992 Presidential Conventions." *FEC Record* 17 (August): 3.

Federal Election Commission. 1991b. "FEC Says Legislative Action Needed to Save Election Program." Press Release, 6 March. Washington, DC.

Federal Election Commission. 1991c. "PAC Activity Falls in 1990 Elections." Press Release, 31 March. Washington, DC.

Federal Election Commission. 1991d. "1990 Congressional Election Spending Drops to Low Point." Press Release, 22 February. Washington, DC.

Feigenbaum, Edward D., and James A. Palmer. 1988. *Ballot Access 1: Issues and Options*. Report prepared for Federal Election Commission, Washington, DC.

Feigert, Frank. 1989. *Canada Votes: 1935–1988*. Durham: Duke University Press.

Ferejohn, John, and Brian Gaines. 1991 RC. "The Personal Vote in Canada." In *Representation, Integration and Political Parties in Canada*, ed. Herman Bakvis. Vol. 14 of the research studies of the Royal Commission on Electoral Reform and Party Financing. Ottawa: RCERPF.

Fitzgerald, Marian. 1983. "Are Blacks an Electoral Liability?" *New Society* 66 (8 December): 394–95.

Fleras, Augie. 1991 RC. "Aboriginal Electoral Districts for Canada: Lessons from New Zealand." In *Aboriginal Peoples and Electoral Reform in Canada*, ed. Robert A. Milen. Vol. 9 of the research studies of the Royal Commission on Electoral Reform and Party Financing. Ottawa: RCERPF.

Fletcher, Frederick J. 1987. "Mass Media and Parliamentary Elections in Canada." *Legislative Studies Quarterly* 12: 341–72.

Fletcher, Frederick J. 1988. "The Media and the 1984 Landslide." In *Canada at the Polls, 1984: A Study of the Federal General Elections*, ed. Howard Penniman. Washington, DC: American Enterprise Institute for Public Policy Research.

Fletcher, Frederick J. 1990. "The Mass Media and Elections in Canada: An Overview." Issue paper prepared for the Royal Commission on Electoral Reform and Party Financing. Ottawa.

Fletcher, Frederick J., and Robert Everett. 1991 RC. "Mass Media and Elections in Canada." In *Media, Elections and Democracy*, ed. Frederick J. Fletcher. Vol. 19 of the research studies of the Royal Commission on Electoral Reform and Party Financing. Ottawa: RCERPF.

Fortin, Pierre. 1991 RC. "Ethical Issues in the Debate on Reform of the *Canada Elections Act*: An Ethicological Analysis." In *Political Ethics: A Canadian*

Perspective, ed. Janet Hiebert. Vol. 12 of the research studies of the Royal Commission on Electoral Reform and Party Financing. Ottawa: RCERPF.

Frizzell, Alan. 1989. "The Perils of Polling." In Alan Frizzell, Jon H. Pammett and Anthony Westell, *The Canadian General Election of 1988*. Ottawa: Carleton University Press.

Frizzell, Alan. 1991. "Report." Carleton University Survey Centre telephone survey conducted for the Royal Commission on Electoral Reform and Party Financing. Ottawa.

Frizzell, Alan. 1991 RC. "In the Public Service: Representation in Modern Canada." In *Drawing the Map: Equality and Efficacy of the Vote in Canadian Electoral Boundary Reform*, ed. David Small. Vol. 11 of the research studies of the Royal Commission on Electoral Reform and Party Financing. Ottawa: RCERPF.

Frizzell, Alan, and Anthony Westell. 1985. *The Canadian General Election of 1984: Politicians, Parties, Press and Polls*. Ottawa: Carleton University Press.

Frizzell, Alan, and Anthony Westell. 1989. "The Media and the Campaign." In Alan Frizzell, Jon H. Pammett and Anthony Westell, *The Canadian General Election of 1988*. Ottawa: Carleton University Press.

Gagnon, Lysiane. 1981. "Journalism and Ideologies in Québec." In *The Journalists*. Vol. 2 of the research studies of the Royal Commission on Newspapers. Ottawa: Minister of Supply and Services Canada.

Gallagher, Michael. 1988. "Conclusion." In *Candidate Selection in Comparative Perspective: The Secret Garden of Politics*, ed. Michael Gallagher and Michael Marsh. London: Sage Publications.

Gallup Poll of Canada. 1943. "Libs, Pro-Cons, and C.C.F. Now Tied in Popular Support, Survey Shows." Toronto: Canadian Institute of Public Opinion.

Gallup Report. 1972. "Voters Give Solid Support to Limit on Campaign Funds." 27 May. Toronto: Canadian Institute of Public Opinion.

Garant, Patrice. 1991a RC. "Political Rights of Public Servants in the Political Process." In *Democratic Rights and Electoral Reform in Canada*, ed. Michael Cassidy. Vol. 10 of the research studies of the Royal Commission on Electoral Reform and Party Financing. Ottawa: RCERPF.

Garant, Patrice. 1991b RC. "The Possibilities of Reopening the Voting Age Issue under the Charter of Rights and Freedoms." In *Youth in Canadian Politics: Participation and Involvement*, ed. Kathy Megyery. Vol. 8 of the research studies of the Royal Commission on Electoral Reform and Party Financing. Ottawa: RCERPF.

Gerstlé, Jacques. 1991 RC. "Election Communication in France." In *Media, Elections and Democracy*, ed. Frederick J. Fletcher. Vol. 19 of the research studies of the Royal Commission on Electoral Reform and Party Financing. Ottawa: RCERPF.

Gibbins, Roger. 1991 RC. "Electoral Reform and Canada's Aboriginal Population: An Assessment of Aboriginal Electoral Districts." In *Aboriginal Peoples and Electoral Reform in Canada*, ed. Robert A. Milen. Vol. 9 of the research studies of the Royal Commission on Electoral Reform and Party Financing. Ottawa: RCERPF.

Gilsdorf, William O., and Robert Bernier. 1991 RC. "Journalistic Practice in Covering Federal Election Campaigns in Canada." In *Reporting the Campaign: Election Coverage in Canada*, ed. Frederick J. Fletcher. Vol. 22 of the research studies of the Royal Commission on Electoral Reform and Party Financing. Ottawa: RCERPF.

Globe and Mail. 1991. "Reform, BQ Gain When Names Listed." 22 April.

Goldenberg, Edie N., and Michael W. Traugott. 1987. "Mass Media and Legislative Contests: Opportunities for Comparative Study." *Legislative Studies Quarterly* 12: 445–56.

Goldstein, Joshua. 1991a. *The Fat Cats' Laundromat: Soft Money and the National Parties 1989–1990*. Washington, DC: Center for Responsive Politics.

Goldstein, Joshua. 1991b. *Gearing Up for '92: Soft Money Fundraising: January 1–June 30, 1991*. Washington, DC: Center for Responsive Politics.

Gould v. *Canada (Attorney General)*, [1984] 1 F.C. 1133 (C.A.), reversing [1984] 1 F.C. 1119 (T.D.); affirmed [1984] 2 S.C.R. 124.

Graber, Doris A. 1991 RC. "The Mass Media and Election Campaigns in the United States of America." In *Media, Elections and Democracy*, ed. Frederick J. Fletcher. Vol. 19 of the research studies of the Royal Commission on Electoral Reform and Party Financing. Ottawa: RCERPF.

Graham, Ron. 1986. *One-Eyed Kings: Promise and Illusion in Canadian Politics*. Toronto: Collins.

Granatstein, J.L. 1982. *The Ottawa Men: The Civil Service Mandarins, 1935–1957*. Toronto: Oxford University Press.

Green, Lyndsay. 1991 RC. "An Exploration of Alternative Methods for Improving Voter Information." In *Media and Voters in Canadian Election Campaigns*, ed. Frederick J. Fletcher. Vol. 18 of the research studies of the Royal Commission on Electoral Reform and Party Financing. Ottawa: RCERPF.

Greene, Ian. 1991 RC. "Allegations of Undue Influence in Canadian Politics." In *Political Ethics: A Canadian Perspective*, ed. Janet Hiebert. Vol. 12 of the research studies of the Royal Commission on Electoral Reform and Party Financing. Ottawa: RCERPF.

Griggs v. *Duke Power Co.* 401 U.S. 424 (1971).

Grondin v. *Ontario (Attorney General)* (1988), 65 O.R. (2d) 427 (H.C.).

Grondin, C.R. 1990. "Redistricting: A Case Study of the 1987 Exercise." Paper prepared for the Royal Commission on Electoral Reform and Party Financing. Ottawa.

Hackett, Robert A. 1991 RC. "Smaller Voices: Minor Parties, Campaign Communication and the News Media." In *Reporting the Campaign: Election Coverage in Canada*, ed. Frederick J. Fletcher. Vol. 22 of the research studies of the Royal Commission on Electoral Reform and Party Financing. Ottawa: RCERPF.

Heintzman, Keith. 1991 RC. "Electoral Competition, Campaign Expenditure and Incumbency Advantage." In *Issues in Party and Election Finance in Canada*, ed. F. Leslie Seidle. Vol. 5 of the research studies of the Royal Commission on Electoral Reform and Party Financing. Ottawa: RCERPF.

Herberg, Edward N. 1989. *Ethnic Groups in Canada: Adaptations and Transitions*. Scarborough: Nelson Canada.

Hiebert, Janet. 1991a RC. "A Code of Ethics for Political Parties." In *Political Ethics: A Canadian Perspective*, ed. Janet Hiebert. Vol. 12 of the research studies of the Royal Commission on Electoral Reform and Party Financing. Ottawa: RCERPF.

Hiebert, Janet. 1991b RC. "Interest Groups and Canadian Federal Elections." In *Interest Groups and Elections in Canada*, ed. F. Leslie Seidle. Vol. 2 of the research studies of the Royal Commission on Electoral Reform and Party Financing. Ottawa: RCERPF.

Hogarth, David, and Bill Gilsdorf. 1991 RC. "The Impact of All-News Services on Elections and Election Coverage." In *Election Broadcasting in Canada*, ed. Frederick J. Fletcher. Vol. 21 of the research studies of the Royal Commission on Electoral Reform and Party Financing. Ottawa: RCERPF.

Hoy, Claire. 1989. *Margin of Error: Pollsters and the Manipulation of Canadian Politics*. Toronto: Key Porter Books.

Hudon, Raymond, Bernard Fournier and Louis Métivier, with the assistance of Benoît-Paul Hébert. 1991 RC. "To What Extent Are Today's Young People Interested in Politics? An Inquiry among 16- to 24-Year-Olds." In *Youth in Canadian Politics: Participation and Involvement*, ed. Kathy Megyery. Vol. 8 of the research studies of the Royal Commission on Electoral Reform and Party Financing. Ottawa: RCERPF.

Hunter, Alfred A., and Margaret A. Denton. 1984. "Do Female Candidates 'Lose Votes'? The Experience of Female Candidates in the 1979 and 1980 Canadian General Elections." *Canadian Review of Sociology and Anthropology* 21: 395–406.

Institute for Political Involvement. 1981. *A Model Corporate Policy on Political Leave for Employees*. Toronto: IPI.

Institute of Public Administration of Canada. 1986. *Statement of Principles Regarding the Conduct of Public Employees.* Toronto: IPAC.

Irvine, William P. 1985. "A Review and Evaluation of Electoral System Reform Proposals." In *Institutional Reforms for Representative Government*, ed. Peter Aucoin. Vol. 38 of the research studies of the Royal Commission on the Economic Union and Development Prospects for Canada. Toronto: University of Toronto Press.

Jackman, Robert W. 1972. "Political Parties, Voting, and National Integration: The Canadian Case." *Comparative Politics* 4: 511–36.

Jackman, Robert W. 1987. "Political Institutions and Voter Turnout in the Industrial Democracies." *American Political Science Review* 81: 405–23.

Jenson, Jane. 1991a RC. "Citizenship and Equity: Variations across Time and in Space." In *Political Ethics: A Canadian Perspective*, ed. Janet Hiebert. Vol. 12 of the research studies of the Royal Commission on Electoral Reform and Party Financing. Ottawa: RCERPF.

Jenson, Jane. 1991b RC. "Innovation and Equity: The Impact of Public Funding." In *Comparative Issues in Party and Election Finance*, ed. F. Leslie Seidle. Vol. 4 of the research studies of the Royal Commission on Electoral Reform and Party Financing. Ottawa: RCERPF.

Johnson, David. 1991 RC. "The Ontario Party and Campaign Finance System: Initiative and Challenge." In *Provincial Party and Election Finance in Canada*, ed. F. Leslie Seidle. Vol. 3 of the research studies of the Royal Commission on Electoral Reform and Party Financing. Ottawa: RCERPF.

Johnston, Richard. 1986. *Public Opinion and Public Policy in Canada: Questions of Confidence.* Vol. 35 of the research studies of the Royal Commission on the Economic Union and Development Prospects for Canada. Toronto: University of Toronto Press.

Johnston, Richard, André Blais, Henry Brady and Jean Crête. 1991. "Letting the People Decide: History, Contingency and the Dynamics of Canadian Elections." Unpublished manuscript made available by the authors. (Forthcoming)

Jolivet v. *Canada* (1983), 48 B.C.L.R. 121 (S.C.).

Kernaghan, Kenneth. 1991 RC. "The Political Rights of Canada's Federal Public Servants." In *Democratic Rights and Electoral Reform in Canada*, ed. Michael Cassidy. Vol. 10 of the research studies of the Royal Commission on Electoral Reform and Party Financing. Ottawa: RCERPF.

Kline, Stephen, Rovin Deodat, Arlene Shwetz and William Leiss. 1991 RC. "Political Broadcast Advertising in Canada." In *Election Broadcasting in Canada*, ed. Frederick J. Fletcher. Vol. 21 of the research studies of the Royal Commission on Electoral Reform and Party Financing. Ottawa: RCERPF.

Kohlberg, L. 1958. "The Development of Modes of Moral Thinking and Choice in the Years Ten to Sixteen." Ph.D. diss., University of Chicago.

Krashinsky, Michael, and William J. Milne. 1991 RC. "Some Evidence on the Effects of Incumbency in the 1988 Canadian Federal Election." In *Issues in Party and Election Finance in Canada*, ed. F. Leslie Seidle. Vol. 5 of the research studies of the Royal Commission on Electoral Reform and Party Financing. Ottawa: RCERPF.

LaCalamita, John. 1984. "The Equitable Campaign: Party Political Broadcasting Regulation in Canada." *Osgoode Hall Law Journal* 22: 543–79.

Lachapelle, Guy. 1991 RC. *Polls and the Media in Canadian Elections: Taking the Pulse*. Vol. 16 of the research studies of the Royal Commission on Electoral Reform and Party Financing. Ottawa: RCERPF.

Landreville, Pierre, and Lucie Lemonde. 1991 RC. "Voting Rights for Inmates." In *Democratic Rights and Electoral Reform in Canada*, ed. Michael Cassidy. Vol. 10 of the research studies of the Royal Commission on Electoral Reform and Party Financing. Ottawa: RCERPF.

Landry, Réjean. 1991 RC. "Inducements Created by the Institution of Representative Democracy: Their Effect on Voters, Political Parties and Public Policy." In *Representation, Integration and Political Parties in Canada*, ed. Herman Bakvis. Vol. 14 of the research studies of the Royal Commission on Electoral Reform and Party Financing. Ottawa: RCERPF.

Leduc, J. 1990. "Getting the Nomination the Key to Equality of Representation: A Case Study of Women Candidates for the Liberal Party of Canada, 1988 Federal Election." MA thesis, Carleton University.

LeDuc, Lawrence. 1991. "Voting for Free Trade? The Canadian Voter and the 1988 Federal Election." In *Politics: Canada*. 7th ed., comp. Paul W. Fox and Graham White. Toronto: McGraw-Hill Ryerson.

Lee, Robert Mason. 1989. *One Hundred Monkeys: The Triumph of Popular Wisdom in Canadian Politics*. Toronto: Macfarlane Walter and Ross.

Lemieux, Vincent. 1991 RC. "Public Sector Ethics." In *Political Ethics: A Canadian Perspective*, ed. Janet Hiebert. Vol. 12 of the research studies of the Royal Commission on Electoral Reform and Party Financing. Ottawa: RCERPF.

Lévesque v. *Canada (Attorney General)* (1985), [1986] 2 F.C. 287 (T.D.).

Liberal Party of Newfoundland and Labrador. 1989. "Partisan Polls Should Be Identified." Press Release, 17 April. St. John's.

Lichtenberg, Judith. 1990. "Introduction." In *Democracy and the Mass Media: A Collection of Essays*, ed. Judith Lichtenberg. Cambridge: Cambridge University Press.

Lijphart, Arend. 1990. "The Political Consequences of Electoral Laws, 1945–85." *American Political Science Review* 84: 481–89.

Lindquist, Evert Anthony. 1989. "Behind the Myth of Think Tanks: The Organization and Relevance of Canadian Policy Institutes." Ph.D. diss., University of California, Berkeley.

Loh, Shirley. 1990. "Population Projections of Registered Indians, 1986–2011." Ottawa: Statistics Canada, Demography Division.

MacBain v. *Canada (Canadian Human Rights Commission)*, [1985] 1 F.C. 856 (C.A.).

McCormick, Peter. 1991. "The Reform Party of Canada: New Beginning or Dead End?" In *Party Politics in Canada*. 6th ed., ed. Hugh G. Thorburn. Scarborough: Prentice-Hall Canada.

McCormick, Peter. 1991 RC. "Provision for the Recall of Elected Officials: Parameters and Prospects." In *Democratic Rights and Electoral Reform in Canada*, ed. Michael Cassidy. Vol. 10 of the research studies of the Royal Commission on Electoral Reform and Party Financing. Ottawa: RCERPF.

MacDermid, Robert. 1991 RC. "Media Usage and Political Behaviour." In *Media and Voters in Canadian Election Campaigns*, ed. Frederick J. Fletcher. Vol. 18 of the research studies of the Royal Commission on Electoral Reform and Party Financing. Ottawa: RCERPF.

Mac Donald, David. 1991 RC. "Referendums and Federal General Elections." In *Democratic Rights and Electoral Reform in Canada*, ed. Michael Cassidy. Vol. 10 of the research studies of the Royal Commission on Electoral Reform and Party Financing. Ottawa: RCERPF.

Macdonald, Doug. 1991 RC. "Ecological Communities and Constituency Districting." In *Drawing the Map: Equality and Efficacy of the Vote in Canadian Electoral Boundary Reform*, ed. David Small. Vol. 11 of the research studies of the Royal Commission on Electoral Reform and Party Financing. Ottawa: RCERPF.

Mackintosh, John P. 1977. *The British Cabinet*. 3d ed. London: Stevens.

MacLean v. *Nova Scotia (Attorney General)* (1987), 35 D.L.R. (4th) 306 (T.D.).

Maclean's/Decima. 1988. "The Voters Reflect: Conflicts in a Postelection Poll." *Maclean's* (5 December): 19.

Magleby, David B., and Candice J. Nelson. 1990. *The Money Chase: Congressional Campaign Finance Reform*. Washington, DC: Brookings Institution.

Mansfield, Harvey, Jr. 1965. *Statesmanship and Party Governments: A Study of Burke and Bolingbroke*. Chicago: University of Chicago Press.

Martin, Patrick, Allan Gregg and George Perlin. 1983. *Contenders: The Tory Quest for Power*. Scarborough: Prentice-Hall Canada.

Massicotte, Louis. 1991 RC. "Party Financing in Quebec: An Analysis of the Financial Reports of Political Parties 1977–1989." In *Provincial Party and*

Election Finance in Canada, ed. F. Leslie Seidle. Vol. 3 of the research studies of the Royal Commission on Electoral Reform and Party Financing. Ottawa: RCERPF.

Meisel, John. 1962. *The Canadian General Election of 1957*. Toronto: University of Toronto Press.

Mellon, H. 1991 RC. "The Evolution of Political Financing Regulation in New Brunswick." In *Provincial Party and Election Finance in Canada*, ed. F. Leslie Seidle. Vol. 3 of the research studies of the Royal Commission on Electoral Reform and Party Financing. Ottawa: RCERPF.

Michaud, Pascale, and Pierre Laferrière. 1991 RC. "Economic Analysis of the Funding of Political Parties in Canada." In *Issues in Party and Election Finance in Canada*, ed. F. Leslie Seidle. Vol. 5 of the research studies of the Royal Commission on Electoral Reform and Party Financing. Ottawa: RCERPF.

Milen, Robert A. 1991 RC. "Aboriginal Constitutional and Electoral Reform." In *Aboriginal Peoples and Electoral Reform in Canada*, ed. Robert A. Milen. Vol. 9 of the research studies of the Royal Commission on Electoral Reform and Party Financing. Ottawa: RCERPF.

Monarchist League of Canada. 1991. "Canada's Crown: Cornerstone of Confederation." Brief submitted to the Citizens' Forum on Canada's Future. Oakville.

Morley, Terry. 1991 RC. "Paying for the Politics of British Columbia." In *Provincial Party and Election Finance in Canada*, ed. F. Leslie Seidle. Vol. 3 of the research studies of the Royal Commission on Electoral Reform and Party Financing. Ottawa: RCERPF.

Morton, W.L. 1967. *The Progressive Party in Canada*. Toronto: University of Toronto Press.

Muldoon v. *Canada*, [1988] 3 F.C. 628.

Mutch, Robert E. 1988. *Campaigns, Congress, and Courts: The Making of Federal Campaign Finance Law*. New York: Praeger.

Mutch, Robert E. 1991 RC. "The Evolution of Campaign Finance Regulation in the United States and Canada." In *Comparative Issues in Party and Election Finance*, ed. F. Leslie Seidle. Vol. 4 of the research studies of the Royal Commission on Electoral Reform and Party Financing. Ottawa: RCERPF.

Nassmacher, Karl-Heinz. 1991. "Citizen Cash: The Impact of Tax Credits, Tax Check-Offs and Matching Funds." Paper prepared for the 15th World Congress of the International Political Science Association, Buenos Aires.

National Citizens' Coalition Inc./Coalition nationale des citoyens inc. v. *Canada (Attorney General)* (1984), 32 Alta L.R. (2d) 249 (Q.B.).

National Media Archive. 1991. "1988 Federal Election Campaign: Source of Statement by Program/Publication." Vancouver: Fraser Institute.

Nevitte, Neil. 1991 RC. "New Politics, the Charter and Political Participation." In *Representation, Integration and Political Parties in Canada*, ed. Herman Bakvis. Vol. 14 of the research studies of the Royal Commission on Electoral Reform and Party Financing. Ottawa: RCERPF.

New York Times (National). 1990. "In a Survey, Americans Wish a Pox on Both Congress and the President." 12 October.

New York Times. 1991. "One Big Problem Is Politics." 31 July.

New Zealand. Royal Commission on the Electoral System. 1986. *Towards a Better Democracy*. Wellington: Government Printer.

Nolan, Michael. 1990. "The Evolution of the Relationship between the Mass Media and Political Parties in the Conduct of Canadian Federal Election Campaigns." Paper prepared for the Royal Commission on Electoral Reform and Party Financing. Ottawa.

Ontario. Ontario Commission on the Legislature. 1974. *Third Report*. Toronto.

Ontario. Ontario Commission on the Legislature. 1975. *Fifth Report*. Toronto.

Ontario Securities Commission. 1990. *Annual Report*. Toronto: OEC.

Padget, Donald. 1991 RC. "Large Contributions to Candidates in the 1988 Federal Election and the Issue of Undue Influence." In *Issues in Party and Election Finance in Canada*, ed. F. Leslie Seidle. Vol. 5 of the research studies of the Royal Commission on Electoral Reform and Party Financing. Ottawa: RCERPF.

Paltiel, Khayyam Z. 1975. "Campaign Financing in Canada and Its Reform." In *Canada at the Polls: The General Election of 1974*, ed. Howard R. Penniman. Washington, DC: American Enterprise Institute for Public Policy Research.

Paltiel, Khayyam Z. 1977. "Party, Candidate and Election Finance." Study no. 22 of the Royal Commission on Corporate Concentration. Ottawa: Minister of Supply and Services Canada.

Pammett, Jon H. 1991 RC. "Voting Turnout in Canada." In *Voter Turnout in Canada*, ed. Herman Bakvis. Vol. 15 of the research studies of the Royal Commission on Electoral Reform and Party Financing. Ottawa: RCERPF.

Pammett, Jon H., and John Myles. 1991 RC. "Lowering the Voting Age." In *Youth in Canadian Politics: Participation and Involvement*, ed. Kathy Megyery. Vol. 8 of the research studies of the Royal Commission on Electoral Reform and Party Financing. Ottawa: RCERPF.

Patterson, Thomas E., and Robert D. McClure. 1976. *The Unseeing Eye: The Myth of Television Power in National Politics*. New York: G.P. Putnam's.

Peers, Frank W. 1969. *The Politics of Canadian Broadcasting 1920–1951*. Toronto: University of Toronto Press.

Pelletier, Alain. 1991 RC. "Politics and Ethnicity: Representation of Ethnic and Visible-Minority Groups in the House of Commons." In *Ethno-Cultural Groups and Visible Minorities in Canadian Politics: The Question of Access,* ed. Kathy Megyery. Vol. 7 of the research studies of the Royal Commission on Electoral Reform and Party Financing. Ottawa: RCERPF.

Pelletier, Réjean. 1991 RC. "The Structures of Canadian Political Parties: How They Operate." In *Canadian Political Parties: Leaders, Candidates and Organization,* ed. Herman Bakvis. Vol. 13 of the research studies of the Royal Commission on Electoral Reform and Party Financing. Ottawa: RCERPF.

Perlin, George. 1991 RC. "Attitudes of Liberal Convention Delegates Towards Proposals for Reform of the Process of Leadership Selection." In *Canadian Political Parties: Leaders, Candidates and Organization,* ed. Herman Bakvis. Vol. 13 of the research studies of the Royal Commission on Electoral Reform and Party Financing. Ottawa: RCERPF.

Pinto-Duschinsky, Michael. 1991 RC. "The Party Foundations and Political Finance in Germany." In *Comparative Issues in Party and Election Finance,* ed. F. Leslie Seidle. Vol. 4 of the research studies of the Royal Commission on Electoral Reform and Party Financing. Ottawa: RCERPF.

Pinto-Duschinsky, Michael, and Shelley Pinto-Duschinsky. 1987. *Voter Registration in England and Wales: Problems and Solutions.* London: Constitutional Reform Centre.

Preyra, Leonard. 1991 RC. "Riding the Waves: Parties, the Media and the 1988 Federal Election in Nova Scotia." In *Reaching the Voter: Constituency Campaigning in Canada,* ed. Frederick J. Fletcher and David V.J. Bell. Vol. 20 of the research studies of the Royal Commission on Electoral Reform and Party Financing. Ottawa: RCERPF.

Pro-Canada Network. 1988. *What's the Big Deal?* Ottawa: Pro-Canada Network.

Pross, A. Paul. 1986. *Group Politics and Public Policy.* Toronto: Oxford University Press.

Qualter, Terence H. 1970. *The Election Process in Canada.* Toronto: McGraw-Hill of Canada.

R. v. Big M Drug Mart Ltd., [1985] S.C.R. 295.

R. v. Bruneau (1963), [1964] 1 O.R. 263 (C.A.); leave to appeal to S.C.C. refused [1964] 1 O.R. 263 note (S.C.C.).

R. v. MacLaren, B.C.S.C., No. CC901670, 30 April 1991.

R. v. Oakes, [1986] 1 S.C.R. 103.

R. v. Publicis communicateur conseil, Que. Prov. Ct., 20 March 1981.

R. v. Risdon, Ont. Prov. Ct., Murphy J., 1978.

R. v. Risdon, Ont. Co. Ct., Whealy J., 24 October 1980.

R. v. Roach (1978), 25 O.R. (2d) 767 (Co. Ct.).

Radio-Television News Directors Association of Canada. 1986. *Code of Ethics.* Thornhill: RTNDAC.

Rawls, John. 1972. *A Theory of Justice.* Oxford: Clarendon Press.

Reference re Alberta Statutes, [1938] S.C.R. 100; affirmed in part [1939] A.C. 117 (P.C.).

Reference re Provincial Electoral Boundaries, [1991] 3 W.W.R. 593 (Sask. C.A.); reversed (*sub nom. Reference re Electoral Boundaries Commission Act, ss. 14, 20 (Sask)*) (1991), 81 D.L.R. (4th) 16 (S.C.C.).

Reform Commission of the Liberal Party of Canada. 1991. *Agenda for Reform.* Interim Report. Ottawa.

Reid, Escott M. 1932. "The Rise of National Parties in Canada." Reprinted in *Party Politics in Canada*. 6th ed., ed. Hugh G. Thorburn. Scarborough: Prentice-Hall Canada.

Roach, Kent. 1991 RC. "One Person, One Vote? Canadian Constitutional Standards for Electoral Distribution and Districting." In *Drawing the Map: Equality and Efficacy of the Vote in Canadian Electoral Boundary Reform*, ed. David Small. Vol. 11 of the research studies of the Royal Commission on Electoral Reform and Party Financing. Ottawa: RCERPF.

Roberts, Geoffrey. 1988. "The German Federal Republic: The Two-Lane Route to Bonn." In *Candidate Selection in Comparative Perspective: The Secret Garden of Politics*, ed. Michael Gallagher and Michael Marsh. London: Sage Publications.

Robinson, Gertrude J., and Armande Saint-Jean, with the assistance of Christine Rioux. 1991 RC. "Women Politicians and Their Media Coverage: A Generational Analysis." In *Women in Canadian Politics: Towards Equity in Representation*, ed. Kathy Megyery. Vol. 6 of the research studies of the Royal Commission on Electoral Reform and Party Financing. Ottawa: RCERPF.

Romanow, Walter I., Walter C. Soderlund and Richard G. Price. 1991 RC. "Negative Political Advertising: An Analysis of Research Findings in Light of Canadian Practice." In *Political Ethics: A Canadian Perspective*, ed. Janet Hiebert. Vol. 12 of the research studies of the Royal Commission on Electoral Reform and Party Financing. Ottawa: RCERPF.

Roth, Lorna. 1991 RC. "CBC Northern Services and the Federal Electoral Process: Problems and Strategies for Improvement." In *Election Broadcasting in Canada*, ed. Frederick J. Fletcher. Vol. 21 of the research studies of the Royal Commission on Electoral Reform and Party Financing. Ottawa: RCERPF.

Rutherford, Paul. 1978. *The Making of the Canadian Media.* Toronto: McGraw-Hill Ryerson.

Rutherford, Paul. 1982. *A Victorian Authority: The Daily Press in Late Nineteenth-Century Canada*. Toronto: University of Toronto Press.

Sancton, Andrew. 1990. "Eroding Representation-by-Population in the Canadian House of Commons: The *Representation Act, 1985*." *Canadian Journal of Political Science* 23: 441–57.

Saunders, Eileen. 1991 RC. "Mass Media and the Reproduction of Marginalization." In *Reporting the Campaign: Election Coverage in Canada*, ed. Frederick J. Fletcher. Vol. 22 of the research studies of the Royal Commission on Electoral Reform and Party Financing. Ottawa: RCERPF.

Sauvageau, Florian. 1981. "French-speaking Journalists on Journalism." In *The Journalists*. Vol. 2 of the research studies of the Royal Commission on Newspapers. Ottawa: Minister of Supply and Services Canada.

Sauvé v. *Canada (Attorney General)* (1988), 66 O.R. (2d) 234 (H.C.).

Sayers, Anthony M. 1991 RC. "Local Issue Space at National Elections: Kootenay West–Revelstoke and Vancouver Centre." In *Reaching the Voter: Constituency Campaigning in Canada*, ed. Frederick J. Fletcher and David V.J. Bell. Vol. 20 of the research studies of the Royal Commission on Electoral Reform and Party Financing. Ottawa: RCERPF.

Scarrow, Howard A. 1962. *Canada Votes: A Handbook of Federal and Provincial Election Data*. New Orleans: Hauser Press.

Scarrow, Howard A. 1964. "Nomination and Local Party Organization in Canada: A Case Study." *Western Political Quarterly* 17 (March): 55–62.

Scarrow, Howard A. 1991 RC. "Apportionment, Districting, and Representation in the United States." In *Drawing the Map: Equality and Efficacy of the Vote in Canadian Electoral Boundary Reform*, ed. David Small. Vol. 11 of the research studies of the Royal Commission on Electoral Reform and Party Financing. Ottawa: RCERPF.

Schoenbach, Klaus. 1991 RC. "Mass Media and Election Campaigns in Germany." In *Media, Elections and Democracy*, ed. Frederick J. Fletcher. Vol. 19 of the research studies of the Royal Commission on Electoral Reform and Party Financing. Ottawa: RCERPF.

SECOR Group. 1990. "The Impact of New Technologies on the Electoral Process and Party Management in Canada." Report prepared for the Royal Commission on Electoral Reform and Party Financing. Ottawa.

Seidle, F. Leslie. 1980. "Electoral Law and Its Effects on Election Expenditure and Party Finance in Great Britain and Canada." D.Phil. diss., Oxford University.

Seidle, F. Leslie. 1988. "The Canadian Electoral System and Proposals for Its Reform." In *Canadian Parties in Transition: Discourse, Organization, and Representation*, ed. Alain G. Gagnon and A. Brian Tanguay. Scarborough: Nelson Canada.

Seidle, F. Leslie, and Khayyam Zev Paltiel. 1981. "Party Finance, the Election Expenses Act, and Campaign Spending in 1979 and 1980." In *Canada at the Polls, 1979 and 1980*, ed. H.R. Penniman. Washington, DC: American Enterprise Institute for Public Policy Research.

Selle, Per, and Lars Svåsand. 1991. "Membership in Party Organizations and the Problem of Decline of Parties." *Comparative Political Studies* 23: 459–77.

Semetko, Holli A. 1991 RC. "Broadcasting and Election Communication in Britain." In *Media, Elections and Democracy*, ed. Frederick J. Fletcher. Vol. 19 of the research studies of the Royal Commission on Electoral Reform and Party Financing. Ottawa: RCERPF.

Simard, Carolle. 1991 RC. "Visible Minorities and the Canadian Political System." In *Ethno-Cultural Groups and Visible Minorities in Canadian Politics: The Question of Access*, ed. Kathy Megyery. Vol. 7 of the research studies of the Royal Commission on Electoral Reform and Party Financing. Ottawa: RCERPF.

Simeon, Richard. 1972. *Federal–Provincial Diplomacy: The Making of Recent Policy in Canada*. Toronto: University of Toronto Press.

Siune, Karen. 1991 RC. "Campaign Communication in Scandinavia." In *Media, Elections and Democracy*, ed. Frederick J. Fletcher. Vol. 19 of the research studies of the Royal Commission on Electoral Reform and Party Financing. Ottawa: RCERPF.

Small, David. 1991 RC. "Enhancing Aboriginal Representation within the Existing System of Redistricting." In *Drawing the Map: Equality and Efficacy of the Vote in Canadian Electoral Boundary Reform*, ed. David Small. Vol. 11 of the research studies of the Royal Commission on Electoral Reform and Party Financing. Ottawa: RCERPF.

Smiley, Donald V. 1980. *Canada in Question: Federalism in the Eighties*. Toronto: McGraw-Hill Ryerson.

Smith, Anthony. 1981. "Mass Communications." In *Democracy at the Polls: A Comparative Study of Competitive National Elections*, ed. David Butler, Howard R. Penniman and Austin Ranney. Washington, DC: American Enterprise Institute for Public Policy Research.

Smith, David E. 1985. "Party Government, Representation and National Integration in Canada." In *Party Government and Regional Representation in Canada*, ed. Peter Aucoin. Vol. 36 of the research studies of the Royal Commission on the Economic Union and Development Prospects for Canada. Toronto: University of Toronto Press.

Smith, Hedrick. 1988. "Congress and the Constant Campaign: Survival Politics and the New Breed." In Hedrick Smith, *The Power Game: How Washington Works*. New York: Random House.

Smith, Jennifer. 1991 RC. "The Franchise and Theories of Representative Government." In *Democratic Rights and Electoral Reform in Canada*, ed. Michael Cassidy. Vol. 10 of the research studies of the Royal Commission on Electoral Reform and Party Financing. Ottawa: RCERPF.

Soderlund, Walter C. 1991. "Mass Media in Canadian Politics: A Survey of Contemporary Issues." In Robert M. Krause and R.H. Wagenberg, *Introductory Readings in Canadian Government and Politics*. Toronto: Copp Clark Pitman.

Soderlund, Walter C., Walter I. Romanow, E. Donald Briggs and Ronald H. Wagenberg. 1984. *Media and Elections in Canada*. Toronto: Holt, Rinehart and Winston of Canada.

Spencer, Beverley. 1988. "Abortion Still an Election Issue." *Leader-Post* (Regina), 16 November.

Spencer, David Ralph, with the assistance of Catherine M. Bolan. 1991 RC. "Election Broadcasting in Canada: A Brief History." In *Election Broadcasting in Canada*, ed. Frederick J. Fletcher. Vol. 21 of the research studies of the Royal Commission on Electoral Reform and Party Financing. Ottawa: RCERPF.

Stanbury, W.T. 1991 RC. *Money in Politics: Financing Federal Parties and Candidates in Canada*. Vol. 1 of the research studies of the Royal Commission on Electoral Reform and Party Financing. Ottawa: RCERPF.

Stasiulis, Daiva K., and Yasmeen Abu-Laban. 1991 RC. "The House the Parties Built: (Re)constructing Ethnic Representation in Canadian Politics." In *Ethno-Cultural Groups and Visible Minorities in Canadian Politics: The Question of Access*, ed. Kathy Megyery. Vol. 7 of the research studies of the Royal Commission on Electoral Reform and Party Financing. Ottawa: RCERPF.

Stewart, Alan. 1991 RC. "Community of Interest in Redistricting." In *Drawing the Map: Equality and Efficacy of the Vote in Canadian Electoral Boundary Reform*, ed. David Small. Vol. 11 of the research studies of the Royal Commission on Electoral Reform and Party Financing. Ottawa: RCERPF.

Stewart, Gordon. 1986. *The Origins of Canadian Politics: A Comparative Approach*. Vancouver: University of British Columbia Press.

Storer v. *Brown* 415 U.S. 724 (1974).

Sutherland, S.L. 1991 RC. "The Consequences of Electoral Volatility: Inexperienced Ministers 1949–1990." In *Representation, Integration and Political Parties in Canada*, ed. Herman Bakvis. Vol. 14 of the research studies of the Royal Commission on Electoral Reform and Party Financing. Ottawa: RCERPF.

Taagepera, Rein, and Matthew S. Shugart. 1989. *Seats and Votes: The Effects and Determinants of Electoral Systems*. New Haven: Yale University Press.

Tanguay, A. Brian, and Barry J. Kay. 1991 RC. "Political Activity of Local Interest Groups." In *Interest Groups and Elections in Canada*, ed. F. Leslie Seidle. Vol. 2 of the research studies of the Royal Commission on Electoral Reform and Party Financing. Ottawa: RCERPF.

Taras, David. 1990. *The Newsmakers: The Media's Influence on Canadian Politics.* Scarborough: Nelson Canada.

Taylor, Allan R. 1991. "When Business and Politics Mix." James C. Taylor Distinguished Lecture in Finance, delivered at the University of Western Ontario, 26 February 1991. *Canadian Speeches/Issues, Informed Thought* 5 (May): 34–40.

Taylor, Charles. 1991. "Shared and Divergent Values." In *Options for a New Canada*, ed. Ronald L. Watts and Douglas M. Brown. Toronto: University of Toronto Press.

Taylor, Paul. 1990. *See How They Run: Electing the President in an Age of Mediaocracy.* New York: Alfred A. Knopf.

Thomas, Paul G. 1991 RC. "Parties and Regional Representation." In *Representation, Integration and Political Parties in Canada*, ed. Herman Bakvis. Vol. 14 of the research studies of the Royal Commission on Electoral Reform and Party Financing. Ottawa: RCERPF.

Thompson-Pyper, Catherine. 1991. "Implications of the 1991 Broadcasting Act for Election Broadcasting." Paper prepared for the Royal Commission on Electoral Reform and Party Financing. Ottawa.

Traugott, Michael W. 1991. "The Impact of Media Polls on the Public." Unpublished manuscript prepared for publication in a book on media polls edited by Thomas E. Mann and Gary R. Orren, to be published by the Brookings Institution. With permission of the author.

Trudel, Pierre, and France Abran. 1991 RC. "The Legal and Constitutional Framework for the Regulation of Election Campaign Broadcasting." In *Election Broadcasting in Canada*, ed. Frederick J. Fletcher. Vol. 21 of the research studies of the Royal Commission on Electoral Reform and Party Financing. Ottawa: RCERPF.

United States. Department of Commerce. Bureau of the Census. 1983. *Congressional District Profiles, 98th Congress: Supplementary Report.* 1980 Census of Population. Washington, DC: Department of Commerce.

Wagenberg, Ronald H., Walter C. Soderlund, Walter I. Romanow and E. Donald Briggs. 1988. "Campaigns, Images and Polls: Mass Media Coverage of the 1984 Canadian Election." *Canadian Journal of Political Science* 21: 117–29.

Ward, Norman. 1963. *The Canadian House of Commons: Representation.* 2d ed. Toronto: University of Toronto Press.

Warhurst, John. 1991 RC. "Campaign Communication in Australian Elections." In *Media, Elections and Democracy*, ed. Frederick J. Fletcher. Vol. 19 of the research studies of the Royal Commission on Electoral Reform and Party Financing. Ottawa: RCERPF.

Wearing, Joseph. 1988. *Strained Relations: Canadian Parties and Voters*. Toronto: McClelland and Stewart.

Wearing, Joseph. 1991. "Regulating Federal Election Spending." In *Politics: Canada*. 7th ed., comp. Paul Fox and Graham White. Toronto: McGraw-Hill Ryerson.

Wearing, Joseph, and Peter Wearing. 1990. "Mother's Milk Revisited: The Effect of Foreign Ownership on Political Contributions." *Canadian Journal of Political Science* 23: 115–23.

Whitaker, Reginald. 1977. *The Government Party: Organizing and Financing the Liberal Party of Canada 1930–58*. Toronto: University of Toronto Press.

Whitehorn, Alan. 1991. "The Communist Party of Canada." In *Party Politics in Canada*. 6th ed., ed. Hugh G. Thorburn. Scarborough: Prentice-Hall Canada.

Willison, Sir John. 1919. *Reminiscences: Political and Personal*. Toronto: McClelland and Stewart.

Winter, James P., ed. 1990. *The Silent Revolution: Media, Democracy, and the Free Trade Debate*. Ottawa: University of Ottawa Press.

Wolfinger, Raymond E. 1974. *The Politics of Progress*. Englewood Cliffs: Prentice-Hall.

Wolinetz, Steven B. 1991. "Party Foundations in the Netherlands." Paper prepared for the Royal Commission on Electoral Reform and Party Financing. Ottawa.

Worcester, Robert M. 1991. *British Public Opinion: A Guide to the History and Methodology of Political Opinion Polling*. Oxford: Basil Blackwell.

Young, Lisa. 1991a RC. "Legislative Turnover and the Election of Women to the Canadian House of Commons." In *Women in Canadian Politics: Towards Equity in Representation*, ed. Kathy Megyery. Vol. 6 of the research studies of the Royal Commission on Electoral Reform and Party Financing. Ottawa: RCERPF.

Young, Lisa. 1991b RC. "Toward Transparency: An Evaluation of Disclosure Arrangements in Canadian Political Finance." In *Issues in Party and Election Finance in Canada*, ed. F. Leslie Seidle. Vol. 5 of the research studies of the Royal Commission on Electoral Reform and Party Financing. Ottawa: RCERPF.